P9-AES-109

REVIEW OF RESEARCH IN EDUCATION

Review of Research in Education is published annually on behalf of the American Educational Research Association, 1430 K St., NW, Suite 1200, Washington, DC 20005, by SAGE Publishing, 2455 Teller Road, Thousand Oaks, CA 91320. Send address changes to AERA Membership Department, 1430 K St., NW, Suite 1200, Washington, DC 20005.

Copyright © 2020 by the American Educational Research Association. All rights reserved. No portion of the contents may be reproduced in any form without written permission from the publisher.

Member Information: American Educational Research Association (AERA) member inquiries, member renewal requests, changes of address, and membership subscription inquiries should be addressed to the AERA Membership Department, 1430 K St., NW, Suite 1200, Washington, DC 20005; fax 202-238-3250; e-mail: members@aera.net. AERA annual membership dues are $215 (Regular Members), $215 (Affiliate Members), $165 (International Affiliates), $65 (Graduate Students), and $40 (Student Affiliates). **Claims:** Claims for undelivered copies must be made no later than six months following month of publication. Beyond six months and at the request of the American Educational Research Association, the publisher will supply missing copies when losses have been sustained in transit and when the reserve stock permits.

Subscription Information: All non-member subscription inquiries, orders, back-issue requests, claims, and renewals should be addressed to SAGE Publishing, 2455 Teller Road, Thousand Oaks, CA 91320; telephone (800) 818-SAGE (7243) and (805) 499-0721; fax: (805) 375-1700; e-mail: journals@sagepub.com; website: http://journals.sage pub.com. **Subscription Price:** Institutions: $419; Individuals: $74. For all customers outside the Americas, please visit http://www.sagepub.co.uk/customercare.nav for information. **Claims:** Claims for undelivered copies must be made no later than six months following month of publication. The publisher will supply missing copies when losses have been sustained in transit and when the reserve stock will permit.

Copyright Permission: To request permission for republishing, reproducing, or distributing material from this journal, please visit the desired article on the SAGE Journals website (journals.sagepub.com) and click "Permissions." For additional information, please see www .sagepub.com/journalspermissions.nav.

Advertising and Reprints: Current advertising rates and specifications may be obtained by contacting the advertising coordinator in the Thousand Oaks office at (805) 410-7763 or by sending an e-mail to advertising@sagepub.com. To order reprints, please e-mail reprint@ sagepub.com. Acceptance of advertising in this journal in no way implies endorsement of the advertised product or service by SAGE or the journal's affiliated society(ies). No endorsement is intended or implied. SAGE reserves the right to reject any advertising it deems as inappropriate for this journal.

Change of Address: Six weeks' advance notice must be given when notifying of change of address. Please send old address label along with the new address to ensure proper identification. Please specify name of journal.

International Standard Serial Number ISSN 0091-732X
International Standard Book Number ISBN 978-1-0718-1886-2 (Vol. 44, 2020, paper)
Manufactured in the United States of America. First printing, March 2020.

Printed on acid-free paper

REVIEW OF RESEARCH IN EDUCATION

Emergent Approaches for Education Research: What Counts as Innovative Educational Knowledge and What Education Research Counts?

Volume 44, 2020

Jeanne M. Powers, Editor
Gustavo E. Fischman, Editor
Margarita Pivovarova, Editor
Arizona State University

AERA
FOUNDED
1916
AMERICAN EDUCATIONAL RESEARCH ASSOCIATION

⑤SAGE

Review of Research in Education

Emergent Approaches for Education Research: What Counts as Innovative Educational Knowledge and What Education Research Counts?

Volume 44

EDITORS

JEANNE M. POWERS
Arizona State University

GUSTAVO E. FISCHMAN
Arizona State University

MARGARITA PIVOVAROVA
Arizona State University

EDITORIAL BOARD

JONI ACUFF
The Ohio State University

DAVID BARRY
The University of Texas at Austin

MILDRED BOVEDA
Florida International University

KATHERINE R. BRUNA
Iowa State University

DEBORAH CARTER
Claremont Graduate University

ALAN DALY
University of California, San Diego

NOAH DE LISSOVOY
The University of Texas at Austin

CHRISTIAN FISCHER
University of California, Irvine

NICHOLE GARCIA
Rutgers University

JUDITH GLAESSER
University of Tübingen

JOSHUA GLAZER
George Washington University

TAUCIA GONZALEZ
University of Wisconsin, Madison

DAVID GREENWOOD
Lakehead University

HANS GRUBER
University of Regensburg

CHARISSE GULOSINO
University of Memphis

KALERVO GULSON
University of New South Wales

SHERRILL HAYES
Kennesaw State University

HEGE HERMANSEN
University of Oslo

NICHOLAS HILLMAN
University of Wisconsin

STEPHEN HUTT
University of Colorado, Boulder

ROMAN LIERA
University of Southern California

JOSEPH MAXWELL
George Mason University

DANIELLE MCNAMARA
Arizona State University

PAUL MORRIS
University College London

BRENDAN O'CONNOR
Arizona State University

ANATOLI RAPOPORT
Purdue University

CHRISTOPHER REDDING
University of Florida

CHRIS TAYLOR
Cardiff University, WISERD

TINA TRUJILLO
University of California, Berkeley

VIVIAN WONG
University of Virginia

AMERICAN EDUCATIONAL RESEARCH ASSOCIATION

Tel: 202-238-3200 Fax: 202-238-3250
http://www.aera.net/pubs

FELICE J. LEVINE
Executive Director

MARTHA YAGER
Managing Editor

JOHN NEIKIRK
Director of Publications

JESSICA SIBOLD
Senior Publications Associate

Contents

Introduction

Moving Beyond the Paradigm Wars: Emergent Approaches for
   Education Research   vii
      Authors: *Margarita Pivovarova, Jeanne M. Powers,*
          and Gustavo E. Fischman

**I. Technological Innovations That Change the Scale and
Scope of Education Research**

1. Research Synthesis Infrastructures: Shaping Knowledge in Education   1
      Authors: *J. W. Hammond, Pamela A. Moss, Minh Q. Huynh,*
          and Carl Lagoze

2. Terminological "Communities": A Conceptual Mapping of Scholarship
   Identified With Education's "Global Turn"   36
      Authors: *Heela Goren, Miri Yemini, Claire Maxwell,*
          and Efrat Blumenfeld-Lieberthal

3. Place Matters: A Critical Review of Place Inquiry and Spatial
   Methods in Education Research   64
      Authors: *Alisha Butler and Kristin A. Sinclair*

4. Geospatial Analysis: A New Window Into Educational Equity,
   Access, and Opportunity   97
      Author: *Casey D. Cobb*

5. Mining Big Data in Education: Affordances and Challenges   130
      Authors: *Christian Fischer, Zachary A. Pardos, Ryan Shaun Baker,*
          Joseph Jay Williams, Padhraic Smyth, Renzhe Yu,
          Stefan Slater, Rachel Baker, and Mark Warschauer

II. Expanding the Boundaries of Education Research

6. Studying the Over-Time Construction of Knowledge in Educational
   Settings: A Microethnographic Discourse Analysis Approach   161
      Authors: *Judith L. Green, W. Douglas Baker, Monaliza Maximo Chian,*
          Carmen Vanderhoof, LeeAnna Hooper, Gregory J. Kelly,
          Audra Skukauskaite, and Melinda Z. Kalainoff

7. Emerging Perspectives on the Co-Construction of Power and
   Learning in the Learning Sciences, Mathematics Education,
   and Science Education   195
      Authors: *Thomas M. Philip and Ayush Gupta*

8. Use of Quasi-Experimental Research Designs in Education Research: Growth, Promise, and Challenges   218
    Authors: *Maithreyi Gopalan, Kelly Rosinger, and Jee Bin Ahn*

9. Linking Quantitative and Qualitative Network Approaches: A Review of Mixed Methods Social Network Analysis in Education Research   244
    Authors: *Dominik E. Froehlich, Sara Van Waes, and Hannah Schäfer*

10. Critical Counter-Narrative as Transformative Methodology for Educational Equity   269
    Authors: *Richard Miller, Katrina Liu, and Arnetha F. Ball*

III. Rethinking What We Know So Far

11. How Administrative Data Collection and Analysis Can Better Reflect Racial and Ethnic Identities   301
    Authors: *Samantha Viano and Dominique J. Baker*

12. Qualitative Comparative Analysis in Education Research: Its Current Status and Future Potential   332
    Authors: *Sebnem Cilesiz and Thomas Greckhamer*

13. Bifurcating Worlds? A Systematic Review of How Visual and Language Data Are Combined to Study Teachers and Their Teaching   370
    Authors: *Rachel E. Schachter, Donald Freeman, and Naivedya Parakkal*

14. Research on Continuous Improvement: Exploring the Complexities of Managing Educational Change   403
    Authors: *Maxwell M. Yurkofsky, Amelia J. Peterson, Jal D. Mehta, Rebecca Horwitz-Willis, and Kim M. Frumin*

About the Editors   434

About the Contributors   435

Cover image: iStock.com/99ultimate

Introduction

Moving Beyond the Paradigm Wars: Emergent Approaches for Education Research

Margarita Pivovarova
Jeanne M. Powers
Gustavo E. Fischman
Arizona State University

In 2002, the National Research Council (NRC) released a report that articulated its vision about education research (Eisenhart & Towne, 2003; Feuer et al., 2002), which focused on scientifically based research methods. The release of the report was followed by an extensive debate and is broadly understood as part of the long-standing "paradigm war"[1] in the field (Fischman & Tefera, 2014; Munoz-Najar Galvez et al., 2019).

Some of the scholars defending the criteria advanced by the report had somewhat traditionally dismissive views of education research "as something of a stepchild, reluctantly tolerated at the margins of academe and rarely trusted by policy makers, practitioners, or members of the public at large" (Lagemann, 2000, p. x). A similar perspective was advanced by Grover Whitehurst, the influential director of the Institute of Education Sciences from 2002 to 2008, who claimed that the

world of education, unlike defense, heath care, or industrial production, does not rest on a strong research base. In no other field are personal experience and ideology so frequently relied on to make policy choices, and in no other field is the research base so inadequate and little used. (Whitehurst, 2007, quoted in Hess, 2008, p. 9)

On the opposite side were those who argued that by defining scientifically based research as primarily based on quantitative approaches, the report devalued some long-standing ways of generating knowledge in education (Erickson & Gutierrez, 2002; St. Pierre, 2006; Willinsky, 2001). For the skeptics, the report was seen as another manifestation of a long-standing pejorative assessment of education scholars as using outdated, ineffective, and narrowly constructed research methods, and slow

Review of Research in Education
March 2020, Vol. 44, pp. vii–xvi
DOI: 10.3102/0091732X20909400
Chapter reuse guidelines: sagepub.com/journals-permissions
© 2020 AERA. http://rre.aera.net

to adapt to new developments. Criticizing federal policies for narrowly defining scientific research in education and arguing for a more inclusive approach to education research, Lather (2004) noted that "in spite of its [NRC's] oft-repeated intentions of balance across multiple methods, objectivity is enshrined and prediction, explanation, and verification override description, interpretation, and discovery" (p. 762).

It is hard to assess to what extent the paradigm war in education research is over (Munoz-Najar Galvez et al., 2019), but we are convinced it is necessary to move beyond it in the service of answering urgent and compelling questions for the field. This move is important because the landscapes where education research occurs have become even more complicated due in part—but not limited to—the emergence of novel knowledge infrastructures, new developments in information and communication technologies, as well as political, scientific, and cultural changes.

We want to highlight two trends. First, the predictions of both sides in the paradigm wars about the devastating effects of what each perceived as the poor research practices of their opponents (Biesta, 2020; Lather, 2004) have not destroyed the field. Indeed, based on the number of scholarly publications, attendance at scientific conferences, and enrollments in graduate programs, it appears evident that education research continues to grow as a field (Levine & Hill, 2015; McCarty, et al., 2017). Second, increased power in data-processing and technological capacities has generated new conceptual and technical challenges for education research.

These two trends have created opportunities for education researchers to (a) reconceptualize existing approaches, (b) adopt and advance methods associated with other fields, and (c) leverage new technologies to expand the capabilities of existing tools.[2] This volume highlights how education research is a sophisticated and robust field, and the diversity and complexity of the ever-shifting contexts for education research, while also featuring some novel ways of analyzing those contexts.

Our goal as editors was to create a volume that will serve as a resource for both novice and experienced education researchers for understanding how innovative methodological approaches might provide more comprehensive explanations into enduring questions, challenge existing theoretical frameworks and paradigms, or address novel challenges in the field of education. The chapters in this volume demonstrate how emerging approaches continue to address the complexities of education research—ethics, politics, diversity, and its interdisciplinary nature, to name a few—all of which make education research "the hardest-to-do science of them all" (Berliner, 2002, p. 18). Some of these approaches can also be regarded as responses to changes in the context of research that showcases how education scholars adapt to new demands and opportunities.

It is probably not surprising that most of the chapters in this volume position emergent methodologies as responses to challenges educational systems face locally, nationally, and internationally. Arguably the most prominent of these challenges[3] is to address unjust gaps in educational access and opportunities. Inspired by Ladson-Billings's (2015) call to "move from justice as theory to justice as praxis," the 2017 volume of *Review of Research in Education* was devoted to how inequities in education research and practice can be disrupted. In this introduction, we show how the chapters in the present volume extend that call and propose new methodological ways to further educational equity and promote social justice.

TECHNOLOGICAL INNOVATIONS THAT CHANGE THE SCALE AND SCOPE OF EDUCATION RESEARCH

A number of chapters in this volume address the way that technological advances have changed the scale of education research. Consider, for example, how new technologies have changed some aspects of teaching and learning. The adoption of assessment and instructional technologies (Halverson & Smith, 2009; Straub, 2009) and online learning at scale have enabled researchers to collect large amounts of data that monitor and record learning activities in online and technology-rich environments. These developments have also fostered the development of new methods of inquiry aimed at understanding these changes and their consequences.

Researchers are developing new methods to adapt to the increased scale of the research context and utilize the opportunity provided by big as well as fine-grained data, and advances in computer-based systems and software packages. Several of our authors describe the emergent methods that respond to these demands. The geographical mapping of educational data and spatial methods of analysis have allowed researchers to identify, document, and assess incidences and patterns of inequality and injustice (Cobb, Chapter 4; Butler & Sinclair, Chapter 3). Using geospatial methods, education scholars are able to examine the distribution of opportunities and access to educational and other resources. Take, for instance, spatial justice—the distribution of opportunity across geographies at multiple scales. As charter schools, vouchers, and inter- or intradistrict choice options have expanded, researchers have used Geographic Information System (GIS) mapping (Cobb, Chapter 4) and other geospatial methods (Butler & Sinclair, Chapter 3) to document how spatial location, locale, and sense of place influence the contexts and outcomes of schooling. These methods have helped us better understand the factors, such as distance between students' residences and schools, that influence the choices students and families make, and to demonstrate the segregating effects of choice.

Similarly, in Chapter 5, Fischer et al. address the challenges of the partial relocation of traditional knowledge infrastructures online by mapping the landscape of big data and their increasing use in education research. Connecting administrative and learning process data using new techniques of data mining allows researchers to understand the mechanisms of education policy effects, reveals the nuances of educational inequities, and provides insights for policymakers.

The availability of large databases, the globalization of networks, and new search engines enabled by high computing power have led to a reconceptualization of how research syntheses are conducted. As Hammond et al. point out in Chapter 1 of this volume, this traditional staple of education research should be regarded not only as a formal methodology but rather also as a process of engagement with "the ecologies of policies, practices, norms, resources, social structures, technologies, and methodologies through which knowledge is produced" (p. 2).

Analyses of big data integrated with natural language processing and network analysis complemented with qualitative analytical methods, is yet another example of how education researchers expand the boundaries of traditional methods. Goren et al. (Chapter 2) demonstrate how a novel way to review and compare large bodies of literatures across disciplines facilitates the identification of interconnections, common trends, and divergences. Yet, alongside this increased scale of data and the technological ability to condense large amounts of information, Philip and Gupta (Chapter 7) and Green et al. (Chapter 6) highlight the continued importance of attending to smaller scale processes occurring within classrooms.

EXPANDING THE BOUNDARIES OF EDUCATION RESEARCH BY BORROWING FROM OTHER DISCIPLINES

Relatedly, new methodological approaches enter education research via interdisciplinary channels as tools and methods prevalent in other fields are adopted and adapted by education researchers. For example, the spatial sciences contributed to understanding how location might perpetuate educational inequality (Cobb, Chapter 4; Butler & Sinclair, Chapter 3), and advances in social network analysis allow researchers to reconceptualize the relationship within and between educational actors and networks (Froehlich et al., Chapter 9). The multidisciplinary nature of geospatial methods and social network analysis provides opportunities to integrate the insights and efforts from other fields to raise new questions and identify otherwise undetected patterns and phenomena. Similarly, Miller et al. (Chapter 10) highlight how education researchers used counternarrative drawn from critical race theory, which has its origins in legal analysis, to highlight how racial inequality has been deeply institutionalized within educational systems and practices.

Another example of the integration and adaptation of methods is the use of quasi-experimental research designs based on naturally occurring experiments to produce causal claims. In the wake of the "credibility revolution" in economics (Angrist & Pischke, 2010) and the strong emphasis on an evidence-based approach to policy and interventions by the government (No Child Left Behind, 2002), an increased number of education researchers have utilized quasi-experimental research designs (Angrist, 2004). In Chapter 8, Gopalan et al. describe the methods and standards for causal inference in education research formalized by the What Works Clearinghouse (WWC). The influence of the WWC standards for evaluation of education interventions in education research is also evident in the analysis of the WWC as one of the major research synthesis infrastructures (Hammond et al., Chapter 1).

Yet another example of merging approaches within the discipline is what Green et al. describe in Chapter 6 as a microethnographic-discourse approach. This logic of inquiry leverages the knowledge and experiences of researchers around the globe in their respective contexts to explore potential common understandings of learning in classrooms. Similar to many chapters in this volume, the guiding principle of the telling case studies analyzed by Green et al. in this chapter is to understand and support the needs of diverse learners in different educational contexts, and to ensure their access to educational opportunities. They also highlight how disciplinary knowledge is an important resource for researchers as they come to understand how students learn in different settings.

Continuing the conversation about learning, Philip and Gupta (Chapter 7) analyze the vertical and horizontal interactions between learners and their environments in math and science settings. Presenting the evidence bases on interaction and microgenetic analyses within the critical social theory framework, Philip and Gupta question the notion that students' engagements with macro-level identities and ideologies in spaces of learning are stable, and underscore the need for explicit analytical attention to intersectionality.

Rethinking What We Know So Far

New approaches to research are often developed by merging existing methodologies between as well as within different types of methods and reconceptualizing traditional ways of asking and answering questions. In education research, as in other social sciences, "the social and cultural contexts of the phenomenon studied are crucial for understanding the operation of causal mechanisms" (Maxwell, 2004, p. 6). This requires approaches that combine a variety of methods and perspectives that allow researchers to examine phenomena from different angles.

Yurkofsky et al. in Chapter 14 utilize the tools of social network analysis to demonstrate the relationships between different continuous improvement methods. In that chapter, authors also rethink the directionality of the connection between practice and research—one of the challenges intrinsic to education research. They point out that the failure of both experimental and implementation paradigms to find policy solutions occurred because these solutions were developed separately from the context-specific problems facing the educators they are meant to serve. The authors argue that researchers should allow practitioners to identify problems and participate in knowledge generation to develop solutions to those problems of practice.

Building appropriate infrastructures for meaningful interactions between researchers and practitioners will foster research that is useful to practice. That said, the success of the infrastructure depends on the willingness of teachers and other practitioners to participate in the research process. Understanding teachers, their teaching, and their thinking is critical if researchers want to engage educational professionals in a more substantive way. Chapter 13 by Schachter et al. introduces a solution to the conceptual and methodological challenge of documenting the relationship between what teachers think and how they act, or between their private and public identities. These identities, or teachers' public and private worlds, can be captured methodologically by visual and language data. Researchers have repeatedly identified the disconnect between the two worlds, what the authors characterize as bifurcation. In the presence of these bifurcating worlds, researchers should balance their use of visual and language data, but this is rare in reality—few studies draw conclusions from equally weighted visual and language data. This raises both methodological and theoretical concerns and suggest the need for more integrative research procedures. The reconceptualization of conventional approaches is also the focus of Froehlich et al. (Chapter 9), who show how traditionally quantitative social network analysis benefits from incorporating mixed-methods and qualitative approaches to research. They also highlight some of the challenges of mixed-methods social network analysis.

Another example of methodological craftsmanship in combining existing methods to uncover new perspectives and illuminate new approaches is the use of counter-narrative (Chapter 10, Miller et al.). As a tool developed to foster education equity, critical counter-narrative borrows from narrative inquiry, autoethnography, and life history and is based on the premises of critical race theory. Critical counter-narrative is a timely and absolutely necessary approach for a society that is becoming increasingly and more openly diverse because it gives power and voice to marginalized communities beyond storytelling. Miller et al. also point to the ways that this rigorous scientific approach serves as a pedagogical tool with the potential to transform teaching practice and how it might be expanded to more effectively promote educational equity.

As showcased by all the chapters in this volume, the interdisciplinary nature of education research requires synthesizing frameworks and methods from different perspectives and suggests that education research in part depends on advancements in other disciplines (NRC, 2002). For example, the review of qualitative comparative analysis (QCA) by Cilesiz and Greckhamer (Chapter 12) spans political science, psychology, sociology, management, and the organizational sciences to show how education researchers can use QCA to reconceptualize causal relationships in complex settings characterized by conjunction, equifinality, and asymmetry. While still not completely embraced by scholars in education, the logic of Boolean algebra is a promising approach to help us better address social inequality by highlighting the complex relationships between the factors associated with disadvantage and privilege through the lens of intersectionality. Cilesiz and Greckhamer show how other fields and disciplines have approached similar questions and encourage education researchers to take advantage of QCA, especially in the area of policy analysis.

The issues we highlight above have also created new challenges for research synthesis as well as ethical issues that researchers will need to consider as they move forward. The instability of research databases such as ProQuest due to frequent updates of search algorithms creates challenges with the replicability of research syntheses (Schachter et al., Chapter 13). Hammond et al. (Chapter 1) emphasized the need for a new approach to the standards of research synthesis that could vary between full flexibility on one end and common standards on the other end. Such an approach requires understanding the mechanisms for quality control among the existing synthesis infrastructures and the accessibility they provide to researchers. Considerations of accessibility versus privacy is one of the central issues in using big data and specifically administrative data. The trade-off researchers face is on the one hand limiting the range of questions to be addressed and on the other hand protecting the subjects of research and their private information (Fischer et al., Chapter 5).

The expanded use of administrative data has also raised questions about the extent to which it allows researchers to adequately address the ways race shapes educational phenomena. As Viano and Baker (Chapter 11) observe, there is a tension between the static racial categories often used in administrative data and the comparatively fluid nature of racial identities. While administrative data could provide researchers with possibilities to analyze the fluidity of racial/ethnic identities and capture the dynamics in how identities are defined, they also highlight a need for a new framework that could address the complexity of the data themselves (Viano & Baker, Chapter 11).

Spatial analysis and the associated use of geographical methods revealed the need to develop new theoretical perspectives as many of the reviewed studies that employ GIS methods are undertheorized in that they use a technique without being accompanied by a clear theory. To address this challenge, Butler and Sinclair (Chapter 3) propose merging GIS and other spatial methods with critical spatial research paradigms and perspectives to explore the experiences of communities that are most often affected by inequity and spatial injustice. Relatedly, in Chapter 13, Schachter et al. note a lack of explicit theorization of the connection between visual and language data and how these two types of information allow researchers to understand the link between teachers' private lives and the public process of teaching.

CONCLUSION

What I am going to argue is that the critical mind, if it is to renew itself and be relevant again, is to be found in the cultivation of a stubbornly realist attitude. (Latour, 2004, p. 231)

Our main motivation and goal when we conceptualized this volume for *Review of Research in Education* was to contribute to "the cultivation of a stubbornly realist attitude." Integral to our realist perspective is the belief that methods and methodological approaches have a peculiar place in the inquiry process—they are often overshadowed by the significance of the research question and the consequences of the answer and solutions to it. Unlike theories and conceptual frameworks or paradigms that set down the motivation, intent, and expectations for systematic inquiry, methods provide systems and principles for carrying out that inquiry. In this volume, the authors brought research methods and methodologies to their well-deserved spotlight.

The chapters in this volume describe approaches that cannot be easily summarized by the traditional distinction of quantitative versus qualitative methods. They highlight how moving beyond the paradigm wars and engaging in key concerns within the field can foster the innovation needed to adapt to the changing environment for education research and advance the field. The different contributions also suggest how we might move beyond the easy temptation of defending sides in the paradigm war to engage with matters of central concern to the field, and this is how innovations and adaptations to the changing environments for modern education research are generated.

The contributions to this volume also foster the dialogue between conceptual perspectives and technical and methodological procedures. There are no perfect methods that will provide effective tools for all educational problems, and as the authors of this volume explicitly showed, testing theoretical ideas require new methods, and new methods call for revising existing conceptualizations and theorizations.

The methods, models, and processes discussed in this volume demonstrate that education researchers are quite adept at adapting and using state-of-the art methods such as natural language processing, geographical methods, and network analysis. This is in sharp contrast with what is often the dismissive perspective that education researchers do not keep up with other fields in how they develop rigorous procedures and adapt new methods.[4] Education researchers not only adapt methods but also develop creative interdisciplinary approaches such as combining video and language data. The interdisciplinary orientation of the field is evident in the multitude of methods used to study educational phenomena, and also in the combinations of these methods. As the authors in this volume demonstrate, these include but are not limited to geospatial data and methods used to study justice, critical social theory combined with the methodological approaches of interaction analysis and microgenetic analysis to understand the dynamics of power and learning, or the use of administrative data or traditional qualitative methods to study race and identity.

Overall, the methods discussed in this volume provide evidence of the strengthening of the interdisciplinary and intersectional perspectives in the field (Tefera et al., 2018). We are also hopeful that our readers will agree that the chapters in this volume reflect Latour's (2004) particular perspective of being critical: "That is generating more ideas than we have received, inheriting from a prestigious critical tradition but not letting it die away, or 'dropping into quiescence' like a piano no longer struck" (p. 248).

NOTES

[1]In its perhaps most neutral definition, the "paradigm war" was a "within-field scientist-to-scientist discussion in which the principal concern was whether research in the field met commonly-accepted scientific standards" (Walters et al., 2009, p. 26). For other, perhaps more critical perspectives, see Anderson and Herr (1999), Bloch (2004), and Moss et al. (2009).

[2]While we divided the chapters thematically for the sake of organization by placing them within one of these themes, all of the chapters bridge more than one of these themes.

[3]Another pressing challenge for education researchers is to recognize that as a field we have a key role in altering the dialogue of educational discourse to more explicitly and extensively address the climate crisis as well as the challenges and affordances for education research of the rapid developments in the fields of artificial intelligence, machine learning, robotics, and brain research. However, we did not receive submissions explicitly addressing these important issues

[4]For example, Maris Vinovskis, a distinguished historian of education, commented that when compared to some of the other social and behavioral disciplines, "Educational research

appears to be relatively backward and underdeveloped . . . second-rate and rather unsophisticated" (Henig, 2008, p. 41, footnotes omitted).

REFERENCES

Anderson, G. L., & Herr, K. (1999). The new paradigm wars: Is there room for rigorous practitioner knowledge in schools and universities? *Educational Researcher, 28*(5), 12–40. https://doi.org/10.3102/0013189X028005012

Angrist, J. D. (2004). American education research changes tack. *Oxford Review of Economic Policy, 20*(2), 198–212. https://doi.org/10.1093/oxrep/grh011

Angrist, J. D., & Pischke, J. S. (2010). The credibility revolution in empirical economics: How better research design is taking the con out of econometrics. *Journal of Economic Perspectives, 24*(2), 3–30. https://doi.org/10.1257/jep.24.2.3

Berliner, D. (2002). Educational research: The hardest science of all. *Educational Researcher, 31*(8), 18–20. https://doi.org/10.3102/0013189X031008018

Biesta, G. (2020). *Educational research: An unorthodox introduction.* Bloomsbury.

Bloch, M. (2004). A discourse that disciplines, governs, and regulates: The national research council's report on scientific research in education. *Qualitative Inquiry, 10*(1), 96–110. https://doi.org/10.1177/1077800403259482

Eisenhart, M., & Towne, L. (2003). Contestation and change in national policy on "scientifically based" education research. *Educational Researcher, 32*(7), 31–38. https://doi.org/10.3102/0013189X032007031

Erickson, F., & Gutierrez, K. (2002). Culture, rigor, and science in educational research. *Educational Researcher, 31*(8), 21–24. https://doi.org/10.3102/0013189X031008021

Feuer, M. J., Towne, L., & Shavelson, R. J. (2002). Scientific culture and educational research. *Educational Researcher, 31*(8), 4–14. https://doi.org/10.3102/0013189X031008004

Fischman, G. E., & Tefera, A. (2014). Qualitative inquiry in an age of educationalese. *Education Policy Analysis Archives, 22*, 7. https://doi.org/10.14507/epaa.v22n7.2014

Halverson, R., & Smith, A. (2009). How new technologies have (and have not) changed teaching and learning in schools. *Journal of Computing in Teacher Education, 26*(2), 49–54. https://files.eric.ed.gov/fulltext/EJ907118.pdf

Henig, J. (2008). The evolving relationship between researchers and public policy. In F. Hess (Ed.), *When research matters: How scholarship influences education policy* (pp. 41–62). Harvard University Press.

Hess, F. (2008). *When research matters: How scholarship influences education policy.* Harvard University Press.

Ladson-Billings, G. (2015). *Just justice* [American Educational Research Association Social Justice in Education Award lecture video]. https://www.youtube.com/watch?v=ofB_tloTYhI

Lagemann, P. (2000). *An elusive science: The troubling history of educational research.* University of Chicago Press.

Lather, P. (2004). Scientific research in education: A critical perspective1. *British Educational Research Journal, 30*(6), 759–772. https://doi.org/10.1080/0141192042000279486

Latour, B. (2004). Why has critique run out of steam? From matters of fact to matters of concern. *Critical Inquiry, 30*(2), 225–248. https://doi.org/10.1086/421123

Levine, F. J., & Hill, L. D. (2015). The field of educational research. In J. D. Wright (Ed.), *International encyclopedia of the social and behavioral sciences* (Vol. 7, pp. 279–288). Elsevier. https://doi.org/10.1016/B978-0-08-097086-8.92156-1

Maxwell, J. A. (2004). Causal explanation, qualitative research, and scientific inquiry in education. *Educational Researcher, 33*(2), 3–11. https://doi.org/10.3102/0013189X033002003

McCarty, T. L., Mancevice, N., Lemire, S., & O'Neil, H. F. (2017). Introduction: Education research for a new century: A renewed vision of interdisciplinarity. *American Educational Research Journal, 54*(1 Suppl.), 5S–22S. https://doi.org/10.3102/0002831216687340

Moss, P. A, Phillips, D. C., Erickson, F. D., Floden, R. E., Lather, P. A., & Schneider, B. L. (2009) Learning from our differences: A dialogue across perspectives on quality in education research. *Educational Researcher, 38*(7), 501–517. https://doi.org/10.3102/001318 9X09348351

Munoz-Najar Galvez, S., Heiberger, R., & McFarland, D. (2019). Paradigm wars revisited: A cartography of graduate research in the field of education (1980–2010). *American Educational Research Journal.* Advance online publication. https://doi .org/10.3102/0002831219860511

National Research Council. (2002). *Scientific research in education.* National Academies Press.

No Child Left Behind Act of 2001, P.L. 107-110, 20 U.S.C. § 6319 (2002).

St. Pierre, E. A. (2006). Scientifically based research in education: Epistemology and ethics. *Adult Education Quarterly, 56*(4), 239–266. https://doi.org/10.1177/0741713606289025

Straub, E. T. (2009). Understanding technology adoption: Theory and future directions for informal learning. *Review of Educational Research, 79*(2), 625–649. https://doi.org /10.3102/0034654308325896

Tefera, A. A., Powers, J. M., & Fischman, G. E. (2018). Intersectionality in education: A conceptual aspiration and research imperative. *Review of Research in Education, 42*(1), vii–xvii. https://doi.org/10.3102/0091732X18768504

Walters, P. B., Lareau, A., & Ranis, S. (Eds.). (2009). *Education research on trial: Policy reform and the call for scientific rigor.* Routledge. https://doi.org/10.4324/9780203928684

Willinsky, J. (2001). The strategic education research program and the public value of research. *Educational Researcher, 30*(1), 5–14. https://doi.org/10.3102/0013189X030001005

Chapter 1

Research Synthesis Infrastructures: Shaping Knowledge in Education

J. W. Hammond
Pamela A. Moss
Minh Q. Huynh
Carl Lagoze
University of Michigan

Research syntheses provide one means of managing the proliferation of research knowledge by integrating learnings across primary research studies. What it means to appropriately synthesize research, however, remains a matter of debate: Syntheses can assume a variety of forms, each with important implications for the shape knowledge takes and the interests it serves. To help shed light on these differences and their stakes, this chapter provides a critical comparative review of six research synthesis infrastructures, entities that support research syntheses through investments they make in synthesis production and/or publication— enabling (and constraining) the ways knowledge takes shape. Identifying our critical cases through purposive selection, we examined research synthesis infrastructure variations with respect to four different kinds of investments they make: in the genres of synthesis they support, in their promotion of synthesis quality, in sponsoring stakeholder engagement, and in creating the conditions for collective work. We draw on this comparison to suggest some of the potential changes and challenges in store for education researchers in future years.

With bodies of research continually expanding, it is arguably impossible for education scholars to "know" every study relevant to an area of interest. Investments in methodologies for integrating learnings from existing research are increasingly crucial for developing and managing knowledge. *Research syntheses* integrate learnings from "primary" empirical research studies to develop theory and to enable more robust conclusions about the phenomena studied. Formal synthesis methodologies only partly account for how syntheses are conducted and reported—much less how they shape

Review of Research in Education
March 2020, Vol. 44, pp. 1–35
DOI: 10.3102/0091732X20907350
Chapter reuse guidelines: sagepub.com/journals-permissions
© 2020 AERA. http://rre.aera.net

knowledge and how we engage with it. Methodologies are embedded in larger socio-technical infrastructures that enable and constrain how we can collectively learn from existing research. Taking stock of research syntheses requires us to engage the *knowledge infrastructures* they participate in: the ecologies of policies, practices, norms, resources, social structures, technologies, and methodologies through which knowledge is produced. In this chapter, we examine *research synthesis infrastructures* (*RSIs*): knowledge infrastructures that subtend and shape the synthesis of research—in turn, enabling and constraining our engagements with(in) it.[1]

Science studies scholars who research *infrastructures* define them as forms of "substrate: something upon which something else 'runs' or 'operates'" (Star & Ruhleder, 1996, p. 112)—for example, the electric grid, a municipal sewage system, or the Internet. Infrastructure

refers to the prior work (be it building, organization, agreement on standards, and so forth) that supports and enables the activity we are really engaged in doing. More particularly, infrastructure refers to those systems, technologies, organizations, and built artifacts that *do not need to be reconsidered at the start of a new venture* [emphasis added]. (Slota & Bowker, 2017, p. 529)

By extension, *knowledge infrastructures* can be understood as "robust networks of people, artifacts, and institutions that generate, share, and maintain specific knowledge about the human and natural worlds [italics removed]" (Edwards, 2010, p. 17; see also Borgman, 2015; Edwards et al., 2013). For well over a century, education scholarship has been supported by knowledge infrastructures that include libraries, publishers, professional organizations, and the Academy itself—with books and journal articles as its primary "knowledge objects" (Bowker, 2017, p. 391). In recent decades, research syntheses have emerged as increasingly important knowledge objects for empirical scholarship: "Synthesis extends the analysis of the characteristics of individual research studies . . . to investigate what they mean as a *collective* body of knowledge," meaning that a research synthesis "generates new knowledge and understanding in response to the review research question" (Thomas, O'Mara-Eves, et al., 2017, p. 182). This work has been described as providing education research an "architecture" (Murphy et al., 2017, p. 3)—an intellectual foundation on which present practices and future developments can depend.

Thanks to the *Review of Educational Research*, journals dedicated to reviewing education research have been around for almost a century, but the modern rise of explicit research synthesis *methodology* can be traced back to the 1970s, when education researchers Feldman (1971) and Light and Smith (1971) highlighted the potential of methodologically explicit integrations of research, and when—in his 1976 AERA (American Educational Research Association) presidential address—Glass advanced a new synthesis methodology in the form of *meta-analysis*, which pools effect sizes across quantitative studies (Glass, 1976; see also Chalmers et al., 2002). Notably, while not invoking the word "infrastructure," Glass followed up this address with a 1977 *Review of Research in Education* article that noted how technical issues of research integration were underpinned by a host of nontechnical factors and forces—among them, access to primary research (e.g., through libraries or databases), disciplinary incentives for undertaking and publishing syntheses, and communal norms and standards for conducting and reporting research (Glass, 1977, pp. 353–354).

Research syntheses have become complexly (and controversially) enmeshed in the disciplinary ecology of education research, with synthesis methodologies and infrastructures emerging (and evolving) in response to political pressures or disciplinary commitments—and with researchers regularly debating about synthesis work in education (e.g., Ginsburg & Smith, 2016; Gough & Thomas, 2016; Green & Skukauskaitė, 2008; Slavin, 2008; Suri & Clarke, 2009; Zawacki-Richter et al., 2020). Following Edwards et al. (2013), an *infrastructural* understanding of synthesis work requires us to investigate how knowledge infrastructures configure the "shape and possibility of knowledge" (p. 15) and to consider whose interests are advanced and whose are constrained, ignored, or hindered by different infrastructural configurations (pp. 14–15). Considerations like these take on particular urgency in the present digital age, when the ubiquity of networked, mobile, and cloud computing promise to disrupt the "control zone" (Lagoze, 2010) within which scholarly results are evaluated, disseminated, and curated (see Borgman, 2015). Big data and automation are augmenting the ways research syntheses can be—and are being—produced and used (see Gough, Thomas, & Oliver, 2019; Snilstveit et al., 2018; White, 2019). As Bowker (2017) notes, "The great potential of the current moment is to re-imagine the engines of knowledge production in ways which produce new forms of alignment" (p. 397). The risk is that these changes will occur without critical reflection on their consequences in time to shift their trajectories. How might we take advantage of these opportunities to enhance our collective learning from research?

We build toward answers to these overarching questions with the following (interrelated) analytical questions about infrastructural investments RSIs make, consistently asked of six RSI cases we review:

- What are the primary *genres* or types of synthesis RSIs invest in?
- How do RSIs invest in promoting or controlling synthesis *quality*?
- In what ways do RSIs invest in outreach to and engagement with *stakeholders*?
- Through what structures and tools do RSIs invest in *collective work*?

Answering these questions empowers us to critically grapple with ways current RSI configurations shape knowledge in education, and (paraphrasing Bowker) to re-imagine the engines of research synthesis production moving forward.

METHODOLOGY AND RSI CASE OVERVIEWS

We examine six RSI cases with instructively different features relevant to our analytical questions. To be considered as a potential case, RSIs had to be active as of 2005, noncommercial (with exceptions made for commercial publishing partnerships), and primarily configured to support the production and dissemination of research syntheses. To select cases, we drew on prior knowledge of prominent organizations sponsoring research syntheses and conducted a more extensive online search, informed by insights from the secondary literature reviewing such organizations (e.g., Green & Skukauskaitė, 2008; Means et al., 2015; Slavin, 2008), from prominent synthesis methodology textbooks (e.g., Booth et al., 2016; Cooper et al., 2019; Gough et al., 2017b), and from the Systematic Review Toolbox— a website that curates synthesis-supporting tools (http://systematicreviewtools .com/). Seeking to illustrate instructive variations in RSI configurations (not an exhaustive overview of the field), we privileged RSIs with longer histories, more explicit guidance, broader recognition, and/or instructively different features. We included not only education-centric RSIs but also health- and social science-centric RSIs, because such RSIs have served as models that education-centric RSIs have regularly been compared with; they also offered alternative configurations from which we could learn. Below, we provide brief overviews of (and reasons for selecting) RSI cases.

Three selected RSI have historically privileged systematic reviews of intervention effectiveness (and, where possible, meta-analysis)—a synthesis genre often colloquially called "what works" reviews—although the latter two RSIs now support reviews addressing other kinds of questions:

- *What Works Clearinghouse (WWC)*, included for its significance in U.S. education. An outgrowth of the 2002 Education Sciences Reform Act, WWC seeks to provide "education decisionmakers" with "access to the best evidence about the effectiveness of education practices, products, programs, and policies . . . by identifying existing research on education interventions, assessing the quality of this research, and summarizing and disseminating the evidence from studies that meet WWC Standards" (What Works Clearinghouse, 2020a, p. 1).
- *Cochrane (formerly the Cochrane Collaboration)*, an international RSI selected for its major historical significance, including as a model against which other RSIs are often compared (e.g., Slavin, 2008). Founded in 1993, Cochrane seeks "to promote evidence-informed health decision making by producing high quality, relevant, accessible systematic reviews and other synthesized research evidence" (Chandler et al., 2019, p. 1).
- *The Campbell Collaboration (Campbell)*, an international RSI founded in 2000 (and closely related to Cochrane), selected because it supports decision-making regarding "the effectiveness of programs, policies, and practices (and, in some instances, closely related topics) in the areas of crime and justice, education, international development, and social welfare" (Campbell Collaboration, 2019, p. 6).[2] Campbell's methodological guidance is now largely coordinated with Cochrane's, but we treat them separately below wherever their infrastructural elements significantly distinguish them.

We selected one RSI, less well known in the United States, because it supports synthesis methodologies that challenge/expand those historically privileged by WWC, Cochrane, and Campbell:

- *The Evidence for Policy and Practice Information and Coordinating Centre (EPPI-Centre)*, founded in 1993 and based in the University College London's Social Science Research Unit, selected for the diversity of synthesis genres and methodologies they support. EPPI-Centre focuses on "complexity and mixed methods reviews to understand research relevant to decision making as well as methods for how that research is used in practice" (EPPI-Centre, n.d., para. 2), supporting "reviews driven by any research questions and including any research methods and types of data" (Gough et al., 2017a, p. 12).[3]

Finally, we included two venerable RSIs because their infrastructural elements depart in significant ways from other selected RSIs:

- *Review of Education Research (RER)*, chosen as one prominent example of the many journals focused on research syntheses. "Since its inception in 1931," editors Murphy et al. (2017) write, "*RER* has stood as a prestigious journal within the field of education, publishing critically important reviews of research focused on educational constructs, processes, and outcomes" (pp. 3–4).
- *The National Academies of Sciences, Engineering, and Medicine (National Academies)*, a private nonprofit that began in 1863 as the National Academy of Sciences, incorporated to "investigate, examine, experiment, and report upon any subject of science or art" (quoted in Feuer & Maranto, 2010, p. 260). National Academies was chosen as a prominent example of the many learned societies that synthesize and publicize scientific knowledge.

Importantly, our selection of RSIs—especially *RER* and National Academies—is broader than is typical for comparative reviews of research synthesis-supporting entities (but see Slavin, 2008, p. 5; Zawacki-Richter et al., 2020). Synthesis methodology scholarship now constitutes an active field, complete with journals (e.g., *Research Synthesis Methods, Systematic Reviews*). Although *RER* and National Academies significantly depart from this tradition (and from more "conventional" RSIs associated with it), they nevertheless produce research syntheses and expand the range of answers to our critical questions. Table 1 provides an overview of the six RSIs.

These RSIs routinely evolve, in ways small and large. Our analysis focuses on each RSI's public documentation (e.g., handbooks, standards, software, policy statements) appearing/referenced on their websites as of January 8, 2020; we also considered external literature providing relevant context and/or commentary, though except where otherwise noted, data regarding RSIs were drawn from their websites (see Table 1). While the issues we raise are (we argue) enduring and forward-looking, the RSI

TABLE 1

Overview of Research Synthesis Infrastructure (RSI) Cases

Name	Founded	Focus and Mission	Website	Primary Review Genre	Primary Guidance Documents[a]	Orientation Toward Quality	Primary Stakeholders	Primary Digital Tools and Automations[b]
The Campbell Collaboration (Campbell)	2000	"The Campbell Collaboration is an international network that supports the preparation and dissemination of high quality systematic reviews of research evidence on the effectiveness of social programs, policies, and practices. The mission of Campbell is to promote positive social change by contributing to better-informed decisions and greater effectiveness for public and private services around the world" (Campbell Collaboration, 2019, p. 5).	https://campbellcollaboration.org/	• Systematic reviews	• *Campbell Systematic Reviews: Policies and Guidelines* (Campbell Collaboration, 2019) • *Methodological Expectations of Campbell Collaboration Intervention Reviews (MECCIR)* (Methods Coordinating Group of the Campbell Collaboration, 2019a, 2019b)	Primarily procedural control	"Campbell systematic reviews are intended to inform policymakers, practitioners, researchers, and other interested parties about the extent, quality, and findings of the available research evidence on the effectiveness of social programs, policies, or practices" (Campbell Collaboration, 2019, p. 7).	• Archie • Web-based effect size calculator • RevMan • Covidence • EPPI-Reviewer
Cochrane	1993	"Cochrane is a global network of health and social care practitioners, researchers, patient advocates, and others, with a mission to promote evidence-informed decision making by producing high quality, relevant, accessible systematic reviews and other synthesized research evidence (www.cochrane.org)" (Chandler et al., 2019, p. 1).	https://www.cochrane.org/	• Systematic reviews	• *Cochrane Handbook for Systematic Reviews of Interventions* (2nd ed.; Higgins, Thomas, et al., 2019) • *Methodological Expectations of Cochrane Intervention Reviews (MECIR)* (Higgins, Lasserson et al., 2019)	Primarily procedural control	"Stakeholders typically include: patients and consumers; consumer advocates; policy makers and other public officials; guideline developers; professional organizations; researchers; funders of health services and research; healthcare practitioners, and, on occasion, journalists and other media professionals" (Lasserson et al., 2019, p. 6).	• Archie • GRADEpro GDT • RevMan • Covidence • EPPI-Reviewer

(continued)

TABLE 1 (CONTINUED)

Name	Founded	Focus and Mission	Website	Primary Review Genre	Primary Guidance Documents[a]	Orientation Toward Quality	Primary Stakeholders	Primary Digital Tools and Automations[b]
The Evidence for Policy and Practice Information and Coordinating Centre (EPPI-Centre)	1993	"The EPPI-Centre's main business is conducting and supporting systematic reviews of social science research relevant to different areas of public policy. . . . The EPPI-Centre provides a system for conducting, storing and disseminating systematic reviews relevant to public policy; searchable registers of reviews and primary research; training programmes to build capacity for undertaking systematic reviews; and web-based systems for national and international collaboration" (Oakley et al., 2005, p. 6).	https://eppi.ioe.ac.uk/	• Systematic reviews	• An Introduction to Systematic Reviews (Gough et al., 2017b)	Primarily conceptual guidance and professional judgment	EPPI-Centre's main stakeholders include not only researchers but also those who have a stake in public policy, generally: "The stakeholders for public services include the people the services are established to serve, the people who manage or work in them, and taxpayers and others who fund them" (Rees & Oliver, 2017, p. 20).	• EPPI-Reviewer
National Academies of Science, Engineering, and Medicine (National Academies)	1863	"For more than 150 years, the Academies have been advising the nation on issues of science, technology, and medicine; ever since an 1863 Congressional charter signed by President Lincoln authorized this non-governmental institution to honor top scientists with membership and to serve the nation whenever called upon. . . . Each year, more than 6,000 of these experts are selected to serve on hundreds of study committees that are convened to answer specific sets of questions. All serve without pay" (National Academies, n.d.-b, "Study Process Overview" section).	https://www.nationalacademies.org/	• Consensus study reports	• Guidelines for the Review of Reports of the National Academies of Sciences, Engineering, and Medicine (National Academies, n.d.-a) • Our Study Processes (National Academies, n.d.-b) • Policy on Committee Composition and Balance and Conflicts of Interest for Committees Used in the Development of Reports (National Academies, 2003)	Primarily conceptual guidance and professional judgment	Within its mission to advise the nation and shape public opinion, National Academies serves not just the general public but also a "complex client base [that] includes federal agencies, private foundations, and the scientific community itself" (Feuer & Maranto, 2010, p. 272).	• None

(continued)

TABLE 1 (CONTINUED)

Name	Founded	Focus and Mission	Website	Primary Review Genre	Primary Guidance Documents[a]	Orientation Toward Quality	Primary Stakeholders	Primary Digital Tools and Automations[b]
Review of Educational Research (RER)	1931	"The *Review of Educational Research* publishes critical, integrative reviews of research literature bearing on education. Such reviews should include conceptualizations, interpretations, and syntheses of literature and scholarly work in a field broadly relevant to education and educational research. . . . *RER* does not publish original empirical research, and all analyses should be incorporated in a broader integrative review" (*Review of Educational Research*, n.d.-a, para. 1).	https://journals.sagepub.com/home/rer	Critical integrative reviews	• *Aims and Scope* (*Review of Educational Research*, n.d.-a) • *Manuscript Submission Guidelines* (*Review of Educational Research*, n.d.-b)	Primarily conceptual guidance and professional judgment	Although the journal *RER* sets out to publish research with "implications for the educational problems and issues affecting our national and global societies" (*Review of Educational Research*, n.d.-a, para. 11), its primary audience is education researchers themselves (i.e., "the broad readership of *RER*") (para. 16).	• None

(continued)

TABLE 1 (CONTINUED)

Name	Founded	Focus and Mission	Website	Primary Review Genre	Primary Guidance Documents[a]	Orientation Toward Quality	Primary Stakeholders	Primary Digital Tools and Automations[b]
What Works Clearinghouse (WWC)	2002	"The WWC is an initiative of the U.S. Department of Education's Institute of Education Sciences (IES), which was established under the Education Sciences Reform Act of 2002. It is an important part of IES's strategy to use rigorous and relevant research, evaluation, and statistics to improve our nation's education system. The mission of the WWC is to be **a central and trusted source of scientific evidence for what works in education.** The WWC examines research about interventions that focus on improving educationally relevant outcomes, including those for students and educators" (WWC, 2020b, p. 1).	https://ies.ed.gov/ncee/wwc/FWW	• Systematic reviews	• *What Works Clearinghouse™: Standards Handbook* (WWC, 2020b) • *What Works Clearinghouse™: Procedures Handbook* (WWC, 2020a)	Primarily procedural control	With particular attention to education policy and practice in the United States, WWC invests its energies in supporting an education-centric stakeholder community (composed of teachers, as well as policymakers and administrators) in "mak[ing] evidence-based decisions" (WWC, n.d.-a).	• None

Note. Bolded text is bold in the original.

[a]The materials cited as "primary guidance documents" represent—as of January 8, 2020—the most recent versions associated with the primary synthesis genres each RSI supports; they do not represent the full diversity of guidance materials that these RSIs develop and/or publish. Additionally, Cochrane, Campbell, EPPI-Centre, and *RER* publish (or link to) methodology articles not listed here; and while Campbell currently adapts and/or links to primary guidance documents produced by Cochrane, the table lists only those documents produced by the RSI in question itself. This column lists only the primary digital tools and automations for supporting synthesis production that were publicized online by the RSIs themselves at the time we are writing this chapter. Additionally, while not captured in this table, Campbell and Cochrane link to the Systematic Review Toolbox (http://systematicreviewtools.com/), which maintains an extensive database of synthesis-supporting tools.

[b]This column lists only the primary digital tools and automations for supporting synthesis production that were publicized online by the RSIs themselves at the time we are writing this chapter. Additionally, while not captured in this table, Campbell and Cochrane link to the Systematic Review Toolbox (http://systematicreviewtools.com/), which maintains an extensive database of synthesis-supporting tools.

comparisons illustrating these issues reflect a snapshot in time. Infrastructure studies sometimes involve network analyses and ethnographic research (e.g., Star & Ruhleder, 1996), including considerations of "infrastructuring"—that is, infrastructure as a function of complex, ongoing processes and design-related activities (e.g., Karasti, 2014; Pipek & Wulf, 2009)—but such research was beyond this review's goals and scope.[4] In analyzing available documentation, we drew on comparative case study research—especially structured, focused comparison (George & Bennett, 2005)— seeking information relevant to our critical questions about *genre, quality, stakeholders*, and *collective work*. For each RSI, we asked a senior scholar who is/was in a leadership role within the RSI to review an earlier draft for accuracy and fairness.

FINDINGS

We contrast how RSIs invest in and shape knowledge by considering

- which primary *genres* of research synthesis they support,
- how they promote and control *quality*,
- how they engage *stakeholders*, and
- how they support *collective work* in knowledge production.

These kinds of investments, examined separately below, are intricately interrelated— a circumstance to which we turn in the Discussion and Conclusion.

Genre

The primary synthesis genres RSIs sponsor represent a priori positions regarding the types of research that should be synthesized and the forms such syntheses should take. Investments in genre can have institutional ramifications for the kinds of research that are funded and rewarded—and thus for the kinds of knowledge that get generated. Apart from National Academies and *RER*, the examined RSIs identified *systematic reviews* as the primary syntheses they support. Generally, a systematic review can be described as "a review of existing research using explicit, accountable rigorous research methods" (Gough et al., 2017a, p. 4)—but across RSIs, what counts as "systematic" can vary significantly (see also Gough & Thomas, 2017). For Cochrane, for instance,

A systematic review attempts to collate all the empirical evidence that fits pre-specified eligibility criteria in order to answer a specific research question. It uses explicit, systematic methods that are selected with a view to minimizing bias, thus providing more reliable findings from which conclusions can be drawn and decisions made. . . . (Lasserson et al., 2019, p. 4)

This emphasis on identifying *all* studies that meet eligibility criteria (i.e., comprehensive or "exhaustive" searching) is more controversial. EPPI-Centre staff caution that "for an 'exhaustive' approach to be manageable, the scope of the review needs to be limited" (G. Brunton et al., 2017, p. 98), with emphasis placed on crafting "a 'reasonable' search strategy" that documents choices made and efforts "to minimise . . . biases"

(p. 100). As an alternative, EPPI-Centre offers *purposive searching*: "identifying studies that contain new conceptualisations of the phenomenon of interest" until the point "of *saturation*," where no new concepts of interest are contributed (G. Brunton et al., 2017, p. 101)—an approach Cochrane also acknowledges for synthesizing qualitative evidence (Noyes et al., 2019, p. 531).

Three RSIs focus largely on systematic reviews of the effects of interventions on designated outcomes (Cochrane, Campbell, WWC)—often colloquially called "what works" reviews (see Gough & Thomas, 2017, p. 53). While intervention reviews are the genre these RSIs privilege (and, thus, our focus here), they each produce other review genres. In addition to reviews of intervention effectiveness, Cochrane lists the following as major review genres it supports: reviews of diagnostic test accuracy, reviews of prognosis, systematic overviews of reviews, and reviews of methodology (Chandler et al., 2019, pp. 4–6).[5] Campbell also sponsors systematic overviews of reviews, methods research papers, and evidence and gap maps that "systematically identify and report the range of research activity in broad topic areas or policy domains" (Saran & White, 2018, p. 5)—with Campbell allowing reviews "on topics . . . closely related to interventions," such as cost-effectiveness, predictive validity, and other associational studies (Campbell Collaboration, 2019, p. 7). The RSI further allows for what it calls "Campbell Innovations"—that is, "novel evidence synthesis types that have not yet been published by the Campbell Collaboration," which receive a "specialized methods peer review" (Campbell Collaboration, 2019, p. 6). Cochrane, Campbell, and WWC also publish documents that are prospective to/derivative of systematic reviews, including review protocols (WWC, Cochrane, Campbell) and reviews of individual studies (WWC). (Except *RER*, all examined RSIs also routinely produce materials translating knowledge for nonspecialist stakeholders; see "Stakeholders.") Notably, alongside its intervention effectiveness reports, WWC publishes *educator's practice guides*—written with practitioners in mind (see "Stakeholders")—which synthesize "rigorous research" (as evaluated against WWC's standards) to provide "recommendations for a coherent approach to a multifaceted problem" (Institute of Education Sciences [IES], 2018, p. 43).

For systematic reviews of interventions, WWC, Campbell, and Cochrane promote comprehensive searching—though WWC adopts a priori restrictions on this process, allowing only for "publicly available" English-language studies (WWC, 2020a, p. 7). These RSIs embrace a methodological hierarchy privileging randomized controlled trials (RCTs): experimental studies randomly assigning participants to intervention and control groups. Because they produce unbiased effect size estimates for studied outcomes, RCTs are treated—within these RSIs—as providing the best evidence for causal conclusions regarding intervention effectiveness. Quasi-experimental (nonrandomized) studies are treated as potentially worthy of inclusion in intervention reviews, provided they meet specified minimal internal validity standards.[6] These RSIs recommend *meta-analysis* (wherever it is possible) as their preferred synthesis method, pooling effect sizes to produce an overall effect size estimate of a (type of) intervention (Campbell Collaboration, 2019; Higgins, Thomas, et al., 2019; WWC, 2020a).

For Campbell and Cochrane (but *not* WWC), studies from other methodological traditions—including qualitative research—are permitted to contextualize quantitative synthesis findings and to address questions supplementary to intervention reviews. Campbell notes that such research "can help paint a richer picture of the intervention, its effects, how or why it produces those effects (or not), and other such features that provide texture and explanatory context to a review" (Campbell Collaboration, 2019, p. 11). Cochrane identifies "synthesis of qualitative evidence" as beneficial to understanding interventions by "increasing understanding of a phenomenon of interest," of the relationship between interventions and the "broader environment" they take place in, of the ways "health conditions and interventions" are perceived and experienced, and of the context-contingent "complexity" of the "impacts and effects" of "interventions and implementation . . . on different subgroups of people" (Noyes et al., 2019, pp. 525–526). Describing "designs for synthesizing qualitative evidence with evidence of the effects of interventions," Cochrane identifies two forms this integration can take: *Sequential reviews*, which integrate qualitative evidence synthesis findings with pre-existing intervention review findings; and *convergent mixed-methods reviews,* when "no pre-existing intervention review exists" and both the (trial-based) intervention review and qualitative evidence synthesis must be conducted and integrated (Noyes et al., 2019, p. 526).

EPPI-Centre contrasts its work with that of Cochrane and Campbell (and, by implication, WWC), privileging different methodologies within its broader definition of "systematic reviews." Encouraging a theory-driven methodological flexibility, EPPI-Centre primarily supports systematic reviews—and related secondary synthesis genres (e.g., maps and overviews of reviews)—that are "driven by any research questions and including any research methods and types of data" (Gough et al., 2017a, p. 12), stressing that synthesis work should be driven by "a 'fit for purpose' approach" (Gough & Thomas, 2017, p. 52), where synthesis methods are calibrated to context-contingent objectives. (Additionally, EPPI-Centre generates publications on synthesis methodology and reviews/primary research studies of evidence use.) EPPI-Centre distinguishes between "aggregative" and "configurative" orientations toward synthesis work—first introduced by Sandelowski et al. (2006)—a key distinction carried throughout their guidance manual *An Introduction to Systematic Reviews*: "The diversity of methods . . . used to bring together ('synthesise') study findings lie on a continuum between approaches that aim to *aggregate* or 'add up' findings from multiple, similar studies; and those that aim to *configure* or 'organise' findings" (Gough et al., 2017a, p. 7). Synthesis approaches with a more aggregative orientation tend to test hypotheses and make inferential claims based on statistical information (as with meta-analysis); approaches with a more configurative orientation tend to generate and explore theory, making inferential claims based on the theory developed (Gough & Thomas, 2017, pp. 62–65). Configurative synthesis approaches highlighted by EPPI-Centre, such as the following, include those developed by its staff and those developed elsewhere:

- *Thematic synthesis*, which "emphasises the development of theory from a starting point of open questions and few secure initial concepts," and "makes no inferential claims based on statistics, but aims to enlighten decision making through the creation of new theory" (Thomas, O'Mara-Eves, et al., 2017, p. 190; see also Thomas & Harden, 2008)
- *Realist synthesis*, which "aims to uncover the (usually) hidden *mechanisms* which cause interventions to result in specific outcomes in specified contexts" (Thomas, O'Mara-Eves, et al., 2017, p. 200; see also Pawson, 2006)
- *Meta-narrative review*, which helps manage plural (and perhaps competing) perspectives concerning "complex and contested topic areas which have been studied by different disciplines and traditions," such that these syntheses "unpack the shared set of concepts, theories and methods within a research tradition and chart how the research conducted within the tradition unfolds and changes over time, highlighting key discoveries and insights" (Thomas, O'Mara-Eves, et al., 2017, p. 202; see also Greenhalgh et al., 2005)
- *Meta-ethnography*, which provides "a way of thinking about drawing conclusions across multiple ethnographic studies" and other sources of qualitative evidence (Thomas, O'Mara-Eves, et al., 2017, p. 195), with meta-ethnographers "systematically comparing conceptual data from primary qualitative studies to identify and develop new overarching concepts, theories, and models," instead of "aggregat[ing] findings" (France et al., 2019, p. 2; see also Noblit & Hare, 1988)

The latter three approaches have standards supporting their enactment or reporting developed by the RAMESES (Realist And Meta-narrative Evidence Syntheses: Evolving Standards) Projects (Wong et al., 2014) and eMERGe (Meta-Ethnography Reporting Guidance) Project (France et al., 2019), respectively. RAMESES scholars Wong et al. (2014) argue that synthesis genres like these can "supplement, extend and in some circumstances replace Cochrane-style systematic reviews" (p. 1).

In contrast to the RSIs above, *RER* includes systematic reviews among the genres it supports but invests in the broader category of *integrative reviews*, which

pull together the existing work on an educational topic and work to understand trends in that body of scholarship. In such a review, the author describes how the issue is conceptualized within the literature, how research methods and theories have shaped the outcomes of scholarship, and what the strengths and weaknesses of the literature are. (*Review of Educational Research*, n.d.-a, para. 2)

Beyond empirical reviews, *RER* supports historical, theoretical, and methodological reviews as well, investing in an inclusive understanding of what counts as data, "including empirical articles, secondary databases, and historical and political archives" (Murphy et al., 2017, p. 4).

For its part, National Academies invests in expert *consensus study reports* and *workshop summaries*, undertaken in response to queries posed by sponsors, such as the U.S. federal government and state agencies. An expert consensus report (our focus here) is simply "a report produced by a committee of experts convened by the National

Academies . . . to study a specific scientific or technological issue of national importance" (National Academies, 2018, para 1). In its public documentation, National
Academies offers no a priori methodological restrictions for these genres, beyond
expecting that report findings be "supported by the scientific evidence and the arguments presented" (National Academies, n.d.-b, "Stage 4" section)—rendering the
methodological scope of its work more implicit (and perhaps less narrowly defined)
than is typical of the RSIs we examined.[7]

Quality

Each examined RSI enacts a conception of synthesis quality, offering explicit recommendations (or requirements) for quality judgments. While no two RSIs make
identical investments, each could be understood as primarily adopting one of two
general approaches to quality we characterize as (a) procedural control or (b) conceptual guidance and professional judgment.

Primarily Procedural Control

For systematic reviews of interventions, WWC, Cochrane, and Campbell maintain highly detailed, centralized control over the process of synthesis development
and reporting, providing easily documented and audited quality assurances.
Prioritizing review topics chosen (with stakeholder input) by the Institute of
Education Services (IES; WWC, 2020a, p. A-2), WWC exerts procedural control at
several review stages: A topic-specific review protocol (containing required features)
is made *before* reviews are conducted, specifying how relevant research should be
searched for and appraised; relevant literature is identified and screened in accordance with protocol requirements; studies included in the synthesis are individually
assessed using standards established in WWC guidance documents; and synthesis
findings are publicized in one or more privileged formats (WWC, 2020a, pp. 1–2).
WWC authors are screened for conflicts of interest, those reviewing individual studies must first be formally trained and certified by the RSI, and review team members
are chosen on the basis of prior WWC-certification and (in the case of team leaders)
perceived methodological and content expertise (WWC, 2020a, pp. C-1–C-5).
WWC reports receive internal review by the IES and a blind external "peer review by
researchers who are knowledgeable about WWC standards and are not staff with the
WWC contractor that prepared the draft publication" (p. C-3)—in addition to "a
final review by IES staff to ensure that any issues have been addressed appropriately,"
after authors have had an opportunity to address reviewer comments (p. C-4).[8]

Cochrane and Campbell coordinate intervention review production through
documents and tools that procedurally regulate synthesis work, including the organizations' primary guidance texts (Higgins, Thomas, et al., 2019; Campbell
Collaboration, 2019), checklists for additional/special considerations (e.g., equity),
and their respective guidelines for review conduct and reporting: the MECIR
(Methodological Expectations of Cochrane Intervention Reviews) and the
MECCIR (Methodological Expectations of Campbell Collaboration Intervention

Reviews), each of which contains close to 200 distinct standards—a level of procedural detail unmatched by any other examined RSI.[9] These RSIs employ required software for protocol and review submission—Review Manager (RevMan)—ensuring a standardized reporting format with limited flexibility (see "Collective Work" section). When reviewing the quality of studies to be included in syntheses, Cochrane expects (and Campbell encourages, where applicable) that authors use the procedurally oriented GRADE (Grading of Recommendations, Assessment, Development and Evaluation) approach—an evidence quality evaluation framework with associated software (GRADEpro GDT [Guideline Development Tool]). For qualitative evidence synthesis, Cochrane promotes use of GRADE-CERQual (Confidence in the Evidence from Reviews of Qualitative research), a related tool for appraising "relevance, methodological limitations, adequacy and coherence . . . to formulate an overall assessment of confidence in the synthesized qualitative finding" (Noyes et al., 2019, p. 537). Thus, as Campbell puts it, "Systematic reviews are developed through a process that helps ensure that they are accurate, methodologically sound, comprehensive, and unbiased" (Campbell Collaboration, 2019, p. 6). And, following Cochrane, the systematic review process seeks "to minimize bias by using explicit, systematic methods documented in advance with a protocol" (Chandler et al., 2019, p. 1)—deviations from which must be justified in the full report.

Cochrane and Campbell also invest in centralized editorial oversight, such that systematic reviews undergo quality evaluation at three stages: when titles (and thereby research questions/topics) for specific reviews are registered, when protocols for those reviews are submitted, and when reports adhering to those protocols are completed (Campbell Collaboration, 2019; Higgins, Thomas, et al., 2019).[10] For Cochrane and Campbell, quality evaluation requires peer review by one or more topic specialists and at least one methodologist, overseen by editorial groups that determine (at each stage) whether and how review production should continue. Cochrane typically provides for named peer review, where reviewers and authors know one another's names; Campbell, by contrast, invests in single-blind peer review, preserving reviewer anonymity. And because, under certain circumstances, Cochrane and Campbell allow copublication of their reviews elsewhere, these reports may undergo peer review more than once.[11]

Primarily Conceptual Guidance and Professional Judgment

Other RSIs offer principles for synthesis conduct while supporting local, context-contingent uptake of those principles (EPPI-Centre)—or else invest primarily in the professional judgment of authors and reviewers (*RER*, National Academies). Supporting reviews that span aggregation-oriented and configuration-oriented genres (see "Genre" section), EPPI-Centre makes clear "there is not an EPPI-Centre method for undertaking reviews; rather there are principles that guide our work" (Gough et al., 2017b, p. 14)—with web-based EPPI-Reviewer software providing (paying subscribers) a flexible resource supporting development of multiple synthesis genres (see "Collective Work" section). Producing many of its systematic reviews at the request of organizational partners (with reviews coauthored, or otherwise supported by,

EPPI-Centre staff), EPPI-Centre has "adapted and adjusted [its] review methods in order to answer the questions asked by [its] stakeholders in meaningful and useful ways" (Gough & Thomas, 2017, p. 52). General principles of methodological quality, tailored for appropriateness to the questions asked, are a function of three primary dimensions: "a review's method (Dimension 1), the nature of its included studies (Dimension 2) and the evidence produced (Dimension 3)," which—taken together— provide "a framework for appraising a review in terms of whether it provides enough evidence, good enough evidence and relevant enough evidence to make evidence claims" (Liabo et al., 2017, p. 253). The reviews EPPI-Centre publishes "have been extensively peer reviewed before being published online, apart from one or two, and the absence of peer review is highlighted where this happens (usually for 'maps' of research, rather than syntheses)," with this review process occasionally overseen by organizations with which EPPI-Centre has partnered: For example, EPPI-Centre's reviews for the U.K. Department of Health are "always independently peer reviewed by up to five reviewers in a process that is managed by NIHR [National Institute for Health Research]" (James Thomas, personal communication, January 7, 2020).

Quality control for National Academies is largely a matter of managing the quality of the authoring committee, with explicit procedures for nomination (and opportunity for public comment on prospective membership) to ensure that the committee embodies a range of expertise and balance of perspectives, unburdened by conflicts of interest (National Academies, 2003). Prior to committee selection for a study, a draft "statement of task, work plan, and budget" is internally reviewed by National Academies (National Academies, n.d.-b, "Stage 1" section). Once constituted, committees are not held to strict a priori reporting requirements and are expected to turn to a variety of sources—among them, "reviews of the scientific literature" (National Academies, n.d.-b, "Stage 3" section). Indeed, while National Academies is chartered to take up "request[s] for scientific advice" and convenes expert committees for this purpose, "the specifics of the study question can be refined and improved by the committee members *after they are appointed*" (Feuer & Maranto, 2010, p. 267). This emphasis on expertise and "flexibility" is shaped by a belief that "complex questions are better defined through deliberation rather than by *a priori* certitudes"—but investments of this kind are not without critical "tradeoffs," regularly discussed within National Academies (Feuer & Maranto, 2010, p. 267). Committee members are permitted to submit brief dissenting opinions as appendices to the consensus report. National Academies reports are submitted to expert reviewers (anonymous, prior to the review's publication), attentive to whether the "report addresses its approved study charge and does not go beyond it," whether report "findings are supported by the scientific evidence and arguments presented," whether "the exposition and organization are effective," and whether "the report is impartial and objective" (National Academies, n.d.-b, "Stage 4" section). Here, the fact that the authoring committee can augment the study question(s) it was charged to investigate can "have its downsides: reviewers asked to judge the extent to which a committee adhered to its 'charge' may find it difficult to respond without more specificity" (Feuer & Maranto, 2010, p. 267). The report committee's response to the reviewers' comments is then audited by "independent report review 'monitors'" prior to the report's publication (The National Academies, n.d.-b, "Stage 4" section).

RER provides an example of a traditional "peer review" evaluation, with quality control almost exclusively invested in editors' and peer reviewers' judgments. To focus its double-blind peer review process, *RER* offers a general set of peer review guidelines addressing quality of the literature reviewed, quality of the analysis, significance of the topic, impact of the article (i.e., usefulness for stakeholders), advancement of the field, style (cautioning against "unexplained jargon and parochialism"), balance and fairness, and purpose (with respect to relevance to education; *Review of Educational Research*, n.d.-a, paras. 8–16). Specific journal editors refine and establish additional priorities for article quality, with recent priorities being not only methodological explicitness and transparency but also "that authors articulate potential avenues for addressing the critical question or problem they interrogated based on the findings they have mapped from the literature" (Murphy et al., 2017, p. 5; see also Murphy et al., 2020). In its online guidance (*Review of Educational Research*, n.d.-b), *RER* recommends that authors consult AERA's *Standards for Reporting on Research in AERA Publications* (which, we note, are intended for primary empirical studies),[12] *Guidelines for Reviewers* (which focus primarily on ethical concerns), and—for "systematic reviews"—the PRISMA Statement: Guidelines for reporting meta-analyses and systematic reviews of intervention effectiveness (Moher et al., 2009), referenced also by Cochrane, Campbell, and EPPI-Centre, among others (see, e.g., Campbell Collaboration, 2019; Gough et al., 2017a; Higgins, Thomas, et al., 2019). *RER* does not mandate where and how reviewers are to make use of these diverse guidelines.[13]

Stakeholders

Rees and Oliver (2017) remind us that the stakeholders for systematic reviews can be any groups affected by or contributing to that review (p. 20), and Suri (2014) notes, "Stakeholders with an interest in educational research . . . include policy-makers, administrators, teachers, funding agencies, researchers, students, parents and the wider community" (p. 2). While all examined RSIs aim to inform/improve policy and/or practice, each configures its investments in stakeholder engagement differently, according to how it (a) structures access to knowledge objects, (b) circumscribes whether/how stakeholders participate in knowledge production, and (c) sponsors "knowledge translation" work: ways to re-mediate (i.e., translate or package) knowledge objects and promote their consumption and uptake.

Access

Stakeholders' (differential) access to RSIs' knowledge objects is a fundamental equity concern with which all RSIs are grappling. All RSIs maintain some sort of searchable database of syntheses (see "Collective Work" section). Campbell and WWC are notable for making all their syntheses, review protocols, and guidance handbooks open access; National Academies also ensures nearly all its reports are available for free download. EPPI-Centre provides free PDF versions of the systematic reviews and primary research reports it participates in producing, in addition to some of the publications on methodology its staff has (co)authored. Cochrane makes its influential guidance documents freely available online but places new syntheses behind a paywall for 12 months, unless authors (or funders) pay for immediate open access. Importantly, the 12-month paywall period currently applies only to review versions published after (or on) February 1, 2013; syntheses published earlier remain behind a paywall (see also Heywood et al., 2018). That said, Cochrane makes several exceptions to its default access restrictions. For instance, some countries pay Cochrane to offer open access to their citizens, and the RSI provides for free access for some countries on the basis of income (see Heywood et al., 2018). Of the RSIs we examined, *RER* currently invests the least in open access, with paywalls for most of the syntheses they publish.

Enfranchising Stakeholders in Knowledge Production

When RSIs actively engage stakeholder/user communities in synthesis production, this involvement tends to take the form of consultation, solicited at one or more stages of the synthesis process. All but *RER* facilitate some form of stakeholder engagement in the review production process—though for some RSIs, stakeholder enfranchisement is limited. EPPI-Centre, for one, recommends stakeholder participation to support several aspects of synthesis work—such as aiding in evidence collection, synthesis oversight, promoting synthesis relevance, and the sharing of syntheses (Rees & Oliver, 2017)—paying particular attention to stakeholder use of synthesis-based evidence (see Gough et al., 2017a).

Of the RSIs examined, Cochrane and Campbell arguably make the most intensive investments in stakeholder enfranchisement. "Cochrane author teams are encouraged to seek and incorporate the views of users, including consumers, clinicians and those from varying regions and settings to develop protocols and reviews" (Cumpston & Chandler, 2019, p. 5). Cochrane reminds its authors that stakeholder engagement can take many forms in addition to synthesis coauthorship: Other "methods for working with consumers and other stakeholders include surveys, workshops, focus groups and involvement in advisory groups"—with the choice of method "typically . . . based on resource availability" (Lasserson et al., 2019, p. 6). A Campbell Policy Brief notes that stakeholder contributions have included "identifying and prioritising review topics, defining review questions and important outcomes, conducting reviews, [enhancing scientific quality through discussion about intervention integrity . . . and transferability], editing review protocols and reports, and disseminating and implementing review findings in practice" (Konnerup & Sowden, 2008, p. 1). Cochrane even maintains multiple web-mediated platforms for stakeholder participation, including the citizen science Cochrane Crowd platform, through which stakeholders can volunteer to identify and characterize/summarize health care–related research (specifically, RCTs), and a related TaskExchange platform, through which stakeholders can volunteer to complete a variety of tasks, such as assessing risk of bias and translating knowledge objects into languages other than English (Cochrane, 2019).

WWC, which contracts out production of its intervention effectiveness reports, offers more limited roles for stakeholders in knowledge production: It consults with policymakers   and   education   association   members   and   provides   occasional opportunities for public feedback, including on potential review topics and proposed modifications to WWC's guidance. It also enfranchises stakeholders to make recommendations regarding potential intervention report topics or studies to review; WWC further provides a public-facing version of its guide for reviewing evidence (to spread popular awareness of the RSI's evaluative processes). The actual review and selection of studies for WWC's database is conducted by official reviewers who have completed a certification process where "typically, individuals with the requisite skills will have an earned doctorate in social science . . . or equivalent" (WWC, n.d.-b, "Becoming a WWC-Certified Reviewer" section).

National Academies circumscribes the roles stakeholders can play in order to "maintai[n] a safe space for deliberations by defending its exemption from federal rules that would otherwise require all meetings to be held in public" (Feuer & Maranto, 2010, p. 270)—a move Feuer and Maranto (2010) argue "can protect *scientific integrity*" (p. 271). While National Academies does not formalize many opportunities for stakeholder participation in knowledge production, "all documents provided by outsiders to . . . [report-authoring] committees are now kept in a so-called 'public access file,' to which the public is welcome, and efforts are made to enable open and public sessions during many phases of committee life" (p. 272). Moreover, authoring committees can themselves be composed of figures other than higher education–affiliated academics/researchers (including K–12 educators, consultants, and nonprofit representatives).

Knowledge Translation

Knowledge translation work supports new and broader publics in consuming and using RSI-produced knowledge, which is often initially authored with specialist audiences in mind. All RSIs, excepting *RER*, routinely publish free policy briefs, evidence bulletins, plain language/executive summaries, and/or snapshots distilling their longer syntheses for stakeholders. In WWC's case, translation efforts like these extend to recommendation-providing free "practice guides" tailored to support educator uptake of "what works," where at least two practitioners serve on the authoring committee (see WWC, 2020a, pp. C-2–C3)—a peer-reviewed genre that relies on and reinforces the evidence hierarchy endorsed within the RSI's intervention reports (see "Genre" section). National Academies also provides open access to a range of knowledge translation documents to accompany their consensus reports, including not only highlights, summaries, and press releases but also report-specific videos, webinars, commissioned reports, and podcasts. It also maintains some general resources (aligned to or informed by National Academies reports), such as teaching materials, interactive infographics, and a question-and-answer platform. Making particularly heavy investments in knowledge translation, Cochrane produces a diversity of free guidance and training resources (e.g., standards for plain language summaries) and has cultivated government partnerships to "increase policy makers' awareness of the value of systematic reviews" and build their "capacity for using research in policy work" (Brennan et al., 2016, p. 26; see also Cochrane, 2019). Cochrane partners with Wikipedia to publicize high quality medical evidence (https://en.wikipedia.org/wiki/Wikipedia:WikiProject_Medicine/Cochrane);

the RSI further produces free podcasts and a synthesis-centric journal club, as well as question-and-answer formatted summaries based on synthesis evidence (though the full texts of these summaries seem not to be open access by default). Importantly, Cochrane, Campbell, and National Academies invest in translating some synthesis-related materials into multiple languages.

Relatedly, in addition to maintaining a centralized website, each RSI provides at least one venue for connecting with stakeholders (e.g., for stakeholders to receive updates or provide feedback). All maintain some kind of mailing list, newsletter, forum, or listserv, and list email addresses or offer online feedback forms; all maintain official social media presences (or have parent organizations that do so); a few maintain synthesis-related blogs with comment functionality (EPPI-Centre) or without it (Campbell, Cochrane, and WWC through its parent, IES), and Cochrane's users can leave comments on reviews, protocols, and editorials published in its library. All but *RER* and National Academies provide for free synthesis production-supporting online training materials, instructional videos, and/or webinars (for more on professional development, see "Collective Work" section). These forms of online outreach establish opt-in relationships with stakeholders, while tending to position RSI-supported knowledge objects as entities stakeholders can consume or respond to, rather than shape.

Collective Work

Given the increasing proliferation of research, attention to how RSIs can facilitate, incentivize, and capitalize on collective work is becoming increasingly crucial. While much of the work entailed in producing individual research syntheses is researcher- or team-specific, RSIs support and sponsor this work by investing in structures to facilitate collective work across time, geography, and research teams (see Gough, Thomas, & Oliver, 2019)—enabling what Bowker (2017) calls a "division of cognitive labor" (p. 398). Here we focus on their investments in creating the social, conceptual, and technical conditions for collective work by providing for (a) coordination across synthesis projects, (b) databases, (c) metadata, (d) professional development, and (e) digital tools and automations to support synthesis work. While these investments enable a shared, common knowledge base that a diversity of researchers can contribute to, draw from, or build on, they also limit the scope of knowledge an RSI can support.

Coordination

By orchestrating which topics are reviewed and by whom, Cochrane and Campbell discourage synthesis duplication so that researchers' efforts are distributed to a greater number of interventions (see Campbell Collaboration, 2019; Cumpston & Chandler, 2019).[14] Campbell, for example, provides reviewers who register a topic with "priority rights to the topic of the systematic review; no other review team will be approved by Campbell for a review on that specific topic as long as the team is making progress toward completing the review" (Campbell Collaboration, 2019, p. 13)—and those reviewers have exclusive rights to update their review within 5 years, "unless the original team explicitly waives their claim on that opportunity" (p. 16). Cochrane registers its review protocols with the international PROSPERO systematic review database (https://www.crd.york.ac.uk/PROSPERO/), a move intended to "reduc[e] duplication of effort, research waste, and promot[e] accountability" (Lasserson et al., 2019, p. 9). Practices that seek to distribute synthesis topics in ways that minimize duplication appear to imply that another qualified author team would arrive at the same conclusions—an assumption that is, perhaps, easier to justify with meta-analysis than with other synthesis genres.[15]

Entities intended to coordinate efforts across RSIs are beginning to take shape. Notably, Evidence Syntheses International (https://evidencesynthesis.org/) "provide[s] a global hub where evidence synthesis organizations meet to build and share capacities, resources and guidance, and enhance and advocate for the synthesis and use of research evidence . . . in all areas of human enterprise" (Gough, Davies, et al., 2019, p. 1). Participating RSIs include Cochrane, Campbell, and EPPI-Centre, advancing a multimethodological orientation to systematic reviews. The STEPP (Statistics for Evidence-Based Policy and Practice) Center at Northwestern University (https://stepp.center/) has similar goals in the context of education and applied social science, although their work seems exclusively oriented to quantitative reviews. STEPP's directors have convened meetings with representatives from several organizations, including WWC and Campbell, "to think about how to get clearinghouses to be better linked with users" (Elizabeth Tipton, personal communication, December 4, 2019). In pursuit of their aims, these entities variously cite and/or link to a diversity of synthesis-supporting resources, including methodological guidance materials, software, and professional development opportunities.

Databases

In addition to databases of syntheses, protocols, and guidance/training materials variously maintained by all RSIs examined (see "Stakeholders" section), three RSIs maintain databases or extractable datasets of primary evidence (e.g., studies, trials) on which researchers can draw to produce new syntheses or audit existing ones. EPPI-Centre provides nine free topic-specific databases (e.g., Bibliomap), partly built from the citations of studies its staff have drawn on when (co)authoring syntheses. WWC offers an open repository of data from individual studies that WWC-certified reviewers have evaluated for quality (in accordance with WWC's RCT-privileging evidence hierarchy). And Cochrane allows subscribers to access its Central Register of Controlled Trials (CENTRAL)—an extensive bibliographic record of RCTs and quasi-experimental studies, identified through a mixture of handsearching (partially via Cochrane Crowd-sourcing) and, more recently, through machine learning–aided searches (see Cochrane, 2019; Marshall et al., 2018).[16]

Metadata

Decisions about how RSIs classify and organize knowledge in their databases relate to decisions around metadata, which are "most simply defined as 'data about data,' [and] are a means to name things, to represent data, and to represent relationships" (Borgman, 2015, p. 66). Investments in metadata shape how patterns (and gaps) in studies and syntheses within topic areas can be made visible, including via evidence and gap maps (see Saran & White, 2018). Well-designed metadata are increasingly important, as the work of synthesizing research increasingly relies on algorithmic tools to search for, select, extract data from, statistically integrate, and generate reports about synthesis-relevant materials. Setting aside the bibliographic metadata (e.g., authors, publication date) they associate with publications, RSIs tend to differ in the primary metadata they invest in to support navigation of (and/or data extraction from) their databases: general keywords or topic area/subject matter focus (all); document genre/type, such as protocol or systematic review (Campbell, Cochrane, EPPI-Centre, WWC); and formalized study and/or synthesis features, such as population or (type of) intervention examined (Cochrane, EPPI-Centre, WWC).

For example, Cochrane's library offers detailed search functionality using MeSH (Medical Subject Headings) and PICO (Population, Intervention, Comparison, Outcome) classification frameworks, in addition to more general topic- and genre-based search functionality. For its part, WWC makes the documents in its synthesis library searchable by topic, synthesis characteristics, and genre, while enabling its primary dataset of individual study evidence to be filtered by formalized features of those studies (e.g., intervention, quality rating). Investments in centralized control over synthesis production (see "Quality" section) may help ensure that metadata are standardized in ways that smooth away some of the dangers of "data friction" (Edwards et al., 2011, p. 669), wherein knowledge objects lack interoperability and are thus ill-formatted for synthesis. A "consistent classification schema"—such as Cochrane's PICO framework—could also enable data to be easily shared between organizations, promoting "more efficient systematic review workflows," such that "duplication of effort was minimised" (Gough, Thomas, & Oliver, 2019, p. 8). "Robust hypotheses require information in standardized formats," Edwards et al. (2013) remind us, adding by way of example, that "the spread of a particular disease around the world cannot be tracked unless everyone is calling it the same thing" (p. 8). Of course, whether and how a phenomenon is (required to be) named has material consequences that can privilege some interests over others (see Bowker & Star, 1999).

Professional Development

WWC, Campbell, Cochrane, and EPPI-Centre each provide formal support for researchers learning to engage in systematic reviews (beyond the formal documentation described in the "Quality" section). For Cochrane and Campbell, professional learning opportunities are available online (e.g., short courses, interactive learning modules, videos) and in a range of face-to-face events. WWC offers training and certification in various aspects of the review process (see "Stakeholders" section) and publishes a list of certified reviewers and organizations, which interested parties may contact for help with (non-WWC sponsored) reviews; it also makes available free online training modules and videos. In addition to offering free instructional videos as well as free software (MetaLight) that provides training in meta-analysis, EPPI-Centre provides a range of professional development services—though these activities typically require external funding. These capacity-building services include direct support and consultations for clients undertaking systematic reviews, as well as EPPI-Centre researcher–led workshops, seminars, college courses, and even two synthesis-related masters of science degrees offered through University College London (which houses EPPI-Centre). Additionally, as noted by one of its current associate editors, *RER* regularly engages with researchers and other stakeholders in "meet the editor" events at the annual conference of its parent entity, AERA (Alicia C. Dowd, personal communication, December 14, 2019)—with access seemingly dependent on conference attendance fees.

Digital Tools and Automations

EPPI-Centre, Cochrane, and Campbell each make available one or more digital tools that automate, facilitate, or otherwise algorithmically augment some aspect of the systematic review process, including synthesis production.[17] These infrastructural investments shape (and often help standardize) the ways in which syntheses can be produced or consumed, while also augmenting the scale at which data(bases) can be mined, mapped, and synthesized (see, e.g., J. Brunton et al., 2017; Snilstveit et al., 2018). Arguably the most flexible software tool is made available by EPPI-Centre (for a subscription fee, after a trial period): the web-based EPPI-Reviewer, a platform for supporting qualitative and quantitative synthesis work through functionalities for "*reference management, study classification* and *data extraction, synthesis,* and general *review management*" (J. Brunton et al., 2017, p. 170). Included among these functionalities are tools to consistently code and classify studies, tools to generate descriptive maps of evidence (e.g., frequency and cross-tabulation visualizations), and machine learning features to automate some parts of the review process.

Both Campbell and Cochrane provide (or link to) a free suite of software tools for their reviewers, aiding them in complying with the myriad procedural requirements that synthesis production in those infrastructures entails. These tools include an information management system (Archie), a review production platform (RevMan), and a data extraction and screening tool (Covidence)—among other tools the RSIs provide access or link to (e.g., EPPI-Reviewer, the Systematic Review Toolbox; see Cumpston & Chandler, 2019). For instance, Cochrane further links to study summarization and evaluation software (GRADEpro GDT); Campbell provides authors with a stand-alone web-based effect size calculator.

Existing technical developments in synthesis automation like these have paved a path for the emergence of *living systematic reviews,* so-called because they are "continually updated, incorporating relevant new evidence as it becomes available" (Elliott et al., 2017, p. 24). Because living reviews represent "an approach to review updating, not a formal review methodology" per se (Thomas, Noel-Storr, et al., 2017, p. 32), their *livingness* can take a number of forms, and be supported by a variety of means—including by machine-based automations (e.g., text-mining and machine-learning algorithms), human-based distributed labor and cognition (e.g., crowdsourcing and task sharing), or some combination of the two (see Elliott et al., 2017; also Marshall & Wallace, 2019; Tsafnat et al., 2014). To date, EPPI-Centre and Cochrane—in addition to the Epistemonikos Foundation (https://www.epistemonikos.cl/), partnered with Cochrane—are among the entities that have begun actively exploring (or, in Cochrane's case, piloting and publishing) living systematic reviews (see, e.g., Cochrane, 2019; Gough et al., 2017b). Though the emergence of living reviews may represent an important change in the RSI status quo, these innovations have—thus far—largely taken advantage of the digital environment to do a more systematic, rapid, and up-to-date job at what RSIs are already doing: producing well-warranted syntheses in accordance with the assumptions they rely on and the aims they endorse. Under current conditions, "the nature of the final synthesis product may not be all that different to what is currently known" (Gough, Thomas, & Oliver, 2019, p. 9).

DISCUSSION: CRITICAL QUESTIONS FOR RSIS IN EDUCATION

Today, the idea that syntheses and the evidence underlying them should be methodologically explicit, accountable, and well-warranted (as is expected of primary research) is not much a matter of debate. The questions confronting us are about *what* kinds of syntheses and synthesis methodologies are valued, about *how* infrastructural choices affect the shape and possibility of knowledge, and about *who* should have access to participate in the production and use of that knowledge. Emerging digital innovations may be creating the conditions for new answers to these questions (see Borgman, 2015). Bowker (2017) teaches us that knowledge infrastructures (e.g., RSIs) change in response to the information ecologies in which they participate: Less centrally planned than emergent, a given "knowledge enterprise . . . will 'learn' from the network of infrastructures it is integrated into" (p. 397). Below, we review some of the complex choices our RSIs comparisons highlight and consider how such infrastructures might "learn."

One tension RSIs must resolve is that between the need for common standards to support collective work and the need for flexibility to enable (local) adaptations (Star & Ruhleder, 1996)—a tension that has been further dimensionalized as between global and local, and between technical and social, ways of addressing problems (see, e.g., Borgman, 2015, pp. 35–39; Bowker, 2017, pp. 392–393). RSI comparisons reveal a fundamental contrast in how this tension has been resolved. One set of RSIs focuses on detailed, centralized standards and production technologies that procedurally regulate synthesis conduct and reporting (Cochrane, Campbell, WWC); another set relies more on professional judgment in synthesis production and evaluation (National Academies, *RER*), or else provides more general frameworks and flexible tools for the development of locally meaningful syntheses (EPPI-Centre). These choices have complex affordances (and limitations) not only for collective work but also for the ability of RSIs to evolve to better meet (or reconsider) their goals in a changing world.

Through investments in centralized, procedurally detailed standards for systematic reviews of interventions (reflecting an RCT-privileging evidence hierarchy), Cochrane and Campbell have been able to catalyze large communities of reviewers and sponsor large numbers of (consistently formatted) reviews—reviews that can be efficiently evaluated, tagged with useful metadata, readily translated/summarized for various stakeholder communities, and efficiently composed (or updated) with the aid of algorithmic tools. To what extent is it the focus on *a* particular methodology—and *this* particular methodology—that enables this kind of progress?

While Cochrane and Campbell are working to expand the types of evidence they allow (including qualitative studies), their syntheses of such evidence remains largely positioned—for now at least—as supplementary to studies of the effectiveness of interventions. This historical choice to privilege a particular type of research question and methodological tradition has constrained what stakeholders can learn from approaches that draw on different methodologies and prioritize different questions. In efforts at promoting evidence-based practice, these limitations can go underacknowledged. Consider, for instance, the description on WWC's homepage:

The What Works Clearinghouse . . . reviews the existing research on different *programs, products, practices,* and *policies* in education. *Our goal* is to provide educators with the information they need to make evidence-based decisions. We focus on the results from *high-quality research* to answer the question 'What works in education?'" (WWC, n.d.-a, para. 1)

Evaluated in light of WWC's evidence hierarchy, this statement can be read as implying that some methodologies (including qualitative ones) are not relevant to WWC's goals—and that these methodologies may disqualify research from being considered "high quality." To the extent that characterizations like this are codified in policy and law, as WWC's evidence hierarchy has been in the Every Student Succeeds Act, their reach risks disenfranchising alternative perspectives from which stakeholders might learn.

Direct challenges to a priori evidence hierarchies can be found in the methodologically pluralist stance taken by EPPI-Centre, in the range of critical synthesis genres supported by *RER*, and in the methodologically flexible consensus reports of National Academies. This press for methodological inclusion is also reflected in the growing attention Cochrane and Campbell pay to qualitative research. The expanded chapter on qualitative research in the recent *Cochrane Handbook* (Higgins, Thomas, et al., 2019), for example, moves toward procedural guidance for synthesizing qualitative evidence—pointing to named frameworks for this work (e.g., GRADE-CERQual, eMERGe) and calling on synthesists to adapt, adopt, or develop alternative guidance where Cochrane's guidance is insufficient (Noyes et al., 2019, pp. 538–539). We also note both that "Campbell launched a working group on stand-alone qualitative evidence synthesis in 2018" (Campbell Collaboration, 2019, p. 11) and that the RSI will consider publishing new/innovative synthesis genres—provided they are "accompanied by a plan and timeline to develop methodological expectation checklists (matching MECCIR, where relevant)" and also "include a discussion of the strengths and limitations of the methods used, and how they could be improved" (Campbell Collaboration, 2019, p. 7). To what extent is detailed procedural control necessary to support high-quality reviews?

Evidence that well-warranted, well-respected reviews can be produced—in volume—under a more flexible model can be found in National Academies' consensus reports, which emphasize careful selection of expert authors, given considerable authority to determine what evidence they synthesize (and how). For the most part, *RER* has similarly resolved infrastructural tensions in favor of the social and local—though the practices warranting its reviews have fewer layers and fewer reviewers than for National Academies. To what extent does this (local, social, flexible) approach require an organization of the stature (and funding resources) of National Academies to warrant the quality of its reports?

RER—with its critical, integrative reviews—creates an important space for syntheses that bring external theory to bear in critiquing a body of empirical research and the methodologies/philosophies on which it draws. While such critical synthesis genres can be methodologically explicit and accountable, enabling rigorous peer review, they raise substantial challenges to the notion that syntheses should seek to yield an objective, replicable set of conclusions on which stakeholders can rely: The conclusions of such syntheses depend on the critical perspectives from which the body of research is reviewed. Thus, stakeholders are instead invited to critically consider the implications of different approaches to research.[18]

It is also worth remembering that shifts toward the local and the social are not without trade-offs. If we are to support collective work in learning from the expanding proliferation of education research and responding to the consequential problems and opportunities research is needed to address, the resolution cannot be abandonment of common standards that enable and sustain shared resources. As Friedman et al. (2017) note, "Without infrastructure, each learning cycle is figuratively a 'tub on its own bottom' requiring its own concepts, methods, tools, and support systems" (p. 19). To the extent education researchers seek to promote evidentiary and methodological pluralism over existing hierarchies *while also supporting collective work*, it seems fair to say that RSIs have much more "learning" still to do.

Furthermore, while methodological transparency is a principle all examined RSIs promote, transparency in *quality evaluation* seems to have attracted less attention or interest. No RSI we examined conducts open quality reviews of the synthesis reports they support; none, in other words, publishes the full record of the formal evaluations their reports accrue on their way to publication. Relatedly, while some RSIs (notably, Cochrane) are expanding opportunities for stakeholders to comment on knowledge objects, no RSI yet provides for the public, crowdsourced evaluation of syntheses by aggregated/accumulated ratings (beyond collecting and publicizing altmetrics, such as the number of times a synthesis has been downloaded or tweeted about). These choices regarding quality evaluation speak to issues of authority over how knowledge is shaped—and by whom. "Systematic reviewing is a tool of democracy," Oakley (2017) argues, stressing that methodological transparency is a matter of politics and power: "Too much reliance is placed on our believing what researchers say they found. In a democratic world, we would rather be in a position to decide for ourselves" (p. xiv). If Oakley (2017) is right, it is arguably also true that in a democratic world, RSIs should position their publics to more richly and deeply participate in synthesis production *and* evaluation. Such a shift depends, of course, on expanding access for the full range of stakeholders—an issue most examined RSIs are investing in or grappling with (as noted above). How can the synthesis of research, viewed as "a public good" rather than "a commodity" (Heywood et al., 2018, p. 131), be made even more publicly accessible—and in what ways can stakeholder publics be further enfranchised in the development of those goods?

There is perhaps particular urgency for us "to re-imagine the engines of knowledge production" (Bowker, 2017, p. 397) at the present moment. Increasingly, RSIs are developing tools to augment or automate synthesis production—developments that may further stabilize (even rigidify) the ways in which syntheses are produced and reported. Edwards et al. (2013) caution that "programmatic efforts to improve science and other knowledge infrastructures have frequently prioritized investments in technical systems over research on how to effectuate equally crucial cultural, social, and organizational transformations" (p. 13). How do we establish common ground (including sufficient commonality in concepts, classifications, and procedures) to enable collective work, without losing the ability to answer important questions that cannot be addressed within a priori evidence hierarchies? As the evidence RSIs synthesize becomes more heterogeneous, what new possibilities for (inter)disciplinary collaboration—between science, social science, and the humanities—can or should be explored (see Teston, 2017, pp. 130–133)? Efforts to support dialogue and resource sharing across RSIs (e.g., Evidence Synthesis International, STEPP) provide promising opportunities for collective learning, but such metacollaboratives are not without risks. It is important we ask: To what extent is the goal to privilege commonality and work toward a synthesis in perspectives—*or* to privilege diversity and seek practices that sustain dialogue and collaboration across different perspectives (see Moss & Haertel, 2016)? What is excluded from consideration? Who gets to be at the table when such decisions are made? Finding a productive and fair balance may be crucial to enabling "learning" in the face of an unknown future.

These are major challenges—*and opportunities*—all RSIs face.

CONCLUSION: THE CHALLENGES (AND OPPORTUNITIES) AHEAD

The future of knowledge in education will assume different shapes, depending on the infrastructural investments made—in emerging tools, methodologies, genres, and social arrangements. The challenge we have presented to our readers is thus both critical and generative: illuminating the consequences of existing infrastructural configurations (whether designed or inherited) *while also* imagining how things might be otherwise. We believe this sort of critical reflection and proactive attention to infrastructural design is urgent. As Bowker (2017) notes, infrastructural shifts of the magnitude that the internet enables are "rare in human history" (p. 394). During this period of "emergence" (p. 393), it is possible to engage in "play and experimentation" supporting intentional design (p. 401)—yet "once the die is cast, the infrastructural choice seems inevitable" (p. 393).

Infrastructures never provide a neutral background that serves everyone's interests equally. They are value-laden, privileging some interests and disenfranchising others.

"The study and practice of knowledge infrastructures therefore require new languages of distributive justice that can map change to consequence in more ethical and effective ways" (Edwards et al., 2013, p. 14); considering these consequences at the time of design is crucial, because well-conceptualized infrastructural changes can "not only provide new maps to known territories—they reshape the geography itself" (Edwards et al., 2013, p. 14; see also Bowker, 2017; Slota & Bowker, 2017). We write at a time when changes in fundamental infrastructures supporting research are both inevitable and tractable. Let's take advantage of it.

ACKNOWLEDGMENTS

We are tremendously grateful to colleagues who reviewed earlier drafts for the accuracy and fairness of our representations of each RSI and to those who offered substantive comments on our arguments, including Alicia Dowd, John Easton, Michael Feuer, David Gough, Jennifer Lawlor, Jane Noyes, James Thomas, Elizabeth Tipton, Vivian Welch, and Geoffrey Wong. We take full responsibility for the many omissions and for any errors remaining. This material is based, in part, upon work supported by the Spencer Foundation (under Grant No. 201900070). Any opinions, findings, and conclusions or recommendations expressed in this material are those of the author(s) and do not necessarily reflect the views of the Spencer Foundation.

NOTES

[1]We are not the first scholars to explicitly discuss research synthesis in light of "infrastructure" (e.g., Gough et al., 2017b; Snilstveit et al., 2018)—though some methodologists have privileged, instead, the vocabulary of "ecosystems" to describe the complex and "dynamic" systems within which syntheses are undertaken and used (Gough, Thomas, & Oliver, 2019, p. 2).

[2]As Campbell's current editor-in-chief notes, "Cochrane and Campbell developed a closer relationship in 2015 . . . when [they] signed a 3 year memorandum of understanding [MOU] to work together on joint advocacy, methods development and other shared interests. This MOU was renewed for 2018–2020" (Vivian A. Welch, personal communication, November 11, 2019).

[3]We are collaborating with EPPI-Centre on a different project.

[4]A senior scholar who reviewed our representation of one RSI emphasized that there is much that goes on in their RSI that is not visible from publicly available documentation.

[5]As of January 8, 2020, Cochrane's library of more than 8,000 reviews has also published eight *qualitative evidence syntheses* (a number not capturing the full range of Cochrane's convergent mixed-methods intervention reviews; see Noyes et al., 2019, p. 526) and one *realist review* (classified as a "prototype" review) that investigates "which interventions work for whom, why and in what circumstances" (Rivas et al., 2019, p. 1). Additionally, while the online version of Cochrane's *Handbook* does not list qualitative reviews as one of its five primary review genres (Chandler, 2019, pp. 4–6; but see Noyes et al., 2019), some pages of Cochrane's website now foreground qualitative reviews as one of the RSI's major review variants (see, e.g., https://www.cochranelibrary.com/about/about-cochrane-reviews/).

[6]Provided they meet required criteria, a variety of RCT variants/non-RCT studies can be considered for inclusion in Cochrane and Campbell intervention reviews (Campbell Collaboration, 2019; Higgins, Thomas, et al., 2019); WWC restricts the studies it reviews to the following four design types: "randomized controlled trial (RCT), quasi-experimental design (QED), regression discontinuity design (RDD), and single-case design (SCD)" (WWC, 2020b, p. 2).

[7]Though our analysis centers on the consensus reports published by National Academies, the RSI further maintains other publications beyond our study's scope, including some dedicated journals for primary research and researcher perspectives (e.g., *Proceedings of the National Academy of Sciences of the United States of America*).

[8]WWC's practice guides "undergo an external peer review process" as well, managed by IES (WWC, 2019a, p. C-4); WWC additionally maintains "quality assurance" teams to respond to specific inquiries/concerns raised regarding reviews (p. C-4).

[9]While we focus our attention here on standards for systematic reviews of interventions, Cochrane and Campbell each provide guidance regarding other knowledge objects, including knowledge translation materials (Cochrane) and evidence and gap maps (Campbell). Cochrane also produces general writing resources, including a style manual. Additionally, Cochrane and Campbell each maintain standing methods groups that produce guidance.

[10]Notably, Heywood et al. (2018) report in their institutional analysis of Cochrane that the RSI's centralized editorial control can extend to the alteration of review content, "overwriting the previous published version—thus destroying public access to the earlier version" (p. 132). Additionally, while closer examination of the rhetorical dimensions of research synthesis is beyond the scope of this review, Teston (2017) provides a helpful discussion of the "complex composing process" (p. 96) undergirding Cochrane Review production and evaluation (pp. 94–133). Regarding Cochrane's procedural control over synthesis production, Teston (2017) reports: "One reviewer stated that the Cochrane Collaboration's guidelines make this process pretty black and white and that the act itself is akin to 'filling in the blanks'" (p. 101).

[11]Cochrane permits copublication in journals with which it has signed agreements; Campbell allows authors to copublish, provided they cite the version published by Campbell and provided the synthesis "remain[s] free for dissemination in any and all media without restriction" (Campbell Collaboration, 2019, p. 17). Campbell further allows for "Campbellization," where reviews first "completed . . . outside of the Campbell editorial process" can be reviewed for potential publication by Campbell (Campbell Collaboration, 2019, p. 15).

[12]Moss chaired the committee that developed these standards.

[13]In the service of making its quality evaluation practices more transparent, *RER* has recently begun publishing new methodological guidance articles regarding synthesis conduct (e.g., Alexander, 2020; Pigott & Polanin, 2020), but these "educative" investments are positioned "to offer supportive, rather than strictly prescriptive, guidance to potential authors and reviewers of *RER*" (Murphy et al., 2020, p. 3). Pigott and Polanin (2020), for example, identify PRISMA as one "helpful framework for meta-analysts to follow when reporting the results of the study" (p. 38).

[14]Of course, any other RSI that selects/designates topics and/or authors could be described as managing the distribution of labor in some way—though of the examined RSIs, only Cochrane and Campbell seem to explicitly endorse and enforce this rationale.

[15]Relatedly, in contrast to the constraints placed on its intervention reports, WWC allows practice guide panels to base their recommendations partly on expert "interpretation" (when research alone is deemed insufficient for "guiding the recommendations"), noting "it is possible that two teams of recognized experts working independently to produce a practice guide on the same topic would come to very different conclusions" (IES, 2018, p. 44).

[16]Although Cochrane restricts access to its database of primary trial data, academic researchers can request to bypass this restriction (James Thomas, personal communication, November 18, 2019). And while the databases maintained by EPPI-Centre and Cochrane include citations for/links to primary evidence, the full texts of these materials are often behind paywalls.

[17]National Academies offers a visualization tool (AcademyScope), but its functionalities are limited to visualizing topical relationships between the RSI's reports. While *RER* neither makes available synthesis-related tools for visualization nor review production, it does (as a

journal currently published by Sage) provide reviewers with access to its required web-based submissions management platform, ScholarOne Manuscripts—as does Campbell, which now publishes its journal through Wiley. This platform, however, merely supports the process of closed peer review and revision, prefiguring some review aspects (e.g., through preset options for reviewers' overall recommendations), and requires minimal reporting elements (e.g., title, author affiliation), certain attestations from authors, and selection of keywords.

[18]Quality guidelines supporting more critical genres include RAMESES standards for meta-narrative reviews (Greenhalgh et al., 2005; Wong et al., 2014) discussed in the "Genre" section, as well as Suri (2014) and colleagues' (e.g., Suri & Clark, 2009) MIRS (methodologically inclusive research synthesis) framework "to support critical reflection among producers and users of research syntheses" (Suri, 2014, pp. 4–5) by drawing attention to the "varied options associated with each decision in the process of a rigorous research synthesis" (p. 4).

REFERENCES

Alexander, P. A. (2020). Methodological guidance paper: The art and science of quality systematic reviews. *Review of Educational Research, 90*(1), 6–23. https://doi.org/10.3102/0034654319854352

Booth, A., Sutton, A., & Papaioannou, D. (2016). *Systematic approaches to a successful literature review* (2nd ed.). Sage.

Borgman, C. L. (2015). *Big data, little data, no data: Scholarship in the networked world.* MIT Press.

Bowker, G. C. (2017). How knowledge infrastructures learn. In P. Harvey, C. B. Jensen, & A. Morita (Eds.), *Infrastructures and social complexity: A companion* (pp. 391–403). Routledge.

Bowker, G. C., & Star, S. L. (1999). *Sorting things out: Classification and its consequences.* MIT Press.

Brennan, S. E., Cumpston, M., Misso, M. L., McDonald, S., Murphy, M. J., & Green, S. E. (2016). Design and formative evaluation of the Policy Liaison Initiative: A long-term knowledge translation strategy to encourage and support the use of Cochrane systematic reviews for informing health policy. *Evidence & Policy, 12*(1), 25–52. https://doi.org/10.1332/174426415X14291899424526

Brunton, G., Stansfield, C., Caird, J., & Thomas, J. (2017). Finding relevant studies. In D. Gough, S. Oliver, & J. Thomas (Eds.), *An introduction to systematic reviews* (2nd ed., pp. 93–122). Sage.

Brunton, J., Graziosi, S., & Thomas, J. (2017). Tools and technologies for information management. In D. Gough, S. Oliver, & J. Thomas (Eds.), *An introduction to systematic reviews* (2nd ed., pp. 145–180). Sage.

Campbell Collaboration. (2019, November 14). *Campbell collaboration systematic reviews: Policies and guidelines* (Version 1.6). https://doi.org/10.4073/cpg.2016.1

Chalmers, I., Hedges, L. V., & Cooper, H. (2002). A brief history of research synthesis. *Evaluation & the Health Professions, 25*(1), 12–37. https://doi-org/10.1177/0163278702025001003

Chandler, J., Cumpston, M., Thomas, J., Higgins, J. P. T., Deeks, J. J., & Clark, M. J. (2019). Introduction. In J. P. T. Higgins, J. Thomas, J. Chandler, M. Cumpston, T. Li, M. J. Page, & V. A. Welch (Eds.), *Cochrane handbook for systematic reviews of interventions* (Version 6.0). Cochrane. https://training.cochrane.org/handbook/current/chapter-i

Cochrane. (2019). *Project Transform: Final report, 2015–2018.* https://community.cochrane.org/sites/default/files/uploads/inline-files/Transform/201910_ProjectTransformReport_FINAL_WEB.pdf

Cooper, H., Hedges, L. V., & Valentine, J. C. (Eds.). (2019). *The handbook of research synthesis and meta-analysis* (3rd ed.). Russell Sage Foundation.

Cumpston, M., & Chandler, J. (2019). Planning a Cochrane review. In J. P. T. Higgins, J. Thomas, J. Chandler, M. Cumpston, T. Li, M. J. Page, & V. A. Welch (Eds.), *Cochrane handbook for systematic reviews of interventions* (Version 6.0). Cochrane. https://training .cochrane.org/handbook/current/chapter-ii

Edwards, P. N. (2010). *A vast machine: Computer models, climate data, and the politics of global warming.* MIT Press.

Edwards, P. N., Jackson, S. J., Chalmers, M. K., Bowker, G. C., Borgman, C. L., Ribes, D., Burton, M., & Calvert, S. (2013). *Knowledge infrastructures: Intellectual frameworks and research challenges.* Deep Blue. http://hdl.handle.net/2027.42/97552

Edwards, P. N., Mayernik, M. S., Batcheller, A. L., Bowker, G. C., & Borgman, C. L. (2011). Science friction: Data, metadata, and collaboration. *Social Studies of Science, 41*(5), 667–690. https://doi.org/10.1177/0306312711413314

Elliott, J. H., Synnot, A., Turner, T., Simmonds, M., Akl, E. A., McDonald, S., Salanti, G., Meerpohl, J., MacLehose, H., Hilton, J., Tovey, D., Shemilt, I., & Thomas, J., & Living Systematic Review Network. (2017). Living systematic review: 1. Introduction— the why, what, when, and how. *Journal of Clinical Epidemiology, 91*, 23–30. https://doi .org/10.1016/j.jclinepi.2017.08.010

EPPI-Centre. (n.d.). *About the EPPI-Centre.* Retrieved January 8, 2020, from https://eppi.ioe. ac.uk/cms/Default.aspx?tabid=63

Feldman, K. A. (1971). Using the work of others: Some observations on reviewing and integrating. *Sociology of Education, 44*(1), 86–102. https://doi.org/10.2307/2111964

Feuer, M. J., & Maranto, C. J. (2010). Science advice as procedural rationality: Reflections on the National Research Council. *Minerva, 48*(3), 259–275. https://doi.org/10.1007/ s11024-010-9152-0

France, E. F., Cunningham, M., Ring, N., Uny, I., Duncan, E. A. S., Jepson, R. G., Maxwell, M., Roberts, R. J., Turley, R. L., Booth, A., Britten, N., Flemming, K., Gallagher, I., Garside, R., Hannes, K., Lewin, S., Noblit, G. W., Pope, C., Thomas, J., . . . Noyes, J. (2019). Improving reporting of meta-ethnography: The eMERGe reporting guidance. *BMC Medical Research Methodology, 19*, Article 25. https://doi.org/10.1186/s12874-018-0600-0

Friedman, C. P., Rubin, J. C., & Sullivan, K. J. (2017). Toward an information infrastructure for global health improvement. *IMIA Yearbook of Medical Information, 26*(1), 16–23. https://doi.org/10.15265/IY-2017-004

George, A. L., & Bennett, A. (2005). *Case studies and theory development in the social sciences.* MIT Press.

Ginsburg, A., & Smith, M. S. (2016, March 15). *Do randomized controlled trials meet the "gold standard"? A study of the usefulness of RCTs in the What Works Clearinghouse.* American Enterprise Institute. https://www.aei.org/research-products/report/do-randomized-controlled-trials-meet-the-gold-standard/

Glass, G. V. (1976). Primary, secondary, and meta-analysis of research. *Educational Researcher, 5*(10), 3–8. https://doi.org/10.2307/1174772

Glass, G. V. (1977). Integrating findings: The meta-analysis of research. *Review of Research in Education, 5*(1), 351–379. https://doi.org/10.2307/1167179

Gough, D., Davies, P., Jamtvedt, G., Langlois, E., Littell, J., Loufti, T., Masset, E., Merlin, T., Pullin, A., Ritskes-Hoitinga, M., Røttingen, J.-A., Sena, E., Stewart, R., Tovey, D., White, H., Yost, J., Lund, H., & Grimshaw, J. (2019). Evidence Synthesis International: Position statement. *Systematic Reviews* [Manuscript submitted for publication]. Retrieved February 10, 2019, from https://evidencesynthesisinternational.files.wordpress.com/2019/10/esi-position-statement-for-esi-website-13th-october-2019.pdf

Gough, D., Oliver, S., & Thomas, J. (2017a). Introducing systematic reviews. In D. Gough, S. Oliver, & J. Thomas (Eds.), *An introduction to systematic reviews* (2nd ed., pp. 1–17). Sage.

Gough, D., Oliver, S., & Thomas, J. (2017b). *An introduction to systematic reviews* (2nd ed.). Sage.

Gough, D., & Thomas, J. (2016). Systematic reviews of research in education: Aims, myths and multiple methods. *Review of Education, 4*(1), 84–102. https://doi.org/10.1002/rev3.3068

Gough, D., & Thomas, J. (2017). Commonality and diversity in reviews. In D. Gough, S. Oliver, & J. Thomas (Eds.), *An introduction to systematic reviews* (2nd ed., pp. 43–70). Sage.

Gough, D., Thomas, J., & Oliver, S. (2019). Clarifying differences between reviews within evidence ecosystems. *Systematic Reviews, 8*, Article 170. https://doi.org/10.1186/s13643-019-1089-2

Green, J. L., & Skukauskaitė, A. (2008). Becoming critical readers: Issues in transparency, representation, and warranting of claims. *Educational Researcher, 37*(1), 30–40. https://doi.org/10.3102/0013189X08314828

Greenhalgh, T., Robert, G., Macfarlane, F., Bate, P., Kyriakidou, O., & Peacock, R. (2005). Storylines of research in diffusion of innovation: A meta-narrative approach to systematic review. *Social Science and Medicine, 61*(2), 417–430. https://doi.org/10.1016/j.socscimed.2004.12.001

Heywood, P., Stephani, A. M., & Garner, P. (2018). The Cochrane Collaboration: Institutional analysis of a knowledge commons. *Evidence & Policy, 14*(1), 121–142. https://doi.org/10.1332/174426417X15057479217899

Higgins, J. P. T., Lasserson, T., Chandler, J., Tovey, D., Thomas, J., Flemyng, E., & Churchill, R. (2019, October). *Methodological expectations of Cochrane intervention reviews (MECIR): Standards for the conduct and reporting of new Cochrane intervention reviews, reporting of protocols and the planning, conduct and reporting of updates.* https://community.cochrane.org/mecir-manual

Higgins, J. P. T., Thomas, J., Chandler, J., Cumpston, M., Li, Tianjing, L., Page, M. J., & Welch, V. A. (Eds.). (2019). *Cochrane handbook for systematic reviews of interventions* (2nd ed.). Wiley Blackwell.

Institute of Education Sciences. (2018, October). Postscript from the Institute of Education Sciences. In S. Graham, A. Bollinger, C. B. Olson, C. D'Aoust, C. MacArthur, D. McCutchen, & N. Olinghouse, *Teaching elementary school students to be effective writers* (Revised ed., pp. 43–44; NCEE 2012-4058). National Center for Education Evaluation and Regional Assistance.

Karasti, H. (2014). Infrastructuring in participatory design. In *Proceedings of the 13th Participatory Design Conference: Research papers* (Vol. 1, pp. 141–150). https://doi.org/10.1145/2661435.2661450

Konnerup, M., & Sowden, A. (2008, February 29). *User involvement in the systematic review process: Campbell Collaboration policy brief.* https://www.campbellcollaboration.org/images/pdf/plain-language/Involvement_in_review_process.pdf

Lagoze, C. J. (2010). *Lost identity: The assimilation of digital libraries into the web* (Publication No. 3396228) [Doctoral Dissertation, Cornell University]. ProQuest Dissertations and Theses Global.

Lasserson, T. J., Thomas, J., & Higgins, J. P. T. (2019). Starting a review. In J. P. T. Higgins, J. Thomas, J. Chandler, M. Cumpston, T. Li, M. J. Page, & V. A Welch. (Eds.), *Cochrane handbook for systematic reviews of interventions* (2nd ed., pp. 3–12). Cochrane.

Liabo, K., Gough, D., & Harden, A. (2017). Developing justifiable evidence claims. In D. Gough, S. Oliver, & J. Thomas (Eds.), *An introduction to systematic reviews* (2nd ed., pp. 251–277). Sage.

Light, R. J., & Smith, P. V. (1971). Accumulating evidence: Procedures for resolving contradictions among different research studies. *Harvard Educational Review, 41*(4), 429–471. https://doi.org/10.17763/haer.41.4.437714870334w144

Marshall, I. J., Noel-Storr, A., Kuiper, J., Thomas, J., & Wallace, B. C. (2018). Machine learning for identifying randomized controlled trials: An evaluation and practitioner's guide. *Research Synthesis Methods, 9*(4), 602–614. https://doi.org/10.1002/jrsm.1287

Marshall, I. J., & Wallace, B. C. (2019). Toward systematic review automation: A practical guide to using machine learning tools in research synthesis. *Systematic Reviews, 8*, Article 163. https://doi.org/10.1186/s13643-019-1074-9

Means, S. N., Magura, S., Burkhardt, J. T., Schröter, D. C., & Coryn, C. L. S. (2015). Comparing rating paradigms for evidence-based program registers in behavioral health: Evidentiary criteria and implications for assessing programs. *Evaluation and Program Planning, 48*, 100–116. https://doi.org/10.1016/j.evalprogplan.2014.09.007

Methods Coordinating Group of the Campbell Collaboration. (2019a, October 28). *Methodological expectations of Campbell Collaboration intervention reviews: Conduct standards.* Campbell Collaboration. https://doi.org/10.4073/cpg.2016.3

Methods Coordinating Group of the Campbell Collaboration. (2019b, October 29). *Methodological expectations of Campbell Collaboration intervention reviews: Reporting standards.* Campbell Collaboration. https://doi.org/10.4073/cpg.2016.4

Moher, D., Liberati, A., Tetzlaff, J., & Altman, D. G., & the PRISMA Group. (2009). Preferred reporting items for systematic reviews and meta-analyses: The PRISMA statement. *Annals of Internal Medicine, 151*(4), 264–269. https://doi.org/10.7326/0003-4819-151-4-200908180-00135

Moss, P. A., & Haertel, E. H. (2016). Engaging methodological pluralism. In D. Gitomer & C. Bell (Eds.), *Handbook of research on teaching* (5th ed., pp. 127–247). American Educational Research Association.

Murphy, P. K., Dowd, A. C., Lloyd, G. M., & List, A. (2020). Transparency in literature syntheses and editorial review: Introducing the methodological guidance paper series. *Review of Educational Research, 90*(1), 3–5. https://doi.org/10.3102/0034654319901128

Murphy, P. K., Knight, S. L., & Dowd, A. C. (2017). Familiar paths and new directions: Inaugural call for manuscripts. *Review of Educational Research, 87*(1), 3–6. https://doi.org/10.3102/0034654317691764

National Academies. (n.d.-a). *Guidelines for the review of reports of the National Academies of Sciences, Engineering, and Medicine.* Retrieved January 8, 2020, from https://www.nationalacademies.org/nasem/na_067075.html

National Academies. (n.d.-b). *Our study process.* Retrieved January 8, 2020, from https://www.nationalacademies.org/studyprocess/

National Academies. (2003, May 12). *Policy on committee composition and balance and conflicts of interest for committees used in the development of reports.* https://www.nationalacademies.org/site_assets/groups/nasite/documents/webpage/na_069688.pdf

National Academies. (2018). *About our expert consensus reports.* Retrieved January 8, 2020, from http://dels.nas.edu/global/Consensus-Report

Noblit, G. W., & Hare, R. D. (1988). *Meta-ethnography: Synthesizing qualitative studies.* Sage.

Noyes, J., Booth, A., Cargo, M., Flemming, K., Harden, A., Harris, J., Garside, R., Hannes, K., Pantoja, T., & Thomas, J. (2019). Qualitative evidence. In J. P. T. Higgins, J. Thomas, J. Chandler, M. Cumpston, T. Li, M. J. Page, & V. A Welch. (Eds.), *Cochrane handbook for systematic reviews of interventions* (2nd ed., pp. 525–545). Cochrane.

Oakley, A. (2017). Foreword. In D. Gough, S. Oliver, & J. Thomas (Eds.), *An introduction to systematic reviews* (2nd ed., pp. xiii-xvi). Sage.

Oakley, A., Gough, D., Oliver, S., & Thomas, J. (2005). The politics of evidence and methodology: Lessons from the EPPI-Centre. *Evidence & Policy, 1*(1), 5–31. https://doi.org/10.1332/1744264052703168

Pawson, R. (2006). *Evidence-based policy: A realist perspective.* Sage.

Pigott, T. D., & Polanin, J. R. (2020). Methodological guidance paper: High-quality meta-analysis in a systematic review. *Review of Educational Research, 90*(1), 24–46. https://doi.org/10.3102/0034654319877153

Pipek, V., & Wulf, V. (2009). Infrastructuring: Toward an integrated perspective on the design and use of information technology. *Journal of the Association for Information Systems, 10*(5), 447–473. https://doi.org/10.17705/1jais.00195

Rees, R., & Oliver, S. (2017). Stakeholder perspectives and participation in reviews. In D. Gough, S. Oliver, & J. Thomas (Eds.), *An introduction to systematic reviews* (2nd ed., pp. 19–41). Sage.

Review of Educational Research. (n.d.-a). *Aims and scope.* Retrieved January 8, 2020, from https://journals.sagepub.com/aims-scope/RER

Review of Educational Research. (n.d.-b). *Manuscript submission guidelines.* Retrieved January 8, 2020, from https://journals.sagepub.com/author-instructions/RER

Rivas, C., Vigurs, C., Cameron, J., & Yeo, L. (2019). A realist review of which advocacy interventions work for which abused women under what circumstances. *Cochrane Database of Systematic Reviews.* https://doi.org/10.1002/14651858.CD013135.pub2

Sandelowski, M., Voils, C. J., & Barroso, J. (2006). Defining and designing mixed research synthesis studies. *Research in the Schools, 13*(1), 29–40.

Saran, A., & White, H. (2018). Evidence and gap maps: A comparison of different approaches (Version 1.0). *Campbell Systematic Reviews, 14*(1), 1–38. https://doi.org/10.4073/cmdp.2018.2

Slavin, R. E. (2008). What works? Issues in synthesizing educational program evaluations. *Educational Researcher, 37*(1), 5–14. https://doi.org/10.3102/0013189X08314117

Slota, S. C., & Bowker, G. C. (2017). How infrastructures matter. In U. Felt, R. Fouché, C. A. Miller, & L. Smith-Doerr (Eds.), *The handbook of science and technology studies* (4th ed., pp. 529–554). MIT Press.

Snilstveit, B., Stevenson, J., Shemilt, I., Clarke, M., Jimenez, E., & Thomas, J. (2018, March). *Timely, efficient, and living systematic reviews: Opportunities in international development* (CEDIL Inception Paper 7). Centre of Excellence for Development Impact and Learning. https://cedilprogramme.org/wp-content/uploads/2018/11/Inception-Paper-7-Birte-Snilsveit-Timely-Efficient-and-living-systematic-reviews.pdf

Star, S. L., & Ruhleder, K. (1996). Steps toward an ecology of infrastructure: Design and access for large information spaces. *Information Systems Research, 7*(1), 111–134. https://doi.org/10.1287/isre.7.1.111

Suri, H. (2014). *Towards methodologically inclusive research syntheses: Expanding possibilities.* Routledge.

Suri, H., & Clarke, D. (2009). Advancements in research synthesis methods: From a methodologically inclusive perspective. *Review of Educational Research, 79*(1), 395–430. https://doi.org/10.3102/0034654308326349

Teston, C. (2017). *Bodies in flux: Scientific methods for negotiating medical uncertainty.* University of Chicago Press.

Thomas, J., & Harden, A. (2008). Methods for the thematic synthesis of qualitative research in systematic reviews. *BMC Medical Research Methodology, 8*, Article 45. https://doi.org/10.1186/1471-2288-8-45

Thomas, J., Noel-Storr, A., Marshall, I., Wallace, B., McDonald, S., Mavergames, C., Glasziou, P., Shemilt, I., Synnot, A., Turner, T., & Elliott, J. (2017). Living systematic reviews: 2. Combining human and machine effort. *Journal of Clinical Epidemiology, 91*, 31–37. https://doi.org/10.1016/j.jclinepi.2017.08.011

Thomas, J., O'Mara-Eves, A., Harden, A., & Newman, M. (2017). Synthesis methods for combining and configuring textual or mixed methods data. In D. Gough, S. Oliver, & J. Thomas (Eds.), *An introduction to systematic reviews* (2nd ed., pp. 181–209). Sage.

Tsafnat, G., Glasziou, P., Choong, M. K., Dunn, A., Galgani, F., & Coiera, E. (2014). Systematic review automation technologies. *Systematic Reviews, 3*, Article 74. https://doi.org/10.1186/2046-4053-3-74

What Works Clearinghouse. (n.d.-a). *Welcome to the What Works Clearinghouse.* https://ies.ed.gov/ncee/wwc/FWW

What Works Clearinghouse. (n.d.-b). *WWC reviewer certification.* Retrieved January 8, 2020, from https://ies.ed.gov/ncee/wwc/Document/237#/Document_237_Becoming

What Works Clearinghouse. (2020a). *What Works Clearinghouse^{TM}: Procedures handbook* (Version 4.1). https://ies.ed.gov/ncee/wwc/Docs/referenceresources/WWC-Procedures-Handbook-v4-1-508.pdf

What Works Clearinghouse. (2020b). *What Works Clearinghouse^{TM}: Standards handbook* (Version 4.1). https://ies.ed.gov/ncee/wwc/Docs/referenceresources/WWC-Standards-Handbook-v4-1-508.pdf

White, H. (2019). The twenty-first century experimenting society: The four waves of the evidence revolution. *Palgrave Communications, 5*, Article 47. https://doi.org/10.1057/s41599-019-0253-6

Wong, G., Greenhalgh, T., Westhorp, G., & Pawson, R. (2014, September). Development of methodological guidance, publication standards and training materials for realist and meta-narrative reviews: The RAMESES (Realist And Meta-narrative Evidence Syntheses–Evolving Standards) project. *Health Services and Delivery Research, 2*(30). https://doi.org/10.3310/hsdr02300

Zawacki-Richter, O., Kerres, M., Bedenlier, S., Bond, M., & Buntins, K. (Eds.). (2020). *Systematic reviews in educational research: Methodology, perspectives and application.* Springer VS.

Chapter 2

Terminological "Communities": A Conceptual Mapping of Scholarship Identified With Education's "Global Turn"

HEELA GOREN
University College London

MIRI YEMINI
Tel Aviv University

CLAIRE MAXWELL
University of Copenhagen

EFRAT BLUMENFELD-LIEBERTHAL
Tel Aviv University

This chapter presents an innovative, cross-disciplinary methodological approach to systematically reviewing and comparing large bodies of literature using big data, Natural Language Processing, network analysis, and supplementary qualitative analysis. The approach is demonstrated through an analysis of the literature surrounding four common concepts within the scholarship related to the global turn in education: 21st-century skills, global citizenship, intercultural competencies, and cosmopolitan education. An analysis is made of each network representing the focal concepts. We also undertake a comparative analysis of topics appearing across the scholarship found on the different concepts. Through this analysis we highlight some benefits of the outlined methodology in identifying overarching themes across bodies of literature, locating differences in how topics are approached within the context of each concept, revealing blind spots and caveats in specific areas of scholarship, and being able to outline distinctive characteristics of the literature related to each concept. Limitations and potential uses of the method are subsequently discussed. This review will be of use to researchers from any field who are interested in novel methodological ways of unpacking and analyzing large bodies of knowledge, as well as scholars embarking on research related to the global turn in education, and finally, policymakers looking to identify which concepts to utilize in their work in this area.

Review of Research in Education
March 2020, Vol. 44, pp. 36–63
DOI: 10.3102/0091732X20909161
Chapter reuse guidelines: sagepub.com/journals-permissions
© 2020 AERA. http://rre.aera.net

Ongoing processes of globalization within education have significantly shaped the goals of schooling, leading to countries adopting a variety of internationalization strategies (Knight, 2004), as well its governance structures. This could be said to constitute the global turn in education, or what Mannion et al. (2011) termed a *curricular global turn.* The global turn in education is more often associated with global governance and its effects on national policy (Meyer & Benavot, 2013), whereas the curricular aspects of it are most often associated with the introduction of new models of citizenship and an emphasis on skills that would prepare students to participate and succeed in a global society through schooling (Bamber, Bullivant, et al., 2018; Mannion et al., 2011; Van der Wende, 2007). Schooling now, more than ever, seeks to prepare students to take part in the "global competition" for future education and employment destinations, participate in "global problem solving," and, broadly, be better equipped to face the challenges that globally connected contemporary societies must engage with (Dill, 2013; Reilly & Niens, 2014; Vidovich, 2004).

Both practitioners and the research literature refer to the multifaceted manifestations of the global turn within schools as promoting "global citizenship education" (GCE), teaching "21st-century skills," developing "intercultural competencies," and offering a "cosmopolitan education." These terms and some others (e.g., international mindedness, education for global competencies, education for world citizenship, education for world competencies, and education for global consciousness) are all used synonymously in many cases (Caruana, 2014; Goren & Yemini, 2017; Kerkhoff, 2017). Policymakers and scholars take into account different contextual factors when choosing which to employ, but they rarely present or justify how this decision is made. Thus, the meanings associated with each term within the context being studied are often unclear and why a particular term has been chosen over another not articulated.

The terms that are adopted differ somewhat. There are those that relate to the curricular aspects of the global turn (e.g., *global citizenship education, education for intercultural skills, education for global competence, cosmopolitan education and education for 21st-century skills*), while others are more prevalent in discussions of the global turn in education governance (e.g., *global education governance, internationalization, policy borrowing*). Meanwhile, in the literature we also find terms that are arguably too broad or too specific (e.g., *multiculturalism, digital literacy*). Such a situation means that when reviewing the literature or analyzing the policy produced, there can be challenges in having a consistent set of terms to compare across, or concepts appear to overlap with one another. To this end, we propose a method that will enable us to navigate these large bodies of knowledge in order to identifying trends in the field and understand how and when different terms are used.

Thus, this chapter has two objectives. First to outline a new approach for reviewing large bodies of literature using an innovative, interdisciplinary methodology integrating the use of Big Data, artificial intelligence (AI) in the form of natural language processing (NLP), and network analysis, alongside qualitative data analysis. Second, we offer a comprehensive analysis of the literature related to the curricular aspects of the global turn in education, which scholars and policymakers can draw on to more carefully situate their work and link their contributions to previous research. We focus on the scholarship related to curricular aspects of the global turn in education rather than work on global governance structures in this chapter, because the similarities between the common terms that demonstrate curricular responses to global processes enable us to better demonstrate the advantages of the comparative aspects of our methodology. In our analysis we focus on the academic scholarship surrounding four concepts that are commonly used in the research on the curricular aspects of the global turn in education (Mannion et al., 2011): 21st-century skills, GCE, education for intercultural competence, and cosmopolitan education. Our methodological approach enables us to identify the central foci of research within each of these four concepts and to, critically, demonstrate their interrelationships. We do this by identifying the topics that are common in the academic scholarship surrounding each of the four concepts for which data were collected, and then qualitatively examining the relationship between the concepts themselves. Through this process we were able to identify some distinctive trends within, and characteristics of, the literature surrounding each of the concepts, as well as capture the overarching themes that are present in each of the networks and that are shared across all or some of them. We conclude by proposing how the methodology presented here could be employed by scholars embarking on research in complex fields, in order to identify core terms, caveats, and strands of research across large bodies of literature both individually, when looking at the literature surrounding a single concept, and comparatively, when examining a broader field.

METHOD

Our method (developed by Blumenfeld-Lieberthal et al., 2017, and partially implemented in Yemini et al., 2019) is based on several stages, namely, data collection, NLP analysis, network creation, network visualization, and supplementary qualitative analysis (see Figure 1 for overview). The main novelty in the methodology described in this chapter is that is it used comparatively, to examine a several bodies of knowledge, in a way that can provide insights that would be difficult to obtain through other methods of systematic review. While other methods that involve NLP use the frequency of words, entities, and phrases, our method is based on identifying the topics each paper is engaged with based on a comparison of the papers to other, categorized texts. Additionally, it presents a hierarchy of these topics, based on the extent with which they appear within individual papers and within these large bodies of literature, thus providing ground for a more nuanced analysis.

Data Collection

We used one of the three largest databases for peer-reviewed education research, the Education Resources Information Center (ERIC), to screen

FIGURE 1
Flowchart Detailing Stages of the Methodology

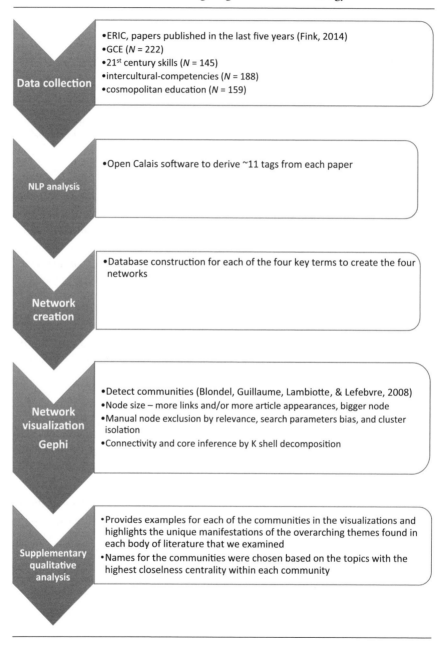

Data collection
- ERIC, papers published in the last five years (Fink, 2014)
- GCE (N = 222)
- 21st century skills (N = 145)
- intercultural-competencies (N = 188)
- cosmopolitan education (N = 159)

NLP analysis
- Open Calais software to derive ~11 tags from each paper

Network creation
- Database construction for each of the four key terms to create the four networks

Network visualization Gephi
- Detect communities (Blondel, Guillaume, Lambiotte, & Lefebvre, 2008)
- Node size – more links and/or more article appearances, bigger node
- Manual node exclusion by relevance, search parameters bias, and cluster isolation
- Connectivity and core inference by K shell decomposition

Supplementary qualitative analysis
- Provides examples for each of the communities in the visualizations and highlights the unique manifestations of the overarching themes found in each body of literature that we examined
- Names for the communities were chosen based on the topics with the highest closeness centrality within each community

academic peer-reviewed papers published in the past 5 years, concentrating on each of the four concepts included in our analysis: GCE ($N = 226$), 21st-century skills ($N = 168$), intercultural competencies ($N = 191$), and cosmopolitan education ($N = 159$). The data collection process followed Fink's (2010) guidelines for systematic reviews, which emphasize rigor and reproducibility. First, we created a list of concepts associated with the global turn through our previous large scale reviews concerning GCE (Goren & Yemini, 2017; Yemini et al., 2019) and other books and reviews of scholarship related to global education and the global turn (i.e., Chu et al., 2017; Meyer & Benavot, 2013). This list of concepts included (in addition to the final four that we address throughout the review) concepts such as internationalization, global governance, digital literacy, multiculturalism, education for world citizenship, education for world competencies, and education for global consciousness. As the first three authors are experienced scholars in this field, we conversed until consensus was reached regarding eight concepts (which we later cut down to four) that we agreed had enough characteristics in common to be examined in a comparative manner: GCE, cosmopolitan education, education for intercultural competencies, 21st-century skills education, education for global competencies, education for world citizenship, education for world competencies, and education for global consciousness. To avoid making conjectures based on small cohorts of articles, we decided to include only search terms (concepts) that yielded at least 100 results, thus resulting in the four selected terms (GCE, 21st-century skills, intercultural competencies, and cosmopolitan education). Underlying our strategy is the assumption that terms that yielded more results are more commonly agreed upon as encapsulating the ideas being worked on within the scholarly community.

The searches were all performed as follows: the concept (with an asterisk for those with different forms such as cosmopolit* to include cosmopolitan and cosmopolitanism) + education; and limited to results published in peer-reviewed journals between 2014 and 2018 (the past 5 years). We created a separate database for each key term and downloaded all papers with an available full text. For papers that did not have an available full text file in ERIC, we searched google scholar and the UCL Explore databases to exhaust all options.

All authors then read the abstracts of the papers to review their relevance for the key term with which they were associated. We excluded papers that we agreed did not actually concentrate on the related key term; two examples of such exclusions are a paper that appeared in the search results for GCE titled "Improving Critical Thinking With Mobile Tools and Apps" (Lin et al., 2014) and one that appeared in the 21st-century skills search results titled "Playing in the Virtual Sandbox: Students' Collaborative Practices in Minecraft" (Davis et al., 2018). Neither of these papers included any meaningful discussion or conceptualizations related to their respective concepts (i.e., definitions, references to relevant scholarship, elaboration on the contribution to the field of research surrounding the concept), so both were removed from the cohort. Following this inclusion/exclusion protocol, the cohort sizes were as follows: GCE, $N = 222$; 21st-century skills, $N = 145$; intercultural competencies, $N = 188$; and cosmopolitan education, $N = 159$.

Key Terms

Due to the complexity of the methodology, in this section we identify and explain the key terms related to the approach to ensure clarity. First, the *concepts* we discuss in this chapter are intercultural competence, GCE, 21st-century skills, and cosmopolitan education. The *network* for each of these concepts is composed of *nodes*, each of which represents a *term* that was identified and derived through the NLP analysis. The topics in the networks are connected by *edges* (which we mostly refer to as *connections*), and the size of each term (node) is determined by its *weighted degree*—the sum of the weight of the edges connected to that node. In each network, there are different *communities*; these identify topics that are densely connected (i.e., frequently appeared in the same paper). The communities therefore represent strands of literature. In the network visualizations, nodes belonging to different communities appear in different colors. Finally, we refer to the *K-core* of each network, which represents the maximal subgroup of the network, in which all nodes are connected to at least k other nodes within this subgroup. In other words, this subnetwork contains the topics that are mostly connected to one another, thus illustrating the key, most central terms used by scholars to explore a specific concept.

NLP Analysis and Network Creation

Once we had assembled the database of all searchable articles, we followed the methodology developed by Blumenfeld-Lieberthal et al. (2017) to continue the analysis. First, we used the Open Calais software developed by Thomson Reuters, which utilizes machine learning and NLP-driven algorithms to derive topics ("social tags") from each of the individual articles in the cohort.[1]

The full text of each paper in each cohort was run through the Open Calais program to extract the metadata of topics or "social tags" representing the subjects comprising its content. The resulting list of topics for each paper (an average of 11 tags per paper) included words that represent the topics the paper addresses and were substantial enough for the software to identify.[2]

While most NLP approaches use the frequency of the words in the text to identify the topics it deals with, Open Calais uses a different algorithm that compares the input text to other, categorized texts, and based on their similarity it determines the main topics of the text. In other words, the topic is identified through its resemblance to other texts that have been classified as engaged with the same topic rather than by the frequency of words that appear within it, or relying on keywords the authors selected for their paper.

Based on the above metadata, we used a co-word methodology (Chavalarias & Cointet, 2008; i.e., linking papers through the co-occurrences of topics to create networks). This process resulted in a categorization scheme with nodes representing the topics, and links denoting co-appearances of two different topics in the same article. The weight of the links represents the number of times two different nodes (topics) appeared in the same article—in other words, the number of articles that were engaged with these two topics.

Network Analysis

Finally, we used the network visualization and exploration software Gephi[3] to perform our analysis and visualize its results. To detect better connected nodes that form communities within our networks (and depict topics that are more closely related to one another within the entire examined corpus), we used the Gephi embedded algorithm based on the Louvain method (Blondel et al., 2008) for community detection. The creation of a cluster or "community" (as they are called throughout this chapter) indicates that the nodes in the same community (represented by the same color in the visualization) are densely linked to the other nodes in the community, and constitute a separate strand of literature. The size of each individual node in the visualization is a function of the number of links the term has and the number of times it appears in the data set (when counted once per article). Thus, larger nodes indicate topics that appear in multiple articles with many other topics.

We omitted from the networks all nodes with a frequency smaller than 2 (i.e., nodes that appeared in only one paper), ensuring that we concentrated on the essential components and relationships in the network (Kumar et al., 2010). This exclusion criterion led to the removal of some names of specific academic institutions and topics related only to a very unique aspect of a particular paper. For example, one paper in the cosmopolitan education network titled "Intersecting Scapes and New Millennium Identities in Language Learning" (Higgins, 2015) used a framework of cosmopolitanism to explore students' engagement in "anime" and "manga" in an introductory university-level Japanese language classroom in Hawaii. Although the paper engages with the topics "anime" and "manga" enough for them to appear as tags, they are unique to its particular focus, and therefore were excluded from the analysis.

Nodes were also omitted if they included the search terms that the network was based on, to prevent them from overtaking the network by dictating the communities due to their high frequencies. For example, the node Education was removed from all of the networks, in addition to its respective unique search terms (i.e., cosmopolitan*, global citizen*, intercultural skill*, 21st-century skill*). In the next stage of the exclusion process, nodes that depicted topics that are very broad and had very high frequencies compared to the rest of the topics in each network were also removed; this includes topics such as Curricula, Curriculum, Teacher, Student, Culture, and Policy. These topics were removed across the networks because they are very broad and hence have co-appearances with many othertopics hence rendering their appearance meaningless in a list of tags. For example, a word like *culture* could appear as a topic derived from over 90% of the articles in a cohort, thus making it appear very large in the visualization, but its appearance does not contribute to the analysis because it is so broad. Next, we removed all the nodes that were not part of the "giant component" (i.e., the largest group of nodes connected to each other directly, or indirectly, that did not have edges connecting them to the rest of the network (meaning they were mentioned exclusively with each other).

After removing the excluded topics we calculated the network density for each of the networks (see Table 1). The network density represents the ratio between the existing and the possible links, that is, the percentage of actual links out of all possible ones.

After analyzing the networks, we applied two different filters in Gephi to reveal (1) the 10 topics with the highest closeness centrality in each network (meaning the nodes that are nearest, on average, to the largest number of other nodes) and (2) the K-core of each network, which includes only topics that were connected to the maximal number k of other nodes in this core. We accomplished the latter by means of the K-shell decomposition[4] using the K-core filter in Gephi. The nodes that comprise the core are those that are most often mentioned together, indicating that they are at the center of discussions within the literature. Because an average of 11 topics appeared in each paper, a K-core of 11 or less in a network indicates that it does not have a strong core and the scholarship is scattered rather than centered on certain central topics.

Supplementary Qualitative Analysis

Due to the descriptive nature of the network analysis and visualizations, we supplemented the analysis using a deductive qualitative approach (Morse & Niehaus, 2009). This allowed us to provide in-depth examples of the analysis for each of the communities in the networks, and, critically, to highlight the distinctive manifestations of the themes we found across all of the networks.

The qualitative analysis was performed as follows: Once we had established the networks, we used the databases created in the second stage (after the use of Open Calais), which included the key topics derived by the program for each article, so as to locate papers that had co-occurrences of topics that were linked in the network. We then read each of those papers fully to get a more nuanced sense of how the topics we were interested in were actually connected within the scholarship. Once we identified the themes that appeared across all of the networks, we once again searched the our databases to locate specific articles that were found by Open Calais to include two or more of the topics associated with each (qualitatively identified) theme. The analysis of these articles is used in this chapter to show the similarities and differences in the appearances of these themes in the context of the literature surrounding each concept, as we demonstrate later in this chapter.

Limitations and Advantages of This Mixed-Methods Approach

The approach we have outlined in this chapter (developed by Blumenfeld-Lieberthal et al., 2017, and partly implemented in Yemini et al., 2019) provides an

TABLE 1
Network Analysis Results by Concept

Concept	No. of Nodes (Frequency > 2)	Representative Topics for Each Community (Highest Closeness Centrality Within the Community)	Network Density	10 Highest Closeness Centrality	Network Core (K-core = X, n = No. of Nodes)
Education for 21st-century skills	111	• Problem solving and creativity • Teaching method and information technology • Active learning and project-based learning • Technology integration and science education	0.109	Active learning Technology integration Project-based learning Inquiry-based learning Science education Literacy Learning environment Information literacy Cooperative learning Problem-based learning	K-core = 14, n = 15
Cosmopolitan education	110	• Cross-cultural studies and linguistics • Social philosophy and discrimination • Critical theory and poststructuralism • Politics and world government • Student exchange and racism	0.112	Politics World government Cultural geography Global citizenship Social philosophy Globalization Citizenship Cultural globalization Global education Critical pedagogy	K-core = 9, n = 39

(continued)

TABLE 1 (CONTINUED)

Concept	No. of Nodes (Frequency > 2)	Representative Topics for Each Community (Highest Closeness Centrality Within the Community)	Network Density	10 Highest Closeness Centrality	Network Core (K-core = X, n = No. of Nodes)
Global citizenship education	140	• Political philosophy and globalization • Critical pedagogy and alternative education • Environmental education and education for sustainable development • Literacy and critical literacy	0.088	Community building Education for sustainable development Environmental education Situated learning Service-learning Transformative learning Alternative education Globalization Political philosophy Critical pedagogy	K-core = 11, n = 26
Intercultural competencies	66	• Critical pedagogy and experiential learning • International education and study abroad • Language education and English as a second or foreign language • Distance education and virtual exchange	0.137	Language education Critical pedagogy English as a second or foreign language Experiential learning Language-teaching methodology Distance education Computer-assisted language learning Bilingual education Second-language acquisition Telecollaboration	K-core = 7, n = 30
Full network	180 (frequency > 5)	• Interculturalism and intercultural competence • Critical pedagogy and global citizenship • Language education and English as a second or foreign language • 21st-century skills and teacher education	0.189	Global citizenship Interculturalism Critical pedagogy Citizenship Global education Intercultural competence Global citizenship education Global studies 21st-century skills Human communication	K-core = 24, n = 46

innovative way of creating an overview of academic fields and concepts, reveal research trajectories and strands, and, specifically through the developments presented in this chapter, comparatively examine the composition of large bodies of literature. Nonetheless, the approach has several limitations that must be taken into account both while reading this chapter and when undertaking similar research endeavors.

First, the use of NLP relies on AI that requires manual adjustments, thus introducing subjectivity to this mostly quantitative approach. One example of such subjectivity is the need to remove some broad topics that would overshadow and shape the network, as explained above; another example lies in the need to remove the search terms, leading to the keyword "citizenship" being eliminated from the GCE network. These decisions shape the data in a way that should not be ignored, but they can be taken into account and therefore we argue the network still provides an accurate portrayal of the discussions found within it. For example, in the 21st-century skills network, we removed the word "skills" from the list of topics in the network—but this did not preclude us from observing the specific types of skills that still appear in the network such as critical thinking and digital literacy.

Another limitation of the methodology is that the interpretations of links that appear in the networks is undertaken post hoc, through focused searches for co-appearances of key words in individual articles; this process includes sampling only some of the relevant articles and inferring some generalizations. For this reason, our interpretations of the network are carefully worded to point to possible explanations and trends rather than empirical claims. In addition, the NLP algorithm employed by Open Calais does not identify sentiment within the text, and as a result the network analysis is not sensitive to whether or not a concept is presented from a critical or noncritical standpoint.

Nevertheless, the combination we employed of the inductive and quantitative method of NLP and network analysis, supplemented by a deductive and qualitative search for explanations of connections, similarities, and differences that were too intricate to observe through the network analysis, provides a rounded and comprehensive picture that cannot be captured without such a mixed-method approach we argue.

Readers should take into account that the methodology we present here was tailored to fit the goals of our research, and as a result some potential uses of the methodology are not demonstrated here. For example, we did not create our database based on the journal in which each article was published, although this can be done and could provide valuable insights into the terminology and concepts employed by the different publication venues. We also did not divide the cohorts of articles into years, which we have previously done using this method (Yemini et al., 2019); doing this would have enabled a review of the scholarship's evolution over time within each concept, but it was determined to be beyond the scope of this chapter.

FINDINGS

The analysis described above produced four networks (one for each concept), each of which is composed of four communities that represent different strands of literature. In this section, we discuss the composition of the individual networks and their communities, offer some examples, and make interpretations of co-appearances of topics that we show to be connected in the networks. We then present some broad findings from our analysis of the full dataset and discuss themes that appeared across the networks. We highlight the distinct manifestations of the themes in each network using examples from the relevant literature, and provide yet further insights about them by drawing on the analysis of the entire network.

Quantitative Metrics and Network Cores

The number of nodes or topics that appeared in more than one article in each network was as follows: 21st-century skills, 111; GCE, 140; cosmopolitan education, 110; intercultural competence, 66. The network density calculation also reflects this variance in that the intercultural competence network is the densest (0.137), indicating it has the highest ratio of potential to actual connections between topics. This distribution also suggests that the discussions in the literature surrounding this concept is slightly more consistent than the others with regard to the topics associated with it or used to describe it. Conversely, the GCE network density is the smallest (0.088), possibly indicating an opposite trend, whereby the GCE body of literature is more complex, with different papers often concentrating on discrete aspects or interpretations of the term.

The K-core values of the networks and the number of topics in each K-core provide some information about the networks' composition (see Figure 2). As explained in the methodology section, the "coreness" of the network is determined by the maximal number of connections in a subnetwork where each node is connected to at least k other nodes. In other words, the K-core includes only the nodes that are mentioned together with all the other nodes in the core most often. By revealing the topics most often mentioned together across the network, the value of K also reveals the extent to which the scholarship is either focused or scattered; a K value that is lower than the average number of topics extracted from each article (11) points to a scattered discussion with relatively small number of connections between topics that appear in different papers. The value of n further illuminates the nature of the discussion, as low values indicate the discussion is more focused around few topics that keep appearing together in different studies. The core of the network of the 21st-century skills has the highest K-core value (K $=$ 14, n $=$ 15), followed by GCE (K $=$ 11, n $=$ 26), cosmopolitan education (K $=$ 9, n $=$ 39), and intercultural competencies (K $=$ 7, n $=$ 30). This means that the scholarship surrounding 21st-century skills is the most consistent and focused, whereas the discussion in the GCE scholarship and even more so that within cosmopolitan education and intercultural competence scholarship are more diverse and a larger number of disparate focal points

FIGURE 2
Visualisation of the Core of Each Network: (A) 21st-Century Skills; (B) Cosmopolitan Education; (C) Global Citizenship Education; (D) Intercultural Skills

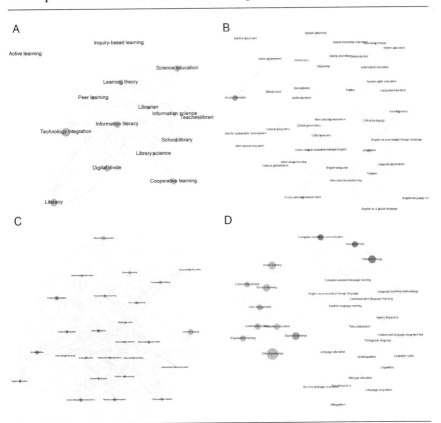

Note. A detailed view of this figure is available in the online journal.

can be identified within each of them. Accordingly, the values of *n* for these last two concepts are the highest (which corresponds to their low K values, and reflects that many studies in these areas focus on topics that are markedly different).

We now turn to describe the results of the analysis for each of the bodies of literature we examined, highlighting the communities that emerged in each network and set out the core of each network. This demonstrates a central benefit of our methodological approach—the ability to identify strands of literature and key topics within large bodies of knowledge.

21st-Century Skills

The 21st-century skills network shows four distinct communities that can be identified as follows: (1) problem solving and creativity, (2) teaching method and information technology, (3) active learning and project based learning, and (4) technology integration and science education.

The clearest observation that can be derived from this network relates to the pervasiveness of topics related to technology, information and communication technologies (ICTs), and digital literacy that are scattered throughout the communities in this network. These concepts are ubiquitous in the 21st-century skills scholarship, with the literature evaluating and researching information literacy and new developments in E-learning options and technologies that now appear at the heart of many institutional attempts to promote this sort of learning and education.

Another distinctive characteristic of this network is the appearance of topics related to the Organisation for Economic Co-operation and Development (OECD) and digital literacy. The community that includes these topics demonstrates that the OECD and the Program for International Student Assessment (PISA), which have begun assessing 21st-century skills and has taken a wide interest in their dissemination, are most commonly mentioned in tandem with topics related to technology and digital skills—even more often than they are mentioned alongside topics like assessment or any nontechnological skills. This may indicate a certain inclination of these organizations to promote a particular type of 21st-century student (Lucas, 2016; O'Leary et al., 2018). This tendency raises some questions about inequality between nations and within them in terms of the digital divide, a research concern that also appears in this community, and highlights the essential role that access to information plays in promoting 21st-century skills (Scalise, 2016; Storksdieck, 2016; Terrazas-Arellanes et al., 2017).

The 21st-century skills network has a K-core value of 14 and contains 15 nodes. The core of this network boils down to two components: information literacy and technology, and forms of learning associated with 21st-century skills. This finding suggests that the main skill associated with 21st-century skills in the scholarship is information literacy, which can be promoted through technology integration (also in this core). The appearance of the digital divide at the core of this network could indicate awareness in the scholarship of the inequality that could be amplified through some initiatives aimed at promoting 21st-century skills, or, alternatively, a view of 21st-century skills education as a way of mitigating the digital divide. The characteristics of this core suggests a focused core, in that most of the topics appear together in different studies.

Broadly, this network is characterized by its concrete nature; all of the communities are closely related to the skills, pedagogies, and motives related to education for 21st-century skills. These is also a noticeable presence of topics related to assessment scattered across the different communities, indicating that it plays a significant role in shaping and dictating the foci of the scholarship—perhaps limiting it in a sense to those aspects that could be said to be measured.

Cosmopolitan Education

The analysis of the cosmopolitan education network reveals that it is multifaceted and complex, encompassing a broad variety of conceptions and associations for this term. The network reveals five communities: (1) cross-cultural studies and linguistics, (2) social philosophy and discrimination, (3) critical theory and poststructuralism, (4) politics and world government, and (5) student exchange and racism. The discussions pervasive in this network are the least focused of all the concept networks we present here, as demonstrated by the characteristics of its core and the variety of concepts within its communities.

The cosmopolitan education network analysis shows that the literature surrounding this concept is more likely to discuss and engage with issues of race, social place, social justice, and inequality than the scholarship related to the other concepts we examined. This network ties the concept of cosmopolitanism to concepts such as intersectionality, cultural/social capital, neoliberalism, employment, and social inequality, pointing to a more critical approach that some scholars have taken (e.g., Groves & O'Connor, 2018; Hull & Stornaiuolo, 2014).

The cosmopolitan education network also included a variety of topics related to global citizenship, globalization, and governance. Cosmopolitanism and global citizenship are often mentioned synonymously, or in tandem, with GCE portrayed as a way to promote cosmopolitanism among students, and global citizenship portrayed as the outcome of cosmopolitan education (Coryell et al., 2014). Internationalization of higher education also appears in this network, indicating that the scholarship surrounding cosmopolitan education in relation to higher education commonly uses GCE as a term that expresses concrete strategies related to internationalization and skill development rather than abstract notions of closeness or empathy (Caruana, 2014; Moskal & Schweisfurth, 2018).

Narrowing the cosmopolitan education network to its core reveals that the discussion is scattered, as the K-core is 9 and it includes 39 nodes. The nodes that comprise the core belong to different communities and include student exchange and higher education from one community, over 10 topics related to world government and global citizenship, two topics related to philosophy (social philosophy and Martha Nussbaum, a key scholar in the field), over 10 topics connected to linguistics and language education, and finally five topics related to intercultural competence. As explained in the methodology, a K-core value under 11 (the average number of topics derived from each paper) points to the lack of a unified core or key topics that can be identified as essential throughout the scholarship.

This network reveals an interesting paradox about cosmopolitan education scholarship—that it can simultaneously be described as philosophical and broad, while at the same time attentive to contextual issues such as positionality and inequality. The core illuminates this finding by showing that the discussion is scattered rather than focused, suggesting these topics would be discussed across distinct strands of the literature.

Global Citizenship Education

Across the full cohort of GCE literature, the network analysis reveals four dominant communities in the research concerning GCE: (1) political philosophy and globalization, (2) critical pedagogy and alternative education, (3) environmental education and education for sustainable development, and (4) literacy and critical literacy. These communities differ in their interconnectedness as well as their relationships with each other, as demonstrated by the density of topics within each community and the thickness of the connecting lines.

The first community centers around globalization and internationalization but also includes cosmopolitanism—a disposition that is seen as synonymous with global citizenship or a desired outcome of GCE in many settings. This community also includes the term *nationalism*, often portrayed as a barrier to GCE or perceived as being at the opposite end of the spectrum (Fernekes, 2016; Rapoport, 2010). GCE appears to be a much more politically charged concept than the other concepts we examined, encompassing topics like politics, world and global governance, neoliberalism, and social inequality. This community also includes topics related to intercultural competence and English as a second language. We infer several observations from the appearance of these topics in the same community. First, language (and specifically English) is often portrayed in the scholarship as a prerequisite for GCE, mirroring neoliberal trends (Aktas et al., 2017; Cho & Mosselson, 2018; Myers, 2016; Wang & Hoffman, 2016). Mastery of the English language is not a subset of skills but rather a separate prerequisite for participation in the Western-dominated global society. Furthermore, the inclusion of intercultural learning in this community rather than the community pertaining to pedagogies also indicates its distinctiveness as a different form or category of GCE, often driven by a rationale that concentrates on social cohesion in light of migration, for example, rather than the cultivation of forms of thinking and concrete skills associated with economically driven forms of GCE. This type of rationale for GCE is well demonstrated by Engel's (2014) analysis of the citizenship education reform in Spain, largely catalyzed by incoming migration. The appearance of human rights, global justice, right to asylum, and forced migration in this community indicates that these issues may appear as broad justifications for GCE, and conceptualized as byproducts of globalization. Articles that discuss human rights as key a concept within this body of literature are often somewhat critical or skeptical of GCE's commitment to human rights education, discussing the complexity of the concept and how this might push ideas related to human rights aside (Fernekes, 2016; Monaghan & Spreen, 2016).

The third community in the GCE network points to a very distinct strand in the GCE scholarship devoted to the definitions and conceptions promoted by UNESCO, which until recently centered heavily on environmental education and education for sustainable development but now also encompass peace education under the umbrella of GCE (Bamber et al., 2016; Bamber, Lewin, & White, 2018; Mochizuki, 2016). The uniqueness of this community shows that these topics are often presented in a way that does not necessarily engage with other forms of GCE in any meaningful manner and is somewhat disconnected from the concrete skills, dispositions, and structures found in the other communities (Mochizuki, 2016). UNESCO's recent integration of GCE into its 2030 Sustainable Development Goals (SDGs) bound the concepts of sustainable development and GCE together in a more meaningful way. However, these notions, our analysis shows, have already been referred to in tandem in the literature long before this (see Bamber et al., 2016). The centrality of these topics in the network is not surprising, as UNESCO's SDGs have now become a driving force and central rationale in much of the GCE scholarship. Indeed, the distinctiveness of this community suggests that these topics are not dispersed throughout the literature and are more likely to appear together. The interrelationships between the topics in this community show the power that international and supranational organizations like UNESCO can hold over academic scholarship, commandeering topics and shaping their meaning in a way that eventually makes them synonymous with the organizations themselves. This raises questions about the balance of power between these bodies and academia, challenging the extent to which NGOs and supranational bodies engage with other academic conceptions when forming their agendas and the nexus of scholarship and practice (as discussed by VanderDussen Toukan, 2018).

The final community in this network connects GCE to literacy and critical literacy, which is also central to the discussions revealed in the 21st-century skills network. This community includes scientific and digital literacy and the digital divide. This community points to a connection between the GCE scholarship and that of 21st century, which is more closely associated with the OECD than with UNESCO. The inclusion of the digital divide in this community points to a potential acknowledgement of the inequality of access, digital or otherwise, related to GCE in the scholarship (e.g., Goren & Yemini, 2017; Mikander, 2016).

The core of the GCE network consists of 26 nodes that come from only two communities and can be centered around two themes: pedagogy and globalization. The nodes related to pedagogy include transformative learning, critical pedagogy, service-learning, and more, whereas the globalization related nodes consist of topics related to interculturalism (intercultural learning, education, competence, etc.), international education, and student exchange.

Overall, the GCE network reflects the breadth of definitions, antecedents, and outcomes associated with this concept (for a review, see Oxley & Morris, 2013), and shows the relationships between these. The analysis also highlights the success of supranational organizations in shaping the scholarship surrounding this topic, suggesting that in the near future this network could undergo significant changes, as the work on such international organizations gathers pace.

Intercultural Competence

The final concept we collected data for is *intercultural competence*. The network for this term posed some challenges, as many of the topics were directly related to the search terms, such as competence, intercultural learning, intercultural communication, and more. These topics were removed, leaving a network that is slightly less dense than the previous ones presented here but that we still consider important and to accurately represent the main strands of literature in this field. The analysis reveals four strands: (1) critical pedagogy and experiential learning, (2) international education and study abroad,

(3) language education and English as a second or foreign language, and (4) distance education and virtual exchange.

The analysis of this network points to a close relationship in the literature between language education and cross-cultural skills and understanding. More broadly, the community demonstrates an assumed connection between the ability to communicate with others as a prerequisite for such understanding (Lau, 2015; Toyoda, 2016).

This network also includes topics related to internationalization and cultural exchange pointing to a strand of the literature on intercultural competence that presents international students and student exchanges as providing opportunities for multicultural experiences at home and abroad (Morales, 2017; Schartner, 2016), while critical works challenge the efficacy of these types of interventions (Almeida et al., 2016; Nguyen, 2017).

The core of the intercultural skills network has K = 7 and includes 30 nodes (that represent 36% of the entire network). This suggests a highly dispersed set of discussions within this concept across the research. There are two main communities that constitute the core, with topics related to critical pedagogy and leaning, and language education. It also includes four topics from other communities: student exchange (from the international education and study abroad community), and three items from the virtual exchange community (virtual exchange, videotelephony, and computer-mediated communication). This suggests that the scholarship surrounding education for intercultural competence is highly oriented toward the assumption that linguistics and speaking the same language as others (or a variety of languages) lie at the heart of this type of education. It also seems to emphasize different forms of pedagogy and learning as ways to accomplish or promote intercultural skills. Additionally, technology, which also appears at the core of the 21st-century skills network, is presented in the literature as an important aspect of enabling or facilitating education for intercultural competence, but the technology-related topics at the core of this network show that scholarly portrayals of technology within this field are limited to ways of facilitating communication, unlike in the 21st-century skills network and scholarship, where mastering the use of technology is portrayed an essential skill students need to acquire in order to compete in the global work force, and the literature most often reflects this through terms such as *digital* and *information* literacy (alongside *employability*, a term unique to the 21st-century skills network).

This network is unique in that it suggests that the literature almost exclusively engages with intercultural competencies as an outcome rather than a means for promoting goals such as tolerance, peace, or social cohesion. This is demonstrated by the fact that each of the communities centers around ways to facilitate the acquisition or development of these competencies (through technology, through language education, through international exchange programs, and through different forms of learning and pedagogy). Although the 21st-century skills network could also be said to reflect a similar pattern, the latter consists of more topics related to outcomes such as employability and digital literacy.

FIGURE 3
Full Network Visualization

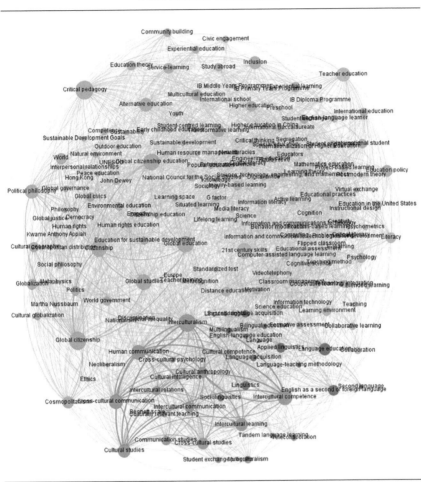

Note. A detailed view of this figure is available in the online journal.

The Scholarly Landscape of the Curricular Global Turn: Examining Thematic Overlap

After collecting the data for each of the networks, we combined the data (without removing the original search terms) into one network, which reveals the relationships between the different concepts and their relative importance in the scholarship surrounding education's global turn (see Figure 3). When dividing the entire database into four communities (using the relevant resolution in the Louvain algorithm), we expected to find four communities that correspond to our four concepts—but this was not the case. The analysis of the full database reveals that the GCE and cosmopolitanism scholarships are quite similar in their foci and share enough connections to be integrated into a single community. It also reveals the opposite about interculturalism (and intercultural competence by association) and 21st-century skills, each of which constitute a distinctive body of knowledge as suggested by their separate communities. Finally, a fourth community in this network is composed only of topics related to linguistics.

To elaborate, because data selection was performed using the same methodology for all the topics combined (rather than separated by concept), the topography of these communities cannot be attributed to the data selection process. As for the communities, the Louvain algorithm we applied through Gephi identifies nodes that are highly connected to one another. The resultant communities suggest that for GCE and cosmopolitanism, the papers that contained these topics had other topics in common as well. Thus, they were joined into a single community. For interculturalism and 21st-century skills, the fact they were could not be united into one community suggests that papers that address these topics address other similar topics as well. In other words, each of these topics had enough unique topics that did not appear in other communities, and therefore, they formed separate communities. Of the 46 topics that form the core of the full network, 30 belong to the community of topics that encompasses GCE and cosmopolitan education and 13 to the community of topics related to intercultural competence, while the other communities (21st-century skills and language education) are nearly absent (three terms altogether). This could be indicative of the relative importance of these topics in the scholarship related to education's global turn. The absence of 21st-century skills from this core corresponds with the focused core of the 21st-century skills network, which indicates that all the topics in the core are very likely to appear together in the same article. It is possible that these topics are unique to the 21st-century skills scholarship, and not engaged with in relation to the other concepts we examined.

The analysis of the full network enables a large-scale overview that sheds light on many of the findings from the individual concept networks and introduces some further insights; it allows us to place topics and themes that appeared across the networks together, and to reveal which of these are most closely connected to one another. This facilitates the unveiling of the topics that stand at the core of the scholarship within this broad area.

Across the individual concept networks, some communities appeared to be very similar, comprising occasionally differing topics but that could be organized around the same theme. We choose to elaborate here on the four most prominent of these themes, in order to analyze how the conceptual context can shape the way that topics are utilized in different bodies of literature. The analysis of our full database (encompassing all the concepts) helps organize and catalogue the topics most likely to be associated with one another. The themes we will elaborate on are language learning, inequality, and technology. These themes were derived qualitatively, by looking for topics that could be organized around the same concept in the individual networks, their highest rated topics (closeness centrality) and cores, and at the entire network.

Language Learning

Language learning and a variety of related topics appeared in all of the networks we produced and analyzed. In the GCE network, "English as a second language" and "language education" appear as topics embedded within in a broad community per-taining to globalization and internationalization, although the term "English language learner" is also present within the network core. This finding suggests that language, and specifically the English language, is a key part of how GCE is portrayed in the scholarship. Ahn (2015), for example, discusses the immense pressures South Korean parents face in taking responsibility for their children's English language learning as part of an assumption that it is crucial for participation in global society and global citizenship. The policy and teacher-training materials Ahn analyses widely support the claim that whereas other skills or dispositions are required for one to become a global citizen, knowledge of the English language is not a subset of skills but rather a separate prerequisite for participation in the Western-dominated global society.

In the 21st-century skills network, the appearance of language education and related topics implies that language acquisition is considered a 21st-century skill in itself (much like it is a prerequisite for GCE); more important, the key position of language education indicates that language classes and programs can be effective plat-forms for 21st-century skill learning. This finding aligns with those of Ashraf et al.'s (2017) study on the effectiveness of 21st-century skills integration within English classroom teaching in Iran.

A similar account of language classrooms as a platform arises from a close exami-nation of the articles that comprise the intercultural competence network (e.g., Toyoda, 2016; Truong & Tran, 2014). The appearance of language acquisition at the core of this network described in the previous section indicates that the literature depicts the ability to communicate with others as the bedrock for the development of intercultural competencies. In a more critical piece, Kubota (2016) presents the social imagery of the study abroad experience and warns against the neoliberal assumptions embedded within it, arguing that language learning and cultural competence in these contexts are unidirectional and reinforce the idea that those coming from non-West-ern countries are the ones who must make allowances and changes.

Finally, in the cosmopolitan education network, language education appears in a community with topics such as neocolonialism and critical theory, suggesting that these matters are discussed in the scholarship with regard to the implications of viewing English as the natural international language and a prerequisite for cos-mopolitan participation (see Groves & O'Connor, 2018). The cosmopolitan edu-cation network also includes articles that refer to languages other than English as forms of cosmopolitan capital, not only in English speaking countries, and not necessarily from a critical standpoint. For example, Yemini and Bar-Netz (2015) showed in a qualitative study of Israeli parents that those whose children studied French as a foreign language in schools explained this choice in terms of cosmopoli-tan capital, as opposed to parents of students who studied Arabic, who explained the choice in pragmatic and ideological terms.

The analysis of the full network shows that topics related to linguistics form a separate community, indicating that they are indeed scattered throughout the literature in a way that cannot be said to be more closely tied to one concept or another. When the full network is reduced to its core, only language education and English as a second or foreign language remain from this community, showing these topics are most central to the scholarship we examined (i.e., the whole database).

Inequality

Social inequality is a theme that appeared in each of the networks except in the intercultural competence network. In the cosmopolitan education network, a full community of topics related to social inequality emerged, as well as topics related to social positionality, such as gender, intersectionality, and discrimination. This finding appears to point to some critical approaches to studying cosmopolitanism. This community reveals a connection between cosmopolitan education and cultural/social capital, neoliberalism, employment, and social inequality that is indicative of a critical strand of literature that emphasizes the inequalities embedded in understandings of and access to cosmopolitan education, which is often associated with privileged groups (Groves & O'Connor, 2018).

In the GCE network, social inequality appears in the community related to political philosophy and globalization, as do global justice, White privilege, and neoliberalism, the latter of which is often associated with the expansion of inequality in the context of GCE (Friedman, 2018). The *digital divide* also emerged as a term in this network, as did *social capital*, pointing to a critical strand of literature that highlights issues of access to, and provision of, GCE and problematizes its perception as a one-size-fits-all approach to accommodating or implementing internationalization-related aspects of the global turn in education (Reynolds, 2015).

In the 21st-century skills network, social inequality does not appear explicitly, although the appearance of segregation and the digital divide imply that the literature addresses this theme in other ways. Mathews and Landorf (2016) discuss the digital divide as one of the main criticisms of massive open online courses, which are presented in the literature as a key platform for learning and teaching 21st-century skills.

Finally, inequality and related topics do not appear in the intercultural competence network at all, indicating certain neutrality or, we might suggest, blind spot in the literature to issues of social justice that might be associated with disparities in access to intercultural competence education among members of different social groups.

In the analysis of the full network, topics related to inequality appear mostly in the community that comprises topics connected to global citizenship and cosmopolitanism, as our qualitative analysis also shows. One exception is the digital divide, which appears in the 21st-century skills community alongside many other technology-related topics. No topics related to inequality appear at the core of the full network, indicating that inequality appears to be peripheral to the scholarship surrounding the curricular global turn in education.

Technology

Technology in general and ICTs specifically appeared in all of the networks apart from cosmopolitan education. The 21st-century skills network involves more topics related to technology than the other networks, including computing, digital literacy, and others. Many articles in this cohort discuss technological proficiency and information literacy as key skills required of 21st-century learners (e.g., Byker & Marquardt, 2016; Ruggiero & Mong, 2015; Scalise, 2016). Others discuss technology integration in the assessment of 21st-century skills, comprising another strand of research that emerged from the network analysis (e.g., O'Leary et al., 2018).

In the GCE and intercultural competencies networks, topics related to technology and ICTs appear alongside and among topics related to 21st-century skills and to intercultural experiences. Technological ways of facilitating communication across cultures and exposure to the world in a variety of ways comprise the majority of instances of this topic's appearance within these two conceptual bodies of literature (e.g., Gardner-McTaggart & Palmer, 2018; Krutka & Carano, 2016).

The absence of topics related to technology in the cosmopolitan education network could suggest that this body of literature is more theoretical than others, and that cosmopolitanism is presented in the literature as a disposition that is attained through actual (rather than virtual) international experiences. This approach is reflected, for example, in Groves and O'Connor's (2018) study of Western expatriates' school choices in Hong Kong. As would be expected, technology and related topics are located in the 21st-century skills community in the full network analysis but are not a part of the network's core, suggesting that discussions of technology are currently still quite peripheral in the scholarship surrounding the skills related to the curricular global turn in education.

CONCLUDING REMARKS

The main contribution of this chapter lies in showing the benefits of the methodological approach we outline, which facilitates the examination of vast bodies of literature in an empirical manner to identify caveats, trends, and strands of literature within them. Additionally, through our analysis, we show how researchers in the field align themselves with particular concepts and how the focus of their research often affects the kinds of topics and issues they engage with. The networks produced through our analysis also provide several key insights for other scholars and for policymakers by illuminating the composition of the literature surrounding four concepts used to demonstrate the curricular global turn in education: 21st-century skills, intercultural competencies, cosmopolitan education, and GCE. This review is the first to comparatively examine the scholarship surrounding these concepts.

We have shown that while some themes and topics appear across the different bodies of literature, their manifestations in the literature can differ when they are related to certain concepts. This demonstrates the broad applicability and range of uses for the methodology presented in this chapter, as the overlap of topics and the plethora of meanings that can be associated with them characterize many areas of research within and beyond the field of education. By performing the network analysis comparatively and supplementing it with a qualitative analysis, we were able to discern the ways in which research is shaped by the prevalent language that is used to describe, define, and legitimize a particular concept and the audience to whom it is directed.

In showing the individual composition of each network, our review also reveals some aspects that are distinctive in the literature surrounding each of the concepts we chose, such as the extent to which they are shaped by supranational organizations. The abundance of mentions of topics related to the OECD, PISA, testing, and assessment in the 21st-century skills network, for example, provides evidence of the successful dissemination of the OECD's educational goals through academic literature. The variety of topics in the GCE network that are associated with UNESCO and its various development goals, as well as the grouping of these topics in the same community as environmental education (a supposedly neutral field of knowledge), similarly points to a successful process of dissemination. Thus, this chapter contributes to a growing body of literature that calls attention to the political, economic, and supranational bodies that can influence the language chosen, theoretical orientation taken, and thus the concepts employed in nationally based policy, practice, and research (e.g., Auld & Morris, 2019; Hamilton, 2017; Kraess, 2018; Lewis, 2019). The newly introduced measurement of global competencies in PISA, alongside the simultaneous inclusion of GCE in UNESCO's SDGs,[5] means that ensuring we have a coherent evidence base, which understands how these terms are differentially engaged with but linked is ever more critical.

Through this review, we aim to engage researchers from other disciplines with this novel methodology, shedding light on a new way to include big data, NLP, and AI in any field. We also hope to consolidate much of the scholarship related to the skills and dispositions associated with the curricular aspects of education's global turn, by providing a blueprint for scholars embarking on related research, enabling them to reflect on the concepts and specific stands of literature to which their work relates, and providing a clear account of the distinctive features and characteristics of each body of literature.

NOTES

[1]http://www.opencalais.com/open-calais-faq/

[2]We do not address the NLP algorithm as it is beyond the scope of this work. However, we conducted a pilot study to verify the resulted topics match qualitative analysis.

[3]https://gephi.org/users/tutorial-visualization/

[4]https://www.ibm.com/support/knowledgecenter/SS3J58_9.0.6/com.ibm.i2.anb.doc/about_k_core.html

[5]https://en.unesco.org/education2030-sdg4/targets

REFERENCES

Ahn, S. (2015). Criticality for global citizenship in Korean English immersion camps. *Language & Intercultural Communication, 15*(4), 533–549. https://doi.org/10.1080/14 708477.2015.1049612.

Aktas, F., Pitts, K., Richards, J., & Silova, I. (2017). Institutionalizing global citizenship. *Journal of Studies in International Education, 21*(1), 65–80. https://doi .org/10.1177/1028315316669815

Almeida, J., Fantini, A., Simões, A., & Costa, N. (2016). Enhancing the intercultural effectiveness of exchange programmes: Formal and non-formal educational interventions. *Intercultural Education, 27*(6), 517–533. https://doi.org/10.1080/14675986.2016.1262190

Ashraf, H., Ahmadi, F., & Hosseinnia, M. (2017). Integrating 21st century skills into teaching English: Investigating its effect on listening and speaking skills. *i-Manager's Journal on English Language Teaching, 7*(4), 35–43. https://doi.org/10.26634/jelt.7.4.13766

Auld, E., & Morris, P. (2019). Science by streetlight and the OECD's measure of global competence: A new yardstick for internationalisation? *Policy Futures in Education,* 147821031881924. https://doi.org/10.1177/1478210318819246

Bamber, P., Bullivant, A., Clark, A., & Lundie, D. (2018). Educating global Britain: Perils and possibilities promoting "national" values through critical global citizenship education. *British Journal of Educational Studies, 66*(4), 433–453.

Bamber, P., Bullivant, A., Glover, A., King, B., & McCann, G. (2016). A comparative review of policy and practice for education for sustainable development/education for global citizenship (ESD/GC) in teacher education across the four nations of the UK. *Management in Education, 30*(3), 112–120. https://doi.org/10.1177/0892020616653179

Bamber, P., Lewin, D., & White, M. (2018). (Dis-)Locating the transformative dimension of global citizenship education. *Journal of Curriculum Studies, 50*(2), 204–230. http://doi .org/10.1080/00220272.2017.1328077

Blondel, V. D., Guillaume, J. L., Lambiotte, R., & Lefebvre, E. (2008). Fast unfolding of communities in large networks. *Journal of Statistical Mechanics, 2008*(10), Article ID: P10008. https://doi.org/10.1088/1742-5468/2008/10/p10008

Blumenfeld-Lieberthal, E., Serok, N., & Milner, E. L. (2017, September 12–14). *Mapping the Smart Cities discourse* [Paper presentation]. International Conference on Smart Cities: Potentials, Prospects and Discontents, Tel Aviv, Israel.

Byker, E. J., & Marquardt, S. (2016). Curricular connections: Using critical cosmopolitanism to globally situate multicultural education in teacher preparation courses. *Journal of Social Studies Education Research, 7*(2), 30–50.

Caruana, V. (2014). Re-thinking global citizenship in higher education: From cosmopolitanism and international mobility to cosmopolitanisation, resilience and resilient thinking. *Higher Education Quarterly, 68*(1), 85–104. https://doi.org/10.1111/hequ.12030

Chavalarias, D., & Cointet, J. P. (2008). Bottom-up scientific field detection for dynamical and hierarchical science mapping, methodology and case study. *Scientometrics, 75*(1), 37–50. https://doi.org/10.1007/s11192-007-1825-6

Cho, H. S., & Mosselson, J. (2018). Neoliberal practices amidst social justice orientations: Global citizenship education in South Korea. *Compare: A Journal of Comparative and International Education, 48*(6), 861–878. https://doi.org/10.1080/03057925.2017.13 64154

Chu, S. K. W., Reynold, R. B., Tavares, N. J., Notari, M., & Lee, C. W. Y. (2017). *21st century skills development through inquiry-based learning: From theory to practice.* Springer.

Coryell, J. E., Spencer, B. J., & Sehin, O. (2014). Cosmopolitan adult education and global citizenship: Perceptions from a European itinerant graduate professional study abroad program. *Adult Education Quarterly, 64*(2), 145–164. https://doi.org/10.1177/0741713 613515067

Davis, K., Boss, J. A., & Meas, P. (2018). Playing in the virtual sandbox: Students' collaborative practices in Minecraft. *International Journal of Game-Based Learning, 8*(3), 56–76. https://doi.org/10.4018/IJGBL.2018070104

Dill, J. S. (2013). *The longings and limits of global citizenship education: The moral pedagogy of schooling in a cosmopolitan age.* Routledge.

Engel, L. C. (2014). Global citizenship and national (re) formations: Analysis of citizenship education reform in Spain. *Education, Citizenship and Social Justice, 9*(3), 239–254. https://doi.org/10.1177/1746197914545927

Fernekes, W. R. (2016). Global citizenship education and human rights education: Are they compatible with US civic education? *Journal of International Social Studies, 6*(2), 34–57.

Fink, A. (2010). *Conducting research literature reviews: From internet to paper* (3rd ed.). Sage.

Friedman, J. Z. (2018). The global citizenship agenda and the generation of cosmopolitan capital in British higher education. *British Journal of Sociology of Education, 39*(4), 436–450. https://doi.org/10.1080/01425692.2017.1366296

Gardner-McTaggart, A., & Palmer, N. (2018). Global citizenship education, technology, and being. *Globalisation, Societies and Education, 16*(2), 268–281. https://doi.org/10.1080/1 4767724.2017.1405342

Goren, H., & Yemini, M. (2017). Global citizenship education redefined: A systematic review of empirical studies on global citizenship education. *International Journal of Educational Research, 82*, 170–183. https://doi.org/10.1016/j.ijer.2017.02.004

Groves, J. M., & O'Connor, P. (2018). Negotiating global citizenship, protecting privilege: Western expatriates choosing local schools in Hong Kong. *British Journal of Sociology of Education, 39*(3), 381–395. https://doi.org/10.1080/01425692.2017.1351866

Hamilton, M. (2017). How international large-scale skills assessments engage with national actors: Mobilising networks through policy, media and public knowledge. *Critical Studies in Education, 58*(3), 280–294. https://doi.org/10.1080/17508487.2017.1330761

Higgins, C. (2015). Intersecting scapes and new millennium identities in language learning. *Language Teaching, 48*(3), 373–389. https://doi.org/10.1017/S0261444814000044

Hull, G. A., & Stornaiuolo, A. (2014). Cosmopolitan literacies, social networks, and "proper distance": Striving to understand in a global world. *Curriculum Inquiry, 44*(1), 15–44. https://doi.org/10.1111/curi.12035

Kerkhoff, S. N. (2017). Designing global futures: A mixed methods study to develop and validate the teaching for global readiness scale. *Teaching and Teacher Education, 65*, 91–106. https://doi.org/10.1016/j.tate.2017.03.011

Knight, J. (2004). Internationalization remodeled: Definition, approaches, and rationales. *Journal of Studies in International Education, 8*(1), 5–31.

Kraess, K. (2018). The cross-Atlantic knowledge divide, or PISA for Development: Should one size ever fit all? *Atlantic Studies, 15*(3), 349–364. https://doi.org/10.1080/1478881 0.2017.1370356

Krutka, D. G., & Carano, K. T. (2016). Videoconferencing for global citizenship education: Wise practices for social studies educators. *Journal of Social Studies Education Research, 7*(2), 109–136.

Kubota, R. (2016). The social imaginary of study abroad: complexities and contradictions. *Language Learning Journal, 44*(3), 347–357. https://doi.org/10.1080/09571736.2016.1 198098

Kumar, R., Novak, J., & Tomkins, A. (2010). Structure and evolution of online social networks. In P. S. Yu, J. Han, & C. Faloutsos (Eds.), *Link mining: Models, algorithms, and applications* (pp. 337–357). Springer.

Lau, S. M. C. (2015). Intercultural education through a bilingual children's rights project: reflections on its possibilities and challenges with young learners. *Intercultural Education, 26*(6), 469–482. https://doi.org/10.1080/14675986.2015.1109774

Lewis, S. (2019). "Becoming European"? Respatialising the European schools system through PISA for Schools. *International Studies in Sociology of Education*. Advance online publication. doi:10.1080/09620214.2019.1624593

Lin, L., Widdall, C., & Ward, L. (2014). Improving critical thinking with interactive mobile tools and apps. *Social Studies and the Young Learner, 26*(4), 10–14.

Lucas, B. (2016). A five-dimensional model of creativity and its assessment in schools. *Applied Measurement in Education, 29*(4), 278–290. https://doi.org/10.1080/08957 347.2016.1209206

Mannion, G., Biesta, G., Priestley, M., & Ross, H. (2011). The global dimension in education and education for global citizenship: Genealogy and critique. *Globalisation, Societies and Education, 9*(3–4), 443–456. https://doi.org/10.1080/14767724.2011.605327

Mathews, S. A., & Landorf, H. (2016). Developing a framework to evaluate the potential of global learning in MOOCs. *New Horizons in Adult Education and Human Resource Development, 28*(4), 3–14. https://doi.org/10.1002/nha3.20157

Meyer, H. D., & Benavot, A. (Eds.). (2013). *PISA, power and policy: The emergence of global educational governance*. Symposium Books.

Mikander, P. (2016). Globalization as continuing colonialism–Critical global citizenship education in an unequal world. *Journal of Social Science Education, 15*(2), 70–79. https://doi .org/10.4119/UNIBI/jsse-v15-i2-1475

Mochizuki, Y. (2016). Educating for transforming our world: Revisiting international debates surrounding education for sustainable development. *Current Issues in Comparative Education, 19*(1), 109–125.

Monaghan, C., & Spreen, C. A. (2016). From human rights to global citizenship education: Peace , conflict and the Post-Cold War era. *International Journal of Educational Sciences, 13*(1), 42–55. https://doi.org/10.1080/09751122.2016.11890439

Morales, A. (2017). Intercultural sensitivity, gender, and nationality of third culture kids attending an international high school. *Journal of International Education Research, 13*(1), 35–44. https://doi.org/10.19030/jier.v13i1.9969.

Morse, J. M., & Niehaus, L. (2009). *Mixed method design: Principles and procedures*. Left Coast Press.

Moskal, M., & Schweisfurth, M. (2018). Learning, using and exchanging global competence in the context of international postgraduate mobility. *Globalisation, Societies and Education, 16*(1), 93–105. https://doi.org/10.1080/14767724.2017.1 387768

Myers, J. P. (2016). Charting a democratic course for global citizenship education: Research directions and current challenges. *Education Policy Analysis Archives, 24*(55), 1–19. https://doi.org/10.14507/epaa.24.2174

Nguyen, A. (2017). Intercultural competence in short-term study abroad. *Frontiers: The Interdisciplinary Journal of Study Abroad, 29*(2), 109–127.

O'Leary, M., Scully, D., Karakolidis, A., & Pitsia, V. (2018). The state-of-the-art in digital technology-based assessment. *European Journal of Education, 53*(2), 160–175. https://doi .org/10.1111/ejed.12271

Oxley, L., & Morris, P. (2013). Global citizenship: A typology for distinguishing its multiple conceptions. *British Journal of Educational Studies, 61*(3), 301–325. https://doi.org/10.1 080/00071005.2013.798393

Rapoport, A. (2010). We cannot teach what we don't know: Indiana teachers talk about global citizenship education. *Education, Citizenship and Social Justice, 5*(3), 179–190. https:// doi.org/10.1177/1746197910382256

Reilly, J., & Niens, U. (2014). Global citizenship as education for peacebuilding in a divided society: structural and contextual constraints on the development of critical dialogic discourse in schools. *Compare: A Journal of Comparative and International Education, 44*(1), 53–76.

Reynolds, R. (2015). One size fits all? Global education for different educational audiences. In R. Reynolds, D. Bradbery, J. Brown, K. Carroll, D. Donelly, K. Ferguson-Patrick, & S. Mcqueen (Eds.), *Contesting and constructing international perspectives in global education* (pp. 27–41). Sense. doi:10.1007/978-94-6209-989-0_3

Ruggiero, D., & Mong, C. J. (2015). The teacher technology integration experience: Practice and reflection in the classroom. *Journal of Information Technology Education, 14*, 161–178. http://www.jite.org/documents/Vol14/JITEv14ResearchP161-178Ruggiero0958.pdf

Scalise, K. (2016). Student collaboration and school educational technology: Technology integration practices in the classroom. *Journal on School Educational Technology, 11*(4), 53–63.

Schartner, A. (2016). The effect of study abroad on intercultural competence: A longitudinal case study of international postgraduate students at a British university. *Journal of Multilingual & Multicultural Development, 37*(4), 402–418. https://doi.org/10.1080/01434632.2015.1073737

Storksdieck, M. (2016). Critical information literacy as core skill for lifelong STEM learning in the 21st century: Reflections on the desirability and feasibility for widespread science media education. *Cultural Studies of Science Education, 11*(1), 167–182.

Terrazas-Arellanes, F., Strycker, L., Walden, E., & Gallard, A. (2017). Teaching with technology: Applications of collaborative online learning units to improve 21st century skills for all. *Journal of Computers in Mathematics and Science Teaching, 36*(4), 375–386.

Toyoda, E. (2016). Intercultural knowledge, awareness and skills observed in a foreign language classroom. *Intercultural Education, 27*(6), 505–516. https://doi.org/10.1080/14675986.2016.1256600

Truong, L. B., & Tran, L. T. (2014). Students' intercultural development through language learning in Vietnamese tertiary education: A case study on the use of film as an innovative approach. *Language & Intercultural Communication, 14*(2), 207–225. https://doi.org/10.1080/14708477.2013.849717

VanderDussen Toukan, E. (2018). Educating citizens of "the global": Mapping textual constructs of UNESCO's global citizenship education 2012–2015. *Education, Citizenship and Social Justice, 13*(1), 51–64. https://doi.org/10.1177/1746197917700909

Van der Wende, M. (2007). Internationalization of higher education in the OECD countries: Challenges and opportunities for the coming decade. *Journal of Studies in International Education, 11*(3–4), 274–289. https://doi.org/10.1177/1028315307303543

Vidovich, L. (2004). Towards internationalizing the curriculum in a context of globalization: Comparing policy processes in two settings. *Compare: A Journal of Comparative and International Education, 34*(4), 443–461. https://doi.org/10.1080/0305792042000294823

Wang, C., & Hoffman, D. M. (2016). Are WE the world? A critical reflection on selfhood and global citizenship education. *Education Policy Analysis Archives, 24*,. https://doi.org/10.14507/epaa.24.2152

Yemini, M., & Bar-Netz, N. (2015). Between Arabic and French in the Israeli education system: Acquisition of cosmopolitan capital in a conflict-ridden society. *Journal of Language, Identity and Education, 14*(3), 179–190.

Yemini, M., Tibbitts, F., & Goren, H. (2019). Trends and caveats: Review of literature on global citizenship education in teacher training. *Teaching and Teacher Education, 77*(1), 77–89.

Chapter 3

Place Matters: A Critical Review of Place Inquiry and Spatial Methods in Education Research

ALISHA BUTLER
University of Maryland, College Park

KRISTIN A. SINCLAIR
Georgetown University

Place is an inescapable aspect of daily life and is intimately linked to our life experiences. An expanding body of research has investigated how place shapes the "geography of opportunity" as well as students', families', and stakeholders' experiences in and around schools. While researchers have begun to investigate the spatial context of education, the notion of place remains somewhat underconceptualized in education research. This chapter draws on an interdisciplinary review of 60 empirical, education-related studies to understand how researchers have accounted for place, the theoretical and conceptual frames in which they ground their work, and their data collection methods. We find that researchers have used place inquiry and spatial methods to investigate diverse education-related phenomena, such as school choice and teaching and learning. Beyond using place to identify and describe inequalities, we argue that place inquiry and spatial methodologies can strengthen the potential of education research to disrupt systems of power and oppression by also advancing our knowledge of the nature of and potential solutions to educational injustice.

Place is an inescapable aspect of daily life and is intimately linked to our life experiences. Places provide the context in which we learn about ourselves and make sense of and connect to our natural and cultural surroundings; they shape our identities, our relationships with others, and our worldviews (e.g., Basso, 1996; Gruenewald, 2003b; Keith & Pile, 1993). Places can reproduce hegemony, ideology, racism, and other forms of oppression. Places can also be sites of resistance; they can function as a setting for people from marginalized backgrounds to escape and resist oppression

Review of Research in Education
March 2020, Vol. 44, pp. 64–96
DOI: 10.3102/0091732X20903303
Chapter reuse guidelines: sagepub.com/journals-permissions
© 2020 AERA. http://rre.aera.net

while building group consciousness and solidarity (Delaney, 2002; Haymes, 1995; hooks, 1990; Lefebvre, 1974). The connection among place, power, and resistance underscores another important feature of place: the link between place and social justice. Justice and injustice both have a spatial expression, or a "consequential geography" (Soja, 2010, p. 1). Justice and injustice shape—and are shaped by—a localized set of changing social, political, and economic conditions. Thus, the pursuit of justice requires an understanding and critical examination of place not as a background to our social lives but as an active agent in shaping our life experiences and institutions.

The centrality of place in shaping our life experiences is also evident in how place influences education and schooling. Place shapes the broader "geography of opportunity" in which schools are situated (Tate, 2008) as well as the experiences of diverse stakeholders, including students, parents, and educators, in and around schools. Yet, while a growing body of theoretical and conceptual work has explored the role of place in education *practice* (e.g., Gruenewald, 2003b), place has been somewhat underconceptualized in education *research* (O. D. Johnson, 2012). Although a growing number of education researchers have embraced "the spatial turn" (Gulson & Symes, 2007) and have drawn on the concepts and tools of geographers in education-related inquiry (Hogrebe & Tate, 2012; Taylor, 2009b), the role of place and its relationship to power, pedagogy, and the social context of schooling is largely undertheorized.

We acknowledge the progress that education researchers, in particular, have made engaging both the theories and tools of geographers. We argue, however, that at this point in time research employing GIS (geographic information system) or other quantitative spatial methods and research engaging critical theories of place exist in parallel in the literature. That is, there are strands of research that employ GIS and spatial methods descriptively—often distilling injustice to places on maps—and research that critically interrogates the systems of power and oppression that exists in places. However, rarely are these two approaches used together. In this chapter, we argue that a methodological approach to education research that integrates spatial methods and sociospatial perspectives would increase the explanatory power of GIS and other spatial methods to not only *describe* injustice but also *interrogate* the systems of power and oppression underlying those injustices.

This chapter investigates how and to what ends education researchers use place in their methodology and methods and aims to deepen our understanding of the potential of place inquiry (Tuck & McKenzie, 2015) to advance our knowledge of the nature of and potential solutions to educational injustice. To accomplish this goal, we describe how researchers have accounted for place in education-related research through both their use of spatial methods as well as through the theoretical and conceptual frames in which they ground their work. Specifically, this chapter addresses the following research questions:

Research Question 1: What types of questions or issue areas have researchers examined using place inquiry?

Research Question 2: What theoretical perspectives have researchers brought to bear when accounting for place?

Research Question 3: What are the implications for the potential of place inquiry to advance equity and social justice?

Our chapter responds to recent calls from scholars across disciplines, including Tuck and McKenzie (2015) and Morrison et al. (2017), to foreground place and spatial perspectives to advance equity, justice, and liberation. To situate our work, we define the concepts, place and space, that guide this chapter and explain how these concepts might help illuminate some of the mechanisms undergirding complex educational and social problems. Next, we describe the methods used to gather literature for this chapter and discuss our findings, which are organized by our research questions. We argue that role of place as a theoretical frame for education research has important implications for the potential of place inquiry and spatial methods to not only help education researchers identify and describe inequities but also challenge and disrupt the systems of power and oppression that produce those inequities.

DEFINING PLACE AND SPACE

At a cursory level, "space" is an abstract, general realm without meaning, while place, on the other hand, is concrete, is particular, and has meaning (Agnew, 1987; Casey, 1996; Cresswell, 2004). The theoretical and conceptual literature often disagrees about what counts as "place" and what counts as "space" and the nature of the relationship between these two concepts. For example, Lefebvre's (1974) theory of social space closely resembles the notions of place discussed in this chapter. He describes space as a social construction imbued with experience and meaning, both of which are a result of the daily activities that happen in a space, the symbols and forms in that space, and the meaning that inhabitants and users make of those places. Broadly speaking, we understand place as a "meaningful location" (Cresswell, 2004): a cultural and ecological entity that includes a location's human scale, social relationships, cultural characteristics, history, natural and geographic landmarks, and built environment (e.g., Basso, 1996).

More specifically, for the purposes of this chapter we draw primarily and liberally on Agnew's (1987) definition of place, alongside Soja's (2010) concept of "spatial justice," to guide our analysis of the literature and resulting implications. Because education practice and policy are shaped by human decision making and behavior— either as individuals or as members of institutions—conceptualizations of place, such as Agnew's (1987), that attend to the dialectical relationships between place and human behavior in the context of power and systems of oppression (e.g., Soja, 2010) may be particularly useful for understanding how place inquiry can help further educational and social justice.

Agnew's (1987) definition of place has three fundamental aspects: (1) a location— that is, a specific fixed point in space where a place exists, (2) a locale—the material setting in which people conduct their lives at that particular location, and (3) a sense of place, or the meaning attached to a particular location and locale. While "location" is a fairly straightforward aspect of place, both locale and sense of place are more complex. For example, the "location" of a place may include both the natural and built environment, while the "locale" encompasses human, cultural, and natural characteristics. Some scholars argue that place should also include virtual sites such as social media, websites, or other online communities that may serve as important "locales" where young people gather and interact (e.g., McKenzie, 2008).

While the location and locale of a place may be the same or similar for everyone, the third characteristic of place, "sense of place," may differ depending on one's social positionality. As Cresswell (2004) explains, "Place is how we make the world meaningful and the way we experience the world. Place, at a basic level, is space invested with meaning in the context of power" (p. 12). This explanation reveals two key dimensions of sense of place. The first is that places are cultural products with different meanings for different people. The attachments people develop to places and the meanings they make of places may vary greatly depending on one's cultural background and positionality; in fact, every person has a unique sense of place (Cresswell, 2004; Dentzau, 2014). The meaning-making dimension also reflects an understanding of place as a cultural construct that is continually made and remade on a daily basis as we perceive and make sense of places (Casey, 1996; Cresswell, 2004; Greenwood, 2012).

The second dimension of sense of place sees place as political. In this understanding, places are political entities that embody and produce systems of power and can perpetuate or resist forces of oppression. Place is the context in which human agency and social structure interact and influence each other. Agnew (1987) draws upon structuration theory to describe place as "process." This theory rejects dichotomous views of behavior as either purely an outcome of individual agency or a result of structural forces. Instead, behavior is "the product of agency as structured by the historically constituted social contexts in which people live their lives—in a word, places" (p. 43). That is, place is central to the formation and maintenance of social structures; it is a "contact zone of cultural contact" (Somerville, 2010, p. 335). As such, places can also be sites of power struggles and resistance and can function as a means of reproducing oppression and hegemony (Feld & Basso, 1996; Lefebvre, 1974) particularly related to race (e.g., Delaney, 2002), class (e.g., Harvey, 1973), and gender (e.g., Massey, 1994), and across multiple intersecting lines of identity (e.g., McKittrick, 2006). Thus, where one stands within the power structure of society can greatly influence the meaning one makes of a place and whether one experiences a place as welcoming, empowering, or a symbol of oppression (e.g., Feld & Basso, 1996; Lefebvre, 1974). The understanding of place described here is not above critique because it is largely rooted in a Western knowledge system and epistemological tradition that "normalizes domination through systems of white supremacy, settler colonialism, heteropatriarchy, and anthropocentrism" (Seawright, 2014, p. 555).

In light of such critiques, this chapter pays careful attention to the extent to which discussions of place account for the role of racism, classism, and sexism in constructing peoples' different meanings and experiences of place as well as the long Indigenous cultural histories and meanings of place (J. Johnson, 2012; Tuck & McKenzie, 2015). Place inquiry that focuses on location and locale alone, on anthropocentrism, and not on the deeper Indigenous history or the broader social context of that location and locale can lead to what Peña (1998) calls "exoticist placemaking": the reinvention of place and its material and symbolic trappings by the "other" (p. 46). That is, education scholars might effectively erase, ignore, or exoticize the complicated cultural history and present of any given place and in doing so may silence potentially valuable place-meanings and reinforce systems of oppression and domination including but not limited to racism and settler colonialism (e.g., Tuck & Yang, 2012). For example, Tuck and McKenzie (2015) point out that maps—a primary data point for place-as-location—are an artifact and production of settler colonialism and thus an incomplete and potentially oppressive spatial tool; for Indigenous people, "places are not always named, do not always appear on maps, do not always have agreed-upon boundaries" (Tuck & McKenzie, 2015, p. 14). That is, this chapter responds to Indigenous scholars' critiques by paying attention to the extent to which researchers account for not just place but land—and the Indigenous histories, presents, and futures of land—in their work (e.g., Bang et al., 2014; Calderon, 2014; Styres et al., 2013).

To summarize, we conceptualize place as a complex interplay of location, locale, and the meaning people make of a location and also as a key component in understanding systems of power. In line with Soja's (2010) explanation of spatial justice, we see "space [as] filled with politics and privileges, ideologies and cultural collisions, utopian ideals and dystopian oppression, justice and injustice, oppressive power and the possibility for emancipation" (p. 103).

PLACE AND SPACE IN EDUCATION RESEARCH

Theoretical frameworks and methodological approaches grounded in place have great potential to unmask deep social, economic, and environmental inequities without the limitations inherent in some traditional approaches (e.g., Tate, 2008). For example, as "transdisciplinary" concepts that span all interpretive perspectives, space and place allow researchers to apply multiple lenses on a particular phenomenon, which may be particularly illustrative for studying complex educational and social problems (Gulson & Symes, 2007; Velez & Solórzano, 2017). As Gulson and Symes (2007) argue, "Drawing on theories of space contributes in significant and important ways to subtle and more sophisticated understandings of the competing rationalities underlying educational policy change, social inequity, and cultural practices" (p. 2). The extent to which education researchers have taken up this call is an open question and a central impetus for this chapter.

During the later years of the 20th century, a "spatial turn" occurred across nearly all the human sciences, wherein scholars began to consider theories of space and place, alongside social and historical perspectives, as equally valuable ways of seeing and interpreting the world (Soja, 2010). While, starting in the mid-1990s, some scholars in environmental and rural education began to push for schools and teachers to engage with young people's places in order to enhance *teaching and learning* (e.g., Orr, 1992, 2004; G. A. Smith & Sobel, 2010; G. A. Smith & Williams, 1999; Theobald, 1997), education *research*, on the other hand, has been slower to take up this "spatial turn" (Gulson & Symes, 2007, p. 1). Many theories driving education research, in fact, have often been despatialized and, as a result, may operate from problematic assumptions, for example, that the children at a particular school are "from families whose neighboring has no social explanation—as if families had been organized into residential groups randomly" (O. D. Johnson, 2012, p. 32). Notably, place—and peoples' relationships to place—have always been central to Indigenous cultures, identities, ways of knowing, and systems of education, long before the "spatial turn" in social theory (Basso, 1996; Cajete, 1994, 1999; Deloria & Wildcat, 2001; see also L. T. Smith, 2012, for a discussion of Indigenous perspectives on and critiques of research methodologies).

More recently, however, as Gulson and Symes (2007) and others have documented (see also Lubienski & Lee, 2017; Taylor, 2009b), researchers have increasingly drawn from the tools of geographers to examine a broad range of education-related questions. Tate (2008), for example, calls on researchers to study the "geography of opportunity," what he defines as the study of patterns of geographic and economic development across spatial and ideological boundaries such as cities and suburbs and how these patterns contribute to and/or reflect educational inequality. In addition to mapping the geography of opportunity, a growing number of scholars have argued for increased attention to place and spatial analyses in education research, particularly in research that intends to advance equity, justice, and liberation (Morrison et al., 2017; Tuck & McKenzie, 2015). Morrison et al.'s (2017) edited volume calls on education researchers to use spatial analyses such as GIS or mapping together with critical race theory (CRT) in a combined methodological approach called critical race spatial analysis (CRSA):

CRSA is an explanatory framework and methodological approach that accounts for the role of race, racism, and white supremacy in examining geographic and social space and that works toward identifying and challenging racism and white supremacy within these spaces as part of a larger goal of identifying and challenging all forms of subordination. . . . CRSA is particularly interested in how structural and institutional factors divide, constrict and construct space to impact the educational experiences and opportunities available to students based on race. (p. 20)

Similarly, Tuck and McKenzie (2015) argue that education researchers have an "ethical imperative" to engage in critical place inquiry grounded in rich theorizations (and methods and methodologies) of place. They define critical place inquiry as follows:

Research that takes up critical questions and develops corresponding methodological approaches that are informed by the embeddedness of social life in and with places, and that seeks to be a form of action in responding to critical place issues such as those of globalization and neoliberalism, settler colonialism, and environmental degradation. (p. 2)

Both of these approaches to education research embody what Soja (2010) calls a "critical spatial perspective"; this chapter intends to examine existing education research in light of these concepts.

Prior to—and following—these theoretical advancements, however, whether and the extent to which researchers have gone beyond simply *doing* geography (Taylor, 2009b) to acknowledging and considering the importance of place in studies of education remain an open and empirical question. While other literature reviews have looked at how researchers have (1) used spatial methods within specific domains of education research such as school choice (e.g., Lubienski & Lee, 2017), (2) argued for the benefits of using GIS mapping in multiple ways within education research broadly (e.g., Taylor, 2007), or (3) called for an increased use of spatial tools in the classroom (e.g., Kerski, 2011), no reviews to date have examined researchers' use of spatial theories, methodologies, and methods across multiple domains and issue areas of education research. Thus, this chapter seeks to bring together fragmented but related streams of literature in order to develop a comprehensive understanding of how researchers have used place inquiry and spatial methods and of the possibilities and challenges of spatial methods to generate insights about education policy, practice, and social contexts.

METHOD

To deepen our understanding of how education researchers investigate and account for place in their research, we identified and analyzed empirical education research that engages in what we will call "place inquiry."[1] For the purposes of this chapter, we define place inquiry as any form of empirical research that collects place-specific data, draws on these data explicitly during data analysis, and/or generates insights that speak back to the role of place in answering research questions in education-related studies. For example, research that falls under this definition may include those studies that are grounded in a theoretical framework drawing on critical theories of place and space but use traditional data collection methods (e.g., ethnographic or case study approaches) as well as research that uses explicitly spatial methods within any methodological or theoretical approach. Some "explicitly spatial" data collection methods, for example, may include GIS, GPS (Global Positioning System), and mapping. These methods are commonly used to study place in other fields such as geography, urban planning, and sociology and have emerged as theoretically promising strategies for education research (Gulson & Symes, 2007; Morrison et al., 2017).

This chapter includes empirical studies of diverse education-related phenomena identified through systematic searches of research databases.[2] Our iterative searches used the following key terms designed to identify relevant studies based on the methodologies or theoretical perspectives employed: critical place inquiry, critical human geography, spatial analysis, participatory mapping, spatial justice, GIS/GPS, photovoice, or mapping. We also employed snowball sampling techniques to identify additional studies cited in authors' bibliographies. The interdisciplinary set of 60 studies included in the chapter were selected because they (a) investigate questions related to education or youths' experiences in and around schools and (b) collect place-specific data through diverse methodologies (e.g., spatial analysis, participatory mapping, archival methods). We included education-related research conducted in the United States and abroad and studies focused on an array of grade levels (e.g., preK–12 in the United States). We use a broad conception of place inquiry and included the work of scholars whose studies are explicitly grounded in theories of space and place as well as researchers who employ spatial methods (e.g., GIS/GPS) whose work is atheoretical or grounded in other frameworks. We excluded studies designed to investigate the effectiveness of GIS and mapping as pedagogical tools in classrooms. See the appendix for a summary of all included studies.

An extensive, interdisciplinary literature base on "neighborhood effects" has investigated whether and how a person's neighborhood affects their life trajectories, such as health and social mobility (Sampson et al., 2002). This research base, for example, often draws on sociodemographic data (e.g., racial and socioeconomic composition of census tracts or block groups) to investigate how environments shape individual and intergenerational outcomes (e.g., Sharkey, 2013; Sharkey & Elwert, 2011). Following Sampson et al.'s (2002) call, a growing number of researchers studying neighborhood effects have begun to account for spatial dimensions of inequality. We excluded studies within the neighborhood effects literature if those studies did not use spatial methods to account for spatial variations or patterns in the effects of social context on the outcome variables of interest.

Our analysis also excludes much of the empirical literature on place-based education (e.g., G. A. Smith, 2002; Sobel, 2004), critical pedagogies of place (e.g., Gruenewald, 2003a), and eco-justice education (e.g., Martusewicz et al., 2014), because researchers in this field do not necessarily collect data specific to the places they are studying, consider the impact of local context in their analyses, or ground their work in spatial theories. Generally speaking, research on place-based education investigates whether and how studying place through a particular lesson, curricular unit, or program might affect student learning (e.g., Zimmerman & Weible, 2017), academic engagement (e.g., Howley et al., 2011; Powers, 2004), place attachment (e.g., Takano et al., 2009), sense of place (e.g., Azano, 2011), environmental stewardship (e.g., Gallay et al., 2016), civic engagement (e.g., Trinidad, 2011), awareness of injustice (e.g., Buxton, 2010; Rubel et al., 2016), or social change (e.g., Owens et al., 2011). This literature base is an important source of evidence as to whether and how *engagement with place through teaching and learning* has the potential to enhance young people's academic and personal development and build stronger bonds between schools and communities. This chapter, however, is concerned with whether and how *engagement with place through research methods and methodologies* might provide particular insights and avenues toward achieving greater educational and social justice.

Once we identified the set of studies for the chapter, each author reviewed all of the pieces and read a subset based on the author's expertise in greater depth. We created a spreadsheet with detailed information for each study, including a brief summary, research questions, methods used, and our reflections on how the authors used concepts of space and place. We then developed a matrix, based on our research questions, to categorize each study's research questions and issue areas addressed in education-related research, the methodological approaches employed, and the theoretical perspectives guiding the analysis. As we discuss in subsequent sections, questions and issue areas spanned education policy (e.g., school choice, school siting policies), the social contexts of education, and youths' perceptions of place. Methodological codes include qualitative (e.g., ethnography and case study methodologies), quantitative (e.g., spatial analysis, regression techniques), and mixed-method approaches. The studies included in this chapter draw on diverse theoretical perspectives, including theories of place and space, to guide analyses.

To identify what education researchers mean when they claim they are using concepts of place and space (Gulson & Symes, 2007), we draw on Agnew's (1987) framework, as described above, of place as location, locale, and sense of place—both the meaning people make of places and place as political—to surface the conceptions of place that emerge in each study. The studies included in this chapter did not always explicitly frame their investigations using one or more aspects of place defined in Agnew's framework. Rather, we use the framework, along with Soja's (2010) concept of spatial justice, as a heuristic to generate insights about how place functions in studies of education-related phenomenon. Once we coded all studies with each category, we looked for patterns within and across categories.

FINDINGS

This section summarizes findings from our review. First, we describe the array of questions for which education researchers have employed place inquiry and spatial methods. Next, we describe the theoretical perspectives—including works that do not draw on clear perspectives—that researchers have brought to bear in their work. Finally, we describe how education researchers have employed place inquiry and spatial methods for advancing equity and social justice.

Questions and Issue Areas Examined

Our analysis identified five broad categories of questions and issue areas that researchers have examined through place inquiry: (1) education policy, (2) the social context of education, (3) the mesosystem, (4) youths' perspectives on and interactions with their environments, and (5) teaching and learning.

Education Policy

Half of the studies reviewed investigated questions broadly related to education policy, such as school choice (e.g., Dougherty et al., 2009; Lubienski et al., 2009; Smrekar & Honey, 2015) and education markets (e.g., Corbett & Helmer, 2017; Davis & Oakley, 2013; Misra et al., 2012; Taylor, 2001, 2009a), how parents and students select schools (Bell, 2007, 2009; Parsons et al., 2000; Phillippo & Griffin,

2016; Reay, 2007), school funding (Ajilore, 2011), teacher labor markets (Jaramillo, 2012), and school closures (Buras, 2013; Ewing, 2018; Good, 2017a, 2017b). We focus our discussion on the literature on school choice—both policy and the experiences of choosing schools—and school closures to reveal how researchers have employed place inquiry to interrogate inequities within education systems.

School choice. Researchers (e.g., Lubienski & Dougherty, 2009; Lubienski & Lee, 2017) have argued that spatial methods hold promise for investigations of school choice because these methods illuminate how place and space shape the realities of school choice policies. Our review, for example, reveals how place inquiry can reveal patterns of inequity in education markets. One assumption guiding the growth of school choice policies (e.g., charter schools and voucher systems) is that they provide all families—regardless of socioeconomic class—the option to choose schools for their children (Viteritti, 1999). A large volume of research has investigated this assumption, and researchers have employed a variety of methodologies to understand access and equity in school choice. Spatial methods can further these discussions by investigating how place and space shape what options are actually available to families (LaFleur, 2016; Lubienski et al., 2009). Pairing spatial and quantitative methods, LaFleur (2016) found that charter schools in Chicago were more likely to be found *near*, not *in*, the highest need communities. By mapping charter school locations against community demographics, this work reveals how school placement might impede the choices economically disadvantaged families can make within a choice market (LaFleur, 2016). Spatial methods can also reveal tensions between the policy aims and realities of school choice policies. In their multimodel study of magnet schools, Smrekar and Honey (2015) found that magnet programs located in communities with large minority populations reflected the demographics of these neighborhoods; conversely, schools located in predominantly White neighborhoods were more racially diverse (Smrekar & Honey, 2015). Through Smrekar and Honey's (2015) analysis, we see how school location has the potential to undermine the stated goals of magnet policies in the studied districts. This strand of work reveals how geography and the spatial distribution of schools shape inequity.

Place inquiry is not limited to questions of geography and school location. Researchers have also used notions of place and space to interrogate the meanings students and parents associate with schools and the implications of those meanings for school selection. Challenging the notion that school selection is a "rational" process, researchers have used place inquiry to demonstrate how geography and perceptions of place influence families' school choice decisions. A pair of studies from Bell (2007, 2009), for example, reveal how the meanings students and parents attach to schools influence whether parents will consider that school as a viable option for their children. Bell (2007), for example, found that parents' perceptions of school quality were based on their perceptions of place—including the neighborhoods in which schools were located. Similarly, Reay (2007) found that place was an important consideration in school selection but that the meanings associated with place were often in flux. She found, for example, while both working-class and middle-class students alike adopted deficit-based narratives about schools located in working-class communities, working-class students' sense of place became more nuanced when they enrolled in these schools. Notably, both Bell's (2007, 2009) and Reay's (2007) studies show that effective place inquiry need not necessarily use spatial methods per se; education researchers can collect and draw inferences about place-specific data using a variety of methodological approaches.

School closures. A growing number of researchers have interrogated the relationship between school closures and spatial injustice. For example, a recent research review on school closures challenges the notion that closing schools is a neutral process and reveals how the process disproportionately affects low-income, racially segregated communities in urban and rural contexts (Tieken & Auldridge-Reveles, 2019). The studies included in this chapter similarly reveal the spatial distribution of closures and surface counternarratives that challenge the myth of closed schools as "failed" places (Ewing, 2018). As Ewing's (2018) study of closures in Chicago reveals, foregrounding place in research on closures reveals what drives resistance to closures and what schools at risk for closure mean to communities. Ewing draws on a "place-sensitive sociological" approach, which foregrounds the importance of place as a key agent in our social lives (see also Shedd, 2015) to capture the importance of schools for residents' day-to-day lives and broader attempts to redefine urban schools not as "failures" but as places of "perseverance and growth" (Ewing, 2018, p. 135). Similar themes emerge in Good's (2017a, 2017b) studies of school closures in Philadelphia. Good integrates spatial methods and qualitative methods to visualize the distribution of closures and the meanings of closures for residents. Good's (2017b) study reveals not only the extent of spatial injustice related to closures but also how residents who resisted closures used their understanding of where closures were happening to comment on racial injustice. Both Ewing's (2018) and Good's (2017b) studies reveal the potential for place inquiry in education research to use both spatial *and* traditional methods. Moreover, both sets of studies reveal the potential of place inquiry to interrogate policy and reveal the consequences of policy decisions for communities.

Social Contexts of Education

Our review identified several studies that employ place inquiry to answer questions about the broader social context of education. Within this strand of research are studies that investigate patterns of inequality and racial segregation (e.g., Saporito & Sohoni, 2007; Sohoni & Saporito, 2009) and how place shapes access to opportunity (Erbstein, 2015; Green, 2015; Hogrebe & Tate, 2017; Jocson & Thorne-Wallington, 2013; B. D. Jones et al., 2015; Rodríguez et al., 2016; Turley, 2009; Wei et al., 2018). Jocson and Thorne-Wallington (2013), for example, used spatial methods to examine access to literacy-rich environments in relation to the spatial distribution of racial and socioeconomic groups in the St. Louis Metropolitan Area. Similarly, Rodríguez et al.

(2016) used place inquiry to explore differential access to early childhood programs and quality teachers in a New Mexico county. Drawing on spatial methods, these studies—and others like them—reveal and visualize the unequal distribution of resources across a given location. Beyond just describing the geography of opportunity, these studies illustrate the underlying links between racial and socioeconomic isolation and the resulting availability—or lack thereof—of educational opportunities in communities.

Mesosystem

Drawing on Bronfenbrenner's (1979) ecological system theory of human development, we use the term *mesosystem* to categorize studies that investigate processes and phenomena that occur across settings or as part of the interactions between settings, such as the journey to and from school and what students may or may not encounter during that journey. This research strand revealed the greatest diversity across disciplines, including studies from the fields of education, criminology, urban studies and planning, and public health. Studies in this category illuminated the critical role of place in shaping human behavior (e.g., Morojele & Muthukrishna, 2012; Schlossberg et al., 2005; Wridt, 2010; S. Y. Yoon et al., 2011). Schlossberg et al. (2005), for example, examined the role of the mobility structure in students' and parents' decisions about how to travel to school. Even when students lived close to their schools, the built environment often created barriers that restricted students' ability to walk or ride their bikes to schools. Similarly, in addition to examining the built environment, Morojele and Muthukrishna (2012) investigated how students' journey to school shaped and was shaped by power dynamics, including gendered role expectations. Boys, for example, were expected to exude strength and protect their female peers on the journey to school.

Shedd (2015) employed a "place-sensitive sociology" to demonstrate how Chicago's transformation into a global city has reinforced inequality (see also Lipman, 2002, 2013). Shedd (2015) focused specifically on how the broader policy context shaped youths' experiences in and outside of schools. For example, she described the significance of crossing neighborhood boundaries on school commutes, a simple act that could endanger youth if they encountered youth from rival neighborhoods.

Youths' Perceptions of Their Environments

Four studies reviewed for this chapter centered on questions about youths' perceptions of and interactions with their environments (Del Vecchio et al., 2017; O'Donoghue, 2007; Power et al., 2014; Schlemper et al., 2018). This strand of work offers insights into how researchers can use place inquiry and spatial methods to answer questions about place's role in shaping our lives. O'Donoghue's (2007) study of the formation of masculinity integrates photovoice and interviews to examine youths' sense of place and, more broadly, youths' senses of self. Similarly, Del Vecchio et al.'s (2017) study of how youth plan for their futures reveals where youth place themselves within society and youth's perceptions of their present and future selves. Notably, this strand of research points to the value of place inquiry and spatial methods for surfacing perspectives that might not emerge through other forms of research. Power et al. (2014) observed that youths' perspectives of their hometowns shifted when they were asked to capture photos of meaningful places compared to when they were asked to describe opportunities in their hometowns in focus groups. In conversations, for example, youth described their hometowns as having few opportunities; yet their photos and descriptions revealed positive perceptions and attachments to their hometowns that participants did not discuss in interviews.

Teaching and Learning

Finally, two studies investigated the role of place in shaping the context of teaching and learning. Blaisdell (2017) employs CRSA to investigate how teachers can reproduce systems of racial domination through what Blaisdell calls "redlining" in their classrooms. Teachers observed in Blaisdell's study made sense of their students based on information about where their students lived. For Blaisdell, place and space are embodied, which can lead individuals to treat others like the places from which people come. For educators, embodied place can lead teachers to marginalize and exclude students of color in the classroom (Blaisdell, 2017). In a second example of place inquiry in studies of teaching and learning, Burnett (2014) investigated how classroom context shapes how students make meaning of what they learn through digital literacy practices. Specifically, she examines the "classroom-ness" of digital learning, which she argues is shaped not only by the physical boundaries of the classroom but also by external environments. That is, students can learn and make meaning from digital practices using both information presented during lessons and their lives outside of class. For example, in making sense of a geography lesson using online maps, students drew on information that was presented in class and knowledge of environments outside of their classrooms (e.g., their neighborhoods). For Burnett, the concept of "classroom-ness" reveals the fluidity of place for student learning.

Together, Blaisdell (2017) and Burnett (2014) demonstrate that place inquiry and spatial methods need not be limited to macro-level geographies (e.g., neighborhoods, cities). Place inquiry and spatial methods also have potential for investigating place at micro-level locations, like classrooms, where systems of power have the potential to shape the contexts in which students learn and grow. The reviewed studies illustrate the utility of place inquiry and spatial methods to examine a diverse set of questions across domains of education and, more broadly, disciplines. Moreover, the studies included in this chapter illustrate how place inquiry and spatial methods can be used on their own or in concert with methods that are common in education research (e.g., case study methods, ethnographic methods). In the next section, we describe the theoretical perspectives that we identified within research employing place inquiry and spatial methods.

Theoretical Perspectives Brought to Bear

This section includes a discussion of the theoretical perspectives undergirding researchers' spatial methods and uses Agnew's (1987) framework of place as location, locale, and sense of place to surface the conceptions of place that emerge across the studies. Our analysis of the 60 studies revealed that the theoretical perspectives used by researchers fell into five main categories: (1) those studies that had no clear theoretical perspective, (2) studies that drew on literature directly related to the phenomenon of study, (3) CRT, (4) critical theories of space and place, and (5) other theories from the fields of geography and sociology.

Unclear Theoretical Perspectives

Approximately a quarter of the studies covered in this chapter had no clear theoretical perspective. All studies that fell into this category were quantitative studies using either broad spatial analyses (e.g., Ajilore, 2011), GIS software (e.g., Schlossberg et al., 2005), regression (e.g., Jaramillo, 2012), or geographically weighted regression (e.g., Fotheringham et al., 2001). The prominent issue areas that these studies addressed were education policy topics such as school choice (e.g., Dougherty et al., 2009) and the geography of opportunity (e.g., Hogrebe & Tate, 2017; Wei et al., 2018) or phenomena in the mesosystem (e.g., Day & Pearce, 2011; S. Y. Yoon et al., 2011). Importantly, the authors of all of these studies focused only on location. Jaramillo (2012), for example, used location-specific variables such as teachers' place of birth, location of matriculating college, and location of their first teaching jobs to demonstrate the existence of teacher labor markets. Even when illuminating inequalities, studies in this category revealed spatial differences in outcomes along race and socioeconomic lines as functions of a particular spot on a map. Sohoni and Saporito (2009), for example, use GIS to analyze differences in racial segregation between neighborhood public schools and their school catchment areas as well as the impact of students attending nonneighborhood schools. In this article, these authors conceptualize place as "school catchment areas"—an identifiable geographic location on a map. Others conceptualize place as a school district (Hogrebe & Tate, 2012, 2017), census tracts (LaFleur, 2016), or the path traveled between school and home (e.g., Schlossberg et al., 2005).

Theories Linked to Phenomenon of Study

A second theoretical category included those studies, about a quarter of all included studies, that drew on literature or theoretical constructs stemming directly from the phenomena of study. For example, several studies drew on the literature on school choice decision-making (e.g., Parsons et al., 2000) or used spatial methods to directly test the logical links in market theories (e.g., Farmer et al., 2019). Again, these studies were nearly all quantitative and fell into the education policy issue area. The aspects of place addressed by the author almost always reflected an understanding of place-as-location, although several studies also considered locale. For example, Taylor's (2009a) study of patterns of school choice, competition, and segregation examined both the role of location (i.e., catchment areas) and the results of parents' choices to move across location boundaries to attend schools. The social interactions—or avoidance of social interactions—inherent in these choices add important nuance to this study's findings. Two studies (Teixeira & Gardner, 2017; Wridt, 2010) in this category used participatory action research to reveal how youths' local context shapes their perspectives of their neighborhoods and opportunities therein. Using a combination of participatory action research and spatial methods such as participatory mapping, these studies captured findings related to location, locale, and sense of place, such as how youth made sense of their changing neighborhood contexts (Teixeira & Gardner, 2017) and where youth saw potential in their communities for physical activity (Wridt, 2010).

Critical Race Theory

Studies in the last three theoretical categories draw from the range of critical approaches advocated for by Morrison et al. (2017) and Tuck and McKenzie (2015). Both sets of authors argue that researchers engaging in place inquiry should employ critical perspectives, such as CRT and those that acknowledge the indigenous history of the land. Three studies, for example, drew upon CRT (Annamma et al., 2014; Blaisdell, 2017; Rodríguez et al., 2016). All of these studies, both quantitative and qualitative, used spatial methods to varying degrees within the context of CRT and illuminate how race and racism shape educational inequality through place. Annamma et al. (2014), for example, used spatial data descriptively to illustrate the links between race, school discipline, and special education policy and the role of state and federal policy, while Blaisdell (2017) took a deep dive into the classroom to investigate how teachers contribute to the racialization of classroom space in the context of White supremacy. Taken together, these three studies demonstrate how critical theoretical perspectives, such as CRT, in combination with spatial methods of data collection and analysis, can be particularly powerful tools for unmasking inequality.

Critical Theories of Space and Place

The largest number of studies, approximately a third of all studies covered, drew on critical theories of space and place, primarily the work of (in order of most often used) Massey (1994, 2005), Soja (2010), Lefebvre (1974), Tuan (1977), and Harvey (1973, 1996, 2008). Most often invoked was Massey's (2005) definition of space not as bound by location but as a sphere of "coexisting heterogeneity" that is a product of interrelations and is always under construction wherein space is "never finished, never closed" (p. 9).

Nearly all studies that used these critical theories to undergird their work were qualitative, two used mixed methods (e.g., Good, 2017b; Jocson & Thorne-Wallington,

2013), and one was quantitative (Tate & Hogrebe, 2018). Studies in this category also included all issue areas, including education policy (e.g., Bell, 2007, 2009; Buras, 2011, 2013; Gulson & Parkes, 2009), teaching and learning (e.g., Burnett, 2014), geography of opportunity (e.g., Erbstein, 2015; Jocson & Thorne-Wallington, 2013), youth perspectives (e.g., Del Vecchio et al., 2017), and social contexts of education (e.g., S. Jones et al., 2016). Additionally, data analyses, discussions, and conclusions in nearly all of the studies in this category suggested an acknowledgment and incorporation of multiple understandings of place, particularly locale and sense of place. Some studies in this category narrowed their focus and applied their critical theoretical lens on the "space" of the classroom. Burnett (2014), for example, discusses the complexities of classroom space and its importance for how students make meaning of their learning.

Most significantly, authors also used these theories to unmask the second dimension of sense of place: how place can function both as a site of oppression and resistance. Gulson and Parkes (2009), for example, in their study of educational policy in Sydney, Australia, emphasize that space functioned as a site of racial oppression and colonialism but also observe "hope and possibility" in marginalized peoples' "performances of space" (p. 277). Similarly, S. Jones et al.'s (2016) study reveals the powerful potential of pairing ethnographic research with a spatial theoretical framework. Their careful place-sensitive data collection methods account for the role that location, locale, and sense of place play in shaping people's experiences and illuminate how place can be both oppressive and sites for building resistance. Buras's (2011, 2013) pair of articles on post-Katrina New Orleans use Harvey's (1973, 2006) conceptions of "accumulation by dispossession" and "the urban space economy" to unmask inequities and identify how systems of oppression and White supremacy work within a particular location and set of social relationships. She also uses critical spatial theories to emphasize how community residents tapped into a local neighborhood school's role in their sense of place to resist governmental efforts to close that school (Buras, 2013).

Geography and Sociology

Finally, six studies drew on other related theories from the fields of geography and sociology, such as theories of children's geographies (e.g., Morojele & Muthukrishna, 2012), place-sensitive sociology (Shedd, 2015), and spatial behavior (Gilespe, 2010). Much like the studies that used critical theories of space and place, these studies are mostly qualitative, reflect a range of issue areas, and address multiple definitions and understandings of place. The studies that use children's geographies or emotional geographies, for example, describe children's social relationships within an emotional experience of a particular geographic location, as well as the role of this place in shaping their personal and cultural identities (e.g., Morojele & Muthukrishna, 2012; Power et al., 2014). Power et al. (2014), for example, examined youth's perceptions of rural environments using interviews and spatial methods. As discussed previously, Power et al. found that youth's attachments to their hometowns surfaced when researchers asked them to take photos of places that were significant to them.

Liberatory Potential of Place Inquiry and Spatial Methods

Using the lens of place in education research has the potential to reveal sources of and potential solutions to inequality in part because place is inherently connected to issues of social justice. As Soja (2010) describes, justice and injustice both have a spatial expression, or a "consequential geography" (p. 1). Soja describes the relation between space, geography, and the social world as a "socio-spatial dialectic," that is, spatiality "[shapes] social relations and societal development just as much as social processes configure and give meaning to the human geographies or spatialities in which we live" (p. 4). Put differently, place and space, as Lipsitz (2011) and others have observed, shape the enactment of social relations and, importantly, the power systems guiding our lives. Spatial and social justice, then, are also inseparable and embedded in a particular, localized set of changing social, political, and economic conditions (Marcuse, 2009; Soja, 2010). Spatial injustice takes two major forms: the involuntary confinement of any group to a limited space and the unequal allocation of resources over space (Marcuse, 2009). Both forms of injustice occur within and across three overlapping and interrelated geographical levels (Soja, 2010): processes of global development, the establishment of political, economic and social boundaries, and the privatization of public space and the disappearance of the commons. Such political spaces can be unjust and also enabling by creating opportunities and foundations for resistance and emancipation.

The relationships among space, social processes, and power, thus, suggest a potential to use spatial methods to critically examine how—to borrow from Lipsitz (2011)—hegemony "takes place" and how places come to exist as sites of domination and resistance. Moreover, the studies included in our analysis provide guidance for the potential of place inquiry and spatial methods for future education- and youth-focused research. At a basic level, as Hogrebe and Tate (2012), Lubienski and Lee (2017), and others have argued, integrating geospatial tools and perspectives into education research can illuminate the central role of context in shaping the perceptions and realities of justice—and injustice—in education. Studies reviewed for this chapter used spatial data collection and analysis tools to illustrate the inequitable distribution of opportunity across local contexts, such as the spatial location of schools (LaFleur, 2016; Lubienski et al., 2009; Smrekar & Honey, 2015), the distribution of learning opportunities across the P–20 education system (Erbstein, 2015; Hogrebe & Tate, 2017, 2012; Rodríguez et al., 2016; Turley, 2009), or the distribution of education resources (B. D. Jones et al., 2015); geospatial tools and perspectives can help visualize patterns of inequality across geographic locations. Furthermore, as we discuss in detail below, place inquiry in education research has the potential to reveal counternarratives of place and how systems of power function in places. By incorporating place inquiry, we argue that researchers studying the context and lived experiences in and around schools can help advance equity, liberation, and social justice.

Interrogating How Domination and Power Function in Places

Place inquiry can reveal how power and domination function in places. As the research analyzed here suggests, studies framed through the lens of CRSA, for example, can generate insights about how places become racialized. As previously discussed, Blaisdell's (2017) study of redlining in classrooms reveals the implicit ways that teachers can create spaces of exclusion within their classrooms. Paralleling Lipsitz's (2011) concept of the "white spatial imaginary," which ascribes moral and economic value to White spaces and devalues Black spaces, Blaisdell (2017) found that educators often unconsciously drew negative inferences about students of color based on the places that they lived. In doing so, these educators risked reproducing racism and white supremacy in their classrooms by managing students in ways that marginalized or excluded them from instruction.

Shedd's (2015) analysis, similarly, reveals how place shapes youths' interactions with surveillance systems and police—both inside and outside of their schools—as well as their perceptions of injustice. In a revealing analysis drawing on survey and spatial data on demographics, Shedd (2015) found that communities with the highest perception of injustice based on police behavior were also the communities with the highest proportions of African American residents. Similarly, students from the two schools with the largest minority populations were also more likely to report more contact with police and perceptions of injustice. These findings reveal the ways in which state actors' desire to "control" certain spaces—in this case, spaces with high proportions of minoritized residents—and the people within them creates systems that reinforce the domination of communities of color. Similarly, Grant et al.'s (2014) historical and contemporary case study of school closing decisions in Chicago illuminates how these decisions perpetuate spatial injustices and imperil minoritized residents' "right to the city" (Lefebvre, 1996).

The oppressive potential of places is not limited to domination based on race. Two studies included in this chapter reveal similar processes for gendered oppression. O'Donoghue (2006, 2007) uses theories of space, place, and masculinity formation, as well as arts-based methodologies, to unearth how schools can function as agents of masculinization. That is, his research on all-boys high schools in Ireland explains how physical spaces in schools embody specific values, beliefs, and attitudes and are the context in which masculinities are performed and produced.

With one exception (Del Vechhio et al., 2017), the studies reviewed for our analysis fall short in their analyses of domination and power in that they fail to acknowledge Indigenous histories—and present—of places while also anthropomorphizing place and ignoring the role of the natural environment. Such omissions perpetuate settler colonialism[3] by failing to acknowledge or account for the Indigenous histories of places, Indigenous peoples' resistance to settlement and claims to land, and the history and ongoing process of colonization (Greenwood, 2009; J. Johnson, 2012; Tuck et al., 2014; Tuck & Yang, 2012; Seawright, 2014). For place inquiry to truly challenge systems of domination and oppression, education scholars should heed Indigenous scholars' call to "front Indigeneity" (J. Johnson, 2012) and "learn to listen to what places are telling us" (Bang et al., 2014, p. 49; see also Tuck & McKenzie, 2015).

Counternarratives of Places

The stories that we tell about places, especially economically disadvantaged or minoritized communities, can reinforce class- and/or race-based oppression (Solórzano & Yosso, 2002). Researchers can inadvertently reify these narratives through studies that emphasize what places or people "lack," what Tuck (2009) calls "damage-centered research" (p. 409). However, researchers can potentially challenge such deficit-based perspectives through the types of place-specific data they collect and how they frame the said data. The literature we reviewed for this chapter suggests that the emergence of these counternarratives may be more likely when place inquiry is paired with asset-based or critical theoretical frames. Green's (2015) study of Detroit, for example, operationalized an asset-based framework to map the opportunities—in addition to the areas of need—present in communities. We also see the emergence of counternarratives in research that centers participants' sense of place. Power et al. (2014) found, for example, that youths' perceptions of their place can vary when they are asked to talk about places that are important to them compared to when they are asked to *show* places of significance. In interviews, youth talked about their hometowns as places with few opportunities. Yet, when asked to take photos of places that were significant to them and describe those places in focus groups, youth's perspectives of their hometowns encompassed a much more positive view of rural spaces and youth's attachments to place. Likewise, Teixeira and Gardner (2017) used participatory mapping to elicit youths' perspectives about their community, which focused not only on areas of challenge in their communities but also on areas of opportunity. Makris's (2015) investigation of how youth living in public housing relate to changing neighborhood contexts also reveals the potential of place inquiry and spatial methods as a complement to other data collection approaches. As part of a larger inquiry on gentrification, Makris (2015) investigates youths' understanding of gentrification and the extent to which they are separate—both physically and metaphorically—from the increased investment occurring elsewhere in the city. Complicating understandings of gentrification and displacement, she found that youth living in public housing are physically separated from development but, through youth-created maps, observed that youth interact with gentrified places and benefit from the proximity to middle-class capital (see also O. D. Johnson, 2012).

Counternarratives of place can also reframe them as sites not just of oppression but also of strength and resistance. One group of studies included in this chapter use critical spatial theories to guide research that illuminates how community residents invoke the deeply personal and historical meanings of their places in order to resist oppression. Buras's (2013) study of school rebuilding in the aftermath of Hurricane Katrina illustrated the shared meanings of place among teachers, administrators, and local activists that enabled local stakeholders to resist district and state takeovers of one elementary school. Similarly, Good's (2017a, 2017b) research on school closings in Philadelphia highlights how residents protested closures using spatial narratives that emphasized schools' historical and contemporary significance to the neighborhood. Gulson and Parkes (2009) demonstrated how the "performances of space" inherent in education policy discourses around the opening of a new school in an Aboriginal neighborhood in Sydney, Australia, can reinforce deficit views of Aboriginal people but also potentially mobilize residents to resist colonialism. They emphasized the "notion of hope and possibility in these 'performances of space'" (p. 277). On a smaller scale, S. Jones et al.'s (2016) postqualitative study of children's experiences in and around an after-school and summer space argued that place and space-making for and with children is a political act that can indoctrinate and oppress children or, more promisingly, can support creativity, curiosity and social critique. Taken together, these two sets of studies—those that center the voices and perspectives of youth and those that highlight the potential for resistance and hope within spaces—demonstrate the power of spatial methods to elicit powerful counternarratives of place that challenge systems of oppression.

CONCLUSION AND IMPLICATIONS

Our analysis reveals the potential for place inquiry and spatial methods to strengthen studies of education-related phenomena. By employing the tools of geographers, researchers studying education can strengthen their analyses by accounting for the many ways spatial location, locale, and sense of place influence the context and outcomes of schooling. However, as Tuck and McKenzie (2015) and others have argued, researchers who use place inquiry must take care to avoid simply using concepts of space and place descriptively—a limitation that we often identified in our analysis, particularly among studies that did not engage critical theories of space and place. While we recognize that such studies reveal important patterns of spatial inequality and injustice, we note that they also tend to distill such patterns to geographic location. The tensions inherent in portraying deep, complex injustices as points on a map speak to a broader conflict between the use of GIS and spatial methods in education research and efforts to reveal socio-spatial dynamics of power and oppression. As E. S. Yoon et al. (2018) and others have noted, a focus on place as location often limits the degree to which education researchers can interrogate power relations. This critique does not mean education researchers should *not* pursue GIS and spatial methods. Instead, as the studies reviewed for this chapter demonstrate, we propose pairing GIS and other spatial methods with critical spatial research paradigms and perspectives that allow for an exploration of the experiences of communities that are most often affected by inequity and spatial injustice. Multimodal research, such as Good's (2017b) study of school closures and quantitative work that incorporates critical theories of space and place (e.g., Tate & Hogrebe, 2018), exemplifies how researchers can use GIS and other quantitative spatial methods while also generating insights about how place shapes—and is shaped by—systems of power and domination. In our efforts to illuminate spatial inequality, however, we must take care to avoid defining places solely by what they "lack" (e.g., Tuck, 2009). As Green (2015), Ewing (2018), and others demonstrate, place inquiry can reveal powerful counternarratives of places and the deep attachments that people have to them.

The studies analyzed in this chapter reveal the potential of place inquiry for advancing social justice within education research. Certainly, inquiries that engage GIS and other spatial methods (e.g., Hogrebe & Tate, 2017) can advance the field's understanding of the distribution of opportunity across geographies at multiple scales; such inquiries make a valuable contribution. However, such inquiries must also go beyond describing the distribution of opportunity. We urge education researchers to conduct place inquiry that draws upon critical theories of place to reveal the ways in which place not only *contains* patterns of inequality but *shapes—and is shaped by*—patterns of inequality and systems of power and domination. Studies such as Blaisdell's (2017) study of redlining in schools reveal the ways in which educational spaces, such as classrooms, and noneducation spaces around schools are not neutral. Rather, schools—as places—shape and are shaped by forces that can oppress individuals from nondominant backgrounds.

The critical spatial perspective described throughout this chapter also gives rise to a call for scholars and researchers to use place as a tool for resisting such forces of oppression. Lefebvre (1996) argued that all people, especially people from historically marginalized backgrounds, have a "right to the city," that is, the right to benefit from equitable distribution of resources, to have access to geographical space, and to "make the city different" (Soja, 2010, p. 99) by challenging forces of homogenization, fragmentation, and uneven development imposed by the state. The overall aim of the struggle for spatial rights is to reclaim the city[4] and related democratic processes from the hands of those in power who develop and remake the city to further their own interests at the expense of marginalized people and the environment (Harvey, 2008; Lefebvre, 1996; Soja, 2010). Harvey (2008) argues that the struggle for spatial justice is not an individual endeavor but requires the "exercise of a collective power to reshape the processes of urbanization" (p. 23). This resistance, however, need not be limited to those who live and make their lives in cities. As Soja (2010) argues, the redistribution of resources and equitable development can, and should, extend to suburban and rural localities and consider how all three localities (urban, suburban, and rural) are interrelated and interdependent.

As this chapter illustrates, education researchers can respond to this call for resistance by using place inquiry and spatial methods to surface patterns of inequality and oppression *as well as* localized opportunities for people and communities to challenge these patterns in the context of education policy and practice. Illuminating patterns of inequality is only the first step; place inquiry and spatial methods have the potential to help education researchers generate explanations for why these patterns exist and how the collective power of individuals can disrupt these patterns. By collecting data about places and listening to the people who occupy those places, education researchers can produce scholarship that moves us toward greater equity and justice in schools and communities.

APPENDIX

Summary of Sources and Analytic Categories

Citation	Phenomena of Study	Issue Area(s)	Methods: General	Methods: Specific	Theoretical Perspective	Conceptions of Place Used by Author
Ajilore (2011)	Spatial variation in the relationship between ethnic heterogeneity and education spending	Education policy, school funding	Quantitative	Spatial analysis	No clear theoretical perspective	Location
Annamma et al. (2014)	Disproportionate assignment of students of color to special education and juvenile justice system and the role of state and federal policy	Education policy, inequality	Qualitative	Archival	Critical race theory, disability critical race theory, critical race spatial analysis	Location
Bell (2007)	The role of space and place in shaping parents' school choices	Education policy, school choice	Qualitative	Interviews	Critical theories of space and place (Lefebvre, Massey, Tuan), Bourdieu's theory of social action	Location, locale, sense of place (meaning)
Bell (2009)	The role of space and place in shaping parents' school choices	Education policy, school choice	Qualitative	Interviews, mapping	Critical theories of space and place (Lefebvre, Massey, Tuan), theories of parental school choice decision-making	Location, locale, sense of place (meaning)
Blaisdell (2017)	How teachers contribute to the racialization of space in the classroom	Teaching and learning, inequality	Qualitative	Ethnography	Critical race theory, racial spaces analysis	Location, locale, sense of place (politics)
Buras (2013)	Community residents' reliance on sense of place to resist school closure and rebuild a local school	Social context of education, school closings	Qualitative	Case study	Critical theories of space and place (Harvey)	Location, locale, and sense of place (meaning and political)
Burnett (2014)	How children make meaning of new technologies in the classroom	Teaching and learning	Qualitative	Case study	Critical theories of space and place (Massey, 2005)	Sense of place (meaning and political)
Cloutier et al. (2007)	Proximity of child pedestrian accidents to schools and relationship to neighborhood characteristics	Mesosystem	Quantitative	GIS, geographically weighted regression	No clear theoretical perspective	Location
Corbett & Helmer (2017)	Rural parents' use of spatialized strategies to protest school closures	Education policy, school closings	Qualitative	Interviews, archival	Grounded theory	Sense of place (meaning)
Davis & Oakley (2013)	Relationship between charter school emergence and urban neighborhood revitalization	Geography of opportunity	Quantitative	Regression, mapping	Grounded in the literature on school reform	Location
Day & Pearce (2011)	The local food environment, specifically locations of fast-food and convenience food outlets around elementary and secondary schools	Mesosystem	Quantitative	Spatial analysis	No clear theoretical perspective	Location
Del Vecchio et al. (2017)	Migrant, DACA-eligible youths' conceptions of and plans for their futures	Youth perspectives	Qualitative	Youth participatory action research	Critical place analysis (Tuck & McKenzie, 2015), theories of refusal	Location, locale, sense of place (meaning)
Dougherty et al. (2009)	Effect of test scores and minority composition on home prices	Education policy, school choice	Quantitative	GIS, regression	No clear theoretical perspective	Location

(continued)

85

APPENDIX (CONTINUED)

Citation	Phenomena of Study	Issue Area(s)	Methods: General	Methods: Specific	Theoretical Perspective	Conceptions of Place Used by Author
Erbstein (2015)	The role of housing patterns in producing segregation, math reform, and other educational opportunities for Latino English Language Learners	Geography of opportunity, inequality	Qualitative	Case study	Critical theories of space and place (Harvey, Lefebvre, Massey)	Location and locale
Ewing (2018)	Local resistance and the role of race, power and history in Chicago school closures	Education policy, school closures	Qualitative	Interviews, discourse analysis	Place-sensitive sociology	Location, locale, sense of place (political)
Farmer et al. (2019)	Impact of heightened school competition through choice policies and charter schools on education market efficiency	Education policy, school choice	Quantitative	GIS, spatial analysis	Market theory	Location
Fataar (2007)	How spatial processes mediate the local implementation of national education reforms	Education policy	Qualitative	Ethnography	Critical theories of space and place (Hart, Lefebvre, Massey)	Location, locale
Fotheringham et al. (2001)	Spatial variations between catchment areas and school performance	Social context of education, student achievement	Quantitative	Spatial analysis, geographically weighted regression	No clear theoretical perspective	Location
Gilespe (2010)	Impact of socialization processes on students' sense of neighborhood and community	Neighborhood context, youth perspectives	Qualitative	Visual	Theories of spatial behavior	Location, locale
Good (2017a)	Community residents' strategies and use of space/place in protesting school closures	Education policy, school closings	Qualitative	Interviews, archival	Critical theories of space (Massey, 2005)	Location, sense of place (meaning and politics)
Good (2017b)	Stakeholders' leveraging of space/place and spatialized inequality in protesting school closures	Education policy, school closings	Mixed	Regression, interviews	Critical theories of space, place, and the city (Harvey, Lefebvre)	Location, locale, sense of place (meaning and politics)
Grant et al. (2014)	Ideological, historical and cultural dimensions of school closing decisions	Education policy, school closings	Qualitative	Archival	Spatial justice (Soja)	Location, locale, sense of place (politics)
Green (2015)	Institutional assets in low-opportunity neighborhoods	Social context of education, geography of opportunity	Quantitative	GIS, spatial analysis	Asset-based community development	Location and locale
Gulson & Parkes (2009)	Interplay of urban renewal, identity, and education policy; racialization of the inner city	Education policy	Qualitative	Interviews, archival	Critical theories of space and place (Massey)	Location, locale, sense of place (politics)
Hogrebe & Tate (2012)	Spatial variations in relationships between school district demographics, financial context, student behavior, and academic performance	Social context of education, student achievement	Quantitative	Spatial analysis, geographically weighted regression	No clear theoretical perspective	Location
Hogrebe & Tate (2017)	Equity in enrollment in advanced math courses across local contexts	Education policy, geography of opportunity	Quantitative	GIS, spatial analysis	No clear theoretical perspective	Location
Jaramillo (2012)	Regional variation in teacher labor markets	Education policy, distribution of teachers	Quantitative	Regression	No clear theoretical perspective	Location
Jocson & Thorne-Wallington (2013)	Spatial inequalities by race and income in distribution of literacy-rich environments	Geography of opportunity	Mixed	Spatial analysis, mapping	Critical theories of space, place and the city (Lefebvre, Harvey, and Soja)	Location
B. D. Jones et al. (2015)	Interdependence of health, education, and place	Social context of education, geography of opportunity	Quantitative	GIS, mapping	Social epidemiology	Location, locale

(continued)

APPENDIX (CONTINUED)

Citation	Phenomena of Study	Issue Area(s)	Methods: General	Methods: Specific	Theoretical Perspective	Conceptions of Place Used by Author
S. Jones et al. (2016)	How a particular place (after-school and summer space for youth) shapes and is shaped by children's experiences	Neighborhood context, children's geographies	Qualitative	Ethnography, archival	Critical theories of space and place (Massey, Soja) and theories of childhood spatialities (Kraftl)	Location, locale, and sense of place (meaning and politics)
LaFleur (2016)	Location of charter schools in relation to demographic characteristics of census tracts	Education policy, charter schools	Quantitative	GIS	No clear theoretical perspective	Location
Lubienski et al. (2009)	How competitive incentives shape the location of school choice options in local education markets	Education policy, education markets	Quantitative	GIS	Theories of organizational and institutional competition	Location
Makris (2015)	Youth responses to gentrification	Mesosystem	Qualitative	Case study, map analysis	Neoliberal policy, capital	Sense of place (meaning)
Misra et al. (2012)	Impact of private school competition on public school efficiency	Education policy, education markets	Quantitative	Regression, mapping	Market theory	Location
Morojele & Muthukrishna (2012)	Children's understanding of their journey to school	Mesosystem, children's geographies	Qualitative	Interviews, mapping	Theories of children's geographies and sociology of childhood	Location, locale and sense of place (meaning)
Murray & Swatt (2013)	Proximity of crime to schools, considering type and level of school	Mesosystem	Quantitative	Spatial analysis	Routine activity theory	Location
O'Donoghue (2006)	How school places and spaces embody and perform masculinity	Social context of education	Qualitative	Visual	Critical theories of space and place (Massey), theories of masculinity formation	Location, locale, sense of place (meaning)
O'Donoghue (2007)	How boys learn about masculinity through the places and spaces of school	Youth perspectives	Qualitative	Visual, focus groups	Critical theories of space and place (Massey, Tuan), theories of masculinity formation	Location, locale, sense of place (meaning)
Parsons et al. (2000)	Patterns of pupil flow across school catchment boundaries	Education policy, school choice	Quantitative	GIS	Grounded in the literature on school choice	Location, locale
Phillippo & Griffin (2016)	Role of social geography in students' school choices	School choice	Qualitative	Case study	Critical theories of space and place (Massey), geography of educational opportunity	Location, locale, sense of place (meaning)
Power et al. (2014)	Youth senses of place and place attachment	Neighborhood context, youth perspectives	Qualitative	Visual, interviews	Grounded in literature on emotional geographies	Sense of place (meaning)
Reay (2007)	How young people perceive and make choices about schools	Social context of education	Qualitative	Interviews	Theories of the geographies of schooling, Sheild's conceptualization of places on the margin	Sense of place (meaning)
Rice et al. (2017)	Patterns in voting for or against a new city-wide school assignment policy	Education policy	Quantitative	GIS, regression	Grounded in the literature on school assignment policies	Location
Rodríguez et al. (2016)	Spatial variations and patterns in access to early childhood programs in quality teachers	Education policy	Quantitative	Spatial analysis	Critical race theory, Latina/o critical race theory	Location

(continued)

APPENDIX (CONTINUED)

Citation	Phenomena of Study	Issue Area(s)	Methods: General	Methods: Specific	Theoretical Perspective	Conceptions of Place Used by Author
Saporito & Sohoni (2007)	Concentration of poverty in neighborhood schools as compared to catchment areas	Education policy	Quantitative	GIS, regression	Grounded in the literature on school choice	Location, locale
Schlemper et al. (2018)	Students' understandings of their neighborhoods, identities, and sense of place	Youth perspectives	Qualitative	Interviews, mapping	Critical geography (Harvey, Caitling)	Location, locale, sense of place (meaning)
Schlossberg et al. (2005)	How students get to and from school and the surrounding mobility infrastructure	Mesosystem	Quantitative	GIS, survey	No clear theoretical perspective (brings in transportation literature)	Location
Shedd (2015)	Youth perceptions of self and justice	Mesosystem	Mixed	Interviews, survey	Geography of exclusion (Sibley), youth perceptions of injustice as informed by a "place-sensitive" sociology	Location, locale, sense of place (meaning and politics)
Smrekar & Honey (2015)	How education policy and parents' preferences shape the racial and socioeconomic integration of magnet schools	Education policy	Qualitative	Interviews, mapping	Grounded in the literature on school choice	Location
Sohoni & Saporito (2009)	Correspondence between public school demographics and demographics of school attendance zones	Education policy	Quantitative	GIS, mapping	No clear theoretical perspective	Location
Talen (2001)	Spatial patterns of elementary schools in a rural area and related variations in access to school	Education policy	Quantitative	Regression, mapping	No clear theoretical perspective	Location
Tate & Hogrebe (2018)	Local variation in school segregation	Education policy	Quantitative	GIS, spatial analysis	Critical theories of space, critical spatial analysis (Soja)	Location
Taylor (2001)	Impact of multiple choice markets on schools	Education policy	Quantitative	GIS, spatial analysis	Spatial construction of education markets and competition	Location, locale
Taylor (2009a)	Patterns of school choice, competition, and racial and socioeconomic segregation	Education policy	Quantitative	GIS, mapping	Grounded in the literature on school choice	Location, locale
Teixeira & Gardner (2017)	Relationships between youth and the built and social environment of their neighborhoods; how those neighborhoods shape youth perceptions of their opportunities	Neighborhood context	Qualitative	Visual	No clear theoretical perspective	Location, locale, sense of place (meaning)
Turley (2009)	Effects of college proximity on students' decision to enroll	Geography of opportunity	Quantitative	Regression, mapping	Grounded in the literature on college choice	Locale
Wei et al. (2018)	Spatial variations in neighborhood effects on students' achievement	Geography of opportunity	Quantitative	Regression, geographically weighted regression	No clear theoretical perspective	Location
Wridt (2010)	The role of neighborhood context in shaping children's perspectives, access and use of community spaces for physical activity	Mesosystem	Qualitative	Participatory action research, mapping	No clear theoretical perspective	Location, locale
S. Y. Yoon et al. (2011)	Spatial variation of students' and parents' behaviors related to their commute to school	Mesosystem	Quantitative	Regression, mapping	No clear theoretical perspective	Location, locale

Note. GIS = geographic information system; DACA = Deferred Action for Childhood Arrivals.

NOTES

[1]Tuck and McKenzie (2015) coined the term *critical place inquiry*. Because our review intends to encompass a wide range of literature that may not necessarily incorporate critical perspectives, we will be using the broader term *place inquiry*.

[2]Databases used to identify literature include Academic Search Ultimate, Education source, ERIC, PsychINFO, SocIndex, and Urban Studies. We replicated all searches in Google Scholar to identify additional studies that may not have been cataloged in academic databases.

[3]Settler colonialism is "a form of colonization in which outsiders come to land inhabited by indigenous peoples and claim it as their own new home" (Tuck et al., 2014, p. 6). It is distinct from other forms of colonialism in that settlers are seeking land and resources, not necessarily labor. Settler colonialism is not a relic of the past but an ongoing activity as settler colonial states, such as the United States, continually ignore their own history as settler states as well as Indigenous peoples' resistance to settlement and claims to land (Tuck et al., 2014).

[4]Lefebvre (1996) argues that the processes of urbanization and the "urban fabric" have influenced communities beyond the city center and blurred the boundaries between "town and country" (p. 118). Thus, the idea of "the right to the city" and related concepts of spatial justice extend to rural as well as urban areas.

REFERENCES

References marked with an asterisk indicate studies included in the meta-analysis.

Agnew, J. (1987). *Place and politics: The geographical meditation of state and society.* Allen & Unwin.

*Ajilore, O. (2011). The impact of ethnic heterogeneity on education spending: a spatial econometric analysis of United States school districts. *Review of Urban & Regional Development Studies, 23*(1), 66–76. https://doi.org/10.1111/j.1467-940X.2011.00178.x

*Annamma, S., Morrison, D., & Jackson, D. (2014). Disproportionality fills in the gaps: Connections between achievement, discipline and special education in the school-to-prison pipeline. *Berkeley Review of Education, 5*(1), 53–87. https://doi.org/10.5070/B85110003

Azano, A. (2011). The possibility of place: One teacher's use of place-based instruction for English students in a rural high school. *Journal of Research in Rural Education, 26*(10), 1–12. https://pdfs.semanticscholar.org/7442/8ce8b1b3d694652ddb37c585 9213104dc887.pdf

Bang, M., Curley, L., Kessel, A., Marin, A., Suzukovich, E. S., III, & Strack, G. (2014). Muskrat theories, tobacco in the streets, and living Chicago as Indigenous land. *Environmental Education Research, 20*(1), 37–55. https://doi.org/10.1080/13504622.20 13.865113

Basso, K. H. (1996). *Wisdom sits in places: Landscape and language among the Western Apache.* University of Minnesota Press.

*Bell, C. A. (2007). Space and place: Urban parents' geographical preferences for schools. *The Urban Review, 39*(4), 375–404. https://doi.org/10.1007/s11256-007-0059-5

*Bell, C. A. (2009). Geography in parental choice. *American Journal of Education, 115*(4), 493–521. https://doi.org/10.1086/599779

*Blaisdell, B. (2017). Resisting redlining in the classroom: A collaborative approach to racial spaces analysis. In D. Morrison, S. A. Annamma, & D. D. Jackson (Eds.), *Critical race spatial analysis: Mapping to understand and address educational inequality* (pp.109–125). Stylus.

Bronfenbrenner, U. (1979). *The ecology of human development: Experiments by nature and design.* Harvard University Press.

*Buras, K. (2011). Race, charter schools, and conscious capitalism: On the spatial politics of whiteness as property (and the unconscionable assault on black New Orleans). *Harvard Educational Review, 81*(2), 296–330. https://doi.org/10.17763/haer.81.2.6l42343qqw360j03

*Buras, K. (2013). 'We're not going nowhere': Race, urban space, and the struggle for King Elementary School in New Orleans. *Critical Studies in Education, 54*(1), 19–32. https://doi.org/10.1080/17508487.2013.741072

*Burnett, C. (2014). Investigating pupils' interactions around digital texts: a spatial perspective on the "classroom-ness" of digital literacy practices in schools. *Educational Review, 66*(2), 192–209. https://doi.org/10.1080/00131911.2013.768959

Buxton, C. A. (2010). Social problem solving through science: An approach to critical, place-based, science teaching and learning. *Equity & Excellence in Education, 43*(1), 120–135. https://doi.org/10.1080/10665680903408932

Cajete, G. (1994). *Look to the mountain: An ecology of indigenous education.* Kivaki Press.

Cajete, G. (1999). Reclaiming biophilia: Lessons from indigenous peoples. In G. Smith & D. Williams (Eds.), *Ecological education in action: On weaving education, environment, and culture* (pp. 189–206). State University of New York Press.

Calderon, D. (2014). Speaking back to Manifest Destinies: A land education-based approach to critical curriculum inquiry. *Environmental Education Research, 20*(1), 24–36. https://doi.org/10.1080/13504622.2013.865114

Casey, E. (1996). How to get from space to place in a fairly short stretch of time: Phenomenological prolegomena. In K. H. Basso & S. Feld (Eds.), *Sense of place* (pp. 13–52). School of American Research Press.

*Cloutier, M., Apparicio, P., & Touez, J. (2007). GIS-based spatial analysis of child pedestrian accidents near primary schools in Montreal, Canada. *Applied GIS, 3*(4), 1–18. https://doi.org/10.4225/03/57E9B71457976

*Corbett, M., & Helmer, L. (2017). Contested geographies: Competing constructions of community and efficiency in small school debates. *Geographical Research, 55*(1), 47–57. https://doi.org/10.1111/1745-5871.12209

Cresswell, T. (2004). *Place: A short introduction.* Blackwell.

*Davis, T., & Oakley, D. (2013). Linking charter school emergence to urban revitalization and gentrification: A socio-spatial analysis of three cities. *Journal of Urban Affairs, 35*(1), 81–102. https://doi.org/10.1111/juaf.12002

*Day, P., & Pearce, J. (2011). Obesity-promoting food environments and the spatial clustering of food outlets around schools. *American Journal of Preventative Medicine, 40*(2), 113–121. https://doi.org/10.1016/j.amepre.2010.10.018

Delaney, D. (2002). The space that race makes. *The Professional Geographer, 54*(1), 6–14. https://doi.org/10.1111/0033-0124.00309

Deloria, V., & Wildcat, D. R. (2001). *Power and place: Indian education in America.* Fulcrum.

*Del Vecchio, D., Toomey, N., & Tuck, E. (2017). Placing photovoice: Participatory action research with undocumented migrant youth in the Hudson Valley. *Critical Questions in Education, 8*(4), 358–376. https://files.eric.ed.gov/fulltext/EJ1159312.pdf

Dentzau, M. W. (2014). The value of place. *Cultural Studies of Science Education, 9*(1), 165–171.

*Dougherty, J., Harrelson, J, Maloney, L., Murphy, D., Smith, R., Snow, M., & Zannoni, D. (2009). School choice in suburbia: Test scores, race, and housing markets. *American Journal of Education, 115*, 523–548. https://doi.org/10.1086/599780

*Erbstein, N. (2015). Placing math reform: locating Latino English learners in math classrooms and communities. *International Journal of Qualitative Studies in Education, 28*(8), 906–931. https://doi.org/10.1080/09518398.2014.974714

*Ewing, E. L. (2018). *Ghosts in the schoolyard: Racism and school closings on Chicago's south side.* University of Chicago Press. https://doi.org/10.7208/chicago/9780226526331.001.0001

*Farmer, S., Poulos, C., & Baber, A. (2019). Challenging the market logic of school choice: A spatial analysis of charter school expansion in Chicago. *Journal of Urban Affairs*, 1–23. https://doi.org/10.1080/07352166.2018.1555437

*Fataar, A. (2007). Educational renovation in a South African "township on the move": A social-spatial analysis. *International Journal of Educational Development*, *27*, 599–612. https://doi.org/10.1016/j.ijedudev.2006.10.019

Feld, S., & Basso, K. (Eds.). (1996). *Senses of place.* School of American Research Press.

*Fotheringham, A., Charlton, M., & Brunsdon, C. (2001). Spatial variations in school performance: A local analysis using geographically weighted regression. *Geographical & Environmental Modeling*, *5*(1), 43–66. https://doi.org/10.1080/13615930120032617

Gallay, E., Marckini-Polk, L., Schroeder, B., & Flanagan, C. (2016). Place-based stewardship education: Nurturing aspirations to protect the rural commons. *Peabody Journal of Education*, *91*, 155–175. https://doi.org/10.1080/0161956X.2016.1151736

*Gilespe, C. (2010). How culture constructs our sense of neighborhood: Mental maps and children's perceptions of place. *Journal of Geography*, *109*, 18–29. https://doi.org/10.1080/00221340903459447

*Good, R. M. (2017a). Histories that root us: Neighborhood, place, and the protest of school closures in Philadelphia. *Urban Geography*, *38*(6), 861–8883. https://doi.org/10.1080/02723638.2016.1182286

*Good, R. M. (2017b). Invoking landscapes of spatialized inequality: Race, class, and place in Philadelphia's school closure debate. *Journal of Urban Affairs*, *39*(3), 358–380. https://doi.org/10.1080/07352166.2016.1245069

*Grant, C., Arcello, A., Konrad, A., & Swenson, M. (2014). Fighting for the "right to the city": Examining spatial injustice in Chicago public school closings. *British Journal of Sociology of Education*, *35*(5), 670–687. https://doi.org/10.1080/01425692.2014.919844

*Green, T. L. (2015). Places of inequality, places of possibility: Mapping "opportunity in geography" across urban school-communities. *The Urban Review*, *47*(4), 717–741. https://doi.org/10.1007/s11256-015-0331-z

Greenwood, D. A. (2009). Place, survivance, and White remembrance: A decolonizing challenge to rural education in mobile modernity. *Journal of Research in Rural Education*, *24*(10), 1–6.

Greenwood, D. A. (2012). A critical theory of place-conscious education. In R. B. Stevenson, M. Brody, J. Dillon, & A. E. J. Wals (Eds.), *International handbook of research on environmental education* (pp. 93–100). Routledge.

Gruenewald, D. (2003a). The best of both worlds: A critical pedagogy of place. *Educational Researcher*, *32*(4), 3–12. https://doi.org/10.3102/0013189X032004003

Gruenewald, D. (2003b). Foundations of place: A multidisciplinary framework for place-conscious education. *American Educational Research Journal*. *40*(3), 619–654. https://doi.org/10.3102/00028312040003619

*Gulson, K., & Parkes, R. (2009). In the shadows of the mission: Education policy, urban space, and the "colonial present" in Sydney. *Race Ethnicity and Education*, *12*(2), 267–280. https://doi.org/10.1080/13613320903178246

Gulson, K. N., & Symes, C. (2007). *Spatial theories of education: Policy and geography matters.* Routledge. https://doi.org/10.4324/9780203940983

Harvey, D. (1973). *Social Justice and the City.* Johns Hopkins University Press.

Harvey, D. (1996). *Justice, nature and the geography of difference.* Blackwell.

Harvey, D. (2006). *Spaces of global capitalism: Towards a theory of uneven geographical development.* New York, NY: Verso.

Harvey, D. (2008). The right to the city. *New Left Review, 53*, 23–40. https://newleftreview
  .org/issues/II53/articles/david-harvey-the-right-to-the-city

Haymes, S. N. (1995). *Race, culture, and the city: A pedagogy for Black urban struggle.* State
  University of New York Press.

*Hogrebe, M., & Tate, W. (2012). Place, poverty and algebra: A statewide comparative spatial
  analysis of variable relationships. *Journal of Mathematics Education, 3*, 12–24. https://
  journals.library.columbia.edu/index.php/jmetc/article/view/746

*Hogrebe, M., & Tate, W. (2017). Exploring educational opportunity with geospatial pat-
  terns in high school Algebra 1 and Advanced Mathematics Courses. In D. Morrison, S.
  A. Annamma, & D. D. Jackson (Eds.), *Critical race spatial analysis: Mapping to understand
  and address educational inequality* (pp. 126–146). Stylus.

hooks, b. (1990). *Yearning: Race, gender, and cultural politics.* South End Press

Howley, A., Howley, M., Camper, C., & Perko, H. (2011). Place-based education at island
  community school. *Journal of Environmental Education, 42*(4), 216–236. https://doi.org/
  10.1080/00958964.2011.556682

*Jaramillo, M. (2012). The spatial geography of teacher labor markets: Evidence from a devel-
  oping country. *Economics of Education Review, 31*, 984–995. https://doi.org/10.1016/j
  .econedurev.2012.07.005

*Jocson, K., & Thorne-Wallington, E. (2013). Mapping literacy-rich environments:
  Geospatial perspectives on literacy and education. *Teachers College Record, 115*(6), 1–24.

Johnson, J. (2012). Place-based learning and knowing: Critical pedagogies grounded in
  Indigeneity. *GeoJournal, 77*(6), 829–836. https://doi.org/10.1007/s10708-010-9379-1

Johnson, O. D. (2012). Toward a theory of place: Social mobility, proximity, and proximal
  capital. In W. Tate (Ed.), *Research on schools, neighborhoods, and communities: Toward
  civic responsibility* (pp. 29–46). American Educational Research Association.

*Jones, B. D., Harris, K., & Tate, W. (2015). Ferguson and beyond: A descriptive epide-
  miological study using geospatial analysis. *Journal of Negro Education, 84*(3), 231–253.
  https://doi.org/10.7709/jnegroeducation.84.3.0231

*Jones, S., Thiel, J., Davila, D., Pittard, E., Woglom, J., Zhou, X., Brown, T., & Snow, M.
  (2016). Childhood geographies and spatial justice: Making sense of place and space-making as political acts in education. *American Educational Research Journal, 53*(4), 1126–
  1158. https://doi.org/10.3102/0002831216655221

Keith, M., & Pile, S. (Eds.). (1993). *Place and the politics of identity.* Routledge.

Kerski, J. (2011). Sleepwalking into the future: The case for spatial analysis throughout education. In K. Donert & M. Lindner-Fally (Eds.), *Learning with geoinformation* (pp. 2–11).
  Wichmann.

*LaFleur, J. (2016). Locating Chicago's charter schools: A socio-spatial analysis. *Education
  Policy Analysis Archives, 24*(33). https://doi.org/10.14507/epaa.24.1745

Lefebvre, H. (1974). *The production of space.* Blackwell.

Lefebvre, H. (1996). *Writings on cities.* Blackwell.

Lipman, P. (2002). Making the global city, making inequality: The political economy and
  cultural politics of Chicago school policy. *American Educational Research Journal, 39*(2),
  379–419. http://doi.org/10.3102/00028312039002379

Lipman, P. (2013). *The new political economy of urban education: Neoliberalism, race, and the
  right to the city.* Taylor & Francis. https://doi.org/10.4324/9780203821800

Lipsitz, G. (2011). *How racism takes place.* Temple University Press.

Lubienski, C., & Dougherty, J. (2009). Mapping educational opportunity: Spatial analysis
  and school choices. *American Journal of Education, 115*(4), 485–491.

*Lubienski, C., Gulosino, C., & Weitzel, P. (2009). School choice and competitive incentives:
  Mapping the distribution of educational opportunities across local education markets.
  American Journal of Education, 115(4), 601–647. https://doi.org/10.1086/599778

Lubienski, C., & Lee, J. (2017). Geo-spatial analyses in education research: The critical challenge and methodological possibilities. *Geographical Research*, *55*(1), 89–99. https://doi .org/10.1111/1745-5871.12188

*Makris, M. (2015). Separate, different, but not isolated: How youth in public housing relate to their gentrified community. In *Public housing and school choice in a gentrified city: Youth experiences of uneven opportunity* (pp. 170–189). Palgrave.

Marcuse, P. (2009). Spatial justice: derivative but causal of social injustice. *Spatial Justice*, *1*(4), 1–6.

Martusewicz, R. A., Edmundson, J., & Lupinacci, J. (2014). *Ecojustice education: Toward diverse, democratic, and sustainable communities* (2nd ed.). Routledge.

Massey, D. (1994). *Space, place, and gender*. University of Minnesota Press.

Massey, D. (2005). *For space*. Sage.

McKenzie, M. (2008). The places of pedagogy: Or, what we can do with culture through intersubjective experiences. *Environmental Education Research*, *14*(3), 361–373. https:// doi.org/10.1080/13504620802194208

McKittrick, K. (2006). *Demonic grounds: Black women and the cartographies of struggle*. University of Minnesota Press.

*Misra, K., Grimes, P., & Rogers, K. (2012). Does competition improve public school efficiency? A spatial analysis. *Economics of Education Review*, *31*, 1177–1190. https://doi .org/10.1016/j.econedurev.2012.08.001

*Morojele, P., & Muthukrishna, N. (2012). The journey to school: Space, geography, and experiences of rural children. *Perspectives in Education*, *30*(1), 90–100.

Morrison, D., Annamma, S. A., & Jackson, D. D. (Eds.). (2017). *Critical race spatial analysis: Mapping to understand and address educational inequity*. Stylus.

*Murray, R. K., & Swatt, M. L. (2013). Disaggregating the relationship between schools and crime: A spatial analysis. *Crime & Delinquency*, *59*(2), 163–190. https://doi.org/ 10.1177/0011128709348438

*O'Donoghue, D. (2006). Situating space and place in the making of masculinities in schools. *Journal of Curriculum and Pedagogy*, *3*(1), 15–33. https://doi.org/10.1080/15505170.20 06.10411569

*O'Donoghue, D. (2007). 'James always hangs out here': making space for place in studying masculinities at school. *Visual Studies*, *22*(1), 62–73. https://doi.org/10 .1080/14725860601167218

Orr, D. W. (1992). *Ecological literacy: Education and the transition to a postmodern world*. State University of New York Press.

Orr, D. W. (2004). *Earth in mind: On education, environment, and the human prospect* (10th anniversary ed.). Island Press.

Owens, P. E., Rochelle, M. L., Nelson, A. A., & Montgomery-Block, K. (2011). Youth voices influencing local and regional change. *Children, Youth and Environments*, *21*(1), 253–274. https://doi.org/10.7721/chilyoutenvi.21.1.0253

*Parsons, E., Chalkley, B., & Jones, A. (2000). School catchments and pupil movements: A case study in parental choice. *Educational Studies*, *26*(1), 33–48. https://doi .org/10.1080/03055690097727

Peña, D. G. (1998). Los animalitos: Culture, ecology, and the politics of place in the Upper Rio Grande. In D. G. Peña (Ed.), *Chicano culture, ecology, politics: Subversive kin* (pp. 25–57). University of Arizona.

*Phillippo, K. L., & Griffin, B. (2016). The social geography of choice: Neighborhoods' role in students' navigation of school choice policy in Chicago. *The Urban Review*, *48*(5), 668–695. https://doi.org/10.1007/s11256-016-0373-x

*Power, N. G., Norman, M. E., & Dupré, K. (2014). Rural youth and emotional geographies: how photovoice and words-alone methods tell different stories of place. *Journal*

of Youth Studies, 17(8), 1114–1129. https://doi.org/10.1080/13676261.2014.88
1983

Powers, A. L. (2004). An evaluation of four place-based education programs. *Journal of Environmental Education, 35*(4), 17–32. https://doi.org/10.3200/JOEE.35.4.17-32

*Reay, D. (2007). "Unruly places": Inner-city comprehensives, middle-class imaginaries and working-class children. *Urban Studies, 44*(7), 1191–1201. https://doi.org/10.1080/00420980701302965

*Rice, L., Henderson, M., & Hunter, M. (2017). Neighborhood priority or desegregation plans? A spatial analysis of voting on San Francisco's student assignment system. *Population Research and Policy Review, 36*(6), 805–832. https://doi.org/10.1007/s11113-017-9435-3

*Rodríguez, C., Amador, A., & Tarango, B. A. (2016). Mapping educational equity and reform policy in the Borderlands: LatCrit spatial analysis of grade retention. *Equity & Excellence in Education, 49*(2), 228–240. https://doi.org/10.1080/10665684.2016.1144834

Rubel, L. H., Lim, V., Hall-Wieckert, M., & Katz, S. (2016). Cash across the city: Participatory mapping and teaching for spatial justice. *Journal of Urban Learning, Teaching, and Research, 12*, 4–14.

Sampson, R. J., Morenoff, J. D., & Gannon-Rowley, T. (2002). Assessing "neighborhood effects": Social processes and new directions in research. *Annual Review of Sociology, 28*(1), 443–478. http://doi.org/10.1146/annurev.soc.28.110601.141114

*Saporito, S., & Sohoni, D. (2007). Mapping educational inequality: Concentrations of poverty among poor and minority students in public schools. *Social Forces, 85*(3), 1227–1253. https://doi.org/10.1353/sof.2007.0055

*Schlemper, M. B., Stewart, V. C., Shetty, S., & Czajkowski, K. (2018). Including students' geographies in geography education: Spatial narratives, citizen mapping, and social justice. *Theory & Research in Social Education, 46*(4), 603–641. https://doi.org/10.1080/00933104.2018.1427164

*Schlossberg, M., Phillips, P. P., Johnson, B., & Parker, B. (2005). How do they get there? A spatial analysis of a "sprawl school" in Oregon. *Planning Practice & Research, 20*(2), 147–162. https://doi.org/10.1080/02697450500414678

Seawright, G. (2014). Settler traditions of place: Making explicit the epistemological legacy of white supremacy and settler colonialism for place-based education. *Educational Studies, 50*(6), 554–572. https://doi.org/10.1080/00131946.2014.965938

Sharkey, P. (2013). *Stuck in place: Urban neighborhoods and the end of progress toward racial equality.* University of Chicago Press. https://doi.org/10.7208/chicago/9780226924267.001.0001

Sharkey, P., & Elwert, F. (2011). The legacy of disadvantage: Multigenerational neighborhood effects on cognitive ability. *American Journal of Sociology, 116*(6), 1934–1981. https://doi.org/10.1086/660009

*Shedd, C. (2015). *Unequal city: Race, schools, and perceptions of injustice.* Russell Sage Foundation.

Smith, G. A. (2002). Place-based education: Learning to be where we are. *Phi Delta Kappan, 83*(3), 584–594. https://doi.org/10.1177/003172170208300806

Smith, G. A., & Sobel, D. (2010). *Place- and community-based education in schools.* Routledge.

Smith, G. A., & Williams, D. R. (Eds.). (1999). *Ecological education in action: On weaving education, culture, and the environment.* State University of New York Press.

Smith, L. T. (2012). *Decolonizing methodologies: Research and Indigenous peoples* (2nd ed.). Zed Books

*Smrekar, C., & Honey, N. (2015). The desegregation aims and demographic contexts of magnet schools: How parents choose and why siting policies matter. *Peabody Journal of Education, 90*(1), 128–155. https://doi.org/10.1080/0161956X.2015.988545

Sobel, D. (2004). *Place-based education: Connecting classroom and community.* The Orion Society.

*Sohoni, D., & Saporito, S. (2009). Mapping school segregation: using GIS to explore racial segregation between schools and their corresponding attendance areas. *American Journal of Education, 115*(4), 569–600. https://doi.org/10.1086/599782

Soja, E. W. (2010). *Seeking spatial justice.* University of Minnesota Press. https://doi.org/10.5749/minnesota/9780816666676.001.0001

Solórzano, D. G., & Yosso, T. J. (2002). Critical race methodology: Counter-storytelling as an analytical framework for education research. *Qualitative Inquiry, 8*(1), 23–44. https://doi.org/10.1177/107780040200800103

Somerville, M. (2010). A place pedagogy for "global contemporaneity." *Educational Philosophy and Theory, 42*(3), 326–344. https://doi.org/10.1111/j.1469-5812.2008.00423.x

Styres, S., Haig-Brown, C., & Blimkie, M. (2013). Towards a pedagogy of Land: The urban context. *Canadian Journal of Education, 36*(2), 34–67.

Takano, T., Higgins, P., & McLaughlin, P. (2009). Connecting with place: Implications of integrating cultural values into the school curriculum in Alaska. *Environmental Education Research, 15*(3), 343–370. https://doi.org/10.1080/13504620902863298

*Talen, E. (2001). School, community, and spatial equity: An empirical investigation of access to elementary schools in West Virginia. *Annals of the Association of American Geographers, 91*(3), 465–486. https://doi.org/10.1111/0004-5608.00254

Tate, W. F. (2008). "Geography of opportunity": Poverty, place, and educational outcomes. *Educational Researcher, 37*(7), 397–411.

*Tate, W. F., & Hogrebe, M. C. (2018). Show me: Diversity and Isolation indicators of spatial segregation within and across Missouri's school districts. *Peabody Journal of Education, 93*(1), 5–22. https://doi.org/10.1080/0161956X.2017.1403170

*Taylor, C. (2001). Hierarchies and "local" markets: The geography of the "lived" market place in secondary education provision. *Journal of Education Policy, 16*(3), 197–214. https://doi.org/10.1080/02680930110041024

Taylor, C. (2007). Geographical information systems (GIS) and school choice: The use of spatial research tools in studying educational policy. In K.N. Gulson & C. Symes (Eds.), *Spatial theories of education: Policy and geography matters* (pp. 77–94). New York, NY: Routledge.

*Taylor, C. (2009a). Choice, competition, and segregation in a United Kingdom urban education market. *American Journal of Education, 115*(4), 549–568. https://doi.org/10.1086/599781

Taylor, C. (2009b). Towards a geography of education. *Oxford Review of Education, 35*(5), 651–669. https://doi.org/10.1080/03054980903216358

*Teixeira, S., & Gardner, R. (2017). Youth-led participatory photo mapping to understand urban environments. *Children and Youth Services Review, 82*, 246–253. https://doi.org/10.1016/j.childyouth.2017.09.033

Theobald, P. (1997). *Teaching the commons: Place, pride, and the renewal of community.* Routledge.

Tieken, M. C., & Auldridge-Reveles, T. R. (2019). Rethinking the school closure research: School closure as spatial injustice. *Review of Educational Research, 89*(6), 917–953. https://doi.org/10.3102/0034654319877151

Trinidad, A. (2011). Sociopolitical development through critical indigenous pedagogy of place: Preparing Native Hawaiian young adults to become change agents. *Hulili: Multidisciplinary Research on Hawaiian Well-Being, 7*, 185–221.

Tuan, Y. (1977). *Space and place: The perspective of experience.* University of Minnesota Press.

Tuck, E. (2009). Suspending damage: A letter to communities. *Harvard Educational Review, 79*(3), 409–427. https://doi.org/10.17763/haer.79.3.n0016675661t3n15

Tuck, E., & McKenzie, M. (2015). *Place in research: Theory, methodology, and methods.* Routledge. https://doi.org/10.4324/9781315764849

Tuck, E., McKenzie, M., & McCoy, K. (2014). Land education: Indigenous, post-colonial, and decolonizing perspectives on place and environmental education research. *Environmental Education Research, 20*(1), 1–23. https://doi.org/10.1080/13504622.2013.877708

Tuck, E., & Yang, K. W. (2012). Decolonization is not a metaphor. *Decolonization: Indigeneity, Education & Society, 1*(1), 1–40. https://clas.osu.edu/sites/clas.osu.edu/files/Tuck%20and%20Yang%202012%20Decolonization%20is%20not%20a%20metaphor.pdf

*Turley, R. N. L. (2009). College proximity: Mapping access to opportunity. *Sociology of Education, 82*(2), 126–146. https://doi.org/10.1177/003804070908200202

Velez, V., & Solórzano, D. (2017). Critical race spatial analysis: Conceptualizing GIS as a tool for critical race research in education. In D. Morrison, S. A. Annamma, & D. D. Jackson (Eds.), *Critical race spatial analysis: Mapping to understand and address educational inequity* (pp. 8–31). Stylus.

Viteritti, J. (1999). *A way out: School choice and educational opportunity.* Brookings Instituition. https://doi.org/10.2307/20080877

*Wei, Y. D., Xiao, W., Simon, C. A., Liu, B., & Ni, Y. (2018). Neighborhood, race and educational inequality. *Cities, 73*, 1–13. https://doi.org/10.1016/j.cities.2017.09.013

*Wridt, P. (2010). A qualitative GIS approach to mapping urban neighborhoods with children to promote physical activity and child-friendly community planning. *Environment and Planning B: Planning and Design, 37*(1), 129–147. https://doi.org/10.1068/b35002

Yoon, E. S., Gulson, K., & Lubienski, C. (2018). A brief history of the geography of education policy: Ongoing conversations and generative tensions. *AERA Open, 4*(4), 1–9. https://doi.org/10.1177/2332858418820940

*Yoon, S. Y., Doudnikoff, M., & Goulias, K. G. (2011). Spatial analysis of propensity to escort children to school in southern California. *Transportation Research Record, 2230*(1), 132–142. https://doi.org/10.3141/2230-15

Zimmerman, H. T., & Weible, J. L. (2017). Learning in and about rural places: Connections and tensions between students' everyday experiences and environmental quality issues in their community. *Cultural Studies of Science Education, 12*(1), 7–3. https://doi.org/10.1007/s11422-016-9757-1

Chapter 4

Geospatial Analysis: A New Window Into Educational Equity, Access, and Opportunity

CASEY D. COBB
University of Connecticut

A robust body of geographic education policy research has been amassing over the past 25 years, as researchers from a variety of disciplinary backgrounds have recognized the value of examining education phenomena from a spatial perspective. In this chapter, I synthesize 42 studies that examine education issues using a geographic information system, or GIS. The review is framed by the major thread that runs through this body of research: educational equity, access, and opportunity. I summarize the research within seven theme-based research topics and offer examples of geospatial analysis as applied to education. The chapter includes a discussion of the major barriers and limitation facing GIS researchers and offers thoughts about the future.

A robust body of "geographic" education policy research has been amassing over the past 25 years. Researchers from a variety of disciplinary backgrounds have persistently highlighted the value of examining education phenomena from a spatial perspective (Bruno, 1996; Cobb, 2003; Gulson & Symes, 2007; Holloway et al., 2010; Kelly, 2019; Lubienski & Dougherty, 2009; Misra et al., 2012; Tate, 2008; Taylor, 2007). Advances in software packages have undoubtedly contributed to the field's emergence—namely, the growing use of "geographic information systems," or GIS.

In this chapter, I review over two decades of education policy research that analyzes data using a GIS. The vast majority of geospatial studies in education directly examine issues of educational equity, access, or opportunity. I summarize the research within theme-based research topics, expound on the geospatial questions that drive this research, and offer examples of geospatial analysis as applied to education.

Review of Research in Education
March 2020, Vol. 44, pp. 97–129
DOI: 10.3102/0091732X20907362
Chapter reuse guidelines: sagepub.com/journals-permissions
© 2020 AERA. http://rre.aera.net

Numerous terms are used in the literature that denote geographic methods of analysis. The most common descriptor is *geospatial analysis*, but this is also referred to as *spatial analysis* or more basically as *GIS research*. No matter the term, all capture the practice of examining phenomena from a geographical perspective. Trained GIS users likely differentiate between what they consider to be *robust geospatial analysis* on one end, and *analysis using a spatial lens*, on the other. It is not my objective here to define or sort through these variations, however. For this review, I focus on education and education policy topics examined, in some manner or another, using geographic techniques. Throughout this chapter I use the terms *GIS education research*, *GIS education policy research*, and *geospatial analysis* virtually interchangeably.

The article begins with an overview of GIS and spatial analysis, including a rundown of common analytic techniques. I then describe the literature under review and the sources from which they derive. The bulk of the chapter is devoted to a synthesis of GIS education research. The synthesis includes summaries of research by thematic topic, as well as a set of questions they aim to address, study contexts, equity concepts, units of analysis, and GIS analytic approaches. Toward the end, I outline commonly applied spatial techniques, identify sources of publicly available GIS data, and discuss the challenges associated with conducting geospatial research. I end with a few thoughts about the future of GIS research in education.

GEOGRAPHIC INFORMATION SYSTEMS

A GIS is a computer-based system that analyzes and displays geographically referenced information.[1] The systems are unique in that geographic features can be linked to relational databases, such as those containing tabular data or narrative accounts in the form of interviews. GIS facilitates the analysis of conventional quantitative and qualitative data, situating those data in a geographic context, and gives greater meaning to inferences about those data. For instance, geospatial data can be used to study the location of features and relationships to other features, the density of features in a given area, the distribution of features across spaces and time, and what is occurring within or nearby features.[2]

In the context of education research, most geospatial data are in what is called "vector" format, which enables representation of point, line, and polygon features. These representations capture features such as schools (points), neighborhood boundaries (lines), or district attendance zones (polygons). GIS analysis allows researchers to examine, visually and through advanced spatial techniques, relationships among quantitative and qualitative data in a geographic context. Spatial analysis can also be conducted historically, as in *spatiotemporal* analysis, which combines the analysis of data across space and time.

One of the advantages of GIS research is that it is inherently multidisciplinary and that it provides a "powerful mechanism for integrating the efforts of the various social sciences" (Goodchild & Janelle, 2004, p. 4). Multiple data sources can be joined with geographic data within a GIS. It is not uncommon for three, four, or more data sets to be joined by a common identifier. Commonly used tabular data include the U.S. Census, American Community Survey of the Census, state agency administrative data sets, National Center for Education Statistics Common Core of Data, researcher-generated data sets, and spatial data from GIS repositories. In many instances spatial data are created through geocoding addresses or boundary lines. Also, once a GIS data set is established, there are opportunities to generate new data fields through interpolation, aggregation of features within areas, or applying various other GIS tools designed to manipulate geospatial data.

The multidisciplinary, integrated nature of GIS offers powerful analytic capabilities. Using GIS, researchers are able to simultaneously explore quantitative and qualitative geospatial data that are seldom considered together. As an example, Tate's (2008) spatial analysis of the St. Louis biotechnical industry demonstrated the influence of geographic "clustering" of high-tech employment on neighborhood employment, poverty, and school performance. Using kernel density calculation and nearest neighbor analysis, Tate produced a series of maps showing the distribution of key economic, demographic, and educational indicators surrounding four biotech clusters in St. Louis. Tate found that the universities, corporations, and industrial parks that constituted the biotechnology initiative were "spatially distributed in a manner that is clustered rather than random," which resulted in an uneven geography of opportunity" in metropolitan St. Louis (pp. 406–407).[3]

OVERVIEW OF GIS ANALYTIC TECHNIQUES

Although GIS came on the scene in education research roughly around the turn of the century, it is still considered an innovative methodology. Geospatial techniques are ever expanding, offering new perspectives on studying issues in education, and thus new ways of knowing. Geospatial databases, tools, and services are becoming more prevalent as well. Even the manner in which geographic based data are created and stored has changed considerably in the past few years. For instance, GIS software now accommodates relational database management systems called geodatabases—a collection of files that can store, query, and manage both spatial and nonspatial data. Another GIS-related innovation has also been the creation of *interactive* spatiotemporal databases, where users can conduct analyses in real time on a variety of variables.

While there are several GIS programs to choose from, one of the more widely used packages is ArcGIS (Environmental Systems Research Institute, 2018). ArcGIS contains ArcMap, which is the primary application used to assemble, edit, and query geospatial data, and to generate maps. ArcMap and its predecessor, ArcView, were the most cited software programs in my review.

A wide variety of spatial analytic tools is offered by ArcMap or other comparable GIS programs. Map generation typically involves downloading an existing map file (in the case of ArcMap, a "shapefile"), geocoding specific points of interest, and adding other pertinent geographic layers of information. Spatial analysis can begin after the geographic data—usually in the form of points, lines, or polygons—are joined to relational tabular databases. It is beyond the scope of this review to go into great detail on digital map making and spatial analysis, but I offer a synopsis of the most common spatial techniques applied by education policy researchers.

Geographical areas, or "polygon features," are often the subject of study in GIS research. Areas are defined by "line features" in GIS, such as attendance zones, census tracks, and political boundaries. Areas lend themselves to internal examination as well as comparison to other areas. Spatial analytic software "allow[s] data from neighboring zones to be compared and aggregated, and areal interpolation tools allow statistics for one set of reporting zones to be estimated from known values for a second, incompatible set of reporting zones" (Goodchild, 1993, as cited in Goodchild & Janelle, 2004, p. 12). A frequently applied GIS tool is *average nearest neighbor analysis* (ANNA), which measures distances from central points and is used to determine whether certain features of a variable demonstrate a statistically significant level of clustering (Allen, 2009, as cited in Schultz, 2014). For example, Gilblom and Sang (2019) used ANNA to assess the degree to which charter schools in Cleveland clustered together and under what geographic conditions. ANNA was used by Schultz (2014) in a similar fashion to assess clustering of high-quality teachers in St. Louis.

Areas also exhibit varying shapes (square, oval, narrow) and sizes with properties and characteristics within them that interact with the surrounding political geography. GIS researchers have examined the shape of school districts in relation to internal and contiguous community demographics. Saporito (2017) and Saporito and Van Riper (2016) investigated the extent to which the shapes of school attendance zones were associated with racial segregation in schools. To make their determination, they tested the "irregularity" of school district shapes across the United States using GIS *compactness measures*.[4]

Kernel density estimates (KDEs) are used to calculate the density of features in a geographic space (e.g., density of schools, crime reports, interstates). Singleton et al. (2011) produced an alternative representation of school catchment areas "using kernel density estimates (KDE) of the areas where a local population of interest is spatially concentrated" (p. 243). They suggest density estimates can be used "to identify the areas within which approximately 50%, 75% or 95% of the pupils live, and who attend a given school" (p. 243). A major advantage of the KDE technique is that it "does not divulge the point locations of any pupils" (p. 243), which can help maintain confidentiality.[5] Singleton et al. (2011) expounded on the utility of the KDE-enhanced map, noting that in "some sense this creates a reasonable approximation of the school catchment, and indeed mirrors hotspot type visualisations that are commonly used in other domains such as crime analysis (Chainey & Ratcliffe, 2005)" (p. 243).

Câmara et al. (2004) employed several advanced spatial techniques to measure social exclusion in Sao Paulo, Brazil. They sought to answer the question whether social exclusion was spatially dependent, or if there were "'pockets' of local variation where social exclusion/inclusion differ[ed] significantly from the overall trends in the city" (p. 229). To do so, they applied global and local *spatial autocorrelation* to identify clusters of social exclusion and inclusion in the city. Spatial autocorrelation is "the tendency for observations that are near each other in space to have similar values" (Goodchild & Janelle, 2004, p. 8). In order to determine the relative influence of various other political, demographic, and community factors, including level of education and crime, Câmara et al. (2004) used *spatial regression techniques*. Finally, they applied spatial tools "to produce trend surfaces for homicide rates in São Paulo" in 1996 and 1999 (p. 236). They generated maps containing district homicide rates and used these data to produce a variogram that "model[ed] the spatial correlation structure, and a surface was interpolated by ordinary *kriging* [emphasis added] (Bailey and Gatrell 1995)" (p. 235).

In many, if not most, studies that employ geospatial analysis, GIS is used as a means to generate space-based data for subsequent statistical analysis. As an example, Collingwood et al. (2018) used GIS to spatially join census data with precinct data in their political analysis of Washington's 2012 charter school initiative—the first voter-approved charter initiative in the United States. They employed a *spatial lag regression model* to draw the conclusion that "the coalition of [charter] supporters cut across usual partisan and demographic cleavages, producing somewhat strange bedfellows" (p. 61). Other analytic tools combine geography and statistics, such as *geographically weighted regression*. Geographically weighted regression assigns observations weights that are inversely related to a distance from a selected location (Goodchild & Janelle, 2004).

Spatiotemporal analysis can be applied to investigate patterns or historical accounts of educational opportunity over time. For example, Reed (2006) studied the racial effects of a 1960 voucher program four years after it was introduced in Alexandria, Virginia. S. Williams and Wang (2014) spatially examined the accessibility of public schools in Baton Rouge, Louisiana, over three successive time periods—1990, 2000, and 2010. They used GIS tools to create a *spatial accessibility index* to gauge students' accessibility to high schools and then compared the accessibilities over time. To learn of other GIS studies adopting a historical perspective, see a summary by Kelly (2019).

S. Williams and Wang's (2014) measure of spatial accessibility expanded upon prior GIS techniques. They note that

[a]ccessibility measures need to account for both spatial and aspatial factors (Wang & Luo, 2005). Spatial accessibility emphasizes the importance of spatial separation between supply (i.e. high schools) and demand (i.e. student population) and how they are connected in space. Aspatial factors include many demographic and socioeconomic variables. In earlier literature, two simple methods are often used to measure spatial accessibility: the distance or travel time from the nearest supply facility termed the proximity method (Wang, 2006, p. 56) and the supply-demand ratio in an area. The former ignores the effect of the service's scarcity, and the latter does not account for interaction between supply and demand across the borders of analysis areas. (p. 1069)

Instead, S. Williams and Wang (2014) employed the

two-step floating catchment area (2SFCA) method (Luo & Wang, 2003), [which] measures spatial accessibility as a ratio of the amount of service supplied to the population in demand of the service, while accounting for the complex interaction between them within a certain distance range. (p. 1069)

In this case, supply was determined by the number of full-time equivalent teachers in each high school, and demand was defined by the number of high school-age students within a 5-mile radius.

A small but growing body of GIS education research is combining geospatial analysis with qualitative inquiry. Indeed, there have been increased calls for moving beyond post-post-positivistic geospatial research and toward more mixed and qualitative methods (Elwood & Cope, 2009; Lubienski & Lee, 2017; Yoon & Lubienski, 2018), as well as the application of critical perspectives in GIS research (Hogrebe & Tate, 2012; Jabbar et al., 2017; Yoon, Gulson, & Lubienski, 2018). Those calls are now being answered, and more qualitative GIS studies have emerged (Bell, 2007; Jabbar et al., 2017; Yoon, Lubienski, & Lee, 2018), including "participatory GIS" (Dunn, 2007; Elwood, 2006; Weiner & Harris, 2008; Yoon & Lubienski, 2018), those that engage marginalized communities and their members (Ghose & Welcenbach, 2018; Hogrebe & Tate, 2012; Kwan & Ding, 2008), or those that are emancipatory in nature (Sui, 2015). Mixed-method approaches invite both etic and emic perspectives, giving deeper accounts of "place" and pushing GIS research to consider not only multiple ways of knowing but also multiple ontologies.

LITERATURE SOURCES AND METHODS OF REVIEW

A systematic review uses "a specific procedure to search the research literature, select the studies to include in their review, and critically evaluate the studies" (Nelson, 2013, p. 139). The GIS education research literature was identified through a set of searches. The search process was highly iterative.

I started by searching various individual literature databases, knowing that search terms can vary among databases. I began by looking at search terms in the thesaurus of the Education Resources Information Center (ERIC) and found descriptors for "GIS" that included geographic information systems, geographic location, and geographic concepts. I also found descriptors for "policy" that included policy analysis, educational policy, policy, and public policy.

I executed my first query in ERIC using a combination of the two concepts and their descriptors above. This search yielded 34 articles published between 1995 and 2018. I did not include any other search delimiters such as earliest date of publication or journal articles (only) because the field is relatively new and small, and I wished to maximize return during this first probe. A scan of the titles and abstracts indicated these articles, books, book chapters, and (the occasional) conference papers and policy documents[6] were in line with my search objectives.

To conduct an even more expansive search, I examined the descriptor and keyword terms associated with each of these articles and conducted additional searches using several more similar terms, such as "geospatial analysis," "spatial analysis," "spatiotemporal analysis," "education research," and "education policy analysis." Because subject terms are invariably different across databases, I amassed a collection of all relevant keyword terms that could potentially detect GIS education research in the databases. I then designed a search string using all the relevant keywords and Boolean logic to search two major databases, ERIC and Scopus. Starting from scratch, these two searches generated over 70 articles. Once again, I examined each article title and abstract, eliminating those off topic and removing duplicates, which left 42 articles.

For the review, I was primarily interested in studies published in peer-reviewed journals. Research not falling in this category was evaluated for its rigor and relevance to the review. Publications that spoke to the use of GIS for school planning and management purposes were eliminated. Studies that focused on geography education, rather than geographic analysis of education, were also removed.

As is often the case, the Boolean searches above did not identify all the relevant literature. Some articles did not include relevant search terms and thus were not detected in the search. Others were simply not stored in the databases I searched. However, I was able to discover several additional studies that were referenced in the original set of publications searched. These new articles and publications were added to my database and downloaded for review. I reached a point of saturation where no new articles were revealing themselves in my collection of studies. To be certain, I also conducted forward searches of what I deemed to be more seminal studies using Google Scholar. In the end, an additional 30 or so articles were identified after the initial database searches. These additions brought the total number of research articles under review to 60. Further inspection reduced the number of empirical analyses using GIS on education-related topics to 42. Most all were published after 2000, and by far the vast majority were journal articles. Thus 42 studies represented the final number of studies that were synthesized here.

Synthesis

I read each study carefully and recorded key features on a spreadsheet. I documented characteristics or themes that I thought would bear upon the review. For instance, for each article I recorded the research topic, publication year, context for the study (e.g., country or city or state), unit or units of analysis, any equity concepts that were applied or generated, types of GIS techniques applied (e.g., geocoding, boundary drawing, dynamic mapping, or other more advanced geospatial techniques such as ANNA), and the role that geospatial methods played in the study. All these data were assembled into a data matrix. Based on an iterative coding process, research topics were grouped into seven research categories: access to education, location studies, local education markets (LEMs), catchment areas, gerrymandering, school choice and segregation, and other resources bearing upon education. Studies were assigned to the research category that best matched the study objective. This is not to say that studies could fit only under one category. To the contrary, about a third of the studies could be secondarily classified under a different theme. For instance, studies that *primarily* focused on gerrymandering or catchment areas were likely to also address questions about spatial access and/or social segregation.

The initial data matrix was condensed into a synthesis matrix (Table 1), which organizes the 42 studies by the seven research themes. Each group of studies is summarized by analytic techniques, study context, equity concepts, and units of analysis. I expound on each of these characteristics below. In Table 1, the number in parentheses represents the tally of studies under each research theme that met that criterion.

Analytic Techniques

Nearly three quarters (28/42) of the studies used GIS to geocode point features, such as school addresses, or line/area perimeters, such as school attendance zones. Another highly used GIS technique was descriptive map analysis, which is also referred to as dynamic mapping. Nearly all studies employed descriptive, dynamic mapping. Less common was the application of advanced GIS techniques—functions that went beyond descriptive map analysis and employed such techniques as kernel density averaging or centroid analysis. Just over one third of the studies (15/42) used some form of advanced spatial analysis, with studies focused on gerrymandering exhibiting the most (4/4). In terms of the role of GIS in each study, a vast majority (32/42) used GIS data to conduct basic quantitative analysis (means, correlations). A relatively smaller portion (16/42) used spatial data as foundation for more sophisticated quantitative analysis, such as multivariate modeling. A third of the studies (13/42) examined spatial data from a longitudinal perspective.

Contexts

The majority of studies, regardless of research theme, were conducted in urban contexts, or "major cities" (Column 3, Table 1). Metropolitan areas were also commonly studied. Only 2 of the 42 studies exclusively involved a rural context. The emphasis on urban contexts is not surprising given that GIS data are most prevalent in those settings and cities also dominate dialogue on education reform. Moreover, spatial studies are more likely to be done in smaller geographical units (cities over counties or states). All 5 studies examining a non-U.S. setting (referred to here as "International") addressed the catchment area topic; the remainder of studies addressed the United States or single states.

Equity Concepts

Given the equity focus in GIS education research, I identified any specific equity concept either explicitly named or implicated in each study. Almost every study that involved educational equity framed it as either "spatial equity" or "geography of opportunity." Given the heavy use of these two terms, I expand on both these concepts in greater detail later in the chapter. Other equity concepts that were identified and listed in Table 1 (under Column 4) actually constituted equity "measures." These

TABLE 1
Synthesis Matrix

Primary Research Theme	Studies	Contexts	Equity Concepts	Units of Analysis (Can Be Multilayered) Primary	Secondary	Analytic Techniques
Access to education	LaFleur (2016) Green et al. (2017) S. Williams & Wang (2014) Talen (2001)	Major city (2) Metro (1) County (1)	Spatial equity/geography of opportunity (4)	School (4) • High school (2) • Elementary (1) • Charter (1)	Census tract (2) Census block (2) Boundary (1)	Geocoded schools or line/area boundaries (3) Measured travel distances (3) Descriptive, dynamic mapping (4) Advanced GIS technique (2) GIS–set up basic quantitative analysis (4) GIS–set up multivariate modeling (2) Longitudinal (1)
Location study	Gulosino & d'Entremont (2011) Saultz & Yaluma (2017) Gilblom & Sang (2019) Saultz et al. (2015) Koller & Welsch (2017) Burdick-Will et al. (2013) Smrekar & Honey (2015)	Major city (5) State (2)	Spatial equity/geography of opportunity (2) Spatial distribution/clustering (4) Spatial "need" index (1) Segregation (3)	School (5) • Elementary (1) • Charter (5) • TPS (2) • Magnet (1)	District zone (2) Census tract (5) Census block (1)	Geocoded schools or line/area boundaries (4) Measured travel distances (2) Descriptive, dynamic mapping (6) Advanced GIS technique (1) GIS–set up basic quantitative analysis (5) GIS–set up multivariate modeling (2) Longitudinal (2)
Local education market	Lubienski et al. (2009) Gulosino & Lubienski (2011) Kamienski (2011) P. A. Jones (2018) Misra et al. (2012) Powers et al. (2017) Bell (2009)	Major city (3) Metro (2) State (1) United States (1)	Spatial equity/geography of opportunity (2) Spatial "need" index (2)	School (4) • Elementary (2) • Charter (3) • TPS (2) • Private (1)	District zone (4) Parent choice set (1) Census tract (3) Census block (1) Boundary (1)	Geocoded schools or line/area boundaries (7) Measured travel distances (2) Descriptive, dynamic mapping (7) Advanced GIS technique (1) GIS–set up basic quantitative analysis (7) GIS–set up multivariate modeling (4) Longitudinal (5)

(continued)

TABLE 1 (CONTINUED)

Primary Research Theme	Studies	Contexts	Equity Concepts	Units of Analysis (Can Be Multilayered)		Analytic Techniques
				Primary	Secondary	
Catchment areas	Chumacero et al. (2011) Rehm & Filippova (2008) Siegel-Hawley (2013) Parsons et al. (2000) Singleton et al. (2011) Taylor (2009)	Major city (1) Metro (2) International (5)	Spatial equity/geography of opportunity (4) Segregation (1)	School (4) • High school (3) • TPS (1) • Private (1)	District zone (4) Parent choice set (2) Student home (1) Census tract (2) Census block (1)	Geocoded schools or line/area boundaries (6) Measured travel distances (3) Descriptive, dynamic mapping (6) Advanced GIS technique (3) GIS–set up basic quantitative analysis (6) GIS–set up multivariate modeling (4) Longitudinal (3)
Gerrymandering	Richards (2014) Richards & Stroub (2015) Saporito & Van Riper (2016) Saporito (2017)	United States (4)	Spatial equity/geography of opportunity (2) Segregation (2)	District zone (4)		Descriptive, dynamic mapping (3) Advanced GIS technique (4) GIS–set up basic quantitative analysis (4) GIS–set up multivariate modeling (3)
School choice and segregation	Gibblom & Sang (2019) Cobb & Glass (1999) Saporito & Sohoni (2006) Archbald et al. (2018) Hogrebe & Tate (2019)	Major city (2) Metro (3) Rural (1) State (1)	Spatial distribution/clustering (2) Segregation (4)	District (1) School (1) • Charter (2) • TPS (1)	District zone (1) Census block (1) Boundary (1) Census tract (1) Modified areal (1)	Geocoded schools or line/area boundaries (3) Descriptive, dynamic mapping (2) Advanced GIS technique (2) GIS–set up basic quantitative analysis (4) GIS–set up multivariate modeling (2) Longitudinal (1)
Other resources bearing upon education	Schultz (2014) Dougherty et al. (2009) Oyana (2011) Schafft et al. (2009) B. D. Jones et al. (2015) Cobb (2019) Gulosino & Maxwell (2018) Miller (2012)	Metro (5) Rural (1) State (2)	Spatial equity/geography of opportunity (6) Spatial distribution/clustering (2) Spatial "need" index (1)	School (2) District zone (1) Teachers (1) College students (1) Census block (1)	Census tract (2) Boundary (1) Municipality (2) School (1)	Geocoded schools or line/area boundaries (5) Measured travel distances (1) Descriptive, dynamic mapping (7) Advanced GIS technique (3) GIS–set up basic quantitative analysis (4) Longitudinal (1)

Note. GIS = geographic information system; TPS = traditional public school. The numbers in parentheses from Column 3 and across indicate the number of studies within the research theme that are implicated. For instance, "Metro (4)" indicates four studies listed to the left were conducted on a "metropolitan" context.

included measures of spatial distribution, clustering, and socioeconomic need. Segregation was also used as a measure of equity (or, rather, inequity). Racial, social, and economic segregation was considered by several studies as problematic to fair and equitable educational opportunity. While some studies conceptualized segregation as spatial (e.g., Hogrebe & Tate, 2019), most used traditional measures such as the dissimilarity index to capture the magnitude of segregation between groups within a spatialized area or location.

Units of Analysis

Identifying units of analysis in GIS research deviates somewhat from conventional notions. GIS research can simultaneously incorporate multiple data layers, often times implicating point data (e.g., schools), perimeter data (e.g., district boundaries), and area data (e.g., census tract socioeconomic status index). Thus I have identified both primary and secondary units of analysis in Columns 5 and 6 of Table 1. "School" was by far the most common unit of analysis, implicated in every research category except gerrymandering. Within "school" were a range of types—charter schools, elementary schools, and private schools. Districts zones and census tracts represented the most popular secondary units of analysis.

PRIMARY RESEARCH THEMES IN GIS EDUCATION RESEARCH

In the following sections, I discuss the seven primary research themes listed in the first column of Table 1. The themes demonstrate the range of topics studied, where those studies took place, and the types of analyses and GIS techniques that were applied. A common thread that ran through much, but not quite all, of this research was an emphasis on educational equity, access, and opportunity.

Access to Education

As noted above, a considerable amount of GIS education research has focused on some aspect of school choice. From "voucher programs to inter- or intra-district open enrollment to private schools, studies of parental decision-making have shown that location proves to be an especially important consideration for families" (Lafleur, 2016, p. 4). Enrollment in schools and school choice invite questions about *access*. Studies on school choice at the K–12 level have examined the delimiting and often-times exclusionary consequences of certain choice policies. Other studies have explored the integrating opportunities afforded by choice, such as through magnet programs or policies that incent diverse schools.

School choice policies notwithstanding, access to education is a theme throughout GIS education policy research. S. Williams and Wang (2014) assessed the spatial accessibility of public high schools in the city of Baton Rouge against the backdrop of community demographic characteristics. They discovered that, over a 20-year period, spatial accessibility to high schools was consistently lower for urban families than for those living in rural or suburban communities. High schools that enrolled large percentages of African American students also exhibited lower accessibility scores in general. The study underscores the significance of "space, place, and race" with regard to spatial access to education.

Talen (2001) assessed the spatial equity of 84 elementary school locations in three West Virginia counties. School access was operationalized "as the total distance or 'travel cost' along a street network between block centroids and elementary schools" (p. 472). Findings revealed considerable inequities in the distribution of travel costs between resident locations and elementary schools. However, the relationship between school access and family socioeconomic status was inconclusive, exhibiting the similar "unpatterned-inequality" (p. 483) found by other accessibility studies.

Jabbar et al. (2017) conducted one of the few GIS studies focused on higher education. They examined the spatial distribution, and hence accessibility, of 4-year-institution options available to community college students in central Texas. In their analysis, they explored the role that geography played in students' choices and disaggregated findings among students from underrepresented backgrounds. GIS was used to trace distances between where community college students lived and the universities they were considering. Geospatial data were complemented by interviews to gain a clearer understanding of how students perceived their options. The researchers found that students' options were geographically constrained and that "for many students, these zones are geographically large, suggesting that interventions and targeted outreach from universities could help students identify and select from greater range of options to enhance higher educational opportunity" (p. 749).

Location Studies

Because charter schools are a relatively new phenomenon (since 1996), they have literally emerged as new real estate across the nation.[7] High costs prevent many from newly constructing and instead new charter schools seek out an existing community or industrial structure. Other charter schools can be "conversion" schools, where existing public schools—and sometimes private schools—reopen as a charter school. Whatever their geographical origins, charter schools strategically position themselves based on place and space. Geospatial studies that examine location and positionality of charter schools all tend to raise important implications for equity and access. Indeed, the location of a charter school can have a strong influence on its student composition (Bifulco, 2014). Location positions also raise questions about equal access for students from different racial and economic backgrounds (Koller & Welsch, 2017).

Education researchers using GIS have the ability to view charter locations spatially and in relation to surrounding neighborhoods and other schools. Location studies can also explore the potential competitive influence of charter schools on LEMs. Many studies on charter location have examined the effects on racial and economic stratification. For example, LaFleur (2016) inspected the location of Chicago charter schools within the context of census tract demographic data. She found that charter schools tended to locate in low-socioeconomic tracts but not the most poverty-stricken ones. The inference is that charter schools may be attempting to maximize their enrollment while balancing their risk of ineffective performance. In other words, enrolling very high-needs students may present educational challenges that bear upon a charter school's performance and threaten its sustainability. LaFleur argues these location patterns may inhibit charter school access to the students in highest need. These findings concerning charters locating in high-needs, but not the highest needs, areas are consistent with conclusions from similar studies. For example, Gulosino and d'Entremont (2011) used dynamic mapping to examine charter school location and enrollment in New Jersey's most densely populated cities. They also found charter schools clustering just outside neighborhoods with high concentrations of African American families, which "suggests that charter schools more closely resemble the racial makeup of adjacent neighborhoods than the ones in which they reside" (p. 19).[8]

Saultz and Yaluma (2017) used GIS to analyze locations of charter schools in Ohio. They generated several maps to examine the location of charter schools "in relation to census tracts poverty rates, 2015–2016 student test scores, traditional public schools, and access (within 5-mile distance) to low-income areas" (p. 463). They reported that charters "seldom locate in tracts with the highest concentrations of poverty or percentages of Black population; they are more apt to locate in city centers" (p. 474). Locations of Ohio charter schools appear to be influenced by a state policy that prioritizes charters in low-performing "challenge" districts, which, the authors argue, is at the expense of offering access to many other high-poverty regions in Ohio. This study provides a good example in which contextual data—in this case information about a state policy—can inform the spatial analysis.

Similarly, Saultz et al. (2015) used GIS to visually examine where newly opened charter schools in New York City positioned themselves. They explored relationships between new charter schools and community characteristics using descriptive statistics, including bivariate correlations. They reported charters opened in low–academic performance regions, most likely trying to attract students seeking another option.

While most charter location studies rely on descriptive techniques and the visual inspection of maps, Gilblom and Sang (2019) used ANNA. ANNA is a specific geospatial technique applied in this case "to measure the spatial distribution of [traditional charter schools] and [traditional public schools] to determine if they have a clustered, random or dispersed spatial pattern" (p. 11). Their analysis of Cleveland Metropolitan School District (CMSD) indicated that locations of traditional charter schools reflect a spatial pattern in which traditional charter schools "are disproportionately located near one another in CMSD as a whole than what would be expected by chance" (p. 17). This finding is significant in that

[w]hile TCS [traditional charter schools] are permitted to open as startup and conversion community schools within all of CMSD, as CMSD has low student performance, they are more clustered on the east side of CMSD. . . . TPS [traditional public schools] cluster less than TCS within CMSD and on the east side, they have a random and independent distribution on the west side that contrasts with the placement of TCS on the west side. (p. 17)

Last, Koller and Welsch (2017) examined charter location decisions using 12 years of panel data from Michigan. They employed newer and, what they contend are, more sophisticated geographic techniques to analyze the location of charter schools. Because charter schools in most cases are not beholden to district boundaries, they are free to draw students from multiple districts. Koller and Welsch developed a distance measure that considered this feature among charters and ignored district boundaries. This strategy allowed them "to map how many charter schools have located near a traditional public school" (p. 160). In essence, their intent was to model the "number of new charter schools who locate near a traditional public school in a given year" against "predictor variables [that include] measures of performance, school policy variables, and student socioeconomic details of the traditional public schools as well as information on the characteristics of the surrounding communities" (p. 164). They geocoded the locations of every charter and traditional public school that existed between 2000 and 2012 and calculated the travel distances between charter and traditional public schools. Travel distances of 5, 10, 15, and 20 miles served as indicators of how "nearby" charters were to traditional publics.[9] Koller and Welsch (2017) combined their GIS data with binomial logistic regression analysis and found that charter schools were more likely to locate in areas with higher median salaries, higher socioeconomic status, lower reading scores, a larger percentage of Black students, and more racial and ethnic diversity.

Geospatial location analyses have not been restricted to the siting of new schools, or even to charter schools, only. Burdick-Will et al. (2013) examined school-level and neighborhood characteristics that explained the closing and opening of Chicago public elementary schools during the late 1990s and 2000s, a period in which market-based reforms became increasingly prominent. They found that schools located in disadvantaged communities were more likely to close but "only because they were also underperforming and under-enrolled schools" (p. 59). In contrast, after controlling for educational demand in their analysis, they reported that new schools tended to open in neighborhoods undergoing economic revitalization and declining White populations.

Smrekar and Honey (2015), in a study of four large districts, found that the placement of magnet schools is critical to their success in serving a racial and economically diverse student population. Their descriptive map analysis revealed that magnet schools located in largely non-White census tracts

tend to reflect the racial composition of the census tract rather than the racial composition and diversity of the district as a whole [while magnets] located in predominantly White census tracts are associated with student enrollments that more closely reflect the racial composition and diversity of the district as a whole. (p. 141)

Local Education Markets

Schools operate in LEMs, with or without the presence of formal school choice programs. Many families make choices about where to live based on perceptions of the schools. Of course, myriad other factors go into decisions about choosing a school, including distance, convenience, real estate, and access to other desired services. Research indicates parents make decisions under a "bounded rationality" (Kahneman, 2003), not necessarily as predicted by classical rational choice theory. The assumptions underlying rational choice theory do not tend to hold up in real LEMs. Markets do not convey perfect information, nor do consumers possess the same knowledge. Generally speaking, parents with more means have more school options available to them (Ball, 2003; Ball & Nikita, 2014).

Moreover, parents are influenced by a broad variety of factors when making school choice decisions. Bell (2007) conceptualized these factors as parental "choice sets" that encompass a variety of geospatial and social influences. Bell (2009) used mixed methods to investigate parent geographic-based decision making in a city rich with school choice options. To do so, she geospatially analyzed 36 parent households, prior schools, choice sets, geographic sets, and final choice of school. Locations were georeferenced and joined with dozens of socioeconomic and housing census tract data. Maps were used in the analysis, which allowed for "a richer, more contextualized understanding of the spatial features of parents' geographic preferences" (p. 501). Bell (2009) found,

Space and place-based preferences shaped and bounded the set of schools [Detroit] parents were willing to consider. These preferences did not play the same role for every parent. Nor were roles stable over the choice process. (p. 519)

There is also evidence that schools can greatly influence supply-side behavior in local markets through locational placement of schools of choice (e.g., Glomm et al., 2005), explicit and soft marketing, and dissuasion of students who require specialized services (Waitoller & Lubienski, 2019), all of which can serve to include or exclude students and families on the demand side.

LEMs are geopolitical spaces that operate in a manner that raises critical questions about access and opportunity. An advantage of GIS research is that "[s]patial analysis allows [researchers] to examine data like admission policies or school demographics in the wider context of neighborhood demographics and in relation to other schools nearby" (Lubienski et al., 2009, p. 613). For example, Lubienski et al. (2009) applied geospatial techniques to analyze how market incentives influenced geography of opportunity in Detroit, the District of Columbia, and New Orleans. Using GIS, they focused on "ways that whole populations of schools may arrange educational opportunities for different communities through location and admissions policies—policy strategies that have spatial attributes (i.e., they are geographically identifiable) in LEMs" (p. 612). Their analysis suggests that market competition induced exclusionary practices, disproportionately affecting students from disadvantaged backgrounds.

In a similar analysis, Gulosino and Lubienski (2011) explored the supply side of market competition, examining trends in the opening, relocating, and closing of public, private, and charter schools in highly segregated Detroit. Their study revealed location patterns across school types relative to socioeconomic and demographic neighborhood contexts. They draw a distinction between certain types of charter schools—for-profit and mission-oriented—and demonstrate different behavior with respect to how they located:

> While profit-oriented charters have an equal presence in high-need areas . . . they essentially avoid areas with students who may be most likely to damage the school's market position. . . . On the other hand, the physical locations of mission-oriented charter schools suggest that they are driven by business opportunities in areas with disadvantaged socioeconomic and demographic characteristics and where the cost of real estate is low. (p. 19)

Two other studies that examined the potential effect of competition brought on by charter schools are also mentioned here. Kamienski (2011) studied the academic performance of elementary charter and traditional public schools in Chicago. He created two sets of comparisons consisting of "competitive" and "noncompetitive" market environments. In order to be competitors, the schools had to provide the "same opportunities for students relative to academic aptitude, cost, and proximity in travel" (p. 164). Proximity in travel was determined by capturing all eligible traditional public schools within a 1-mile radius of each charter school.[10]

The geospatial strategy served as a means to a subsequent hierarchical linear model analysis to compare test performance among schools. The results showed that charter schools, on average, exhibited higher student test gains than proximal traditional public schools but that competition effects were negligent. The Herfindhahl index was used as a measure of competition within each LEM; none of the index values reached thresholds indicative of increased competition.

In a similar fashion, P. A. Jones (2018) used GIS to identify a set of charter–traditional public school comparison groups. P. A. Jones's interest was to study the potential effect of charter school competition on public school district revenues across the nation using measures of distance and density derived from the district centroid rather than from individual schools.

Extending conventional measures of market competition, Misra et al. (2012) established a school competition index to assess the effects of competition on school performance. They used GIS to generate competition index scores for primary and high schools in Mississippi and then applied them to an econometric model to predict school proficiency ratings on state exams. The index is spatially related, measuring the level of competition each public school faced from proximal private schools of similar grade level. The authors noted that "in addition to the number of competitors, knowing the size of competitors and distance between them is important to measure the competitive pressure" (p. 1180). They drew concentric circles around each public school of increasing expanse (i.e., 5-, 15-, and 25-mile radii) to capture various market sizes. Various calculations with respect to distance and number of schools were made within each circle to generate competition indexes and ultimately draw conclusions about market competition and potential contributing factors. The authors also included schools in their model from four other states that fell along the Mississippi border, so as not to restrict their sample to Mississippi only. They claimed that competition from private schools increased proficiency rates on state exams in Mississippi primary and high schools.

Powers et al. (2017) used descriptive maps to explore the relationship between charter school location and interdistrict mobility among students in Arizona elementary schools. Maps allowed them to simultaneously track movement both across districts and between districts and charter schools. Their analysis determined that interdistrict mobility generated and sustained local educational markets more so than charter school choice.

Catchment Areas

A considerable amount of GIS research on school attendance boundaries has been published (Chumacero et al., 2011; Gulosino & Lubienski, 2011; Rehm & Filippova, 2008; Siegel-Hawley, 2013; Singleton et al., 2011; Taylor, 2009; Yoon, Gulson, & Lubienski, 2018; Yoshida et al., 2009). Many of these studies use GIS techniques to establish hypothetical catchment areas that are later used to model their effects on student sorting and access to schools. Lubienski and Lee (2017) find that "GIS research on school attendance boundaries has identified how [those boundaries] are playing a decisive role in enrolment, often gerrymandered by race, employment, and household income with respect to housing patterns" (p. 92).

Singleton et al. (2011) used a kernel density tool to articulate school catchment areas under the choice program in England and Wales. Following the 1998 Education Reform Act, parents in England and Wales are free to choose their preferred schools. One problem is that demand exceeds supply, particularly among higher quality schools.

[T]here are inevitably more applications to popular schools, such as those with particularly high average attainment, than places at them. . . . A variety of mechanisms have evolved to manage these rates of oversubscription, the most widely used of which is to favour pupils living in close proximity to an oversubscribed school. (p. 241)

Singleton et al. (2011) examined whether this preference for enrolling students nearest the oversubscribed schools resulted in inequities and social stratification across the region. Their findings confirmed that "[t]hrough this geographic selection process, choice is spatially sorted and access to the best schools is often crucially dependent upon where parents live" (p. 241). In a similar analysis, Parsons et al. (2000) examined intercatchment movements among secondary students in an economically diverse local education area (LEA) in the United Kingdom. The LEA comprised both rural and urban schools. Their objective was to examine the degree to which parents chose to enroll their children outside of the assigned catchment area and to uncover any patterns in student movement across catchment boundaries. They found that about a third of Year 7 students moved outside their assigned catchments (with most occurring in urban schools) and that middle class students were least likely to enroll outside their catchment. Their findings were discussed in relation to the LEA's student assignment protocol, which, among other factors, prioritized a student's physical distance from school in making assignment decisions.

Gerrymandering

Geographic techniques have also been used extensively to examine gerrymandering of school attendance boundaries and to address implications for school segregation. Siegel-Hawley (2013) studied a southern suburban district undergoing rezoning and the building of new schools due to substantial growth in the district, particularly among underrepresented minority students. She used GIS to illustrate the effects of three different zoning options on racial composition of high schools. In the end, the zoning policy that was ultimately adopted by policymakers was the option that had the largest adverse effect on racial isolation.

Using the School Attendance Boundary Information System (SABINS),[11] which consists of GIS data of thousands of school attendance zones from 2009–2010, Richards (2014) analyzed over 15,000 attendance zones in 663 U.S. school districts. She discovered that gerrymandering generally increases racial segregation, particularly in areas undergoing rapid demographic changes. In contrast, gerrymandering occurring in the few districts under court-ordered desegregation experienced a reduction in segregation. In a similar SABINS-based analysis, Richards and Stroub (2015) measured school attendance zones along the two spatial dimensions of *dispersion* (how elongated the boundary presented) and *indentation* (how irregular the perimeter of the boundary presented). They found that school attendance zones were gerrymandered nearly as much as legislative districts. The educational gerrymandering was also increasing over time and exacerbating racial and socioeconomic inequities (Richards, 2017).

In their analysis of SABINS data, Saporito and Van Riper (2016) reported that most U.S. school districts are compactly shaped or square-like. Such shapes tend to mimic the racial homogeneity of the surrounding area, without much variation. In contrast, although relatively rare, irregularly shaped districts tended most always to be racially diverse, which, according to them, is contradictory to many other claims that oddly shaped districts reflect historical gerrymandering for the purposes of exclusion. Similarly, Saporito (2017) found evidence that irregularly shaped districts— again, which are often associated with gerrymandering—do not necessarily contribute to increased levels of economic segregation. From his analysis of 2009–2010 SABINS data, Saporito (2017) learned just the opposite. He summarized,

I find that on average, school districts with irregularly shaped attendance zones have *lower levels* of income segregation, net of income segregation within districts' residential areas. These findings completely contradict claims that school districts "typically" draw irregularly shaped attendance zones to exacerbate income segregation. . . . I suggest that focus should shift to comparing income segregation in schools with income segregation in residential areas. (p. 1346)

School Choice and Segregation

GIS studies on school choice and segregation use a range of spatial techniques, including dynamic mapping analysis (Cobb & Glass, 1999; Siegel-Hawley, 2013; Taylor, 2009), modified areal measures such as composite population counts (Hogrebe & Tate, 2019), and ANNA and density modeling (Gilblom & Sang, 2019). Others use GIS to supplement or directly support multilevel statistical models (Saporito & Sohoni, 2006) or to track changes over time (Archbald et al., 2018). For instance, Saporito and Sohoni (2006) used a GIS to test whether private schools contributed to racial segregation in urban districts. They constructed geographic databases (including digitized attendance boundaries) for the 22 largest school districts in the United States. The GIS was layered with federal databases containing statistical information on public and private schools. They compared the racial composition of schools with the racial composition of school-aged children living in the same attendance boundary. Taylor (2009) conducted a spatial systems analysis, inspecting socioeconomic segregation within several local markets or "competition spaces" (p. 554) in the United Kingdom.

One of the earliest geospatial studies on school choice was conducted on Arizona charter schools. Cobb and Glass (1999) examined the ethnic composition of Arizona charter schools in relation to nearby traditional public schools. They used GIS to geocode 586 school addresses onto a digital map of Arizona, and spatially joined these data with administrative data from the state department of education as well as census tract data. Their comparative analysis between charter schools (55 urban, 57 rural) and nearby traditional public schools revealed that nearly half of the charter schools exhibited evidence of substantial ethnic separation.

Cobb and Glass (1999) discussed the advantages of using spatial analysis over traditional statistical methods, noting that common measures of segregation and equity, such as the dissimilarity index, Gini coefficient, and Lorenz curve, are highly sensitive to school size and poorly equipped to discern between-school segregation. Similarly, Hogrebe and Tate (2019) noted limitations of global segregation measures that "do not provide information about patterns of segregation that occur in and across local contexts" (p. 3). Instead, they argue that localized measures of segregation, such as those developed by Oka and Wong (2014), better capture how different groups are distributed across space.

More recently, highly sophisticated geospatial analyses have been carried out by Hogrebe and Tate (2019), who mapped two local spatial measures of segregation (isolation-exposure, evenness-clustered) in metro St. Louis. Using this technique, they found that "in regions that appear diverse and where individuals and groups are potentially exposed to each other, there may also be areas or neighborhoods where individuals or groups are isolated" (p. 11). Their findings have implications for student transfer plans that are aimed at desegregating and improving the educational conditions for disadvantaged students.

Other Resources Bearing Upon Education

Because GIS research directly implicates the contextual elements of space and place, it lends itself to multidimensional, interdisciplinary accounts of education phenomena. This final category of GIS research includes spatial analyses that explore the influence of a broader range resources on educational outcomes. My review surfaced GIS research examining teacher quality, housing costs, and other resources that bear upon education.

Schultz (2014) spatially analyzed characteristics among teachers in Missouri. She used maps to illustrate the geographic distribution of high-quality teachers and ANNA to examine the existence of clustering of those teacher characteristics. Findings indicated that highly-qualified teachers were clustered in schools with lower levels of poverty and students of color.[12]

Dougherty et al. (2009) explored the relationship between school performance, race, and housing markets in a 10-year study of a Connecticut suburb. They estimated the impact of school test scores and racial composition on home sales, while controlling for various house and residential characteristics. GIS allowed them to spatially link each home sale to the nearest school attendance line shared by two elementary schools.[13] They found that both test scores and race were statistically related to home prices, but the effect of tests decreased "while race became nearly seven times more influential over our decade-long period of study" (p. 542). Their study raised major implications for educational inequity, to which the authors credit GIS for affording "better tools with which to measure and demonstrate its existence and perhaps growing influence" (p. 545).

Other geospatial studies have examined the distribution of resources linked to education and, more specifically, child development. Hogrebe (2012) has encouraged the expanded application of geographical perspectives in research on urban schools, neighborhoods, and communities. Oyana (2011) tracked access to high-speed internet in rural southern Illinois and found significant geographic disparities. Schafft et al. (2009) analyzed spatial access to grocery stores and health food stores in rural Pennsylvania, establishing the link between food deserts and obese school children. B. D. Jones et al. (2015) examined residential segregation, education, and health disparities in their comprehensive geospatial analysis of metropolitan St. Louis. Miller (2012) mapped "educational opportunity zones" in two adjacent urban neighborhoods in Pittsburgh, Pennsylvannia.

Cobb (2019) employed social epidemiology case analysis (Tate & Striley, 2010) to document the spatial distribution of key housing, economic, health, and educational indicators in greater Hartford, Connecticut. Similar to the findings reported by B. D. Jones et al. (2015), Cobb's (2019) analysis revealed substantial disparities in the spatial distribution of these resources across the racially and economically stratified Hartford region. Despite earnest school desegregation efforts in and around Hartford, resident children of color are disproportionately affected by a highly fragmented sociopolitical geography. The geographic fragmentation has very real and significant consequences for those who live in the region. Marginalized families living in high-poverty neighborhoods have restricted access to health care and education, are exposed to health risks, and lack opportunities for upward mobility through home ownership.

Gulosino and Maxwell (2018) used GIS to investigate voluntary preschool programs in Tennessee's largest and most populous county. They explored the "bounded" nature of voluntary prekindergarten programs within particular neighborhoods and reported the following:

[T]he benefits conferred by proximity or geographic accessibility to urban preschools contribute to the provision of Pre-K services, thus highlighting the role of spatial/locational perspective as an important lens for evaluating public school choice programs in low-opportunity neighborhoods. This study thus echoes long-standing concerns about how choice might create a nearly closed loop of systemic disadvantage in cases where there is limited capacity and choice is essentially limited to the immediate neighborhood, thus deepening inequality of educational opportunities. (p. 27)

A last example comes from Brazil, where Câmara et al. (2004) employed several advanced spatial techniques to measure social exclusion/inclusion in the city of São Paulo.

QUESTIONS UNDERLYING GIS EDUCATION RESEARCH

Several important geospatial questions appear to drive the scholarly dialogue about educational equity, access, and opportunity. Such questions are both specific to and cut across the research categories surfaced by the review. Table 2 provides a list of the types of questions raised within each research theme. These questions and more have been addressed by scholars interested in studying education from a geospatial perspective. Collectively, they rely and expand on concepts of educational equity, access, and opportunity from a spatial perspective. I expound on these concepts in more depth below.

Spatial Equity and the Geography of Opportunity

Given the strong interconnections between place, space, and resources, spatial analysis is uniquely equipped to examine, and improve our understanding of, educational equity, access, and opportunity. Spatial analysis can not only assist researchers in testing a priori hypotheses but also reveal instantiations of unfairness and injustice through spatial inaccessibility or exclusion. As evidenced above, spatial analysis can serve to raise new questions surrounding fairness and access; it can identify otherwise undetected problems and phenomena that bear upon justice and equity in education. GIS scholarship has thus examined the geographic distribution of opportunity (Reece, Gambhir, Olinger, et al., 2009; Reece, Gambhir, powell, & Grant-Thomas, 2009) and access to education resources and health care (B. D. Jones et al., 2015). And still other studies using GIS have combined it with critical and narrative analyses to reveal power dynamics and give voice to those often marginalized in the politicized

TABLE 2

Underlying Research Questions in GIS Education Research

Primary Research Theme	Example Driving Research Questions
Access to education	How does geography impact families' decisions to participate in school choice options that require them to send their child to a school further from home?
	In what ways do social, racial, and economic characteristics of space (e.g., neighborhood wealth) impact student access to schools?
	Do children from different backgrounds have equitable access to the same quality schools?
Location studies	What space and place[a] factors are associated with the location of new schools (particularly charter schools)?
Local education markets	To what extent do local education markets bring about competition and improve low-performing schools?
	Does school choice competition through school choice markets offer more or less access to disadvantaged students?
Catchment areas	How does the geography of attendance zones and catchment boundaries influence access to educational opportunity?
	In what ways do school catchment areas enhance or constrain educational opportunity?
Gerrymandering	Does gerrymandering of attendance zones result disproportionately affect students of color or students in poverty? How so?
School choice and segregation	To what extent do physical and social contexts affect school choice patterns (e.g., how programs operate and how consumers and suppliers make choices?)
	How does how geography impact families' decisions to participate in school choice options?
Other resources bearing upon education	How do other geospatial resources, such as teacher labor markets and housing, bear upon educational equity and access?
	Is the spatial distribution of health, social, and educational services equitably distributed?

[a]Space has to do with the physical features of geography, such as distance and travel time. Place refers to the meanings people ascribe to specific spaces or geographic locations (Bell, 2009).

arena of education (e.g., Kwan & Ding, 2008; Kwan & Schwanen, 2009). A large body of GIS research has examined school choice, a set of policies, that when contextualized in the spaces in which they play out, raises questions about who has choices, who exercises them, and to what ends (e.g., Lubienski & Dougherty, 2009).

From the very outset GIS education research has been aimed at issues of access, such as the spatial distribution of preschool services in Wales (Webster & White, 1997) and the accessibility to public playgrounds (Talen & Anselin, 1998). These early investigations examined spatial equity, or what Soja (2010) later referred to as "spatial justice" and Tate (2008) called the "geography of opportunity." The geography of opportunity implies where one lives has a direct effect on their life opportunities (Briggs, 2005; Galster & Killen, 1995; Rosenbaum, 2008). In the United States in particular, space and place are heavily shaped by race and income (Pastor, 2001). Geography of opportunity has thus been directly implicated in race-based studies of urban housing desegregation efforts such as the Gautraux and Moving to Opportunity programs (Galster, 2011), health disparities (Acevedo-Garcia et al., 2008; Osypuk & Acevedo-Garcia, 2010; D. R. Williams & Collins, 2001), and crime (Peterson & Krivo, 2010; Squires & Kubrin, 2006). Geography of opportunity has also served as a useful lens for examining educational equity (Green, 2015; Hillman, 2016; Tate, 2008), as where children reside is strongly associated with their educational opportunities and outcomes. Residential segregation stubbornly mimics public school segregation along the lines of race and wealth (Massey, 2001). Thus a child living in a high-poverty community is more likely to attend a school with fewer resources than a child living in a wealthier neighborhood.

Soja (2010) noted a distinct shift in the social sciences toward the acceptance and application of postmodern and critical human geography, what he referred to as the "spatial turn" (p. 13). Edward Soja is a renowned geographer and activist-scholar who studied the city of Los Angeles over the past four decades (Soja & Chouinard, 1999). He was a pioneer in examining the social conditions of a city using the lens of spatial justice (Woessner, 2010). For him, spatial justice has to do with "control over how the spaces in which we live are socially produced" (Soja, 2010, p. 7, quoted in Chatterton, 2010). Woessner credits Soja for teaching modern geographers that "place and justice go together" and that to "talk about spatial (in)justice is to acknowledge, first and foremost, that (in)justice is the product of spatial forces as much as social or historical ones" (Woessner, 2010, p. 603). Although it remains a developing field, the spatial analysis of education—and the application of GIS techniques—is perhaps amidst its own "spatial turn."

GEOSPATIAL ANALYSIS IN THE CONTEXT OF TRADITIONAL EDUCATION RESEARCH: BARRIERS AND CHALLENGES

Geospatial analyses rely heavily on spatial depictions of evidence through maps and mapping techniques. The use of maps can present problems for researchers interested in publishing in traditional print journals. There are at least three barriers to entry. Space is the first limitation. Restrictions on page limits and even use of figures by some journals can dissuade authors seeking tenure from even engaging in this research, let alone submitting it to upper-tier print journals. The second major limitation is maps are best interpreted using color schemes, and color figures can be cost-prohibitive with print journals. Last, the traditional journals, which tend to remain print only, are overseen by editors and editorial boards who are themselves likely heavily influenced by the norms of traditional research paradigms. Many GIS studies rely on descriptive techniques (although this is rapidly changing as new spatial tools are being applied or spatial analyses are being supplemented by traditional methods such as hierarchical linear modeling), and this is often seen, at least in the quantitative research realm, as severely limiting if not unsophisticated. For an enlightening critique of geospatial analysis in education, see Lubienski and Lee (2017).

Although GIS data are becoming more plentiful and accessible, challenges still remain with respect to data availability and quality (see the appendix for an overview of spatial data sources available to GIS education researchers). Sometimes data are not complete for a specific geographic area (e.g., all student attendance zones have not been digitized). There can also be problems with merging relevant data sets with GIS data in the absence of common identifiers. These are technical but very real challenges within a field that is highly labor-intensive already.

A good portion of education research is dependent upon individual-level, administrative data, which even when available often contains only limited sociodemographic information on individuals. Fortunately, GIS provides an opportunity to address this by combining anonymous data at the spatial point rather than relying on the need for nonanonymized data linkage (a practice that carries greater risks of breaching confidentiality).

Although mixed-methods GIS research is a promising arena, Yoon, Gulson, and Lubienski (2018) caution that there are practical challenges "associated with collecting and analyzing multiple sources of data and maintaining methodological coherence" (p. 5). And furthermore,

[w]hile researchers intend to make smooth transitions and connections between qualitative and quantitative data, such intentions may get derailed because of issues of data availability and access (e.g., school division data availability/permission) or because themes emerging from the qualitative data may go in directions other than what a researcher initially planned. (p. 5)

These challenges and barriers for researchers notwithstanding, GIS remains an extremely powerful and illuminating research paradigm.

One important caution to our field: While spatial analysis has the power to reveal significant inequity, researchers must be wary of perpetuating deficit orientations with respect to marginalized populations and communities. In addition to exposing and capturing magnitudes of spatial injustice, geospatial research should also foster an asset perspective. Referencing their opportunity map analysis of Connecticut, Boggs and Dabrowski (2017) implored others to "use the mapping to . . . transcend assumptions about neighborhoods" (p. iii). Offering insight into community assets and the social and cultural capital of "othered" populations serves to disrupt normative perspectives on such constructs as the "urban poor" or "impoverished communities."

THE FUTURE OF GIS IN EDUCATION RESEARCH

The future of geospatial analysis in education research looks promising. A growing cadre of researchers are acquiring GIS skills, more spatial data are being made available, and GIS software is now offered under numerous packages, including some that are web-based and free. More opportunities afforded by technology and researcher imagination abound, such as using global positioning systems (GPS) to collect geospatial data. For instance, Helbich (2017) studied Dutch children's commute to school by having participants wear GPS devices as belts. Bürgi et al. (2016) were able to monitor the spatial physical activity patterns of primary school children living under varying economic conditions—pattern data that were supplemented by interviews with children and their caregivers to enhance understanding of the connection between social capital, socioeconomic status, and physical activity.

Another dynamic GIS approach is "exploratory spatial data analysis," a practice rooted in the principles of "a more interactive and visual approach to statistical analysis" (Goodchild & Janelle, 2004, p. 7) originated by Tukey (1977) and others. Kelly (2019) calls for more historical analyses using GIS, encouraging researchers to "reap the benefits of considering time and space simultaneously" (p. 11). Earlier I briefly discussed mixed-methods approaches to GIS, which opens up even more epistemological possibilities. Qualitative, participatory, emancipatory, and critical GIS offer powerful methods to generate and act upon new understandings. A geospatial perspective enriches nearly any form of inquiry and offers an inimitable lens to study issues that bear upon educational equity, access, and opportunity.

APPENDIX

Accessing Geospatial Data for Education Policy Research

The availability of research-ready, geospatial data for education policy research has expanded in the past decade or so, but there is still room to grow. GIS data for the physical sciences are far more ubiquitous than for the social sciences. In this section, I offer a brief overview of spatial data sources for education researchers.

One of the more positive developments was the origination of SABINS. SABINS was developed through a grant from the National Science Foundation and includes nearly 24,000 school attendance zone boundaries for the 2009–2010 and 2010–2011 school years (The College of William and Mary and the Minnesota Population Center, 2011). According to Saporito and Van Riper (2016), the 2009–2010 SABINS database contains attendance zone data for over 90% of the largest 350 school districts in the United States. In addition, hundreds of GIS data sets at the city, county, and state levels are publicly available. One useful resource is census.gov, which has linked census data to geographic databases at various geographic levels. A quick search on many city, state, and federal government websites will turn up repositories of GIS data, now in several new formats and part of larger "geodatabases."

The most commonly tapped resource for U.S.-based GIS education researchers is the U.S. Census. Census.gov houses mapping data, including cartographic boundary files, TIGER (Topologically Integrated Geographic Encoding and Referencing) line shapefiles, and geodatabases, and of course census data. The TIGER line shapefiles and geodatabases do not include demographic data, but they do have geographic entity codes, or GEOIDs, that can be spatially joined to demographic census data. The TIGER geodatabases are sourced from a commercial entity, Environmental Systems Research Institute (ESRI).

Although a for-profit corporation, ESRI provides free access to hundreds of spatial data sets. ESRI is an international supplier of GIS software, web-based GIS, and geodatabase management applications. They offer online access to base maps and thematic layer data, including layers for states, counties, zip codes, and the U.S. Census, that accompany their popular ArcGIS desktop software.

Another source for publicly available spatial data is *data.gov*. Using the two keyword filters, "education" and "geospatial data," a recent search of data.gov turned up 30 datasets. After removing duplicates and several data sets that were irrelevant, there were at least three resources of interest to GIS education researchers. They included school district boundary files,[14] school locations,[15] and school neighborhood poverty estimates.[16]

To obtain more detailed and context-specific spatial data, researchers should search the websites for state governments, cities, and universities. State-based GIS data are typically housed in a state agency (e.g., Department for Energy and Environmental Protection). Most major cities now have geographic data offices, although these tend to focus on urban planning and transportation. Many universities host or provide links to publicly available GIS data—especially regional data—through a GIS lab, center, or geography department.

A handful of other national clearinghouses offer access to various types of spatial data, such as the Geospatial Platform (geoplatform.gov). The Geospatial Platform was created by federal agencies; state, local, and Tribal governments; the private sector; and academia. It provides online access to federally maintained geospatial data, services, and applications, although not to a considerable amount of education-related data. Researchers interested in historical accounts of education phenomena may wish to explore the National Historical Geographic Information System, which offers boundary files for years from 1790 through the present and for all levels of the U.S. Census, states, counties, tracts, and block group.

ORCID iD

Casey D. Cobb (iD) https://orcid.org/0000-0001-6573-2390

NOTES

[1]https://www.usgs.gov/

[2]https://researchguides.library.wisc.edu/GIS

[3]See Figure 3 in Tate (2008, p. 404) for a depiction of the four biotech clusters.

[4]See Corcoran and Saxe (2014) for a math-based, and Dopp and Godfrey (2012) for a map-based, discussion on the relative merits of measures of compactness for detecting gerrymandering.

[5]See Figure 4 in Singleton et al. (2011, p. 244) for an illustration of this benefit.

[6]For textual simplicity and because the vast majority of scholarship was published in a peer-reviewed journal, I refer to them all as "articles" hereafter.

[7]Of course, the one exception is online or virtual charter schools, which have no physical presence. That said, virtual charters still can "locate" themselves in terms of which students may have access to them or to which populations they market themselves.

[8]For illustrations, see Maps 6 and 7 in Gulosino and d'Entremont (2011, pp. 20–21)

[9]See Figure 1 in Koller and Welsch (2017, p. 164) for a depiction of school locations and travel times.

[10]See Figure 3 in Kamienski (2011, p. 169) for an illustration of the selection of schools and comparisons groups.

[11]Source: The College of William and Mary and Minnesota Population Center (2011).

[12]For graphic representations, see Figures 1 and 2 in Schultz (2014, pp. 12–13).

[13]See Figure 3 in Dougherty et al. (2009, p. 533).

[14]Derived from the National Center for Education Statistics Education Demographic and Geographic Estimate program.

[15]Latitude and longitude point locations from the National Center for Education Statistics Common Core of Data (CCD). The CCD contains annually updated administrative and fiscal data on all public schools, school districts, and state education agencies in the United States.

[16] The School Neighborhood Poverty estimates are based on school locations from the most recent CCD data and family income data from the U.S. Census Bureau's American Community Survey.

REFERENCES

Acevedo-Garcia, D., Osypuk, T. L., McArdle, N., & Williams, D. R. (2008). Toward a policy-relevant analysis of geographic and racial/ethnic disparities in child health. *Health Affairs, 27*(2), 321–333. https://doi.org/10.1377/hlthaff.27.2.321

Archbald, D., Hurwitz, A., & Hurwitz, F. (2018). Charter schools, parent choice, and segregation: A longitudinal study of the growth of charters and changing enrollment patterns in five school districts over 26 years. *Education Policy Analysis Archives, 26*(22). https://doi.org/10.14507/epaa.26.2921

Ball, S. J. (2003). *Class strategies and the education market.* Routledge. https://doi.org/10.4324/9780203218952

Ball, S. J., & Nikita, D. P. (2014). The global middle class and school choice: A cosmopolitan sociology. *Zeitschrift für Erziehungswissenschaft, 17*(3), 81–93. https://doi.org/10.1007/s11618-014-0523-4

Bell, C. A. (2007). Space and place: Urban parents' geographical preferences for schools. *The Urban Review, 39*(4), 375–404. https://doi.org/10.1007/s11256-007-0059-5

Bell, C. (2009). Geography in parental choice. *American Journal of Education, 115*(4), 493–521. https://doi.org/10.1086/599779

Bifulco, R. (2014). Charter school location: Evidence and policy implications. In G. K. Ingram & D. A. Kenyon (Eds.), *Education, land, and location* (pp. 243–266). Lincoln Institute of Land Policy.

Boggs, E., & Dabrowski, L. (2017, September). *Out of balance: Subsidized housing, segregation, and opportunity in Connecticut.* Open Communities Alliance. http://www.ctoca.org/outofbalance

Briggs, X. (2005). *The geography of opportunity: Race and housing choice in metropolitan America.* Brookings Institution Press.

Bruno, J. E. (1996). Use of geographical information systems (GIS) mapping procedures to support educational policy analysis and school site management. *International Journal of Educational Management, 10*(6), 24–31. https://doi.org/10.1108/09513549610151677

Burdick-Will, J., Keels, M., & Schuble, T. (2013). Closing and opening schools: The association between neighborhood characteristics and the location of new educational opportunities in a large urban district. *Journal of Urban Affairs, 35*(1), 59–80. https://doi.org/10.1111/juaf.12004

Bürgi, R., Tomatis, L., Murer, K., & de Bruin, E. D. (2016). Spatial physical activity patterns among primary school children living in neighbourhoods of varying socioeconomic status: A cross-sectional study using accelerometry and global positioning system. *BMC Public Health, 16*(1), 1–12. https://doi.org/10.1186/s12889-016-2954-8

Câmara, G., Sposati, A., Koga, D., Monteiro, A. M., Ramos, F. R., Camargo, E., & Fuks, S. D. (2004). Mapping social exclusion and inclusion in developing countries. In M. F. Goodchild & D. G. Janelle (Eds.), *Spatially integrated social science* (pp. 223–238). Oxford University Press.

Chatterton, P. (2010). Seeking the urban common: Furthering the debate on spatial justice. *City, 14*(6), 625–628. https://doi.org/10.1080/13604813.2010.525304

Chumacero, R. A., Gómez, D., & Paredes, R. D. (2011). I would walk 500 miles (if it paid): Vouchers and school choice in Chile. *Economics of Education Review, 30*(5), 1103–1114. https://doi.org/10.1016/j.econedurev.2011.05.015

Cobb, C. D. (2003). Geographic methods and policy: Using geographic information systems to inform education policy. *Educational Research Quarterly, 27*(1), 28–39.

Cobb, C. D. (2019). A geographic account of economic, health, and educational disparities in Hartford's *Sheff* region. *Humboldt Journal of Social Relations, 41*, 84–100.

Cobb, C. D., & Glass, G. V. (1999). Ethnic segregation in Arizona charter schools. *Education Policy Analysis Archives, 7*(1). https://doi.org/10.14507/epaa.v7n1.1999

The College of William and Mary and the Minnesota Population Center. (2011). *School Attendance Boundary Information System (SABINS): Version 1.0.* University of Minnesota.

Collingwood, L., Jochim, A., & Oskooii, K. A. R. (2018). The politics of choice reconsidered: Partisanship, ideology, and minority politics in Washington's charter school initiative. *State Politics & Policy Quarterly, 18*(1), 61–92. https://doi.org/10.1177/1532440017748569

Corcoran, C., & Saxe, K. (2014). Redistricting and district compactness. *The Mathematics of Decisions, Elections, and Games, Providence: American Mathematical Society*, 1–16. https://doi.org/10.1090/conm/624/12476

Dopp, K. A., & Godfrey, N. (2012). Legislative redistricting–compactness and population density fairness. *Available at SSRN 1945879.* https://doi.org/10.2139/ssrn.1945879

Dougherty, J., Harrelson, J., Maloney, L., Murphy, D., Smith, R., Snow, M., & Zannoni, D. (2009). School choice in suburbia: Test scores, race, and housing markets. *American Journal of Education, 115*(4), 523–548. https://doi.org/10.1086/599780

Dunn, C. E. (2007). Participatory GIS—a people's GIS? *Progress in Human Geography, 31*(5), 616–637. https://doi.org/10.1177/0309132507081493

Elwood, S. (2006). Critical issues in participatory GIS: Deconstructions, reconstructions, and new research directions. *Transactions in GIS, 10*(5), 693–708. https://doi.org/10.1111/j.1467-9671.2006.01023.x

Elwood, S., & Cope, M. (2009). Qualitative GIS: Forging mixed methods through representations, analytical innovations, and conceptual engagements. In M. Cope & S. Elwood (Eds.), *Qualitative GIS: A mixed methods approach* (pp. 1–12). Sage. https://doi.org/10.4135/9780857024541.n1

Environmental Systems Research Institute. (2018). *ArcGIS 10.6.*

Galster, G. C. (2011). The mechanism(s) of effects: Theory, evidence and policy implications. In M. van Ham, D. Manley, N. Bailey, L. Simpson, & D. Maclennan (Eds.), *Neighbourhood effects research: New perspectives.* Springer.

Galster, G. C., & Killen, S. P. (1995). The geography of metropolitan opportunity: A reconnaissance and conceptual framework. *Housing Policy Debate, 6*(1), 7–43. https://doi.org/10.1080/10511482.1995.9521180

Ghose, R., & Welcenbach, T. (2018). "Power to the people": Contesting urban poverty and power inequities through open GIS. *Canadian Geographer/Le Géographe Canadien, 62*(1), 67–80. https://doi.org/10.1111/cag.12442

Gilblom, E. A., & Sang, H. I. (2019). Schools as market-based clusters: Geospatial and statistical analysis of charter schools in Ohio. *Education Policy Analysis Archives, 27*(15). https://doi.org/10.14507/epaa.27.4091

Glomm, G., Harris, D., & Lo, T.-F. (2005). Charter school location. *Economics of Education Review, 24*(4), 451–457. https://doi.org/10.1016/j.econedurev.2004.04.011

Goodchild, M. F., & Janelle, D. G. (2004). Thinking spatially in the social sciences. In M. F. Goodchild & D. G. Janelle (Eds.), *Spatially integrated social science* (pp. 3–22). Oxford University Press.

Green, T. L. (2015). Places of inequality, places of possibility: Mapping "opportunity in geography" across urban school-communities. *The Urban Review, 47*(4), 717–741. https://doi.org/10.1007/s11256-015-0331-z

Green, T. L., Sánchez, J. & Germain, E. (2017). Communities and school ratings: Examining geography of opportunity in an urban school district located in a resource-rich city. *The Urban Review, 49*(5), 777–804. https://doi.org/10.1007/s11256-017-0421-1

Gulosino, C., & d'Entremont, C. (2011). Circles of influence: An analysis of charter school location and racial patterns at varying geographic scales. *Education Policy Analysis Archives, 19*. https://doi.org/10.14507/epaa.v19n8.2011

Gulosino, C., & Lubienski, C. (2011). School's strategic responses to competition in segregated urban areas: Patterns in school locations in metropolitan Detroit. *Education Policy Analysis Archives, 19*(13). https://doi.org/10.14507/epaa.v19n13.2011

Gulosino, C., & Maxwell, P. (2018). A comprehensive framework for evaluating Shelby County School District's voluntary preschool program: The challenges of equity, choice, efficiency, and social cohesion. *Urban Education.* Advance online publication. https://doi.org/10.1177/0042085918801885

Gulson, K. N., & Symes, C. (2007). *Spatial theories of education: Policy and geography matters.* Routledge. https://doi.org/10.4324/9780203940983

Helbich, M. (2017). Children's school commuting in the Netherlands: Does it matter how urban form is incorporated in mode choice models? *International Journal of Sustainable Transportation, 11*(7), 507–517. https://doi.org/10.1080/15568318.2016.1275892

Hillman, N. W. (2016). Geography of college opportunity: The case of education deserts. *American Educational Research Journal, 53*(4), 987–1021. https://doi.org/10.3102/0002831216653204

Hogrebe, M. C. (2012). Adding geospatial perspective to research on schools, communities, and neighborhoods. In W. Tate IV (Ed.), *Research on schools, neighborhoods, and communities: Toward civic responsibility* (pp. 151–159). Rowman & Littlefield.

Hogrebe, M. C., & Tate, W. F., IV. (2012). Geospatial perspective: Toward a visual political literacy project in education, health, and human services. *Review of Research in Education, 36*(1), 67–94. https://doi.org/10.3102/0091732X11422861

Hogrebe, M. C., & Tate, W. F. (2019). Residential segregation across metro St. Louis school districts: Examining the intersection of two spatial dimensions. *AERA Open, 5*(1). https://doi.org/10.1177/2332858419837241

Holloway, S., Hubbard, P., Jöns, H., & Pimlott-Wilson, H. (2010). Geographies of education and the significance of children, youth and families. *Progress in Human Geography, 34*(5), 583–600. https://doi.org/10.1177/0309132510362601

Jabbar, H., Sánchez, J., & Epstein, E. (2017). Getting from here to there: The role of geography in community college students' transfer decisions. *The Urban Review, 49*(5), 746–776. https://doi.org/10.1007/s11256-017-0420-2

Jones, B. D., Harris, K. D., & Tate, W. F. (2015). Ferguson and beyond: A descriptive epidemiological study using geospatial analysis. *Journal of Negro Education, 84*(3), 231–253. https://doi.org/10.7709/jnegroeducation.84.3.0231

Jones, P. A. (2018). The influence of charter school competition on public school district revenues across the U.S. *Journal of Education Finance, 43*(4), 327–359.

Kahneman, D. (2003). Maps of bounded rationality: Psychology for behavioral economics. *American Economic Review, 93*(5), 1449–1475. https://doi.org/10.1257/000282803322655392

Kamienski, A. (2011). Competition: Charter and public elementary schools in Chicago. *Journal of School Choice, 5*(2), 161–181. https://doi.org/10.1080/15582159.2011.576573

Kelly, M. G. (2019). A map is more than just a graph: Geospatial educational research and the importance of historical context. *AERA Open, 5*(1). https://doi.org/10.1177/2332858419833346

Koller, K., & Welsch, D. M. (2017). Location decisions of charter schools: an examination of Michigan. *Education Economics, 25*(2), 158–182. https://doi.org/10.1080/09645292.2016.1203866

Kwan, M., & Ding, G. (2008). Geo-narrative: Extending geographic information systems for narrative analysis in qualitative and mixed-method research. *The Professional Geographer, 60*(4), 443–465. https://doi.org/10.1080/00330120802211752

Kwan, M., & Schwanen, T. (2009). Quantitative revolution 2: The critical (re)turn. *The Professional Geographer, 61*(3), 283–291. https://doi.org/10.1080/00330120902931903

LaFleur, J. C. (2016). Locating Chicago's charter schools: A socio-spatial analysis. *Education Policy Analysis Archives, 24.* https://doi.org/10.14507/epaa.24.1745

Lubienski, C., & Dougherty, J. (2009). Mapping educational opportunity: Spatial analysis and school choices. *American Journal of Education, 115,* 485–491. https://doi.org/10.1086/599783

Lubienski, C., Gulosino, C., & Weitzel, P. (2009). School choice and competitive incentives: Mapping the distribution of educational opportunities across local education markets. *American Journal of Education, 115*(4), 601–647. https://doi.org/10.1086/599778

Lubienski, C., & Lee, J. (2017). Geo-spatial analyses in education research: The critical challenge and methodological possibilities. *Geographical Research, 55*(1), 89–99. https://doi.org/10.1111/1745-5871.12188

Massey, D. S. (2001). Residential segregation and neighborhood conditions in US metropolitan areas. In N. J. Smelser, W. J. Wilson, & F. Mitchell (Eds.), *America becoming: Racial trends and their consequences* (Vol. 1, pp. 391–434). National Academies Press.

Miller, P. (2012). Mapping educational opportunity zones: A geospatial analysis of neighborhood block groups. *Urban Review, 44*(2), 189–218. https://doi.org/10.1007/s11256-011-0189-7

Misra, K., Grimes, P. W., & Rogers, K. E. (2012). Does competition improve public school efficiency? A spatial analysis. *Economics of Education Review, 31*(6), 1177–1190. https://doi.org/10.1016/j.econedurev.2012.08.001

Nelson, L. K. (2013). *Research in communication sciences and disorders.* Plural.

Oka, M., & Wong, D. W. (2014). Capturing the two dimensions of residential segregation at the neighborhood level for health research. *Frontiers in Public Health, 2,* 118. https://doi.org/10.3389/fpubh.2014.00118

Osypuk, T. L., & Acevedo-Garcia, D. (2010). Beyond individual neighborhoods: A geography of opportunity perspective for understanding racial/ethnic health disparities. *Health & Place, 16*(6), 1113–1123. https://doi.org/10.1016/j.healthplace.2010.07.002

Oyana, T. J. (2011). Exploring geographic disparities in broadband access and use in rural southern Illinois: Who's being left behind? *Government Information Quarterly, 28*(2), 252–261. https://doi.org/10.1016/j.giq.2010.09.003

Parsons, E., Chalkley, B., & Jones, A. (2000). School catchments and pupil movements: A case study in parental choice. *Educational Studies, 26*(1), 33–48. https://doi.org/10.1080/03055690097727

Pastor, M. (2001). Geography and opportunity. In N. J. Smelser, W. J. Wilson, & Mitchell (Eds.), *America becoming: Racial trends and their consequences* (Vol.1, pp. 435–468). National Academies Press.

Peterson, R. D., & Krivo, L. J. (2010). *Divergent social worlds: Neighborhood crime and the racial-spatial divide.* Russell Sage Foundation.

Powers, J. M., Topper, A. M., & Potterton, A. U. (2017). Interdistrict mobility and charter schools in Arizona: Understanding the dynamics of public school choice. *Journal of Public Management & Social Policy, 25*(3), 56–87.

Reece, J., Gambhir, S., Olinger, J., Martin, M., & Harris, M. (2009). *People, place and opportunity: Mapping communities of opportunity in Connecticut.* Kirwan Institute for the Study of Race and Ethnicity, Ohio State University.

Reece, J., Gambhir, S., powell, j. a., & Grant-Thomas, A. (2009). *The geography of opportunity: Building communities of opportunity in Massachusetts.* Kirwan Institute for the Study of Race and Ethnicity, Ohio State University.

Reed, D. S. (2006). *Vouchers, desegregation and the segregationist academies: A spatial examination of the racial effects of school vouchers, in Alexandria, VA, 1960-1964* [Paper presentation]. American Political Science Association Policy History Conference, Charlottesville, VA, United States.

Rehm, M., & Filippova, O. (2008). The impact of geographically defined school zones on house prices in New Zealand. *International Journal of Housing Markets and Analysis, 1*(4), 313–336. https://doi.org/10.1108/17538270810908623

Richards, M. P. (2014). The gerrymandering of school attendance zones and the segregation of public schools: A geospatial analysis. *American Educational Research Journal, 51*(6), 1119–1157. https://doi.org/10.3102/0002831214553652

Richards, M. P. (2017). Gerrymandering educational opportunity. *Phi Delta Kappan, 99*(3), 65–70. https://doi.org/10.1177/0031721717739597

Richards, M. P., & Stroub, K. J. (2015). An accident of geography? Assessing the gerrymandering of public school attendance zones. *Teachers College Record, 117*(7), 1–32.

Rosenbaum, E. (2008). Racial/ethnic differences in asthma prevalence: the role of housing and neighborhood environments. *Journal of Health and Social Behavior, 49*(2), 131–145. https://doi.org/10.1177/002214650804900202

Saporito, S. (2017). Shaping income segregation in schools: The role of school attendance zone geography. *American Educational Research Journal, 54*(6), 1345–1377. https://doi.org/10.3102/0002831217724116

Saporito, S., & Sohoni, D. (2006). Coloring outside the lines: Racial segregation in public schools and their attendance boundaries. *Sociology of Education, 79*(2), 81–105. https://doi.org/10.1177/003804070607900201

Saporito, S., & Van Riper, D. (2016). Do irregularly-shaped school attendance zones contribute to racial segregation or integration? *Social Currents, 3*(1), 64–83. https://doi.org/10.1177/2329496515604637

Saultz, A., Fitzpatrick, D., & Jacobsen, R. (2015). Exploring the supply side: Factors related to charter school openings in NYC. *Journal of School Choice, 9*(3), 446–466. https://doi.org/10.1080/15582159.2015.1028829

Saultz, A., & Yaluma, C. B. (2017). Equal access? Analyzing charter location relative to demographics in Ohio. *Journal of School Choice, 11*(3), 458–476. https://doi.org/10.1080/15582159.2017.1345239

Schafft, K. A., Jensen, E. B., & Hinrichs, C. C. (2009). Food deserts and overweight schoolchildren: Evidence from Pennsylvania. *Rural Sociology, 74*(2), 153–177. https://doi.org/10.1111/j.1549-0831.2009.tb00387.x

Schultz, L. M. (2014). Inequitable dispersion: Mapping the distribution of highly qualified teachers in St. Louis metropolitan elementary schools. *Education Policy Analysis Archives, 22*(90). https://doi.org/10.14507/epaa.v22n90.2014

Siegel-Hawley, G. (2013). Educational gerrymandering? Race and attendance boundaries in a demographically changing suburb. *Harvard Educational Review, 83*(4), 580–612. https://doi.org/10.17763/haer.83.4.k385375245677131

Singleton, A. D., Longley, P. A., Allen, R., & O'Brien, O. (2011). Estimating secondary school catchment areas and the spatial equity of access. *Computers, Environment and Urban Systems, 35*(3), 241–249. https://doi.org/10.1016/j.compenvurbsys.2010.09.006

Smrekar, C., & Honey, N. (2015). The desegregation aims and demographic contexts of magnet schools: How parents choose and why siting policies matter. *Peabody Journal of Education, 90*(1), 128–155. https://doi.org/10.1080/0161956X.2015.988545

Soja, E. W. (2010). *Seeking spatial justice.* University of Minnesota Press. https://doi.org/10.5749/minnesota/9780816666676.001.0001

Soja, E. W., & Chouinard, V. (1999). Thirdspace: Journeys to Los Angeles & other real & imagined places. *Canadian Geographer, 43*(2), 209–212.

Squires, G. D., & Kubrin, C. E. (2006). *Privileged places: Race, residence, and the structure of opportunity.* Lynne Rienner.

Sui, D. (2015). Emerging GIS themes and the six senses of the new mind: is GIS becoming a liberation technology? *Annals of GIS, 21*(1), 1–13. https://doi.org/10.1080/19475683.2014.992958

Talen, E. (2001). School, community, and spatial equity: An empirical investigation of access to elementary schools in West Virginia. *Annals of the Association of American Geographers, 91*(3), 465–486. https://doi.org/10.1111/0004-5608.00254

Talen, E., & Anselin, L. (1998). Assessing spatial equity: An evaluation of measures of accessibility to public playgrounds. *Environment and Planning A: Economy and Space, 30*(4), 595–613. https://doi.org/10.1068/a300595

Tate, W. F. (2008). "Geography of opportunity": Poverty, place, and educational outcomes. *Educational Researcher, 37*(7), 397–411. https://doi.org/10.3102/0013189X08326409

Tate, W. F., & Striley, C. (2010). Epidemiology and education research: Dialoguing about disparities. *Teachers College Record.* http://www.tcrecord.org/Content.asp?ContentId=16036

Taylor, C. M. (2007). Geographical information systems (GIS) and school choice: The use of spatial research tools in studying educational policy. In K. N. Gulson & C. Symes (Eds.), *Spatial theories of education: Policy and geography matters* (pp. 77–93). Routledge.

Taylor, C. (2009). Choice, competition, and segregation in a United Kingdom urban education market. *American Journal of Education, 115*(4), 549–568. https://doi.org/10.1086/599781

Tukey, J. W. (1977). *Exploratory data analysis.* Pearson.

Waitoller, F. R., & Lubienski, C. (2019). Disability, race, and the geography of school choice: Toward an Intersectional analytical framework. *AERA Open, 5*(1). https://doi.org/10.1177/2332858418822505

Webster, C. J., & White, S. (1997). Child-care services and the urban labour market. Part 2: Modelling the relationships between child-care service accessibility and labour-market participation. *Environment and Planning A: Economy and Space, 29*(9), 1675–1695. https://doi.org/10.1068/a291675

Weiner, D., & Harris, T. M. (2008). Participatory geographic information systems. In J. P. Wilson & A. S. Fotheringham (Eds.), *The handbook of geographic information science* (pp. 466–480). Blackwell. https://doi.org/10.1002/9780470690819.ch26

Williams, D. R., & Collins, C. A. (2001). Racial residential segregation: A fundamental cause of racial disparities in health. *Public Health Reports, 116*(5), 404–415. https://doi.org/10.1016/S0033-3549(04)50068-7

Williams, S., & Wang, F. (2014). Disparities in accessibility of public high schools in metropolitan Baton Rouge, Louisiana 1990-2010. *Urban Geography, 35*(7), 1066–1083. https://doi.org/10.1080/02723638.2014.936668

Woessner, M. (2010). A new ontology for the era of the New Economy: On Edward W. Soja's *Seeking Spatial Justice. City, 14*(6), 601–603. https://doi.org/10.1080/13604813.2010.525080

Yoon, E. S., Gulson, K., & Lubienski, C. (2018). A brief history of the geography of education policy: Ongoing conversations and generative tensions. *AERA Open, 4*(4). https://doi.org/10.1177/2332858418820940

Yoon, E. S., & Lubienski, C. (2018). Thinking critically in space: Toward a mixed-methods geospatial approach to education policy analysis. *Educational Researcher, 47*(1), 53–61. https://doi.org/10.3102/0013189X17737284

Yoon, E. S., Lubienski, C., & Lee, J. (2018). The geography of school choice in a city with growing inequality: The case of Vancouver. *Journal of Education Policy, 33*(2), 279–298. https://doi.org/10.1080/02680939.2017.1346203

Yoshida, A., Kogure, K., & Ushijima, K. (2009). School choice and student sorting: Evidence from Adachi Ward in Japan. *Japanese Economic Review, 60*(4), 446–472. https://doi.org/10.1111/j.1468-5876.2008.00462.x

Chapter 5

Mining Big Data in Education: Affordances and Challenges

CHRISTIAN FISCHER
University of Tübingen

ZACHARY A. PARDOS
University of California, Berkeley

RYAN SHAUN BAKER
University of Pennsylvania

JOSEPH JAY WILLIAMS
University of Toronto

PADHRAIC SMYTH
RENZHE YU
University of California, Irvine

STEFAN SLATER
University of Pennsylvania

RACHEL BAKER
MARK WARSCHAUER
University of California, Irvine

The emergence of big data in educational contexts has led to new data-driven approaches to support informed decision making and efforts to improve educational effectiveness. Digital traces of student behavior promise more scalable and finer-grained understanding and support of learning processes, which were previously too costly to obtain with traditional data sources and methodologies. This synthetic review describes the affordances and applications of microlevel (e.g., clickstream data), mesolevel (e.g., text data), and macrolevel (e.g., institutional data) big data. For instance, clickstream data are often used to operationalize and understand knowledge, cognitive strategies, and behavioral

Review of Research in Education
March 2020, Vol. 44, pp. 130–160
DOI: 10.3102/0091732X20903304

Chapter reuse guidelines: sagepub.com/journals-permissions
© 2020 AERA. http://rre.aera.net

processes in order to personalize and enhance instruction and learning. Corpora of student writing are often analyzed with natural language processing techniques to relate linguistic features to cognitive, social, behavioral, and affective processes. Institutional data are often used to improve student and administrational decision making through course guidance systems and early-warning systems. Furthermore, this chapter outlines current challenges of accessing, analyzing, and using big data. Such challenges include balancing data privacy and protection with data sharing and research, training researchers in educational data science methodologies, and navigating the tensions between explanation and prediction. We argue that addressing these challenges is worthwhile given the potential benefits of mining big data in education.

In recent decades, the increased availability of big data has led to new frontiers in how we monitor, understand, and evaluate processes in educational contexts and has informed decision making and efforts to improve educational effectiveness. Although no single unified definition exists, big data are generally characterized by high volume, velocity, and variety in the digital era (Laney, 2001; Ward & Barker, 2013). Compared with earlier generations of data collected through considerable human effort, the prevalent use of digital tools in everyday life generates an unprecedented amount of data (volume) at an increasing speed (velocity) and from different modalities and time scales (variety; Laney, 2001; Ward & Barker, 2013). Thus, these data require considerable computing resources and alternative analytical methodologies to process and interpret. The National Academy of Education (2017) states that "in the educational context, big data typically take the form of administrative data and learning process data, with each offering their own promise for educational research" (p. 4).

The emergence of big data in education is attributed to at least two major trends in the digital era. First, the recording and storing of institutional data in traditional settings have become increasingly digitized, resulting in vast amounts of standardized student information. Specifically, student information systems (SIS) have been widely adopted to store and organize student profile information (e.g., demographics, academic background) and academic records (e.g., course enrollment and final grades) in schools. These data traditionally encompass decades of students at an institution, with an institution's SIS making it possible to manage and analyze those data at scale. Second, learning behaviors that were challenging to record in face-to-face classrooms can now be partially captured by learning management systems (LMS). In most cases, LMS are used by instructors to distribute instructional materials, manage student assignments, and communicate with students. From clicks on course modules to revisions of an essay submission, these time-stamped logs easily amount to thousands of data points for an individual student. Beyond SIS and LMS, the variety of innovations in digital learning environments enrich new pedagogical possibilities and, in the meantime, collect students' digital footprints. This diversity leads to heterogeneous and multimodal data in large volumes.

A broad range of data mining techniques can be utilized for big data in education, which Baker and Siemens (2014) broadly categorize into prediction methods, including inferential methods that model knowledge as it changes; structure discovery algorithms, with emphasis on discovering the structures of content and skills in an educational domain and the structures of social networks of learners; relationship mining, including sequential pattern mining and correlation mining; visualization; and discovery with models, including using models in subsequent analyses.

With their volume, velocity, and variety, all these "big data" represent a high-value perspective on learner behavior for multiple fields of education research. Questions that were either costly or even impossible to answer before these data sources were available can now be potentially addressed. Digital traces of student actions promise a more scalable and finer-grained understanding of learning processes. By combining behavioral data with surveys or psychological scales, researchers can map action sequences to cognitive traits and test whether observed behavioral traces align with theoretical assumptions and refine theories at a granular level. This rich information has the potential to help understand the mechanisms of specific policy effects and to address policy-relevant issues. For example, connecting administrative and learning process data can unveil nuances about educational inequities and inform actions in faster feedback cycles. The goal of finding effective instructional approaches comparable with one-to-one tutoring has been sought after for decades, and the magnitude of learning process data makes it possible to personalize learning experiences in new ways.

Framework for the Review

This review describes the affordances of big data use in education at three broad levels relevant to educational contexts: the *microlevel* (e.g., clickstream data), *mesolevel* (e.g., text data), and *macrolevel* (e.g., institutional data).

Microlevel big data are fine-grained interaction data with seconds between actions that can capture individual data from potentially millions of learners. Most microlevel data are collected automatically during interactions between learners and their respective learning environments, which include intelligent tutoring systems, massive online open courses (MOOCs), simulations, and games.

Mesolevel big data include computerized student writing artifacts systematically collected during writing activities in a variety of learning environments ranging from course assignments to online discussion forum participation, intelligent tutoring systems, and social media interactions. Notably, mesolevel data affords opportunities to naturally capture raw data on learners' progressions in cognitive and social abilities, as well as affective states.

Macrolevel big data comprise data collected at the institutional level. Examples of macrolevel data include student demographic and admission data, campus services data, schedules of classes and course enrollment data, and college major requirement and degree completion data. While macrolevel data are generally collected over multiyear time spans, they are infrequently updated, often only once or twice per term (e.g., course schedule information, grade records).

Notably, these micro-/meso-/macrolevel categorizations should not be viewed as strictly distinct levels as there can be considerable overlap within each data source. For example, keystroke logs in intelligent tutoring systems represent microlevel data that could provide insights on writing behavior (e.g., burst writing, editing processes). In turn, the content and linguistic features of written texts represent mesolevel data that could be analyzed with natural language processing (NLP) approaches. Similarly, social media interactions often entail microlevel time stamps (and sometimes location information), in addition to the mesolevel contents of each posting. Also, social media data frequently allow researchers to analyze the mesolevel relational positioning between users. Another example is college application materials. Essays are frequently a standard component of university application processes, which provide both mesolevel text data and macrolevel institutional data.

Literature Search

Given the fast-growing nature of relevant research, our synthetic review is primarily based on the literature of the past 5 years (2014–2018), while building on several review and synthesis papers (e.g., Baker & Yacef, 2009; Baker & Siemens, 2014; Pardos, 2017). More specifically, the research communities that examine big data in education increasingly focus on providing policy-relevant insights into education and learning in a variety of learning contexts. Thus, we mostly draw on refereed conference proceedings and peer-reviewed journals from these communities, including the International Conference on Learning Analytics and Knowledge, the International Conference on Educational Data Mining, the International Conference on Artificial Intelligence in Education, the ACM (Association for Computing Machinery) Conference on Learning at Scale, the *International Journal of Artificial Intelligence in Education*, the *Journal of Educational Data Mining, IEEE Transactions on Learning Technologies*, and the *Journal of Learning Analytics*. However, seminal papers from other outlets that are not primarily outlets for big data research (and thus not part of the above list) were also considered based on the authors' expertise in their respective areas.

Papers included for consideration had to be original empirical studies that analyzed real-world data. Thus, papers that described simulation studies, replication studies, and meta-analytic studies were not included in this synthetic review. We did not consider papers that solely report on methodological improvements or conceptual papers. Also, the research needed to be situated in a formal or informal educational context. For instance, research studies that focused on students, teachers, classrooms, learning platforms, schools, or universities were eligible for inclusion in this synthetic review. Regarding analytical strategies, studies that were included needed to have used data mining techniques, rather than just qualitative methods or descriptive statistical analyses. Data needed to be digitally recorded and/or archived at scale. In most cases, this excluded traditionally summative educational data (e.g., surveys, test performance) and new digitized data that were currently less feasible to collect at scale (e.g., data from audio, visual, physiological, and neural sensors).

For each paper, we read the abstract and data set description (if provided) to decide whether they fit the inclusion criteria of this review. Then, the studies were examined to verify that they did not meet the exclusion criteria. The remaining studies were categorized as micro-, meso-, and macrolevel studies. Notably, a study could be assigned more than one category. In total, we identified 370 papers eligible for the section on microlevel big data, 175 for mesolevel big data, and 57 for macrolevel big data, as well as about 200 short papers. Papers included in the list of potentially eligible studies were carefully reviewed by experts on the author team in their respective area of expertise to identify and synthesize larger conceptual themes.

MICROLEVEL BIG DATA

Microlevel big data in education consist of data that can occur at the granularity of seconds between actions. Although multimodal data are increasingly commonly used in learning analytics (Ochoa & Worsley, 2016), the majority of microlevel data used in education consist of data produced by exchanges between learners and data collection platforms in MOOCs, intelligent tutoring systems, simulations, and serious games. This type of data includes information about both the learner's actions and the context in which those actions occur. Often, this type of data is not large in terms of numbers of students—in many cases only hundreds of students are considered—but the volume of data they produce is often quite large, ranging from tens of thousands to millions of data points. In some cases, models are developed for and applied to hundreds of thousands of students, bringing the total data size to billions of data points.

The nature and grain size of microlevel clickstream data make such data well suited to situations where direct intervention might be useful, such as providing students with scaffolding or feedback based on their cognitive or affective states or moving students to a new topic on a knowledge component when they are ready. The scale of clickstream data also facilitates their use across large numbers of contexts and situations, such as studying the development of student learning and engagement over the scale of months or differentiating between student groups who are too rare to show up in small samples.

Microlevel data are often used to detect cognitive strategies, affective states, or self-regulated learning (SRL) behaviors, and they are sometimes validated based on real-time observations of student actions (Botelho et al., 2017; DeFalco et al., 2018; Pardos et al., 2014) or retrospective hand coding of data subsets (Gobert et al., 2012). Then, these detectors are used to study the construct of interest (Pardos et al., 2014; Sao Pedro et al., 2014; Tóth et al., 2014) and drive automated intervention (Aleven et al., 2016; DeFalco et al., 2018; Moussavi et al., 2016). This two-step process necessitates the identification of constructs of interest, either through quantitative coding or by obtaining labels in another fashion (e.g., self-report), and the construction of a machine-learned model that can accurately identify the presence or absence of the construct.

In this section, we review research that used microlevel data to operationalize and understand (a) knowledge components, (b) metacognition and self-regulation, and (c) affective states, as well as to evaluate (d) student knowledge. We also consider how microlevel data mining can identify (e) actionable knowledge to enhance instruction and learning and (f) how to personalize digital educational resources.

Identifying Knowledge Components

There has been considerable prior work on using microlevel data to make inferences about how student performance relates to complex cognitive skills within learning activities. Complex cognition has historically been difficult to infer at scale, but new data mining methods made it possible to model and track it over time. Hundreds of students typically generate vast numbers of interactions, ranging from magnitudes of ten thousand to millions of interactions. Automated detectors that identify students' behavioral patterns have been developed and applied to data sets to identify the degree to which students transferred their knowledge of scientific inquiry between domains and to improve outcomes, driving automated scaffolding aimed at improving students' ability with these skills (Moussavi et al., 2016; Sao Pedro et al., 2014). This work was followed by considerable interest in studying problem-solving strategies. For instance, Tóth et al. (2014) studied problem solving within the MicroDYN learning environment and clustered how student strategies developed and shifted over time. Similarly, Bauer et al. (2017) examined problem-solving approaches in the scientific discovery game *Foldit*, which tasks users with identifying protein structures, a biology research task that is difficult to do in a fully automated fashion. By using visualization to understand the clickstream data produced within the game, the authors identified several common problem-solving strategies and associated these strategies with players' performances. Bauer and colleagues noted that understanding these approaches could be used to provide scaffolding that could improve the quality of players' solutions.

Identifying Metacognitive and SRL Skills

Within the educational data mining community, many researchers have also studied metacognition and SRL. These constructs often examine the learner's ability to self-regulate learning processes (Roll & Winne, 2015), behaviors that are especially relevant in less structured systems such as LMS and MOOCs. Samples ranged from ten to tens of thousands of students and included up to 100 million interactions. Educational data mining approaches to examining SRL often involve modeling the processes and actions that students undertake within learning environments to identify possible scaffolds to encourage learning, which system developers and designers may use to improve user interfaces and experiences (Aleven et al., 2016; Roll & Winne, 2015).

Microlevel clickstream data are uniquely positioned to provide detailed information on students' temporal and sequential patterns of behaviors based on specific actions students undertake and the system design components students utilize. For instance, Park et al. (2017) explored the development and validation of an effort regulation measure using clickstream data on students' previewing and reviewing of course materials. Students who increased their efforts to review course materials were more likely to pass the course, whereas students who decreased their efforts were less likely to pass the course. Similarly, Park et al. (2018) developed and validated a time management measure that identifies student procrastination and regularity of procrastination based on student clickstream data in online courses with periodic deadlines. Students who received As had significantly higher time management skills (i.e., regular nonprocrastinators) than B grade students (i.e., irregular procrastinators/ irregular nonprocrastinators), who had significantly higher time management skills than C/D/F grade students (i.e., regular procrastinators).

There has also been considerable research into SRL within the Betty's Brain teachable agent and learning management platform for middle school science (Biswas et al., 2016; Segedy et al., 2015). In Betty's Brain, students are tasked with teaching a computer agent (Betty) by producing causal maps and models describing science phenomena. Students' ability to teach Betty is evaluated by a second computer agent, Mr. Davis, who gives Betty quizzes and grades her performance based on how well the student instructed Betty. The Betty's Brain platform provides SRL support to students through both computer agents. For instance, Segedy et al. (2015) clustered SRL behaviors and investigated their associations with student learning in key domain-specific concepts.

Many studies investigated metacognitive and SRL skills in Cognitive Tutors, an intelligent tutoring system for mathematics. A prominent line of SRL research targets help-seeking skills (Aleven et al., 2016). Researchers used microlevel data to develop models of instructional hand-offs (Fancsali et al., 2018), which use student help-seeking behavior and SRL practices to understand how students transition between using different learning resources. For example, Ogan et al. (2015) investigated how help-seeking strategies correlate with learning, using the same learning system and content in different translations. Lu and Hsiao (2016) studied how student behavior during programming correlates to their help seeking within discussion forums and determined that more successful learners read posts in a deeper fashion than less successful learners.

Identifying Affective States

Microlevel data allow us to make inferences about "noncognitive" constructs surrounding engagement, motivation, and affect. The most thoroughly studied constructs are *academic emotions*, also referred to as affective states: frustration, confusion, boredom, and engaged concentration (sometimes called *flow*). Affective states inspired work on developing affect detectors for various learning environments, including intelligent tutoring systems, puzzle games, and first-person simulations (Botelho et al., 2017; DeFalco et al., 2018; Hutt et al., 2019; Pardos et al., 2014;

Sabourin et al., 2011). Detectors are frequently trained on data from hundreds of students with tens of thousands of actions prior to their deployment. Increasingly, this work uses multiple data sources combining quantitative field observations (trained coders observing student behavior during learning and taking systematic notes) and microlevel log data in the development and validation of detectors.

The capacity of educational data mining techniques to identify affective states affords utilization of affective detectors to provide real-time feedback, scaffolding, and interventions to learners. For example, DeFalco et al. (2018) used affective detectors in a military training game to address student frustration as students worked through a combat casualty care skill simulation, TC3Sim, for the U.S. Army. By integrating affective detectors into the game itself, TC3Sim was able to provide feedback messages to students when frustration was identified, leading to improved student learning from pretest to posttest.

Evaluating Student Knowledge

An early application of microlevel clickstream data is the evaluation of student knowledge based on sets of correct and incorrect responses to problems, known as knowledge inference or latent knowledge estimation. Three popular methods are Bayesian knowledge tracing (BKT; Corbett & Anderson, 1995), performance factors analysis (PFA; Pavlik et al., 2009), and deep knowledge tracing (DKT; Khajah et al., 2016). These methodologies use distinct frameworks to infer the degree to which students master given skills. The increasing availability of public data sets such as the Cognitive Tutor and ASSISTments platforms, with data sets often as large as thousands or tens of thousands of students and millions of interactions, has helped this work move forward.

BKT, the oldest of these three approaches, estimates student mastery using a Hidden Markov Model to estimate four parameters for each unique skill contained within the data: the probability that a given student mastered a given skill before the first opportunity to practice that skill; the probability that a student reaches mastery of a skill after the last opportunity to practice but before the next one; the probability that a student who has not mastered a skill will guess on a given opportunity to practice; and the probability that a student who has mastered a skill will answer a given opportunity to practice with an incorrect answer. The parameters of BKT describe qualities of the skill being learned, such as how likely students are to guess at this skill or student prior knowledge. Over the past five years, this framework was expanded to include item difficulty estimates (González-Brenes et al., 2014), answers with partial correctness (Ostrow et al., 2015), and a wider number of possible states for specific knowledge components (Falakmasir et al., 2015). BKT studies support basic research, including on affect detectors, and underpin adaptivity through several learning platforms, such as the Cognitive Tutor (e.g., Liu & Koedinger, 2017).

While BKT uses a Hidden Markov Model to infer student knowledge, PFA (Pavlik et al., 2009) uses logistic regression to estimate three parameters for each unique skill within the data: the degree to which correct answers are associated with better future performance; the degree to which incorrect answers are associated with better future performance; and the overall ease or difficulty of the skill being estimated. These parameters produce an outcome logit, the probability that a student has mastered a given skill, given the responses up to that point. Compared with BKT, PFA parameters provide less information on the initial knowledge state of learners on a given skill and the predisposition of learners to guess or make careless errors. However, PFA parameters provide insight on the relative difficulty of skills and the relative learning associated with correct and incorrect answers. Extensions of PFA are an active area of research—for instance, to investigate the relative predictive value of recent performance versus older performance (Galyardt & Goldin, 2015), to investigate individual differences in learning rate (Liu & Koedinger, 2015), and to better understand mastery criteria (Käser et al., 2016).

In the past 5 years, DKT has emerged as a popular alternative to BKT and PFA. DKT uses recurrent neural networks to model skill knowledge and mastery, producing a vector of the probability of mastery associated with each opportunity to practice a skill. Compared with the other approaches, DKT is generally more effective at predicting student correctness during learning (Khajah et al., 2016; Yeung & Yeung, 2018), but it has not been used extensively in the real world due to limitations around interpretability and stability of estimates (Yeung & Yeung, 2018).

Using Data for Actionable Knowledge

Big data are also used to understand the effectiveness of administrative decisions and educational interventions. Big data models can predict *when* actions need to be taken for students, such as identifying when students are disengaging from online courses (Le et al., 2018). For instance, Whitehill et al. (2015) analyzed more than 2 million data points generated by more than 200,000 students taking 10 MOOC courses from HarvardX to develop detectors of whether a student would stop course work. These detectors were then used as the basis of interventions that improved student engagement.

In other circumstances, big data have been utilized to discover *what* actions are effective, such as analyzing the larger-scale randomized experiments or randomized controlled trials (Liu et al., 2014; Liu & Koedinger, 2017). Approaches such as reinforcement learning (a subfield of machine learning and artificial intelligence) can create a new paradigm for educational experimentation that attempts to determine which interventions or conditions are effective, and for which students, and to scale those interventions to future students (Liu et al., 2014; Shen & Chi, 2016). Such dynamic experiments estimate the probability that certain conditions are effective, dynamically reweighting randomization so as to present more effective conditions to future students, converging over time to a better instructional policy for each student (Rafferty et al., 2018).

Clustering Student Profiles and Discovering How to Personalize

Actionable knowledge can be gained from assessing which actions are appropriate for different subgroups or profiles of students. Prior research examined hundreds of students in school settings, as well as tens of thousands of students in MOOCs. Examples include identifying how different student groups work through a learning simulation as part of an experimental standardized test (Bergner et al., 2014), modeling how different student groups have different strategies emerge over time in their use of online course resources (Gasevic et al., 2017), and identifying distinct patterns of engagement in MOOCs (Guo & Reinecke, 2014; Kizilcec et al., 2013).

Knowledge of subgroups can inform interventions tailored to different student groups. For instance, recurrent neural networks approaches are used to recommend a timely course page predicted to be relevant to learners given their pattern of engagement (Pardos et al., 2017). Similarly, reinforcement learning can be used to design effective strategies (e.g., problem solving, worked examples) for low- versus high-knowledge learners (Shen & Chi, 2016). These methods have been used to discover how best to sequence practice problems by testing out many different sequences with large numbers of observations from each student (Clement et al., 2015).

Affordances and Challenges of Microlevel Big Data

As this section shows, there are many ways in which microlevel big data have been used in education. Microlevel data are often voluminous, a single student may produce thousands or tens of thousands of data points. It thus becomes possible to analyze phenomena that may take place over a matter of seconds. Affect, for instance, is often detected at a 20-second grain size (Botelho et al., 2017; DeFalco et al., 2018; Pardos et al., 2014), but the resultant detectors can then be used to analyze behavior over the course of an entire year (Pardos et al., 2014; Slater et al., 2016). Analyses at the microlevel lend themselves to models that are relatively easy to apply in interventions. Microlevel big data are, however, not without limitations. Since microlevel big data are easy to collect, many research projects focus solely on them, potentially neglecting important related phenomena that are more coarse-grained. For example, the student knowledge modeling work has focused almost entirely on optimizing immediate prediction, raising possible concerns that these models may be less effective at inferring robust learning that will persist over time (Corbett & Anderson, 1995; Pardos et al., 2014, are notable exceptions). Thus, the ease of collecting microlevel big data does not remove the importance of connecting brief phenomena with longer trends in a learner's development.

MESOLEVEL BIG DATA

Mesolevel big data primarily relate to corpora of writing. The availability of systematically collected computerized student writing artifacts at scale is growing as academic writing moves from paper to digital texts. Whereas one-time national assessments like the ACT/SAT examinations previously constituted a rare opportunity to gather large writing corpora, submissions of student assignments to LMS made large corpora of writing accessible.

Besides course assignments, textual data can originate from online discussion forums, intelligent tutoring systems, website databases, programming code, and many other sources. Each mesolevel data point is usually collected in time periods that range from minutes to hours. However, an individual may engage in writing activities with varying frequency and regularity. For instance, a student may submit writing assignments every week to LMS over a term to complete a class but may engage in social media interactions with varying intensity over the course of multiple years in the course of a degree program.

Prominent approaches to analyzing text data at scale use NLP tools to automate analytical processes. Linguistic tools can indicate the clusters of lexical, syntactic, or morphological features in student writing; the patterns of collaborative writing in cloud-based corpora; or the quality of student writing normed on corpora of essays previously scored by human graders. For instance, Coh-Metrix (McNamara & Graesser, 2012) reports on linguistics primarily related to text difficulty by measuring components aligned to discourse comprehension including narrativity, syntactic simplicity, word concreteness, referential cohesion, and deep cohesion. Similarly, the Linguistic Inquiry and Word Count tool (Pennebaker et al., 2015) measures psychological constructs including confidence, leadership, authenticity, and emotional tone. Other approaches include social network analysis to generate inferences about relational positionings, and grouping approaches such as k-means clustering.

In this section, we review research studies that use mesolevel data to provide insights into (a) cognitive processes (e.g., cognitive functioning, knowledge, and skills), (b) social processes (e.g., discourse and collaboration structures), (c) behavioral processes (e.g., learner engagement and disengagement), and (d) affective processes (e.g., sentiment, motivation).

Supporting and Evaluating Cognitive Functioning

Studies related to cognitive processes have focused on supporting and evaluating learners' cognitive functioning, knowledge, and skills, as well as providing instructors with support (e.g., automated student feedback, automated assignment grading). In recent years, the ability to automate evaluations of student learning expanded from multichoice formats to student writing samples. These studies typically utilize writing samples of hundreds or thousands of students as well as reading comprehension data sets with hundreds of thousands of interactions. Numerous studies demonstrate that evaluation of student writing can be automated to substantially reduce human effort in grading essays in a range of subjects (e.g., Allen et al., 2018; Allen & McNamara, 2015; Head et al., 2017; Lan et al., 2015). For instance, Lan et al. (2015) examined how to automatically grade open-response questions in mathematics. In this work, mathematical solutions for four open-response problems were converted into numerical features, which were then clustered into incorrect, partially correct, and correct solutions. Based on instructor grade assignments for each cluster, the student solutions were then automatically graded. Studies found students' overall linguistic abilities to be associated with student performance in mathematics and other disciplines (e.g., Crossley et al., 2018; Wang, Yang, et al., 2015). For instance, Crossley et al. (2018) examined the associations between students' mathematical self-concept, interest in mathematics, written interactions with the learning platform, and performance indicators in a blended-learning mathematics program. In particular, Crossley and colleagues found that NLP-derived features were associated with students' mathematical identity (self-concept, interest, value) and mathematics ability. These findings encourage the design of early-warning systems that flag students who are at greater risk of underperforming to instructors. In large lecture courses, these systems may be able to help instructors better identify students who need additional support.

In addition to evaluations of student work, researchers have developed support systems that automate feedback to learners and provided hints to support learning in a variety of domains. For instance, Price et al. (2016) developed a Contextual Tree Decomposition algorithm to provide students working on programming assignments in an intelligent tutoring system with hints on their next steps. These automatically generated hints effectively guide students toward correct solutions of the programming tasks.

Oher research examined how to support instructors with developing assessments by automating the process to evaluate and generate questions. For instance, Wang et al. (2018) used recurrent neural networks models to automatically generate open-response questions from textbooks based on the Stanford Question Answering Dataset. Similarly, Harrak et al. (2018) used clustering approaches on medical school lecture questions to provide instructors with suggestions for in-class feedback.

Supporting and Examining Social Processes

Recent studies analyzed dialogue, discussions, and collaboration patterns from online discussion forums, intelligent tutoring systems, and video transcripts to examine social processes. These studies may use thousands of students with up to a few million interactions. For instance, Hecking et al. (2016) examined MOOC discussion forum data and found that social and semantic structures influenced interaction patterns and community formation processes. Similarly, Gelman et al. (2016) analyzed user interactions on Scratch, an informal learning environment for block-based programming language. Much like in physical spaces, interest-driven subcommunities emerged over time. Besides fully online learning environments, blended-learning formats also provide opportunities for students to engage in collaborative learning. For example, Scheihing et al. (2018) studied a microblogging platform to identify differences in student interaction patterns. In classroom settings, transcript data from video recordings can be used to automate classifications of classroom discourse structures. For instance, Cook et al. (2018) examined classroom recording transcripts, utilizing speech recognition and NLP to detect a characteristic of effective teaching, the proportion of authentic questions asked in a class session. This finding is mirrored in research that examines and classifies dialogue sequences in intelligent tutoring systems (Dzikovska et al., 2014).

Detecting Behavioral Engagement

Studies related to behavioral engagement analyzed student course engagement and resource-seeking behavior, often utilizing hundreds of thousands of interactions from up to tens of thousands of students. For example, Epp et al. (2017) examined communication behavior in online discussions, with a particular emphasis on student pronoun use. They found that students in instructor-facilitated courses demonstrated higher levels of interaction and used more personal pronouns, whereas students in peer-facilitated courses exhibited lower levels of engagement and used fewer personal pronouns. Atapattu and Falkner (2018) used NLP on MOOC lecture videos to find that discourse features of the lecture video content are related to student interactions with the videos (e.g., pausing, seeking). Joksimović et al. (2015) examined course-related participation patterns of MOOC students on Twitter, Facebook, and blogs. They found that the topics discussed were similar across social media platforms and that the most prominent topics emerged relatively early in the course.

To better support resource-seeking behavior, Yang and Meinel (2014) mined textual metadata from lecture video audio tracks to assist users in their video-browsing and search behavior. Similarly, Peralta et al. (2018) developed a recommendation system that uses metadata to support teachers in the exploration of learning resources on an online platform. Also, Slater et al. (2016) evaluated the quality of mathematics problems that were mostly developed by teachers and submitted to an intelligent tutoring system. Notably, Slater et al. examined students engaging in mathematics problems to detect the relationships between semantic features of the problems and student learning or engagement, which could guide teachers in both their mathematics problem selection in classrooms and their development of new mathematics problems.

Examining Affective Constructs

Studies that investigated affective constructs examined learners' self-concept, sentiment, and motivation while engaging in learning opportunities, often examining hundreds or thousands of students. For instance, Crossley et al. (2018) used data from an online tutoring environment by employing NLP tools to identify the relationships of learners' linguistic ability with their mathematics identity (e.g., math value, interest, and self-concept). Similarly, Allen et al. (2016) utilized NLP to derive the writing characteristics of essays and related them to the affective states of engagement and boredom. In MOOC settings, Wen et al. (2014) utilized discussion forum data in Coursera courses to examine learners' sentiment toward the courses and to identify the relationships between sentiment and course dropout.

Investigating learners' motivations for enrollment in MOOCs, Crues et al. (2018) examined the responses to open-ended questions about course expectations during MOOC enrollment processes and their relationship with age and gender. Using latent Dirichlet allocation and correspondence analysis, they identified 26 reasons for course enrollment, which were associated with learners' age but not their gender. Similarly, Reich et al. (2015) used structural topic modeling to uncover patterns of semantic meaning in unstructured text in order to understand students' enrollment motivation in an educational policy course.

Affordances and Challenges of Mesolevel Big Data

As outlined in this section, mesolevel big data provide several affordances to researchers. Text data can provide insight into students' understanding, their views on various topics, and even their emotional affect. Such data can also give information on relationships and networks within an online community. Studies that use textual analysis may help instructors design courses and activities to improve student engagement and to facilitate peer-to-peer learning (e.g., Atapattu & Falkner, 2018; Gelman et al., 2016; Slater et al., 2016). However, the applicability of various tools (e.g., Coh-Metrix and Linguistic Inquiry and Word Count) has not been tested extensively in all educational settings (Fesler et al., 2019). Researchers cannot ignore contextual factors such as the stimuli to which students are responding. If researchers do not pay attention to unique contextual factors, techniques for analyzing mesolevel big data might result in inaccurate inferences. Such errors are particularly dangerous when tied to important outcomes such as student grades (e.g., Lan et al., 2015).

MACROLEVEL BIG DATA

Macrolevel big data are collected over multiyear time spans, with low rates of collection relative to the other levels. For instance, university-wide institutional data include student demographic and admission data, course enrollment and grade records, course schedule and course descriptions, degree and major requirement information, and campus living data. These data are infrequently updated, at most every few weeks and often only once or twice per term. For instance, student demographic information is usually collected only once and only updated per student request. Nonetheless, such data can afford administrators opportunities to engage in data-driven decision making to improve administrative decision making, enhance student experiences, and improve college or K–12 success.

In this section, we focus on three common application areas of macrolevel data that have emerged in the literature: (a) early-warning systems, also known as early-alert systems; (b) course guidance and information systems; and (c) administration-facing analytics.

Early-Warning Systems

Traditionally, signs that students may be at risk of dropping a course or dropping out of a program are first responded to when students reach out to an instructor or adviser. The affordance of data-driven early-warning systems is that preemptive support is possible given the availability and utilization of decades of institutional big data, often consisting of tens of thousands of students combined with predictive modeling. Studies assessed real-world deployments of early-warning systems; however, a challenge remains of selecting the appropriate institutional response and types of information to convey to students in order to effectively increase their chances of success (Chaturapruek et al., 2018; Jayaprakash et al., 2014). Notably, a financial evaluation of deployed early-warning systems concluded that setting up early-warning systems and deploying their interventions was cost-effective (Harrison et al., 2016).

Early applications of institutional early-warning systems predicted and responded to course-level failure. Marist College piloted a system that predicted students' likelihood of failing a course based on LMS session data, academic standing, demographics, and standardized test scores (Jayaprakash et al., 2014). Candidate predictive models were trained to predict course failure. The most accurate model was used in a real-time controlled study to trigger an intervention for any students who were predicted to fail a course. For students in the experimental condition, the system dispatched an email alerting them that they were at risk of failing the course and describing resources they could seek to receive support (Harrison et al., 2016; Jayaprakash et al., 2014). The intent of the intervention was to increase the flagged students' chances of success in the course; however, the results were mixed. A statistically significant increase in average course grade of 2 to 5 percentage points was observed in the experimental condition over the control. However, about 7% to 11% more students in the experimental condition withdrew from the course compared with students in the control condition (Jayaprakash et al., 2014).

Course Guidance and Information Systems

Course information and guidance systems have emerged as a complement to early-warning systems. Instead of responding to early signs of trouble in a class, they instead aim to help students select their courses. An example of a deployed system is AskOski at University of California, Berkeley, which uses historic enrollments and machine learning to suggest courses across campus that may be relevant to students' interests and links them to the campus degree audit system to give personalized recommendations of courses that would satisfy students' unmet graduation requirement (Pardos, Fan, et al., 2019). Another deployed system, Stanford's CARTA system, surfaces historic course grade distributions, course evaluations, and common courses taken before and after a course (Chaturapruek et al., 2018). As with the early-warning intervention at Marist, unintended results were observed in CARTA's surfacing of course grade distributions, leading to one-quarter reduction in grade point average (GPA) for students encouraged to use the system. These findings underscore the importance of understanding how different types of information affect student choices, agency, and success.

Off-line experiments applying machine learning to predict student course grades have been increasingly commonplace in the literature (O'Connell et al., 2018; Ren et al., 2017; Sweeney et al., 2016). As data sources and techniques for achieving high accuracy in this prediction task become established, the methodological question shifts toward using models to support students in achieving their desired performance. Nascent work (Jiang et al., 2019) has investigated if recommendations for preparation courses outside of the standard prerequisites can be data mined from historical course enrollment and performance data. Furthermore, degree-level and institution dropout, particularly within the first semester, has been frequently studied (Aguiar et al., 2014; Chen et al., 2018; Gray et al., 2016; Zhang & Rangwala, 2018). For example, Gray et al. (2016) predicted which students are likely to earn a failing-level GPA in the first semester based on course selection, age, and prior academic performance in secondary school. On-time versus over-time graduation expectations have also been modeled. Hutt et al. (2018) predicted college-level outcomes from macrolevel data even before a student arrives on campus. Using a national data set, Hutt and colleagues investigated the use of binary classification models to predict whether students would graduate within 4 years, using 166 features as predictor variables, including student demographics, standardized test scores, academic achievement, and institution-level graduation rates.

Administration-Facing Data Analytics

Méndez et al. (2014) argue that "simple techniques applied to readily-available historical academic data" (p. 148) can provide valuable inside perspectives of educational institutions' programs. Institutional data sets typically contain decades of data from hundreds of thousands of students accumulating millions of course enrollments. Relatively straightforward data visualization, exploration, and -modeling techniques can be quite useful, and more advanced methods are not necessary to extract useful information, although such techniques are less popular in the literature, which often emphasizes the development and application of more complex methodologies. For instance, Méndez and colleagues extracted insights from course outcome data in a computer science program by utilizing the included estimation of course dependence via pairwise linear correlation of grades for the same student across pairs of courses, inference of curriculum coherence via factor analysis of student grades across multiple courses, and identification of dropout paths via sequence mining of the course paths of students who dropped out. This combination of techniques provided insights that were obvious retrospectively but hidden otherwise. For example, many dropouts occurred early in student trajectories due to failing courses in basic science (rather than computer science), suggesting that focusing tutorial resources on these science courses might help increase retention rates. Work has also extended from identifying relationships between courses within an institution to identifying such relationships across institutions. Pardos, Chau, et al. (2019) used classical and neural networks–based natural language techniques to analyze course catalog descriptions and enrollment records from a 2-year and a 4-year institution to identify similar courses between them. Their investigation attempted to increase the quantity and quality of course pairs, or articulations, where transfer students would be guaranteed course credit. They found that while the course descriptions provided the most powerful signal of similarity, patterns of enrollment around the course (i.e., who took the course and which other courses they took) were nearly as valuable as the descriptions in identifying similarities across institutions.

Koester et al. (2017) aimed for the "transcript of the future" by using macrolevel data to generate a richer description of a student's academic experience as an alternative to traditional GPA and course grade information. They modeled student–grade pairs as linear combinations of student and course fixed effects and explored estimated student and course effects, identifying various aggregated patterns in enrollment and outcome data. This illustrates that even relatively limited institutional data (records of course outcomes for student–course pairs) can potentially provide a wealth of information about students, courses, and majors. Similarly, Mahzoon et al. (2018) focused on information contained in sequences of student course outcomes to build sequential descriptors of student academic performance across terms from college entrance to graduation, providing a basis for visualizations and automatically generated narratives about student trajectories. This approach derived sequential signatures for each student to predict on-time graduation, concluding that temporal information as a student progresses through college is important in predicting student outcomes.

In addition, course information captured in course syllabi and curricula can be mined for potentially insightful information. For example, Sekiya et al. (2015) analyzed computer science degree curricula across 10 U.S. universities, focusing on online syllabi (available from course webpages) for each computer science course. With topic modeling, Sekiya and colleagues automatically extracted clusters of words in the form of topics or "knowledge areas," where each university's syllabus could be characterized as a distribution over knowledge areas. This approach provides a systematic framework for quantitative comparative analysis and visualization of syllabi across universities, leading to insights about emphases in education across different universities—the use of automated text analysis techniques here is essential given the volume and complexity of the data involved. Davis et al. (2018) analyzed learning design components across 177 MOOCs consisting of more than 78,000 learning components (e.g., assets with which learners interact—videos, problems, html pages, etc.). Sequences of activities were abstracted via "lecture → discussion → assessment" by clustering transition probabilities and sequence mining to generate insights about common sequential learning patterns across multiple courses. While this analysis is relatively new, it has the potential to provide novel insights, for example, by linking thematic aspects of course design with measurements of student activity and performance.

Affordances and Challenges of Macrolevel Big Data

This section highlights the promise of bringing more advanced statistical techniques to bear on extant data sets. Universities routinely collect reams of course-taking and student performance data, but until recently these data were rarely used for institutional reforms or to improve student decision making. By analyzing these data, and making data and analyses available to students, schools can meaningfully improve outcomes. Importantly, public access to these data may also improve equity. Whereas course-taking information was historically available only through social networks, such as fraternities and sororities, more open access may have a democratizing effect by giving all students equal access.

However, benefits of these data sources may be limited in several ways. First, schools' contexts are unique, and applying the same analysis across schools may yield unreliable findings. For example, curricular requirements across majors or schools can affect student course taking, and knowledge of these requirements can affect inferences from analyses. Second, if students have goals not captured by institutional data, such as employment outcomes, the available data may provide limited guidance. Joining multiple sources of data, such as employment records or students' social activities on and off campus, could improve researchers' ability to make inferences but may also raise concerns about student privacy. Finally, as with all types of big data, it is uncertain how students may use the information from these analyses to change their behavior. As Chaturapruek et al. (2018) found, informational interventions may have unintended consequences on student behavior and student outcomes.

CHALLENGES

Though data mining offers numerous potential benefits for education research, there are also many challenges to be overcome to achieve those benefits. We summarize them below in three main areas: accessing, analyzing, and using big data.

Accessing Big Data

Educational data exist in a wide array of formats across an even wider variety of platforms. In almost all cases, these platforms were developed for other purposes, such as instruction or educational administration, rather than for research. Many commercial platform providers, such as educational software companies, have no interest in making their data available publicly. Other companies make their data available in a limited way but have not invested resources to facilitate access to data for research. Only a small number of platforms, such as Cognitive Tutor and ASSISTments, have made high-quality data broadly available.

By contrast, Google makes available the API (Application Programming Interface) of its widely used Google Docs program so that third-party companies can create extensions and other products that use or integrate with the software. It also allows users to view the history of their writing process in individual documents they have written or collaborated on down to 4-second increments; these documents can also be shared with others, who can also view those histories. The combination of open API and document history should, in theory, allow users to analyze metadata from large sets of writing data, for example, all documents written by students and teachers in a school district under a Google Docs site domain. In principle, though, writing the software to extract and analyze the data is a hugely complicated task. Some university and commercial groups have taken small steps in this direction, including the Hana Ohana research lab at University of California, Irvine, which has developed tools for analyzing collaboration history on individual Google Docs (Wang, Olson, et al., 2015), and the private company Hapara (2019), which mines school district data for patterns related to time and amount of student writing, but these are very partial solutions to what largely remains an out-of-reach treasure of student writing data. In addition, even platforms that make their data available may require programming skills to extract the data. Though many education researchers are familiar with statistical software such as R or Stata, far fewer know programming languages superior for data extraction, such as Python.

Finally, and most important, the availability of data is complicated by privacy issues. Parents, educators, and others are rightly concerned about companies' ability to mine large amounts of sensitive student data and act in ways that are not necessarily focused on bettering individual students' futures. Fears have been raised that student data that are inappropriately shared or sold could be used to stereotype or profile children, contribute to tailored marketing campaigns, or lead to identity theft (Strauss, 2019). Data privacy issues are exacerbated in K–12 settings, where students are children and participation in educational activities is mandatory.

Though the risks of sharing student data generate the most publicity, there are also risks to *not* sharing student data. Colorado has the strictest student data–sharing policies in the United States, according to the Parent Coalition for Student Privacy (2019). Yet data sharing is so strict that, according to the Right to Know (2019) coalition (see also Meltzer, 2019; Schimke, 2019), the public is robbed of the information necessary to evaluate the performance of schools and educational programs in the state and their impact on diverse students.

Finding the right balance between individual privacy and the public interest is very challenging. This is, in part, because the large amount of data available in big data sets makes it very difficult to prevent the "reidentification" of de-identified data, even if all direct identifiers are removed. It is thus impossible to combine maximal privacy with maximal utility. Instead, educational institutions and researchers face a choice between maximizing privacy and limiting the utility of the data set or maximizing utility but leaving the data subject to possible reidentification with sufficient effort (Nelson, 2015).

The challenges of sharing mesolevel data are even greater, since there is an unlimited number of ways in which students can reveal their identity in their writing. Addressing these challenges requires different kinds of strategies for different audiences and purposes. The U.S. Family Education and Privacy Act allows schools and institutions to share data with organizations conducting studies for the purpose of improving instruction. Organizations such as the Inter-University Consortium for Political and Social Research host data sets with a wide range of restrictions. Data sets that favor utility (but sacrifice maximal privacy) can be made available to other research teams that are governed by institutional review board protocols, while data sets that limit utility but maximize privacy can be shared with the general public. Of course, even groups that are inclined to make data available for research may be hesitant to do so due to the extra steps and expenses required to ensure an appropriate level of de-identification.

Analyzing Big Data

As with accessing big data, analyzing big data also poses challenges regarding researchers' skills. As noted above, few education researchers know key programming languages used for data science, such as Python. Education research graduate programs seldom offer instruction in the data-clustering, -modeling, and prediction techniques used to analyze big data.

Even for researchers with such skills, error rates and noise pose additional challenges. For example, although predictive models can provide systematic improvements in prediction quality on average over base rates, high error rates may indicate the occurrence of significant exogenous factors at play not captured even in large amounts of data. When such predictive results facilitate the decision making of instructors or institutional policymakers, these errors may harm students' short-term learning or long-term success. In addition, large data sets with large numbers of predictor variables may result in models that are quite complex and difficult to interpret and that may not necessarily help stakeholders more than simpler models. This suggests that predicting student outcomes at a macro, "long time scale" level is inherently difficult and relationships between predictors and "downstream outcomes" can be complex, with many different factors affecting student outcomes that may potentially not be measured.

One way to mitigate these challenges is to combine macrolevel data with micro- or mesolevel data. For instance, Aguiar et al. (2014) exemplified how nonmacro data can be useful in predicting student outcomes. The authors investigated different data sources for predicting student dropout of engineering courses at Notre Dame after their first term, treated as a binary classification problem. In terms of institutional (macro) data sources, the authors used predictor variables based on academic performance (i.e., SAT scores, first-term GPA) and demographics (i.e., gender, income group). Microlevel predictor variables included online student engagement during the first college term. The results were strikingly clear: Online engagement variables had significantly more predictive power than academic performance or demographic variables across a variety of classification models. Similarly, Miller et al. (2015) found that predictive models constructed to predict learning outcomes for students taking undergraduate computer science courses could benefit significantly from including online student interaction data. These studies indicated that the addition of predictors based on noninstitutional data (e,g., online engagement data) can provide significant additional predictive power beyond that of institutional data alone.

Using Big Data

Finally, even if we successfully access and analyze big data, additional issues arise related to how such data are used. As education researchers increasingly turn to data mining, they will have to confront the tension between explanation and prediction. Yarkoni and Westfall (2017) discuss this tension in detail in relationship to the field of psychology. They argue that psychology's focus on explaining the causes of behavior has led the field to be populated by research programs that provide intricate theories but have little ability to accurately predict future behaviors. They further suggest that increased focus on prediction using data mining and machine learning techniques can ultimately lead to a greater understanding of behavior.

We also believe that this is true in education research, as seen in the example of Connor's (2019) research on her Assessment2Instruction (A2i) professional support system for reading instruction. Literacy research has been marked by the so-called reading wars between advocates of code-focused (e.g., phonics) versus meaning-focused (e.g., comprehension) instruction. Though a consensus has emerged over time on the critical value of the former, how much it should be supplemented by the latter is a continued debate. Connor's team tackled this issue in a highly creative way, adding a less-talked-about but also important question: Are elementary students best served by individualized (child managed) or whole-class (teacher managed) instruction?

The research team collected vast amounts of data on how much time children spent in (a) code- versus meaning-focused and (b) child- versus teacher-managed reading instruction, as well as (c) children's progression in reading proficiency throughout the year. Data mining techniques were used to develop and refine models indicating what combinations of instruction work best for children at different levels of proficiency and at different points in the school year (Connor, 2019). These models were developed into a software recommender system (A2i) that would assist teachers with grouping students to receive the types of instruction best suited to their needs. Randomized controlled trials were used to compare reading achievement in classrooms using A2i with that in classrooms teaching reading without it, finding strong positive effects for the former. This project thus not only built a valuable predictive tool that can guide teachers and improve literacy outcomes but also added explanatory value as to the differential contributions of code- versus meaning-focused and child- versus teacher-managed instruction.

Finally, in using big data, it is critically important to examine and address potential issues of bias, particularly when algorithms associated with big data lead to predictions and/or policy. For example, much attention has been focused on the potential for racial bias in predictive algorithms used in policing (e.g., Brantingham et al., 2018). The European Union Agency for Fundamental Rights (2018) provides a well-justified set of recommendations for how to minimize bias in big data–derived algorithms. These include ensuring maximum transparency in the development of algorithms, conducting fundamental rights impact assessments to identify potential biases and abuses in the application of and output from algorithms, checking the quality of data collected and used, and ensuring that the development and operation of the algorithm can be meaningfully explained.

Recommendations

Meeting these challenges will require rethinking both how we develop education researchers and the kinds of research practices our research community favors. Curricula in graduate schools of education overwhelmingly favor research methods that fall within one of two major paradigms: quantitative measurement and hypothesis testing or interpretive qualitative research. Analyzing big data draws on an alternate research paradigm to those used in computational social sciences. Only a handful of doctoral programs in education offer the kinds of research training necessary to develop the educational data sciences of the future, and even fewer offer instruction related to the ethical, moral, and privacy dimensions of working with big data. Partnering with other programs across campus, from computer science, data science, or other fields, is a possibility, but in most universities, there is too little interdisciplinary training across these fields and education. In addition, both faculty and graduate students in computer science and data science are incentivized to focus their research on original contributions to important theoretical challenges and techniques in those fields, rather than on applications of data science in other areas, such as education.

To address this challenge, we need to create broader pipelines of talented data scientists focused on education research. This can be through curricular reform within education graduate programs and/or improved interdisciplinary training across the education and computer/data science fields. Federally funded doctoral and postdoctoral training programs in educational sciences would be one very valuable step in this direction.

Mining big data in education challenges not only how we prepare education researchers, but also what kinds of research practices we engage in. Traditional models of education research privilege the sole author, who gets extra rewards in the hiring, tenure, and promotion process; discourage collaboration between junior and senior scholars because such collaboration taints junior scholars as supposedly lacking independence; and favor hoarding of data, so that investigators reap all the rewards from the data without diminishing their value through sharing. In contrast, research projects that involve data mining typically privilege team science, with junior and senior scholars, and open science, so that large data sets can be combined and reused for new analyses and replication. Of course, there are many reasons to support open science even within the traditional quantitative and qualitative education research paradigms, but the value of adopting open science practices is even more pressing as we transition to conducting more educational data science.

The Sloan Equity and Inclusion in STEM Introductory Courses, launched by the University of Michigan, exemplifies the value of open science for new kinds of education research. Faculty at 10 large research universities connect through parallel and combined data analyses and continuous exchange of speakers and graduate student researchers to explore and improve instructional practices and outcomes in foundational STEM (science, technology, engineering, and mathematics) courses reaching hundreds of thousands of students. Open sharing of data and team science will be hallmarks of this important research initiative. Perhaps not surprisingly, the project was initiated by a professor of physics and astronomy, a discipline where large-scale open team science is much more common than in education.

CONCLUSION

The availability of big data offers exciting new threads of research and the opportunity to add additional perspective to existing threads in education. All types of big data in education offer affordances and challenges. The sheer amount of microlevel data make big data methods a powerful tool for analyzing learner processes, but that power can lead researchers to ignore broader and potentially more important patterns that cannot be measured at the microlevel. Mesolevel data provide a deep window into cognitive processes by examining individuals' writing, but they are prone to many of the broader challenges of using automated tools for writing measurement (e.g., Raczynski & Cohen, 2018). Macrolevel data can be valuable for taking the broadest look at student persistence and achievement, but the smaller size and coarse measurements of macrolevel data sets may make it difficult to identify the finergrained mechanisms at play (e.g., Scott-Clayton, 2015).

The limitations of each of these types of big data can be minimized, and the benefits amplified, if future research is triangulated either with the remaining types of big data or with more traditional forms of quantitative or qualitative analysis. Through recording, accessing, analyzing, and utilizing multiple types of data, we can better understand and respond to individual learner behavior as it manifests in the increasingly pervasive digital realm. Furthermore, the ubiquity of big data suggests an increased emphasis on preparing students in educational graduate programs to utilize data science methods as well as a committed push toward open science and research structures that favor collaborative teams, to improve our field's capacity for mining big data for education research. Given the potential benefits of mining big data in education, it is worth our effort to begin addressing these challenges.

ACKNOWLEDGMENTS

This work is supported by the National Science Foundation through the EHR Core Research Program, Award 1535300. The views contained in this article are those of the authors and not of their institutions or the National Science Foundation.

ORCID iDs

Christian Fischer 🆔 https://orcid.org/0000-0002-8809-2776
Zachary A. Pardos 🆔 https://orcid.org/0000-0002-6016-7051

REFERENCES

Aguiar, E., Chawla, N. V., Brockman, J., Ambrose, G. A., & Goodrich, V. (2014). Engagement vs performance: Using electronic portfolios to predict first semester engineering student retention. In *Proceedings of the Fourth International Conference on Learning Analytics and Knowledge* (pp. 103–112). Association for Computing Machinery. https://doi .org/10.1145/2567574.2567583

Aleven, V., Roll, I., McLaren, B. M., & Koedinger, K. R. (2016). Help helps, but only so much: Research on help seeking with intelligent tutoring systems. *International Journal of Artificial Intelligence in Education*, 26(1), 205–223. https://doi.org/10.1007/s40593-015-0089-1

Allen, L., Likens, A. D., & McNamara, D. S. (2018). A multi-dimensional analysis of writing flexibility in an automated writing evaluation system. In *Proceedings of the 8th International Conference on Learning Analytics and Knowledge* (pp. 380–388). Association for Computing Machinery. https://doi.org/10.1145/3170358.3170404

Allen, L., & McNamara, D. S. (2015). You are your words: Modeling students' vocabulary knowledge with natural language processing tools. In *Proceedings of the 8th International Conference on Educational Data Mining* (pp. 258–265), Madrid, Spain. https://pdfs .semanticscholar.org/3f55/697498e911f1a020ad3b75ba6982e16fe69b.pdf

Allen, L., Mills, C., Jacovina, M. E., Crossley, S., D'Mello, S., & McNamara, D. S. (2016). Investigating boredom and engagement during writing using multiple sources of information: The essay, the writer, and keystrokes. In *Proceedings of the Sixth International Conference on Learning Analytics and Knowledge* (pp. 114–123). Association for Computing Machinery. https://doi.org/10.1145/2883851.2883939

Atapattu, T., & Falkner, K. (2018). Impact of lecturer's discourse for student video interactions: Video learning analytics case study of MOOCs. *Journal of Learning Analytics*, 5(3), 182–197. https://doi.org/10.18608/jla.2018.53.12

Baker, R. S., & Siemens, G. (2014). Educational data mining and learning analytics. In R. K. Sawyer (Ed.), *Cambridge handbook of the learning sciences* (2nd ed., pp. 253–274). Cambridge University Press.

Baker, R., & Yacef, K. (2009). The state of educational data mining in 2009: A review and future visions. *Journal of Educational Data Mining*, 1(1), 3–17. https://doi.org/10.5281/ zenodo.3554657

Bauer, A., Flatten, J., & Popović, Z. (2017). Analysis of problem-solving behavior in open-ended scientific-discovery game challenges. In X. Hu, T. Barnes, A. Hershkovitz, & L. Paquette (Eds.), *Proceedings of the 10th International Conference on Educational Data Mining* (pp. 32–39), Wuhan, China. https://pdfs.semanticscholar.org/fa02/2ca5d9b1f53 64d5346ce0a6ee1cff0976840.pdf

Bergner, Y., Shu, Z., & von Davier, A. (2014). Visualization and confirmatory clustering of sequence data from a simulation-based assessment task. In *Proceedings of the 7th International Conference on Educational Data Mining* (pp.177–184). International Educational Data Mining Society. https://pdfs.semanticscholar.org/b0da/eb27f2982ced-8ab9fc6646edc33abad04742.pdf

Biswas, G., Segedy, J. R., & Bunchongchit, K. (2016). From design to implementation to practice a learning by teaching system: Betty's Brain. *International Journal of Artificial Intelligence in Education*, 26(1), 350–364. https://doi.org/10.1007/s40593-015-0057-9

Botelho, A. F., Baker, R. S., & Heffernan, N. T. (2017). Improving sensor-free affect detection using deep learning. In E. André, R. Baker, X. Hu, M. T. Rodrigo, & B. du Boulay (Eds.), *Artificial intelligence in education* (Vol. 10331, pp. 40–51). Springer. https://doi .org/10.1007/978-3-319-61425-0_4

Brantingham, P. J., Valasik, M., & Mohler, G. O. (2018). Does predictive policing lead to biased arrests? Results from a randomized controlled trial. *Statistics and Public Policy, 5*(1), 1–6. https://doi.org/10.1080/2330443X.2018.1438940

Chaturapruek, S., Dee, T. S., Johari, R., Kizilcec, R. F., & Stevens, M. L. (2018). How a data-driven course planning tool affects college students' GPA: Evidence from two field experiments. In *Proceedings of the Fifth Annual ACM Conference on Learning at Scale*. Association for Computing Machinery. https://doi.org/10.1145/3231644.3231668

Chen, Y., Johri, A., & Rangwala, H. (2018). Running out of STEM: A comparative study across STEM majors of college students at-risk of dropping out early. In *Proceedings of the 8th International Conference on Learning Analytics and Knowledge* (pp. 270–279). Association for Computing Machinery. https://doi.org/10.1145/3170358.3170410

Clement, B., Roy, D., Oudeyer, P.-Y., & Lopes, M. (2015). Multi-armed bandits for intelligent tutoring systems. *Journal of Educational Data Mining, 7*(2), 20–48. https://doi.org/10.5281/zenodo.3554667

Connor, C. M. (2019). Using technology and assessment to personalize instruction: Preventing reading problems. *Prevention Science, 20*(1), 89–99. https://doi.org/10.1007/s11121-017-0842-9

Cook, C., Olney, A. M., Kelly, S., & D'Mello, S. (2018). An open vocabulary approach for estimating teacher use of authentic questions in classroom discourse. In *Proceedings of the 11th International Conference on Educational Data Mining* (pp. 116–126), Raleigh, NC. International Educational Data Mining Society. https://pdfs.semanticscholar.org/1a75/8415f51474b9943faea5b506f98cadba1d15.pdf

Corbett, A. T., & Anderson, J. R. (1995). Knowledge tracing: Modeling the acquisition of procedural knowledge. *User Modelling and User-Adapted Interaction, 4*(4), 253–278. https://doi.org/10.1007/BF01099821

Crossley, S., Ocumpaugh, J., Labrum, M., Bradfield, F., Dascalu, M., & Baker, R. S. (2018). Modeling math identity and math success through sentiment analysis and linguistic features. In *Proceedings of the 11th International Conference on Educational Data Mining* (pp. 11–20), Raleigh, NC. International Educational Data Mining Society. https://pdfs.semanticscholar.org/6153/3632ce351c2b34486645dec7ea58d7186289.pdf

Crues, R. W., Bosch, N., Anderson, C. J., Perry, M., Bhat, S., & Shaik, N. (2018). Who they are and what they want: Understanding the reasons for MOOC enrollment. In *Proceedings of the 11th International Conference on Educational Data Mining* (pp. 177–186), Raleigh, NC. International Educational Data Mining Society. https://pdfs.semanticscholar.org/a794/99a5e1e87a7bdbdf70df2127d78f5cc0182d.pdf

Davis, D., Seaton, D., Hauff, C., & Houben, G.-J. (2018). Toward large-scale learning design: Categorizing course designs in service of supporting learning outcomes. In *Proceedings of the Fifth Annual ACM Conference on Learning at Scale* (pp. 1–10). Association for Computing Machinery. https://doi.org/10.1145/3231644.3231663

DeFalco, J. A., Rowe, J. P., Paquette, L., Georgoulas-Sherry, V., Brawner, K., Mott, B. W., Baker, R. S., & Lester, J. C. (2018). Detecting and addressing frustration in a serious game for military training. *International Journal of Artificial Intelligence in Education, 28*(2), 152–193. https://doi.org/10.1007/s40593-017-0152-1

Dzikovska, M., Steinhauser, N., Farrow, E., Moore, J., & Campbell, G. (2014). BEETLE II: Deep natural language understanding and automatic feedback generation for intelligent tutoring in basic electricity and electronics. *International Journal of Artificial Intelligence in Education, 24*(3), 284–332. https://doi.org/10.1007/s40593-014-0017-9

Epp, C. D., Phirangee, K., & Hewitt, J. (2017). Talk with me: Student behaviours and pronoun use as indicators of discourse health across facilitation methods. *Journal of Learning Analytics, 4*(3), 47–75. https://doi.org/10.18608/jla.2017.43.4

European Union Agency for Fundamental Rights. (2018). *#BigData: Discrimination in data-supported decision making.* https://doi.org/10.1163/2210-7975_HRD-9992-20180020

Falakmasir, M., Yudelson, M., Ritter, S., & Koedinger, K. (2015). Spectral Bayesian knowledge tracing. In *Proceedings of the 8th International Conference on Educational Data Mining.* International Educational Data Mining Society. https://pdfs.semanticscholar.org/0e15/52be96b2d2829c5c62288851b9b139e3e9b6.pdf

Fancsali, S. E., Yudelson, M. V., Berman, S. R., & Ritter, S. (2018). Intelligent instructional hand offs. In *Proceedings of the 11th International Conference on Educational Data Mining* (pp. 198–207), Raleigh, NC. International Educational Data Mining Society. https://pdfs.semanticscholar.org/9bf6/1bd5c6a3a7f65e52a4a8ec8928857b5a1af6.pdf

Fesler, L., Dee, T., Baker, R., & Evans, B. (2019). Text as data methods for education research. *Journal of Research on Educational Effectiveness, 12*(4), 707–727. https://doi.org/10.1080/19345747.2019.1634168

Galyardt, A., & Goldin, I. (2015). Move your lamp post: Recent data reflects learner knowledge better than older data. *Journal of Educational Data Mining, 7*(2), 83–108. https://doi.org/10.5281/zenodo.3554671

Gasevic, D., Jovanovic, J., Pardo, A., & Dawson, S. (2017). Detecting learning strategies with analytics: Links with self-reported measures and academic performance. *Journal of Learning Analytics, 4*(2), 113–128. https://doi.org/10.18608/jla.2017.42.10

Gelman, B. U., Beckley, C., Johri, A., Domeniconi, C., & Yang, S. (2016). Online urbanism: Interest-based subcultures as drivers of informal learning in an online community. In *Proceedings of the Third ACM Conference on Learning at Scale* (pp. 21–30). Association for Computing Machinery. https://doi.org/10.1145/2876034.2876052

Gobert, J. D., Sao Pedro, M. A., Baker, R. S. J. D., Toto, E., & Montalvo, O. (2012). Leveraging educational data mining for real-time performance assessment of scientific inquiry skills within microworlds. *Journal of Educational Data Mining, 4*(1), 111–143. https://doi.org/10.5281/zenodo.3554645

González-Brenes, J., Huang, Y., & Brusilovsky, P. (2014). General features in knowledge tracing to model multiple subskills, temporal item response theory, and expert knowledge. In *Proceedings of the 7th International Conference on Educational Data Mining* (pp. 84–91), University of Pittsburgh. International Educational Data Mining Society. https://pdfs.semanticscholar.org/0002/fab1c9f0904105312031cdc18dce358863a6.pdf

Gray, G., McGuinness, C., Owende, P., & Hofmann, M. (2016). Learning factor models of students at risk of failing in the early stage of tertiary education. *Journal of Learning Analytics, 3*(2), 330–372. https://doi.org/10.18608/jla.2016.32.20

Guo, P. J., & Reinecke, K. (2014). Demographic differences in how students navigate through MOOCs. In *Proceedings of the First ACM Conference on Learning at Scale Conference* (pp. 21–30). Association for Computing Machinery. https://doi.org/10.1145/2556325.2566247

Hapara. (2019). *Hapara Analytics.* https://hapara.com/analytics/

Harrak, F., Bouchet, F., Luengo, V., & Gillois, P. (2018). PHS profiling students from their questions in a blended learning environment. In *Proceedings of the 8th International Conference on Learning Analytics and Knowledge* (pp. 102–110). Association for Computing Machinery. https://doi.org/10.1145/3170358.3170389

Harrison, S., Villano, R., Lynch, G., & Chen, G. (2016). Measuring financial implications of an early alert system. In *Proceedings of the Sixth International Conference on Learning Analytics and Knowledge* (pp. 241–248). Association for Computing Machinery. https://doi.org/10.1145/2883851.2883923

Head, A., Glassman, E., Soares, G., Suzuki, R., Figueredo, L., D'Antoni, L., & Hartmann, B. (2017). Writing reusable code feedback at scale with mixed-initiative program synthesis.

In *Proceedings of the Fourth (2017) ACM Conference on Learning @ Scale—L@S '17* (pp. 89–98). https://doi.org/10.1145/3051457.3051467

Hecking, T., Chounta, I.-A., & Hoppe, H. U. (2016). Investigating social and semantic user roles in MOOC discussion forums. In *Proceedings of the Sixth International Conference on Learning Analytics and Knowledge* (pp. 198–207). Association for Computing Machinery. https://doi.org/10.1145/2883851.2883924

Hutt, S., Gardener, M., Kamentz, D., Duckworth, A. L., & D'Mello, S. K. (2018). Prospectively predicting 4-year college graduation from student applications. In *Proceedings of the 8th International Conference on Learning Analytics and Knowledge* (pp. 280–289). Association for Computing Machinery. https://doi.org/10.1145/3170358.3170395

Hutt, S., Grafsgaard, J. F., & D'Mello, S. K. (2019). Time to scale: Generalizable affect detection for tens of thousands of students across an entire school year. In *Proceedings of the 2019 CHI Conference on Human Factors in Computing Systems*. Association for Computing Machinery. https://doi.org/10.1145/3290605.3300726

Jayaprakash, S. M., Moody, E. W., Lauría, E. J. M., Regan, J. R., & Baron, J. D. (2014). Early alert of academically at-risk students: An open source analytics initiative. *Journal of Learning Analytics*, *1*(1), 6–47. https://doi.org/10.18608/jla.2014.11.3

Jiang, W., Pardos, Z. A., & Wei, Q. (2019). Goal-based course recommendation. In *Proceedings of the 9th International Conference on Learning Analytics and Knowledge* (pp. 36–45). Association for Computing Machinery. https://doi.org/10.1145/3303772.3303814

Joksimović, S., Kovanović, V., Jovanović, J., Zouaq, A., Gasevic, D., & Hatala, M. (2015). What do cMOOC participants talk about in social media? A topic analysis of discourse in a cMOOC. In *Proceedings of the Fifth International Conference on Learning Analytics and Knowledge* (pp. 156–165). Association for Computing Machinery. https://doi.org/10.1145/2723576.2723609

Käser, T., Klingler, S., & Gross, M. (2016). When to stop? Towards universal instructional policies. In *Proceedings of the Sixth International Conference on Learning Analytics and Knowledge* (pp. 289–298). Association for Computing Machinery. http://dx.doi.org/10.1145/2883851.2883961

Khajah, M., Lindsey, R. V., & Mozer, M. C. (2016). How deep is knowledge tracing? In *Proceedings of the 9th International Conference on Educational Data Mining* (pp. 94–101), Raleigh, NC. International Educational Data Mining Society. https://arxiv.org/pdf/1604.02416.pdf

Kizilcec, R. F., Piech, C., & Schneider, E. (2013). Deconstructing disengagement: Analyzing learner subpopulations in massive open online courses. In *Proceedings of the Third International Conference on Learning Analytics and Knowledge* (p. 170). Association for Computing Machinery. https://doi.org/10.1145/2460296.2460330

Koester, B. P., Fogel, J., Murdock, W., Grom, G., & McKay, T. A. (2017). Building a transcript of the future. In *Proceedings of the Seventh International Learning Analytics and Knowledge Conference* (pp. 299–308). Association for Computing Machinery. https://doi.org/10.1145/3027385.3027418

Lan, A. S., Vats, D., Waters, A. E., & Baraniuk, R. G. (2015). Mathematical language processing: Automatic grading and feedback for open response mathematical questions. In *Proceedings of the Second ACM Conference on Learning at Scale* (pp. 167–176). Association for Computing Machinery. https://doi.org/10.1145/2724660.2724664

Laney, D. (2001). 3D data management: Controlling data volume, velocity and variety. *META Group Research Note*, *6*(70), 1.

Le, C. V., Pardos, Z. A., Meyer, S. D., & Thorp, R. (2018). Communication at scale in a MOOC using predictive engagement analytics. In M. Mavrikis, K. Porayska-Pomsta, & R. Luckin (Eds.), *Proceedings of the 19th International Conference on Artificial Intelligence in Education* (pp. 239–252). Springer. https://doi.org/10.1007/978-3-319-93843-1_18

Liu, R., & Koedinger, K. R. (2015). Variations in learning rate: Student classification based on systematic residual error patterns across practice opportunities. In *Proceedings of the 8th International Conference on Educational Data Mining*. International Educational Data Mining Society. https://pdfs.semanticscholar.org/0b57/0c5a732552bb50d80eafe1122a3 ef52bad23.pdf

Liu, R., & Koedinger, K. R. (2017). Closing the loop: Automated data-driven cognitive model discoveries lead to improved instruction and learning gains. *Journal of Educational Data Mining*, *9*(1), 25–41. https://doi.org/10.5281/zenodo.3554625

Liu, Y. E., Mandel, T., Brunskill, E., & Popovic, Z. (2014). Trading off scientific knowledge and user learning with multi-armed bandits. In *Proceedings of the 7th International Conference on Educational Data Mining* (pp. 161–168). International Educational Data Mining Society. https://pdfs.semanticscholar.org/029a/3f34047890e2a399094c3755c0c 162aae664.pdf

Lu, Y., & Hsiao, I. H. (2016). Seeking programming-related information from large scaled discussion forums, help or harm? In *Proceedings of the 9th International Conference on Educational Data Mining*. International Educational Data Mining Society. https://pdfs .semanticscholar.org/dc76/33aae5a8a99c2abac1c927617187cfefa7eb.pdf

Mahzoon, M. J., Maher, M. L., Eltayeby, O., Dou, W., & Grace, K. (2018). A sequence data model for analysing temporal patterns of student data. *Journal of Learning Analytics*, *5*(1), 55–74. https://doi.org/10.18608/jla.2018.51.5

McNamara, D. S., & Graesser, A. C. (2012). Coh-Metrix: An automated tool for theoretical and applied natural language processing. In P. M. McCarthy & C. Boonthum-Denecke (Eds.), *Applied natural language processing and content analysis: Identification, investigation and resolution* (pp. 188–205). IGI Global.

Méndez, G., Ochoa, X., & Chiluiza, K. (2014). Techniques for data-driven curriculum analysis. In *Proceedings of the Fourth International Conference on Learning Analytics and Knowledge* (pp. 148–157). Association for Computing Machinery. https://doi.org/ 10.1145/2567574.2567591

Meltzer, E. (2019, May 29). *How are Colorado schools doing? Advocates say the state still holds back too much data*. https://chalkbeat.org/posts/co/2019/05/29/how-are-colorado-schools-doing-advocates-say-the-state-still-holds-back-too-much-data/

Miller, L. D., Soh, L.-K., Samal, A., Kupzyk, K., & Nugent, G. (2015). A comparison of educational statistics and data mining approaches to identify characteristics that impact online learning. *Journal of Educational Data Mining*, *7*(3), 117–150.

Moussavi, R., Gobert, J., & Sao Pedro, M. (2016). The effect of scaffolding on the immediate transfer of students' data interpretation skills within science topics. In *Proceedings of the 12th International Conference of the Learning Sciences* (pp. 1002–1005), Singapore. International Society of the Learning Sciences. https://doi.dx.org/10.22318/icls2016.157

National Academy of Education. (2017). *Big data in education: Balancing the benefits of educational research and student privacy: Workshop summary*.

Nelson, G. S. (2015). Practical implications of sharing data: A primer on data privacy, anonymization, and de-identification. In *Proceedings of the SAS® Global Forum 2015 Conference*. SAS Institute. https://support.sas.com/resources/papers/proceedings15/1884-2015.pdf

Ochoa, X., & Worsley, M. (2016). Augmenting learning analytics with multimodal sensory data. *Journal of Learning Analytics*, *3*(2), 213–219. https://doi.org/10.18608/ jla.2016.32.10

O'Connell, K., Wostl, E., Crosslin, M., Berry, T. L., & Grover, J. P. (2018). Student ability best predicts final grade in a college algebra course. *Journal of Learning Analytics*, *5*(3), 167–181. https://doi.org/10.18608/jla.2018.53.11

Ogan, A., Walker, E., Baker, R., Rodrigo, Ma. M. T., Soriano, J. C., & Castro, M. J. (2015). Towards understanding how to assess help-seeking behavior across cultures. *International*

Journal of Artificial Intelligence in Education, 25(2), 229–248. https://doi.org/10.1007/s40593-014-0034-8

Ostrow, K., Donnelly, C., Adjei, S., & Heffernan, N. (2015). Improving student modeling through partial credit and problem difficulty. In *Proceedings of the Second ACM Conference on Learning at Scale* (pp. 11–20). Association for Computing Machinery. https://doi.org/10.1145/2724660.2724667

Pardos, Z. A. (2017). Big data in education and the models that love them. *Current Opinion in Behavioral Sciences, 18*, 107–113. https://doi.org/10.1016/j.cobeha.2017.11.006

Pardos, Z. A, Baker, R. S. J. D., San Pedro, M., Gowda, S. M., & Gowda, S. M. (2014). Affective states and state tests: Investigating how affect and engagement during the school year predict end-of-year learning outcomes. *Journal of Learning Analytics, 1*(1), 107–128. https://doi.org/10.18608/jla.2014.11.6

Pardos, Z. A., Chau, H., & Zhao, H. (2019). Data-assistive course-to-course articulation using machine translation. In J. C. Mitchell & K. Porayska-Pomsta (Eds.), *Proceedings of the 6th ACM Conference on Learning at Scale*. Association for Computing Machinery. https://doi.org/10.1145/3330430.3333622

Pardos, Z. A., Fan, Z., & Jiang, W. (2019). Connectionist recommendation in the wild: On the utility and suitability of neural networks for personalized course guidance. *User Modeling and User-Adapted Interaction, 29*(2), 487–525. https://doi.org/10.1007/s11257-019-09218-7

Pardos, Z. A., Tang, S., Davis, D., & Le, C. V. (2017). Enabling real-time adaptivity in MOOCs with a personalized next-step recommendation framework. In C. Thille & J. Reich (Eds.), *Proceedings of the 4th ACM Conference on Learning at Scale* (pp. 23–32). Association for Computing Machinery. https://doi.org/10.1145/3051457.3051471

Parent Coalition for Student Privacy. (2019). *The state student privacy report card: Grading the states on protecting student data privacy.* https://www.studentprivacymatters.org/wp-content/uploads/2019/01/The-2019-State-Student-Privacy-Report-Card.pdf

Park, J., Denaro, K., Rodriguez, F., Smyth, P., & Warschauer, M. (2017). Detecting changes in student behavior from clickstream data. In *Proceedings of the Seventh International Conference on Learning Analytics and Knowledge* (pp. 21–30). Association for Computing Machinery. https://doi.org/10.1145/3027385.3027430

Park, J., Yu, R., Rodriguez, F., Baker, R., Smyth, P., & Warschauer, M. (2018). Understanding student procrastination via mixture models. In *Proceedings of the 11th International Conference on Educational Data Mining*. International Educational Data Mining Society. https://pdfs.semanticscholar.org/67a4/027404642fad7f9baf0c5d76dea14c99f563.pdf

Pavlik, P., Cen, H., & Koedinger, K. R. (2009). Performance factors analysis: A new alternative to knowledge tracing. In *Proceedings of the 2009 Conference on Artificial Intelligence in Education* (pp. 531–538). Association for Computing Machinery. https://dl.acm.org/doi/10.5555/1659450.1659529

Pennebaker, J. W., Boyd, R. L., Jordan, K., & Blackburn, K. (2015). *The development and psychometric properties of LIWC2015.* University of Texas-Austin.

Peralta, M., Alarcon, R., Pichara, K., Mery, T., Cano, F., & Bozo, J. (2018). Understanding learning resources metadata for primary and secondary education. *IEEE Transactions on Learning Technologies, 11*(4), 456–467. https://doi.org/10.1109/TLT.2017.2766222

Price, T. W., Dong, Y., & Barnes, T. (2016). Generating data-driven hints for open-ended programming. In *Proceedings of the 9th International Conference on Educational Data Mining* (pp. 191–198), Raleigh, NC. International Educational Data Mining Society. https://pdfs.semanticscholar.org/7800/c7981659f2fafbe1a6966ce43f7ca9460f48.pdf

Raczynski, K., & Cohen, A. (2018). Appraising the scoring performance of automated essay scoring systems—Some additional considerations: Which essays? Which human raters? Which scores? *Applied Measurement in Education, 31*(3), 233–240. https://doi.org/10.1080/08957347.2018.1464449

Rafferty, A. N., Ying, H., & Williams, J. J. (2018). Bandit assignment for educational experiments: Benefits to students versus statistical power. In C. Penstein Rosé, M. Mavrikis, R. Martínez-Maldonado, K. Porayska-Pomsta, H. U. Hoppe, B. McLaren, R. Luckin, & B. du Boulay (Eds.), *Artificial intelligence in education* (Vol. 10948, pp. 286–290). Association for Computing Machinery. https://doi.org/10.1007/978-3-319-93846-2_53

Reich, J., Tingley, D., Leder, J., Roberts, M. E., & Stewart, B. M. (2015). Computer-assisted reading and discovery for student-generated text in massive open online courses. *Journal of Learning Analytics, 2*(1), 156–184. https://doi.org/10.18608/jla.2015.21.8

Ren, Z., Ning, X., & Rangwala, H. (2017). Grade prediction with temporal course-wise influence. In *Proceedings of the 10th International Conference on Educational Data Mining* (pp. 48–55), Wuhan, China. International Educational Data Mining Society. https://arxiv.org/pdf/1709.05433.pdf

Right to Know. (2019). *Report card for education transparency and access.* http://rightoknowco.org/report-cards/

Roll, I., & Winne, P. H. (2015). Understanding, evaluating, and supporting self-regulated learning using learning analytics. *Journal of Learning Analytics, 2*(1), 7–12. https://doi.org/10.18608/jla.2015.21.2

Sabourin, J., Mott, B., & Lester, J. (2011). Modeling learner affect with theoretically grounded dynamic Bayesian networks. In S. D'Mello (Ed.), *Proceedings of the Fourth International Conference on Affective Computing and Intelligent Interaction* (pp. 286–295). Springer.

Sao Pedro, M., Jiang, Y., Paquette, L., & Baker, R. S. (2014). Identifying transfer of inquiry skills across physical science simulations using educational data mining. In *Proceedings of the 11th International Conference of the Learning Sciences* (pp. 222–229), Boulder, CO. International Society of the Learning Sciences. https://pdfs.semanticscholar.org/0ca7/cfc8e4575225162dd02c9ff64372158b030b.pdf

Scheihing, E., Vernier, M., Guerra, J., Born, J., & Carcamo, L. (2018). Understanding the role of micro-blogging in B-learning activities: Kelluwen experiences in Chilean public schools. *IEEE Transactions on Learning Technologies, 11*(3), 280–293. https://doi.org/10.1109/TLT.2017.2714163

Schimke, A. (2019, September 10). *How are Colorado's kindergarteners doing? With hidden data, it's hard to tell.* https://chalkbeat.org/posts/co/2019/09/10/how-are-colorados-kindergarteners-doing-with-hidden-data-its-hard-to-tell/

Scott-Clayton, J. (2015). The shapeless river: Does a lack of structure inhibit students' progress at community colleges? In B. L. Castleman, S. Baum, & S. Schwartz (Eds.), *Decision making for student success* (pp. 114–135). Routledge.

Segedy, J. R., Kinnebrew, J. S., & Biswas, G. (2015). Using coherence analysis to characterize self-regulated learning behaviours in open-ended learning environments. *Journal of Learning Analytics, 2*(1), 13–48. https://doi.org/10.18608/jla.2015.21.3

Sekiya, T., Matsuda, Y., & Yamaguchi, K. (2015). Curriculum analysis of CS departments based on CS2013 by simplified, supervised LDA. In *Proceedings of the Fifth International Conference on Learning Analytics and Knowledge* (pp. 330–339). Association for Computing Machinery. https://doi.org/10.1145/2723576.2723594

Shen, S., & Chi, M. (2016). Aim low: Correlation-based feature selection for model-based reinforcement learning. In *Proceedings of the 9th International Conference on Educational Data Mining* (pp. 507–512), Raleigh, NC. International Educational Data Mining Society. https://pdfs.semanticscholar.org/0acc/f1cf5015eb7cb7059b1b977991c1a9249e1a.pdf

Slater, S., Baker, R., Ocumpaugh, J., Inventado, P., Scupelli, P., & Heffernan, N. (2016). Semantic features of math problems: Relationships to student learning and engagement. In *Proceedings of the 9th International Conference on Educational Data Mining* (pp. 223–230), Raleigh, NC. International Educational Data Mining Society. https://pdfs.semanticscholar.org/df3e/9da476337def1021b12e03ab9959f9fd43d7.pdf

Strauss, V. (2019, September 11). Is New York State about to gut its student data privacy law? *Washington Post.* Retrieved from https://washingtonpost.com/education/2019/09/11/is-new-york-state-about-gut-its-student-data-privacy-law/

Sweeney, M., Lester, J., Rangwala, H., & Johri, A. (2016). Next-term student performance prediction: A recommender systems approach. *Journal of Educational Data Mining, 8*(1), 22–51. https://doi.org/10.5281/zenodo.3554603

Tóth, K., Rölke, H., Greiff, S., & Wüstenberg, S. (2014). Discovering students' complex problem solving strategies in educational assessment. In *Proceedings of the 7th International Conference on Educational Data Mining*, London, UK. https://pdfs.semanticscholar.org/1baf/8106de777bd369cbc7eb4e1d8c6689aed420.pdf

Wang, D., Olson, J. S., Zhang, J., Nguyen, T., & Olson, G. M. (2015). DocuViz: Visualizing collaborative writing. In *Proceedings of the 33rd Annual ACM Conference on Human Factors in Computing Systems* (pp. 1865–1874). Association for Computing Machinery. https://doi.org/10.1145/2702123.2702517

Wang, X., Yang, D., Wen, M., Koedinger, K., & Rosé, C. P. (2015). Investigating how student's cognitive behavior in MOOC discussion forums affect learning gains. In *Proceedings of the 8th International Conference on Educational Data Mining*. International Educational Data Mining Society. https://pdfs.semanticscholar.org/21af/f1b2e4f-fe5fbf86f3c4648315474ce271f1e.pdf

Wang, Z., Lan, A. S., Nie, W., Waters, A. E., Grimaldi, P. J., & Baraniuk, R. G. (2018). QG-net: A data-driven question generation model for educational content. In *Proceedings of the Fifth Annual ACM Conference on Learning at Scale* (pp. 1–10). Association for Computing Machinery. https://doi.org/10.1145/3231644.3231654

Ward, J. S., & Barker, A. (2013). *Undefined by data: A survey of big data definitions.* https://arxiv.org/pdf/1309.5821.pdf

Wen, M., Yang, D., & Rosé, C. P. (2014). Sentiment analysis in MOOC discussion forums: What does it tell us? In *Proceedings of the 7th International Conference on Educational Data Mining* (pp. 130–137), London, England. International Educational Data Mining Society. https://pdfs.semanticscholar.org/3190/0b62fabf7da87573e93e473dd72cc68f24fa.pdf

Whitehill, J., Williams, J. J., Lopez, G., Coleman, C. A., & Reich, J. (2015). Beyond prediction: First steps toward automatic intervention in MOOC student stopout. In *Proceedings of the 8th International Conference on Educational Data Mining*, Madrid, Spain. International Educational Data Mining Society. http://dx.doi.org/10.2139/ssrn.2611750

Yang, H., & Meinel, C. (2014). Content based lecture video retrieval using speech and video text information. *IEEE Transactions on Learning Technologies, 7*(2), 142–154. https://doi.org/10.1109/TLT.2014.2307305

Yarkoni, T., & Westfall, J. (2017). Choosing prediction over explanation in psychology: Lessons from machine learning. *Perspectives on Psychological Science, 12*(6), 1100–1122. https://doi.org/10.1177/1745691617693393

Yeung, C.-K., & Yeung, D.-Y. (2018). Addressing two problems in deep knowledge tracing via prediction-consistent regularization. In *Proceedings of the Fifth Annual ACM Conference on Learning at Scale* (pp. 1–10). Association for Computing Machinery. https://doi.org/10.1145/3231644.3231647

Zhang, L., & Rangwala, H. (2018). Early identification of at-risk students using iterative logistic regression. In C. Penstein Rosé, M. Mavrikis, R. Martínez-Maldonado, K. Porayska-Pomsta, H. U. Hoppe, B. McLaren, R. Luckin, & B. du Boulay (Eds.), *Artificial intelligence in education* (Vol. 10947, pp. 613–626). Association for Computing Machinery.

Chapter 6

Studying the Over-Time Construction of Knowledge in Educational Settings: A Microethnographic Discourse Analysis Approach

JUDITH L. GREEN
University of California, Santa Barbara

W. DOUGLAS BAKER
Eastern Michigan University

MONALIZA MAXIMO CHIAN
University of Hong Kong

CARMEN VANDERHOOF
LEEANNA HOOPER
GREGORY J. KELLY
Pennsylvania State University

AUDRA SKUKAUSKAITE
University of Central Florida

MELINDA Z. KALAINOFF
United States Military Academy

This review presents theoretical underpinnings supporting microethnographic-discourse analytic (ME/DA) approaches to studying educational phenomena. The review is presented in two parts. Part 1 provides an analytic review of two seminal reviews of literature that frame theoretical and methodological developments of microethnography and functions language in classrooms with diverse learners. Part 2 presents two telling case studies that illustrate the logic-of-inquiry of (ME/DA) approaches. These telling case studies make transparent how theoretical considerations of cultural perspectives on education inform decisions regarding research methodology. Telling Case Study 1 makes transparent the logic-of-inquiry undertaken to illustrate how microanalyses of discourse and action among participants in a physics class provided an empirical grounding for identifying how different

Review of Research in Education
March 2020, Vol. 44, pp. 161–194
DOI: 10.3102/0091732X20903121
Chapter reuse guidelines: sagepub.com/journals-permissions
© 2020 AERA. http://rre.aera.net

groups undertook a common task. This case study shows how ethnographically informed discourse analyses formed a foundation to theoretically identify social processes of knowledge construction. Telling Case Study 2 makes transparent multiple levels of analysis undertaken to examine ways that creative processes of interpretation of art were communicated and taken up in an art studio class across multiple cycles of activity. Taken together, these telling case studies provide evidence of how ME/DA provides a theoretically grounded logic-of-inquiry for investigating complex learning processes in different educational contexts.

In the past six decades, researchers within and across disciplines have sought to develop theoretically grounded approaches to investigate and theorize the complex and developing social, communicative, and academic experiences of learners as they engage in local and situated *cycles of activity*, in and across times, events, and configurations of participants in formal and informal educational contexts. Many of these developing lines of research have sought to provide ways of responding to the calls of *Review of Research Education* (*RRE*) editors to *reconsider long-accepted findings, the nature of data and analysis, and existing theoretical frameworks and paradigms.* Today, as evidenced by this call, the process is ongoing.

The challenges facing researchers seeking to address this call were captured by a set of international dialogues over the past two decades. For example, Candela et al. (2004) report on dialogues over 3 days among 35 international scholars, guided by a range of theoretical perspectives and methodological processes, who were asked to address the following: *What in the world happens in classrooms from qualitative research perspectives?* Each participant brought a history of ongoing research focusing on classroom processes and practices that shape socially, culturally, linguistically, and academically diverse students' opportunities for learning in classrooms in different national contexts.

Given this diversity of perspectives and methodologies, Candela et al. (2004) urged the participants to explore potential common understandings of learning in classrooms and the possibility of interconnecting their lines of research. This request led to a series of unanticipated challenges:

We faced the initial difficulty of defining what "classrooms" are, have been, or will become. This led to a discussion of the various links between classrooms and their social contexts, which posed the problem of working on various spatial and temporal scales. The topic of learning was a constant preoccupation, as we considered that researchers still lack tools to connect specific teaching practices with student outcomes over time, and simultaneously to account for learning in other, non-classroom spaces. (p. 692)

They further framed an analytic problem of methodological actions in past research in the following way:

There was agreement that studies focused on the "play-script transcript" version of fragments of teacher-student interactions do not exhaust the complex nature of classroom activities and processes, as has already been shown in a variety of studies. Focusing on classrooms, while also reconstructing within them the influence of processes from the surrounding world, became one of the challenges of a new research agenda. (p. 693)[1]

These challenges also pointed to the need for transparency in presenting the logics of inquiry guiding the lines of research.

In 2006, after a 2-year development process that included a taskforce and public debates, the American Educational Research Association (AERA) recognized the need for transparency in reporting the *logic of inquiry* guiding a research process by publishing the "Standards for Reporting Empirical Social Science Research in AERA Publications."[2] These standards framed a research logic of inquiry as follows:

> Reports of empirical research should be transparent; that is, reporting should make explicit the logic of inquiry and activities that led from the development of the initial interest, topic, problem, or research question; through the definition, collection, and analysis of data or empirical evidence; to the articulated outcomes of the study. . . . These standards are therefore intended to promote empirical research reporting that is warranted and transparent. (p. 33)[3]

The arguments framed in this introduction provide a foundation for our approach to presenting the microethnographic discourse analytic logic of inquiry that has guided studies in classrooms at different levels of schooling as well as in different disciplines and (inter)national contexts. In this chapter, we will make transparent the theoretical, epistemological, methodological, analytical, and reporting processes and practices that guide the logic of inquiry of ME/DA as an epistemology (cf. Kelly, 2006).

GOALS FOR PRESENTING ME/DA AS AN EMERGENT LOGIC OF INQUIRY

Our goals for presenting this microethnographic discourse approach are two-fold, given that microethnographic discourse analysis (ME/DA) is an interdisciplinary logic of inquiry that has developed over the past four decades through the contributions of a growing range of international and interdisciplinary researchers and educators.[4] Our first goal is to present an analytic review of two seminal reviews of literature published in the first decade of *RRE*, which frame theoretical and methodological developments in microethnography (Smith, 1978) and the functions of language in classrooms with diverse learners (Guthrie & Hall, 1983).

Through this process, we identify how ME/DA is situated in these historical and developing lines of research. Additionally, we will make transparent to readers new to these lines of inquiry, as well as to experienced researchers, what has been learned about ethnographic and discourse lines of research from these two historical reviews.

Our goal in taking this approach is to make transparent a process that ME/DA researchers have undertaken: an "*if . . . then . . .* " logic. This epistemological process, as we will demonstrate, supports an exploration of the relationships among theories, epistemologies, and methodologies that frame particular actions central to constructing warranted accounts of learning as a communicative (discourse) and social process in classrooms (Heap, 1985, 1991, 1995).

By engaging in an *if–then* logic of analysis, as we analyzed the conceptual processes and theories inscribed by Smith (1978) and Guthrie and Hall (1983), we identified theoretical and methodological arguments to explore how they relate to, and inform, the developing microethnographic discourse analytic logic of inquiry presented in this chapter. We asked ourselves the following interrelated set of questions. *If* we take this theoretical perspective or methodological process, *then* what are the conceptual perspectives we need to consider in our own research? What actions in the conduct of our research does this entail? How do these theoretical and methodological processes identified relate (or not) to those guiding the developing the microethnographic discourse analytic logic of inquiry? And finally, how do they inform the conduct of ME/DA research in different disciplinary and social contexts in and out of schools?

The *if–then* approach also demonstrates a conceptual stance central to ME/DA research, whether in situ, in constructing data sets from archived records, or in reading the published work of others (Green et al., 2015; Skukauskaite & Grace, 2006). This stance is framed by Heath (1982) as *stepping back from ethnocentrism*—that is, *stepping back from the known* to learn from others' perspectives, a stance that guides an anthropological approach to ethnography, and thus to ME/DA (see also Green & Castanheira, 2019; Green et al., 2012; Heath & Street, 2008).

Our second goal is to present two *telling case studies* (Mitchell, 1984) of how a microethnographic discourse analytic logic of analysis was undertaken by two researchers (Kelly and Baker, contributing authors to this intergenerational author team). Through the (re)presentation and (re)examination of the decisions and actions that Kelly (Kelly et al., 2001) and Baker (2001; Baker & Green, 2007) undertook in their microethnographic discourse analytic studies in two different, discipline-based secondary Advanced Placement classrooms (Physics and Visual Arts), we demonstrate how the microethnographic discourse analytic logic of inquiry informed an *iterative, recursive, and abductive process of analyses of opportunities for learning* afforded to and being constructed by members of these two classes.

Our adoption of the telling case studies[5] is grounded in the theoretical developments in social and linguistic anthropology that have informed members of the ME/DA research community in the past four decades.[6] Underlying the adoption of telling case studies is the following argument by Mitchell (1984), who defined anthropological case studies as

the detailed presentation of ethnographic data related to some sequence of events from which the analyst seeks to make some theoretical inference. The events themselves may relate to any level of social organization: a whole society, some section of a community, a family or an individual. (p. 238)

In this argument, what becomes evident is that the goal of *telling case studies*, from an anthropological perspective, is the construction of theoretical understandings of how actors in particular social contexts draw on and/or make present to others local and situated processes and practices as they engage in particular events in and across times with particular configurations of participants.

By tracing the actions of particular actors and analyzing the sequence of events through particular theoretical lenses, the anthropologically guided ethnographer seeks to develop valid connections among actions, objects, actors, and activities to construct theoretical understandings of what is being interactionally, socially, discursively, and situationally accomplished by participants. The process that the ethnographer engages in, therefore, is one of *analytic induction* (not deduction, or a priori defined phenomena); that is, by undertaking a set of analytic processes, the ethnographer seeks to make theoretically valid (i.e., grounded) connections between and among the phenomena analyzed (Corsaro & Heise, 1990).

This definition of case studies, as *telling cases of analytic induction*, therefore frames the goals of ME/DA researchers as well as how they *bound units of analysis* and *make theoretically valid connections* between and among phenomena of classroom life that are the focus of such research (Green et al., 2012; Heath & Street, 2008). This conceptual process, as we will demonstrate through these two telling case studies by Kelly and Baker, supports analysis of what constitutes a process of *analytic induction* of what is being constructed in the moment-by-moment and over-time discourse and the interactions of students with their teacher in purposefully designed cycles of activity at different levels of scale.[7]

In taking a telling case approach, we also seek to address one additional set of challenges identified through international conversations that this chapter addresses. In ongoing dialogues undertaken over 10 years, Kumpulainen et al. (2009) and researchers from AERA and EARLI (European Association of Research on Learning and Instruction) identified the following challenge facing researchers seeking to undertake new and developing research studies in classrooms:

> What has become clear among the research community is that although great accomplishments have been achieved in research on social interaction in learning and instruction, we still lack a coherent understanding of how methodologies illuminate learning and education as a social process and also how these conceptual tools "work" in empirical studies . . . [and that] there is a need for opportunities to discuss and demonstrate how these methodologies are used, how they become alive in the actual research studies of classroom interaction. (p. 1)

Through the telling case studies approach, we will make transparent how the exploration of what was happening in the two Advanced Placement classes (not classrooms) required an iterative, recursive, and abductive logic of analyses guided by a microethnographic discourse analytic logic of inquiry.

The first telling case study (re)constructs the logic of analysis that Kelly developed (i.e., a microethnographic discourse analytic logic in use) to examine how students in four self-selected groups interpreted and undertook a guided physics assignment in a high school Advanced Placement Physics Lab (Kelly et al., 2001). The second telling case study (re)constructs Baker's analyses of how students in an intergenerational (Grades 9–12) Advanced Placement Studio Arts class, with students who had participated from 1 to 4 years (Baker, 2001; Baker & Green, 2007), engaged in learning studio art processes and practices.

These telling case studies also make transparent how the analytic logic constructed by these researchers supported their investigations of how and in what ways particular learning processes, practices, and conceptual knowledge were introduced to, and constructed with, students in these classes. By holding the level of schooling (secondary education) constant and varying the academic area of study (Physics and Visual Arts), we seek to make transparent how ME/DA, as a logic of inquiry, can be undertaken to examine social, epistemological, and communicative processes, practices, and conceptual systems in different educational contexts (Kelly, 2016a, 2016b).

ANALYSIS OF FOUNDATIONAL REVIEWS OF THE ROOTS OF MICROETHNOGRAPHY AND FUNCTIONS OF LANGUAGE IN *RRE*: 1973 TO 1983

In this section, guided by the arguments about transparency in reporting perspectives presented above, we trace the roots of the core principles guiding microethnographic and discourse lines of research that were introduced by Smith (1978) and Guthrie and Hall (1983) in the first decade of *RRE* (1973–1983). These historical reviews provide a foundation for understanding the roots of, and thus situating, ME/DA in the theoretical and methodological development of studies of the social construction of learning in classroom contexts.[8]

To step back from our current understanding of the lines of research known as ME/DA, we posed the following questions of Smith (1978) and Guthrie and Hall (1983):

- How and in what ways did the author(s) bound the review?
- What actions and conceptual perspectives were inscribed in the research identified?
- What issues were raised through the review process to inform readers about challenges and issues to consider in engaging in a particular research logic of inquiry?
- What directions for future research were identified?

Through this analytic process, we also investigated the challenges or methodological concerns raised by these authors, which we then triangulated (Denzin, 1978; Green & Chian, 2018) with actions, theories, and processes of the microethnographic discourse analytic logic of inquiry.

Smith (1978) and the Roots of Ethnography/Microethnography in Education

In his chapter titled "An Evolving Logic of Participant Observation, Educational Ethnography, and Other Case Studies," Smith (1978) frames his goals as follows:

To provide a context and logic for the discussion of the genre of research that is becoming known by such varied labels as educational ethnography, participant observation, qualitative observation, case study, or field study. (p. 316)

We identified a challenge facing researchers in this early period that converges with the challenges presented in the introduction to this chapter. Smith (1978) argued that although there was an emerging body of research across different traditions, there was limited understanding of the processes involved in the *evolving logic of participant observation* and other ethnographic processes or phases of research.

Therefore, in this section, we focus on the roots of the theoretical and conceptual processes that Smith identified as central to engaging in ethnographic research by 1978. The researchers identified were guided by different conceptual traditions[9] grounded in anthropological and sociological perspectives on ethnography. They included educational ethnographers as well as scholars in other social science disciplines. The lines of research in education identified by Smith focused on different dimensions of education as a social phenomenon: schools and communities (e.g., Spindler, 1963; Wolcott, 1967), school and interorganizational educational systems (e.g., Lutz, 1962; Smith, 1977), schools (Rist, 1973), classrooms (Cazden et al., 1972; Delamont, 1976; Rist, 1973; Smith & Geoffrey, 1968), and curriculum and program evaluation (e.g., Smith & Carpenter, 1972), among others.

Smith (1978) further argued that although these studies constituted a growing body of work, there was a parallel body of work focusing on what was entailed in engaging in participant observation. The processes identified at the time (1978 and earlier) were based on reflexive processes, represented by what he framed as the researcher's "creative processes in learning from a fieldwork project" (p. 329). This state of affairs, he argued, required further exploration to make transparent what constituted this social science approach as a methodology. To support this argument, Smith identified phases of ethnographic studies that he and others had experienced:

- Identifying the origins of the problem
- Identifying major seminal bodies of work that frame methodological processes and issues
- Developing awareness of competing theories
- Identifying the multiple phases required in designing and engaging in a study
- Developing guiding models and theories
- Constructing ways of recording the researcher's thinking, decision making, and interpretive asides during phases
- Engaging in conscious searching of records to construct data and literature to inform analyses as well as interpretation of records and analyses

Smith also introduced what he termed as "new ethnographies," which shifted the focus from a more holistic study of a group or community to analyses of audio and video tapes of classroom events, a direction that he framed as *microethnography*.

This argument foreshadowed Mitchell's (1984) arguments about multiple ethnographic studies that focus on different levels and participants in societies. Smith's chapter also foreshadowed Agar's (1994, 2006a) argument of ethnography as an iterative, recursive, and abductive process, in which decisions are made throughout an ethnographic study. This process, Agar (2006a) argues, requires the ethnographer to *step back* and begin to trace the pathways leading to, and roots of, the processes being experienced by the ethnographer (and participants) to develop a grounded understanding from the *point of view of participants*—that is, the *perspectives*, not perceptions, of insiders (participants in the event).

As a part of his presentation of processes and practices in the conduct of ethnographic inquiry, Smith (1978) identified ways of framing decisions in phases of analyses and writing. The following sets of decisions and actions also frame a process of transparency in reporting on the conceptual decisions guiding the researcher's logic of inquiry that we drew on in the two telling case studies that follow:

- Make transparent how "the case" is an instance of a class of events.
- Present an initial overview of the process of analysis.
- Describe the process of concept formation.
- Describe how outliers (to a set/class of events) were addressed.
- Present a discussion of ways of clustering the multiple dimensions identified in participant observation and analyses.
- Describe the data level(s) that raise issues of access.

As indicated in these actions, a key issue Smith identified was the need to define *what constitutes a case* within a class of events—that is, what the case is a *case of* (e.g., a color, an action, a place for particular actions) and what will be included as an instance of a particular phenomenon.[10] He indicated that the ethnographer needs to consider outliers that are beyond the set of cultural processes in a particular class of phenomena (a set of cases) and what issues outliers raise for reporting on the different classes (sets)—that is, *what is included* and *what is not*, and *what questions* outliers raise about the claims being made.

Smith (1978) also included *concept formation as a process* and thus framed a conceptual argument that an ethnographic approach does not start with, or is limited to, what is observed and analyzed in predefined (a priori) ways based on prior research. Rather, this process involves a principled approach to *clustering* the multiple dimensions that were identified through an in-time and over-time analysis of such phenomena. This process Smith further describes as involving *multiple levels of data construction at different levels of analytic time and social scale*. Through different forms and levels of analyses, Smith argues, ethnographers construct *classes* (i.e., sets of phenomena) and develop ways of clustering them to build warranted accounts of the phenomena and processes being studied.

In examining the *issues and directions* Smith inscribed, our authorial team identified the importance of making transparent what counts as access to particular educational sites and how access is (re)negotiated with particular actors at particular levels of an organization. Smith argued that if there are limits to access, then the data presented are suspect. His review also led him to conclude that there is minimal overlap in reference citations across research traditions focusing on observation in classrooms as well as language related to school performance, a point also made more than two decades later by Candela et al. (2004) and Kumpulainen et al. (2009).

Readers of Smith's chapter, therefore, are afforded a unique opportunity to develop a deep history of ethnographic inquiry in education and other disciplines, which makes visible differences among ethnography *of* education, undertaken by researchers in other disciplines; ethnography *in* education, undertaken by education researchers to address areas relevant to educators; and ethnography *for* education, designed to support transformation in education to address issues of equity of access for diverse learners (cf. Bloome et al., 2018; Dixon et al., 2000; Green & Bloome, 1997).

Guthrie and Hall (1983) on the Functions of Language in Classrooms

We selected Guthrie and Hall (1983) for two reasons. First it provides a four-decade review (1950–1983) that parallels the history of ethnographic research by Smith (1978). Like Smith, Guthrie and Hall (1983) examined developing theoretical and methodological directions central to studies on how language functions to support and/or constrain learning in classrooms with linguistically, culturally, socially, and academically diverse students. Second, they complement and expand Green's (1983) *RRE* review of 10 National Institute of Education–funded studies of how language use in classrooms and other education settings was supported and/or constrained by actions of teachers with students as well as how students learned academic and social processes in classrooms (Cazden, 1986, 1988, 2017; Cazden et al., 1972; Gage, 1974). The lines of research Guthrie and Hall (1983) inscribe in their review are central to understanding the microethnographic studies of the 1960s to 1980s and the microethnographic discourse analytic logic of inquiry underlying Kelly's and Baker's telling case studies, which follow this section. They also link this developing line of research to the perspectives on ethnographic research identified in Smith (1978), as (re)presented in the following:

One approach to the study of children's language use in and out of classrooms has been known variously as microethnography (Erickson & Shultz, 1977, 1981), constitutive ethnography (Mehan, 1979), or ethnographic monitoring (Hymes, 1981). There are other types of research labeled microethnography, notably the method devised and employed by Smith & Geoffrey (1968), and Rist (1973). However, here we are concerned with the system of microethnography incorporating a sociolinguistic perspective and focus. (p. 64)

In Table 1, we present a detailed description of the key concepts and processes that Guthrie and Hall (1983) identified at the intersection of microethnography and sociolinguistics, concepts central to the telling case studies by Kelly and Baker presented in the next section of this chapter.

As indicated in Table 1, the concepts presented frame how social interaction, as a multidimensional phenomenon, like language (cf. Halliday, 1973), can be characterized as a set of options (Gumperz, 1972, 1977). From their perspective on interaction, Guthrie and Hall (1983) frame the following:

In the mutual construction of their discourse, actors select what they want to say next (semantic options), how to say it (social options), and the form it will take (linguistic options). They even exercise options about

TABLE 1

Analytic Constructs Derived From Guthrie and Hall (1983)

Phenomena to explore to understand how language functions in classrooms
- Examining the effects of situation and context on human speech performance in different contexts of use
- Examining situation constraints on language use and how they influence the performance of children
- Identifying ways to assess the abilities of the child/student more fairly
- Identifying and delineating the social factors contributing to variability in speech and school performance
- Exploring the conditions in which the formality of a situation influences observed performance
- Identifying the social context of a situation
- Identify the social context of interactions
- Identifying whether the situation represents rather stable patterns constructed across times, events, and configurations of participants
- Social context may be thought of as the immediate environment of interactions or as a more dynamic level of situation

Conceptual perspectives that guide research from a microethnographic perspective
- Participant structures are patterned or expected ways in which interactions are arranged and undertaken in
  - whole-group patterns of instruction
  - small-group patterns of instruction, or seat work
  - individual interactions with material resources constructed in and/or brought to the classroom
- Participation structures develop in particular local and situated contexts and will differ in terms of ways of speaking, getting to speak, getting turns at talk, who can speak, and so on
- Constructs defining interactions in the classroom may differ in terms of
  - whether context is, or is not, conceptualized as created by the ways in which people organize their interactions
  - how interactions and/or discourse is transcribed, analyzed, and interpreted and (re)presented in writing
  - how people are viewed as contexts for one another, or not
  - how the conceptual framework guiding the research examines everything people say and do in the course of an interaction to identify the ways in which they signal changes in context
- Contextualization cues that support meaning construction include
  - paralinguistics (pitch, stress, intonation, pause, juncture)
  - nonverbal actions, proxemics, kinesics, gesture, eye gaze, and spatial orientations
  - references to present, past, and future processes, events, and actions/interactions, and so on
  - visual dimensions, including multimodal resources used by, referenced, and constructed in the interactions
- Social interaction is a multidimensional process and subject to constraints on several levels (social, cultural, and situational)

what to attend to, how to interpret their environment, and how to define what is going on. At the basis of these choices is a series of factors that can act as constraints. At the most general level, these include social and cultural facts such as social status and cultural norms. At the most-narrow level are facts that are within the interaction itself, such as prosodic and phonological variations. (p. 59)

They further argue that constraints also operate at the local level and that these constraints (e.g., norms and/or rules for participation) are always in context. These levels of constraint do not act in isolation; rather, they are interdependent and mutually interacting and are experienced in terms of situation, social context, and task. Moreover, "the influence of any constraint depends on the actor's consciousness, which lies at the center of all social interaction" (p. 61).

If we extend the conceptual arguments about language and interaction (re)presented in Table 1, *then* it becomes important to consider what influences how students will interpret what is being proposed to them in and through the interactions, as well as how they interpret what is required to participate (Bloome & Egan-Robertson, 1993; Bloome et al., 2005; Green & Wallat, 1981b; Gumperz, 1981; Lin, 1993). Thus, in Table 1, we (re)present core constructs that are central to understanding why Guthrie and Hall (1983) frame the following *limits to research*, focusing on particular moments in classrooms: "The complexities of human interaction are so great that one cannot, with confidence, point to independent variables within a particular situation as having caused any observed differences" (p. 63).

In their chapter, therefore, Guthrie and Hall (1983) provide a rich review of conceptual arguments about how different researchers have theorized language, interaction, contexts, social processes, consciousness, and personal interpretations, among other human processes that influence what can be made available to and interpreted by (or not) students in and across times, events, cycles of activity, and configurations of different actors. The challenges that Guthrie and Hall raise converge with those framed by the education researchers presented previously and lay a foundation for understanding the decisions and actions that guided Kelly and Baker in the (re)examination and (re)presentations of their telling case studies, as demonstrated in the next section.

TELLING CASE STUDIES: MAKING TRANSPARENT MICROETHNOGRAPHIC DISCOURSE ANALYTIC LOGICS IN USE

As the telling case studies presented in this section will make transparent, the concepts and processes presented in both Smith (1978) and Guthrie and Hall (1983) are central to the microethnographic discourse analytic logic of inquiry. Additionally, they inform the iterative, recursive, abductive logic of analyses undertaken by Kelly and Baker.

Telling Case Study 1: Common Task, Uncommon Take-Up

In this telling case study, we describe the multifaceted and multilevel approach to analysis undertaken by Kelly and his team of sociolinguistic-based analysts (Crawford and Green) to trace the ways students in his Advanced Placement Physics Lab were introduced to new technology-based processes. These laboratory processes were designed by Kelly to guide the students' work in four small groups (teams) as they engaged in explorations of physics concepts and processes explained in more detail later. Thus, through this telling case study, we (re)construct the actions that Kelly took as designer and instructor of the laboratory experiences as well as researcher.

This telling case study (re)examines Kelly et al.'s (2001) original study that focused on identifying the actions, interactions, discourse, and ways used by students to negotiate the technology-oriented physics task. Kelly's goal for the original study was to develop an understanding of how students constructed common knowledge (Edwards & Mercer, 1987; Mercer & Hodgkinson, 2008) of a physics problem and the epistemic processes and practices involved in undertaking the problem.

To step back from the presentation of different analyses undertaken by his research team, Kelly and colleagues (2001) (re)analyzed the original published report to make transparent the logic of analysis that they undertook to examine how and in what ways each group of students engaged in the following actions:

- How students formed self-selected teams of three to four people
- How each team interpreted the task
- The ways in which each team engaged with the technology for collecting sources of data related to the physics problem inscribed in the guide constructed by Kelly in his multiple roles of designer, instructor, and research team leader
- How the participants in the team negotiated what knowledge of physics was critical to accomplishing this task and whose knowledge was accepted (or not) as these Advanced Placement students engaged with the problem over time

As this telling case study will make transparent, to examine what forms of common knowledge as well as how common and individual knowledges were being proposed, recognized, and taken up (or not) in the process of learning from the technology-enabled physics problem, Kelly and the sociolinguistic/microethnographic research team undertook multiple levels of analyses, including the following:

- Constructing multiple forms of transcripts to *map* and thus create texts, which were then analyzed to seek evidence of how the developing task and events identified were being constructed by the different groups, in order to develop an empirical/grounded understanding of the group's interpretation of the developing tasks.
- Tracing student interactions, actions, and discourse to examine how and under what conditions, and in what ways, the students proposed and thus displayed (or not) understandings of scientific knowledge and epistemic processes and practices.
- Engaging in contrastive analyses across groups that required different forms of (re)presentation of what was being constructed in and across times and interactions among the members of each team.

- Developing theoretical understandings of what constituted common knowledge across groups as well as individual student knowledge and collective knowledge within groups.

Although these multiple levels of analyses were limited to examining one laboratory experience (1 day), Kelly's telling case study, with its close focus on developing segments of classroom life within and across groups, was designed to provide readers with an opportunity to examine critical dimensions of the microethnographic discourse analytic logic of inquiry. It also creates a foundation for understanding studies in Kelly's larger program of research, which have been undertaken over the past two decades. This program of research has led to the identification of new and previously unexamined dimensions of processes in classrooms that shape students' access to, and understandings of, knowledge and epistemic practices of science and engineering within and across different levels of school and classroom contexts (e.g., Kelly, 2008a, 2008b, 2016b; Kelly & Cunningham, 2017; Kelly & Licona, 2018).

Situating the Physics Lab Study Within an Ongoing Program of Research

In this section, we (re)construct Kelly's logic of analysis to demonstrate how the analysis of micro-moments of interaction led to the identification of various ways in which the students sought to propose, communicate, evaluate, and legitimize knowledge claims in their small groups. Underlying these processes was Kelly's background in physics, which led to the importance of examining how the local and situated processes and practices related to ways of knowing physics as a discipline.

This process involved multiple angles and forms of analyses in the original study, not just a single transcript analysis (Alexander, 2015). These analytic processes involved examining different phenomena as they were being constructed, including the following: analysis of teachers' discursive work, analysis of available texts (guide sheet) by student take-up, analysis of student engagement with the technologies (i.e., computer probes using software that embody concretized physics and mathematics knowledge), and students' interactional and discourse processes within and across particular phases of the developing events of the lab session.

In constructing this telling case study of his logic of inquiry, Kelly (re)analyzed the transcripts archived from his team's earlier work to further explore how the local and situated epistemic practices were formed in this endogenous community, in ways that reflect the processes and practices of science communities in general. Specifically, through this (re)analysis, Kelly makes transparent how he and his team examined how the laboratory community (students, with their teacher) constructed, extended, modified, and changed their understandings of the physical phenomena.

Kelly's Logic of (Re)Analysis of Epistemic Practices and Knowledge Construction

To establish the context and make transparent the affordances Kelly created as designer and instructor of the laboratory experiences, we now foreground his goals for the design of this laboratory task for the Advanced Placement physics students. In this way, we make *visible* what is often an *invisible*, or unexamined, context in studies of teaching-learning processes, when studies solely focus on *what is happening in a particular event*, a concern that will be further explored in Telling Case Study 2 by Baker.

Kelly's goals for his design were grounded in his understanding of the epistemic processes and practices as well as conceptual knowledge of the discipline of physics: to provide the students with opportunities to recognize the affordances of the real-time graphing capabilities of the computer-based laboratory, to create situations that encourage interpretation (i.e., to "talk science") across different media, and to produce representations of physical phenomena. The students were encouraged to make sense of the physical events (linear and oscillatory motion) through a series of verbal and written prompts (teacher lab guide sheet, student talk), symbols (real-time, computer-generated graphs), and embodied motion (students' imitation of motion through the physical movement of their hands).

Kelly engaged a discourse analysis team (Crawford and Green) to support the analyses of how students made sense of the science. Working together, this team produced a series of timelines and transcripts that served as *graphic (re)presentations* of different dimensions of the social processes and epistemic consequences entailed in the students' actions and meaning-making processes. For example, the team created timelines (see Figure 1; Kelly et al., 2001, figure 3, p. 144) to examine how four small student groups organized their time to accomplish the academic tasks framed by the teacher's lab guide sheet.

Analyses of these timelines (a visual text of developing activity flow) provided a basis for examining the question "On what was time spent, by whom and in what ways, leading to what progression of understanding of concepts and processes?" This level of analysis, a *mesolevel* focusing on actions being undertaken, formed a foundation for *contrastive analyses* across groups, and thus for examining how the *common task* was taken up *uncommonly* by each group. As Figure 1 demonstrates, this approach to contrasting a group's take-up and engagement in this task, (re)presented as timelines, reveals the ways the students' initial thinking, false starts, and knowledge claims were embedded in sequences of activity. It also makes transparent how the time spent engaging in particular elements of the lab guide sheet differed across groups, leading to different potentials of future understandings of these physics concepts.

To examine the students' interactions at a more *microlevel*, the analysts created transcripts of talk and action (cf. Green & Kelly, 2019; Green & Wallat, 1981b) that (re)presented discourse beyond the speech mode. This approach to (re)presenting discourse and the interpretive processes being proposed, recognized, and interactionally accomplished by the participants included *recognizing and examining the signs and symbols used by the students in the activities, the proxemics* (the distances between and among group members and artifacts), and *the prosody* (pitch, stress, intonational contour, pause, and juncture) *of the conversations* (e.g., Bloome & Theodorou, 1988;

FIGURE 1
Timelines of Four Physics Student Groups With Phase Unit Activities Marked

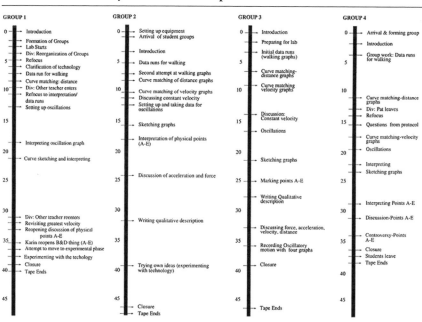

Source. From Kelly et al. (2001, Figure 3, p. 144). Reprinted with permission.

Gumperz & Herasimchuk, 1972). Figure 2 (Kelly et al., 2001) provides an illustrative example of one of these transcript formats that supported multiple levels of analysis, drawing on different inscriptions of discourse and configurations of participants, and the developing interactional processes.

While a complete set of transcripts constructed and analyzed is beyond the scope of this chapter (see additional transcripts in Kelly et al., 2001), Figure 2 provides a focused exploration of how the analysis team created graphic texts that (re)presented particular levels of information that served to contextualize the discourse processes.

For example, Figures 1 and 2 (Figures 3 and 7, respectively, in the original publication; Kelly et al., 2001) were designed to provide a basis for examining how the group came together and the sequences of decisions and actions leading to the production of knowledge claims and engagement in epistemic practices (Kelly, 2016b; Kelly & Chen, 1999). This level of sociolinguistic analysis was informed by the following microethnographic question: *How and in what ways were the students engaging in and with the technology-generated texts as well as the actions and verbal/nonverbal interactions within the group?* Importantly, the transcription process shown in Figure 2 made it possible to identify the nonverbal communication, the eye gaze, and the proxemics of the groups, and thus their orientations to particular dimensions of the lab task (cf. Bloome & Theodorou, 1988; Green & Bridges, 2018; Gumperz, 1982).

FIGURE 2
Sequence of Interpretation of the Meaning of Constant Velocity Across Visual and Symbolic Forms

line #	actor	talk (MU)	nonverbals	referent
1072	Sue	think about	reading from guide sheet	
1073		constant velocity		
1074		and talk it over in your group		
1075	Sue	constant velocity		physics
1076		looks like a		knowledge
1077		straight line		
1078	Fran	right		
1079		but		
1080		you have a	pause after "a"	
1081	Pat	no	gesturing in the air showing	physical
1082		you could be going	possible motion; (no real-	movement
1083		different	time data collected, but	
1084		further away	previously recorded data	
1085		or something	remained on the screen)	
1086		and have the same velocity		
1087		so it wouldn't =be= a straight line		
1088	Sue	=yeah =but you	gesturing and pointing to	
1089		it'd have to be a straight=line=	the computer	
1090	Pat	=it would be going=		
1091	Sue	it would have to be	tracing a possible graphical	hypothetical
1092		that way	representation	data
1093		this way	and pointing to the	
1094		that way	computer screen	
1095		that way		
1096	Pat	yeah		
1097	Fran	so it		physics
1098		would always have to be a straight line		knowledge
1099		it couldn't be anything		
1100	Sue	it couldn't be curved		physics
1101		that's like		knowledge
1102		changing		
1103	Pat	well		
1104		you know		
1105		but you could		
1106		go		
1107		da	moving hand back and forth	physical
			to show possible movement	movement
			(no data collected)	

(continued)

FIGURE 2 (CONTINUED)

1108	Sue	like on her		
1109	Pat	and then come back		
1110		and still be going		
1111	Sue	=but no=		
1112	Fran	=but that =	moving hand and pointing	physics
1113		moment of change	to notebook	knowledge
1114		when you go to turn it		
1115	Sue	that's acceleration		physics
1116		change in direction		knowledge
1117		is acceleration		
1118		this is		
1119		what		
1120		you're		
1121		seeing		

Note. The transcription shows the verbal exchanges (transcribed in message units), the nonverbal communication, and the referent for the verbal and nonverbal exchanges.
Source. From Kelly et al. (2001, Figure 7, p. 155). Reprinted with permission.

In creating the text in Figure 2, the analysts provide evidence of how this form of transcription created a foundation for exploring how the participants' use of *reference* and *gestures* was critical to identifying the developing actions and texts being constructed by them in and across time and flow of activity in this developing event. By analyzing the video record in concert with this approach to transcribing, these researchers were able to develop *inferences about the referents* of the students' multimodal (Gumperz, 1981) conversations at *important junctures* in the conversations. This analytic process, therefore, laid a foundation for examining the *complex meaning-making process* that involved the coordination of *words*, *symbols*, and *objects* as they were developing in and across phases of the group work.

Through the different levels of analysis of discourse and interactions, the analysts were able to develop an evidence-based narrative that traced the students' reasoning as they worked through the laboratory exercises. What these levels of analysis made possible to understand, and develop warranted accounts of, is that the students working in small groups did not always, or even often, come to a common interpretation without considerable discourse and interactional work. The analyses included the ways in which different members within a particular student group reopened topics, a process that led the analysts to develop evidence of the variations in students' understandings of the physics topics. By examining *key referents to physics concepts* in the conversations of particular students across the groups, the analysts were able to identify the subset of students who articulated the canonical knowledge in the moment, and for whom resolution was achieved among the group members.

These figures and descriptions of the actions of the research team made transparent how the microethnographic discourse analytic logic of analysis supported the team in identifying social processes of learning the disciplinary knowledge of physics. Thus, in Telling Case 1, we presented a logic of analysis undertaken by Kelly et al. (2001) that made transparent how ME/DA, as a logic of inquiry and analysis, theoretically and conceptually framed a multifaceted and multileveled approach to analysis, to trace sources of common knowledge as they were being constructed (Edwards & Mercer, 1987; Mercer & Hodgkinson, 2008) in and through the discourse, actions, and understandings within and across groups (Guthrie & Hall, 1983).

The telling case study also provides evidence for the importance of reporting on how and why iterative processes of ethnographic analyses were necessary to *examine how knowledge claims were asserted, considered, tested, (re)formulated, and revised* by the students in each group. This telling case study of the analytic processes undertaken by Kelly and his research team, therefore, frames the importance of an iterative, recursive, and abductive process central to tracing developing differences in the social construction of events and knowledge within and across groups. The research team thus engaged in the epistemic practices of ME/DA to understand the ways in which the students were learning through engagement in the epistemic practices of physics.

Telling Case Study 2: Analyzing the Social Construction of Studio Artist Processes and Practices

In Telling Case Study 2, we (re)construct the analytic logic of analysis that Baker (2001) undertook to examine how intergenerational participants (1–4 years in the program) were afforded opportunities to develop understandings of creative processes in an Advanced Placement high school Studio Art class. As in Telling Case Study 1, we present the logic of analysis for exploring opportunities for learning that raised additional analytic issues and for further demonstrating the iterative, recursive, and abductive processes of the microethnographic discourse analytic logic in use. Specifically, we focus on developing a theoretical and empirical argument for the necessity of examining an often invisible mediating factor of classroom life: the developing histories and perspectives of students and teachers across times and events.

Through this (re)analysis of Baker's (2001) original study and subsequent studies (e.g., Baker et al., 2008; Baker & Green, 2007), we unfold the reflexive processes that Baker undertook through a multilayered process of (re)analyzing archived records. In exploring Baker's reflexive analytic process, we identified a shift from his original focus on the teacher and the opportunities for learning she provided through her discursive actions to a focus on the communicative processes of students with their teacher. In this way, Baker shifted from the role of *observer-as-analyst* to one of *hearer/listener-as-analyst* (cf. Bakhtin, 1986).

This shift in focus, as we demonstrate in this section, supported a (re)examination of the histories of class members, and their views on core discipline-based practices. Through this process, Baker raises questions about what an outsider (the researcher) may or may not be able to see, hear, or understand (e.g., the embedded social and disciplinary assumptions of particular classroom practices). By examining a key event from the 2-year ethnographic study, the third cycle of *public critique*, we foreground how, and in what ways, Baker identified the discipline-based practices that were being constructed in the class (e.g., an iteration of public critique). Additionally, by examining the developing processes and practices for conducting and participating in this event, we demonstrate how Baker then engaged in a process of *backward mapping* (Agar, 2006b). His goal through this form of mapping was to identify the sources of differences in the teacher's actions and discourse that shaped how she engaged students with different histories in successfully participating as artists in public critique.

Importantly, the telling case offers a second example of how the logic of ME/DA led a researcher to develop theoretically and empirically grounded claims about how the teacher—and, in this case, some of the experienced students—provided access to students for learning local disciplinary knowledge, processes, and practices. Specifically, we will (re)present the layers of analyses undertaken to examine the roots of observed differences in two students' performance of *public critique*, a 3-day event. This cycle of critique provided the students with an opportunity to present a series of drawings to the teacher and peers, engage in a public conversation about the artifacts (i.e., drawings) constructed by each presenter, and examine the processes and practices used to construct them.

What is important to note for this telling case study is that Baker was entering the second year of a 2-year ethnographic study in a field outside of his disciplinary background (English language arts). Therefore, in many ways, he represented a second-year student in the intergenerational (1–4 years of participation) Advanced Placement Studio Art class taught by an experienced (29 years) Visual Arts teacher. We present this telling case study to raise issues of *limits to certainty*, when interpretations by the analyst do not match the teacher's interpretation of student performances, based on the teacher's knowledge of the history of the students in the class (particularly points of entry) as well as of the disciplinary expectations within and beyond the class (Baker & Green, 2007).

Through Baker's telling case study, we (re)construct the key components of Baker's logic in use and reflect on many of the points Guthrie and Hall (1983) argue for in Table 1. For example, we explore how Baker's initial analysis of the student performances led to a "rich point" (Agar, 1994), an unexpected moment that requires further examination to gain understanding. We also explore how his lack of knowledge of particular social contextual factors of the situation became visible only after he engaged in further discussions with the teacher about the students. By challenging his initial assumptions of the discursive patterns that he had identified and by (re)considering a collaborative analysis, he (Baker, 2001; Baker & Green, 2007) recognized the *limits to certainty*. This process of analysis led to the following questions:

- What analytic processes guide researchers-as-observers in interpreting what is happening, particularly in considering the perspective of participants (*insiders*)?

- Moreover, what background knowledge of the teacher's/teachers' and students' histories is critical to consider in order to understand what the ethnographer, as an outsider, is seeing, hearing, and understanding and, thus, is able to develop as warranted accounts of the phenomena under study (Heap, 1995)?

Entering the Studio Art Class: Historical Roots

Baker and the studio art teacher, and one her colleagues, originally met during a summer institute designed for teachers (the National Writing Project), and through their dialogues, Baker grew interested in how the *creative process* was introduced to an intergenerational group of students by this studio art teacher. Their mutual interest in the creative process led to ongoing conversations and the 2-year collaboration in which Baker recorded classroom life on video and in field notes (cf. Corsaro, 1981, cited in Evertson & Green, 1986; see also Emerson et al., 2011) during his cycles of observation: the first 2 days of the class, continuous days each week, and whole cycles of activity across the 2 years of public critique. Through this process of entering each observation day, recording the flow of events in field notes and videos, and archiving and analyzing these records of classroom life, Baker strived to achieve his goal of gaining an insider's perspective (understanding) of what constituted studio art and the work of artists in this classroom community.

During the first year of the ethnographic study, Baker conducted a series of interviews with volunteer students. During an interview, one of the students stated, "If you want to know about the [studio] art class, you need to see [public] critique" (Field Notes, February 9, Year 1). Therefore, Baker, in consultation with the teacher, elected to begin the second year by entering and observing how the teacher initiated the class prior to and on the first day of the school year to trace the construction of the role that public critique played in the development of the student artists. Baker began video recording and writing field notes, focusing on the ways in which the teacher initiated developing events and cycles of activity in the class (Green & Meyer, 1991). These included materials, processes, and practices—particularly the social, semiotic (Gee & Green, 1998), and language (Bloome & Egan-Robertson, 1993) systems—as they were proposed, recognized, acknowledged, and interactionally accomplished by students with different histories in this course (cf. Bloome et al., 2005). The archived video records and Baker's field notes were a basis for him to construct an *index* for his developing archive (Corsaro, 1985; cf. Green, Chian, Stewart & Couch, 2017).

Baker began a multifaceted process of transcribing archived video records by using an approach that members of his microethnographic discourse analytic community frame as *running records* of the developing class (times and flow of events and first drafts of transcriptions). These running records and field notes afforded Baker mesolevel opportunities to (re)construct the developing chains of events (shifts in activities), which were being constructed each day—a process that led to the construction of *event maps* of each day (cf. Baker et al., 2008; Green & Wallat,

1981b). An event map is a mesolevel, graphic (re)presentation of the flow of activity (see Figure 3) at particular levels of scale that include columns for clock time and for observational notes on the analysis of discursive and interactional signals of transitions from one event to the next. In constructing these event maps, as well as writing field notes, Baker identified the boundaries of events and created a second layer of field notes that included theoretical, methodological, and personal notes, which reflected his growing understanding of what was happening and what was being constructed in and across moment-by-moment and over-time interactions of the teacher with students, and students with others (cf. Corsaro, 1985, cited in Evertson & Green, 1986).

This process led Baker to construct notebooks organized by days that included running records, event maps, classroom transcripts, and other artifacts (e.g., handouts). Baker also charted when the teacher invited speakers from earlier iterations of the course (e.g., alumni) to share stories and confirm discipline-based practices with the students. This process of *indexing* different records as they were collected provided a historical grounding for (re)visiting the developing history of the class as well as for adding reflexive notes (links to theory, hypotheses, methodological processes, etc.) for further consideration and analysis both in and over time.

Figure 3 presents a multilayered map of the history of the teacher and the placement of Baker's years in her class as part of the teacher's personal history as well as the history of the students participating for the first time each year (Timeline 1). This figure (the teacher's and the program's history timeline) formed an anchor for situating the 2 years of Baker's ethnographic study of the class within this Visual Arts program (indicated by the years that are shaded in gray).

This level of analysis led Baker to seek deeper understandings of how students with different histories (years in the class, 1–4 years) understood and presented their work as artists during the cycle of activity in November titled *public critique*, an event in which students as artists engaged with others in the class in a form of public evaluation of their work.

Such critique, as Baker and the students learned over developing cycles of critique (presented in Figure 3), is a common practice of the studio art world, as framed by the teacher as she introduced intertextually tied cycles of activity (Bloome & Egan-Robertson, 1993) across the first 3 months of the class (see the timeline of cycles in Figure 3). In these intertextually tied events, she framed for the students how what they were engaging in was part of the world of studio art that they were seeking to enter. In this way, the teacher made the walls of the class permeable to support the students in developing visions of future sites for their work as artists.

What is also visible in the *swing-out timelines* (a term in Baker's ME/DA community) is how Baker (re)presented the interconnections of the developing events in particular cycles of activity at particular levels of analytic scale. The swing-out timelines constitute a process for *situating part-whole relationships of times and events* to *locate* the point in the history of the class being analyzed. This *zooming in* and *zooming out* create a process that maintains the laminated (multilayered) and historical

FIGURE 3
Timelines Leading to Cycles of Activity of *Public Critique*

LIFE HISTORY OF CLASS: TIMELINE OF INTERGENERATIONAL STUDIO ART CLASS (1997–2000)

Teacher 29 years of teaching	1996–1997 (5% of students enter)	1997–1998 (12% of students enter)	1998–1999 (35% of students enter)	1999–2000 (53% of students enter)

ENTERING THE FIELD: TIMELINE OF THE ETHNOGRAPHY 1998–2000

Academic Year One (1998–1999)	Academic Year Two (1999–2000)

Event Map of First Day of Class

9/2 FIRST DAY OF SCHOOL: INITIATING CYCLES

Clock Time (Videotape time)	Running Record of Phases (phase numbers on left)	Running Record of Events (line numbers)
9:09–9:18 (00:00:01–00:10:01)	1. T preparing (talks to researcher) 2. T explaining letters from past students to present students	1. T preparing before students arrive (1–79)
9:18–9:22 (00:10:02–00:13:56)	1. T talking about class preparation 2. T instructing students to pick up two index cards and select a workbench	2. Students arriving; T greeting students at door (80–134)
(9:22–9:30) (00:13:57–00:21:04)	1. Students writing two questions, etc. 2. T giving each student an envelope 3. Students passing back index cards	3. T taking roll and initiating "index card activity" (134–235)

(continued)

FIGURE 3 (CONTINUED)

Time	Activities	Summary
(9:30–9:44) (00:22:32–00:36:14)	1. *T presenting overview day and program 2. Introducing Disney video 3. Playing Disney video 4. Explaining links with video	4. T welcoming, presenting agenda and introducing self and program (236–686)
6 min. (00:28:28–00:34:28)		4a. Disney video (442–621)
9:44–9:55 (00:36:15–00:47:24)	1. T reading letters from: D, M, A, C 2. T explaining connections	5. T reading and commenting on excerpts from letters of past students (687–1063)
9:55–10:00 (00:47:26–53:01)	1. T assigning letter of intent 2. Handout; quoting Z. Hurston 3. "Student agendas"	6. T assigning: Read letter from past student and write letter of intent (1064–1243)
10:00–10:09 (00:53:03–01:01:40)	1. T introducing sketchbooks 2. Notebooks: connection to AP and areas of concentration 3. Folders: Value of handouts 4. Fee: Cost of some of the materials	7. T presenting four needs for class (1234–1568)
10:09–10:15 (01:02:04–01:08:18)	1. Mini-chalk festival with kids 2. Visit from superintendent 3. Presentations from students who attended art summer school 4. "Film Festival"; 5. "Breakfast Club"; 6. "Fashion Show"	8. T discussing "Highlights" of upcoming year (1569–1792)

*T initiates cycles of friendly sharing: "tomorrow I'll have a short activity that's kind of a creative activity" (lines 332–334) (occurs on 9/3)

HISTORY OF CYCLES OF CRITIQUE

Framing class 9/2: James enters	Friendly Sharing 9/10, 13	Gentle Critique 9/22–24	Maya enters 10/11	Deep Critique 11/16–19

Note. Modified from Baker and Green (2008).

contexts of particular events and frames empirical ways of interconnecting particular levels of analysis (Green et al., 2012).

As indicated in Figure 3, Baker added a *running record* of the developing phases of actions that the teacher presented to the students on the first day of school as practices for being artists. In this analysis, he focused on the teacher's ways of initiating a discourse of studio art as well as foreshadowing future events in which the students would participate, thus creating *intertextual* (Bloome & Egan-Robertson, 1993) and *intercontextual* (Bloome et al., 2005; Floriani, 1993; Heras, 1993; Yeager et al., 1998) (re)presentations of processes and events. Baker also included quotations within this timeline to foreground the observed *intertextual/intercontextual references* as well as the *material resources* that the teacher drew on (e.g., a video of an art event, letters from previous students) to introduce what counted as, and constituted, being an artist in this intergenerational program (cf. Durán & Szymanski, 1995; Putney et al., 1999). Additionally, Baker (re)presented cycles of critique that included the public critique in November.

In his original study, Baker (2001) had identified differences in student performance during public critique of two students, and through a conversation with the teacher, he learned that these students were both first-year students in the class. As indicated in Figure 3, the two students, Maya and James (pseudonyms), were both seniors in high school but first-year students in this class and program. As also indicated in this timeline of the cycles of critique, through a *backward* and *forward* mapping of the critique cycles, Baker identified Maya's point of entry into the class as 1 month into the school year, while James entered on the first day. This process of tracing points of entry provided information that was not observable in Baker's live observation of the students' performance or in his initial analysis of what he was hearing or seeing. This multilevel process of analysis led Baker to a deeper understanding that what he had heard and observed in each performance was related to the two students' levels of access to the developing processes of drawing techniques, materials, and practices of critique. That is, Baker learned that Maya did not have the same level of experience with critique as a practice as James.

A complete analysis of the differences in their performances is beyond the scope of this chapter (see Baker, 2001). What is important to report about the analysis is that when Baker engaged with the teacher in a conversation about the two students' performances, and the differences observed in the teacher's responses to them, the teacher made visible that she was aware of what Maya had, and had not, experienced and that her interactions with Maya were designed to support Maya in undertaking critique for the first time (see Baker in Green et al., in press). Furthermore, Baker also learned that James was only a first-year student, although Baker had presumed that James was a more experienced student based on the discourse and actions he had observed during James's presentation of his drawings. That is, James's discourse reflected the teacher's discourse that Baker, as observer-participant (Spradley, 1980/2016), had initially analyzed from the beginning of the school year. Because Baker had been transcribing and mapping the flow of activity for each day from the beginning of the school year, he expected to hear discourse of the drawing techniques that the teacher had introduced and descriptions of the creative process and other practices modeled by the teacher that the students had experienced within and across earlier intertextually tied cycles of activity.

Baker's growing understanding of the roots of the differences between Maya's and James's performances of public critique was further extended when, at a later point in time, he engaged with the teacher in a *conversation of process* that focused on his interpretation of his observations of the performance of different students across the 3 days of critique. The teacher led Baker to understand the need to know the history of the students, not simply to base his interpretations on what he saw and heard in the moment, particularly given that some students had been there for 4 years and he had only been part of this intergenerational studio art class for 2 years. In other words, Baker, like the students, was developing understandings of, and knowledge about, what was being proposed, recognized, acknowledged, and interactionally accomplished by students with different years of experience with the processes, practices, and discourse of studio art (cf. Bloome et al, 2005).

For Baker, this growing awareness of what was observable by the teacher in contrast to Baker as a researcher (outsider) raised a question of *access* similar to that framed by Smith (1978). That is, it raised questions about *access to what?* Access, Baker learned, involved developing understandings of the history of participants in observed events, and discourse from different points of view, often information not directly recorded in field notes, on video, or during interviews. Baker's telling case study, therefore, provides a grounding for examining and questioning what constitutes insider (i.e., emic) knowledge (cf. Heath, 1983; Heath & Street, 2008). Although Baker was alerted by a student to the importance of critique for the class, his telling case further demonstrates how a microethnographic discourse analytic logic of inquiry supported multiple levels of analysis and, at times, new data collection and (re)analyses, which proved critical to developing theoretically grounded interpretations of the developing processes and practices within the studio art class.

Thus, Baker's and Kelly's telling case studies demonstrate why no single analysis, or theoretical perspective, is sufficient to understand how students develop disciplinary knowledge of concepts, processes, and practices through educational opportunities afforded them in classrooms (Kelly, 2016b). That is, Baker's, like Kelly's, telling case study frames the importance of understanding the goals of the research and what each study provides educators and researchers (cf. Kaur, 2012; Morine-Dershimer, 2013; Nuthall, 2007). This issue, as Candela et al. (2004) and Kumpulainen et al. (2009) argue, constitutes the basis for a new research agenda, one that supports deeper understandings of the complex and developing lives of learners in different educational contexts.

Closing and Opening: On What Was Learned From the Telling Case Studies

Kelly's and Baker's telling case studies provide a basis for understanding the ongoing and developing nature of ME/DA-based knowledge construction as framed by

Smith (1978), Guthrie and Hall (1983), and others. Kelly and Baker also demonstrate the critical need to understand the history of the participants as well as the relationship of the researcher with members of the ongoing community in which the researcher seeks to gain entry. Through these processes, the ethnographer-as-learner seeks to understand what members need know, understand, and interpret in order to participate in *culturally relevant ways* in a developing culture-in-the-making (cf. Bloome et al., 2018; Collins & Green, 1992; Green et al., 2012; Heath, 1982; Heath & Street, 2008; Walford, 2008; Yeager et al., 2009).

By presenting these two telling case studies, we created a foundation for understanding the need for *triangulating different angles of vision* on a particular event (participants, researchers, teacher) as well as undertaking multiple levels of analyses to construct warranted understandings of what was being observed and understood by the researcher (Green & Chian, 2018; Heap, 1995). We also made transparent the chains of decisions, actions, and theories that were guided by a microethnographic discourse analytic logic that constituted the particular approach to microethnography, that is, *interactional ethnography*, undertaken by Kelly and Baker (cf. Castanheira et al., 2000; Green & Bridges, 2018; Kelly & Green, 2019).

From the interactional ethnographic perspective, each level of analysis, as Smith (1978) and Mitchell (1984) argue, forms a basis for tracing a particular sequence of events at some level of society (an individual, a small group, a class) to learn from members what is required to participate in what Hymes (1972) framed as a "bit of life." Moreover, this complex iterative, recursive, and abductive logic of inquiry supports identification of previously unexamined dimensions of classroom life as experienced by particular participants. It also provides a basis for engaging different participants in *conversations of processes* that need to be understood to gain emic or insider understandings of what is being heard, seen, and thus observed. These telling case studies, therefore, make visible how microethnography is an *epistemological approach*, which supports researchers in studying a particular group or phenomenon within a particular social context (e.g., literacy practices, epistemic processes and practices that constitute disciplinary knowledge, and equity of access to particular opportunities for learning in local contexts as well as across national contexts; Anderson-Levitt & Rockwell, 2017; Bloome et al., 2018; Garcez, 2008, 2017; Green & Bloome, 1997; Heath & Street, 2008; Skukauskaite et al., 2017; Smith, 1978).

Furthermore, the fact that Baker and Kelly had extensive archives, which supported multiple levels of (re)analysis, makes clear how archived records can support multiple studies at different points in time and, thus, the development of deeper theories of learning through multifaceted iterative, recursive, and abductive research processes (Green et al., 2015; Green et al., 2017). These telling case studies make it apparent how one study may lead to the need for further analyses and the creation of new data sets to construct an intertextual *web of understandings* that lead to deeper theoretically and empirically grounded claims (Heap, 1995) about what counts as learning processes and practices for particular participants engaged in particular events with particular configurations of actors at particular points in time within particular communities of learners.

Finally, by tracing the historical roots of ME/DA studies of the functions of language in classrooms, we also make visible the depth of recurrent issues in research that have led to the current epistemological approaches. In this way, we reiterate the editors' call for this volume of *RRE* to address how ME/DA, as an emergent approach over the past four decades, builds on, and extends, the ways of studying recurring issues of student access to learning opportunities in the changing educational world of the 21st century.

ORCID iD

Judith L. Green https://orcid.org/0000-0002-3379-6733

NOTES

[1]Issues arguing that data are not found but produced have been framed by Ellen (1984), Clifford and Marcus (1985/2010), and Cole and Zuengler (2007). This argument includes issues of how to transcribe social and cultural events and actors (Bucholtz, 2000) given the different theoretical traditions of discourse analysis. For contrasts among the different theories of discourse and conversation analysis in classrooms, see McDermott et al. (1978), Heap (1995), Cummings and Wyatt-Smith (2001), Wyatt-Smith and Cumming (2001), Blommaert and Jie (2010), Rampton et al. (2015), Rex et al. (2006), and Markee (2015).

[2]Three years later, in 2009, AERA published "Standards for Reporting on Humanities-Oriented Research in AERA Publications" in *Educational Researcher*.

[3]For a contrastive analysis of the *status of claims* associated with different research traditions, see Heap (1995).

[4]For conceptual developments in microethnographic discourse-analytic studies of classroom interactions and their consequences in different educational spaces, see, for example, Green and Wallat (1981a), Gilmore and Glatthorn (1982), Bloome et al. (2005), Rex (2006), Bridges et al. (2015), Green and Castanheira (2019), Kelly and Green (2019), and Bloome et al. (in press). For conceptual review articles on microethnography that situates ME/DA research, see Garcez (2008, 2017), Spindler (2000), Spindler and Spindler (1982), McCarty (2005, 2014), Street (1984, 2005, 2013), and Green and Bridges (2018).

[5]For discussions of the different conceptual and philosophical perspectives on case study research in education, see Harrison et al. (2017).

[6]The roots include theoretical arguments grounded in the social and linguistic anthropological theories of Bateson (Birdwhistell, 1977; Brockman, 1977), Geertz (1983), Spradley (1980/2016), Ellen (1984), Street (2005), and Agar (1994, 2006a, 2006b), among others. Within education research, we draw on conceptual developments in linguistic and social anthropology, and ethnography of communication framing microethnographic research in schools and communities (e.g., Bloome et al., 2005; Egan-Robertson & Bloome, 1998; Erickson, 2004; Gilmore & Glatthorn, 1982; Gumperz, 1981, 1982, 1986; Heath, 1982, 1983; Heath & Street, 2008; Hymes, 1972, 1982; Rex, 2006; Sheridan et al., 2000; Trueba & Wright, 1981).

[7] For studies focusing on different sites, levels of human and time scale, and phenomena of interest from a common logic of inquiry, see Castanheira et al. (2000), Rex (2006), Carter (2007), Newell et al. (2017), Bloome et al. (2019), and Kelly and Green (2019). For

explorations of the theories guiding ethnographies across national borders in Latin America, see Anderson-Levitt and Rockwell (2017).

[8] For a three-decade review that complements these seminal reviews, see Ball (2002) and subsequent reviews in the next two decades of *RRE*.

[9] The work inscribed in Smith is primarily grounded in U.S. contexts of ethnography. For sociological and international perspectives, see Heap (1985), Atkinson (1990/2014), Walford (2008), Beach (2017), Skukauskaite et al. (2017), and Anderson-Levitt and Rockwell (2017).

[10] See Spradley (1980/2016) on semantic relationships, domain analysis, and taxonomic construction.

REFERENCES

Agar, M. (1994). *Language shock: Understanding the culture of conversation.* Quill.

Agar, M. (2006a). Culture: Can you take it anywhere? *International Journal of Qualitative Methods, 5*(2), 1–12. https://doi.org/10.1177/160940690600500201

Agar, M. (2006b). An ethnography by any other name. *Forum: Qualitative Sozialforschung/ Forum: Qualitative Social Research, 7*(4), Article 37. http://www.qualitative-research.net/fqs

Alexander, R. J. (2015). Dialogic pedagogy at scale: Oblique perspectives. In L. Resnick, C. Asterhan, & S. Clarke (Eds.), *Socializing intelligence through academic talk and dialogue* (pp. 429–439). American Educational Research Association.

American Educational Research Association. (2006). Standards for reporting on empirical social science research in AERA publications. *Educational Researcher, 35*(6), 33–40. https://doi.org/10.3102/0013189X035006033

American Educational Research Association. (2009). Standards for reporting humanities-oriented research in AERA publications. *Educational Researcher, 28*(6), 481–486. https://doi.org/10.3102/0013189X09341833

Anderson-Levitt, K. M., & Rockwell, E. (2017). *Comparing ethnographies: Local studies of education across the Americas.* American Educational Research Association.

Atkinson, P. (2014). *The ethnographic imagination: Textual constructions of reality.* Routledge. (Original work published 1990)

Baker, D., & Green, J. (2007). Limits to certainty in interpreting video data: Interactional ethnography and disciplinary knowledge. *Pedagogies: An International Journal, 2*(3), 191–204. https://doi.org/10.1080/15544800701366613

Baker, D., Green, J., & Skukauskaite, A. (2008). Video-enabled ethnographic research: A microethnographic perspective. In G. Walford (Ed.), *How to do educational ethnography* (pp. 77–114). Tufnell Press.

Baker, W. D. (2001). *Artists in the making: An ethnographic investigation of discourse and literate practices as disciplinary processes in a high school advanced placement studio art classroom* (Unpublished doctoral dissertation). University of California-Santa Barbara.

Bakhtin, M. M. (1986). *Speech genres and other late essays* (V. W. McGee, Trans.). University of Texas Press. (Original work published 1979)

Ball, A. F. (2002). Three decades of research on classroom life: Illuminating the classroom communicative lives of America's at-risk students. *Review of Research in Education, 26*(1), 71–111. https://doi.org/10.3102/0091732X026001071

Beach, D. (2017). International trends and developments in the ethnography of education. *Acta Paedagogica Vilnensia, 39*(2), 15–30. https://doi.org/10.15388/ActPaed.2017.39.11455

Birdwhistell, R. L. (1977). Some discussion of ethnography, theory, and method. In J. Brockman (Ed.), *About Bateson* (pp. 101–141). E. P. Dunon.

Blommaert, J., & Jie, D. (2010) *Ethnographic fieldwork: A beginners guide.* Multilingual Matters.

Bloome, D., Beauchemin, F., Brady, J., Buescher, E., Kim, M.-Y., & Schey, R. (2018). Anthropology of education, anthropology in education, and anthropology for education. In H. Callan (Ed.), *The international encyclopedia of anthropology* (pp. 1–10). John Wiley.

Bloome, D., Carter, S. P., Christian, B. M., Otto, S., & Shuart-Faris, N. (2005). *Discourse analysis and the study of classroom language and literacy events: A microethnographic perspective*. Lawrence Erlbaum.

Bloome, D., Castanheira, M. L., Leung, C., & Rowsell, J. (2019). *Retheorizing literacy practices: Complex social and cultural contexts*. Routledge.

Bloome, D., & Egan-Robertson, A. (1993). The social construction of intertextuality in classroom reading and writing lessons. *Reading Research Quarterly, 28*(4), 305–333. https://doi.org/10.2307/747928

Bloome, D., Newell, C., Hirvela, A., & Lin, T.-J., with Brady, J., Ha, S. Y., Swak, S., Seymour, M., Thanos, T., VanDerHeide, J., & Wynhoff Olsen, A. (in press). *Dialogic literacy argumentation in high school language arts classrooms*. Routledge.

Bloome, D., & Theodorou, E. (1988). Analyzing teacher-student and student-student discourse. In J. L. Green & J. O. Harker (Eds.), *Multiple perspective analyses of classroom discourse* (Vol. 28, pp. 217–248). Ablex.

Bridges, S. M., Green, J., Botelho, M. G., & Tsang, P. C. S. (2015). Blended learning and PBL: An interactional ethnographic approach to understanding knowledge construction in-situ. In A. Walker, H. Leary, C. E. Hmelo-Silver, & P. A. Ertmer (Eds.), *Essential readings in problem-based learning: Exploring and extending the legacy of Howard S. Barrows* (pp. 107–130). Purdue University Press.

Brockman, J. (Ed.). (1977). *About Bateson: Essays on Gregory Bateson*. E. P. Dunon.

Bucholtz, M. (2000). The politics of transcription. *Journal of Pragmatics, 32*(10), 1439–1465. https://doi.org/10.1016/S0378-2166(99)00094-6

Candela, A., Rockwell, E., & Coll, C. (2004). What in the world happens in classrooms? Qualitative classroom research. *European Educational Research Journal, 3*(3), 692–713. https://doi.org/10.2304/eerj.2004.3.3.10

Carter, S. P. (2007). Reading all that White crazy stuff: Black young women unpacking Whiteness in a high school British literature classroom. *Journal of Classroom Interaction, 41*(2), 42–54.

Castanheira, M. L., Crawford, T., Dixon, C. N., & Green, J. (2000). Interactional ethnography: An approach to studying the social construction of literate practices. *Linguistics and Education, 11*(4), 353–400. https://doi.org/10.1016/s0898-5898(00)00032-2

Cazden, C. (1986). Classroom discourse. In M. C. Wittrock (Ed.), *The handbook of research on teaching* (3rd ed., pp. 432–463). MacMillan.

Cazden, C. (1988). *Classroom discourse: The language of teaching and learning*. Heinemann.

Cazden, C., John, V., & Hymes, D. (Eds.). (1972). *Functions of language in the classroom*. Teachers College Press.

Cazden, C. B. (2017). *Communicative competence, classroom interaction, and educational equity: The selected works of Courtney B. Cazden*. Routledge.

Clifford, J., & Marcus, G. E. (Eds.). (2010). *Writing culture: The poetics and politics of ethnography*. University of California Press. (Original work published 1985)

Cole, K. M., & Zuengler, J. (2007). *The research process in classroom discourse analysis*. Routledge.

Collins, E., & Green, J. (1992). Learning in classroom settings: Making and breaking a culture. In H. Marshall (Ed.), *Redefining learning: Roots of educational reform* (pp. 59–86). Ablex.

Corsaro, W. A. (1981). Entering the child's world: Research strategies for field entry and data collection. In J. Green & C. Wallat (Eds.), *Ethnography and language in educational settings* (pp. 117–146). Ablex.

Corsaro, W. A. (1985). *Friendship and peer culture in the early years*. Ablex.

Corsaro, W. A., & Heise, D. R. (1990). Event structure models from ethnographic data. In C. Clegg (Ed.), *Sociological methodology* (pp. 1–27). Basil Blackwell.

Cummings, J., & Wyatt-Smith, C. (Eds.). (2001). *Literacy and the curriculum: Success in senior secondary school*. Australian Council for Educational Research.

Delamont, S. (1976). *Interaction in the classroom*. Methuen.

Denzin, N. (1978). *The research act: A theoretical introduction to research methods*. Aldine.

Dixon, C. N., Green, J., Yeager, B., Baker, W. D., & Franquiz, M. (2000). "I used to know that:" What happens when reform gets through the classroom door. *Bilingual Education Research Journal, 24*(1&2), 113–126. https://doi.org/10.1080/15235882.2000.10162754

Durán, R., & Szymanski, M. (1995). Cooperative learning interaction and construction of activity. *Discourse Processes, 19*(1), 149–164. https://doi.org/10.1080/01638539109544909

Edwards, D., & Mercer, N. (1987). *Common knowledge: The development of understanding in the classroom*. Methuen/Routledge.

Egan-Robertson, A., & Bloome, D. (Eds.). (1998). *Students as researchers of culture and language in their own communities*. Hampton.

Ellen, R. F. (Ed.). (1984). *Ethnographic research: A guide to general conduct*. Academic Press.

Emerson, R. M., Fretz, R. I., & Shaw, L. L. (2011). *Writing ethnographic fieldnotes* (2nd ed.). University of Chicago Press.

Erickson, F. (2004). *Talk and social theory: Ecologies of speaking and listening in everyday life*, Polity Press.

Erickson, F., & Shultz, J. (1977). When is a context? *ICHD Newsletter, 1*(4), 5–10. https://doi.org/10.1525/pol.1977.1.4.1

Erickson, F., & Shultz, J. (1981). When is context? Some issues and methods in the analysis of social competence. In J. Green & C. Wallat (Eds.), *Ethnography and language in educational settings* (Vol. 5, pp. 147–150). Ablex.

Evertson, C. M., & Green, J. L. (1986). Observation as inquiry and method. In M. Wittrock (Ed.), *Handbook of research on teaching* (3rd ed., pp. 162–213). American Educational Research Association.

Floriani, A. (1993). Negotiating what counts: Roles and relationships, texts and contexts, content and meaning. *Linguistics and Education, 5*(3–4), 241–274. https://doi.org/10.1016/0898-5898(93)90002-R

Gage, N. L. (1974). *Teaching as a linguistic process in a cultural setting* (ERIC 111 806). National Institute of Education.

Garcez, P. M. (2008). Microethnography in the classroom. In N. Hornberger & D. Corson (Eds.), *Encyclopedia of language and education: Vol. 8. Research methods in language and education* (pp. 257–271). Springer.

Garcez, P. M. (2017). Microethnography in the classroom. In K. A. King & N. H. Hornberger (Eds.), *Encyclopedia of language and education: Vol. 10. Research methods in language and education* (pp. 436–466). Springer.

Gee, J. P., & Green, J. L. (1998). Discourse analysis, learning, and social practice: A methodological study. *Review of Research in Education, 23*, 119–169. https://doi.org/10.2307/1167289

Geertz, C. (1983). *Local knowledge: Further essays in interpretive anthropology*. Basic Books.

Gilmore, P., & Glatthorn, A. (Eds.). (1982). *Children in and out of school: Ethnography and education*. Praeger.

Green, J. (1983). Research on teaching as a linguistic process: A state of the art. *Review of Research in Education, 10*, 151–254. https://doi.org/10.2307/1167138

Green, J., & Bloome, D. (1997). Ethnography and ethnographers in education: A situated perspective. In J. Flood, S. B. Heath, & D. Lapp (Eds.). *Handbook of research on teaching literacy through the communicative and visual arts* (pp. 181–202). Simon & Schuster MacMillan.

Green, J., Brock, C., Baker, D., & Harris, P. (in press). Positioning theory for learning in discourse. In N. Nasir, C. Lee, R. Pea, & M. Royston (Eds.), *Reconceptualizing learning in the 21st century: The handbook of the cultural foundations of learning.* Routledge.

Green, J., & Castanheira, M. (2019). Revisiting the relationship between, ethnography, discourse and education. *Caletroscópio, 7*(1), 10–55.

Green, J., Castanheira, M., Skukauskaite, A., & Hammond, J. (2015). Developing a multi-faceted research process: An ethnographic perspective for reading across traditions. In N. Markee (Ed.), *Handbook of classroom discourse and interaction* (pp. 26–43). Wiley-Blackwell.

Green, J., & Chian, M. (2018). Triangulation. In B. Frey (Ed.), *The SAGE encyclopedia of educational research, measurement, and evaluation.* Sage. https://dx.doi.org/10.4135/978150 6326139.n711

Green, J., Skukauskaite, A., & Baker, B. (2012). Ethnography as epistemology: An introduction to educational ethnography. In J. Arthur, M. I. Waring, R. Coe, & L. V. Hedges (Eds.), *Research methodologies and methods in education* (pp. 309–321). Sage.

Green, J., & Wallat, C. (Eds.). (1981a). *Ethnography and language in educational settings.* Ablex.

Green, J., & Wallat, C. (1981b). Mapping instructional conversations: Sociolinguistic ethnography. In J. Green & C. Wallat (Eds.), *Ethnography and language in educational settings* (pp. 161–208). Ablex.

Green, J. L., & Bridges, S. M. (2018). Interactional ethnography. In F. Fischer, C. E. Hmelo-Silver, S. R. Goldman, & P. Reimann (Eds.), *International handbook of the learning science* (pp. 475–488). Routledge.

Green, J. L., Chian, M., Stewart, E., & Couch, S. (2017). What is an ethnographic archive an archive of? A telling case of challenges in exploring developing interdisciplinary programs in higher education. *Acta Paedagogica Vilnensia, 39*(2), 112–131. https://doi .org/10.15388/ActPaed.2017.39.11485

Green, J. L., & Kelly, G. L. (2019). Appendix A: How we look at discourse: Definitions of sociolinguistic units. In G. J. Kelly & J. L. Green (Eds.), *Theory and methods for sociocultural research in science and engineering education* (pp. 264–270). Routledge.

Green, J. L., & Meyer, L. (1991). The embeddedness of reading in classroom life: Reading as a situated process. In C. Baker & A. Luke (Eds.), *Research methodologies and methods in education* (pp. 309–321). Sage.

Gumperz, J. J. (1972). *Introduction.* In J. J. Gumperz & D. Hymes (Eds.), *Directions in sociolinguistics: The ethnography of communication* (pp. 1–25). Holt, Rinehart & Winstron.

Gumperz, J. J. (1977). Socio-cultural knowledge in conversational inference. In M. Saville-Troike (Ed.), *Twentieth annual roundtable monograph series on language and linguistics* (pp. 191–212). Georgetown University Press.

Gumperz, J. J. (1981). Conversational inference and classroom learning. In J. Green & C. Wallat (Eds.). *Ethnography and language in educational settings* (pp. 3–24). Ablex.

Gumperz, J. J. (1982). *Discourse strategies.* Cambridge University Press.

Gumperz, J. J. (1986). Interactive sociolinguistics on the study of schooling. In J. Cook-Gumperz (Ed.), *The social construction of literacy* (pp. 45–68). Cambridge University Press.

Gumperz, J. J., & Herasimchuk, E. (1972). The conversational analysis of social meaning: A study of classroom interaction. In R. Shuy (Ed.), *Sociolinguistics: Current trends and prospects* (pp. 99–134). Georgetown University Press.

Guthrie, L. F., & Hall, W. (1983). Discontinuities/continuities in the functions of language and use of language. *Review of Research in Education, 10*, 55–77. https://doi.org /10.2307/1167135

Halliday, M. A. K. (1973). *Explorations in the functions of language.* Edward Arnold.

Harrison, H., Birks, M., Franklin, R., & Mills, J. (2017). Case study research: Foundations and methodological orientations. *Forum: Qualitative Social Research, 18*(1), Article 19.

Heap, J. (1985). Discourse in the production of classroom knowledge: Reading lessons. *Curriculum Inquiry, 15*(3), 245–279. https://doi.org/10.1080/03626784.1985.110759 66

Heap, J. L. (1991). A situated perspective of what counts as reading. In C. D. Baker & A. Luke (Eds.), *Towards a critical sociology of reading pedagogy* (pp. 103–139). John Benjamin.

Heap, J. L. (1995). The status of claims in "qualitative" educational research. *Curriculum Inquiry, 25*(3), 271–292. https://doi.org/10.1080/03626784.1995.11076182

Heath, S. B. (1982). Ethnography in education: Defining the essentials. In P. Gilmore & A. A. Glatthorn (Eds.), *Children in and out of school: Ethnography and education* (pp. 33–55). Center for Applied Linguistics.

Heath, S. B. (1983). *Ways with words: Language, life, and work in communities and classrooms.* Cambridge University Press.

Heath, S. B., & Street, B. V. (2008). *On ethnography: Approaches to language and literacy research.* Teachers College Press.

Heras, A. (1993). The construction of understanding in a sixth-grade bilingual classroom. *Linguistics and Education, 5*(3–4), 241–274. https://doi.org/10.1016/0898-5898(93) 90002-R

Hymes, D. (Ed.). (1972). *Reinventing anthropology.* Pantheon Books.

Hymes, D. (1981). Ethnographic monitoring. In H. T. Trueba, G. P. Guthrie, & K. H.-P. Au (Eds.), *Culture and the bilingual classroom: Studies in classroom ethnography* (pp. 56–68). Newbury House.

Hymes, D. (1982). What is ethnography? In P. Gilmore & A. A. Glatthorn (Eds.), *Children in and out of school: Ethnography and education* (pp. 21–32). Center for Applied Linguistics.

Kaur, B. (Ed.). (2012). *Understanding teaching and learning: Classroom research revisited.* Sense.

Kelly, G., & Chen, C. (1999). The sound of music: Constructing science as sociocultural practices through oral and written discourse. *Journal of Research in Science Teaching, 36*(8), 883–915. https://doi.org/10.1002/(SICI)1098-2736(199910)36:8%3C883::AID-TEA1%3E3.0.CO;2-I

Kelly, G., Crawford, T., & Green, J. L. (2001). Common task and uncommon knowledge: Dissenting voices in the discursive construction of physics across small laboratory, *Linguistics and Education, 12*(2), 135–174. https://doi.org/10.1016/S0898-5898(00)00046-2

Kelly, G. J. (2006). Epistemology and educational research. In J. Green, G. Camilli, & P. Elmore (Eds.), *Handbook of complementary methods in education research* (pp. 33–55). Lawrence Erlbaum.

Kelly, G. J. (2008a). Inquiry, activity, and epistemic practice. In R. Duschl & R. Grandy (Eds.), *Teaching scientific inquiry: Recommendations for research and implementation* (pp. 99–117, 288–291). Sense.

Kelly, G. J. (2008b). Learning science: Discursive practices. In A.-M. de Mejia & M. Martin-Jones (Eds.), *Encyclopedia of language and education: Vol. 3. Discourse and education* (pp. 329–340). Springer.

Kelly, G. J. (2016a). Learning science: Discourse practices. In S. Wortham, D. Kim, & S. May (Eds.), *Encyclopedia of language and education: Vol. 3. Discourse and education* (pp. 1–15). Springer.

Kelly, G. J. (2016b). Methodological considerations for the study of epistemic cognition in practice. In J. A. Greene, W. A. Sandoval, & I. Braten (Eds.), *Handbook of epistemic cognition* (pp. 393–408). Routledge.

Kelly, G. J., & Cunningham, C. (2017). Engaging in identity work through engineering practices in elementary classrooms. *Linguistics and Education, 39,* 48–59. https://doi.org/10.1016/j.linged.2017.05.003

Kelly, G. J., & Green, J. L. (Eds.). (2019). *Theory and methods for sociocultural research in science and engineering education.* Routledge.

Kelly, G. J., & Licona, P. (2018). Epistemic practices and science education. In M. Matthews (Ed.), *History, philosophy and science teaching: New research perspectives* (pp. 139–165). Springer.

Kumpulainen, K., Hmelo-Silver, C., & César, M. (2009). *Investigating classroom interactions: Methodologies in action.* Sense.

Lin, L. (1993). Language of and in the classroom: Constructing the patterns of social life. *Linguistics and Education, 5*(3–4), 241–274. https://doi.org/10.1016/0898-5898(93)90002-R

Lutz, F. (1962). *Social systems and school districts* (Unpublished doctoral dissertation). Washington University.

Markee, N. (Ed.). (2015). *Handbook of classroom discourse and interaction.* Wiley-Blackwell.

McCarty, T. (2005). Indigenous epistemologies and education: Self-determination, anthropology, and human rights. *Anthropology & Education Quarterly, 36*(1), 1–7. https://doi.org/10.1525/aeq.2005.36.1.001

McCarty, T. (2014). Ethnography in educational linguistics. In M. Bigelow & J. Ennser-Kananen (Eds.), *The Routledge handbook of educational linguistics* (pp. 23–37). Routledge.

McDermott, R. P., Gospodinoff, K., & Aron, J. (1978). Criteria for an ethnographically adequate description of concerted activities and their contexts. *Semiotica, 24*(3–4), 245–275. https://doi.org/10.1515/semi.1978.24.3-4.245

Mehan, H. (1979). *Learning lessons.* Harvard University Press.

Mercer, N., & Hodgkinson, S. (Eds.). (2008). *Exploring talk in school: Inspired by the work of Douglas Barnes.* Sage.

Mitchell, C. J. (1984). Typicality and the case study. In R. F. Ellen (Ed.), *Ethnographic research: A guide to general conduct* (pp. 238–241). Academic Press.

Morine-Dershimer, G. (2013). Classroom management and classroom discourse. In C. Evertson & C. Weinstein (Eds.), *Handbook of classroom management: Research, practices and contemporary issues* (Chapter 6). Routledge. https://doi.org/10.4324/9780203874783

Newell, G., Bloome, D., & the Argumentative Writing Project. (2017). Teaching and learning literary argumentation in high school English language arts classrooms. In D. Appleman & K. Hinchman (Eds.), *Adolescent literacy: A handbook of practice-based research* (pp. 379–397). Guilford Press.

Nuthall, G. (2007). *The hidden lives of learners.* New Zealand Education Research Association.

Putney, L., Green, J. L., Dixon, C., Durán, R., & Yeager, B. (1999). Consequential progressions: Exploring collective-individual development in a bilingual classroom. In C. Lee & P. Smagorinsky (Eds.), *Constructing meaning through collaborative inquiry: Vygotskian perspectives on literacy research* (pp. 86–126). Cambridge University Press.

Rampton, B. M. H., Maybin, J., & Roberts, C. M. (2015). Theory and method in linguistic ethnography. In J. Nell, S. Shaw, & F. Copland (Eds.), *Linguistic ethnography: Interdisciplinary explorations* (pp. 14–20). Palgrave Macmillan.

Rex, L. A. (2006). *The discourse of opportunity: How talk in learning situations supports and constrains.* Hampton.

Rex, L. A., Steadman, S. C., & Graciano, M. K. (2006). Researching the complexity of classroom interaction. In. J. Green, G. Camilli, & P. Elmore (Eds.), *Handbook of complementary methods in education research* (pp. 727–772). Lawrence Erlbaum.

Rist, R. (1973). *The urban school: A factory for failure: A study of education in American society.* MIT Press.

Sheridan, D., Street, B. V., & Bloome, D. (2000). *Writing ourselves: Mass observation and literacy practices.* Hampton.

Skukauskaite, A., & Grace, E. (2006). On reading and using the volume: Notes to students. In. J. Green, G. Camilli, & P. Elmore (Eds.). *Handbook of complementary methods in education research* (pp. xxi–xxiv). Lawrence Erlbaum.

Skukauskaite, A., Rupsiene, L., Player Koro, C., & Beach, D. (2017). Rethinking educational ethnography: Methodological quandaries and possibilities. *Acta Pedagogica Vilnensia, 39,* 9–14. https://doi.org/10.15388/ActPaed.2017.39.11451

Smith, L. (1977). Effective teaching: A qualitative inquiry in aesthetic education. *Anthropology and Education Quarterly, 8*(2), 127–129. https://doi.org/10.1525/aeq.1977.8.2.05x1408d

Smith, L. M. (1978). An evolving logic of participant observation, educational ethnography, and other case studies. *Review of Research in Education, 6*(1), 316–377. https://doi.org/1 0.3102/0091732X006001316

Smith, L. M., & Carpenter, P. C. (1972). *General reinforcement project: Qualitative observation and interpretation.* CEMREL.

Smith, X., & Geoffrey, X. (1968). *Learning beyond the school. International perspectives on the schooled society.* Routledge.

Spindler, G. (Ed.). (1963). *Education and culture: Anthropological approaches.* Holt, Rinehart & Winston.

Spindler, G.. (Ed.). (2000). *Fifty years of anthropology and education 1950–2000: A Spindler anthology.* Lawrence Erlbaum.

Spindler, G., & Spindler, L. (1982). Do anthropologists need learning theory? *Anthropology and Education Quarterly, 13*(2), 109–124. https://doi.org/10.1525/aeq.1982.13.2.05x1828h

Spradley, J. P. (2016). *Participant observation.* Holt, Rinehart, & Winston. (Original work published 1980)

Street, B. V. (1984). *Literacy in theory and practice.* Cambridge University Press.

Street, B. V. (2005). Foreword. In D. Bloome, S. Power Carter, B. M. Christian, S. Otto, & N. Shuart-Faris (Eds.), *Discourse analysis and the study of classroom language and literacy events: A microethnographic perspective* (pp. ix–xii). Lawrence Erlbaum.

Street, B. V. (2013). Anthropology and education. *Teaching Anthropology, 3*(1), 57–60.

Trueba, H. T., & Wright, P. G. (1981). On ethnographic studies and multicultural education. *NABE Journal, 5*(2), 29–56. https://doi.org/10.1080/08855072.1981.10668403

Walford, G. (Ed.). (2008). *How to do educational ethnography* (pp. 77–114). Tufnell Press.

Wolcott, H. F. (1967). *A Kwakiutl village and school.* Holt, Rinehart & Winston.

Wyatt-Smith, C., & Cumming, J. (2001). Examining the literacy-curriculum relationship. *Linguistics and Education, 11*(4), 295–312. https://doi.org/10.1016/S0898-5898(00) 00028-0

Yeager, B., Floriani, A., & Green, J. L. (1998). Learning to see learning in the classroom: Developing an ethnographic perspective. In D. Bloome & A. Egan-Robertson (Eds.), *Students as researchers of culture and language in their own communities* (pp. 115–139). Hampton Press.

Yeager, B., Green, J., & Castanheira, M. (2009). Two languages one community: On the discursive construction of community in bilingual classrooms. In K. Kumpulainen & M. Cesar (Eds.), *Social interactions in multicultural settings* (pp. 235–268). Sense.

Chapter 7

Emerging Perspectives on the Co-Construction of Power and Learning in the Learning Sciences, Mathematics Education, and Science Education

THOMAS M. PHILIP
University of California, Berkeley

AYUSH GUPTA
University of Maryland, College Park

In this chapter, we examine a significant shift in research in the learning sciences, mathematics education, and science education that increasingly attends to the co-construction of power and learning. We review articles in these fields that embody a new sense of theoretical and methodological possibilities and dilemmas, brewing at the intersections of critical social theory and the methodological approaches of interaction analysis and microgenetic analysis. We organize our review into three thematic categories: (1) the dynamic construction of identity and ideology, (2) attending to the organization of a learning environment, and (3) leveraging and repurposing tools. Reading across these thematic areas, we identify and outline a burgeoning subfield that we term critical interaction and microgenetic analysis. *By bringing this collection of articles together, this chapter provides collective epistemic and empirical weight to claims of power and learning as co-constituted and co-constructed through interactional, microgenetic, and structural dynamics. In our conclusions, we suggest six analytical commitments that are important to hold when engaging in critical interaction and microgenetic analysis.*

In *Identity and Agency in Cultural Worlds*, Dorothy Holland and her colleagues (2001) highlight the tensions in privileging an analysis of socially determining forces on one hand or individual human agency on the other. As they elucidate, an emphasis on societal structures tends to gloss over people's agency, creativity, and ingenuity, and a prioritization of individual agency often erases historical, social,

Review of Research in Education
March 2020, Vol. 44, pp. 195–217
DOI: 10.3102/0091732X20903309
Chapter reuse guidelines: sagepub.com/journals-permissions
© 2020 AERA. http://rre.aera.net

political, economic, and cultural constraints. Along with Erickson (2004), Goodwin (1994, 2007), McDermott (1993), Wortham (2004), and others, they represent a swell of scholarship in anthropology that has emphasized the importance of simultaneously attending to the moment-to-moment improvisations as people interact with each other and their environment, and the ever present societal and local curtailments on human activity. The scholarship we reviewed in this chapter, as a collective, takes up and further extends this challenge with particular attention to learning: How does one theorize and study learning at a level of analysis where structure, context, and agency co-constitute each other?

Taken as a whole, the articles seek to move beyond assertions that historical, social, political, and economic processes shape and influence individuals in some underspecified or overly deterministic manner. Similarly, they are not content with post hoc narratives to substantiate claims that a certain dynamic of power was salient in a particular setting. They seek to empirically show how tools, representations, artifacts, resources, practices, bodies, and the design of learning environments are all imbued with histories of power and contestation *and* that people creatively employ and transform these elements to reify, nudge, perturb, alter, and/or transform existing relationships of power. The micro, meso, and macro, in this sense, cannot be fully disentangled. They are co-constituted, but forefront differences in scale, both temporal and spatial. This dynamic relationship stresses that analyses must not only attend to how macrolevel structures and ideologies afford and constrain microlevel interactions but should also attend to how the macrolevel outcomes, in part, arise from the accretion of microlevel interactions where people are always repurposing tools, reimagining themselves, renegotiating relationships, and improvising with practices and ideologies that may appear otherwise static and inevitable.

More specifically, we examine a significant shift in research in the learning sciences, mathematics education, and science education that embodies a new sense of theoretical and methodological possibilities and dilemmas, brewing at the intersections of critical social theory and the methodological approaches of interaction analysis and microgenetic analysis. Fine-grained analyses of learning have demonstrated rich and varied trajectories of sensemaking, participation, and becoming but have struggled to adequately capture historical, social, political, and economic processes of power. Similarly, research on power in educational settings often missed the mark on cojoining their links with learning into a "multidimensional, multilayered portrait of human activity" that shifted "away from models of reproduction and essentialism" (Nasir & Hand, 2006, pp. 468–469). The scholarship we reviewed has unequivocally taken up the charge to develop new theoretical and methodological tools to study the co-construction of power and learning. We address the following question:

How do emerging approaches to studying learning that integrate (1) microgenetic and/or interaction analysis approaches, and (2) theoretical frameworks from critical social theory, uniquely contribute to equity in education by conceptualizing and addressing power as simultaneously constructed in interaction and place and situated in history and society?

Reading across the literature we reviewed, we name what we see as the emerging subfield of *critical interaction and microgenetic analysis*. Before discussing our literature selection process and analytical strategy, we begin by defining key terms to help frame the analysis that follows.

ESSENTIAL TERMS

Power

Given that others have written tomes about the construct of power, we cannot fathom providing a conclusive definition of the term in a few lines. The dictionary definition is a helpful starting point: "the capacity or ability to direct or influence the behavior of others or the course of events" (New Oxford American Dictionary, n.d.). We also interpret power as the ability to alter or maintain the physical, social, structural, cultural, and political conditions, resources, and/or opportunities of individuals and collectives (Baldwin, 2013; Collins & Bilge, 2016; Davis, 1983; hooks, 2014). From our perspective, power is co-constructed at multiple scales—historically and structurally at the macrolevel, at the organizational and institutional levels, at the interactional level, and in and through the bodies of individuals themselves. At each of these levels, power is simultaneously coercive with the threat of force and violence and also ideological in that it exists as assumptions of "commonsense" and practices taken to be "normal" (Foucault, 1979; Gramsci, 1971; Hall, 1996). The operation and outcomes of power are sometimes aligned across these levels and contradictory at other times.

Interaction and Microgenetic Analyses

Researchers who employ interaction and microgenetic analyses are diverse in terms of their disciplines and the specific methods they employ. However, there are certain commitments that characterize these approaches. Researchers who employ interaction analysis share the premise that "knowledge and action are fundamentally social in origin, organization, and use, and are situated in particular social and material ecologies" (Jordan & Henderson, 1995, p. 41). As Jordan and Henderson (1995) further elaborate, "This view implies a commitment to grounding theories of knowledge and action in empirical evidence, that is, to building generalizations from records of particular, naturally occurring activities, and steadfastly holding . . . theories accountable to that evidence" (p. 41). The interdisciplinary methods that characterize interaction analysis empirically investigates "the interaction of human beings with each other and with objects in their environment" through close attention to "talk, nonverbal interaction, and the use of artifacts and technologies, identifying routine practices and problems and the resources for their solution" (p. 39).

While the roots of interaction analysis "lie in ethnography (especially participant observation), socio-linguistics, ethnomethodology, conversation analysis, kinesics, proxemics, and ethology" (Jordan & Henderson, 1995, p. 39), we see microgenetic analysis as an important parallel set of methods that has its roots in psychology and cognitive science. Microgenetic approaches accentuate fine-grained processes of learning and change that occur "at the smallest observable time scales" (Parnafes & diSessa, 2013, p. 7). They seek a "moment-by-moment explanatory account of learning in particular contexts" and "conceptual resolution" that yields "very fine distinctions in meaning" that must be tracked (Parnafes & diSessa, 2013, p. 7). For Siegler (2006), microgenetic approaches are characterized by the following methodological commitments:

1. Observations span the period of rapidly changing competence.
2. Within this period, the density of observations is high, relative to the rate of change.
3. Observations are analyzed intensively, with the goal of inferring the representations and processes that gave rise to them.

Similar to the use of the term *critical* in fields such as critical discourse analysis (Fairclough, 1995), we seek to identify a body of work that has implicitly or explicitly linked interaction and microgenetic analyses with an examination of power. Critical interaction and microgenetic analysis forefronts that moment-by-moment processes of learning and change, and the interactions of human beings with each other and with objects in their environment, reflexively co-construct "wider social and cultural structures, relations, and processes" and "struggles over power" (Fairclough, 1995, p. 132).

LITERATURE SELECTION AND METHODS

We focus on the fields of the learning sciences, mathematics education, and science education given the overreliance in these fields on "static categories and group labels" that fail to account for the "socially and politically constructed nature of power" (Martin, 2009, p. 295). To bound this review, we examined articles published from January 2007 to March 2019 (the time of writing) from four leading journals in each of these fields. While some journals ultimately yielded few or no articles, we include them below to highlight the absences and silences across the field. The journals we reviewed are listed below and the final number of articles that met our inclusion criteria is indicated in parentheses:

- *Learning sciences: Cognition and Instruction* (5); *The Journal of Learning Sciences* (12); *Mind, Culture and Activity* (3); and *Human Development* (0)
- *Mathematics education: Educational Studies in Mathematics* (1); *Journal for Research in Mathematics Education* (3); *Mathematical Thinking and Learning* (2); and *ZDM: Mathematics Education* (0)
- *Science education: Cultural Studies of Science Education* (11); *Journal of Research in Science Teaching* (5); *International Journal of Science Education* (0); and *Science Education* (7).

To select relevant articles for review, we read through the titles and abstracts of each article that was published in these journals in the 12-year span we reviewed. In this phase, we included articles that used power as one dimension of analysis. We operationalized attention to power as analytically examining at least one system or structure of oppression, such as racism, sexism, heterosexism, patriarchy, ableism, classism, linguicism, and immigration status. In the second phase, we closely read each of the articles initially selected with a filter for whether or not they used microgenetic and/or interaction analysis. We included articles that were resonant with the methodological commitments of these approaches, even when they did not explicitly state the use of these approaches. The use of the second inclusion criteria severely narrowed the pool of articles that were finally included in this review. To elaborate, in the first phase, we identified numerous articles that centrally engaged power as a dimension of analysis. However, these articles relied largely on post hoc interview data or thick ethnographic descriptions but were not attuned toward interaction or microgenetic approaches. The inclusion of the second criterion yielded the set of articles that we finally included in this review.

We coded each of the articles (Jesson et al., 2011) for methodological approaches, significant methodological innovation, theoretical grounding, theoretical contribution, and study contexts. Given the diversity of theoretical and methodological approaches across the articles, we organized the articles into three thematic categories:

1. The dynamic construction of identity and ideology
2. Attending to the organization of a learning environment
3. Leveraging and repurposing tools

For each category, we characterized how the sets of articles contributed to the integration of interaction analysis and/or microgenetic analysis with critical social theory and highlighted and discussed exemplar illustrations of fusing interaction analysis and/or microgenetic analysis with critical social theory. Our categorization does not imply that articles included in one thematic area cannot or do not speak to the other thematic areas. Instead, our intention is to elevate themes that were prominent across different subsets of articles.

THEMES IN THE LITERATURE REVIEWED

Below, we elaborate on the three thematic categories that emerged in the literature we reviewed. In our representation of the themes, we provide a short overview of each article. We took this approach since the articles varied substantially in theoretical frameworks, methods, and disciplines and were only put in conversation by us given our focus on simultaneously attending to power and learning. Given the immense diversity within a relatively small body of literature, we felt it essential to represent the core findings of each article. As we elaborate in the discussion section below, this chapter provides collective epistemic and empirical weight to the understanding of power and learning as co-constituted and co-constructed through interactional, microgenetic, and structural dynamics by putting these articles in dialogue with each other.

The Dynamic Construction of Identity and Ideology

A distinct and shared characteristic of the articles in this review is that they explicitly emphasized the moment-to-moment co-construction of power, identities, ideologies, and learning. This approach stands in contrast to perspectives that have assumed that learning takes place on the substrate of relatively stable and durable identities, ideologies, and forms of status and power. Critiquing these perspectives, Wood (2013) has argued that the most prevalent approaches "lack the sensitivity to account for variability" in who students are across time and place (Wood, 2013). As Wood (2013) argues, assumptions about stability often function to mask or render invisible variations in students' identities. She highlighted the need to attend to "micro-identities," or "identities enacted in a moment of time," in addition to the more common focus on "macro-identities," or "relatively stable, long-term constructions of who a person is" (p. 776).

By using positioning theory (Davies & Harré, 1999), Wood examined how dramatically students' identities could shift across a single classroom lesson. Her analysis identified the "offered position(s)" and "enacted position(s)" in each relevant turn of talk in one group of fourth-grade students interacting during a mathematics lesson. While most work on identity has ample caveats about multiplicity and variability, the typical reliance on interview data or summative narrations of participant observations often does not show the empirical basis or consequences of these theoretical conjectures. Wood demonstrated how close attention to micro-interactions among participants brings multiplicity and variability in identities to the fore, even across short timescales. Making a more explicit connection between possible micro-identities and macro-identities, Gamez and Parker (2017) used the construct of "micro-figured worlds" to study the subtle ethnic, racial, class, gender, and linguistic inequalities that emerged in two small groups. By focusing on two multilingual learners, they draw attention to the significance these subtle distinctions made in the groups and how they might differentially affect students from the "same" presumed identity category.

Through the lens of ideology, Philip (2011), Philip et al. (2016), and Philip et al. (2018) draw attention to the micro-interactions through which ideological stances are taken by participants, taken up by others, and contested and co-constructed in interaction. They demonstrate how participants' ideological stances construct oneself and others in the moment. Similar to Wood (2013), they show the large amount of variation that can be glossed over through accounts of ideology that emphasize stability and durability. In particular, Philip et al. (2018) studied an undergraduate engineering ethics course and showed how presumptions of relative ideological stability is better understood as an interactional achievement between participants that involve moments of ideological expansion and convergence. They define ideological convergence as "the narrowing of the field of ideological stances that are salient and seen as useful as individuals participate in a joint activity" and ideological expansion as an "analogous broadening of the ideological field" (Philip et al., 2018, p. 185). They trace expansions and convergences using Du Bois's (2007) stance triangle, arguing that stances both evaluate an object and aligns or dis-aligns the stance taker to other participants. Their work troubles assumptions about the necessary salience of certain ideologies like American nationalism or the differential value attributed to civilians of different nationalities; they demonstrate how the participants had to co-construct relevant local ideological meanings, which drew on available macrolevel ideologies as well as their locally relevant identities as engineering students, Americans and non-Americans, ethical actors, and so on.

The methodological diversity in the approaches taken by Wood (2013) and Philip et al. (2018) is further reflected in Orlander Arvola (2014) who examines middle school classroom discursive practices during a lesson on human genitals. Drawing on practical epistemology analysis (Wickman, 2004), Orlander Arvola (2014) shows how the teachers and students co-constructed specific meanings through verbalizing, tacit or explicit acceptance of a prior utterance, and/or filling in the gaps and connections left unsaid in a prior utterance. The inclusion and exclusion of particular knowledges and their significance were outcomes of interactional negotiations between the teacher and the students. While the teachers' moves emphasized learning basic facts about human anatomy, students' wonderings connected them to their own experiences, blending gender and sexuality. Thus, "basic facts" reemerged in this discourse as contextual and imbued with cultural-political meaning. Linked to dominant ideologies, the facts-focused discourse also tended to center male anatomy and heteronormativity, with the discussion of female anatomy as derivative and deviating from male anatomy. Even with these reinscriptions of dominant ideology, Orlander Arvola shows that students' questions challenged hegemonic normalizations of gender and epistemology, creating a more expansive and tangled discursive space. Similarly, Hale (2015) shows how the status and identity of being a "special education" student was acknowledged, accepted, contested, and rejected through students who participated in cogenerative dialogue with their peers and teacher.

The distinctive contribution of Wood (2013), Hale (2015), Orlander Arvola (2014), and the work by Philip and his colleagues is showing *how* identity and ideology are co-constructed in interaction between participants within the particularities of context. To be clear, the theoretical underpinning of their work relies heavily on the prior contributions of critical theorists and critical feminist scholars. The novel contribution of this body of work is the development and deployment of methodological tools, such as micro-identities and ideological convergence, which empirically make visible and accentuate the dynamic processes through which identity and ideology are co-constructed. These detailed, microgenetic, and interactional examinations of the processes of co-construction are then poised to further nuance, contextualize, and complicate the theories on which they build. They caution us against the tendency to slip into claims that the historical, structural, and ideological aspects of power are simply embedded in the organization of a learning environment, that they inherently exist in tools, resources, and human bodies and are waiting to be activated. Rather, in analyses, such as Philip et al.'s (2018) examination of nationalism within the context of an undergraduate classroom, these researchers empirically show how it is in interactions that the cultural and historical traces of power are rendered visible, remade, and/or challenged. This approach shifts the lens from efforts to change the macro-identities of students or the presumably stable ideologies of teachers and students to nuanced attention to the interactions between participants through which micro-identities and microcontestations of ideology emerge in spaces of learning.

Another set of articles in this category emphasized the co-constructed nature of disciplines, like mathematics and science. Rahm's (2007) analysis of conversations among teenage youth in a summer gardening program documented that male participants distinguished between different kinds of scientific work along racial lines and female participants constructed the differences in scientific work along gendered lines. Through these utterances, Rahm argues, the youths' own gendered and racialized selves in relation to science were constructed and made visible. Similarly, Archer et al. (2010) examined how in elementary school students' discourse about what counted as science, there emerged a distinction between science in elementary school and "real" or "grown-up" science. Students co-constructed the science that they did in school as "safe," "immature," and not real science. Such science was contrasted with real science that was dynamic, unpredictable, and involved taking risks (including physical risks) and was taught at higher grade levels or practiced by professional scientists. Drawing on poststructural theorizations of gender (Butler, 1990), Archer et al. (2010) argue that these discourses layer "school" versus "real" science with gendered meanings, with masculinity mapped more strongly onto real and grown-up science.

Complementing Rahm's (2007) and Archer et al.'s (2010) studies of how students conceived of science, Due (2014) examines the practices in a science classroom that positioned students differentially. Due illustrated how girls, in observed physics group work, tended to focus more on understanding, expressed uncertainty, and asked more questions, constructing themselves as responsible students but also putting them at risk for being positioned as less competent in physics. Boys, on the other hand, had a larger range of positionalities available to them, from an irresponsible student, to playful, to being a competent and competitive student in physics, and, as a result, their contributions were less frequently questioned by self or peers. While there were contestations to these positionalities in some groups, in most cases, they limited the ways in which female students could come to see themselves as competent physics learners or as having trajectories that allowed for more central participation in the physics community of practice (Lave & Wenger, 1991). Due (2014) argues that these cases illustrate that "theories concerning 'situated learning' (Lave & Wenger, 1991) must be supplemented with theories about power relations" (p. 457). Similarly, Archer et al. (2017) drew on critical discourse (Burman & Parker, 1993) and gender theory (Butler, 1990) to show how power is organized within talk and the social implications of particular constructions. They document how the everyday actions that are celebrated or considered exemplary in the science classroom are often masculine and aggressive, demonstrating what they call "muscular intellect." The celebration of these performances legitimizes them, narrowing the possibilities for who gets to be seen as a science person (Carlone et al., 2014).

In a similar vein, Ideland and Malmberg (2012) compare the discourses that students from a Swedish urban middle school and a Swedish suburban middle school engaged in during same-gender focus group discussions on body and health. They note that the positionalities that were available and taken up by students in terms of being a good student were entangled with their conceptualization of gender performance. Girls at the urban school questioned the normative characterizations of body and health, resisted stereotyped notions of Muslim girls from immigrant and low-income families as weak and passive, and created and made available alternate versions of femininity through "othering" the stereotype.

These studies show local constructions of science and their alignments with dominant representations of race and gender in science rather than assuming the inevitability of gendered and racialized exclusion in science. While the resonance between the local construction of science and its hegemonic representation is disheartening in both studies, they problematize assumptions of top-down determinism and suggest the possibilities of localized constructions that are robust enough to mitigate or resist the effects of dominant ideologies.

Talk and action in science classrooms thus embody cultural understandings and norms of gender, class, and disciplinary identities and epistemologies, constituting the "doing" of specific aspects of identity (Butler, 1990; Paechter, 2007). These discourses simultaneously constrain and enable what participants can do and say, the positionalities available to them (Foucault, 1979), and, ultimately, who gets positioned by self and others as legitimately belonging in science (Carlone et al., 2014). Identity, thus, is not conceptualized as an internal sense of self but as constituted in and remade by interactions and participation in local cultural practices (Esmonde, 2009; Nasir & Hand, 2006).

Much of the work in this category examines shifts in identity and ideology across relatively short timescales. Notable exceptions, Gresalfi et al. (2009) and Carlone et al. (2015) show that microlevel interactions have the potential to sediment into more durable identities over time. In their analysis of competence, Gresalfi et al. (2009) shift the lens of analysis from an individual and individual traits to the social organization of a classroom by considering the system of competence that gets constructed as students and teachers negotiate the following:

(1) the kind of mathematical agency that the task and the participation afford, (2) what the students are supposed to be accountable for doing, and (3) whom they need to be accountable to in order to participate successfully in the classroom activity system. (p. 52)

They thus bring attention to the "interaction between the opportunities that a student has to participate competently and the ways that individual takes up those opportunities" (Gresalfi et al., 2009, p. 50).

Carlone et al. (2015) study girls' identity development in elementary grade science classrooms. While they do not attend to micro-interactions in detail over very short timescales, they attended to "patterns of girls' discursive performances of femininity in school science from fourth to seventh grade" (p. 478). They collected field notes, interviews with students and teachers, and videos of classrooms. They analyzed these data for academic performances like "good student," and particular performances of femininity often associated with distancing from a scientific identity such as pleasing adults and making one self submissive or invisible. Their analysis honed in on one student, Mirabel, over the course of 3 years of schooling. They show how her identity shifted from being one of the class's "smartest science students" and from being actively engaged in Grade 4 to being constructed as "flighty" and a "social butterfly" whose interest in "girly stuff took [her] away from intellectual engagements" in Grade 5. By Grade 6, Carlone et al. argued that Mirabel was playing with a more "heterosexualized identity" and positioned herself as helpless and in need of assistance. In their assessment, by sixth grade, Mirabel played up heteronormative sexual performances and downplayed her academic side, using her agency to "walk away from her possibilities in science in favor of her primary social goal to fit in with peers" (p. 485). The authors situate these changes in the performances of Mirabel and other girls within "classroom organizational, ideological and interpersonal structures," particularly narrow constructions of who is good at science. They argue that Mirabel's fifth- and sixth-grade classrooms put severe constraints on Mirabel's agency, leaving her without a "viable academic/scientific subject position" that allowed her to still fit in, encouraging her to choose to be "more social and girly," a social position that afforded recognition from her peers and teacher.

Reading this body of work prompts us to examine how hegemonies of race, gender, and class (and other dominant power structures) are co-constructed within classroom interactions and "acquire" (McDermott, 1993) learners and/or the discipline through discourse and participation structures. They also present openings that have potential to disrupt these hegemonies. The articles in the next section take up the question of whether and how the organization of the learning environment more broadly reproduces and/or challenges these hegemonies.

Attending to the Organization of a Learning Environment

This set of studies is more diverse with overlapping attention to the organization of a learning environment. At one end of the spectrum are infrastructural elements that embody relationships of power. As an example, Archer et al. (2016) studied the design of particular exhibits at a museum and how students interacted with these spaces. Their discourse analytic approach looked for "how power is organized within (the boys') talk" to draw out "the social implications of particular constructions" (p. 451). Their analysis asked the following: "What is the talk doing? What is being normalized or defended? Where is the locus of power within a particular construction—whose interests are being asserted? Who or what is being othered? What is normalized or closed down?" (p. 451). In their data, Archer et al. identified performances and tropes of masculinity and the ways in which they were supported or challenged by others. They attended to how these forms of masculinities existed in relationship to performances of science identity and intersections with classed and racialized discourses. Their analysis suggests that the design of the exhibits promoted masculine displays of "laddishness" by certain boys visiting the museum. In some cases, such performance of gender also opened up opportunities for the boys to engage in science discussions. Archer et al.'s (2016) analysis draws on poststructural gender theory to show how "hegemonic masculinity is normalized within the museum space," shaping who gets to do science in that space and how. Similarly, Dawson (2014) studied interactions between museum staff and visitors from low-income racial minority backgrounds within the context of the design of exhibits and the assumptions and practices embedded in museums. Through this examination, Dawson highlighted differences in the cultural, linguistic, economic, and social capital (Bourdieu, 1998) of the visitors and how they were co-constructed through assumptions built into the exhibits and modes of interaction. The organization of the learning space led to a form of symbolic violence (Bourdieu, 1990) that tended to exclude visitors from low-income backgrounds or made it more difficult for them to identify with the museum space.

Archer et al.'s (2016) analysis forefronts infrastructure such as the physical environment and the "stereotypically masculine objects in the museum" that emphasized competition and "afforded boys a platform from which to assert performances of hegemonic masculinity" (p. 468). The organization of a learning environment is not only physical, it also entails how the shared activity is locally structured to collectively address certain types of problems. Horn (2007) highlighted the problems of practice that teachers encounter and how they solve these problems in consultation with their colleagues. In particular, she showed how conceptions of students, mathematics as a subject, and teaching are all embedded and interactionally reconstructed in teacher's daily work. She explored how the conversational category systems at schools mediated the ways in which teachers took responsibility for students' learning at one school site and how they constructed students to be at the root of the problem at another school site. Methodologically, Horn studied the categorization of students and its relation to teachers' practices and their conceptions of their subject through a unit of analysis she termed *episode of pedagogical reasoning*—"units of teacher-to-teacher talk in which teachers exhibit their understanding of an issue in their practice" (p. 46). Horn's work shifts the focus from the presumed beliefs of individual teachers (and efforts to change them) to the collective meaning making that emerges from the everyday practices of teachers.

Related to Horn's (2007) problem of practices, Jackson's (2011) inquiry demonstrates the implications for students when sites of learning are organized such that knowledge and practices flow in one direction, particularly between sites with differential forms of power. In her study, Jackson extensively observed one student, Timothy, at home and eventually in his school context. At home, Jackson observed a collective effort on the part of Timothy's parents to arrange and rearrange situations for him to successfully complete his homework, given the consequences that noncompletion presented for him at school. Yet Timothy's teacher attributed his challenges with homework first to a presumed disability and then to "coddling" on the part of his parents. Jackson argued that the student's shortcomings in the classroom were produced not only in the classroom but also through the teacher's unwarranted interpretation of what was happening at home. Jackson's study suggests the importance of examining how different sites of learning are organized and interact with each other.

The organization of a learning environment can also be relational. Bruna and Vann (2007) and Bruna (2010) suggest that a friendly relationship between the teacher and the students can allow students to interject with their ideas and questions, leading to the transformation of the activity system. Takeuchi (2016) takes on this theme more substantively. Takeuchi documents that when English language learners work with friends in small-group problem-solving activities, they had access to a wider range of roles, including that of an expert. In teacher-assigned groups, the same students were positioned as incapable and their contributions were often not recognized, which limited their opportunities to learn.

Differences in epistemologies and the values attributed to different practices also play a role in organizing a learning environment. Bruna and Vann (2007) and Bruna (2010) examine the experiences of immigrant middle-school students of Mexican origin in their science classroom. Focusing on a lesson on pig dissection, Bruna and Vann (2007) show how the framing of the lesson by the teacher was situated in the race and class divisions of the town whose main industry was a meatpacking plant with majority White administrators and majority Mexican immigrant workers. The teacher–student interactions, the structure of the activity, the tools involved, and the knowledges forefronted, reified this racial and classed framing. The organization of the classroom made it difficult for students to draw on their personal experiences and community knowledge as epistemic sources. These authors demonstrate through their analyses that power is never fully deterministic and that the intersectional nature of power allows students to position themselves and get positioned by others along multiple axes. For instance, Bruna (2010) further developed this analysis to show moments when the class's normative patterns were resisted and temporarily transformed by a student, who drew on his transnational cultural resources and his recognized proficiency in English.

As in Bruna (2010), many of the articles in this cluster (Andrée, 2012; LópezLeiva et al., 2013; Meacham, 2007; Puvirajah et al., 2012) show how shifts in the activity system allowed for the emergence of different positionalities and possibilities for authoring different selves. For example, LópezLeiva et al. (2013) showed how a shift in attending to and elaborating on English language learners' hybrid linguistic resources (from judging or dis-acknowledging them) allowed students to make sense of complex mathematical ideas around probability and to author identities as competent mathematics learners. In their study of a dual-language after-school mathematics program, they examined when students decided to work in mostly Spanish or English, the strategies they employed across these instances, and "patterns across groups in how the students' multidimensionality was accounted for and legitimized as well as how students and their facilitators participated [. . .] during probability problem-solving tasks" (p. 924). Puvirajah et al. (2012) examined how the shift in the activity system from a science classroom to the context of a robotics competition reduced the power imbalance between students and teachers, opening up ways in which to participate that more closely mirrored professional science practices.

Resonant with articles in the previous category, Jackson and Seiler (2017, 2018) emphasized the co-construction of disciplines and identities. They draw on the figured worlds framework (Holland et al., 2001) alongside critical discourse analysis (Gee, 2011) to examine how students who enter postsecondary science through non-traditional journeys ("latecomers") struggle to find ways to achieve status as "good student" or "being good in science" in the classroom. They argue that the elitism of science as constructed in the figured world of the institution and the dominance of teacher-centered and sink-or-swim cultural models of learning made it more difficult for latecomers to science to author science identities. In the 2017 article, Jackson and Seiler highlight two cases where the "latecomer" student subverted the dominant models to gain status as a student and a science learner. In their 2018 article, they showed how a similar transformation in status and affinity to science could be achieved collectively by a group of students through online dialogue, by building solidarity, and by recognizing the value of asking questions.

Further problematizing static conceptions of disciplines, Rosebery et al. (2010) develop the construct of epistemological heterogeneity. They highlighted through their study of a class of third and fourth graders how classrooms are "spaces in which whole systems of meaning or ways of seeing the world come into contact with one another in both planned and unplanned ways" (p. 337). They drew attention to how "instructional encounters" can be designed with "the aim of fostering contact among varied languages and points of view to generate learning of disciplinary ways of seeing the world" (p. 351). Rosebery et al.'s theorization of learning as heterogeneous meaning making is resonant with Van Horne and Bell's (2017) study of the design of a high school biology classroom that engaged youth in culturally expansive epistemic practices of science. The design of the classroom provided youth with multiple entry points that supported the development of their disciplinary science identities and their possible future selves. Their analysis examined how particular subject positions became meaningful to participants within the setting they studied. Van Horne and Bell coded for how students "were positioned to engage in specific kinds of work over time, the kinds of persons that were related to that work, and a tracing of the self-reflection and social recognition work that unfolded over time" (pp. 452–453). They also paid particular attention to the outside expertise students brought to bear to disciplinary practices and how it was meaningful or not to their goals within the setting.

While the articles above problematize the exclusionary practices of "Western science" in schools, Bang and Marin (2015) and Marin and Bang (2018) examine the new possibilities that emerge when Indigenous ways of knowing are centered. Marin and Bang (2018) explored a Native American family's experience on a walk in an urban forest preserve and how learning unfolded in this place. They make "an argument for walking, reading, and storying land as a methodology for learning about and making relationships with the natural world" (p. 111). Their analysis is situated within a deep recognition of the complex ecological challenges facing the globe. They suggest that making progress on these ecological challenges "requires attending to the microgenetic processes that give rise to human-nature relationships in activity and practice" (p. 113). Drawing on design-based work rooted in a framework of Indigenous ways of knowing, Bang and Marin's (2015) study of everyday parent-child interactions led them to argue that organizing learning environments so that they "expand the boundaries of reality and possible futures for students is both vital and possible" (p. 542). They argued that normative practices create moments of interaction that tend to reinscribe inequalities while demonstrating the political and ethical significance of reorganizing talk-in-interaction for practices such as "memory traces."

The articles in this section considered the organization of the learning environment as a whole, which includes the physical space, the available resources, the organization of social relationships, particular types of performances and recognitions, and access to resources. While the articles in the first section highlighted the moment-to-moment co-constructions of identities and ideologies, articles in this section take a slightly broader unit of analysis—the organization of the learning environment. They highlight how the mesolevel organization mediates the contact of micro-interactional processes with macrocategories and constructs. In the section below, we explicitly highlight a set of articles that focuses on how tools are used, adapted, and refashioned to exercise power.

Leveraging and Repurposing Tools

The set of articles in this category explored how representational, meditational, and discursive tools afforded opportunities and constraints through which power and learning were co-constructed. In particular, Rubel et al. (2016), Rubel et al. (2017), Hostetler et al. (2018), and Philip et al. (2016) explore how these co-constructions emerge within the context of new digital technologies. Rubel et al. (2017) and Philip et al. (2016) draw attention to how representations of data through maps are interpreted through ideological systems where space is highly racialized. They show how disciplinary meaning making about the data was integrally connected to students' meaning making about themselves as sociopolitical actors and about systems of power in which they lived and moved. Their analysis at the level of turns of talk—drawing from Goodwin's (2007) participation framework in the case of Philip et al. (2016) and Morris's (2013) map reading framework in the case of Rubel et al.—demonstrate the opportunities for disciplinary learning and learning about power that were afforded and limited by the use of the representations. These pieces add to a rich tradition of scholarship that has emphasized that tools and representations embody power and politics. They trace how these representations are leveraged and contested in interaction to co-construct opportunities for learning and meaning making about power.

Hostetler et al.'s (2018) work highlights the use of new digital tools to create representations that allow learners to take on the perspectives of others. Their agent-based computational models of ethnocentrism and racial segregation allowed preservice teachers to "discuss critical socio-political issues in the classroom without forcing themselves to reveal their personal experiences or assumptions" (p. 145). They argue that once the learner locates themselves in the simulation, they identify with a certain type of agent and in turn construct the remaining agents as "others." By attending to the learning opportunities afforded through this set of tools and representations, the authors show the range of empirically informed discussions that learners engage in as they consider, through a process of objectification, the perspectives of the multiple agents in the simulation. Reasoning about the world of computational agents afforded opportunities for the learners to "build discourses that included critical perspectives, debate relevant conflicts, and develop nuanced understandings of the underlying socio-political-economic mechanisms that may be responsible for the emergence of ethnocentric behavior" (p. 140).

Emphasizing the importance of mediational tools, Lewis (2014, 2017) examined the construction of mathematical learning disabilities (MLDs). Based on her analysis of tutoring interactions with two students with MLDs, she showed that standard instructional representations most commonly used in mathematics classrooms are inaccessible for these students and thus co-construct the MLDs. She conjectured that the *re*-mediation (Gutiérrez et al., 2009) of tools to account for and build on students' understandings might expand learning opportunities for students with MLDs. Lewis's (2014, 2017) work demonstrates that an interactional analysis that focuses on the affordances and limitations of mediational tools for different students can elucidate the co-construction of forms of power such as ability and disability. With similar attention to mediational tools, Oliveira et al. (2014) examined how the representation of animal death in elementary school read-aloud sessions through lenses of predation or as an agentless outcome was viewed as natural and morally good, while representations of animal death as pollution-related were viewed as unnatural and immoral. Oliveira et al. demonstrated that representations of death mediate relationships of power between humans and other forms of life. Similarly, Oliveira et al. (2012) analyzed how "specific textual elements in the design of environmental dilemmas (types of prompts used, decision-makers' identities, statements of intentionality and outcome, moral complexity, values of nature, and social representation or cultural images of animals)" prompted either nonadversarial argumentation between students or argumentation that involved contestations over sexual identities, combative disagreement, and "conflict resolution on social rather than rational grounds" (p. 869). As another example, Buchholz et al. (2014) documented the culturally embedded gendered meanings of tools, which were reinscribed and renegotiated in interactions between students in an e-textile maker environment. Their analysis examines how the use of these tools opened up opportunities for students to learn and access positions of leadership.

A second category of tools that we examined was discursive in nature. These discursive tools, both social and disciplinary, were leveraged to co-construct status in classrooms and negotiate relationships of power among students and between teachers and students. Engle et al. (2014) trace the contributions of one student in a mathematics classroom. Through a framework that highlighted (a) the negotiated merit of each participant's contributions, and each participant's (b) degree of intellectual authority, (c) access to the conversational floor, and (d) degree of spatial privilege, the authors demonstrate that influence in argumentation emerged dynamically through social interactions. Their analysis showed that while the normative quality of the focus student's arguments was lower than that of his peers, his arguments garnered more influence because of his perceived intellectual authority and his ability to "command the interactional space and conversational floor" (Langer-Osuna, 2017, p. 240; see also Langer-Osuna, 2015, 2016).

Similarly, Bishop (2012) closely examined the discourse patterns in small-group interactions. Her framework draws attention to (a) using an authoritarian voice, (b) making statements of superiority or inferiority, (c) using face-saving moves, (d) building solidarity and providing encouragement, and (e) controlling problem-solving strategies. Her analysis of two students, Teri and Bonnie, showed that through Teri's "control of discourse at the microlevel and their repeated and joint positioning of Bonnie as mathematically incapable with little to contribute, the girls enacted their respective identities of 'smart' and 'dumb'" (p. 66). Bishop's analysis shows how microlevel patterns in students' discourse shaped the mathematical identities they enacted.

Distinct from Engle et al. (2014) and Bishop (2012), Schoerning et al. (2015) documented the power asymmetry between the teacher and the student by attending to "language markers related to power and agency, including both non-grammatical factors such as tone and tempo of speech as well as the characteristics and qualities of that speech's dialog" (p. 244). They show how it was ameliorated over time, in the case they studied, through "an immersion approach" to argument-based inquiry, where "students develop questions, design experiments, gather data, and generate evidence to support claims that address their initial questions" (p. 254). Schoerning et al. showed that by "actively inverting some of the conventions of formal language" (p. 256), teachers can create new avenues for access and power for their students and engage them as stakeholders who are more able to engage in argumentative aspects of disciplinary negotiation. Highlighting intersections of power, Enyedy et al. (2008) showed the unintended consequences of the practice of revoicing students' contributions in a multilingual classroom and how this discursive tool operated at the intersection of linguistic and racial forms of power to inadvertently marginalize the African American students in the class.

Bridging the multiple tools across both categories, Vossoughi (2014) made an explicit link between artifacts developed in a learning environment and the deepening of the collective analysis of social problems in her study of an educational setting designed for high school–aged migrant students. She attended to how "social analytic artifacts"—"tools or habits of mind that deepen and propel the collective analysis of social problems"—were made and appropriated in real-time talk and interaction (p. 353). She analyzed "how classroom discourse, printed texts, and social relations created an environment where social analytic artifacts were codeveloped and appropriated over time" (p. 353).

Collectively, these articles draw attention to tools as imbued with power and with the potential to be contested and repurposed for different goals. Rubel et al. (2016), Rubel et al. (2017), Hostetler et al. (2018), and Philip et al. (2016) made evident the emergent possibilities and challenges of new digital tools and representations as they enter learning environments. Lewis (2014, 2017), Oliveira et al. (2014), and Buchholz et al. (2014) reminded us of the ways in which power is deeply embedded in the tools and representations that mostly go unquestioned as well as the importance of remediating them toward more equitable and just purposes. Engle et al. (2014), Bishop (2012), and Schoerning et al. (2015) highlighted how discursive tools are deployed constantly to enforce and challenge power and status. Finally, Vossoughi (2014) explicitly attends to how tools can be codeveloped toward collective social analysis and political learning. Collectively, these articles remind us of the dynamic nature of the organization of learning environments and of learners' agency in these spaces. In these articles, tools, which could be linguistic tools, digital technologies, representations, etc., become the locus or site where macrocategories and constructs are entangled with microlevel interactions.

DISCUSSION

In his article, "Researching race in mathematics education," Martin (2009) pointed out a troubling contradiction between the conceptualization of race across fields of inquiry. His critique of undertheorization and overly simplistic methods of analysis echo a recurring theme across the articles we reviewed—the risks of assuming the salience of labels and categories a priori in an analysis, without attention to how they take and give meaning through interaction. Martin's assessment can be extended more broadly:

> Although [group-based identities and categories] are characterized in the sociological and critical theory literatures as socially and politically constructed with structural expressions, most studies of differential outcomes in . . . education begin and end their analyses . . . with static . . . categories and group labels used for the sole purpose of disaggregating data. (p. 295)

The articles we reviewed underscore the steadily growing scholarship in the learning sciences, mathematics education, and science education that has seriously engaged with sociological and critical perspectives to conceptualize and study power. Acknowledging that we included an additional criterion of microgenetic and interactional analysis to Martin's call, the relatively small number of articles we identified, however, and their complete absence or near absence in leading journals in the field speak to the persistence of the underlying shortcoming Martin named in 2009. Yet they also highlight a burgeoning significant subfield that we term *critical interaction and microgenetic analysis*.

It is not uncommon that claims made in rich qualitative studies, such as those we examine here, are minimized as isolated cases (see Flyvbjerg, 2006). By bringing this set of articles together, this chapter provides collective epistemic and empirical weight to claims of power and learning as co-constituted and co-constructed through interactional, microgenetic, and structural dynamics. Reading across the thematic areas we identified, the assembled literature points to the importance of *simultaneously* holding the following analytical commitments in critical interaction and microgenetic analysis:

1. Attending to and foregrounding variability in learners' identities and their ideological stances.
2. Establishing links between moment-to-moment variability in learners' identities, the ideological stances they take, and the forms of relative durability in these constructs over time, place, and settings.
3. Emphasizing the co-construction of power, identity, and ideology through participants' interactions, and how disciplines such as mathematics and science are co-constructed as ideological (racialized, gendered, classed, etc.) through interactional processes.
4. Examining how dynamics of power, identity, ideology, and disciplinary sense making are afforded or constrained by (a) the design of the learning environment, (b) the propensities of architecture and infrastructure to promote particular interactions, and/or (c) the relationships that are likely and that are possible in a setting.
5. Seeking an understanding of the continuities and discontinuities of identities and ideologies in learners' lives across multiple sites.
6. Analyzing how representational and discursive tools are used, contested, and/or repurposed by learners as they negotiate powered relationships.

We certainly resonate with Martin's (2009) call for the learning sciences, mathematics education, and science education to more fully engage critical social theory. And, we reverberate with Nasir and Hand's (2006) provocation for how theories of learning, particularly sociocultural theories, can contribute to social theory. While relatively small in size, the body of scholarship we reviewed begins to illustrate the possibilities of such integration. The microgenetic and interactional analyses bring into relief the particularities of context, making visible the limits, edges, and horizons of more abstracted theories of power. They add nuance to, contextualize, and complicate the theories of power, identity, and ideology on which they build.

In this review, we put in conversation with each other various bodies of research on learning that integrated methods of microgenetic and/or interaction analysis with frameworks of power. Collectively, these articles provide a nascent empirical basis for understanding the dynamic relationship between macrolevel structures and ideologies and microlevel interactions: The macrolevel structures and ideologies afford and constrain microlevel interactions where people are always repurposing tools, reimagining themselves, renegotiating relationships, and improvising with practices and ideologies; these microlevel repurposings, imaginings, negotiations, and improvisations cumulatively shape the local emergence of ideologies and structures. Taken together, this body of scholarship makes visible the limitations of assuming the stability of macrolevel identities and ideologies in spaces of learning or of imposing them onto an environment based solely on post hoc interviews or summative narrations of observations.

As a group, the articles illustrate that interactions, the myriad microtransactions among people and between people and their environments, are sites for "becoming," where identity and ideological work happen. In learning environments, microgenetic processes of identity and ideology are about becoming particular kinds of learners and particular kinds of persons in the world: gendered, raced, classed, (dis)abled, and so on. If race, class, gender, competence, ability, sexuality, disciplinary, and/or professional identity are all constructions locally emergent from culturally historically situated microlevel interactions, then, taken together, these articles suggest that (a) deep engagement with intersectionality (Collins & Bilge, 2016) is essential to better understand power in interaction and (b) a fine-grained attention to power in interaction will further the theoretical and methodological horizons of intersectionality. While the articles we reviewed conceptualize ideology and identity as emergent constructions, only a few (e.g., Gamez & Parker, 2017) took an explicit analytical attention to intersectionality—a pressing area for future work.

The articles reviewed also underscore that all interactions in learning environments are political and ethical, and all learning environments are sites of politics and ethics. Taken together, the articles give added meaning to the claim that all teaching and learning are political, ethical, and ideological, accentuating that each moment of teaching and learning is consequential as teachers and students continually and jointly renegotiate power and possibility in every interaction (Philip, 2019). This recognition alerts us to the need for a more elaborate toolkit of attentional, linguistic, and interactional repertoires to collectively co-organize spaces where participants are more likely to engage "epistemological heterogeneity" (Rosebery et al., 2010) and "ideologically converge" (Philip et al., 2018) toward more just and equitable interactions.

ORCID iD

Thomas M. Philip https://orcid.org/0000-0002-9879-0965

REFERENCES

Andrée, M. (2012). Altering conditions for student participation and motive development in school science: Learning from Helena's mistake. *Cultural Studies of Science Education*, *7*(2), 425–438. https://doi.org/10.1007/s11422-011-9314-x

Archer, L., Dawson, E., Dewitt, J., Godec, S., King, H., Mau, A., Nomikou, E., & Seakins, A. (2017) Killing curiosity? An analysis of celebrated identity performances among teachers and students in nine London secondary science classrooms. *Science Education*, *101*(5), 741–764. https://doi.org/10.1002/sce.21291

Archer, L., Dawson, E., Seakins, A., DeWitt, J., Godec, S., & Whitby, C. (2016). "I'm being a man here": Urban boys' performances of masculinity and engagement with science during a science museum visit. *Journal of the Learning Sciences*, *25*(3), 438–485. https://doi.org/ 10.1080/10508406.2016.1187147

Archer, L., DeWitt, J., Osborne, J., Dillon, J., Willis, B., & Wong, B. (2010). "Doing" science versus "being" a scientist: Examining 10/11-year-old schoolchildren's constructions of science through the lens of identity. *Science Education*, *94*(4), 617–639. https://doi .org/10.1002/sce.20399

Baldwin, J. (2013). *The fire next time*. Vintage.

Bang, M., & Marin, A. (2015). Nature-culture constructs in science learning: Human/ non-human agency and intentionality. *Journal of Research in Science Teaching*, *52*(4), 530–544. https://doi.org/10.1002/tea.21204

Bishop, J. P. (2012). "She's always been the smart one. I've always been the dumb one": Identities in the mathematics classroom. *Journal for Research in Mathematics Education, 43*(1), 34–74. https://doi.org/10.5951/jresematheduc.43.1.0034

Bourdieu, P. (1990). *The logic of practice* (R. Nice, Trans.). Stanford University Press.

Bourdieu, P. (1998). *Practical reason.* Polity Press.

Bruna, K. R. (2010). Mexican immigrant transnational social capital and class transformation: Examining the role of peer mediation in insurgent science. *Cultural Studies of Science Education, 5*(2), 383–422. https://doi.org/10.1007/s11422-009-9232-3

Bruna, K. R., & Vann, R. (2007). On pigs and packers: Radically contextualizing a practice of science with Mexican immigrant students. *Cultural Studies of Science Education, 2*(1), 19–59. https://doi.org/10.1007/s11422-006-9041-x

Buchholz, B., Shively, K., Peppler, K., & Wohlwend, K. (2014). Hands on, hands off: Gendered access in crafting and electronics practices. *Mind, Culture, and Activity, 21*(4), 278–297. https://doi.org/10.1080/10749039.2014.939762

Burman, E., & Parker, I. (1993). *Discourse analytic research: Repertoires and readings of texts in action.* Routledge.

Butler, J. (1990). *Gender trouble.* Routledge.

Carlone, H. B., Johnson, A., & Scott, C. M. (2015). Agency amidst formidable structures: How girls perform gender in science class. *Journal of Research in Science Teaching, 52*(4), 474–488. https://doi.org/10.1002/tea.21224

Carlone, H. B., Scott, C. M., & Lowder, C. (2014). Becoming (less) scientific: A longitudinal study of students' identity work from elementary to middle school science. *Journal of Research in Science Teaching, 51*(7), 836–869. https://doi.org/10.1002/tea.21150

Collins, P. H., & Bilge, S. (2016). *Intersectionality.* Wiley.

Davies, B., & Harré, R. (1999). Positioning and personhood. In R. Harré & L. van Langenhove (Eds.), *Positioning theory* (pp. 32–52). Blackwell.

Davis, A. Y. (1983). *Women, race, and class.* Vintage.

Dawson, E. (2014). "Not designed for us": How science museums and science centers socially exclude low-income, minority ethnic groups. *Science Education, 98*(6), 981–1008. https://doi.org/10.1002/sce.21133

Du Bois, J. W. (2007). The stance triangle. In R. Englebretson (Ed.), *Stancetaking in discourse: Subjectivity, evaluation, interaction* (pp. 139–182). John Benjamins. https://doi.org/10.1075/pbns.164.07du

Due, K. (2014). Who is the competent physics student? A study of students' positions and social interaction in small-group discussions. *Cultural Studies of Science Education, 9*(2), 441–459. https://doi.org/10.1007/s11422-012-9441-z

Engle, R. A., Langer-Osuna, J. M., & McKinney de Royston, M. (2014). Toward a model of influence in persuasive discussions: Negotiating quality, authority, privilege, and access within a student-led argument. *Journal of the Learning Sciences, 23*(2), 245–268. https://doi.org/10.1080/10508406.2014.883979

Enyedy, N., Rubel, L., Castellón, V., Mukhopadhyay, S., Esmonde, I., & Secada, W. (2008). Revoicing in a multilingual classroom. *Mathematical Thinking and Learning, 10*(2), 134–162. https://doi.org/10.1080/10986060701854458

Esmonde, I. (2009). Mathematics learning in groups: Analyzing equity in two cooperative activity structures. *Journal of the Learning Sciences, 18*(2), 247–284. https://doi.org/10.1080/10508400902797958

Erickson, F. (2004). *Talk and social theory: Ecologies of speaking and listening in everyday life.* Polity Press.

Fairclough, N. (1995). *Critical discourse analysis: The critical study of language.* Routledge.

Flyvbjerg, B. (2006). Five misunderstandings about case-study research. *Qualitative Inquiry, 12*(2), 219–245. https://doi.org/10.1177/1077800405284363

Foucault, M. (1979). *The history of sexuality: Vol. 1. An introduction.* Allen Lane.

Gamez, R., & Parker, C. A. (2017). Becoming science learners: A study of newcomers' identity work in elementary school science. *Science Education, 102*(2), 377–413. https://doi.org/10.1002/sce.21323

Gee, J. P. (2011). *How to do discourse analysis: A toolkit.* Routledge. https://doi.org/10.4324/9780203850992

Goodwin, C. (1994). Professional vision. *American Anthropologist, 96,* 606–633. https://doi.org/10.1525/aa.1994.96.3.02a00100

Goodwin, C. (2007). Participation, stance and affect in the organization of activities. *Discourse & Society, 18*(1), 53–73. https://doi.org/10.1177/0957926507069457

Gramsci, A. (1971). *Prison notebooks.* International Publishers.

Gresalfi, M., Martin, T., Hand, V., & Greeno, J. (2009). Constructing competence: An analysis of student participation in the activity systems of mathematics classrooms. *Educational Studies in Mathematics, 70*(1), 49–70. https://doi.org/10.1007/s10649-008-9141-5

Gutiérrez, K. D., Morales, P. Z., & Martinez, D. C. (2009). Re-mediating literacy: Culture, difference, and learning for students from nondominant communities. *Review of research in education, 33*(1), 212–245. https://doi.org/10.3102/0091732X08328267

Hale, C. (2015). Urban special education policy and the lived experience of stigma in a high school science classroom. *Cultural Studies of Science Education, 10*(4), 1071–1088. https://doi.org/10.1007/s11422-013-9548-x

Hall, S. (1996). The problem of ideology: Marxism without guarantees. In D. Morley & K. Chen (Eds.), *Stuart Hall: Critical dialogues in cultural studies* (pp. 25–46). Routledge.

Holland, D., Lachiotte, W. S., Jr., Skinner, D., & Cain, C. (2001). *Identity and agency in cultural worlds.* Harvard University Press.

hooks, b. (2014). *Teaching to transgress.* Routledge. https://doi.org/10.4324/9780203700280

Horn, I. S. (2007). Fast kids, slow kids, lazy kids: Framing the mismatch problem in mathematics teachers' conversations. *Journal of the Learning Sciences, 16*(1), 37–79. https://doi.org/10.1207/s15327809jls1601_3

Hostetler, A., Sengupta, P., & Hollett, T. (2018). Unsilencing critical conversations in social-studies teacher education using agent-based modeling. *Cognition and Instruction, 36*(2), 139–170. https://doi.org/10.1080/07370008.2017.1420653

Ideland, M., & Malmberg, C. (2012). Body talk: Students' identity construction while discussing a socioscientific issue. *Cultural Studies of Science Education, 7*(2), 279–305. https://doi.org/10.1007/s11422-012-9381-7

Jackson, K. (2011). Approaching participation in school-based mathematics as a cross-setting phenomenon. *Journal of the Learning Sciences, 20*(1), 111–150. https://doi.org/10.1080/10508406.2011.528319

Jackson, P. A., & Seiler, G. (2017). Identity work in the college science classroom: The cases of two successful latecomers to science. *Science Education, 101*(5), 716–740. https://doi.org/10.1002/sce.21290

Jackson, P. A., & Seiler, G. (2018). I am smart enough to study postsecondary science: A critical discourse analysis of latecomers' identity construction in an online forum. *Cultural Studies of Science Education, 13*(3), 761–784. https://doi.org/10.1007/s11422-017-9818-0

Jesson, J. K., Matheson, L., & Lacey, F. M. (2011). *Doing your literature review: Traditional and systematic techniques.* Sage.

Jordan, B., & Henderson, A. (1995). Interaction analysis: Foundations and practice. *Journal of the Learning Sciences, 4*(1), 39–103. https://doi.org/10.1207/s15327809jls0401_2

Langer-Osuna, J. M. (2015). From getting "fired" to becoming a collaborator: A case of the coconstruction of identity and engagement in a project-based mathematics classroom. *Journal of the Learning Sciences, 24*(1), 53–92. https://doi.org/10.1080/10508406.2014.944643

Langer-Osuna, J. M. (2016). The social construction of authority among peers and its implications for collaborative mathematics problem solving. *Mathematical Thinking and Learning, 18*(2), 107–124. https://doi.org/10.1080/10986065.2016.1148529

Langer-Osuna, J. M. (2017). Authority, identity, and collaborative mathematics. *Journal for Research in Mathematics Education, 48*(3), 237–247.

Lave, J., & Wenger, E. (1991). *Situated learning: Legitimate peripheral participation.* Cambridge University Press. https://doi.org/10.1017/CBO9780511815355

Lewis, K. E. (2014). Difference not deficit: Reconceptualizing mathematical learning disabilities. *Journal for Research in Mathematics Education, 45*(3), 351–396. https://doi.org/10.5951/jresematheduc.45.3.0351

Lewis, K. E. (2017). Designing a bridging discourse: Re-mediation of a mathematical learning disability. *Journal of the Learning Sciences, 26*(2), 320–365. https://doi.org/10.1080/10508406.2016.1256810

LópezLeiva, C. A., Torres, Z., & Khisty, L. L. (2013). Acknowledging Spanish and English resources during mathematical reasoning. *Cultural Studies of Science Education, 8*(4), 919–934. https://doi.org/10.1007/s11422-013-9518-3

Marin, A., & Bang, M. (2018). "Look it, this is how you know": Family forest walks as a context for knowledge-building about the natural world. *Cognition and Instruction, 36*(2), 89–118. https://doi.org/10.1080/07370008.2018.1429443

Martin, D. B. (2009). Researching race in mathematics education. *Teachers College Record, 111*(2), 295–338.

McDermott, R. (1993). The acquisition of a child by a learning disability. In S. Chaiklin & J. Lave (Eds.), *Understanding practice.* Cambridge University Press. https://doi.org/10.1017/CBO9780511625510.011

Meacham, S. S. (2007). The educational soundscape: Participation and perception in Japanese high school English lessons. *Mind, Culture, and Activity, 14*(3), 196–215. https://doi.org/10.1080/10749030701316334

Morris, K. (2013). *Map reading framework* [Unpublished manuscript]. Department of Teaching, Learning, Policy, & Leadership, University of Maryland.

Nasir, N. S., & Hand, V. M. (2006). Exploring sociocultural perspectives on race, culture, and learning. *Review of Educational Research, 76*(4), 449–475. https://doi.org/10.3102/00346543076004449

New Oxford American Dictionary. (n.d.) https://www.oxfordreference.com/

Oliveira, A. W., Akerson, V. L., & Oldfield, M. (2012). Environmental argumentation as sociocultural activity. *Journal of Research in Science Teaching, 49*(7), 869–897. https://doi.org/10.1002/tea.21020

Oliveira, A. W., Reis, G., Chaize, D. O., & Snyder, M. A. (2014). Death discussion in science read-alouds: Cognitive, sociolinguistic, and moral processes. *Journal of Research in Science Teaching, 51*(2), 117–146. https://doi.org/10.1002/tea.21132

Orlander Arvola, A. (2014). "What if we were in a test tube?" Students' gendered meaning making during a biology lesson about the basic facts of the human genitals. *Cultural Studies of Science Education, 9*(2), 409–431. https://doi.org/10.1007/s11422-012-9430-2

Paechter, C. (2007). *Being boys; being girls: Learning masculinities and femininities.* McGraw-Hill Education.

Parnafes, O., & diSessa, A. A. (2013). Microgenetic learning analysis: A methodology for studying knowledge in transition. *Human Development, 56*(1), 5–37. https://doi.org/10.1159/000342945

Philip, T. M. (2011). An "ideology in pieces" approach to studying change in teachers' sense-making about race, racism, and racial justice. *Cognition and Instruction, 29*(3), 297–329. https://doi.org/10.1080/07370008.2011.583369

Philip, T. M. (2019). Principled improvisation to support novice teacher learning. *Teachers College Record, 121*(6). https://www.tcrecord.org/Content.asp?ContentId=22739

Philip, T. M., Gupta, A., Elby, A., & Turpen, C. (2018). Why ideology matters for learning: A case of ideological convergence in an engineering ethics classroom discussion on drone warfare. *Journal of the Learning Sciences, 27*(2), 183–223. https://doi.org/10.1080/1050 8406.2017.1381964

Philip, T. M., Olivares-Pasillas, M. C., & Rocha, J. (2016). Becoming racially literate about data and data-literate about race: Data visualizations in the classroom as a site of racial-ideological micro-contestations. *Cognition and Instruction, 34*(4), 361–388. https://doi .org/10.1080/07370008.2016.1210418

Puvirajah, A., Verma, G., & Webb, H. (2012). Examining the mediation of power in a collaborative community: Engaging in informal science as authentic practice. *Cultural Studies of Science Education, 7*(2), 375–408. https://doi.org/10.1007/s11422-012-9394-2

Rahm, J. (2007). Youths' and scientists' authoring of and positioning within science and scientists' work. *Cultural Studies of Science Education, 1*(3), 517–544. https://doi.org/10.1007/ s11422-006-9020-2

Rosebery, A. S., Ogonowski, M., DiSchino, M., & Warren, B. (2010). "The coat traps all your body heat": Heterogeneity as fundamental to learning. *Journal of the Learning Sciences, 19*(3), 322–357. https://doi.org/10.1080/10508406.2010.491752

Rubel, L. H., Hall-Wieckert, M., & Lim, V. Y. (2017). Making space for place: Mapping tools and practices to teach for spatial justice. *Journal of the Learning Sciences, 26*(4), 643–687. https://doi.org/10.1080/10508406.2017.1336440

Rubel, L. H., Lim, V. Y., Hall-Wieckert, M., & Sullivan, M. (2016). Teaching mathematics for spatial justice: An investigation of the lottery. *Cognition and Instruction, 34*(1), 1–26. https://doi.org/10.1080/07370008.2015.1118691

Schoerning, E., Hand, B., Shelley, M., & Therrien, W. (2015), Language, access, and power in the elementary science classroom. *Science Education, 99*(2), 238–259. https://doi .org/10.1002/sce.21154

Siegler, R. (2006). Microgenetic studies of learning. In D. Kuhn & R. Siegler (Eds.), *Handbook of child psychology: Cognition, perception, and language* (6th ed., Vol. 2, pp. 464–510). Wiley.

Takeuchi, M. A. (2016). Friendships and group work in linguistically diverse mathematics classrooms: Opportunities to learn for English language learners. *Journal of the Learning Sciences, 25*(3), 411–437. https://doi.org/10.1080/10508406.2016.1169422

Van Horne, K., & Bell, P. (2017). Youth disciplinary identification during participation in contemporary project-based science investigations in school. *Journal of the Learning Sciences, 26*(3), 437–476. https://doi.org/10.1080/10508406.2017.1330689

Vossoughi, S. (2014). Social analytic artifacts made concrete: A study of learning and political education. *Mind, Culture, and Activity, 21*(4), 353–373. https://doi.org/10.1080/10749 039.2014.951899

Wickman, P. O. (2004). The practical epistemologies of the classroom: A study of laboratory work. *Science Education, 88*(3), 325–344. https://doi.org/10.1002/sce.10129

Wood, M. (2013). Mathematical micro-identities: Moment-to-moment positioning and learning in a fourth-grade classroom. *Journal for Research in Mathematics Education, 44*(5), 775–808. https://doi.org/10.5951/jresematheduc.44.5.0775

Wortham, S. (2004). The interdependence of social identification and learning. *American Educational Research Journal, 41*(3), 715–750. https://doi.org/10.3102/000283120 41003715

Chapter 8

Use of Quasi-Experimental Research Designs in Education Research: Growth, Promise, and Challenges

MAITHREYI GOPALAN [ID]
KELLY ROSINGER
JEE BIN AHN [ID]
The Pennsylvania State University

In the past few decades, we have seen a rapid proliferation in the use of quasi-experimental research designs in education research. This trend, stemming in part from the "credibility revolution" in the social sciences, particularly economics, is notable along with the increasing use of randomized controlled trials in the strive toward rigorous causal inference. The overarching purpose of this chapter is to explore and document the growth, applicability, promise, and limitations of quasi-experimental research designs in education research. We first provide an overview of widely used quasi-experimental research methods in this growing literature, with particular emphasis on articles from the top ranked education research journals, including those published by the American Educational Research Association. Next, we demonstrate the applicability and promise of these methods in enhancing our understanding of the causal effects of education policies and interventions using key examples and case studies culled from the extant literature across the pre-K–16 education spectrum. Finally, we explore the limitations of these methods and conclude with thoughts on how education researchers can adapt these innovative, interdisciplinary techniques to further our understanding of some of the most enduring questions in educational policy and practice.

We need rigorous causal inference research to understand what works in the field of education. Following best practices from medical research, randomized controlled trials (RCTs) have become widely regarded as the "gold standard" for establishing causal evidence in education. While RCTs in education have increased dramatically over the years, some educational topics may not be amenable to RCTs either because they are too expensive, especially in larger place-based or policy-driven

Review of Research in Education
March 2020, Vol. 44, pp. 218–243
DOI: 10.3102/0091732X20903302
Chapter reuse guidelines: sagepub.com/journals-permissions
© 2020 AERA. http://rre.aera.net

interventions, or unethical in some cases. This has led to a simultaneous increase in the use of "as-if" random experiments or experiments naturally occurring in the world to establish causal evidence.

The increasing use of quasi-experimental research designs (QEDs) in education, brought into focus following the "credibility revolution" (Angrist & Pischke, 2010) in economics, which sought to use data to empirically test theoretical assertions, has indeed improved causal claims in education (Loeb et al., 2017). However, more recently, scholars, practitioners, and policymakers have questioned if the enthusiasm about RCTs and QEDs has narrowed the focus of research to less important topics. Have they crowded out high-quality descriptive analyses that attempt to make sense of often complex real-world topics that are not amenable to the simple exogenous shocks/variations needed for quasi-experiments (Deaton & Cartwright, 2018; Pritchett, 2018)? Furthermore, the external validity of causal claims made from QEDs and RCTs has not been a focus in the literature until more recently (Tipton & Olsen, 2018)—that is, "Are the results of analyses from specific studies generalizable to other populations not exposed to the intervention/policy?"

In this chapter, we provide an integrative review of the growth of QEDs in education research, their applicability and promise in improving causal inference, and ongoing challenges that exist in adapting these innovative methods in education research with an eye toward informing policy and practice.

WHAT ARE QUASI-EXPERIMENTAL RESEARCH DESIGNS?

To understand the causal effect of any policy or intervention, researchers strive to establish an appropriate counterfactual, or what would have happened in the absence of the policy or intervention, to provide a baseline from which causal effects can be estimated. RCTs are considered the "gold standard" of causal inference because of their ability to create a valid counterfactual by withholding treatment on a random set of subjects—known as the control group. In an educational RCT, subjects—students, classrooms, teachers, schools, or districts—are assigned to treatment and control groups based purely on chance. When treatment is randomly assigned, we can confidently claim that the treatment is the most plausible driver of the outcome. Because it is essential to rule out alternative explanations for an observed outcome to make a causal claim, random assignment ensures that treatment is not systematically related to other observable or unobservable factors. As a result, differences in outcomes can be attributed to the treatment rather than other factors systematically related to receipt of treatment.

However, it is often not feasible to conduct an RCT, especially in some educational settings. One of the most prohibitive barriers to conducting an RCT is the cost associated with many educational interventions. For example, changing classroom sizes requires substantial resources: reducing class size by just one student would cost an estimated $12 billion a year nationwide (Chingos & Whitehurst, 2011). RCTs also raise ethical concerns because some students are denied educational interventions that may be beneficial, while others receive interventions that have not yet been rigorously evaluated.

Quasi-experimental research designs, as the name suggests, use nonexperimental (or non-researcher-induced) variation in the main independent variable of interest, essentially mimicking experimental conditions in which some subjects are exposed to treatment and others are not on a random basis. Regression discontinuity, instrumental variables, differences-in-differences, two-way fixed effects, and other QEDs exploit nonrandom but plausibly exogenous (or as-if random) variation in key parameters to establish causality. The reliability of causal claims and estimates varies across these designs and depends on how close the study conditions are to an experiment. QEDs improve our understanding of the causal effects of various educational policies and interventions by focusing on internal validity—did the policy or intervention being studied cause a significant change in the observed outcome (and if so by how much)—thereby yielding an unbiased estimate of the average treatment effect (Campbell, 1957).

There are a number of threats to internal validity that QEDs try to eliminate in different ways, as is appropriate for each design. The main threat QEDs aim to eliminate is selection bias: the fact that students, districts, schools, or colleges that select into treatment may be different from those who do not select into treatment. Parents, students, or school administrators who are more informed, motivated, or in need of interventions that can improve outcomes may be more likely to opt into an educational program. The factors that lead them to select into treatment, however, are also likely connected to educational outcomes, making it difficult to isolate causal effects. QEDs attempt to exploit exogenous shocks that assign treatment to some and not to others on an as-if random basis—for example, policies that apply to one district and not the neighboring district, or thresholds that determine scholarship criteria based on a score or index that assigns treatment (i.e., scholarship) to students just above the score cutoff—that arguably can be used to establish causality.

QED studies that attempt to mitigate selection bias and reduce threats to internal validity receive the second-highest rating of causal evidence, behind well-conducted RCTs, according to the Institute of Education Sciences' (IES) What Works Clearinghouse (WWC) design standards (U.S. Department of Education, 2017).[1] The *hierarchy of evidence* in terms of the strengths and reliability of findings from studies using QEDs is still evolving and is an active line of research exploration.

TRENDS IN THE USE OF QUASI-EXPERIMENTAL RESEARCH DESIGNS IN EDUCATION RESEARCH

To examine the patterns and trends in the use of QEDs in education research, we followed a systematic search process to identify previous literature using such designs. To begin, we made the following list of the terms associated with QEDs: *quasi-experiment, natural experiment, difference-in-difference, regression discontinuity, instrumental variable, fixed effect, exogenous variation, two-way fixed effect, within sample comparison, synthetic control method, propensity score matching, sibling comparison,* and *comparative interrupted time series.*[2] We used the ProQuest Education Database[3] to search for articles that included any of the keywords in the title, abstract, or subject headings. To narrow our search, we restricted our search to peer-reviewed journals and used the time frame 1995 to 2018. The initial ProQuest Education Database search offered 2,704 search results from 100 scholarly journals.

Because the search results were from a wide range of social science disciplines beyond education, we narrowed the focus to articles published in 15 top education research journals, including all American Educational Research Association (AERA) journals that publish empirical studies. The list includes *AERA Open, American Educational Research Journal, American Journal of Education, Economics of Education Review, Educational Evaluation and Policy Analysis, Education Finance and Policy, Educational Researcher, Journal of Educational and Behavioral Statistics, Journal of Educational Psychology, Journal of Higher Education, Journal of Research on Educational Effectiveness, Research in Higher Education, Review of Higher Education, Sociology of Education,* and *Teachers College Record.* We included these journals in our search not only because they are top-tier journals but also because they represent a broad cross section of education research and are venues in which evaluations of policies that use QEDs are likely to be found. This search offered 632 results (see the supplemental appendix in the online version of the journal for extended bibliography of all these articles).

Figure 1 presents the trend in the use of QEDs (as operationalized by our search terms) in our selected set of journals between 1995 and 2018. The primary axis provides the total number of articles that use the relevant search terms described above and the secondary axis provides the proportion of all articles published in the above 15 journals that use those relevant search terms.

Our systematic search results indicate that while education research incorporated QEDs in the 1990s, they did not become popular until the past decade. The use of quasi-experimental terms has increased substantially over time. Until 2008, less than 20 articles using QED methods (as identified by the search terms) were published every year. Beginning 2009, we see an increasing trend with more than 100 articles using QEDs published in 2018. There is an upward trend in the total number of articles published by these journals over the same period as well. Despite this overall growth, we can see that the share of articles using QEDs has clearly gone up over this time period as well (plotted on the secondary axis).

There are several factors that likely contributed to the exponential growth of QEDs in education research. First, increasing accessibility of data, including micro-level data and large-scale longitudinal surveys collected by the federal and state governments, is key. Data accessibility led the growth of quasi-experimental approaches in economics (Angrist & Pischke, 2010; Panhans & Singleton, 2017) and likely also had similar influence on education research.

Second, increasing demand for rigorous policy evaluation has contributed to the increase in the use of QEDs in education research. Strong emphasis on an evidence-based approach to policy and interventions by the government alongside corresponding

FIGURE 1

Number and Proportion of Articles Using Quasi-Experimental Research Designs Between 1995 and 2018 in 15 Education Journals

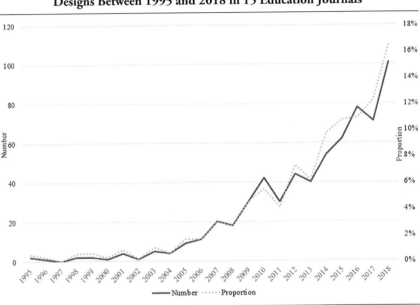

demand from grant-making agencies have also led to the rapid growth of QEDs in education research. For example, IES' grant application requirements include the need for rigorous evidence that meets the WWC standards for evidence. Also, the Every Student Succeeds Act in 2015 defined the term *evidence-based* and recommended that state educational agencies, local educational agencies, schools, educators, and partner organizations select and use evidence-based practices. The Every Student Succeeds Act distinguishes between evidence-based practices with strong, moderate, and promising evidence based on the strength of research design, and QEDs were determined to generate moderate evidence.

Finally, the increasing demand for rigor has also been accompanied by an expansion in methodological training, especially, in quantitative methods at schools of education. For example, a quick glance at the number of training grants provided to graduate schools of education by IES since its formation in 2002 illustrates the growth (see https://ies.ed.gov/funding/grantsearch/index.asp?mode=2&sort=1&order=1&all=1&search=ProgramName&slctProgram=82). Together, increased data accessibility, improved methodological training, and the growing need for transparent and credible policy evaluations with an emphasis on evidence-based policy in recent years seem to have triggered the growth of QEDs in education research.

To evaluate the relative popularity of various QED methods, we tabulated the number of articles that used each of the search terms that we used in our systematic search within the top education research journals (Table 1).

TABLE 1

Number of Articles Using QEDs by Method Between 1995 and 2018 in 15 Education Journals

Year	Quasi-Experiment	Natural Experiment	Difference in Difference	Regression Discontinuity	Instrumental Variable
1995–1999	2	0	0	0	3
2000–2004	3	1	1	0	4
2005–2009	13	8	8	9	26
2010–2014	34	11	30	41	47
2015–2018	49	21	59	77	39
Total	101	41	98	127	119

Year	Fixed Effect	Exogenous Variation	Two-Way Fixed Effects	Sibling Comparisons	Synthetic Control Methods
1995–1999	2	0	0	0	0
2000–2004	7	1	0	0	0
2005–2009	33	3	0	0	0
2010–2014	42	8	0	1	0
2015–2018	65	12	0	1	0
Total	149	24	0	2	0

Year	Propensity Score Matching	Within-Sample Comparison	Comparative Interrupted Time Series
1995–1999	0	0	0
2000–2004	0	0	0
2005–2009	10	0	0
2010–2014	30	0	3
2015–2018	35	0	8
Total	75	0	11

Note. The categorization of articles across these search terms is not mutually exclusive. For example, a study could include two key words such as quasi-experiment and difference in difference in the title, abstract, or article keywords. QEDs = quasi-experimental research designs.

Regression discontinuity (RD) and difference-in-difference (DID) methods are most commonly used in education research.[4] The use of fixed effects is also common. Within the context of quasi-experiments, the use of two-way fixed effects is equivalent empirically to conducting DID with more than two time periods.[5] The popularity of RD design in education research is not surprising. For example, in his review of the history of RD design, Cook (2008) describes how this design first originated in education by psychologists of education—Thistlethwaite and Campbell (1960) before being rediscovered and popularized in statistics and economics around 1995.

TABLE 2
Number of Articles Using QEDs by Topic Between 1995 and 2018 in 15 Education Journals

Year	Early Childhood Education	K–12 Education	Higher Education	Methodology	Other Topics
1995–1999	0	5	0	2	0
2000–2004	0	9	2	4	0
2005–2009	1	51	20	9	8
2010–2014	4	127	55	17	5
2015–2018	13	181	105	7	6
Total	18	372	182	41	19

Note. QEDs = quasi-experimental research designs.

Because several topics of inquiry within education are especially amenable to the use of RD design, it is not surprising that this method is widely used. Indeed, the WWC provides specific standards for evaluating studies using RD design in education research given its increasing use. Second, federalism, especially educational federalism in the United States, where states have tremendous power over education policies makes the use of DID possible and pertinent in education research. Because several educational polices are rolled out by (and across) states over time, this enables researchers to use pre-post designs with nonequivalent comparison groups to understand and evaluate the effects of such policies. Sibling comparison designs and family fixed effects designs seem less common in education research.

While a comprehensive description of the full range of QEDs is beyond the scope of this chapter, in the next section, we include a brief overview of two of the most popular methods—RD and DID (two-way fixed effect designs can be thought of as an extension of the DID). Other QEDs—such as matching techniques and instrumental variables, while also popular—are not described in greater depth in this review due to space constraints (see Stuart, 2010, for a detailed discussion of matching techniques, and Bettinger, 2010, for a detailed discussion of instrumental variables).

Next, we manually coded the articles in terms of the level of education that each article focused on broadly (Table 2).

We find that most of the articles focused on K–12 or higher education: 372 (approximately 59%) articles dealt with topics within K–12 education and 182 (approximately 29%) articles focused on higher education. Relatively few articles covered the issue of early childhood education (ECE); 18 articles, which only accounted for approximately 3% of the total. One reason for this trend in ECE could be that RCTs are still the dominant method used to understand the effects of ECE. Furthermore, several studies using QEDs in ECE have been published in other social science journals. We highlight a few QEDs used in ECE to describe the potential of QEDs to enhance causal evidence research in this domain.

Studies using QEDs in K–12 and higher education have focused on a wide range of topics. For example, within K–12 education, QEDs have been used to analyze the impact of school accountability policies such as the No Child Left Behind Policy Act (NCLB), school finance, class size reductions, school choice, and several other policy changes. Similarly, in higher education, QEDs have been used to assess the impact of financial aid, college selectivity, remedial education, and several other funding/accountability policies on student outcomes. Given the breadth and volume in the use of QEDs in K–12 and higher education, an immersive review of the use of QEDs in these two domains is beyond the scope of this chapter. Therefore, after providing an overview of two commonly used QEDs in the next section, we use specific case studies to highlight how research using QEDs has enhanced our understanding of the impact of certain educational interventions and policies in these domains.

OVERVIEW OF COMMONLY USED QUASI-EXPERIMENTAL RESEARCH DESIGNS IN EDUCATION RESEARCH
Regression Discontinuity Designs

Regression discontinuity designs seem to occupy the top slot when it comes to mimicking an experiment as closely as possible, and the WWC prioritizes evidence from well-conducted RD designs among QEDs. As a result, RD designs have received wide acceptance and use in education research. RD is appropriate for situations in which the eligibility to treatment is defined based on a cutoff on a continuous score or index. For example, a number of states and higher education institutions have enacted merit scholarship programs that provide financial aid to students above some academic eligibility threshold, such as Georgia's HOPE scholarship program that historically covered a portion of college costs for students with a 3.0 high school grade point average (GPA) or higher (see Dynarski, 2002, for more detailed discussion of the HOPE scholarship). Therefore, a student's probability of receiving aid, or "treatment," jumps discontinuously along the variable used in making treatment eligibility decisions. Because students who are just around the eligibility cutoff (e.g., students with a GPA of 3.02 vs. 2.98 when the eligibility cutoff is 3.0) are likely to be similar in observable and unobservable ways, this results in an as-if random experiment in which students just above the cutoff receive aid and students just below the cutoff do not.

The plausibly exogenous variation in who gets treated—those just above the cutoff—can be used to estimate the causal effect of the treatment with those just below the cutoff serving as the counterfactual. In such an RD design, the effect of an intervention is estimated as the difference in the average outcomes between the treatment and the control group members around a narrow threshold of the cutoff, after adjusting statistically for the relationship between the outcomes of interest and the variable used to decide eligibility and thereby the treatment. The estimated effect is known as the "local average treatment effect" and can be generalized only to students at the margin of the cutoff (e.g., students immediately above and below the cutoff value).

For an example of a study that uses an RD design to evaluate the impact of a merit scholarship program on student outcomes, see Curs and Harper (2012).

The variable used to assign subjects to treatment or control groups is commonly referred to as the "forcing," "assignment," or "running" variable. To estimate causal effects using RD, the cutoff value of the forcing variable must not be used for assigning other policies or interventions (e.g., remediation or satisfactory academic progress interventions based on GPA). For instance, an RD design will not establish causality if a 2.5 GPA cutoff value is used for both a scholarship program and for maintaining satisfactory academic progress; in this case, researchers will not be able to identify whether any changes in outcomes around the threshold are the result of the scholarship or interventions provided for students who fail to maintain satisfactory academic progress.

Difference-in-Differences Designs

The DID design is becoming increasingly popular in education policy research as well. Conceptually, in the DID design, researchers try to explore the effect of a policy or intervention that affects a group of students, schools, districts, or states at a point in time but not others at the same point in time in a naturally occurring setting. Researchers compare the outcomes of the groups differentially exposed to the treatment across pre- and posttreatment time periods to estimate the causal effects of policies. The posttreatment observations for units that never received treatment serve as the counterfactual, or what would have happened to treatment outcomes in the absence of treatment, and are used to estimate the average treatment effect. The main identifying assumption in a DID design is that the trends in outcomes for treated and control groups are parallel, or common, prior to treatment and that these trends would have remained parallel in the absence of treatment. The post-treatment trend in the control group (the one that does not experience treatment) is the counterfactual in a DID design and is what establishes causality. Disciplines use different terminology for the same general research design: where applied econometrics refers to this design as DID, psychology refers to it as comparative interrupted time series.

While the term *DID* in the past was used to specifically refer to analysis of two groups (treatment vs. control groups) and two time periods (pre- vs. posttreatment), it can be extended to multiple groups and multiple periods. Indeed, the use of group- and time-fixed effects, also known as the two-way fixed effects parameterization, is an extension of the DID that makes a similar common trend assumption to estimate causal effects of interest. This two-way fixed effect extension allows for more flexibility when treatment adoption occurs (i.e., states or districts that adopt policies in different years) and allows researchers to study variation in policy impact over time. Increasingly, event study analyses are used to supplement (or replace) traditional DID designs. In an event study analysis, a researcher adds leads and lags to the treatment variable to examine possible changes in outcomes in 1, 2, 3 (and possibly more) years prior to treatment and 1, 2, 3 (and possibly more) years after treatment. The leads on the treatment variable allow researchers to examine whether there are anticipatory effects of policies (e.g., whether degree production changes prior to the implementation of differential pricing based on a student's college major), which could indicate that trends in outcomes were not parallel prior to treatment. Lags allow researchers to examine delayed responses to treatment, for instance, if pricing policies take several years to influence degree production in particular majors. See Stange (2015) for an application of this event study analysis.

CASE STUDIES OF QUASI-EXPERIMENTAL RESEARCH IN EDUCATION

We organize the case studies thematically, beginning with ECE research and ending with postsecondary research, to showcase the breadth in the substantive topics in which QEDs have been influential. Through these examples, we illustrate how such methodological advances have challenged and/or enhanced our knowledge regarding educational policy and practice. We draw on several classic studies (published in journals across the social sciences exploring education, broadly defined) that have used QEDs based on our background knowledge in addition to the studies included in our literature search ($N = 632$). We acknowledge that our selection and discussion of specific case study topics, while not exhaustive, nevertheless attempts to strike a balance between breadth and depth for an integrative review.

Early Childhood Education

Recent advances in developmental science aided by a deeper understanding of brain architecture have highlighted early childhood as a particularly sensitive period for promoting children's cognitive and socioemotional development (National Research Council & Institute of Medicine Committee on Integrating the Science of Early Childhood Development, 2000). Such advances combined with economic cost-benefit analyses suggesting high returns to early childhood investment and dynamic complementarities (the notion that "skills beget skills") of early childhood skills (Heckman, 2006) have resulted in a rapid growth of publicly supported ECE programs across the country. According to recent estimates, student enrollment in ECE programs has more than doubled between 2002 and 2018 (Friedman-Krauss et al., 2018). Several observational studies have documented a positive *correlation* between children's attendance in high-quality ECE programs and various outcomes—including academic achievement, behavioral skills, and health (Duncan & Magnuson, 2013; Magnuson et al., 2007).

Despite enthusiasm from researchers and policymakers, questions regarding the efficacy of ECE programs in improving short- and long-term outcomes for children remains. Meta- and re-analysis of studies that used rigorous natural experiments provide mixed evidence (Barnett et al., 2018; McCoy et al., 2017; Morris et al., 2018; van Huizen & Plantenga, 2018). Specifically, the reduction of positive gains (also known as fade-out) made by children who attended ECE in the elementary school years and the reemergence of positive effects in adolescence and beyond has been widely debated. Because children attend ECE programs on a nonrandom basis—that is, parents choose ECE programs for their children—selection bias remains a concern when comparing ECE participants and nonparticipants. Several experimental methods and QEDs have been adopted to disentangle the causal evidence of ECE. We focus on studies that use QEDs to illustrate the applicability of these methods in this context.

For example, a common QED used to unpack the causal effect of ECE programs is the use of sibling- or family-fixed effects (Currie & Thomas, 1995; Deming, 2009). By comparing the outcomes of siblings within a family (such that one of the siblings was an ECE participant and the other was not), shared family-level characteristics can be controlled for as much as possible to isolate the true effect of ECE participation. Studies that use family-fixed effects find that participation in ECE programs improves college attendance and completion, improves health, and reduces criminal justice involvement (Carneiro & Ginja, 2014; Deming, 2009; Garces et al., 2002).

Second, given that the rollout of publicly funded ECE programs across different counties in the country was mostly random, researchers have exploited this "as-if" random variation in the timing of a child's exposure to ECE to estimate the causal effect of ECE on longer run outcomes (Johnson & Jackson, 2019; Thompson, 2017). These studies use a DID design to compare differences in children's outcomes of interest (e.g., achievement, behavior, and other long-term outcomes) between children who were exposed to ECE programs and those who were not, before and after ECE exposure. Similarly, as-if random variation in the timing of state subsidization of kindergarten has also been used in a DID framework to isolate the effect of kindergarten enrollment on student outcomes (Dhuey, 2011).

Finally, studies have also used RD designs to study the effect of ECE programs (Carneiro & Ginja, 2014; Gormley et al., 2005; Jenkins et al., 2016; Weiland & Yoshikawa, 2013). Because early ECE programs such as Head Start had eligibility requirements for participation (based on age, family income, household characteristics, state of residence, year, and others), researchers could compare the outcomes of children who were just above and below the threshold of eligibility using RD to estimate the average treatment effect. However, there have also been concerns raised regarding the use of an age-based RD design (Lipsey et al., 2015) in the ECE literature that later studies have begun to address.

In all, researchers find similar patterns as those observed in well-conducted RCTs. While smaller, local programs such as the Abecadarian and Perry preschool programs were high-quality programs that showed impressive positive results on a wide variety of student outcomes (that nevertheless faded out in elementary school years but reemerged in adolescence), publicly funded, larger ECE programs show smaller but significant effects on long-run student outcomes. Collectively, these studies have improved our understanding of the causal effects of ECE tremendously and encourage continued experimentation and analysis (see Phillips et al., 2017).

K–12 Education

In K–12 education policy, one of the most enduring questions regarding the link between school spending and students' educational outcomes is being increasingly addressed by studies using QEDs. Ever since the Coleman et al. (1966) report published findings suggesting the lack of significant relationship between school spending and student outcomes, there has been a long line of influential literature that was skeptical about the benefits of increased school spending on students' educational outcomes (Hanushek, 1997, 2003). However, most of these past studies suffered from methodological limitations arising from the use of observational data from convenience samples comprising data from few school districts or states and regression models that failed to account for selection bias. While studies observed heterogeneous effects (some positive, some negative, and some found no effect) of spending on key student outcomes even in this past literature (Hedges et al., 1994), none of the observed effects can be treated as causal estimates.

Because historically, local property taxes accounted for a large part of a K–12 school's spending (Howell & Miller, 1997), and the property tax base was typically higher in localities with higher home values, local financing of schools contributed to affluent districts spending more per student compared with poorer localities. Furthermore, given the persistent patterns of residential- and school-segregation by race and socioeconomic status, the link between contemporaneous school spending and student outcomes is likely to be biased in many ways that regression models even with extensive covariate adjustment are unlikely to correct.

Ideally, to reach the "gold standard" of causal inference, one would want to run an RCT where randomly selected school districts received money to spend while others did not. Comparing student outcomes in districts that received the money with student outcomes in similar districts that did not receive the random allocation of money after a set period of time would provide the most rigorous causal estimate of spending on student outcomes of interest. Yet such an experiment would remain a thought experiment at best given the ethical and logistical considerations it entails.

However, in the 1970s, lawsuits challenging the widespread disparity in within-state per-pupil spending across schools and districts resulted in court-ordered school finance reforms across the country. States implementing these court-ordered school finance reforms primarily tweaked their school spending formulas to mitigate inequality in spending. This weakened the positive correlation between per-pupil spending and district-level socioeconomic status/wealth, which was much higher in a school-funding regime that relied on property taxes in the local area. In other words, some school districts' spending changes in response to exogenous events, such as court-ordered school finance reforms, present a natural experiment—school districts that had low per-pupil spending prior to the reforms increased their spending in states that enacted the reforms in comparison with similar districts in states that did not pass reforms. As a result, these exogenous spending changes could be isolated and used to estimate causal effects of spending using DID designs. This new line of literature comparing a range of short- and long-run student outcomes in those districts where spending increased versus those where spending stayed the same gives us some of the first causal estimates of school spending on student outcomes (Candelaria & Shores, 2019; Jackson et al., 2016; Lafortune et al., 2018).

These studies find that school spending improved student test scores (Lafortune et al., 2018), the overall number of years of completed education, wages, and high school graduation rates (Candelaria & Shores, 2019), and reduced the incidence of adult poverty (Jackson et al., 2016). Cumulatively, these studies also show that the positive effects of increases in per-pupil spending were driven by spending on teacher salaries, longer school days, and reduced student-teacher ratios (Jackson et al., 2016).

However, not all kinds of increases in school spending are related to improved educational outcomes. For example, studies using RD have found that increases in capital spending may not have such similar positive effects (Cellini et al., 2010; Martorell et al., 2016). Capital spending increases in schools and districts come from specific capital campaigns that are initiated by the local districts using referendums. Martorell et al. (2016) analyzed nearly 1,400 capital bond program referenda comparing districts where the referenda resulted in a narrow approval or failure. Because districts that barely passed or failed capital bonds passage are likely to be similar in most respects other than the "treatment," selection bias into the treatment could be minimized. Studies using RD have also found that noninstructional spending on school counselors in Alabama causally reduced the frequency of disciplinary incidents (Reback, 2010). In all, there is clear, converging evidence that school spending matters. More important, "how" money is spent matters even more, especially for students who were exposed to unequal school resources (also see Jackson, 2018, for a more immersive review on this topic).

Higher Education

Since the mid-2000s, state legislators have increasingly implemented policies that link public funding for public colleges and universities to student outcomes in an effort to improve educational attainment rates by holding higher education institutions more accountable for outcomes. To date, at least 30 states have implemented some version of performance-based funding (PBF) policy, including most recently California, which passed legislation that will link $2.5 billion in funding for the state's community colleges to institutional performance (Fain, 2018). By linking a portion of state funding to student outcomes, PBF policies are intended to improve graduation rates—nationwide, just 60% of students who began college in 2009 had completed a degree 6 years later (National Student Clearinghouse, 2018)—and increase the number of degree and certificate holders as an effort to boost economic and workforce development within adopting states.

Descriptive reports that examine student outcomes before and after the implementation of PBF policies have highlighted generally positive impacts on degree completion in the 2- and 4-year college sectors, at least in states that tie a moderate amount of funds to performance (e.g., Callahan et al., 2017; Conklin et al., 2016). While these reports offer insight into trends and relationships between state funding policies and student outcomes, some lack a comparison group of states (ones that do not adopt PBF policies) against which to compare outcomes. With no counterfactual (i.e., no approximation of what would have happened if a PBF policy had not been adopted), the resulting estimates could be biased by broader demographic and labor market trends occurring at the same time.

As PBF policies have grown in popularity over the past 10 to 15 years, the staggered adoption of policies across states offers a natural experiment in which some public institutions are subject to PBF in a given year while others are not. Researchers have used this variation in PBF adoption over time to employ a DID framework, in which outcomes are observed before and after policy implementation in both adopting and nonadopting states, to evaluate their impact and generate causal estimates of PBF policies on a range of outcomes. Since PBF adoption may not be completely exogenous—that is, states with lower college completion rates may adopt PBF policies in an effort to boost degree production—many of these studies estimate DID models with multiple comparison groups, such as all other non-PBF states, states in a regional compact, neighboring states, or matching techniques to test whether findings are sensitive to which states are included in the nontreatment group (i.e., which states are used to construct the counterfactual).

Although Dougherty et al. (2016) note that PBF policies have encouraged institutions to offer additional supports to students, quasi-experimental analyses of PBF policies have largely failed to find clear positive impacts on actual degree production. DID analyses of individual state's PBF policies largely indicate that they have had null and, in some cases, even negative effects on degree production (Hillman et al., 2014; Hillman et al., 2015; Umbricht et al., 2017). When impacts on student outcomes have been positive in DID analyses, it has largely been among certificate production, findings that have been documented in Washington for short-term certificates (Hillman et al., 2015) and in Tennessee (Hillman et al., 2018). This boost in certificate production without concurrent increases in 2- and 4-year degrees raises concerns about the long-term impact of PBF policies since the returns for certificates are lower on average than those for associate's or bachelor's degrees (Belfield & Bailey, 2017). National DID analyses of multiple state PBF policies largely confirm null or negative findings from individual state studies for associate's (Li & Kennedy, 2018; Tandberg et al., 2014) and bachelor's (e.g., Tandberg & Hillman, 2014) degree production and an increase in short-term certificates (Li & Kennedy, 2018). One study found evidence that more recent PBF policies—those that tie performance funds to a college's base funding rather than providing performance funds as an additional bonus—have a modest positive effect on degree production (Rutherford & Rabovsky, 2014).

At the same time, the movement toward tying state funds to colleges' and universities' performance has also raised equity concerns. Primarily, if colleges respond to PBF by altering admissions, recruiting, or financial aid practices to expand enrollment among students with a high likelihood of completing a degree, they may limit access for low-income, adult, and underrepresented minority students, groups that have lower graduation rates on average. DID analyses indicate that the implementation of PBF policies increased selectivity at 4-year colleges in Indiana (Umbricht et al., 2017), which could threaten access for underrepresented students. A multistate study found that public institutions in PBF states receive less Pell Grant revenue after implementation, potentially indicating a preference among colleges that are subject to PBF for higher income students who are more likely to graduate (Kelchen & Stedrak, 2016).

Policymakers have responded to the concerns about limiting college access by including equity premiums or bonuses for colleges that enroll and/or graduate at-risk students. DID analyses demonstrate that such equity premiums can support access and success, at least among some underrepresented groups in higher education (e.g., Gándara & Rutherford, 2017; Kelchen, 2018). A more recent study found no changes in enrollment among historically underrepresented students at community colleges even in states with equity provisions (Kelchen, 2019). Understanding the impact of PBF policies on student outcomes is critical given the amount of funds at stake and the potential unintended consequences.

DID analyses have provided fairly strong and consistent evidence that PBF policies may not be meeting their intended goals, although new research indicates that equity metrics can help offset unintended consequences by supporting access and success for at-risk students. However, institutional, student, and broader state financial and economic factors appear to be more important in shaping educational outcomes than tying institutional funds to performance (Rutherford & Rabovsky, 2014).

In all, the above case studies of various points in the educational pipeline clearly document the power of QEDs in illuminating the causal effects of educational policies and interventions across the pre-K–16 spectrum. While in some cases, they uncover clear causal patterns, in others, they help clarify, extend, and/or add much needed nuance to findings uncovered by other observational research methods to enhance our understanding of policy impacts.

CHALLENGES AND LIMITATIONS IN QUASI-EXPERIMENTAL RESEARCH DESIGN APPLICATION
Methodological Limitations

The allure of using QEDs is clearly driven by the power and promise of these approaches in estimating internally valid, unbiased causal effects of a wide range of educational interventions and policies. Yet the validity of the results from studies based on these designs is intrinsically tied to the underlying assumptions and the strength of those assumptions. For example, the parallel trends assumption inherent in DID designs are central to the validity of the estimated effects (see Wing et al., 2018, for a review of the robustness checks necessary to rigorously defend these assumptions). New research also indicates additional analyses, and sensitivity checks are needed for DID designs when treatment varies over time (as often happens when states and districts implement new policies; Goodman-Bacon, 2018). Additionally, other policy changes or interventions that occur at the same time as the treatment under study can confound the estimated effect in a DID design. Because researchers rely on observational data for DID (and other quasi-experimental analyses), there is always the possibility that other unobserved changes that occur simultaneously could drive changes in outcomes rather than the treatment of interest. In RD designs, the practice of including higher order polynomials of the running variable to capture nonlinearity has been a common practice. Recently, however, statisticians have shown how those terms might introduce other biases to the estimates (Gelman & Imbens, 2019).

While these shortcomings are not direct criticisms of QED methods per se, it is important to consider these carefully as we continue to adapt QEDs in educational policy and practice. Given the relatively short period of time over which QEDs have been developed and applied across the social sciences, methodologists and empirical researchers continue to expand our understanding of the underlying assumptions in these designs and the impact those assumptions have on estimating valid causal effects. Education researchers aspiring to use these methods must stay abreast of methodological advances if we hope to build a high-quality evidence base of "what works" and understand the intended and unintended consequences of educational policy and interventions.

Second, a methodological limitation often raised against QEDs (as well as RCTs) is that while the studies are able to estimate valid causal effects when identifying assumptions are met, they are unable to unpack the mechanisms underlying the over-all treatment effects—that is, *how* the changes in outcomes occur. Good descriptive studies and in-depth qualitative studies have a clear role to play in this regard (Loeb et al., 2017). We discuss the need for good quality descriptive studies in the subsequent section.

External Validity and Generalizability

Despite the promise of QEDs in generating internally valid estimates of causal effects, one of the major concerns underlying these approaches is whether the estimated effects from the analytic samples using these designs are generalizable to other populations of interest—both across space and time. This generalizability concern is referred to as external validity (Campbell, 1957). For example, in evaluating the effectiveness of charter schools, several researchers have relied on "lottery studies." Given that many charter schools experience oversubscription (more interest than available seats), some students are admitted to charter schools based on a random lottery. By comparing the learning outcomes of students who win the lottery with those students who lose the lottery and thereby attend traditional public schools, such studies attempt to reduce selection bias given that both lottery winners and losers "selected into" charter schools. These studies have shown null effects overall in terms of learning outcomes in math and reading for charter school students, but significantly high positive effects for some subgroups of students attending high-quality charter schools (see Cohodes, 2018, for a review). However, the lottery approach suffers from a generalizability concern. It is possible to estimate a lottery effect only when a school is oversubscribed and has good administrative data on all lottery applicants available. Such schools may be quite different from an average charter school on several dimensions—such as size, location, student composition, or quality. Thus, findings based on lottery results may not generalize to the entire population of charter schools.

Similarly, studies using RD estimate what is known as the local average treatment effect based on an analytical sample that includes only a small number of observations on either side of the running variable cutoff used to determine treatment eligibility. Because the analytical sample right around the cutoff is not generalizable to the overall population of interest in many ways, the results from RD studies have limited external validity. Active methodological and applied empirical research to expand the external validity of RD designs is currently under way (Wing & Bello-Gomez, 2018). Yet external validity is an important limitation that we need to wrestle with as we continue to adapt these methods in education research.

At the same time, it is important to recognize that concerns regarding external validity are not limited to studies using QEDs alone. For example, similar critiques are leveled against the use of RCTs and experimental research more generally (Schanzenbach, 2012; Stuart et al., 2017). Alternatively, in some instances, studies using QEDs may have *higher* external validity as compared with those using RCTs because QED studies often test interventions or policies in real-world settings. Studies using QEDs can also be conducted in diverse settings where policy variation is observed, which provides opportunities to improve external validity. Therefore, the costs, benefits, and trade-offs between internal and external validity when using these approaches must be evaluated more rigorously to move research forward in this area. Furthermore, internal and external validity require a sharper focus with increased skepticism raised by the "replicability crisis"—instances where results from several classic studies in social psychology and other social sciences have not been replicated on newer, larger samples (Open Science Collaboration, 2015). Critiques such as publication bias (publication of studies that find significant effects as opposed to null effects), underpowered analytical samples, and a narrowed focus on null-hypothesis testing must be grappled with in research that uses QEDs as well.

Crowding Out Descriptive Studies

With the proliferation of the use of QEDs across the social sciences, scholars are also raising concerns regarding the trade-offs inherent in the overreliance on the use of these methods for research and practice more broadly (Deaton & Cartwright,

2018; Pritchett, 2018). First, a concern stemming from one side of this debate is if the search for clever identification strategies that rely on discontinuities and policy variations is limiting the kinds of research questions researchers ask and answer (Ruhm, 2018). Rather than letting the quest to answer policy-relevant research questions of interest using the most appropriate method drive the mode of inquiry, has the chase for exogenous shocks (i.e., search for "as-if" random/natural experiments) driven the questions that are being asked, answered, and published? In other words, similar to the axiom—form follows function—in research, should not the research methods and designs follow the research question and topic of inquiry rather than the other way around?

Education researchers must seriously engage in these discussions just as several social science disciplines are grappling with these issues. For example, a sharp focus on empirical methods to improve causal social science research may at times ignore the theoretical foundations on which research is built. Education research that uses QEDs must be encouraged to adopt practices to mitigate such trade-offs. To build cumulative knowledge, empirical research must help falsify, extend, and/or develop new theoretical predictions, especially in an applied social science field such as education.

Simultaneously, some experts have also raised concerns regarding whether the implicit incentive structures of academic publishing that favored RCTs and QEDs in recent years have crowded out the publication of good descriptive studies (McKenzie, 2018). High-quality descriptive studies are often required to describe key aspects of social phenomena. Recent guidance on how descriptive studies can be planned and executed with high empirical rigor hopefully encourages the publication of both stand-alone descriptive research studies and studies that use descriptive analyses in conjunction with RCTs and QEDs (Loeb et al., 2017).

Descriptive and qualitative studies help generate hypotheses and paint an important contextual picture that is integral for quantitative scholars who hope to identify natural experiments and apply QEDs to test and evaluate causal hypotheses. Therefore, we underscore the need to embrace methodological plurality, especially in education research where the "how" and "why" are just as important as "does the policy/intervention have a positive/negative effect?" and the magnitudes of the effects. Furthermore, advanced machine-learning methods and other data science approaches that favor predictive validity more than estimation of partial causal estimates must also be embraced by education researchers.

Limited Guidance on Policy Implementation and Design

One additional concern over the growing use of QEDs in education research is that they frequently offer limited guidance on policy implementation and design. QEDs lend themselves to binary measures—whether a policy or intervention existed in a given place at a given time. But policy is often much more nuanced than that. For instance, NCLB was implemented differently in each state, essentially resulting in 50 versions of NCLB (Wong et al., 2018), but many studies treat it as a single homogeneous policy across states. Similarly, PBF policies for public colleges and universities vary from state to state, with some states tying as much as 85% of state appropriations for public colleges to institutional performance while others tie less than 5% to similar metrics. Analyses that treat policies as a homogeneous group when in fact substantial differences exist in implementation may fail to offer helpful guidance for policymakers (see Kelchen et al., 2019, for a more detailed discussion of these issues).

Relatedly, another criticism often raised against an overreliance on QEDs and, more generally, the causal inference research movement has been the limited guidance such research offers educational policy design and implementation (Polikoff & Conaway, 2018). Polikoff and Conaway (2018) argue that even when causal evidence exists, such research by itself may not provide sufficient guidance to policymakers that can inform specific policy design or implementation tweaks. Their recommendation is to increase the dissemination of expert-led, nontechnical, research syntheses that will invariably involve some subjective judgments on the cumulative evidence available to guide policymakers. A recent consensus statement authored by some of the most prominent ECE researchers is a classic example of such a research syntheses (Phillips et al., 2017). In that report, the authors evaluate the "state of scientific knowledge" available from RCTs, QEDs, and other research approaches when analyzing the effect of early childhood education on a variety of student outcomes.

OVERCOMING LIMITATIONS: A PATH FORWARD

It is increasingly clear from our trend analysis as well as the deeper case study reviews that QEDs have been embraced by the education research community. Yet concerns regarding how education research that incorporates such innovative techniques can be effectively used to inform future research, policy, and practice linger. A path forward necessarily involves a thoughtful integration of these approaches within the larger toolkit of education research. We offer some specific recommendations for such integration to flourish.

First, as our trend analysis reveals, despite substantial growth over time, only a small percentage of studies published in the top education research journals use QEDs. This leaves a lot of room for the increased use of these methods. Encouraging the use of these methods must, however, be accompanied with a call for an increase in the use of additional within-study robustness checks of results (Duncan et al., 2014). Using alternative specification checks, providing valid arguments defending the specific assumptions on which these designs' ability to tease causal inference rests, and including tests that rule out plausible alternative explanations for observed causal effects become ever more important if these methods are increasingly adopted. Furthermore, quantitative scholars must be encouraged to use and refine theoretical frameworks as they continue to test specific hypotheses using QEDs.

Encouraging greater dialogue between qualitative and quantitative scholarship in education research has the potential to improve both types of research in education (Schudde, 2018). The notion of counterfactual thinking encouraged by the causal inference movement could be adapted in comparative analysis and inform case selections by qualitative researchers (Plümper et al., 2019). On the other hand, in education, more nuanced counterfactual models that explore how control groups' behavior and performance evolves over time using qualitative and quantitative methods must be incorporated in evaluations (Lemons et al., 2014). In-depth qualitative research exploring the mechanisms and theories of change underlying the policy and interventions under study can enhance the quality of studies that use QEDs. Mixed-methods research can also help promote such integration. Studies using QEDs can therefore effectively complement the education research enterprise in several ways with an eye toward improving evidence-based practice and policy.

Finally, most of the challenges we identified above are not limited to just QEDs. Rather, these are challenges that the education sciences face in an effort to ensure that research does not get increasingly disconnected from actual policy design and implementation. It is therefore important to promote the publication of research syntheses using empirical meta-analytical techniques as well as integrative systematic reviews that can evaluate the "state of knowledge" that combines research evidence from a larger body of evidence that includes studies that use QEDs as well as other research methodologies. Developing and enhancing systematic frameworks for assessing the quality of evidence in education that includes these new techniques must be a priority for education research.

CONCLUSION

The rapid growth in the use of QEDs across the social sciences and more specifically in education research is undeniable. In this chapter, we synthesized literature that uses QEDs across the pre-K–16 education spectrum to examine how the use of these methodologies has improved our knowledge and understanding of educational policy issues. In doing so, it seems rather clear that studies using QEDs have significantly improved our understanding of causal relationships in education. Specifically, these methods have been integral in highlighting the strength and magnitude of causal effects of key educational policies and interventions on well-defined student outcomes and, in some cases, have clearly demonstrated unintended consequences of certain education policies and interventions.

However, as is common in any burgeoning literature, there is tension between an overreliance in the use of these methods and the trade-offs that their use entails. Program evaluation literature has long emphasized the trade-off between internal and external validity in social science research (Campbell, 1957). Studies using QEDs (and RCTs) have privileged internal over external validity in education research as well. While scholars, practitioners, and funding agencies grapple with this trade-off, methodologists are increasingly working to improve these methods to provide insights for generalizability (Tipton, 2014; Tipton & Olsen, 2018). Furthermore, the growth of machine learning and data science in education research is another trend that scholars need to engage with when adapting these techniques to inform policy and practice. It is, however, clear that these innovative approaches can be embraced enthusiastically (but also thoughtfully) to extend our knowledge of educational policies and interventions that strive to go beyond correlational approximations.

Indeed, leaders in the field have noted how far researchers have come in improving rigor in education research (Hedges, 2018). But the increasing shift toward QEDs has some challenges: "Purist devotion to experimental and strong quasi-experimental designs made good sense when we were fighting an uphill battle for increased rigor" (Singer, 2018, p. 23). However, now that QEDs are well-established in education research, it seems ever more important to adopt methodological plurality. Simultaneously, at this time of "replication crisis" in the social sciences, we need to be increasingly cautious and humble about the limits of "evidence and how certain that evidence might be" (Hedges, 2018, p. 18).

Ongoing methodological innovations and the increasing availability of large-scale education data make the use of QEDs and other rigorous observational methods ever more possible. This chapter aimed to illustrate the promise as well as challenges and limitations inherent in adapting QEDs to inform education research, policy, and practice.

ACKNOWLEDGMENTS

We thank John Cheslock, two anonymous reviewers, and the editors for helpful feedback on earlier drafts of this chapter.

ORCID iDs

Maithreyi Gopalan 🆔 https://orcid.org/0000-0002-1013-0672
Jee Bin Ahn 🆔 https://orcid.org/0000-0001-9087-4892

NOTES

[1]Only well-conducted RCTs with low levels of sample attrition receive the highest rating for evidence by the WWC.

[2]These search terms include a broadly accepted set of terms to identify QEDs used in social science. While some of these terms have gained more popularity over time, and are more common in some social science fields such as economics, we believe that these search terms are fairly expansive and capture most of the studies published in the top journals in education that use QEDs.

[3]Information on three of the target journals: *AERA Open, Economics of Education Review*, and *Education Finance and Policy*, which were not included in ProQuest Education Database was collected from SAGE Open Access Journals, ScienceDirect Journals, and ERIC, respectively. Also, note that *AERA Open* is a relatively new journal that began publishing in 2015.

[4]Instrumental variable approaches are also used in education research but mostly by economists. More than half of the 119 articles using these approaches were published in a single journal—*Economics of Education Review*.

[5]Studies identified by the search include those that use fixed effects just as a covariate in their analysis. While this method reduces omitted variable bias to some extent, these studies cannot be considered quasi-experimental in a strict sense. Yet we included "fixed effects" in our search term to be as expansive as possible to ensure our review erred on the side of inclusion rather than exclusion.

REFERENCES

Angrist, J., & Pischke, J.-S. (2010). The credibility revolution in empirical economics: How better research design is taking the con out of econometrics. *Journal of Economic Perspectives, 24*(2), 3–30. https://doi.org/10.3386/w15794

Barnett, W. S., Jung, K., Friedman-Krauss, A., Frede, E. C., Nores, M., Hustedt, J. T., Howes, C., & Daniel-Echols, M. (2018). State prekindergarten effects on early learning at kindergarten entry: An analysis of eight state programs. *AERA Open, 4*(2), Article 2332858418766291. https://doi.org/10.1177/2332858418766291

Belfield, C., & Bailey, T. (2017). *The labor market returns to sub-baccalaureate college: A review* (Center for Analysis of Postsecondary Education and Employment Working Paper). https://ccrc.tc.columbia.edu/media/k2/attachments/labor-market-returns-sub-baccalaureate-college-review.pdf

Bettinger, E. (2010). Instrumental variables. In B. McGaw, P. Peterson, & E. Baker (Eds.), *International encyclopedia of education* (3rd ed., Vol. 8). Elsevier.

Callahan, M. K., Meehan, K., & Shaw, K. M. (2017). *Impact of OBF on student outcomes: Tennessee and Indiana*. Research for Action.

Campbell, D. T. (1957). Factors relevant to the validity of experiments in social settings. *Psychological Bulletin, 54*(4), 297–312. http://dx.doi.org/10.1037/h0040950

Candelaria, C. A., & Shores, K. A. (2019). Court-ordered finance reforms in the adequacy era: Heterogeneous causal effects and sensitivity. *Education Finance and Policy, 14*(1), 31–60. https://doi.org/10.1162/EDFP_a_00236

Carneiro, P., & Ginja, R. (2014). Long-term impacts of compensatory preschool on health and behavior: Evidence from Head Start. *American Economic Journal: Economic Policy, 6*(4), 135–173. https://doi.org/10.1257/pol.6.4.135

Cellini, S. R., Ferreira, F., & Rothstein, J. (2010). The value of school facility investments: Evidence from a dynamic regression discontinuity design. *Quarterly Journal of Economics, 125*(1), 215–261. https://doi.org/10.1162/qjec.2010.125.1.215

Chingos, M., & Whitehurst, G. (2011). *Class size: What research says and what it means for state policy*. Brookings Institution. https://www.brookings.edu/research/class-size-what-research-says-and-what-it-means-for-state-policy/

Cohodes, S. (2018, February 1). *Charter schools and the achievement gap*. https://futureofchildren.princeton.edu/news/charter-schools-and-achievement-gap

Coleman, J., Campbell, E., Hobson, C., McPartland, J., Mood, A., Weinfield, F., & York, R. (1966). *Equality of educational opportunity*. U.S. Department of Health, Education, and Welfare, Office of Education. https://eric.ed.gov/?id=Ed012275

Conklin, K. D., Snyder, M., Stanley, J., & Boelscher, S. (2016). *Rowing together: Aligning state and federal investments in talent to common outcomes*. https://www.ecs.org/wp-content/uploads/ECS_FundingReports_HCM_F.pdf

Cook, T. D. (2008). "Waiting for life to arrive": A history of the regression-discontinuity design in psychology, statistics and economics. *Journal of Econometrics, 142*(2), 636–654. https://doi.org/10.1016/j.jeconom.2007.05.002

Currie, J., & Thomas, D. (1995). Does Head Start make a difference? *American Economic Review, 85*(3), 341–364. https://www.jstor.org/stable/2118178

Curs, B. R., & Harper, C. E. (2012). Financial aid and first-year collegiate GPA: A regression discontinuity approach. *The Review of Higher Education, 35*(4), 627–649. https://doi.org/10.1353/rhe.2012.0040

Deaton, A., & Cartwright, N. (2018). Understanding and misunderstanding randomized controlled trials. *Social Science & Medicine, 210*, 2–21. https://doi.org/10.1016/j.socscimed.2017.12.005

Deming, D. (2009). Early childhood intervention and life-cycle skill development: Evidence from Head Start. *American Economic Journal: Applied Economics, 1*(3), 111–134. https://doi.org/10.1257/app.1.3.111

Dhuey, E. (2011). Who benefits from kindergarten? Evidence from the introduction of state subsidization. *Educational Evaluation and Policy Analysis, 33*(1), 3–22. https://doi .org/10.3102/0162373711398125

Dougherty, K. J., Jones, S. M., Lahr, H., Pheatt, L., Natow, R. S., & Reddy, V. (2016). *Performance funding for higher education.* Johns Hopkins University Press.

Duncan, G..J., Engel, M., Claessens, A., & Dowsett, C. J. (2014). Replication and robustness in developmental research. *Developmental Psychology, 50*(11), 2417–2425. https:// doi.org/10.1037/a0037996

Duncan, G. J., & Magnuson, K. (2013). Investing in preschool programs. *Journal of Economic Perspectives, 27*(2), 109–132. https://doi.org/10.1257/jep.27.2.109

Dynarski, S. (2002). The behavioral and distributional implications of aid for college. *American Economic Review, 92*(2), 279–285. https://doi.org/10.1257/000282802320189401

Fain, P. (2018). *As California goes?* https://www.insidehighered.com/news/2018/06/12/calif-finalizes-performance-funding-formula-its-community-colleges

Friedman-Krauss, A. H., Barnett, W. S., Weisenfeld, G. G., Kasmin, R., DiCrecchio, N., & Horowitz, M. (2018). *The state of preschool 2017.* National Institute for Early Education Research.

Gándara, D., & Rutherford, A. (2017). Mitigating unintended impacts? The effects of premiums for underserved populations in performance-funding policies for higher education. *Research in Higher Education, 59*(6), 681–703. https://doi.org/10.1007/s11162-017-9483-x

Garces, E., Thomas, D., & Currie, J. (2002). Longer-term effects of Head Start. *American Economic Review, 92*(4), 999–1012. https://doi.org/10.1257/00028280260344560

Gelman, A., & Imbens, G. (2019). Why high-order polynomials should not be used in regression discontinuity designs. *Journal of Business & Economic Statistics, 37*(3), 447–456. https://doi.org/10.1080/07350015.2017.1366909

Goodman-Bacon, A. (2018). *Difference-in-differences with variation in treatment timing* (Working Paper No. 25018). https://doi.org/10.3386/w25018

Gormley, W. T. Jr., Gayer, T., Phillips, D., & Dawson, B. (2005). The effects of universal pre-K on cognitive development. *Developmental Psychology, 41*(6), 872–884. https://doi .org/10.1037/0012-1649.41.6.872

Hanushek, E. A. (1997). Assessing the effects of school resources on student performance: An update. *Educational Evaluation and Policy Analysis, 19*(2), 141–164. https://doi.org/ 10.3102/01623737019002141

Hanushek, E. A. (2003). The failure of input-based schooling policies. *Economic Journal, 113*(485), F64–F98. https://doi.org/10.1111/1468-0297.00099

Heckman, J. J. (2006). Skill formation and the economics of investing in disadvantaged children. *Science, 312*(5782), 1900–1902. https://doi.org/10.1126/science.1128898

Hedges, L. V. (2018). Challenges in building usable knowledge in education. *Journal of Research on Educational Effectiveness, 11*(1), 1–21. https://doi.org/10.1080/19345747.2 017.1375583

Hedges, L. V., Laine, R. D., & Greenwald, R. (1994). An exchange: Part I. Does money matter? A meta-analysis of studies of the effects of differential school inputs on student outcomes. *Educational Researcher, 23*(3), 5–14. https://doi.org/10.3102/0013189X023003005

Hillman, N. W., Hicklin Fryar, A., & Crespín-Trujillo, V. (2018). Evaluating the impact of performance funding in Ohio and Tennessee. *American Educational Research Journal, 55*(1), 144–170.

Hillman, N. W., Tandberg, D. A., & Fryar, A. H. (2015). Evaluating the impacts of "new" performance funding in higher education. *Educational Evaluation and Policy Analysis, 37*(4), 501–519. https://doi.org/10.3102/0162373714560224

Hillman, N. W., Tandberg, D. A., & Gross, J. P. (2014). Performance funding in higher education: Do financial incentives impact college completions? *Journal of Higher Education, 85*(6), 826–857. https://doi.org/10.1353/jhe.2014.0031

Howell, P. L., & Miller, B. B. (1997). Sources of funding for schools. *Future of Children, 7*(3), 39–50. https://doi.org/10.2307/1602444

Jackson, C. K. (2018). *Does school spending matter? The new literature on an old question.* Paper presented at the Fall 2018 Bronfenbrenner Center for Translational Research Conference. https://works.bepress.com/c_kirabo_jackson/38/

Jackson, C. K., Johnson, R. C., & Persico, C. (2016). The effects of school spending on educational and economic outcomes: Evidence from school finance reforms. *Quarterly Journal of Economics, 131*(1), 157–218. https://doi.org/10.1093/qje/qjv036

Jenkins, J. M., Farkas, G., Duncan, G. J., Burchinal, M., & Vandell, D. L. (2016). Head Start at Ages 3 and 4 versus Head Start followed by state pre-K: Which is more effective? *Educational Evaluation and Policy Analysis, 38*(1), 88–112. https://doi.org/10.3102/0162373715587965

Johnson, R., & Jackson, C. K. (2019). Reducing inequality through dynamic complementarity: Evidence from Head Start and public school spending. *American Economic Journal: Economic Policy, 11*(4), 310–349. https://doi.org/10.3386/w23489

Kelchen, R. (2018). Do performance-based funding policies affect underrepresented student enrollment? *Journal of Higher Education, 89*(5), 702–727. https://doi.org/10.1080/0022 1546.2018.1434282

Kelchen, R. (2019). Exploring the relationship between performance-based funding design and underrepresented student enrollment at community colleges. *Community College Review, 47*(4), 382–405. https://doi.org/10.1177/0091552119865611

Kelchen, R., Rosinger, K. O., & Ortagus, J. C. (2019). How to create and use state-level policy data sets in education research. *AERA Open, 5*(3), Article 2332858419873619. https://doi.org/10.1177/2332858419873619

Kelchen, R., & Stedrak, L. J. (2016). Does performance-based funding affect colleges' financial priorities? *Journal of Education Finance, 41*(3), 302–321. https://doi.org/10.1353/jef.2016.0006

Lafortune, J., Rothstein, J., & Schanzenbach, D. W. (2018). School finance reform and the distribution of student achievement. *American Economic Journal: Applied Economics, 10*(2), 1–26. https://doi.org/10.1257/app.20160567

Lemons, C. J., Fuchs, D., Gilbert, J. K., & Fuchs, L. S. (2014). Evidence-based practices in a changing world: Reconsidering the counterfactual in education research. *Educational Researcher, 43*(5), 242–252. https://doi.org/10.3102/0013189X14539189

Li, A. Y., & Kennedy, A. I. (2018). Performance funding policy effects on community college outcomes: Are short-term certificates on the rise? *Community College Review, 46*(1), 3–39.

Lipsey, M. W., Weiland, C., Yoshikawa, H., Wilson, S. J., & Hofer, K. G. (2015). The prekindergarten age-cutoff regression-discontinuity design: Methodological issues and implications for application. *Educational Evaluation and Policy Analysis, 37*(3), 296–313. https://doi.org/10.3102/0162373714547266

Loeb, S., Dynarski, S., McFarland, D., Morris, P., Reardon, S., & Reber, S. (2017). *Descriptive analysis in education: A guide for researchers* (No. NCEE 2017-4023; p. 53). U.S. Department of Education, Institute of Education Sciences, National Center for Education Evaluation and Regional Assistance.

Magnuson, K. A., Ruhm, C., & Waldfogel, J. (2007). Does prekindergarten improve school preparation and performance? *Economics of Education Review, 26*(1), 33–51. https://doi.org/10.1016/j.econedurev.2005.09.008

Martorell, P., Stange, K., & McFarlin, I. (2016). Investing in schools: Capital spending, facility conditions, and student achievement. *Journal of Public Economics, 140*, 13–29. https://doi.org/10.1016/j.jpubeco.2016.05.002

McCoy, D. C., Yoshikawa, H., Ziol-Guest, K. M., Duncan, G. J., Schindler, H. S., Magnuson, K., Yang, R., Koepp, A., & Shonkoff, J. P. (2017). Impacts of early childhood education on medium- and long-term educational outcomes. *Educational Researcher, 46*(8), 474–487. https://doi.org/10.3102/0013189X17737739

McKenzie, D. (2018, September 4). Have descriptive development papers been crowded out by impact evaluations? *World Bank Blogs.* https://blogs.worldbank.org/impactevaluations/have-descriptive-development-papers-been-crowded-out-impact-evaluations

Morris, P. A., Connors, M., Friedman-Krauss, A., McCoy, D. C., Weiland, C., Feller, A., Page, L., Bloom, H., & Yoshikawa, H. (2018). New findings on impact variation from the Head Start impact study: Informing the scale-up of early childhood programs. *AERA Open, 4*(2), Article 2332858418769287. https://doi.org/10.1177/2332858418769287

National Research Council & Institute of Medicine Committee on Integrating the Science of Early Childhood Development. (2000). *From neurons to neighborhoods: The science of early childhood development* (J. P. Shonkoff & D. A. Phillips, Eds.). National Academies Press. http://www.ncbi.nlm.nih.gov/books/NBK225557/

National Student Clearinghouse. (2018). *Completing college.* https://nscresearchcenter.org/signaturereport16/

Open Science Collaboration. (2015). Estimating the reproducibility of psychological science. *Science, 349*(6251), aac4716–aac4716. https://doi.org/10.1126/science.aac4716

Panhans, M. T., & Singleton, J. D. (2017). The empirical economist's toolkit from models to methods. *History of Political Economy, 49*(Supplement), 127–157. https://doi.org/10.1215/00182702-4166299

Phillips, D. A., Lipsey, M. W., Dodge, K. A., Haskins, R., Bassok, D., Burchinal, M. R., Duncan, G. J., Dynarski, M., Magnuson, K. A., & Weiland, C. (2017). *Puzzling it out: The current state of scientific knowledge on pre-kindergarten effects: A consensus statement* (p. 16). Brookings Institution.

Plümper, T., Troeger, V. E., & Neumayer, E. (2019). Case selection and causal inferences in qualitative comparative research. *PLOS ONE, 14*(7). https://doi.org/10.1371/journal.pone.0219727

Polikoff, M., & Conaway, C. (2018). Getting beyond 'did it work?': Proposing a new approach to integrate research and policy [The Brookings Institution]. *Brookings Brown Center Chalkboard.* https://www.brookings.edu/blog/brown-center-chalkboard/2018/09/25/getting-beyond-did-it-work-proposing-a-new-approach-to-integrate-research-and-policy/

Pritchett, L. (2018). *Lant Pritchett Talk: "The debate about RCTs in development is over. We won. They lost."* Retrieved September 11, 2018, from http://www.nyudri.org/events-index/2018/2/22/lant-pritchett-talk-the-debate-about-rcts-in-development-is-over-we-won-they-lost

Reback, R. (2010). Noninstructional spending improves noncognitive outcomes: Discontinuity evidence from a unique elementary school counselor financing system. *Education Finance and Policy, 5*(2), 105–137. https://doi.org/10.1162/edfp.2010.5.2.5201

Ruhm, C. J. (2018). *Shackling the identification police?* (Working Paper No. 25320). https://doi.org/10.3386/w25320

Rutherford, A., & Rabovsky, T. (2014). Evaluating impacts of performance funding policies on student outcomes in higher education. *Annals of the American Academy of Political and Social Science, 655*(1), 185–208. https://doi.org/10.1177/0002716214541048

Schanzenbach, D. W. (2012). Limitations of experiments in education research. *Education Finance and Policy, 7*(2), 219–232. https://doi.org/10.1162/EDFP_a_00063

Schudde, L. (2018). Heterogeneous effects in education: The promise and challenge of incorporating intersectionality into quantitative methodological approaches. *Review of Research in Education, 42*(1), 72–92. https://doi.org/10.3102/0091732X18759040

Singer, J. D. (2018). Even more challenges in building usable knowledge in education. *Journal of Research on Educational Effectiveness*, *11*(1), 22–24. https://doi.org/10.1080/1934574 7.2017.1402397

Stange, K. (2015). Differential pricing in undergraduate education: Effects on degree production by field. *Journal of Policy Analysis and Management*, *34*(1), 107–135. https://doi .org/10.1002/pam.21803

Stuart, E. A. (2010). Matching methods for causal inference: A review and a look forward. *Statistical Science*, *25*(1), 1–21. https://doi.org/10.1214/09-STS313

Stuart, E. A., Bell, S. H., Ebnesajjad, C., Olsen, R. B., & Orr, L. L. (2017). Characteristics of school districts that participate in rigorous national educational evaluations. *Journal of Research on Educational Effectiveness*, *10*(1), 168–206. https://doi.org/10.1080/1934574 7.2016.1205160

Tandberg, D. A., & Hillman, N. W. (2014). State higher education performance funding: Data, outcomes, and policy implications. *Journal of Education Finance*, *39*(3), 222–243.

Tandberg, D. A., Hillman, N., & Barakat, M. (2014). State higher education performance funding for community colleges: Diverse effects and policy implications. *Teachers College Record*, *116*(12), 1–31.

Thistlethwaite, D. L., & Campbell, D. T. (1960). Regression-discontinuity analysis: An alternative to the ex post facto experiment. *Journal of Educational Psychology*, *51*(6), 309–317. https://doi.org/10.1037/h0044319

Thompson, O. (2017). Head Start's long-run impact: Evidence from the program's introduction. *Journal of Human Resources*, 0216-7735r1. https://doi.org/10.3368/jhr.53.4 .0216.7735R1

Tipton, E. (2014). How generalizable is your experiment? An index for comparing experimental samples and populations. *Journal of Educational and Behavioral Statistics*, *39*(6), 478–501. https://doi.org/10.3102/1076998614558486

Tipton, E., & Olsen, R. B. (2018). A review of statistical methods for generalizing from evaluations of educational interventions. *Educational Researcher*, *47*(8), 516–524. https://doi .org/10.3102/0013189X18781522

Umbricht, M. R., Fernandez, F., & Ortagus, J. C. (2017). An examination of the (un) intended consequences of performance funding in higher education. *Educational Policy*, *31*(5), 643–673. https://doi.org/10.1177/0895904815614398

U.S. Department of Education. (2017). *Standards handbook* (Version 4.0). What Works Clearinghouse. https://ies.ed.gov/ncee/wwc/Docs/referenceresources/wwc_standards_ handbook_v4.pdf

van Huizen, T., & Plantenga, J. (2018). Do children benefit from universal early childhood education and care? A meta-analysis of evidence from natural experiments. *Economics of Education Review*, *66*, 206–222. https://doi.org/10.1016/j.econedurev.2018.08.001

Weiland, C., & Yoshikawa, H. (2013). Impacts of a prekindergarten program on children's mathematics, language, literacy, executive function, and emotional skills. *Child Development*, *84*(6), 2112–2130. https://doi.org/10.1111/cdev.12099

Wing, C., & Bello-Gomez, R. A. (2018). Regression discontinuity and beyond: Options for studying external validity in an internally valid design. *American Journal of Evaluation*, *39*(1), 91–108. https://doi.org/10.1177/1098214017736155

Wing, C., Simon, K., & Bello-Gomez, R. A. (2018). Designing difference in difference studies: Best practices for public health policy research. *Annual Review of Public Health*, *39*(1), 453–469. https://doi.org/10.1146/annurev-publhealth-040617-013507

Wong, V. C., Wing, C., Martin, D., & Krishnamachari, A. (2018). Did states use implementation discretion to reduce the stringency of NCLB? Evidence from a database of state regulations. *Educational Researcher*, *47*(1), 9–33. https://doi.org/10.3102/00131 89X17743230

Chapter 9

Linking Quantitative and Qualitative Network Approaches: A Review of Mixed Methods Social Network Analysis in Education Research

Dominik E. Froehlich
University of Vienna

Sara Van Waes
University of Antwerp

Hannah Schäfer
University of Vienna

Social network analysis (SNA) is becoming a prevalent method in education research and practice. But criticism has been voiced against the heavy reliance on quantification within SNA. Recent work suggests combining quantitative and qualitative approaches in SNA— mixed methods social network analysis (MMSNA)—as a remedy. MMSNA is helpful for addressing research questions related to the formal or structural side of relationships and networks, but it also attends to more qualitative questions such as the meaning of interactions or the variability of social relationships. In this chapter, we describe how researchers have applied and presented MMSNA in publications from the perspective of general mixed methods research. Based on a systematic review, we summarize the different applications within the field of education and learning research, point to potential shortcomings of the methods and its presentation, and develop an agenda to support researchers in conducting future MMSNA research.

Beginning in the 1990s, education researchers, policy makers, and practitioners have become interested in relationships and collaboration in educational settings. In response, social network analysis (SNA) was proposed as a theoretical and methodological framework, offering theory and tools to explore relationships in depth. Compared to then existing approaches for studying interactions and

Review of Research in Education
March 2020, Vol. 44, pp. 244–268
DOI: 10.3102/0091732X20903311

Chapter reuse guidelines: sagepub.com/journals-permissions
© 2020 AERA. http://rre.aera.net

interdependencies among, for example, teachers or pupils, SNA allows one to capture these relationships in a more nuanced way, by focusing on the patterns and qualities of relationships (Borgatti et al., 2009). SNA offers valuable insights into whether and to what degree interactions and collaboration take place in education. Another key strength of SNA is that it offers several tools to visualize relationships (Hogan et al., 2007), which creates opportunities for visual analysis and feedback aimed at improving practice. No other methodological framework is as focused on the in-depth exploration of relationships and structures in learning and instruction (Moolenaar, 2012; Sweet, 2016).

The surge in SNA publications across the academic disciplines is largely driven by quantitative SNA studies (Freeman, 2004). Despite its merits, authors such as Fuhse and Mützel (2011) or Hollstein (2011) have criticized this formalized approach to network analysis for a lack of attention to the qualitative aspects of relationships. Recent work addresses these concerns by combining quantitative and qualitative approaches in SNA to what we call mixed methods social network analysis (MMSNA; Froehlich, Rehm, et al., 2020; Hollstein, 2014). MMSNA is helpful for addressing research questions related to the formal or structural side of relationships and networks, but it also attends to questions related to the actual content and meaning of interactions, the day-to-day variability of social relationships, the developments of nodes and ties, and agency (Crossley, 2010; Crossley & Edwards, 2016).

In this chapter, we describe how researchers have applied and presented MMSNA in publications from the perspective of general mixed methods research. Based on a systematic review, we (a) summarize the different applications within the field of education and learning research, (b) point to potential shortcomings of the methods and its presentation, and (c) develop an agenda to support researchers in conducting future MMSNA research. We tailored the review for a diverse audience. For social network and mixed method researchers, the review details the use of mixed methods within SNA, sets forward a framework for quality reporting practices, and hints at potential pitfalls. For education researchers, the review illustrates how MMSNA is being applied when studying relationships and collaboration within educational settings.

BACKGROUND

Social Network Theory and Analysis

Networks are a way of thinking about social systems that focus our attention on the web of relationships that surrounds actors. Networks are composed of actors (*nodes*) and their relationships (*ties*). Actors can be individuals, for example, pupils in a classroom or teachers in a school, or collectivities, such as teams, organizations, or countries. Ties include relationships or transfers such as conversations between pupils or information exchanges among teachers. The central focus of social network theory is on relationships among actors to explain actor and network outcomes. Over the years, there have been discussions about whether social network theory is an actual "theory," a collection of methods, or a metaphor (Wellman, 1988). Initially, many social capital theorists drew on SNA as a methodological approach and a means to capturing relevant features of interaction only. Today, several scholars argue that this claim is not a valid stance anymore (Borgatti et al., 2014; Brass et al., 2014). To date, a solid body of work has been developed, comprising theoretical concepts such as structural holes (Burt, 1992), centrality (Freeman, 1978), the strength of ties (Granovetter, 1973), and structural equivalence (Lorrain & White, 1971). Network researchers use the tools offered by SNA to study the relationships and structural features of social networks (Wellman, 1983).

A Social Network Perspective in Education Research

The urge to capitalize on relationships, interaction, and collaboration within educational settings is reflected by a growing number of concepts, such as communities of practice, organizational shared and collaborative learning, and professional (learning) communities (Louis & Marks, 1998; McLaughlin & Talbert, 2006; Wenger et al., 2002). Indeed, researchers have established the usefulness of SNA in examining the role of relationships for student achievement (Daly et al., 2014; Pil & Leana, 2009), teacher learning (Baker-Doyle, 2015; Fox et al., 2011), reform and improvement (Moolenaar et al., 2012; Penuel et al., 2016), policy implementation (Coburn et al., 2012; Frank et al., 2011), leadership (Daly & Finnigan, 2011; Spillane & Shirrell, 2017), and professional development programs (Baker-Doyle & Yoon, 2010; Hofman & Dijkstra, 2010; Penuel et al., 2012).

These new lines of research have led to greater interest in the research on relationships in education. However, also conceptual and methodological challenges exist with this approach that SNA attempts to overcome. For example, the focus on particular communities can be limiting, as a student or teacher is often embedded in a network of relationships that span subgroups and include individuals inside and outside institutional boundaries (Penuel et al., 2009; Spillane, 2005). Also, the growing body of research on relationships has concentrated on social interactions. One problem of the extant literature is the precision of measurement (Coburn et al., 2012). Often, an "average" of a relationship between one individual and the rest of the group is being measured, for instance, how many times a teacher reports a certain interaction, irrespective of the specific interaction partner. A more fine-grained exploration of interaction, taking a relational view, could yield a better understanding of these phenomena.[1]

Mixed Methods SNA

The nature of SNA within discussions about quantitative, qualitative, and mixed methodologies is ambiguous. Most researchers consider SNA a formal or quantitative technique (Crossley & Edwards, 2016; Hollstein, 2014). This definition is in stark contrast to the historical roots of social network analysis, which are qualitative (Freeman, 2004). Onwuegbuzie and Hitchcock (2015) highlight the potential to integrate qualitative and quantitative methods of network research and describe the method as quantitative-dominant crossover mixed analysis. Put differently, they view it as an inherently mixed analysis.

An increasing number of social network researchers makes use of mixed methods to generate their findings (Froehlich, Rehm, et al., 2020). This surge in interest has come with the realization that quantitative (or formal) and qualitative SNA each have their respective sets of strengths and weaknesses (Crossley, 2010). For example, qualitative SNA often lacks an overview of the structural properties of a network. Conversely, quantitative network analysis is often too abstract to consider the content being exchanged, the fluctuations of the relationships over time, or the role of agency (Crossley, 2010). This makes MMSNA relevant in gauging the social complexities found within education and learning research.

We define MMSNA as any SNA study drawing from both qualitative and quantitative data or using qualitative and quantitative methods of analysis. This definition is in line with definitions of mixed methods in general (Johnson et al., 2007; Johnson & Onwuegbuzie, 2004). These different methods need to be thoughtfully integrated. This can mean studies (a) that mix within SNA or (b) that include SNA as one element in the overall research design. In the former, qualitative and quantitative relational data are being used or qualitative and quantitative social network analytic approaches are being applied. The latter includes any mixed methods study featuring one component of SNA such as triangulating quantitative SNA with nonrelational, qualitative data.

Describing MMSNA Studies

In his seminal article "Describing Mixed Methods Research," Guest (2013) states that "two dimensions are enough [to describe mixed methods designs]—the *timing* and the *purpose* of integration" (p. 147). These two dimensions thus form the basis for this review. But for any review, it is important not only to look at what is being done but also to assess the quality of research (cf. Siddaway et al., 2019). Therefore, we assess the quality of mixing in addition to the purpose(s) of mixing and its timing.

Purpose(s) of Mixing in MMSNA

Every use of mixed methods has a specific *purpose of mixing*, which is based on the researchers' wish to raise the scope, power, and/or quality of their study (Schoonenboom et al., 2018). In this review, we follow the perspective of Schoonenboom et al. (2018) by focusing on "purposes of mixing at a detailed level" (p. 272). To aid the aggregation of the data for this review, we use three major categories of purposes of mixing: follow-up, comparison, and development. If the purpose is *follow-up*, methods are being used to expand on findings, for example, to aim for more generalizable findings, to find explanations for results, or to replicate findings. For example, researchers might combine a quantitative analysis using survey data with qualitative analysis of interviews "intended to deepen the understandings of the structural network analysis findings" (Rodway, 2015, p. 8). *Comparison* as a purpose refers to answering complementary research questions and triangulations throughout the research process. Last, *development* as a purpose for mixing aims at further informing the main research through a prestudy. For example, researchers may conduct cognitive interviews to improve a survey instrument or a sampling procedure.

Timing in MMSNA

Mixed methods research, in general, and MMSNA, in particular, is characterized by design features related to timing. *Timing* has two dimensions (Schoonenboom & Johnson, 2017):

- *Simultaneity*: A case of mixing is concurrent when both elements involved are performed in parallel (Dingyloudi & Strijbos, 2018), and it is sequential when one element follows the other (Liou & Daly, 2014).
- *Dependence*: A case of mixing is independent when both elements involved are performed without mutual influence (Dingyloudi & Strijbos, 2018), and it is dependent when one element influences the outcome of performance of the other element (Liou & Daly, 2014).

Quality in MMSNA

Hong et al. (2018) developed the Mixed Methods Appraisal Tool (MMAT) as a review tool for mixed studies in 2006 and since then have repeatedly improved it. The MMAT serves as a validated appraisal tool for the methodological quality of either qualitative, quantitative, or mixed methods studies. The MMAT questionnaire has two parts. Two preliminary screening questions confirm the suitability of the study to be evaluated using the MMAT. Next, five criteria for assessing mixed methods studies are applied to studies that include at least one qualitative and one quantitative method. We present the specificities of the coding procedure in the Method section.

METHOD

In this review, we follow the PRISMA statement[2] (Moher et al., 2009) and other texts describing the state of the art of doing literature reviews (Siddaway et al., 2019; Van Tulder et al., 2003) to identify and screen records, check their eligibility, and code them. This literature is then evaluated to answer the guiding question of this chapter of how MMSNA is being applied in contemporary education research. This process is depicted in Figure 1.

Identification of Records

We have followed two major strategies for identifying relevant literature. The first and arguably most important strategy involves the search in scientific databases with

FIGURE 1
Overview of the Search Process

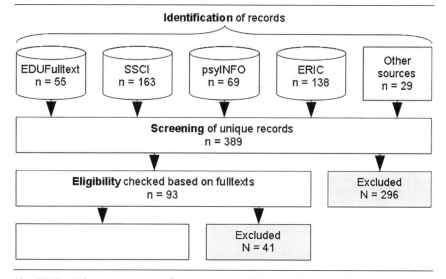

Note. ERIC = Education Resources Information Center; SSCI = Social Sciences Citation Index.

a predefined set of keywords. We focused on databases commonly referenced in learning and education: Education Resources Information Center, Education Full Text, PsycARTICLES, PsycINFO, and the Social Sciences Citation Index. PsycARTICLES was later dropped from the search to safeguard consistency, as the search terms turned out to be very imprecise for this database. Discussions with peers in the field confirmed that these are the most relevant databases for this review.

We searched these databases using three blocks of search terms that are connected to each other through "AND" operators. Figure 2 shows the lists of search terms.

In addition to this search, we followed a set of alternative strategies for identifying relevant literature to produce a comprehensive list of records. This includes back-tracking,[3] forward-tracking,[4] and consulting peers. Neither back-tracking nor forward-tracking returned additional records. This most likely has to do with the nature of the review that is not focused on a content-related theme, which would produce a narrative that could be traced in the reference list, but on a method. The consultation of peers, where we addressed colleagues and an international, informal research group about SNA in learning and education produced a list of 29 records before deleting duplicates.

Screening of Records

After the initial identification of 454 potentially relevant records, we created one database that contained the meta-information, including titles and abstracts, from all

FIGURE 2
Search Terms

Social Network Analysis	social network analysis* OR SNA or social network* or network analysis*
	AND
Mixed Methods	mixed method* OR MMMR OR (qualitative OR unstructured interview* OR open interview* OR semi-structured interview* OR focus group* OR grounded theory OR grounded theories OR et*nogra* OR phenomelogic* OR hermeneutic* OR life history* OR life stor* OR participant observation* OR open interview OR thematic analyses OR content analyses OR observational methods OR constant comparative method OR field notes OR field study OR audio recording) AND (regression OR QAP OR MR-QAP OR ERGM OR SABM))
	AND
Thematic focus on Learning and Edu.	learning* OR education* OR development* OR instruction*

identified texts. First, we screened this list for duplicates and deleted 65 records. For the remainder of 389 records, two of the authors screened the titles and abstracts to make an initial decision about the relevance of the records. Relevance was determined based on four inclusion criteria. Specifically, the record needed

1. To report empirical research; conceptual contributions or reviews were excluded
2. To apply SNA based on our loose definition of MMSNA described in the background section
3. To use qualitative and quantitative data or apply qualitative and quantitative methods of data analysis
4. To be situated in education

During screening we excluded 296 records for an initial pool of 93 potential studies. To safeguard reliability of this process, a subset of 14 randomly selected records was coded by all authors and two independent researchers. Exact Kappa (Conger, 1980) was calculated. The result of $\kappa = .75$ ($p < .01$) indicated substantial agreement among the coders.

Eligibility of Records

For all records that passed the screening stage, the complete texts were accessed to confirm eligibility. For the vast majority of records, the reading of the full texts confirmed the initial assessment in the screening phase. One important deviation was found in methodologically oriented texts (e.g., Martínez et al., 2006) that—strictly speaking—did fulfill all inclusion criteria, but were found to be too shallow in the reporting of the empirical results for our purpose. Since this made a thorough review infeasible, these records were excluded. Also, for two records, no complete text could be retrieved, so they were excluded from further review. In total, 41 texts were removed from the literature review after reading the complete texts for a final list of 52 studies to be reviewed. With 52 studies left from an initial pool of 389 records, the precision of the search amounts to 13%. This number is rather low given that the term *social network* is used in very different ways, most notably in terms of social network sites, which cannot be excluded from the search because relevant research may be carried out using social networking site data. We kept the search rather broad to have greater confidence in not having filtered out relevant studies.

Coding of Included Studies

Three authors coded the following information of each of the eligible texts: publication meta-data, an assessment of the methodological quality of the empirical analysis, and features of the research design and integration. Next to this, memos and qualitative comments were written during the coding procedure.

Publication Meta-Data

Information required for documentation purposes, such as the names of the authors, the publication date, the publication type, and so forth, were coded. Additionally, we coded the theme and context of the article on a broad level.

Purpose(s) of Mixing in MMSNA

In line with our theoretical background, we have categorized the studies based on their purpose(s) of mixing in terms of follow-up, comparison, and development (Schoonenboom et al., 2018). This was done based on the research design, and we did not rely on authors' statements about what they perceived as the purpose(s) of mixing.[5]

Timing in MMSNA

The two dimensions of timing—simultaneity and dependency—were coded for each study. This information was used to form four types of research: parallel and dependent, parallel and independent, sequential and dependent, and sequential and independent. Both design features have been defined and described in the background section. This cross tabulation helped examine the relationships between the dimensions of timing.

Quality in MMSNA

The methodological quality was rated according to the MMAT evaluation instrument (Hong et al., 2018). The MMAT provides five methodological quality criteria to evaluate mixed method studies that are rated as either 1 = *present/yes* or 0 = *not present/no*. Specifically, we coded whether

1. The purpose for applying a mixed methods approach has been stated.
2. The different components of the study were effectively integrated to provide a response to the research question. As integration is considered an essential component of mixed method research, the MMAT suggest to closely inspecting the used methods to integrate qualitative and quantitative phases, results, and data.
3. Meta-interference, the overall conclusion arrived at through integrating each of the methods' inferences (Teddlie & Tashakkori, 2009), added value.
4. Divergences and inconsistencies between quantitative and qualitative results occurred and were adequately addressed.
5. The quality criteria of each applied method was adhered to. The MMAT considers high-quality components without exception as a requirement for mixed methods studies of good quality.

Reliability of the Coding Procedure

The coding was again checked in terms of reliability. This time, three of the authors simultaneously coded three records. The result of $\kappa = .62$ ($p < .01$) indicated that there was substantial agreement between the coders' ratings.

RESULTS

Table 1 summarizes the studies reviewed including information about the theme, identified purpose and timing according to the previously mentioned categories, and the overall score on the MMAT. The table also illustrates the breadth of themes that MMSNA was used to research. In terms of context, it was often applied in K–12 (23 studies, 44%), higher education (18 studies, 35%), or school administration (three studies, 6%).

Purpose(s) of Mixing in MMSNA

We evaluated the major purposes of mixing.[6] In 32 studies (62%), the purpose of mixing was identified as follow-up. Of almost equal prominence, 21 studies (40%) used different methods for the purpose of comparison. In eight studies (15%), follow-up and comparison were simultaneously present as the purposes of mixing. Four studies (8%) used one method to develop another. In four studies (8%) the purpose remained unclear, even after reading the full text.

We also intended to check for congruence between the purpose(s) of mixing identified by us and the purpose(s) stated by the respective study authors. Given that the vast majority of studies did not allow to us to observe the authors' thinking and line of argumentation (see Quality in MMSNA below), the alignment between what the authors stated and what was done could not be coded.

TABLE 1
Overview of the Included Studies

#	Study	Theme	Context	Purpose			Timing	MMAT Score
				F	C	D		
1	Ardoin et al. (2017)	Peer trust in environmental education	K-12	—	✓	—	SD	3
2	Baird et al. (2014)	Interactive decision making	Administration	✓	✓	—	PI	3
3	Baker-Doyle & Petchauer (2015)	Teacher preparation for licensure exam	K-12	✓	✓	—	SD	3
4	Bozkurt & Keefer (2018)	Learning communities in MOOCs	Various	—	—	✓	SD	0
5	Bozkurt et al. (2016)	Learning communities in MOOCs	Various	✓	✓	—	SD	5
6	Carhill-Poza (2015)	Student–peer interaction and language learning	HE	✓	✓	—	SI	4
7	Cornelissen et al. (2014)	School–university research networks	Various	✓	—	—	PD	5
8	Cornelissen et al. (2015)	Development, sharing, and usage of research-based knowledge	HE	✓	—	—	SD	5
9	Cross et al. (2009)	Interagency collaboration	K-12	✓	✓	—	PI	3
10	Daly & Finnigan (2010)	Communication and knowledge networks	Administration	✓	—	—	SD	5
11	Daly & Finnigan (2011)	Communication and knowledge networks	Administration	✓	—	✓	SD	5
12	Daly et al. (2010)	School reform	Administration	✓	—	—	SD	5
13	Dingyloudi & Strijbos (2018)	Peer feedback	HE	✓	✓	—	PI	2
14	Finnigan & Daly (2012)	Organizational learning and improvement	Administration	✓	—	—	SD	4
15	Finnigan et al. (2013)	District reform	K-12	✓	—	—	SD	5
16	Goggins et al. (2011)	Online group formation	HE	✓	✓	—	PI	4
17	Häussling (2010)	Social positions in class	K-12	✓	✓	—	PI	5
18	Hoffman & Silverberg (2015)	Peer interaction	HE	—	—	—	SI	0
19	Honeychurch et al. (2017)	Community development in MOOCs	K-12	✓	—	✓	SD	1
20	Hopkins & Spillane (2014)	Support of beginning teachers	K-12	✓	—	—	PI	4
21	Hopkins et al. (2015)	District infrastructure and language learning	K-12	—	—	—	PI	3
22	Kellogg et al. (2014)	Teacher-peer support in MOOCs	K-12	?	?	?	PI	1
23	Kortemeyer & Kortemeyer (2018)	Student collaboration	HE	✓	—	—	PI	1
24	Langhout et al. (2014)	Relational empowerment	K-12	—	✓	—	SI	1
25	Lee et al. (2014)	Interracial peer relationships	K-12	?	?	?	SI	1
26	Liou & Daly (2014)	Professional learning communities	K-12	✓	✓	—	PI	5

(continued)

TABLE 1 (CONTINUED)

#	Study	Theme	Context	Purpose F	Purpose C	Purpose D	Timing	MMAT Score
27	Liou et al. (2014)	Distributed leadership and data-driven professional networks	K-12	?	?	?	SD	3
28	Lu & Churchill (2014)	Collaborative learning	HE	—	✓	—	SD	5
29	Penuel et al. (2009)	Teacher professional communities	K-12	✓	—	—	PI	5
30	Pifer (2011)	Departmental networks	HE	✓	—	—	SD	5
31	Rienties & Hosein (2015)	Teacher interaction in academic development	HE	—	✓	—	SD	5
32	Rienties & Kinchin (2014)	Interactions in academic development	HE	—	✓	—	PI	4
33	Rienties et al. (2014)	Computer-mediated communication	HE	✓	✓	—	SD	3
34	Rienties et al. (2013)	Student intercultural learning interactions	HE	—	—	—	SD	3
35	Rienties et al. (2015)	Cross-cultural learning	HE	—	✓	—	SD	4
36	Risser (2013)	Twittering in mentoring relationships	K-12	—	—	✓	PD	3
37	Rodriguez-Medina et al. (2018)	Friendship relationships and autism	K12	—	✓	—	PI	3
38	Rodway (2015)	Research brokering networks	Health	✓	—	—	SD	2
39	Sánchez et al. (2011)	Mentoring relationships	K-12	✓	—	—	SI	5
40	Schiff et al. (2015)	Teacher collaboration	K-12	✓	—	—	SD	5
41	Smith (2010)	Learning communities	HE	✓	—	—	SI	0
42	Smith (2015)	Student learning communities	HE	✓	—	—	PI	5
43	Spillane et al. (2015)	Intra- and interschool interactions	K-12	✓	—	—	SD	5
44	Spillane et al. (2018)	Teacher performance	K-12	✓	—	—	SD	4
45	Tirado et al. (2015)	Discussion fora in writing environments	HE	?	?	?	PD	3
46	Ugurlu (2016)	Interorganizational collaboration in districts	K-12	✓	✓	—	SD	5
47	Van Gasse et al. (2017)	Teacher interaction	Various	✓	—	—	SD	5
48	Van Waes et al. (2015)	Teacher interaction in academic development	HE	—	✓	—	PI	5
49	Vanwynsberghe et al. (2014)	Support of social media experts	Library	✓	—	—	SD	1
50	Wise & Cui (2018)	Learning communities in MOOCs	HE	✓	—	—	SD	3
51	Wong-Hooker (2016)	Teacher collaboration in special education	K-12	—	✓	—	SD	5
52	Yessis et al. (2013)	Interorganizational relationships and brokering	Health	—	✓	—	SD	0

Note. Abbreviations in context: HE = higher education; abbreviations for the purposes: F = follow-up. C = comparison, D = development. MMAT = Mixed Methods Appraisal Tool; PD = parallel and dependent; PI = parallel and independent; SD = sequential and dependent; SI = sequential and independent; MOOC = massive open online course.

TABLE 2
Overview of Timing

	Parallel	Sequential
Dependent	3 (6%)	28 (54%)
Independent	15 (29%)	6 (12%)

Timing in MMSNA

Eighteen studies (35%) contained parallel designs. One example is the study by Dingyloudi and Strijbos (2018), who collected and analyzed quantitative social network data and video data in parallel. An example of a sequential MMSNA design is Rodway (2015), where a quantitative, sociocentric strand of survey research was executed before a qualitative investigation. Thirty-one studies (60%) used methods that were dependent on each other. However, this number for dependency needs to be interpreted with caution, as it represents a frequency count that does not say anything about the strength of the dependency. "Dependency" often referred to a minor interface between the two methods only. For example, researchers used metrics derived from sociocentric network data to inform the qualitative data collection through purposeful sampling procedures or by using network maps as interview material (e.g., Daly & Finnigan, 2010).

As described above, we aggregated these data into four types (see Table 2). Designs that combined sequential timing with dependency (28 studies, 54%) or parallel timing with independency (15 studies, 29%) made up the vast majority of the sample. This was to be expected in so far that sequential designs that are dependent rather than independent make better use of the information that is already available in the research project, which naturally leads to a higher prevalence. Likewise, parallel timing is more complex in its implementation when the methods are referring to each other (i.e., dependency).

Quality in MMSNA

Concerning the quality of the studies, we comment on our observations regarding the five aspects of the MMAT. First, we observed whether the purpose of mixing was explicitly stated. Of the 52 studies, 38 (73%) made their purpose(s) of mixing explicit, while in more than one quarter of the reviewed studies, the researchers did not state their reasons for using quantitative and qualitative data and/or methods. Even for those that did, this discussion was often short and most often referred to "triangulation" or a "case study" without more detailed explanations.

Second, when it came to the integration of the different methods used in a MMSNA design, we looked at whether the methods were effectively integrated to answer the posed research question. For most studies (42 studies, 81%), this was done in a sufficiently clear manner. Third, compared to the above figure of integration of 81%, the adequate integration of outputs ("meta-inference") was only present in 27 studies (52%). In other words, often, the information gained in one strand of research was not used at all or not sufficiently integrated with the other findings when forming conclusions. This is a missed opportunity to improve the quality of integration and of the overall study.

Fourth, another opportunity to enhance the quality of MMSNA studies is the discussion of how the findings from the quantitative and qualitative data relate to each other. For 36 studies (69%), there were either no differences to be discussed or these divergences were adequately addressed in the discussion. This means that 31% failed to address conflicting findings in meaningful ways. It is important to note that—in line with the coding instructions of the used instrument—we only coded "absence" when differences were observed but not discussed.

Fifth, concerning the overall adherence to quality criteria, we coded 35 studies (68%) as being in line with the quality criteria associated with each of the methods being used. While this number is high compared to the other metrics coded in this review, it is important to note that meeting methodological quality criteria should be a lower level indicator of quality for a study; it does not say anything about the effectiveness of integration or the actual answering the research question. Associated with this criterion, one comment that was often repeated in the memos we wrote during the coding process was that the word limitations of journals made it difficult for authors to comply with the reporting standards of the underlying methods.

Few studies explicitly addressed convergences or divergences and (in)consistencies between results. Most studies discussed the different methods' findings next to each other and had little or no mixing in the Discussion section. One positive example is the study by Spillane et al. (2018), which integrated the outputs of the different data—interviews with teachers, network surveys, student test scores, and teacher performance data—to investigate how teacher performance predicts interaction. The authors discussed how the interview data offered additional interpretative power on how the school district's educational infrastructure influenced teachers' notions about expert teachers. They also addressed how student test scores did not support findings in predicting expert teaching performance and how the interview data helped to inform this finding.

Post Hoc Observations

In this section, we present two post hoc observations that were not part of the deductive coding scheme but that nevertheless seem important. During coding, we observed that many of the MMSNA studies used network maps as a way to illustrate the findings. For instance, Hoffman and Silverberg's (2015) study on peer interactions in a higher education setting used a network map for the single purpose of illustrating instances of joint work in student collaboration. However, visuals were also used in several studies as feedback to participants or as a basis to develop interventions. For example, Rienties and Kinchin (2014) showed network maps to participants in a professional development program and asked participants to reflect on the patterns and structures as part of a free-response exercise. Van Waes et al. (2015) used a concentric circle method (Hogan et al., 2007; Van Waes & Van den Bossche, 2020) to provide feedback about change over time in personal teaching networks during interviews. The visuals of the personal network maps were used to gain insight into supporting and constraining mechanisms for network change as a complement to longitudinal network surveys. This visual approach (also see Shannon-Baker & Edwards, 2018; Shannon-Baker & Hilpert, 2020) to MMSNA may offer a basis for the design of network interventions where the network awareness of participants is being fostered (Palonen & Froehlich, 2020; Van Waes et al., 2018).

Another post hoc observation is related to the point of integration. The point of integration is the stage of research where two methods are brought together (Schoonenboom & Johnson, 2017). Often, two methods were connected at the sampling stage. Specifically, the quantitative, often sociometric data were used to inform the selection of participants for further, in-depth, and often egocentric data collection (e.g., Rienties & Kinchin, 2014). Other prominent points of integration were at the stages of results/analysis (e.g., Rodríguez-Medina et al., 2018) or in the discussion/conclusion (e.g., Hopkins & Spillane, 2014).

DISCUSSION AND CONCLUSION

As outlined in the introduction, this systematic review aims to (a) give an overview of the different applications of MMSNA within the field of education and learning research, (b) point to challenges of the methods and their presentation, and (c) develop an agenda to support researchers in conducting future MMSNA research. We will now discuss these three themes.

Applications of MMSNA in Education and Learning Research

Overall, our review showed mixing of various methods and data in the eligible MMSNA studies. The surveyed literature shows a great variety of different data sources and analytical methods being used. For example, Häussling (2010) analyzed video recordings of classroom interactions using SNA to uncover social structures, dynamics such as interaction sequences, and the emotional expressions involved. These data were triangulated with responses on networks surveys and interviews. Bokhove (2018) argues how a mixed method approach to classroom interaction may benefit from an SNA lens. He modeled temporal interactions of students and teachers in the classroom combining SNA and video data. However, we did not find examples of mixed data obtained with alternative devices, such as tracking interactions with sociometric badges (Kim et al., 2012). Although we observed some variety in terms of data sources and methods, researchers used network surveys and qualitative interviews most frequently. Similarly, the versatility of MMSNA is illustrated by the range of the themes addressed in the studies we reviewed, which cover diverse topics such as school reform (Daly & Finnigan, 2010), learning in MOOCs (Wise & Cui, 2018), informal mentoring (Risser, 2013), or trust (Ardoin et al., 2017).

Challenges of MMSNA Linked to a Future Research Agenda

We also identified challenges in conducting and reporting MMSNA research from which we try to derive an agenda for further MMSNA research. We recommend to (a) further explore the richness of MMSNA designs, (b) improve reporting practices concerning purpose and design, (c) increase integration, and (d) attends to validity issues identified in MMSNA research.

Variability of MMSNA Designs

We have noted a hegemony of a few MMSNA designs in terms of timing. This is interesting when considering the plethora of different topics and research questions present in the reviewed studies. In consequence, this raises the question whether the designs have indeed been properly fitted to the specific research questions at stake, or whether the designs of published studies have been used overused as blueprints. This observation also extends to the purpose(s) of mixing coded in the studies. While we could name very different purposes of mixing we also noted that *explanation*, a variant of follow-up, and *triangulation*, a variant of comparison, were especially prevalent. This complements the findings of Froehlich (2020b) that show a similar trend in MMSNA when it comes to the pairing of specific methods. As such, future research could tap into the richness offered by novel combinations of methods of social network research. For instance, qualitative methods could be used to inform quantitative data collection and analysis. This is especially true for more advanced quantitative techniques such as exponential random graph models or stochastic actor-based model, which play a large role in contemporary quantitative SNA research, but did not appear in the reviewed MMSNA studies.

Improving Reporting

We found that over one quarter of the observed MMSNA studies did not explicate their purpose(s) of mixing. Given that mixing has no value on its own, it is important to communicate the rationale for using multiple methods to the readers. We urge authors of future MMSNA studies to explicate their purpose(s) of mixing and the reasoning behind it. The studies that did report the purpose of mixing often did so in an overly concise manner. The reviewed MMSNA studies used labels such as *case study* or *triangulation* without clarifying what these terms meant in the context of the studies. We recommend to explain the arguments behind mixing rather than just labelling them.

As an example, we present the study of Cornelissen et al. (2014). The authors studied partnerships between schools and universities using a social network perspective to find out in what ways knowledge generated from students' research is developed, shared, and used in their observed school-university network. The authors describe their approach as a longitudinal multimethod case study design and used a purposeful sampling procedure to identify four cases: two students and their respective research advisors. Data were collected via questionnaires and selected cases were queried at multiple time points about their personal networks. Additionally, logs were collected and interviews conducted. The researchers analyzed the data at the ego, dyad, and whole network levels. Describing this research design as a case study may be appropriate, but it does not adequately characterize the actual richness of the mixing involved. A more detailed description about the reasons that have led to the design could be helpful in developing an even more nuanced research design. Specifically, the authors' interest in studying multiple units of analysis at the same time presents an immediate reason to interweave qualitative and quantitative approaches to network analysis. This is because both approaches have complementary strengths and weaknesses. The higher level questions related to structures could not easily be answered with qualitative methods, whereas quantitative methods often cannot process the details going on at the lower levels of units of analysis. These include why a dyad is functional or not or what an individual's history is in relation to the network (Froehlich, Mejeh, et al., 2020).

Design decisions such as the timing of a specific study should also be explicated. Take the study of Spillane et al. (2018), in which the design is made very explicit: "Our analysis is based on data from a longitudinal, mixed methods study that used a sequential explanatory mixed methods design" (p. 590). Specifically, they used a sequential design as they sampled people for interviews based on network survey results. They purposefully sampled teaching staffs in schools to maximize variation in formal position, social network position (e.g., more or less central in their schools' mathematics network), and level (primary or upper grade teachers). They also explicitly state their purpose of mixing: "We sought to interview a broad range of staff, to maximize opportunities for verification (or contradiction) of our theorizing about school staff interactions about mathematics instruction" (p. 591). These statements allow the reader to make inferences about sequence, dependence, and the purpose. Additionally, they provide information about the underlying argumentation.

Another interesting observation regarding reporting practices focuses on the research questions. While all sampled studies used mixed methods, not all studies reflected this in their research questions. While this is certainly not needed for some purposes of mixing, it may point to a lack of alignment between the research questions and the research design. For some studies, it may help pose a research question that transcends the scope of one individual method or research done at one level of analysis. As mentioned in the background section, qualitative and quantitative methods of SNA are complementary and this should be reflected in the research questions (Plano Clark & Badiee, 2010).

Increasing Integration

While some form of integration did happen in most studies, one avenue for further improvement of MMSNA could be a more explicit focus on meta-inferences (Teddlie & Tashakkori, 2009). This means that combined interpretations should be formulated based on both qualitative and quantitative findings. Meta-inferences show the added value of mixing over two separate studies more clearly and emphasize the purpose of mixing. Also, the explicit discussion of divergent findings could help improve integration within MMSNA. The majority of the sampled studies either did not identify any divergent findings worthy of being discussed or did not adequately address such findings. Another suggestion for increased integration was offered by Toraman and Plano Clark (2020), who recommend the thoughtful use of joint displays, where qualitative and quantitative results are presented in one figure or table.

Considering Validity

Analysis of the coding indicated that one third of all samples studies did not adhere to the basic validity requirements of the methods used. Importantly, this does not refer to validity requirements of MMSNA—which still need to be developed and agreed upon—but rather on the individual methods used in the design. There are two pathways in addressing this challenge. A part of the problem could be competence-related. Given that SNA is a complex method to begin with, this complexity increases when embedding it into a mixed methods design. Therefore, it is advisable to strengthen human capital within the authorship teams, either by increasing individuals' methodological competencies or by adding co-authors with the specific competences in demand.

The root of the problem of validity presented above may also be institutional. We noted that the word limitations of journals and other publication outlets are one potential reason why the authors of many studies in this review (30%) failed to meet the quality criteria of the underlying qualitative and quantitative methods. In general, this is a frequently discussed problem in the mixed methods literature (Leech, 2012). However, we argue that this issue is exacerbated when presenting MMSNA research for two major reasons. First, quantitative approaches to SNA tend to be perceived as more technically challenging and in need of more elaborated methodological explanations. This could be traced back to the methodological training of researchers, which is often focused on statistics at the expense of other quantitative methods (cf. Froehlich, Mamas, et al., 2020). Reporting about qualitative procedures is by no means less problematic. Here, it is our impression that the problem lies in the rather vague guidelines of how to do qualitative SNA. While some exceptions exist—most notably the work of Herz et al. (2015) on qualitative structural analysis—a common language of doing and reporting qualitative SNA is absent (Froehlich, 2020a). Further research may mitigate this problem by developing a clearer conceptualization of how to execute and report qualitative SNA. As SNA is becoming more and more visible especially in the educational domain (Daly, 2010; Moolenaar, 2012;

Sweet, 2016), it is our hope that the basic approaches to analyzing social networks will require less argumentation—and hence alleviate this challenge.

General Conclusion

We have written this review based on the observation that SNA is becoming a standard method of education research, but that purely quantitative SNA approaches are often found to be too superficial for many of the phenomena studied in this field. While the call for MMSNA was voiced by the books of Domínguez and Hollstein (2014) and Froehlich, Rehm, et al. (2020), information about why and how MMSNA is being used in research practice did not exist. In this review, we studied—among others—the purpose(s) of mixing and the designs used as presented in contemporary education research. Through the systematically gathered data and the presentation of illustrative examples, we elaborated on how researchers may use MMSNA to study relationships and interactions within educational settings. This contributes to further research in two ways. First, we have proposed an agenda for further research that tackles the challenges identified through the review. Put differently, we laid out a plan of how MMSNA as a research approach could be improved collectively. Second, and on the level of an individual researcher, this chapter may provide guidance throughout the research process by providing a reference to what has worked well before and what did not.

ORCID iDs

Dominik E. Froehlich https://orcid.org/0000-0002-9991-2784

Sara Van Waes https://orcid.org/0000-0003-3789-7838

NOTES

[1] Cf. Barton's (1968) "sociological meatgrinder" argument.

[2] The PRISMA statement (Preferred Reporting Items for Systematic Reviews and Meta-Analyses) delineates a checklist containing the minimum of required "items deemed essential for transparent reporting of a systematic review" and can be used for as a guideline for interdisciplinary systematic reviews.

[3] Identifying relevant texts from the reference lists of relevant records from the database search.

[4] Identifying relevant texts that cited relevant records from the database search.

[5] Whether such information was provided by the study authors was part of the quality assessment of the MMAT.

[6] The numbers add up to more than 100% as one study can have multiple purposes of mixing.

REFERENCES

Ardoin, N. M., DiGiano, M. L., O'Connor, K., & Podkul, T. E. (2017). The development of trust in residential environmental education programs. *Environmental Education Research*, *23*(9), 1335–1355. https://doi.org/10.1080/13504622.2016.1144176

Baird, J., Plummer, R., Haug, C., & Huitema, D. (2014). Learning effects of interactive decision-making processes for climate change adaptation. *Global Environmental Change*, *27*, 51–63. https://doi.org/10.1016/j.gloenvcha.2014.04.019

Baker-Doyle, K. J. (2015). Stories in networks and networks in stories: A tri-modal model for mixed-methods social network research on teachers. *International Journal of Research & Method in Education, 38*(1), 72–82. https://doi.org/10.1080/17437 27X.2014.911838

Baker-Doyle, K. J., & Petchauer, E. (2015). Rumor has it: Investigating teacher licensure exam advice networks. *Teacher Education Quarterly, 42*(3), 3–32.

Baker-Doyle, K. J., & Yoon, S. A. (2010). Making expertise transparent: Using technology to strengthen social networks in teacher professional development. *Social Network Theory and Educational Change, 2010,* 115–126.

Barton, A. H. (1968). Survey research and macro-methodology. *American Behavioral Scientist, 12*(2), 1–9. https://doi.org/10.1177/000276426801200201

Bokhove, C. (2018). Exploring classroom interaction with dynamic social network analysis. *International Journal of Research & Method in Education, 41*(1), 17–37.

Borgatti, S. P., Brass, D. J., & Halgin, D. S. (2014). Social network research: Confusions, criticisms, and controversies. In D. J. Brass, G. Labianca, A. Mehra, D. S. Halgin, & S. P. Borgatti (Eds.), *Research in the sociology of organizations* (Vol. *40,* pp. 1–29). Emerald. https://doi.org/10.1108/S0733-558X(2014)0000040001

Borgatti, S. P., Mehra, A., Brass, D. J., & Labianca, G. (2009). Network analysis in the social sciences. *Science, 323*(5916), 892–895. https://doi.org/10.1126/science.1165821

Bozkurt, A., Honeychurch, S., Caines, A., Maha, B., Koutropoulos, A., & Cormier, D. (2016). Community tracking in a cMOOC and nomadic learner behavior identification on a connectivist rhizomatic learning network. *Turkish Online Journal of Distance Education, 17*(4), Article 1. https://doi.org/10.17718/tojde.09231

Bozkurt, A., & Keefer, J. (2018). Participatory learning culture and community formation in connectivist MOOCs. *Interactive Learning Environments, 26*(6), 776–788. https://doi.org /10.1080/10494820.2017.1412988

Brass, D. J., Borgatti, S. P., Halgin, D. S., Labianca, G., & Mehra, A. (2014). *Contemporary perspectives on organizational social networks.* http://search.ebscohost.com/login.aspx?direc t=true&scope=site&db=nlebk&db=nlabk&AN=705225

Burt, R. S. (1992). *Structural holes: The structure of social capital competition.* Harvard University Press.

Carhill-Poza, A. (2015). Opportunities and outcomes: The role of peers in developing the oral academic English proficiency of adolescent English learners. *Modern Language Journal, 99*(4), 678–695. https://doi.org/10.1111/modl.12271

Coburn, C. E., Russell, J. L., Kaufman, J. H., & Stein, M. K. (2012). Supporting sustainability: Teachers' advice networks and ambitious instructional reform. *American Journal of Education, 119*(1), 137–182. https://doi.org/10.1086/667699

Conger, A. J. (1980). Integration and generalization of kappas for multiple raters. *Psychological Bulletin, 88*(2), 322–328. https://doi.org/10.1037/0033-2909.88.2.322

Cornelissen, F., Daly, A. J., Liou, Y.-H., van Swet, J., Beijaard, D., & Bergen, T. C. M. (2014). More than a master: Developing, sharing, and using knowledge in school–university research networks. *Cambridge Journal of Education, 44*(1), 35–57. https://doi.org/ 10.1080/0305764X.2013.855170

Cornelissen, F., Daly, A. J., Liou, Y.-H., Van Swet, J., Beijaard, D., & Bergen, T. C. (2015). Leveraging the relationship: Knowledge processes in school–university research networks of master's programmes. *Research Papers in Education, 30*(3), 366–392. https://doi.org/1 0.1080/02671522.2014.919522

Cross, J. E., Dickmann, E., Newman-Gonchar, R., & Fagan, J. M. (2009). Using mixed-method design and network analysis to measure development of interagency collaboration. *American Journal of Evaluation, 30*(3), 310–329. https://doi .org/10.1177/1098214009340044

Crossley, N. (2010). The social world of the network: Combining qualitative and quantitative elements in social network analysis. *Sociologica, 1*. https://doi.org/10.2383/32049

Crossley, N., & Edwards, G. (2016). Cases, mechanisms and the real: The theory and methodology of mixed-method social network analysis. *Sociological Research Online, 21*(2), 1–15. https://doi.org/10.5153/sro.3920

Daly, A. J. (2010). *Social network theory and educational change.* Harvard Education Press.

Daly, A. J., & Finnigan, K. S. (2010). A bridge between worlds: Understanding network structure to understand change strategy. *Journal of Educational Change, 11*(2), 111–138. https://doi.org/10.1007/s10833-009-9102-5

Daly, A. J., & Finnigan, K. S. (2011). The ebb and flow of social network ties between district leaders under high-stakes accountability. *American Educational Research Journal, 48*(1), 39–79. https://doi.org/10.3102/0002831210368990

Daly, A. J., Moolenaar, N. M., Bolivar, J. M., & Burke, P. (2010). Relationships in reform: The role of teachers' social networks. *Journal of Educational Administration, 48*(3), 359–391. https://doi.org/10.1108/09578231011041062

Daly, A. J., Moolenaar, N., Der-Martirosian, C., & Liou, Y.-H. (2014). Accessing capital resources: Investigating the effects of teacher human and social capital on student achievement. *Teachers College Record, 116*(7).

Dingyloudi, F., & Strijbos, J.-W. (2018). Just plain peers across social networks: Peer-feedback networks nested in personal and academic networks in higher education. *Learning, Culture and Social Interaction, 18*, 86–112. https://doi.org/10.1016/j.lcsi.2018.02.002

Domínguez, S., & Hollstein, B. (2014). *Mixed methods social networks research: Design and applications* (S. Domínguez & B. Hollstein, Eds.). Cambridge University Press.

Finnigan, K. S., & Daly, A. J. (2012). Mind the gap: Organizational learning and improvement in an underperforming urban system. *American Journal of Education, 119*(1), 41–71. https://doi.org/10.1086/667700

Finnigan, K. S., Daly, A. J., & Che, J. (2013). Systemwide reform in districts under pressure: The role of social networks in defining, acquiring, using, and diffusing research evidence. *Journal of Educational Administration, 51*(4), 476–497. https://doi.org/10.1108/09578231311325668

Fox, A., Wilson, E., & Deaney, R. (2011). Beginning teachers' workplace experiences: Perceptions of and use of support. *Vocations and Learning, 4*(1), 1–24. https://doi.org/10.1007/s12186-010-9046-1

Frank, K. A., Zhao, Y., Penuel, W. R., Ellefson, N., & Porter, S. (2011). Focus, fiddle, and friends: Experiences that transform knowledge for the implementation of innovations. *Sociology of Education, 84*(2), 137–156.

Freeman, L. C. (1978). Centrality in social networks conceptual clarification. *Social Networks, 1*(3), 215–239. https://doi.org/10.1016/0378-8733(78)90021-7

Freeman, L. C. (2004). *The development of social network analysis.* http://aris.ss.uci.edu/lin/book.pdf

Froehlich, D. E. (2020a). Exploring social relationships in "a mixed way": Mixed structural analysis. In D. E. Froehlich, M. Rehm, & B. C. Rienties (Eds.), *Mixed methods social network analysis: Theories and methodologies in learning and education* (pp. 126–138). Routledge.

Froehlich, D. E. (2020b). Mapping mixed methods approaches to social network analysis in learning and education. In D. E. Froehlich, M. Rehm, & B. C. Rienties (Eds.), *Mixed methods social network analysis: Theories and methodologies in learning and education* (pp. 13–24). Routledge.

Froehlich, D. E., Mamas, C., & Schneider, H. W. (2020). Automation and the journey to mixed methods social network analysis. In D. E. Froehlich, M. Rehm, & B. C. Rienties

(Eds.), *Mixed methods social network analysis: Theories and methodologies in learning and education* (pp. 219–230). Routledge.

Froehlich, D. E., Mejeh, M., Galey, S., & Schoonenboom, J. (2020). Integrating units of analysis: Applying mixed methods social network analysis. In D. E. Froehlich, M. Rehm, & B. C. Rienties (Eds.), *Mixed methods social network analysis: Theories and methodologies in learning and education* (pp. 38–48). Routledge.

Froehlich, D. E., Rehm, M., & Rienties, B. C. (2020). Mixed methods social network analysis. In D. E. Froehlich, M. Rehm, & B. C. Rienties (Eds.), *Mixed methods social network analysis: Theories and methodologies in learning and education* (pp. 1–10). Routledge.

Fuhse, J., & Mützel, S. (2011). Tackling connections, structure, and meaning in networks: Quantitative and qualitative methods in sociological network research. *Quality & Quantity*, *45*(5), 1067–1089. https://doi.org/10.1007/s11135-011-9492-3

Goggins, S. P., Laffey, J., & Gallagher, M. (2011). Completely online group formation and development: Small groups as socio-technical systems. *Information Technology & People*, *24*(2), 104–133. https://doi.org/10.1108/09593841111137322

Granovetter, M. S. (1973). The strength of weak ties. *American Journal of Sociology*, *78*(6), 1360–1380. https://doi.org/10.1086/225469

Guest, G. (2013). Describing mixed methods research: An alternative to typologies. *Journal of Mixed Methods Research*, *7*(2), 141–151. https://doi.org/10.1177/1558689812461179

Häussling, R. (2010). Allocation to social positions in class: Interactions and relationships in first grade school classes and their consequences. *Current Sociology*, *58*(1), 119–138. https://doi.org/10.1177/0011392109349286

Herz, A., Peters, L., & Truschkat, I. (2015). How to do qualitative structural analysis: The qualitative interpretation of network maps and narrative interviews. *Forum Qualitative Sozialforschung/Forum: Qualitative Social Research*, *16*(1). https://doi.org/10.17169/fqs-16.1.2092

Hofman, R. H., & Dijkstra, B. J. (2010). Effective teacher professionalization in networks? *Teaching and Teacher Education*, *26*(4), 1031–1040. https://doi.org/10.1016/j.tate.2009.10.046

Hoffman, S. J., & Silverberg, S. L. (2015). Training the next generation of global health advocates through experiential education: A mixed-methods case study evaluation. *Canadian Journal of Public Health*, *106*(6), e442–e449. https://doi.org/10.17269/CJPH.106.5099

Hogan, B., Carrasco, J. A., & Wellman, B. (2007). Visualizing personal networks: Working with participant-aided sociograms. *Field Methods*, *19*(2), 116–144. https://doi.org/10.1177/1525822X06298589

Hollstein, B. (2011). Qualitative approaches to social reality: The search for meaning. In J. Scott & P. J. Carrington (Eds.), *The Sage handbook of social network analysis* (pp. 404–416). Sage.

Hollstein, B. (2014). Mixed methods social networks research: An introduction. In S. Domínguez & B. Hollstein (Eds.), *Mixed methods social networks research: Design and applications* (pp. 3–34). Cambridge University Press.

Honeychurch, S., Bozkurt, A., Singh, L., & Koutropoulos, A. (2017). Learners on the periphery: Lurkers as invisible learners. *European Journal of Open, Distance and E-Learning*, *20*(1), 192–212. https://doi.org/10.1515/eurodl-2017-0012

Hong, Q. N., Gonzalez-Reyes, A., & Pluye, P. (2018). Improving the usefulness of a tool for appraising the quality of qualitative, quantitative and mixed methods studies, the Mixed Methods Appraisal Tool (MMAT). *Journal of Evaluation in Clinical Practice*, *24*(3), 459–467. https://doi.org/10.1111/jep.12884

Hopkins, M., Lowenhaupt, R., & Sweet, T. M. (2015). Organizing English learner instruction in new immigrant destinations: District infrastructure and subject-specific school practice. *American Educational Research Journal*, *52*(3), 408–439.

Hopkins, M., & Spillane, J. P. (2014). Schoolhouse teacher educators: Structuring beginning teachers' opportunities to learn about instruction. *Journal of Teacher Education, 65*(4), 327–339. https://doi.org/10.1177/0022487114534483

Johnson, R. B., & Onwuegbuzie, A. J. (2004). Mixed methods research: A research paradigm whose time has come. *Educational Researcher, 33*(7), 14–26.

Johnson, R. B., Onwuegbuzie, A. J., & Turner, L. A. (2007). Toward a definition of mixed methods research. *Journal of Mixed Methods Research, 1*(2), 112–133. https://doi.org/10.1177/1558689806298224

Kellogg, S., Booth, S., & Oliver, K. (2014). A social network perspective on peer supported learning in MOOCs for educators. *International Review of Research in Open and Distributed Learning, 15*(5), 263–289. https://doi.org/10.19173/irrodl.v15i5.1852

Kim, T., McFee, E., Olguin, D. O., Waber, B., & Pentland, A.(2012). Sociometric badges: Using sensor technology to capture new forms of collaboration. *Journal of Organizational Behavior, 33*(3), 412–427. https://doi.org/10.1002/job.1776

Kortemeyer, G., & Kortemeyer, A. F. (2018). The nature of collaborations on programming assignments in introductory physics courses: A case study. *European Journal of Physics, 39*(5), 055705. https://doi.org/10.1088/1361-6404/aad511

Langhout, R. D., Collins, C., & Ellison, E. R. (2014). Examining relational empowerment for elementary school students in a yPAR program. *American Journal of Community Psychology, 53*(3–4), 369–381. https://doi.org/10.1007/s10464-013-9617-z

Lee, M., Madyun, N., Lam, B. O., & Jumale, M. (2014). School contexts and "acting white" peer networks of Somali immigrant youths in an Afrocentric charter school. *Schools, 11*(1), 122–155. https://doi.org/10.1086/675752

Leech, N. L. (2012). Writing mixed research reports. *American Behavioral Scientist, 56*(6), 866–881. https://doi.org/10.1177/0002764211433800

Liou, Y.-H., & Daly, A. J. (2014). Closer to learning: Social networks, trust, and professional communities. *Journal of School Leadership, 24*(4), 753–795. https://doi.org/10.1177/105268461402400407

Liou, Y.-H., Grigg, J., & Halverson, R. (2014). Leadership and the design of data-driven professional networks in schools. *Journal of Educational Leadership and Management, 2*(1), 29–73. https://doi.org/10.4471/ijelm.2014.08

Lorrain, F., & White, H. C. (1971). Structural equivalence of individuals in social networks. *Journal of Mathematical Sociology, 1*(1), 49–80. https://doi.org/10.1080/0022250X.1971.9989788

Louis, K. S., & Marks, H. M. (1998). Does professional community affect the classroom? Teachers' work and student experiences in restructuring schools. *American Journal of Education, 106*(4), 532–575. https://doi.org/10.1086/444197

Lu, J., & Churchill, D. (2014). The effect of social interaction on learning engagement in a social networking environment. *Interactive Learning Environments, 22*(4), 401–417.

Martínez, A., Dimitriadis, Y., Gómez-Sánchez, E., Rubia-Avi, B., Jorrín-Abellán, I., & Marcos, J. A. (2006). Studying participation networks in collaboration using mixed methods. *International Journal of Computer-Supported Collaborative Learning, 1*(3), 383–408. https://doi.org/10.1007/s11412-006-8705-6

McLaughlin, M. W., & Talbert, J. E. (2006). *Building school-based teacher learning communities: Professional strategies to improve student achievement* (Series on school reform Book 45). Teachers College Press.

Moher, D., Liberati, A., Tetzlaff, J., Altman, D. G., & PRISMA Group. (2009). Preferred reporting items for systematic reviews and meta-analyses: The PRISMA statement. *PLOS Medicine, 6*(7), e1000097. https://doi.org/10.1371/journal.pmed.1000097

Moolenaar, N. M. (2012). A social network perspective on teacher collaboration in schools: Theory, methodology, and applications. *American Journal of Education, 119*(1), 7–39. https://doi.org/10.1086/667715

Moolenaar, N. M., Sleegers, P. J. C., & Daly, A. J. (2012). Teaming up: Linking collaboration networks, collective efficacy, and student achievement. *Teaching and Teacher Education, 28*(2), 251–262. https://doi.org/10.1016/j.tate.2011.10.001

Onwuegbuzie, A. J., & Hitchcock, J. H. (2015). Advanced mixed analysis approaches. In S. Hesse-Biber & R. B. Johnson (Eds.), *The Oxford handbook of multimethod and mixed methods research inquiry* (pp. 275–295). Oxford University Press.

Palonen, T., & Froehlich, D. E. (2020). Mixed methods social network analysis to drive organizational development. In D. E. Froehlich, M. Rehm, & B. C. Rienties (Eds.), *Mixed methods social network analysis: Theories and methodologies in learning and education* (pp. 87–100). Routledge.

Penuel, W. R., Bell, P., Bevan, B., Buffington, P., & Falk, J. (2016). Enhancing use of learning sciences research in planning for and supporting educational change: Leveraging and building social networks. *Journal of Educational Change, 17*(2), 251–278. https://doi.org/10.1007/s10833-015-9266-0

Penuel, W. R., Riel, M., Krause, A. E., & Frank, K. A. (2009). Analyzing teachers' professional interactions in a school as social capital: A social network approach. *Teachers College Record, 111*(1), 124–163. https://eric.ed.gov/?id=EJ826000

Penuel, W. R., Sun, M., Frank, K. A., & Gallagher, H. A. (2012). Using social network analysis to study how collegial interactions can augment teacher learning from external professional development. *American Journal of Education, 119*(1), 103–136. https://doi.org/10.1086/667756

Pifer, M. J. (2011). Intersectionality in context: A mixed-methods approach to researching the faculty experience. *New Directions for Institutional Research, 2011*(151), 27.

Pil, F. K., & Leana, C. (2009). Applying organizational research to public school reform: The effects of teacher human and social capital on student performance. *Academy of Management Journal, 52*(6), 1101–1124. https://doi.org/10.5465/amj.2009.47084647

Plano Clark, V. L. & Badiee, M. (2010). Research questions in mixed methods research. In A. Tashakkori & C. Teddlie (Eds.), *Sage handbook of mixed methods in social and behavioral research* (pp. 275–304). Sage. https://doi.org/10.4135/9781506335193.n12

Rienties, B., & Hosein, A. (2015). Unpacking (in) formal learning in an academic development programme: A mixed-method social network perspective. *International Journal for Academic Development, 20*(2), 163–177. https://doi.org/10.1080/1360144x.2015.1029928

Rienties, B., Johan, N., & Jindal-Snape, D. (2015). Bridge building potential in cross-cultural learning: A mixed method study. *Asia Pacific Education Review, 16*(1), 37–48. https://doi.org/10.1007/s12564-014-9352-7

Rienties, B., & Kinchin, I. (2014). Understanding (in)formal learning in an academic development programme: A social network perspective. *Teaching and Teacher Education, 39*(2014), 123–135. https://doi.org/10.1016/j.tate.2014.01.004

Rienties, B., Tempelaar, D., Giesbers, B., Segers, M., & Gijselaers, W. (2014). A dynamic analysis of why learners develop a preference for autonomous learners in computer-mediated communication. *Interactive Learning Environments, 22*(5), 631–648. https://doi.org/10.1080/10494820.2012.707127

Risser, H. S. (2013). Virtual induction: A novice teacher's use of Twitter to form an informal mentoring network. *Teaching and Teacher Education, 35*(2013), 25–33. https://doi.org/10.1016/j.tate.2013.05.001

Rodríguez-Medina, J., Rodríguez-Navarro, H., Arias, V., Arias, B., & Anguera, M. T. (2018). Non-reciprocal friendships in a school-age boy with autism: The ties that build? *Journal of Autism and Developmental Disorders, 48*(9), 2980–2994. https://doi.org/10.1007/s10803-018-3575-0

Rodway, J. (2015). Connecting the dots: Understanding the flow of research knowledge within a research brokering network. *Education Policy Analysis Archives, 23*(123). https://doi.org/10.14507/epaa.v23.2180

Sánchez, B., Esparza, P., Berardi, L., & Pryce, J. (2011). Mentoring in the context of Latino youth's broader village during their transition from high school. *Youth & Society, 43*(1), 225–252. https://doi.org/10.1177/0044118x10363774

Schiff, D., Herzog, L., Farley-Ripple, E., & Iannuccilli, L. T. (2015). Teacher networks in Philadelphia: Landscape, engagement, and value. *Penn GSE Perspectives on Urban Education, 12*(1).

Schoonenboom, J., & Johnson, R. B. (2017). How to construct a mixed methods research design. *KZfSS Kölner Zeitschrift Für Soziologie Und Sozialpsychologie, 69*(Suppl. 2), 107–131. https://doi.org/10.1007/s11577-017-0454-1

Schoonenboom, J., Johnson, R. B., & Froehlich, D. E. (2018). Combining multiple purposes of mixing within a mixed methods research design. *International Journal of Multiple Research Approaches, 10*(1), 271–282. https://doi.org/10.29034/ijmra.v10n1a17

Shannon-Baker, P., & Edwards, C. (2018). The affordances and challenges to incorporating visual methods in mixed methods research. *American Behavioral Scientist, 62*(7), 935–955. https://doi.org/10.1177/0002764218772671

Shannon-Baker, P., & Hilpert, J. C. (2020). Visual methods and representations in mixed methods (and) social network research: A discussion. In D. E. Froehlich, M. Rehm, & B. C. Rienties (Eds.), *Mixed methods social network analysis: Theories and methodologies in learning and education* (pp. 49–57). Routledge.

Siddaway, A. P., Wood, A. M., & Hedges, L. V. (2019). How to do a systematic review: A best practice guide for conducting and reporting narrative reviews, meta-analyses, and meta-syntheses. *Annual Review of Psychology, 70*(1), 747–770. https://doi.org/10.1146/annurev-psych-010418-102803

Smith, R. A. (2010). *"Only connect": A mixed methods study of how first-year students create residential academic and social networks.* Syracuse University.

Smith, R. A. (2015). Magnets and seekers: A network perspective on academic integration inside two residential communities. *Journal of Higher Education, 86*(6), 893–922. https://doi.org/10.1353/jhe.2015.0033

Spillane, J. P. (2005). Distributed leadership. *Educational Forum, 69*(2), 143–150. https://doi.org/10.1080/00131720508984678

Spillane, J. P., Hopkins, M., & Sweet, T. M. (2015). Intra-and interschool interactions about instruction: Exploring the conditions for social capital development. *American Journal of Education, 122*(1), 71–110. https://doi.org/10.1086/683292

Spillane, J. P., & Shirrell, M. (2017). Breaking up isn't hard to do: Exploring the dissolution of teachers' and school leaders' work-related ties. *Educational Administration Quarterly, 53*(4), 616–648. https://doi.org/10.1177/0013161X17696557

Spillane, J. P., Shirrell, M., & Adhikari, S. (2018). Constructing "experts" among peers: Educational infrastructure, test data, and teachers' interactions about teaching. *Educational Evaluation and Policy Analysis, 40*(4), 586–612. https://doi.org/10.3102/0162373718785764

Sweet, T. M. (2016). Social network methods for the educational and psychological sciences. *Educational Psychologist, 51*(3–4), 381–394. https://doi.org/10.1080/00461520.2016.1208093

Teddlie, C., & Tashakkori, A. (2009). *Foundations of mixed methods research: Integrating quantitative and qualitative approaches in the social and behavioral sciences.* Sage.

Tirado, R., Hernando, Á., & Aguaded, J. I. (2015). The effect of centralization and cohesion on the social construction of knowledge in discussion forums. *Interactive Learning Environments, 23*(3), 293–316. https://doi.org/10.1080/10494820.2012.745437

Toraman, S., & Plano Clark, V. L. (2020). Reflections about intersecting mixed methods research with social network analysis. In D. E. Froehlich, M. Rehm, & B. C. Rienties (Eds.), *Mixed methods social network analysis: Theories and methodologies in learning and education* (pp. 175–188). Routledge.

Ugurlu, Z. (2016). The effect of the position of educational organizations within the social network on their collaboration levels. *Universal Journal of Educational Research, 4*(12A), 226–254. https://doi.org/10.13189/ujer.2016.041328

Van Gasse, R., Vanlommel, K., Vanhoof, J., & Van Petegem, P. (2017). The impact of collaboration on teachers' individual data use. *School Effectiveness and School Improvement, 28*(3), 489–504. https://doi.org/10.1080/09243453.2017.1321555

Van Tulder, M., Furlan, A., Bombardier, C., & Bouter, L. (2003). Updated method guidelines for systematic reviews in the Cochrane collaboration back review group. *Spine, 28*(12), 1290–1299. https://doi.org/10.1097/01.BRS.0000065484.95996.AF

Van Waes, S., De Maeyer, S., Moolenaar, N. M., Van Petegem, P., & Van den Bossche, P. (2018). Strengthening networks: A social network intervention among higher education teachers. *Learning and Instruction, 53*, 34–49.

Van Waes, S., & Van den Bossche, P. (2020). Around and around: The concentric circles method as powerful tool to collect mixed method network data. In D. E. Froehlich, M. Rehm, & B. C. Rienties (Eds.), *Mixed methods social network analysis: Theories and methodologies in learning and education* (pp. 159–174). Routledge.

Van Waes, S., Van den Bossche, P., Moolenaar, N. M., Stes, A., & Van Petegem, P. (2015). Uncovering changes in university teachers' professional networks during an instructional development program. *Studies in Educational Evaluation, 46*(2015), 11–28. https://doi.org/10.1016/j.stueduc.2015.02.003

Vanwynsberghe, H., Boudry, E., Vanderlinde, R., & Verdegem, P. (2014). Experts as facilitators for the implementation of social media in the library? A social network approach. *Library Hi Tech, 32*(3), 529–545. https://doi.org/10.1108/lht-02-2014-0015

Wellman, B. (1983). Network analysis: Some basic principles. *Sociological Theory, 1*(1), 155–200. https://doi.org/10.2307/202050

Wellman, B. (1988). Structural analysis: From method and metaphor to theory and substance. In B. Wellman & S. D. Berkowitz (Eds.), *Structural analysis in the social sciences: Vol. 2. Social structures: A network approach* (pp. 19–61). Cambridge University Press.

Wenger, E., McDermott, R. A., & Snyder, W. (2002). *Cultivating communities of practice: A guide to managing knowledge.* Harvard Business Press.

Wise, A. F., & Cui, Y. (2018). Learning communities in the crowd: Characteristics of content related interactions and social relationships in MOOC discussion forums. *Computers & Education, 122*(2018), 221–242. https://doi.org/10.1016/j.compedu.2018.03.021

Wong-Hooker, A. M. (2016). *How the formal and informal social networks of special education teachers shape their practice* [PhD Thesis, UC San Diego]. https://eric.ed.gov/?id=ED570587

Yessis, J., Riley, B., Stockton, L., Brodovsky, S., & Von Sychowski, S. (2013). Interorganizational relationships in the Heart and Stroke Foundation's Spark Together for Healthy Kids™: Insights from using network analysis. *Health Education & Behavior, 40*(1 Suppl.), 43S–50S. https://doi.org/10.1177/1090198113490724

Chapter 10

Critical Counter-Narrative as Transformative Methodology for Educational Equity

RICHARD MILLER

KATRINA LIU
University of Nevada, Las Vegas

ARNETHA F. BALL
Stanford University

Counter-narrative has recently emerged in education research as a promising tool to stimulate educational equity in our increasingly diverse schools and communities. Grounded in critical race theory and approaches to discourse study including narrative inquiry, life history, and autoethnography, counter-narratives have found a home in multicultural education, culturally sensitive pedagogy, and other approaches to teaching for diversity. This chapter provides a systematic literature review that explores the place of counter-narratives in educational pedagogy and research. Based on our thematic analysis, we argue that the potential of counter-narratives in both pedagogy and research has been limited due to the lack of a unified methodology that can result in transformative action for educational equity. The chapter concludes by proposing critical counter-narrative as a transformative methodology that includes three key components: (1) critical race theory as a model of inquiry, (2) critical reflection and generativity as a model of praxis that unifies the use of counter-narratives for both research and pedagogy, and (3) transformative action for the fundamental goal of educational equity for people of color.

Since its formulation for education by Ladson-Billings and Tate (1995), critical race theory (CRT) has provided a powerful framework for articulating the needs of and demands for educational equity in U.S. education, and has demonstrated great success in shifting the terms of debate over the increasingly diverse student population from a community deficit model to one of community strengths. Among

Review of Research in Education
March 2020, Vol. 44, pp. 269–300
DOI: 10.3102/0091732X20908501
Chapter reuse guidelines: sagepub.com/journals-permissions
© 2020 AERA. http://rre.aera.net

the tools CRT provides educators and researchers is the collection and analysis of stories in support of demands for educational equity. Within a framework of CRT these "counter-narratives" have emerged as powerful data sources to present the voices of marginalized communities—but have we stopped at the storytelling? Based on the long and difficult struggle for educational equity, we need to further understand how counter-narratives can be used as a research methodology for educational equity. While there is an increasing number of students of color in our K–12 schools, there are also historical and continuing problems of inequity for students of color.[1] These inequities appear in patterns of low achievement and graduation rates (Ford & Moore, 2013; Ladson-Billings, 2006; Milner, 2012a), high suspension and expulsion rates (Carter et al., 2017; Skiba et al., 2002; Skiba et al., 2011), limited access to highly qualified teachers (Zeichner, 2014), and increased presence of these students in the school-to-prison pipeline (Skiba et al., 2014; H. Wilson, 2014). These practices of inequity and the resulting experiences of institutional racism are captured in counter-narratives voiced by students of color and their teachers. In order to prevent continuing inequitable practices in K–12 schools, the most important next step is to address them through teaching and teacher education. This chapter provides a review of the literature focusing on the use of counter-narratives in research on K–12 education and teacher education—with a critical eye toward assessing the methodological strengths and weaknesses of counter-narrative in achieving equity for students of color. We use the following research questions to guide our study:

Research Question 1: How have researchers used counter-narratives in education research and practice?

Research Question 2: To what extent have counter-narratives helped transform education practices to advance the goals of educational equity for people of color?

REVIEW METHOD

Our research included four phases. In the first phase, we surveyed approximately 250 articles in critical legal studies (CLS) and CRT of education to refresh our understanding of the theoretical underpinnings of counter-narrative in relation to educational equity and the transfer of the approach from legal education research and advocacy. In the second phase, we surveyed approximately 500 examples of educational literature and categorized three related approaches to storytelling and narratives in support of educational equity: (1) critical storytelling, (2) counterstory(ies), and (3) counter-narrative(s). These three approaches arose in the mid- to late 1990s but in different disciplines, with the first serious use of "critical storytelling" appearing in social work (Cooper, 1994), of "counterstories" in Latino/a Studies (Delgado Bernal, 1998; Villenas et al., 1999), and of counter-narratives in critical pedagogy (Lather, 1998). All three approaches were quickly adopted in education (Yosso, 2006). Although there are minor differences between the approaches, they are all grounded in a combination of critical theory and discourse theory, particularly CRT, critical feminism, and narrative inquiry. As such, we use *counter-narrative* as a covering term for all three approaches in our writing.

Informed by the historical development of counter-narratives in research, we then conducted the third phase of our literature research by using the three key phrases of counter-narrative(s), critical storytelling, and counterstory(ies) in the main educational databases (ERIC and Education FullText, and Education: A Sage Collection) as well as the much broader collections in JSTOR. Guided by our research questions, we further developed three criteria to narrow down the results. First, the definition of counter-narratives must be directly framed by CRT of education (excluding literature that uses "counter-narratives" in a generic way). Second, the research must have been conducted in the contexts of K–12 education and teacher education (excluding literature on counter-narratives in other fields such as medicine and law). Third, the research must be empirically based (excluding literature based in opinion or focused on policy prescriptions). Using counter-narrative(s), critical storytelling, and counterstory(ies), searching ERIC generates 239 peer-reviewed journal articles; searching Education FullText generates 228 peer-reviewed journal articles; searching Education: A Sage Collection generates 139; and finally, searching JSTOR produced a result of 292 peer-reviewed journal articles. There were significant overlaps in the search results. We then read through these articles carefully to exclude the ones that did not match our three criteria, which narrowed our results to 60 empirical journal articles for this review.

Finally, we conducted a systematic analysis of the 60 articles with the method of thematic analysis (Clarke & Braun, 2013), guided by the theoretical framework of CRT of education (Ladson-Billings & Tate, 1995), with a specific attention to the element of social action as an important legacy of CLS (Delgado, 1995a; Matsuda, 1995). We treated the 60 empirical journal articles as qualitative data and identified patterns through a rigorous process of data familiarization, data coding, and theme development and revision to answer the two research questions we raised. In the rest of this chapter, we first provide a historical analysis of how counter-narratives are conceptualized in CLS and CRT of education, followed by a systematic literature analysis of counter-narrative research in K–12 and teacher education. We end this chapter by proposing critical counter-narrative as a transformative methodology that has the potential to unify CRT as a model of inquiry, critical reflection and generativity as a model of praxis, and transformative action as a fundamental goal to achieve educational equity for students of color.

COUNTER-NARRATIVE IN CRITICAL LEGAL STUDIES

Counter-narratives and their application through CRT of education come out of an earlier movement in legal scholarship and practice, CLS, as does CRT itself (Ladson-Billings & Tate, 1995). As with a number of other efforts to address inequality in the United States, such as Social Security and Workman's Compensation, the locus of CLS was the University of Wisconsin–Madison (Altemeyer, 1958; Hoeveler, 1976). First taking shape as a conference in 1967, CLS quickly grew into a heterogeneous set of theories and practices that shared goals more than methodologies or even political standpoints (Russell, 1986, p. 4). From the beginning, however, CLS scholars and activists problematized normative concepts and practices of law by calling into question the most basic elements of laws and the application of laws, attempting to demonstrate the ideological basis of their justification by non-CLS scholars. Sometimes the questioning is rooted in poststructuralist close reading of legal texts; other times it comes out of empirical examination of laws in vivo. CRT then grew out of CLS as scholars of color, including Derrick Bell, Richard Delgado, Mari Matsuda, and Patricia Williams, began to build legal interventions by focusing on the lived experience of the law rather than on either legal texts or precedents.

The need to examine the lived experience of the law, and to make those experiences the basis for social change, stimulated CRT scholars to develop the practice of counter-narrative. Delgado and Matsuda, in particular, made significant use of counter-narratives in detailing the experience of Latinx and Asian Americans in a variety of legal situations (e.g., Delgado 1989, 1990, 1995b, 1996, 1999; Matsuda, 1991, 1993, 1995). It is important to remember, however, that collecting counter-narratives and presenting them in a new context is not just a scholarly pursuit for these scholars: Doing so in court is advocacy and action, and as such itself bears transformational potential. Legal concepts such as "disparate impact" allow for a counter-narrative, for example, of policing minor crimes, to be used in legislatures and the courts to change legal practice. It is not clear that counter-narratives in education can be as effective in transforming structures and practices as they have been in law, and even there the efficacy of counter-narrative in mobilizing community voices for issues such as environmental racism has not generally translated into legal victories (Foster, 2005). Nevertheless, the importance of counter-narrative in recentering the experience of marginalized communities impels us to consider how storytelling of this kind might generate action.

COUNTER-NARRATIVE IN CRITICAL RACE THEORY OF EDUCATION

One important tenet of CRT is recognizing and valuing the experiences and voices of people of color. In their groundbreaking work on critical race theory of education, Ladson-Billings and Tate (1995) defined counter-narratives as "naming one's own reality" or "voice" by critical race theorists through "parables, chronicles, stories, counterstories, poetry, fiction and revisionist histories to illustrate the false necessity and irony of much of current civil rights doctrine" (p. 56). Delgado (1995a) described counter-story as a "counter-reality that is experienced by subordinate groups, as opposed to those experiences of those in power" (p. 194). Critical race theorists and scholars continue to argue for the importance of drawing on experiences and voices of people of color. Ladson-Billings (2003) pointed out eloquently that "CRT understands that our social world is not fixed; rather, it is something we construct with words, stories, and silences" (p. 11). Solórzano and Yosso (2002) stated that "critical race theory recognizes that the experiential knowledge of people of color is legitimate, appropriate, and critical to understanding, analyzing, and teaching about racial subordination" (p. 26). Many critical theorists and educators have provided similar definitions, such as "counter-storytelling is a means of exposing and critiquing normalized dialogues that perpetuate racial stereotypes" (DeCuir & Dixson, 2004, p. 27), counter-narratives as stories that challenge widespread beliefs and discourses (Solórzano & Yosso, 2001), or counter-narratives as "perspectives that run opposite or counter to the presumed order and control" (Stanley, 2007, p. 14). In general, counter-narratives are important means to document and share how race influences the educational experiences of people of color, whose stories counter the stories of the privileged that are considered normal and neutral.

Delgado (1989) suggested three reasons for naming one's own reality in legal discourse: (1) much of social reality is socially constructed, (2) stories provide members of outgroups a vehicle for psychic self-preservation and for lessening their own subordination, and (3) stories help members of ingroups enrich their own reality—through the dialectic process of telling and listening to stories "we can overcome ethnocentrism and the unthinking conviction that our way of seeing the world is the only one" (p. 2439). Despite the differences in definitions, critical theorists and scholars in education seem to agree upon Delgado and colleagues' rationale for counter-narratives: Counter-narratives are able to achieve educational equity by giving voices to silenced and marginalized populations aimed at informing and educating dominant and elite groups, geared toward the ultimate goal of revealing the truth that "our society is deeply structured by racism" (Delgado, 1990, p. 98). Fairbanks (1996), for instance, argued that by giving voice to previously silenced groups, and by describing the diversity of their experiences, readers gain insight into their own practices, experiences, and biases.

In addition, counter-narrative holds promise to expose, analyze, and critique the racialized reality in which those experiences are contextualized, silenced, and perpetuated. For example, DeCuir and Dixson (2004) focused on exposing and critiquing normalized dialogs, while Delgado (1995a) emphasized the process of analyzing the myths, presuppositions, and received wisdoms that make up the common culture about race. Solórzano and Yosso (2002) pointed out that counterstories help readers critique unfair practices and pinpoint transformative possibilities from the standpoint of traditionally silenced voices. These efforts, indeed, push forward research and practice in educational equity because the "voice" component of CRT, according to Ladson-Billings and Tate (1995), provides a means to communicate the experiences and realities of the oppressed—"a first step on the road to justice" (p. 58). They also called for our attention to the notion that "the voice of people of color is required for a complete analysis of the educational system" (p. 58). Ladson-Billings (1998) further argued that "adopting and adapting CRT for educational equity means that we will have to expose racism in education *and* propose radical solutions for addressing it" (p. 22). To that end, we need to further explore the concept of counter-narrative and the role it plays in educational equity by supporting the development of solutions and actions.

RECONCEPTUALIZING CRITICAL COUNTER-NARRATIVE

Revisiting the goals of CLS on which CRT of education was founded, we see that the ultimate goals of both remain the same: "CRT works toward the end of eliminating racial oppression as part of the broader goal of ending all forms of oppression" (Matsuda, et. al., 1993, p. 6). Based on a comprehensive review of scholarship in CRT of education, Dixson and Rousseau (2005) observed the core value of CLS that centers on action and argue that "this element of CRT in legal studies must be translated to CRT in education" (p. 23). More specifically, they urged that "in addition to uncovering the myriad ways that race continues to marginalize and oppress people of colour, identifying strategies to combat these oppressive forces and acting upon those strategies is an important next step within CRT" (p. 23). Earlier critical race theorists have observed the inseparable relationship between reflection and social action in CRT striving toward equity (e.g., Calmore, 1995; Crenshaw, 1988; Lawrence, 1992; Matsuda, 1995; Matsuda et al., 1993). Calmore (1995), for example, stated that CRT

finds its finest expression when it . . . serves as "fuel for social transformation." In that sense, our efforts must, while directed by critical theory, extend beyond critique and theory to lend support to the struggle to relieve the extraordinary suffering and racist oppression that is commonplace in the life experiences of too many people of color. (p. 317)

Calmore (1995) is arguing for counter-narrative as a *praxis* that Freire (2000) defined in his *Pedagogy of the Oppressed*: "reflection and action directed at the structures to be transformed" (p. 126). He further argued that through praxis those who are oppressed can acquire critical awareness of their own conditions but, more important, of their "struggle for liberation." Freire (2000) specifically cautioned that the experiences of the oppressed must lead them to become subjects of transformation; their experiences cannot be objects of somebody else's praxis (p. 127). Habermas (1968/1971) also linked reflection and action closely, stating "we have made this interlocking of knowledge and interest clear through examining the category of 'actions' that coincide with the 'activity' of reflection, namely that of emancipatory actions" (p. 212).

According to Liu (2015), sharing, reflection, and action constitute a hermeneutic process because "by reflecting on one's actions there can be new knowledge and illumination of one's interests that can, in turn, inform new action" (p. 140). Built on the scholarship of critical theorists such as Habermas, Mezirow's (1990, 2000) transformative theory proposed the interlocking connection between critical theory and transformative learning. For Mezirow, we need to address "the question of the justification for the very premises on which problems are posed or defined in the first place" (Mezirow, 1990, p. 12) based on socially or personally distorted assumptions. This process is exactly what Ladson-Billings and Tate (1995) proposed as a complete analysis of the education system. Mezirow (1990) further pointed out that this type of analysis by and of itself does not lead to transformation; "acting upon these emancipatory insights, a praxis is also necessary" (p. 354). The transformation requires, according to Ball (2009), a generative framework supporting agency, efficacy, and advocacy on the part of teachers, students, and the community as a whole.

Counter-narrative, an important praxis in CRT, promises to bridge reflection and social action in achieving educational equity. However, we argue that we need to (re)center emancipatory action in conceptualizing and implementing counter-narratives. Delgado and Stefancic (1992) clearly explained the limits of sharing and listening to counter-narratives:

> The belief that we can somehow control our consciousness despite limitations of time and positionality we call the *empathic fallacy* [emphasis added] . . . believing that we can enlarge our sympathies through linguistic means alone. By exposing ourselves to ennobling narratives, we broaden our experience, deepen our empathy, and achieve new levels of sensitivity and fellow-feeling. We can, in short, think, talk, read, and write our way out of bigotry and narrow-mindedness, out of our limitations of experience and perspective. As we illustrate, however, we can do this only to a very limited extent. (p. 1261)

Based on the critical scholarship above, we see an imperative need to underscore the importance of transformative action in the conceptualization of counter-narrative. Building on and extending previous scholars' definitions, we propose the following definition of critical counter-narrative:

> Critical counter-narrative is a methodology for critically analyzing the racialized social reality in the education system and society by narrating the authentic lived experiences of people of color, searching for and acting upon emancipatory solutions, and transforming the educational system in order to provide equitable education for people of color.

Therefore, it is the transformative action and its ultimate outcome of enhancing educational equity that we focus on in our systematic review of research on counter-narratives in education. We return to our definition of critical counter-narrative as a methodology at the end of this chapter to provide a comprehensive description of the key components in it.

COUNTER-NARRATIVE IN EDUCATION RESEARCH

In this section, we provide the findings of our thematic analysis to answer research question one. Specifically, we found three primary types of applications of counter-narrative in education research: (1) counter-narrative as theoretical or methodological framing, (2) counter-narrative as research method, and (3) counter-narrative as a pedagogical tool in teaching and teacher education.

Counter-Narratives as Theoretical or Methodological Framing

Counter-Narrative as Theoretical Framing

Although some researchers do not ascribe theoretical significance to counter-narrative, or at least do not address it as such in their writing, others lay claim to counter-narrative as a theoretical framing, often explicitly placed within the broader framework of CRT. For example, many authors explain their approach through descriptions of CRT and the importance of storytelling by Delgado and Stefancic (2001), Ladson-Billings (1998), and Solórzano and Yosso (2002). Some choose only a portion of the scholars associated with counter-narrative to make their claims. For example, Amos (2016) cited Solórzano and Yosso (2009) in discussing the privileging of the voices of people of color (p. 44), while Ellison and Solomon (2019) cited Delgado and Stefancic (2001) and DeCuir and Dixson (2004) in laying out the basic thrust of counter-narrative (p. 224). Finally, N. A. Williams and Ware (2019) took the approach of citing Solórzano and Yosso (2002) in describing their mix of counter-narrative and autoethnography, while simultaneously disavowing their intent to use CRT as a theoretical framework, or indeed in proposing modifications to either CRT or counter-narrative (p. 89).

Education scholars also tend to reference the description of CRT laid out by Matsuda (1991) and Matsuda et al. (1993), usually in the form of a list of features developed by Solórzano and Yosso (2002). For example, Shiller (2018) and Ellison and Solomon (2019) used the list and elide reference to Matsuda (p. 224), whereas Cook and Dixson (2013) drew directly from Matsuda to identify the major themes of CRT as well as to explain the importance of counter-narrative in conveying the experience of life in the United States "from the bottom" (p. 1239). Of all the scholars reviewed here, Cook and Dixson (2013) provided the deepest genealogy of both CRT and counter-narrative, clearly tracing both back to CLS in a section titled "The Centrality of Story in CRT and Method" (pp. 1242–1243).

One important purpose of counter-narrative for theoretical framing is to bring into scholarship the lives and experiences of "those people whose experiences are not often told (i.e., those on the margins of society)" (Solórzano & Yosso, 2002, p. 34) with the aim of critiquing dominant narratives such as deficit thinking. Milner (2012b) explained,

A counter-narrative provides space for researchers to disrupt or to interrupt pervasive discourses that may paint communities and people, particularly communities and people of color, in grim, dismal ways. Indeed, counter-narratives can be used as an analytic tool to counter dominant perspectives in the literature such as discourses that focus on negative attributes, qualities, and characteristics of Black teachers. (p. 28)

Similarly, Flennaugh et al. (2017), referencing Matsuda (1993), suggested that "the idea of counter-storytelling and the inclusion of narratives as a mode of inquiry offer a methodology grounded in the particulars of the social realities and lived experiences of these students" (p. 212).

However, the terminology used to describe the theoretical role of CRT in general, and counter-narrative more specifically, tends to be more evocative than technical. For example, Caton (2012), citing Ladson-Billings (1998) and Delgado and Stefancic (2001), referred to CRT as a "conceptual lens," and counterstorytelling as CRT's "method" (p. 1062). Motha and Vargese (2018), working from Solórzano and Yosso (2002), used the same idea of a theoretical lens for their counterstorytelling study of

Miller et al.: Critical Counter-Narrative

women faculty of color (p. 507). Similarly, in their examination of deficit discourse concerning historically Black colleges and universities, K. Williams et al. (2019) described counter-narrative as an "approach" that should not be assigned "an inflated value in social justice scholarship," noting fundamental limitations suggested by Delgado and Stefancic's (1992) notion of the empathic fallacy, detailed earlier.

Counter-Narrative as Methodological Framing

In addition to presenting counter-narrative as a generalized theoretical frame, a small number of the authors we surveyed argue for counter-narrative as full methodology. The most influential example is Solórzano and Yosso's (2002) "Critical Race Methodology: Counter-Storytelling as an Analytical Framework for Education Research." This work proposes counterstorytelling as an analytical framework for education research, arguing that the result is a "critical race methodology." Key to their argument is the idea that critical race scholars themselves create counter-narratives, a notion that is not congruent with all approaches to counter-narrative but that is certainly arguable. Drawing on Strauss and Corbin's (1990) notion of theoretical sensitivity and Delgado Bernal's (1998) idea of cultural intuition, Solórzano and Yosso (2002) specified four data sources for the counter-stories that critical race methodology researchers construct: "(a) the data gathered from the research process itself, (b) the existing literature on the topic(s), (c) our own professional experiences, and (d) our own personal experiences" (p. 34).

Scholars who incorporate Solórzano and Yosso's critical race methodology tend to use standard qualitative methods for data collection, typically a combination of semi-structured interviews and field observations, with the resultant data coded to produce a thematic analysis. There are several exceptions. Mensah (2019) combined counter-narrative with co-autoethnography in a longitudinal study. Chapman (2007), Lynn (2006), and Ngunjuri (2007) used the idea of portraiture, and multiple scholars employed composite counter-narratives (Cook & Dixson, 2013; Juárez & Hayes, 2010; 2015; Tafari, 2018), originally presented as the central analytical method for critical race methodology (Solórzano & Yosso, 2002). Milner (2008) and Lynn (2006) both intended to differentiate research methodology from methods. Specifically, Lynn (2006) articulated, "Methodology . . . is what guides our thinking about our research . . . Method, on the other hand, describes the specific practices used to collect data" (p. 2502). Citing Lynn (2006), Milner (2008) stated, "Narrative and counter-narrative are the methodologies that framed my research. They were analytic tools that I used to make sense of matters in the study; they guided my rationales, decision-making, and thinking" (p. 1577). What remains unclear is how counter-narrative serves as a research methodology as opposed to counter-narrative as theoretical framing.

Counter-Narrative as Research Method

In addition to the efforts to establish counter-narrative as a theoretical or methodological framing, many scholars have made use of counter-narrative as a research method. For example, Love's (2004) CRT analysis of "achievement gap" narratives argued for the value of collecting and retelling counter-narratives "to change the form and content of research and conversations about events, situations, and societal participation" (p. 232). In making this claim, Love relied on scholars such as Solórzano and Yosso (2002) and Delagado Bernal and Villalpando (2002), who positioned counter-narrative as a vital tool to center analysis on the experiences of people of color within systems conditioned by racism and ethnocentrism. In other words, counter-narrative can be an important data collection method for CRT scholarship, particularly in service to educational equity. Our review indicates two approaches to using counter-narrative as a research method: (1) eliciting narratives from research participants that are conceived of by either the participants or the researchers (or both) as counter to majoritarian narratives and (2) eliciting data of various types from participants that the researchers use to construct a counter-narrative. It is not always clear from the statement of methods typical to research articles which approach a given study uses, but it always becomes clear through reading the findings and discussion. We call the first the *whole narrative* approach, and the second the *narrative factors* approach.

In a piece titled "Counter-Narrative as Method: Race, Policy and Research for Teacher Education," Milner and Howard (2013) provided the clearest discussion of the whole narrative approach. After rehearsing the history and basic thrust of CRT, Milner and Howard turned to the use of narrative in education research beginning with the development of narrative inquiry by Connelly and Clandinin (1990). They emphasized that collecting narratives of lived experience and naming that experience are important not just for storytellers but for listeners as well, which makes the narratives vital to pedagogy as well as research (p. 540). With that background, Milner and Howard then turned specifically to counter-narrative and its importance in CRT for conveying the voices of people of color and for disrupting normative narratives such as ideas of meritocracy. For Milner and Howard, then, and for the whole narrative approach to counter-narrative, the two goals of using authentic narratives are (1) to convey the voices of those underrepresented in research and (2) to make use of these voices as analytical devices to identify and critique majoritarian narratives, especially those that target people of color.

Within the broad category of the whole narrative approach, data collection and analysis methods vary considerably. Auerbach (2002) and Kraehe (2015), for example, used personal narratives to develop ethnographic case studies, while Castro-Sálazar and Bagely (2010) used a life history approach. Berry (2008) employed a phenomenological approach to analyze collected counter-narratives; Lee (2009) and C. M. Wilson (2016) used guided interviews and written reflection papers to stimulate counter-narratives, whereas Milner (2008) deliberately elicited counter-narratives among his participants. Romero et al. (2009) collected youth voices with the intent to construct counter-narratives; Cammarota and Romero (2011), working with students in Tucson Unified School District (TUSD), assisted participants trained in CRT to generate poetic counter-narratives that then form the basis for individual or collective action. Morris (2008) used an analytic review of literature on *Brown v. Board of Education* to tell the counterstory of Black schools before and after that decision, while Mungo (2013) did much the same using thematically coded interviews with six participants in the Civil Rights era. Occasionally, researchers adopt first-person narratives to construct their own counter-narratives. For example, Rodríguez and Greer (2017) constructed their counter-narratives to shed light on the experiences of men of color who grew up in complex community and schooling environments.

In contrast to the whole narrative approach, the narrative factors approach treats participant narratives as one data source among several from which the researcher constructs counter-narrative. The result may be closer to a thematic analysis rooted in CRT than a full counter-narrative, or it may proceed to the composite counter-narrative discussed below. Several scholars describe the overall process of the narrative factors approach. The clearest explanation is in DeCuir and Dixson (2004), in which they used the words of their participants to construct counter-narratives to common majoritarian narratives identified by CRT. In other words, the researchers themselves created counter-narratives, taking the words of their participants as "an illustration of the salience of race and racism in education" (DeCuir & Dixson, 2004, p. 29). For example, Vaught (2012) created a set of counter-narratives regarding the racial identity and categorization of Sa'moan high school students using formal and informal interviews with a broad range of participants, ethnographic observations in the school, and analysis of official documents from the school and the district. However, Vaught was clear that the goal was not to transmit the stories of Sa'moan high school students. Rather, "This is a story about the ways in which institutions and their members construct race. Therefore, I am not paying paramount attention to the stories of Sa'moan students and adults, but including them as they reflect the institutional dynamics" (Vaught, 2012, p. 578). Sealey-Ruiz (2013), on the other hand, although using a similar coding and narrative analysis method as Vaught, was less clear about the motivation for avoiding participant-generated narrative in favor of researcher-constructed counter-narrative. Shiller (2018) took a somewhat different approach, employing counter-narrative in a participant action research project that included the group generation of counter-narrative by the participants through "collected mapping" of interview materials (p. 34). The result, framing school closures in Black neighborhoods in Baltimore in terms of settler colonialism, was then used to advocate at the city level against further school closures. Shiller's approach represented a potentially fruitful amalgam of the whole narrative and narrative factors approaches, ensuring that the participants create the counter-narratives but doing so through analysis rather than pure storytelling.

Finally, because Solórzano and Yosso (2002), working from CLS scholars such as Bell (1987, 1992, 1996) and Delgado (1995a, 1995b, 1996), developed composite counterstorytelling into a key method in their critical race methodology, it merits special attention. In this method, researchers construct literary narratives based on the experiences of the participants and the researchers themselves, creating composite "characters" that represent the collective voice of a marginalized group. Often counterstorytelling begins much like other counter-narrative approaches, with interviews, field observations, written materials, and the like. As Solórzano and Yosso (2002) explained, once the data have been compiled, the researchers create composite characters to help tell the counterstory. Thus, although grounded in the voices of the participants like other forms of counter-narrative, the resulting counterstory puts those voices in dialog with the researchers' knowledge and experience, including their own experiences as members of a marginalized group (p. 34). The result, although created through literary procedures and with literary devices, is not intended to be taken as "fiction" (p. 36). Cook and Dixson (2013) indicated that in addition to emphasizing the shared issues faced by all participants rather than the specific details of individual participants' experiences, composite characters may also protect the privacy—and therefore safety—of participants (p. 1246).

Counter-Narrative as Pedagogical Tool

Finally, counter-narrative has been used as a pedagogical tool in K–12 teaching and in teacher education programs. Some have directed K–12 students to create their own personal counter-narratives, while others have provided already constructed counter-narratives to K–12 students, preservice teachers, or in-service teachers in efforts to counter deficit thinking and colorblindness. Mensah (2019), on the other hand, used longitudinal co-autoethnography to employ counter-narrative as both pedagogy and research tool in a teacher education program. Our review of counter-narrative as a pedagogical tool crosses areas of teaching in K–12 contexts and teacher education programs. Since counter-narrative is an important tenet of CRT, critical theorists consider the construction of counter-narratives an educational outcome of both critical pedagogy and critical literacy (Beach et al., 2010), but there are important differences in specific implementations.

K–12 Teaching and Teacher Professional Development

In K–12 teaching and in-service teacher professional development, having participants identify or construct counter-narratives appears to be the dominant model, whether the participants are students or teachers (Anderson, 2017; Degener, 2018; Godley & Loretto, 2013; Kersten, 2006). Battey and Franke (2015) examined how a math teacher professional development program used counter-narrative to support teachers in gathering counterevidence to challenge dominant deficit narratives about students of color by identifying examples of successful students, and redirecting teachers away from blaming students and toward new approaches to supporting their success. This example shows that when used as a pedagogical tool and implemented in classroom teaching, counter-narrative can produce transformation in teachers' practice. As the authors concluded, this practice of fostering counter-narratives is not about "talking in general"; instead, it is about "embedding stories in the practice of teaching" (p. 456) so that teachers not only challenge deficit thinking about students of color but also take actions to change their teaching practices to better support them to succeed.

In a series of articles beginning in 2008, Cammarota and colleagues reported research on the Social Justice Education Project (SJEP) in the TUSD before the Arizona legislature passed the anti–ethnic studies House Bill 2281 in 2010 that eliminated the program (Cammarota, 2008, 2014; Cammarota & Romero, 2011; Romero et al., 2009). Using CRT as a foundation to the educational praxis in the project, the authors supported high school students to construct counter-narratives through youth participatory action research. The ultimate purpose of this project, according to Cammarota (2008), was for the students to study and attempt to change their social contexts by facilitating the "organizing of stakeholders and constituents for taking direct action to transform practice, policies, and conditions in school sites" (p. 48). In order to engage the students—primarily Chicano/a—one approach the program used was to encourage students to adopt a CRT framework and document the influence of race on their education. The pedagogical process, according to Cammarota (2014), included students selecting themselves as primary subjects of the record, observing their own social context (school, community, family, etc.), reflecting on what they were observing, and creating counterstories through reflective journals or poetry.

Teacher Education Context

In contrast to the K–12 context, teacher educators tend to provide premade counter-narratives to preservice teachers in an effort to counter specific master narratives. For example, Buchanan and Hilburn (2016) used the documentary *Which Way Home* as an immigration counter-narrative, exploring how this film influenced preservice teachers' thinking regarding immigration. The authors found that preservice teachers were able to grapple with immigration counterstories and demonstrated shifts in their thinking about immigration. Similarly, Glenn (2012) used counter-narratives found in young adult novels with the intent to prompt preservice English teachers to think more acutely about their understandings of race within and beyond the text. Ball (2006, 2009), in a multisite, international longitudinal study, provided counter-narratives in the form of published literacy autobiographies to preservice teachers in the United States and South Africa, then teachers produced and shared their own literacy autobiographies and wrote biographies of their students in order to increase their metacognitive awareness of the critical role of literacy in their lives and in the lives of their students.

On the other hand, there are a small number of teacher educators eschewing the use of prepared counter-narratives. Salinas et al. (2016) guided Latina prospective teachers in a bilingual social studies methods course to produce a collection of counter-narratives to address the omission and distortion of history that "reveal a rich legacy of agency and activism that is pronounced by the voices of Tejanas/Chicanas like Marta Cotera and Gloria Anzaldua" (p. 280). Battey and Franke (2015) also helped in-service math teachers develop counter-narratives to be used in classroom teaching to challenge deficit narratives of students of color. In both of these examples, teacher educators scaffolded the creation of counter-narratives and guided their use in interpreting or modifying curriculum. This interest in producing change in the classroom leads us to the findings for Research Question 2.

EVIDENCE FOR TRANSFORMATION OF EDUCATION PRACTICES

Research Question 2 asks us to go beyond the employment of counter-narrative in research and pedagogy and consider to what extent counter-narratives in those contexts enhanced transformations in education practices to advance the goals of educational equity. In short, what actions have been taken beyond crafting and reporting counter-narratives? In answering Research Question 2, our analysis reveals that except for a small portion of research emphasizing emancipatory action as part of the practice of counter-narrative, much research focuses on reporting the counter-narratives themselves, or on changing participants' perceptions or attitudes, with little discussion of the need for follow-up actions in classrooms, schools, or communities. As a consequence, there is limited evidence demonstrating the transformation of educational practices to advance the goals of educational equity for students of color. As Cochran-Smith et. al (2015), Liu and Ball (2019), and others have observed, many teacher education researchers focus on changes in teacher attitudes and perceptions toward students of color, paying little attention to exploring actual change in their teaching practices. This focus is also true of much of the research and pedagogy employing counter-narrative. Buchanan and Hilburn (2016), for example, reported shifting preservice teachers' intentions for future teaching such as becoming informed about social issues like immigration and committing to learning about students' backgrounds, cultures, and experiences. Similarly, Glenn (2012) reported that after exposure to literature on immigrant life experiences, preservice teachers expressed a willingness to reconsider their assumptions about people of color and claimed heightened awareness of Whiteness. However, neither study attempted to further analyze whether these reported changes in attitude resulted in changed teaching practices.

A subset of researchers have articulated the importance of counter-narrative as a stepstone to further dialog and action (King & Pringle, 2019; Rodríguez & Greer, 2017; C. M. Wilson, 2016). For example, Rodríguez and Greer (2017) envisioned "a series of ways that our counter-narratives can be used to engage students and communities, spur dialogue and action, and shape policy and practice at all levels" (p. 118). Salinas et al. (2016) also argued that in framing the historical counter-narratives written by the future Latina teachers within the typology of resistance (Solórzano & Bernal, 2001), "a political, collective, conscious" (Solórzano & Bernal, 2001, p. 320) effort for inclusivity and clarity was made explicit.

However, some researchers such as Ball (2000, 2006, 2009) and Cammarota and Romero (2011) did provide further data to analyze how transformative action was carried out by the participants in teaching students of color. For example, scholars who use a participatory action research framework for their research and pedagogy have been able to go beyond "hearts and minds" and report efforts to make change. Cammarota and colleagues required action on the part of their participants as an essential element of the TUSD Social Justice Education Project. In one of the studies, Cammarota and Romero (2011) reported a student creating a counter-narrative through poetry responding to his experience having a Mexican flag patch taken away by school security labeling it a "gang symbol." As part of the requirement of the participatory action research in the Social Justice Education Project, the student recited his poetry in front of teachers, administrators, and district officials, leading the principal to make a new policy to allow students to display "appropriate cultural symbols" at school. Similarly, in Shiller (2018), participants used collaboratively created counter-narratives to advocate against school closures in Black neighborhoods in Baltimore.

SUMMARY OF COUNTER-NARRATIVE IN EDUCATION RESEARCH AND PRACTICE

In sum, the comprehensive review above demonstrates that counter-narrative in education research has produced invaluable knowledge to reveal the racialized reality in our educational system. Counter-narrative provides great opportunities for students and teachers of color to voice their oppressed experiences that can lead to further critical analysis of the educational system and the society at large by both people of color and the White majority. Our review, on one hand, further demonstrates that there is a lack of emphasis on the transformative actions in research on counter-narratives as well as in the pedagogical process of facilitating counter-narratives. By action, we mean "emancipatory actions" articulated by Mezirow (2000) and Habermas (1971). Specifically, when educators facilitate students to construct counter-narratives, there needs to be a framework to guide the sharing and using of the counter-narratives. In addition to the current practice that primarily focuses on sharing counter-narratives, we argue that educators need to guide the students to further use counter-narratives to analyze the educational system and society at large and search for and implement alternative solutions that may generate new ways to enhance equity for people of color.

On the other hand, our review reveals a lack of clarity in using counter-narratives in education research. Most researchers collect stories shared by people of color, and these stories, in many cases, become data analyzed through the lens of CRT. Therefore the counter-narratives in most cases function as a research method—"the specific practices to collect data" (Lynn, 2006, p. 2502). Researchers such as Solórzano and Yosso (2002), Lynn (2006), and Milner (2012a) push us to see counter-narrative beyond a research method, as a methodology, which inspires us to further build on their work by developing a model of counter-narrative as a methodology. When conducting research on counter-narratives, in addition to collecting counter-narratives as data and analyzing them as content, we should employ a comprehensive framework to focus on whether or not counter-narratives move beyond the sharing stage and into transformative action.

CRITICAL COUNTER-NARRATIVE AS TRANSFORMATIVE METHODOLOGY FOR EDUCATIONAL EQUITY

A quarter century into CRT of education and counter-narrative implementation in education practice and research, racial inequity inside and outside schooling has persisted, if not intensified. This inequity is evident through the resegregation of neighborhood schools (Frankenberg & Orfield, 2012; Orfield & Yun, 1999), a tripling of the wealth gap between White and non-White families (Shapiro et al., 2013), and the elimination of opportunities for students of color to learn beyond the basic skills needed to improve performance on high-stakes standardized tests (Holmes, 2012). As a consequence, 4-year high school graduation rates and college attendance for students of color still lag behind their White peers'. The median net worth of African American families is more than $236,000 lower than their White peers, both resulting from and in turn creating fewer opportunities for their children to participate in the education system (Shapiro et al., 2013, pp. 1–2). All of these have created an inequity loop that perpetuates negative experiences and outcomes for students of color.

Given the racial inequities revealed by counter-narratives in education research, how can we build upon the insights from the counter-narratives in order to address those inequities? Examining the history of counter-narrative in CRT in education versus CLS reveals a clear difference: In CLS, uncovering and sharing counter-narratives is by and of itself advocacy—action with the goal of transforming the legal system. As Crenshaw et al. (1995) asserted, one of the core values of CLS is "the desire to not merely understand the vexed bond between law and racial power but to *change* it" (p. xiii). Matsuda et. al. (1993) similarly described CRT in legal studies as "work that involves both action and reflection. It is informed by active struggle and in turn informs the struggle" (p. 3). Bringing the lived experience of the law for people of color into the legal discourse can shape the interpretation of the law directly, even when it does not affect the letter of the law. In education, however, uncovering, analyzing, and retelling counter-narratives do not, in themselves, generate change in the same way. Our review of the literature therefore supports the warning by Dixson and Rousseau (2005) that "this element of CRT in legal studies [action] must be translated to CRT in education" (p. 23)—or as Ladson-Billings (1998) argued earlier, "We will have to expose racism in education *and* propose radical solutions for addressing it" (p. 22).

In short, counter-narrative can affect change in the educational system, but only if the sharing and analysis of counter-narrative form the basis for transformative action, moving beyond counter-narrative as data and toward counter-narrative as praxis—"the process of reflection and action directed at the structures to be transformed" (Freire, 2000, p. 126). In response, we offer here a comprehensive transformative methodology based on critical reflection and generative change (Liu & Ball, 2019), with the crucial work of praxis carried out by counter-narrative. We begin with a brief description of the essential features of a methodology, then focus on the specific model of our transformative methodology.

ESSENTIAL COMPONENTS OF A RESEARCH METHODOLOGY

In research on counter-narrative, as well as more broadly, the term *methodology* is frequently used as a synonym for *methods*, which in turn is usually a synonym for *data collection and analysis*. The terms are not synonymous, however, and some of the scholars we have already discussed earlier—notably Milner (2008), Lynn (2006), Solórzano and Yosso (2002)—have suggested that counter-narrative can go beyond its role in data collection and analysis and become a research methodology. Nevertheless, as we have seen, the relationship of the elements of previous models of counter-narrative as a methodology are not clearly stated. We argue that this lack of clarity actually stems from some fuzziness in the definitions of methodology in these previous models. To have a clear sense of a methodology of counter-narrative requires a clear sense of the definition of methodology itself, but this has been largely absent.

Cordeiro et al. (2017) saw methodology itself as the unifying element to theory, methods, assumptions, and actions of research:

> From a theoretical perspective a methodology poses the theoretical framework of the research or project in order to increase understanding of what stance the researcher is taking when designing the research. . . . The methodology puts forth the philosophical assumptions that underlie the science. The methods of the research are . . . the tools and processes that are used to carry out the research and are often driven by the methodology. The methods spell out the "action" of the research, the techniques that are used to gather and analyze data. It answers how the research actually gets accomplished and answers the research question(s). (p. 399)

From this standpoint, methodology is typically understood as a broad concept that encompasses methods along with "the values and justifications behind a particular characterization" of method (https://plato.stanford.edu/entries/scientific-method/). Examining multiple models of scientific inquiry suggests that methodology typically unifies three core elements: (1) theoretical models of the inquiry process, (2) praxis appropriate to the different stages of the inquiry process, and (3) broad goals for the whole enterprise. These three elements form a hermeneutic in which the theoretical model of inquiry determines praxis and goals, the goals inform the theoretical model and praxis, and praxis acts as the intermediary between theoretical model and goals.

This definition of methodology suggests that the previous uses of counter-narrative in education we reviewed above, as well as the specific ideas of methodology by Lynn (2006), Milner (2008), and Solórzano and Yosso (2002), lack the hermeneutic linkages between theory, methods, and goals, and especially the mediating element of praxis. We suggest that this problematic construction inhibits the ability of CRT and counter-narrative-based research in education to build upon the undeniable strengths of counter-narrative and achieve transformation of the educational system. Therefore we propose a methodology rooted in CRT, employing counter-narrative and extending the existing approaches, that unifies the following three essential elements: (1) CRT as a theoretical model of inquiry, (2) a praxis model of critical reflection and generative change, and (3) transformative action for the fundamental goal of educational equity for people of color.

CRITICAL RACE THEORY AS A MODEL OF INQUIRY

CRT, since its inception within CLS through to its uptake in education, has clearly informed the underlying assumptions, methods of data collection and analysis, and also the broad goals of much research in education. CRT has been adopted widely by researchers to investigate racism and education inequalities. For example, CRT clearly points out that racism is "a normal fact of daily life in U.S. society that is neither aberrant nor rare" (Taylor, 2009, p. 4) and that racism is endemic, pervasive, widespread, and ingrained in society (Milner, 2007). Working from these basic theoretical points, Dixson and Rousseau (2005) identified eight constructs in CRT that scholars use to analyze race and racism: (1) Whiteness as Property, (2) Intersectionality, (3) Critique of Liberalism and Colorblindness, (4) Interest-Convergence, (5) Racial Realism, (6) Restrictive versus Expansive Notions of Equality, (7) Voice/Counterstory, and (8) Social Change. Although some scholars argue that CRT lacks "the systemic structure" (Trevino et al., 2008, p. 9) necessary to form strong analytic tools that can promote action (Rogers & Jaime, 2010), this assertion clearly is not borne out by our literature review on counter-narrative, several examples of which did result in action. The question, then, is how CRT functions as the model of inquiry for a research methodology, which requires establishing a hermeneutic relationship with both a praxis and the broad goals of educational equity.

CRITICAL REFLECTION AND GENERATIVE CHANGE AS A MODEL OF PRAXIS FOR CRITICAL COUNTER-NARRATIVE

As Milner (2012b) observed, "From critical race theory perspectives, knowledge can and should be generated through narratives and counter-narratives that emerge from and with people of color" (p. 28). Inspired by earlier calls put forward by Ladson-Billings (1999) for "proposing racial solutions" and Dixson and Rousseau (2005) for acting upon those proposals, Liu and Ball (2019) proposed a framework for transformative teacher education by synthesizing critical reflection for transformative learning (Liu, 2015) with the model of generative change for educational equity (Ball, 2009). In this section, we first briefly review critical reflection for transformative learning and generative change and then demonstrate how the synthesized model is a praxis (Freire, 2000) central to constructing a methodology for counter-narrative.

CRITICAL REFLECTION FOR TRANSFORMATIVE LEARNING

Critical reflection is a hermeneutic approach that involves repeated reexamination of one's assumptions about knowledge and understanding, particularly those that are socially, politically, or culturally based (Liu & Ball, 2019). Important as critical reflection in learning, Mezirow (1990, 2000) and other scholars such as Brookfield (1995) and Habermas (1968/1971) have pointed out that reflection itself cannot lead to transformative learning—it is the emancipatory action, the *praxis* based upon reflective insights, that leads to transformation. Liu (2015), building upon Dewey (1933), Mezirow (1990, 2000), and Habermas (1968/1971) and working from Brookfield's stages of critical reflection (1995), developed a full hermeneutic model of critical reflection for transformative learning, including a cycle of six steps—from assumption analysis to reflection on reflection-based action, and asserting an ultimate goal of educational equity (see Figure 1; from Liu & Ball, 2019).

THE MODEL OF GENERATIVE CHANGE

Building on the work in psychology of Erikson (1963), Epstein (1996), and Franke et al. (2001), and influenced by Bandura's (1977, 1997) self-efficacy theories in teacher education, Ball (2009) combined generativity theory and teacher efficacy in a model designed to prepare teachers to believe in their potential to affect positive change in the lives of their students and to think in generative ways about how to incorporate creative transformative action in their classroom practices. Figure 2 illustrates the model of generative change as a series of steps by which individuals move from metacognitive awakening to their own sense of efficacy to becoming transformative intellectuals (Giroux, 1988) able to reshape curriculum, pedagogy, and institutional structures and practices, resulting in teachers who are *agents of change* rather than *objects of change*—teachers who forge new relationships between teachers and students, schools and communities (Figure 2).

THE SYNTHESIZED MODEL OF PRAXIS FOR CRITICAL COUNTER-NARRATIVE

Recognizing significant congruence between the two models, with the hermeneutic steps of the one linking with the generative steps of the other, Liu and Ball (2019) combined the two approaches into a unified framework for promoting the transformation of schools and communities as well as the transformation of learning among teachers and students: critical reflection and generative change. However, beyond the broad ideas of reflection, critique, and so forth, the combined model does not articulate specific key methods for accomplishing the goal of educational equity. In conducting the review of counter-narrative laid out above, we recognized that, along with the practice of counter-narrative, the combined model provides a powerful praxis—"reflection and action directed at the structures to be transformed" (Freire, 2000, p. 126)—for achieving educational equity. This combined model, animated

FIGURE 1
Hermeneutic Cycle of Critical Reflection for Transformative Learning

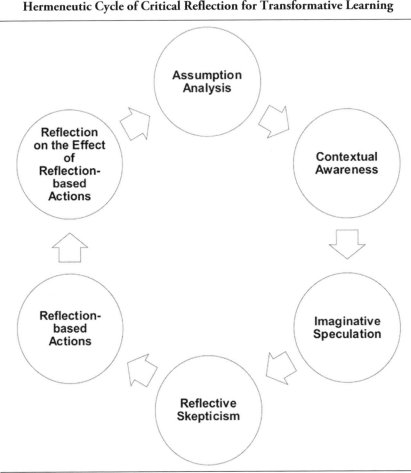

Source. Reprinted from Liu & Ball, 2019, p. 91.

via counter-narrative, stimulates the generation of new knowledge and action through five stages, each one of which represents both cognitive development and greater social engagement.

In summary form (see Figure 3), the process begins with the *narrativization* of personal learning experiences (Ball, 2009) and *assumption analysis* (Liu, 2015) coupled with *awakening* (Ball, 2009), focusing on the development of metacognitive awareness and subsequent critical analysis of individual and social assumptions (Ball, 1998; Mezirow, 2000) embedded in counter-narratives. From there,

FIGURE 2
Model of Generative Change

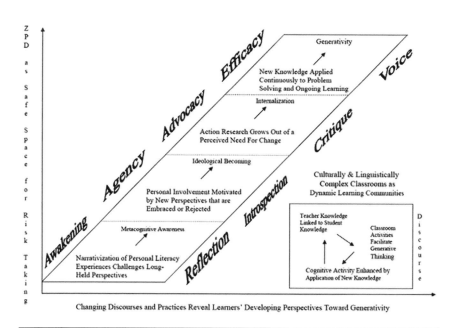

Source. Reprinted from Ball (2009).

participants begin to explore theoretical, historical, cultural, and political factors underpinning distorted assumptions they may hold. Through *introspection* (Ball, 2009) and a *contextual analysis* (Liu, 2015) of these experiences, participants develop a sense of *agency* and an intellectually grounded "ideological becoming" (Bakhtin, 1981; Freedman & Ball, 2004). In the third step, with the foundation of their counter-narratives, participants engage a series of *imaginative speculations* tempered by *reflective skepticism* generated by their counter-narratives in an effort to develop and *advocate* alternatives to the reality in which they find themselves, building upon introspection and critique that leads to what Vygotsky (1978) referred to as *internalization*. During the fourth step, participants generate new knowledge through problem-solving, implement *reflection-based actions* that result from their experiences, and develop a sense of *efficacy*, setting the stage for the final stage of *generativity*, further *reflection on their actions*, and further *generation* of new knowledge, new actions, and new worldviews.

While each stage of the model is vitally important, Step 3 is critical to this discussion because it is here that the process pivots outward from counter-narrative as a

FIGURE 3
Critical Reflection and Generativity: A Model of Praxis
for Critical Counter-Narrative

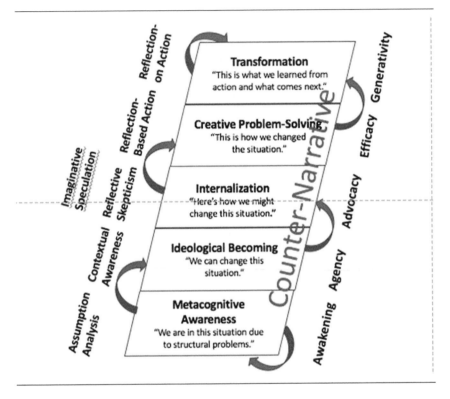

focus on the individual to counter-narrative as the basis for the consideration and generation of *action* in the school and the community. However, it is important to note that counter-narrative is a vital element at every stage in the process, forming the backbone of the praxis that links CRT as the animating theory and generative transformation for educational equity as the ultimate goal. Figure 3 presents a visualization of this model of praxis.

In short, incorporating critical counter-narrative into the combined model enables us to elevate the framework in Liu and Ball (2019) into the praxis for a full methodology to achieve educational equity by not just grounding personal reflection and awareness in CRT theory and method but also fueling the pivot from the individual out toward society in the marginalized voices revealed through counter-narrative. The movement from voice to agency is fueled through the dialectic process of critical reflection, counter-narrative, and generative action for transformative change—the creative and destructive halves of the dialectic (Delgado, 1989)—that provides blueprints for change, then subjects those blueprints to the same critical consideration that produced them in the first instance.

THE GOAL OF TRANSFORMING EDUCATIONAL SYSTEMS AND PRACTICES FOR EDUCATIONAL EQUITY

The final element required for a methodology is the overall goal of the entire inquiry process, supported by the theoretical framework and pursued through the praxis. In the case of critical counter-narrative the goal is educational equity for all students. In identifying this goal, we are not going outside the bounds of other CRT applications in education or, for that matter, much of the previous counter-narrative research and pedagogy. However, here we explicitly identify it as the goal of a coherent methodology grounded in CRT and pursued through the praxis of critical counter-narrative. As such, it is a subgoal of the larger goal of CRT as a whole, "eliminating racial oppression as part of the broader goal of ending all forms of oppression" (Matsuda et. al., 1993, p. 6). It should be clear from our review of the literature that this goal is at least implicit in previous and current counter-narrative research and pedagogy, even in studies that do not go beyond the production or identification of counter-narrative, because the theoretical and methodological framing of counter-narrative assumes a master narrative that denies educational equity.

In any case, making educational equity the explicit goal of a critical counter-narrative methodology encourages the praxis to focus on transformative action. This is particularly important in mentoring teacher education students who have much greater structural incentive to speak and write in support of educational equity than in taking action to achieve it (Liu, 2015, 2017; Thomas & Liu, 2012). For example, focusing on the elicitation or construction of counter-narratives through this praxis means that, whether emphasizing research or pedagogy, participants have in mind not just historical or current inequities but also ideas to address those inequities, and are encouraged to avoid empty discussion, euphemisms, and blame-shifting (Gao et al., 2019). Participants also have incentives to subject their counter-narratives and ideas to the same rigorous critical reflection they use in dealing with the initial majoritarian narratives, which not only enhances the quality of the resulting ideas but also further reinforces the habits of critical reflection for generative transformation. In short, clarifying the end goal of the critical counter-narrative methodology as educational equity strengthens the praxis and efficacy of the methodology as well as contributing to the larger CRT theoretical framework.

The three elements of the critical counter-narrative methodology thus form a hermeneutic process in which the CRT theoretical model of inquiry conditions the critical reflection and generativity for transformative praxis, the praxis reformulates the goals of educational equity, the goals inform reformulation of the praxis, and the reformulated praxis informs reflection on the theoretical model of inquiry. Figure 4 visualizes critical counter-narrative as a methodology for educational equity.

FIGURE 4
Critical Counter-Narrative as a Transformative Methodology
for Educational Equity

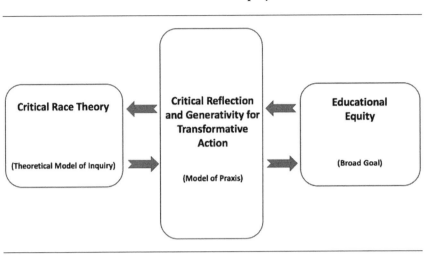

CONCLUSION AND IMPLICATIONS

In this chapter, we have reviewed the application of counter-narratives in education research and pedagogy as a tool to stimulate educational equity for students of
color. Based on a thematic analysis focused on education and research in K–12 and
teacher education contexts, we argue that the potential of counter-narrative to achieve
educational equity remains limited by the lack of a unified methodology, including a
central praxis and clear goals to support action beyond the collection or construction
of counter-narratives. It is crucial to observe that far from criticizing the current
practice of counter-narrative itself, whether the whole narrative or the narrative factors approach, the introduction and development of these practices have been very
effective at bringing the voices of marginalized communities into education research
and pedagogy. However, with the exception of projects clearly designed from the
ground up to result in action (notably the participatory action research–based projects in Tucson and Baltimore; Ball, 2006, 2009; and a few others), there is limited
evidence that bringing in voice has led to transformation in the educational system or
substantial change in teachers' classroom practices. We therefore proposed critical
counter-narrative as a transformative methodology for educational equity, including
three key components: (1) CRT as a model of inquiry, (2) critical reflection and generativity as a model of praxis that unify the use of counter-narratives for both research
and pedagogy, and (3) transformative action for the fundamental goal of educational
equity for people of color.

The implications of this critical counter-narrative methodology begin with reinforcing the call to go beyond telling stories. Yet we must also go beyond calling for change and move into action by examining research and pedagogy using counter-narrative to implement the methodology. We have been piloting critical counter-narrative methodology in our teacher education courses and have the following suggestions for other teacher educators who wish to make use of it in their own courses. First, although an initial step toward awakening can begin with preservice and in-service teachers being given counter-narratives as a discussion point on majoritarian narratives, having participants transition to developing their own counter-narratives is necessary to avoid the common pitfalls of avoiding serious discussion of race and racism, the substitution of abstract concepts for concrete issues, and the practices already identified in CRT research, such as colorblindness, the discourse of meritocracy, and so forth. Second, having preservice and in-service teachers help their own students in K–12 classrooms identify majoritarian narratives and develop counter-narratives will further enable real awareness and growth, particularly when coupled with concrete efforts to connect the teachers with the communities surrounding their schools. Finally, it is important for teacher educators to reframe the talk about counter-narratives so as to stimulate critical reflection on the ultimate goal of educational equity, and what actions, grounded in CRT, could proceed from the knowledge generated by the counter-narratives. In other words, helping the participants develop their agency as well as their voices, and encouraging them to come up with alternative solutions and further take actions to implement them, will more effectively promote generative transformative action inside and outside the classroom.

ORCID iDs

Katrina Liu https://orcid.org/0000-0002-0082-2253
Arnetha F. Ball https://orcid.org/0000-0001-5085-9719

NOTE

[1]Since 2014, White students account for less than half of the total U.S. K–12 public school student population (Institute of Education Sciences, 2016, Table 7, p. 48).

REFERENCES

Altemeyer, A. J. (1958). The Wisconsin Idea and social security. *The Wisconsin Magazine of History, 42*(1), 19–25.

Amos, Y. T. (2016). Wanted and used: Latina bilingual education teachers at public schools. *Equity & Excellence in Education, 49*(1), 41–56. https://doi.org/10.1080/10665684.2015.1122557

Anderson, L. (2017). "I'm known:" Building relationships and helping students construct counter-narratives on the west side of Chicago. *Annals of the American Academy of Political and Social Science, 673*(1), 98–115. https://doi.org/10.1177/0002716217723613

Auerbach, S. (2002). "Why do they give the good classes to some and not to others?" Latino parent narratives of struggle in a college access program. *Teachers College Record, 10*(7), 1369–1392. https://doi.org/10.1111/1467-9620.00207

Bakhtin, M. M. (1981). *The dialogic imagination: Four essays* (M. Holmquist, Ed.; C. Emerson & M. Holmquist, Trans.). University of Texas Press.

Ball, A. F. (1998). The value of recounting narratives: Memorable learning experiences in the lives of inner-city students and teachers. *Journal of Narrative Inquiry, 8*(1), 1–30. https://doi.org/10.1075/ni.8.1.07bal

Ball, A. F. (2000). Preparing teachers for diversity: Lessons learned from the U.S. and South Africa. *Teaching and Teacher Education, 16*(4), 491–509. https://doi.org/10.1016/S0742-051X(00)00007-X

Ball, A. F. (2006). *Multicultural strategies for education and social change: Carriers of the torch in the United States and South Africa.* Teachers College Press.

Ball, A. F. (2009). Toward a theory of generative change in culturally and linguistically complex classrooms. *American Educational Research Journal, 46*(1), 45–72. https://doi.org/10.3102/0002831208323277

Bandura, A. (1977). Self-efficacy: Toward a unifying theory of behavioral change. *Psychological Review, 84,* 191–215. https://doi.org/10.1037/0033-295X.84.2.191

Bandura, A. (1997). *Self-efficacy: The exercise of control.* Freeman.

Battey, D., & Franke, M. (2015). Integrating professional development on mathematics and equity: Countering deficit views of students of color. *Education and Urban Society, 47*(4), 433–462. https://doi.org/10.1177/0013124513497788

Beach, R., Campano, G., Edmiston, B., & Borgmann, M. (2010). *Literacy tools in the classroom: Teaching through critical inquiry grades 5-12.* Teachers College Press.

Bell, D. (1987). *And we will not be saved: The elusive quest for racial justice.* Basic Books.

Bell, D. (1992). *Faces at the bottom of the well: The permanence of racism.* Basic Books.

Bell, D. (1996). *Gospel choirs: Psalms of survival for an alien land called home.* Basic Books.

Berry, R. Q., III. (2008). Access to upper-level mathematics: The stories of successful African American middle school boys. *Journal for Research in Mathematics Education, 39*(5), 464–488. https://www.jstor.org/stable/pdf/40539311.pdf?seq=1

Brookfield, S. (1995). *Becoming a critically reflective teacher.* Jossey-Bass.

Buchanan, L. B., & Hilburn, J. (2016). Riding la Bestiá: Preservice teachers' responses to documentary counter-stories of U.S. immigration. *Journal of Teacher Education, 67*(5), 408–423. https://doi.org/10.1177/0022487116660153

Calmore, J. (1995). Critical race theory, Archie Shepp, and fire music: Securing an authentic intellectual life in a multicultural world. In K. Crenshaw, N. Gotanda, G. Peller, & K. Thomas (Eds.), *Critical race theory: the key writings that formed the movement* (pp. 315–329). New Press.

Cammarota, J. (2008). The cultural organizing of youth ethnographers: Formalizing a praxis-based pedagogy. *Anthropology & Education Quarterly, 39*(1), 45–58. https://doi.org/10.1111/j.1548-1492.2008.00004.x

Cammarota, J. (2014). Challenging colorblindness in Arizona: Latina/o students' counter-narratives of race and racism. *Multicultural Perspectives, 16*(2), 79–85. https://doi.org/10.1080/15210960.2014.889569

Cammarota, J., & Romero, A. (2011). Participatory action research for high school students: Transforming policy, practice, and the personal with social justice education. *Educational Policy, 25*(3), 488–506. https://doi.org/10.1177/0895904810361722

Carter, P. L., Skiba, R., Arredondo, M. I., & Pollock, M. (2017). You can't fix what you don't look at: Acknowledging race in addressing racial discipline disparities. *Urban Education, 52*(2), 207–235. https://doi.org/10.1177/0042085916660350

Castro-Sálazar, R., & Bagley, C. (2010). "Nideaquíni from there." Navigating between contexts: Counter-narratives of undocumented Mexican students in the United States. *Race Ethnicity and Education, 13*(1), 23–40. https://doi.org/10.1080/13613320903549651

Caton, M. T. (2012). Black male perspectives on their educational experiences in high school. *Urban Education, 47*(6), 1055–1085. https://doi.org/10.1177/0042085912454442

Chapman, T. K. (2007). Interrogating classroom relationships and events: Using portraiture and critical race theory in education research. *Educational Researcher, 36*(3), 3–69. https://doi.org/10.3102/0013189X07301437

Clarke, V., & Braun, V. (2013). Teaching thematic analysis: Overcoming challenges and developing strategies for effective learning. *The Psychologist, 26*(2), 120–123.

Cochran-Smith, M., Villegas, A. M., Abrams, L., Chavez-Moreno, L., Mills, T., & Stern, R. (2015). Critiquing teacher preparation research: An overview of the field, Part II. *Journal of Teacher Education, 66*(2), 109–121. https://doi.org/10.1177/0022487114558268

Connelly, F. M., & Clandinin, D. J. (1990). Stories of experience and narrative inquiry. *Educational Researcher, 19*(5), 2–14. https://doi.org/10.3102/0013189X019005002

Cook, D. A., & Dixson, A. D. (2013). Writing critical race theory and method: A composite counterstory on the experiences of black teachers in New Orleans post-Katrina. *International Journal of Qualitative Studies in Education, 26*(10), 1238–1258. https://doi.org/10.1080/09518398.2012.731531

Cooper, L. (1994). Critical storytelling in social work education. *Australian Journal of Adult and Community Education, 34*(2), 131–141.

Cordeiro, L., Baldini Soares, C., & Rittenmeyer, L. (2017). Unscrambling method and methodology in action research traditions: Theoretical conceptualization of praxis and emancipation. *Qualitative Research, 17*(4), 395–407. https://doi.org/10.1177/1468794116674771

Crenshaw, K. (1988). Race, reform, and retrenchment: Transformation and legitimation in antidiscrimination law. *Harvard Law Review, 101*(7), 1331–1387. https://doi.org/10.2307/1341398

Crenshaw, K., Gotanda, N., Peller, G., & Thomas, K. (Eds.). (1995). *Critical race theory: The key writings that formed the movement.* New Press.

DeCuir, J. T., & Dixson, A. D. (2004). "So when it comes out, they aren't that surprised that it is there:" Using critical race theory as a tool of analysis of race and racism in education. *Educational Researcher, 33*(5), 26–31. https://doi.org/10.3102/0013189X033005026

Degener, R. M. (2018). Title IX story club: Creating possibilities for minoritized middle school girls in physical activity. *Journal of Adolescent & Adult Literacy, 62*(2), 195–203. https://doi.org/10.1002/jaal.870

Delgado, R. (1989). Storytelling for oppositionists and others: A plea for narrative. *Michigan Law Review, 87*(8), 2411–2441. https://doi.org/10.2307/1289308

Delgado, R. (1990). When a story is just a story: Does voice really matter? *Virginia Law Review, 76*(1), 95–11. https://doi.org/10.2307/1073104

Delgado, R. (Ed.) (1995a). *Critical race theory: The cutting edge.* Temple University Press.

Delgado, R. (1995b). *The Rodrigo chronicles: Conversations about America and race.* New York University Press.

Delgado, R. (1996). *The coming race war? And other apocalyptic tales of America after affirmative action and welfare.* New York University Press.

Delgado, R. (1999). *When equality ends: Stories about race and resistance.* Westview.

Delgado, R., & Stefancic, J. (1992). Images of the outsider in American law and culture: Can free expression remedy systemic social ills. *Cornell Law Review, 77*, 1258–1297.

Delgado, R., & Stefancic, J. (2001). *Critical race theory: An introduction.* New York University Press.

Delgado Bernal, D. (1998). Using a Chicana feminist epistemology in educational research. *Harvard Educational Review, 68*(4), 555–582. https://doi.org/10.17763/haer.68.4.5wv1034973g22q48

Delgado Bernal, D., & Villalpando, O. (2002). An apartheid of knowledge in academia: The struggle over the "legitimate" knowledge of faculty of color. *Equity & Excellence in Education, 35*(2), 169–180. https://doi.org/10.1080/713845282

Dixson, A. D., & Rousseau, C. K. (2005). And we are still not saved: Critical race theory in education ten years later. *Race Ethnicity and Education, 8*(1), 7–27. https://doi.org/10.1080/1361332052000340971

Ellison, T. L., & Solomon, M. (2019). Counter-storytelling vs. deficit thinking around African American children and families, digital literacies, race, and the digital divide. *Research in the Teaching of English, 53*(3), 223–244.

Epstein, R. (1996). *Cognition, creativity, and behavior.* Praeger.

Erikson, E. H. (1963). *Childhood and society* (2nd ed.). Norton.

Fairbanks, C. (1996). Telling stories: Reading and writing research narratives. *Journal of Curriculum and Supervision, 11*(4), 320–340.

Flennaugh, T. K., Howard, T. C., Malone, M., Tunstall, J., Keetin, N., & Chirapuntu, T. (2017). Authoring student voices on college preparedness: A case study. *Equity & Excellence in Education, 50*(2), 209–221. https://doi.org/10.1080/10665684.2017.1301840

Ford, D. Y., & Moore, J. L. (2013). Understanding and reversing underachievement, low achievement, and achievement gaps among high-ability African American males in urban school contexts. *Urban Review, 45*(4), 399–415. https://doi.org/10.1007/s11256-013-0256-3

Foster, S. R. (2005). Critical race lawyering: Forward. *Fordham Law Review, 73*(5), 2027–2039.

Franke, M., Carpenter, T., Levi, L., & Fennema, E. (2001). Capturing teachers' generative change: A follow-up study of professional development in mathematics. *American Educational Research Journal, 38*, 653–689. https://doi.org/10.3102/00028312038003653

Frankenberg, E., & Orfield, G. (2012). *The resegregation of suburban schools: A hidden crisis in American education.* UCLA Civil Rights Project.

Freedman, S. W., & Ball, A. (2004). Ideological becoming: Bakhtinian concepts to guide the study of language. In A. Ball & S. W. Freedman (Eds.), *Bakhtinian perspectives on language, literacy, and learning* (pp. 3–33). Cambridge University Press. https://doi.org/10.1017/CBO9780511755002.001

Freire, P. (2000). *Pedagogy of the oppressed* (30th ed.). Continuum International.

Gao, S., Liu, K., & McKinney, M. (2019). Learning formative assessment in the field: Analysis of conversations between preservice teachers and their classroom mentors. *International Journal of Mentoring and Coaching in Education, 8*(3), 197–216. https://doi.org/10.1108/IJMCE-10-2018-0056

Giroux, H. A. (1988). *Teachers as intellectuals: Toward a critical pedagogy of learning.* Greenwood.

Glenn, W. J. (2012). Developing understandings of race: Preservice teachers' counter-narrative (re)constructions of people of color in young adult literature. *English Education, 44*(4), 326–253.

Godley, A. J., & Loretto, A. (2013). Fostering counter-narratives of race, language, and identity in an urban English classroom. *Linguistics and Education, 24*(3), 316–327. https://doi.org/10.1016/j.linged.2013.03.006

Habermas, J. (1971). *Knowledge and human interests* (J. J. Shapiro, Trans.). Beacon Press. (Original work published 1968)

Hoeveler, J. D., Jr. (1976). The university and the social gospel: The intellectual origins of the "Wisconsin Idea." *Wisconsin Magazine of History, 59*(4), 282–298.

Holmes, S. L. (2012). *An investigation of No Child Left Behind and its primary purpose to close the achievement gap* (Unpublished EdD dissertation). Northern Arizona University.

Institute of Education Sciences. (2016, April). *Projections of education statistics to 2023.* U.S. Department of Education National Center for Education Statistics.

Juárez, B. G., & Hayes, C. (2010). Social justice is not spoken here: Considering the nexus of knowledge, power and the education of future teachers in the United States. *Power and Education, 2*(3), 233–252. https://doi.org/10.2304/power.2010.2.3.233

Juárez, B. G., & Hayes, C. (2015). On being named a Black supremacist and a race traitor: The problem of White racial domination. *Urban Review, 47*(2), 317–340. https://doi .org/10.1007/s11256-014-0294-5

Kersten, J. (2006). Why's everyone White? Moving toward critical pedagogy in an elementary classroom. *Journal of Urban Learning, Teaching, and Research, 2,* 35–44.

King, N. S., & Pringle, R. M. (2019). Black girls speak STEM: Counterstories of informal and formal learning experiences. *Journal of Research in Science Teaching, 56*(5), 539–569. https://doi.org/10.1002/tea.21513

Kraehe, A. M. (2015). Sounds of silence: Race and emergent counter-narratives of art teacher identity. *Studies in Art Education, 56*(3), 199–213. https://doi.org/10.1080/00393541.2 015.11518963

Ladson-Billings, G. J. (1998). Just what is critical race theory and what's it doing in a nice field like education? *International Journal of Qualitative Studies in Education, 11*(1), 7–24. https://doi.org/10.1080/095183998236863

Ladson-Billings, G. J. (1999). Preparing teachers for diverse student populations: A critical race theory perspective. *Review of Research in Education, 24*(1), 211–247. https://doi.org /10.3102/0091732X024001211

Ladson-Billings, G. J. (2003). It's your world, I'm just trying to explain it: Understanding our epistemological and methodological challenges. *Qualitative Inquiry, 9*(1), 5–12. https:// doi.org/10.1177/1077800402239333

Ladson-Billings, G. J. (2006). From the achievement gap to the education debt: Understanding achievement in U.S. schools. *Educational Researcher, 35*(7), 3–12. https://doi.org/10.310 2/0013189X035007003

Ladson-Billings, G., & Tate, W. (1995). Toward a critical race theory of education. *Teachers College Record, 97*(1), 47–68.

Lather, P. (1998). Critical pedagogy and its complicities: A praxis of stuck places. *Educational theory, 48*(4), 487–497. https://doi.org/10.1111/j.1741-5446.1998.00487.x

Lawrence, C. (1992). The word and the river: Pedagogy as scholarship as struggle. *Southern California Law Review, 65,* 2231-2298.

Lee, T. (2009). Language, identity, and power: Navajo and Pueblo young adults' perspectives and experiences with competing language ideologies. *Journal of Language, Identity, and Education, 8*(5), 307–320. https://doi.org/10.1080/15348450903305106

Liu, K. (2015). Critical reflection as a framework for transformative learning in teacher educa- tion. *Educational Review, 67*(2), 135–157. https://doi.org/10.1080/00131911.2013.83 9546

Liu, K. (2017). Creating a dialogic space for prospective teacher critical reflection and trans- formative learning. *Reflective Practice, 18*(6), 805–820. https://doi.org/10.1080/146239 43.2017.1361919

Liu, K., & Ball, A. F. (2019). Critical reflection and generativity: Toward a framework of transformative teacher education for diverse learners. *Review of Research in Education, 43*(1), 68–105. https://doi.org/10.3102/0091732X18822806

Love, B. J. (2004). *Brown* plus 50 counter-storytelling: A critical race theory analysis of the "majoritarian achievement gap" story. *Equity & Excellence in Education, 37*(3), 227–246. https://doi.org/10.1080/10665680490491597

Lynn, M. (2006). Education for the community: Exploring the culturally relevant practices of Black male teachers. *Teachers College Record, 108*(12), 2497–2522. https://doi.org/10.1111/j.1467-9620.2006.00792.x

Matsuda, M. J. (1991). Voices of America: Accent, antidiscrimination law, and a jurisprudence for the last reconstruction. *Yale Law Journal, 100*(5), 1329–1407. https://doi.org/10.2307/796694

Matsuda, M. J. (1993). Public response to racist speech: Considering the victim's story. In M. J. Matsuda, C. R. Lawrence III, R. Delgado, & K. Williams Crenshaw (Eds.), *Words that wound: Critical race theory, assaultive speech, and the first amendment* (pp. 17–52). Westview. https://doi.org/10.4324/9780429502941-2

Matsuda, M. (1995). Looking to the bottom: Critical legal studies and reparations. In K. Crenshaw, N. Gotanda, G. Peller, & K. Thomas (Eds). *Critical race theory: The key writings that formed the movement* (pp. 63–79). New Press.

Matsuda, M., Lawrence, C., Delgado, R., & Crenshaw, K. (Eds.). (1993). *Words that wound: critical race theory, assaultive speech and the first amendment*. Westview.

Mensah, F. M. (2019). Finding voice and passion: Critical race theory methodology in science teacher education. *American Educational Research Journal, 56*(4), 1412–1456. https://doi.org/10.3102/0002831218818093

Mezirow, J. (Ed.). (1990). *Fostering critical reflection in adulthood: A guide to transformative and emancipatory learning*. Jossey-Bass.

Mezirow, J. (2000). *Learning as transformation: Critical perspectives on a theory in progress*. Jossey Bass.

Milner, H. R., IV. (2007). Race, culture, and researcher positionality: Working through dangers seen, unseen, and unforeseen. *Educational Researcher, 36*(7), 388–400. https://doi.org/10.3102/0013189X07309471

Milner, H. R., IV. (2008). Disrupting deficit notions of difference: Counter-narratives of teachers and community in urban education. *Teaching and Teacher Education, 24*(6), 1573–1598. https://doi.org/10.1016/j.tate.2008.02.011

Milner, H. R., IV. (2012a). Beyond a test score: Explaining opportunity gaps in educational practice. *Journal of Black Studies, 43*(6), 693–718. https://doi.org/10.1177/0021934712442539

Milner, H. R. (2012b). Challenging negative perceptions of Black teachers. *Educational Foundations, 26*(1–2), 27–46.

Milner, H. R. IV., & Howard, T. C. (2013). Counter-narrative as method: Race, policy and research for teacher education. *Race Ethnicity and Education, 16*(4), 536–561. https://doi.org/10.1080/13613324.2013.817772

Morris, J. E. (2008). Research, ideology, and the Brown decision: Counter-narratives to the historical and contemporary representation of Black schooling. *Teachers College Record, 110*(4), 713–732.

Motha, S., & Vargese, M. (2018). Rewriting dominant narratives of the academy: Women faculty of color and identity management. *Race Ethnicity and Education, 21*(4), 503–517. https://doi.org/10.1080/13613324.2016.1248826

Mungo, S. (2013). Our own communities, our own schools: Educational counter-narratives of African American civil rights generation students. *Journal of Negro Education, 82*(2), 111–122. https://doi.org/10.7709/jnegroeducation.82.2.0111

Ngunjuri, F. W. (2007). Painting a counter-narrative of African womanhood: Reflections on how my research transformed me. *Journal of Research Practice, 3*(1), 1–13.

Orfield, G., & Yun, J. T. (1999). *Resegregation in American schools*. Harvard University Press. https://civilrightsproject.ucla.edu/research/k-12-education/integration-and-diversity/resegregation-in-american-schools/orfiled-resegregation-in-american-schools-1999.pdf

Rodríguez, L. F., & Greer, W. (2017). (Un)Expected scholars: Counter-narratives from two (boys) men of color across the educational pipeline. *Equity & Excellence in Education, 50*(1), 108–120. https://doi.org/10.1080/10665684.2016.1256004

Rogers, C. A., & Jaime, A. M. (2010). Listening to the community: Guidance from Native community members for emerging culturally responsive educators. *Equity & Excellence in Education, 43*(2), 188–201. https://doi.org/10.1080/10665681003719657

Romero, A., Arce, M. S., & Cammarota, J. (2009). A Barrio pedagogy: Identity, intellectualism, activism, and academic achievement through the evolution of critically compassionate intellectualism. *Race Ethnicity and Education, 12*(2), 217–233.

Russell, J. S. (1986). The critical legal studies challenge to contemporary mainstream legal philosophy. *Ottawa Law Review, 18*(1), 1–24.

Salinas, C. S., Fránquiz, M. E., & Rodríguez, N. N. (2016). Writing Latina/o historical narratives: Narratives at the intersection of critical historical inquiry and LatCrit. *Urban Review, 48*(2), 264–284. https://doi.org/10.1007/s11256-016-0355-z

Sealey-Ruiz, Y. (2013). Learning to resist: Educational counter-narratives of Black college reentry mothers. *Teachers College Record, 115,* 1–31.

Shapiro, T., Meschede, T., & Osoro, S. (2013). *The roots of the widening racial wealth gap: Explaining the Black-White economic divide* (Research and Policy Brief). Brandeis University Institute on Assets and Social Policy.

Shiller, J. (2018). The disposability of Baltimore's Black communities: A participatory action research project on the impact of school closings. *Urban Review, 50*(1), 23–44. https://doi.org/10.1007/s11256-017-0428-7

Skiba, R. J., Arredondo, M. I., & Williams, N. T. (2014). More than a metaphor: The contribution of exclusionary discipline to a school-to-prison pipeline. *Equity & Excellence in Education, 47*(4), 546–564, https://doi.org/10.1080/10665684.2014.958965

Skiba, R. J., Horner, R. H., Chung, C., Rausch, M. K., May, S. L., & Tobin, T. (2011). Race is not neutral: A national investigation of African American and Latino disproportionality in school discipline. *School Psychology Review, 40*(1), 85–107.

Skiba, R. J., Michael, R. S., Nardo, A. C., & Peterson, R. L. (2002). The color of discipline: Sources of racial and gender disproportionality in school punishment. *Urban Review, 34*(4), 317–342. https://doi.org/10.1023/A:1021320817372

Solórzano, D. G. (1997). Images and words that wound: Critical race theory, racial stereotyping, and teacher education. *Teacher Education Quarterly, 24*(3), 5–19. https://www.jstor.org/stable/23478088

Solórzano, D. G., & Bernal, D. D. (2001). Examining transformational resistance through a critical race and LatCrit theory framework: Chicana and Chicano students in an urban context. *Urban Education, 36*(3), 308–342. https://doi.org/10.1177/0042085901363002

Solórzano, D. G., & Yosso, T. J. (2001). Critical Race and LatCrit theory and method: Counter-storytelling. *Qualitative Studies in Education, 14*(4), 471–495. https://doi.org/10.1080/09518390110063365

Solórzano, D. G., & Yosso, T. J. (2002). Critical race methodology: Counter-storytelling as an analytical framework for education research. *Qualitative Inquiry, 8*(1), 23–44. https://doi.org/10.1177/107780040200800103

Solórzano, D. G., & Yosso, T. J. (2009). Critical race methodology: Counter-storytelling as an analytical framework for educational research. In E. Taylor, D. Gilborn, & G. Ladson-Billings (Eds.), *Foundations of critical race theory in education* (131–147). Routledge.

Stanley, C. A. (2007). When counter narratives meet master narratives in the journal editorial-review process. *Educational Researcher, 36*(1), 14–24. https://doi.org/10.3102/0013189X06298008

Strauss, J., & Corbin, A. (1990). *Basics of qualitative research: Grounded theory procedures and techniques.* Sage.

Tafari, D. N. H. (2018). "Whose world is this?": A composite counterstory of Black male elementary school teachers as Hip-Hop other fathers. *Urban Review, 50*(5), 795–817. https://doi.org/10.1007/s11256-018-0471-z

Taylor, E. (2009). The foundations of critical race theory in education: An introduction. In E. Taylor, D. Gilborn, & G. Ladson-Billings (Eds.), *Foundations of critical race theory in education* (pp. 1–13). Routledge.

Thomas, M., & Liu, K. (2012). The performance of reflection: A grounded analysis of prospective teachers' eportfolios. *Journal of Technology and Teacher Education, 20*(3), 305–330.

Trevino, A. J., Harris, M. A., & Wallace, D. (2008). What's so critical about critical race theory? *Contemporary Justice Review, 11*(1), 7–10. https://doi.org/10.1080/10282580701850330

Vaught, S. E. (2012). "They might as well be Black": The racialization of Sa'moan high school students. *International Journal of Qualitative Studies in Education, 25*(5), 557–582. https://doi.org/10.1080/09518398.2010.538746

Villenas, S., Dehyle, D., & Parker, L. (1999). Critical race theory and praxis: Chicano(a)/Latino(a) and Navajo struggles for dignity, educational equity, and social justice. In L. Parker, D. Dehyle, & S. Villenas. (Eds.) *Race is . . . race isn't: Critical race theory and qualitative studies in education* (pp. 31–52). Westview. https://doi.org/10.4324/9780429503504-3

Vygotsky, L. S. (1978). *Mind and society.* Harvard University Press.

Williams, K., Burt, B., Clay, K., & Bridge, B. (2019). Stories untold: Counter-narratives to anti- Blackness and deficit-oriented discourse concerning HBCUs. *American Educational Research Journal, 56*(2), 556–599. https://doi.org/10.3102/0002831218802776

Williams, N. A., & Ware, C. (2019). A tale of two "halfs:" Being black, while being biracial. *International Journal of Qualitative Studies in Education, 32*(1), 85–106. https://doi.org/10.1080/09518398.2018.1548036

Wilson, C. M. (2016). Enacting critical care and transformative leadership in schools highly impacted by poverty: An African American principal's counter narrative. *International Journal of Leadership in Education, 19*(5), 557–577. https://doi.org/10.1080/13603124.2015.1023360

Wilson, H. (2014). Turning off the school-to-prison pipeline. *Reclaiming Children and Youth, 23*(1), 49–53.

Yosso, T. J. (2006). *Critical race counterstories along the Chicana/Chicano educational pipeline.* Routledge.

Zeichner, K. (2014). The struggle for the soul of teaching and teacher education. *Journal of Education for Teaching, 40*(5), 551–568. https://doi.org/10.1080/02607476.2014.956544

Chapter 11

How Administrative Data Collection and Analysis Can Better Reflect Racial and Ethnic Identities

SAMANTHA VIANO
George Mason University

DOMINIQUE J. BAKER
Southern Methodist University

Measuring race and ethnicity for administrative data sets and then analyzing these data to understand racial/ethnic disparities present many logistical and theoretical challenges. In this chapter, we conduct a synthetic review of studies on how to effectively measure race/ethnicity for administrative data purposes and then utilize these measures in analyses. Recommendations based on this synthesis include combining the measure of Hispanic ethnicity with the broader racial/ethnic measure and allowing individuals to select more than one race/ethnicity. Data collection should rely on self-reports but could be supplemented using birth certificates or equivalent sources. Collecting data over time, especially for young people, will help identify multiracial and American Indian populations. For those with more complex racial/ethnic identities, including measures of country of origin, language, and recency of immigration can be helpful in addition to asking individuals which racial/ethnic identity they most identify with. Administrative data collection could also begin to incorporate phenotype measures to facilitate the calculation of disparities within race/ethnicity by skin tone. Those analyzing racial/ethnic disparities should understand how these measures are created and attempt to develop fieldwide terminology to describe racial/ethnic identities.

Advances in the use of comprehensive administrative data sets have allowed researchers to answer significant questions focused on educational policy and practice (Connelly et al., 2016; Figlio et al., 2017). Mirroring these advancements is a growing literature that problematizes conventional racial and ethnic (R/E) categories by developing theoretical models that include additional layers of individual

Review of Research in Education
March 2020, Vol. 44, pp. 301–331
DOI: 10.3102/0091732X20903321
Chapter reuse guidelines: sagepub.com/journals-permissions
© 2020 AERA. http://rre.aera.net

identity (Ladson-Billings, 2012; Monroe, 2013; Pang et al., 2011), a movement spurred by the acknowledgment that R/E has been undertheorized in education research (King, 2016). While, arguably, those working on both of these advances in the literature have similarly equity-minded goals, combining these two approaches remains a challenge (Dixon-Román, 2017). Administrative data sets—information gathered about an entire population of individuals often collected by the government (Figlio et al., 2017)—tend to include a limited range of categories for R/E, and quantitative researchers often utilize even fewer of these categories in analysis (e.g., combining smaller R/E groups into an "other" category) to create parsimonious models (Denton & Deane, 2010; Ladson-Billings, 2012). At the same time, some critical race theorists, building on a theory that has been discussed for over a hundred years (DuBois, 1899; Jones, 1998),[1] suggest that quantitative analysis is unsuitable for studying inequality and outcomes based on R/E due to the history of the development of statistics in conjunction with racist movements like eugenics (Covarrubias & Vélez, 2013; Gillborn et al., 2018; Zuberi & Bonilla-Silva, 2008).

Prior research on the use of R/E in the social sciences has often focused on the actual collection and categorization of R/E data (e.g., Denton & Deane, 2010) and how participants are categorized into R/E groups, with less attention paid to how researchers then use those categorizations in their analyses. In this synthesis, we compile the knowledge and insights from this literature to further the field's understanding of how to measure R/E in administrative data and then analyze these data to understand trends and disparities by R/E. For the purposes of this study, we use the definition of administrative data used by Figlio et al. (2017). Administrative data sets in education are collected by schools across the K–16 pipeline (a) that include a census of all students (and possibly employees) in that school or institution, (b) that are collected for administrative purposes, and (c) with the school, institution, or their management organizations "owning" the data (though researchers can apply for access). Since administrative data are a census of all students, they provide the opportunity for additional analysis focused on all students beyond the capacity of analysis of survey data. Collecting and analyzing administrative data about R/E are important for education researchers and administrators to be able to address the unique needs of different student groups, particularly in light of the persistent disparities in the experiences and outcomes of certain students.

The goal of this chapter is to create a resource for both researchers with access to administrative data and practitioners managing administrative data systems. While quantitative researchers tend to utilize R/E measures from administrative data sets without recognizing the flaws in these measures, we will review reasons for concern and suggestions for improving the validity and reliability of these measures. The ultimate purpose of this study is to challenge theorists and methodologists to develop new frameworks that will be more sensitive to complicated R/E identities while also being plausible for those using administrative data sets. The following section acts as the guiding framework for this review through summarizing a broad overview of contemporary perspectives on the measurement and analysis of quantitative data on R/E. We juxtapose the overall approaches of those who study critical race theory and their views on quantitative R/E measurement with traditional quantitative researchers. We then describe how we utilize these viewpoints as a conceptual framework guiding our review followed by a description of our methods and results.

IMPORTANT CHALLENGES IN MEASUREMENT AND ANALYSIS OF RACE/ETHNICITY

Both individual R/E identities and R/E categories are constantly shifting and culture dependent (Denton & Deane, 2010; Liebler et al., 2017; Mihoko Doyle & Kao, 2007). Those who collect data on R/E grapple with questions like whether to ask about a person's color (e.g., Black) or someone's ethnic background (e.g., African American; Davis et al., 2012). There is also considerable heterogeneity in how administrative data sets account for those with multiple racial identities. Measurement and missing data issues create challenges in analyzing R/E data. Below, we review three perspectives on R/E measurement and analysis that help inform our subsequent systematic review: (1) a critical view of quantitative measurement and analysis of R/E most notably from the critical race theory community, (2) the perspective of quantitative researchers who engage in research on R/E, and (3) contemporary scholarship seeking to combine critical race theory with quantitative methods, specifically the developments around a QuantCrit framework. We recognize that each perspective includes several additional viewpoints and epistemologies. As we outline these perspectives to provide background for the larger literature review, we focus on providing a generalized overview.

Critical Race Theory and Measurement/Analysis of Race/Ethnicity

Many scholars have written about the inherent flaws in using quantitative methods to research R/E (e.g., Zuberi, 2001). The most prominent and historical argument traces back to the roots of the development of statistics itself. Francis Galton is known as one of the most influential statisticians in the modern era having invented some of the core tools of quantitative analysis including correlations. A half cousin to Charles Darwin, Galton sought to extend the theory of evolution into modern human reproduction by using quantitative analysis (Roberts, 2011). Galton was the founder of the eugenics movement and justified the movement by utilizing statistics to create the illusion that science backed up its tenets. To Galton, the measurability of race was for nefarious purposes—to prove his hypothesis that some races were superior to others (Covarrubias & Vélez, 2013; Sablan, 2019; Zuberi, 2001). The destruction that was caused by the eugenics movement, including genocide, mass sterilization, and pseudo-scientifically based subjugation, and its continued legacy today in the White nationalism movement cannot be denied. In education, eugenics was influential in the creation of many common policies that persist today, including tracking and test score–based college admissions (Stoskopf, 1999; Winfield, 2007)—both policies that evidence indicates continue to privilege White students over students of color (e.g., Dixon-Román, 2017; Grissom & Redding, 2015; Kobrin et al., 2007; Santelices & Wilson, 2010). Responding to the popularity of eugenics-based arguments, some of the earliest writing from W. E. B. DuBois pointed out that statistical arguments of racial inferiority ignored significant heterogeneity within Black populations as well as systemic racism (DuBois, 1899). While DuBois himself utilized quantitative data to create some of the first data visualizations (see Battle-Baptiste & Rusert, 2018), in *White Logic: White Methods*, Zuberi and Bonilla-Silva (2008) argue that the eugenics-based thinking that underlies all statistical analyses was infused within the academy such that physical and social sciences themselves have aided in the continuation of racial stratification as both scientifically legitimate and socially acceptable (Zuberi & Bonilla-Silva, 2008). Even though eugenics itself was disavowed decades ago within the academy, it remains difficult to utilize the statistical tools created by eugenicists to study R/E in ways that do not lead to perpetuating that inequality.

Scientists have now come to the consensus that race is not biological; it is socially constructed (Covarrubias & Vélez, 2013; N. M. Garcia et al., 2018; Gillborn et al., 2018; Ladson-Billings, 2012). R/E has salience for individuals only to the extent that they can self-identify with a particular R/E identity or that others categorize them with one. In addition, R/E self-identification is variable, depending on a variety of elements within the context, such as macropolitical environment or age of the individual (e.g., Liebler et al., 2017; Mihoko Doyle & Kao, 2007; Roberts, 2011). Therefore, the extent to which those who manage administrative data and analyze these data conceptualize the socially constructed and mutable nature of R/E and how it conflicts with how the individuals in the data self-identify determines how useful the data actually are.

Critical race theory in education positions structural inequality, racism, and White supremacy as inherent aspects of educational system/outcomes, acting as a framework for conceptualizing research and interpreting findings on R/E inequality (Ladson-Billings, 1998; Ladson-Billings & Tate, 1995). Stemming from the eugenics-based arguments, critical race theorists have identified three challenges to the use of quantitative measurement and analysis of R/E: claims of neutrality/objectivity, lack of discussion/recognition of power and structural aspects of racism, and White dominance in the academy. One of the central tenets of critical race theory is that any study of R/E is subjective and context dependent. This directly contradicts the argument that quantitative research is neutral, objective, and generalizable (Carbado & Roithmayr, 2014; N. M. Garcia et al., 2018; Gillborn et al., 2018; Sablan, 2019). Critical race theorists argue that quantitative research cannot be as neutral and objective as is claimed because quantitative researchers make many decisions about measurement and analysis that remain as artifacts in their results (Covarrubias & Vélez, 2013; Zuberi & Bonilla-Silva, 2008). Quantitative research also tends to focus on R/E as an individual experience. Critical race theorists recognize that racism is also structural, organizational, and institutional in addition to individual (Carbado &

Roithmayr, 2014; N. M. Garcia et al., 2018; Gillborn et al., 2018; Sablan, 2019; Tatum, 2017). Traditional quantitative researchers tend to ignore these more structural elements, focusing more on aggregating individual trends using unclear definitions of R/E.

Quantitative Perspectives on Measurement and Analysis of Race/Ethnicity

There has been little engagement between critical race theory and quantitative scholarship (Covarrubias & Vélez, 2013; Sablan, 2019). As Ladson-Billings (2012) wrote, education researchers have typically utilized R/E with a lack of attention or understanding that the categories they utilize are superficial and constructed using naïve understandings of class and race that are then imbued with deficit-oriented markers of inferiority and superiority. While some quantitative researchers raise concerns about valid and reliable measures of R/E (which we will review in this synthesis), the most prominent concerns have to do with the statistical properties of power, precision, and parsimony. These properties are all separate and intricately linked when using frequentist statistics. While none of these concepts determine the validity of a model's results, they are all important aspects of modeling decisions that can affect interpretation. All three are linked in some way to the sample size used in a study. Within the broader U.S. population (excluding studies of subsamples of students), the more complexity the researcher allows for the R/E identity of the sample, the lower the sample size. Therefore, navigating issues with power, precision, and parsimony can create barriers in the minds of some quantitative researchers to allowing additional complexity within R/E measures.

Negotiating the Two Perspectives: QuantCrit and Challenges to Quantitative Orthodoxy

A community of scholars has been purposefully attempting to combine critical race theory with quantitative research methods, calling this methodology QuantCrit (Sablan, 2019). The goal of these efforts is to create a space for quantitative research that engages with critical race theory authentically. To do so, QuantCrit scholars start by recognizing the flaws in quantitative research that quantitative researchers do not typically address (Covarrubias & Vélez, 2013; N. M. Garcia et al., 2018; Gillborn et al., 2018; Sablan, 2019). First, as noted above, R/E is socially constructed, and quantitative research needs to recognize that race is not biologically determined and static (Covarrubias & Vélez, 2013; N. M. Garcia et al., 2018; Gillborn et al., 2018). Second, QuantCrit work needs to differentiate itself from other quantitative research by taking a clearly subjective stance; recognizing that the analyst cannot be separated from the analysis is an essential component of QuantCrit (Covarrubias & Vélez, 2013). QuantCrit scholars also suggest that work should recognize the structural elements of racism (Carbado & Roithmayr, 2014; N. M. Garcia et al., 2018; Gillborn et al., 2018; Sablan, 2019). This work also needs to recognize that research and training for quantitative analysis almost exclusively occurs within White spaces, and this will be reflected in the analysis in some conscious or unconscious way (Covarrubias & Vélez, 2013; Zuberi & Bonilla-Silva, 2008). Finally, QuantCrit needs to take an assets-oriented perspective instead of a deficit-oriented perspective (Sablan, 2019). Through either directly conducting research that avoids these pitfalls and/or being cognizant of these challenges, many are beginning to conduct research on R/E from a critical race theory perspective using quantitative methods.

HOW THESE PERSPECTIVES INFORM THIS SYNTHESIS

This systematic review recognizes the perspectives of critical race theorists, including founders of the QuantCrit framework, and other quantitative researchers. The measurement of R/E has typically lacked the degree of validity to which all parties would aspire. For this review, we seek literature that attempts to improve the validity of measurement and analysis of R/E with a particular focus on insights that are applicable to administrative data systems. We do not explicitly focus on applying QuantCrit or critical race theory to this study, we seek to be more informed by multiple perspectives on the validity and reliability of measures of R/E with a focus on administrative data.

As is recognized by QuantCrit scholars, estimates from administrative systems like the U.S. Census can help define racial inequity (Sablan, 2019). We focus on administrative data for its potential to influence policymaking and address inequality, and our review includes research that pertains directly to administrative data collection. Unlike sampling-based survey data sets, administrative data have to be collected in an efficient manner and cannot rely on weighting to account for small samples of certain R/E groups. At the same time, deciding on measures is challenging because often administrative data sets are compared with each other. How to collect and measure R/E in administrative data is a distinct challenge from analyzing survey data, especially when comparing across systems that use different R/E measures. In this review, we focus on studies that address one or both of the following questions:

1. How can scholars measure R/E in administrative data sets in the United States that takes into account how individuals self-identify, multiple identities, and shifting identities?
2. How can scholars include R/E in analyses of administrative data sets in the United States that are able to take into account multiple identities, shifting identities, and small R/E subgroups?

METHOD

We conducted searches of the Google Scholar and ProQuest databases and supplemented these searches by reviewing references lists of the resulting articles. For both searches, we used the following search terms: "race OR ethnic OR ethnicity OR racial" and "quantitative OR administrative OR classification OR measure OR measuring OR 'secondary data.'" The use of administrative databases in education dramatically increased in the past 15 years due to legislative pressure and incentives for states to maintain these databases as well as growing technological capacity to house and analyze these data. To reflect this shift, we bound our search to only include studies from 2001 to 2019 (the passage of the No Child Left Behind Act; McGuinn, 2015).[2] We focused on peer-reviewed studies for this synthesis because we are not as concerned with publication bias since the studies in this review do not rely on significant effects to increase chances of publication. This restriction was included in the ProQuest search (this could not be included in the Google Scholar search). Finally, we restricted our search to only include articles written in English.

We used three different phases of review to arrive at the final set of articles for the current study. In the first phase, we conducted the search outlined above in both ProQuest and Google Scholar. The ProQuest search resulted in 808 articles and the Google Scholar search resulted in 1,085 articles for a total of 1,893. The lead author compiled these searches into a single document, which included the article's title, authors, publication date, and abstract, if available. A group of four researchers jointly reviewed a small set of the articles (30) to determine which articles needed to be excluded based on the exclusion criteria (whether the article included discussion of quantitative data measurement and classification of R/E categories, was published in a peer-reviewed journal, and was written in English). Then the four researchers met and discussed their selections to create a shared understanding of which articles should be excluded. Once consensus was met, the four researchers split all of the compiled list of results into equal sections and reviewed the articles for exclusion. This resulted in 1,714 articles being excluded. These articles were excluded for the following reasons: duplicate of another article already included (190), not being written in English (16), no discussion of quantitative data measurement (220), no classification of R/E (1,224), and not being peer reviewed (283). These numbers do not sum to 1,708 as several articles fit into multiple categories for exclusion. The first author then reviewed this final list for any improperly excluded articles. This added back 18 articles.

In the second phase of the review, the resulting 197 articles were reviewed by the authors for the additional exclusion criteria of articles that do not include the U.S. context (58), focus on racial identity formation (specifically the psychometric properties and usefulness of Multigroup Ethnic Identity Measure), or utilize technology incompatible with administrative data collection (e.g., facial recognition technology; 15). This round of the review resulted in 73 articles being excluded and 124 articles included in the analytical set.

In the third, and final, phase of the review process, the two authors and one trained graduate assistant split the list of all of the final articles and read each article. During the review of the full articles, we again evaluated articles based on the exclusion restrictions while also noting additional literature that the articles highlighted as critical to R/E classification and administrative data analysis. Through this process, we added an additional 21 articles to the literature review. At this phase, an additional 90 articles were excluded. We excluded these articles for the following reasons: no inclusion of quantitative data measurement (12),[3] no discussion of the classification of R/E (15),[4] no U.S. context (24), the discussion of R/E classification is not applicable to administrative databases (36),[5] and the article was not peer reviewed (12). These numbers do not sum to 90 as several articles fit into multiple categories for exclusion. Therefore, at the end of the final phase of review, we included 55 articles in the current study.

During the third phase of review, the authors wrote analytical summaries of each included article. Once this was completed, the first author reviewed all the summaries and created categories for the emergent themes across the articles. The second author then reviewed this analysis, refined the category definitions, and reviewed the category classification of all articles. The first author then reviewed the second author's revisions and incorporated them into the final analysis.

RESULTS

Based on our review of the literature, we found the overarching themes of (1) measuring R/E, (2) missing R/E data, and (3) analysis including R/E data. We discuss each theme along with key challenges to the use of R/E measures.

Measuring Race/Ethnicity

One clear pattern across the 55 studies included in this research synthesis was the heterogeneity in approaches to measuring R/E. Between changes over time, differences across populations, and methodological choices, measuring R/E was conceptualized in dozens of ways across the 55 studies. For instance, see Table 1 for an illustration of how R/E measures have changed over time in one data set (N. M. Garcia & Mayorga, 2018). In this section, we review several themes in measuring R/E, including universal measures, federal agency guidance, pan-ethnicity measurement challenges, reliability and validity of measures, and considering alternative measurement approaches.

Universal Measures of Race/Ethnicity

Several studies advocated for a universal measurement system for R/E (Buescher et al., 2005; Idossa et al., 2018; Mays et al., 2003; Moscou et al., 2003). Among the suggestions, successful universal R/E measurement system would rely on self-reporting, include comprehensive options for ethnic identification, and have clearly defined R/E terms (Idossa et al., 2018; Moscou et al., 2003). Mays et al. (2003) specifically suggested that the federal government develops a universal R/E taxonomy that has consistent classification categories that are mutually exclusive, includes categories that are consistent with how individuals think of themselves, and facilitates reliable responses from individuals and valid analytical methods (Mays et al., 2003). When

TABLE 1
The Freshmen Survey: Racial/Ethnic Survey Question 1965–2014

Year	Question	Racial/Ethnic Category
1965–1968	What is your racial background? (Circle one/mark one)	• Caucasian • Negro • American Indian • Oriental • Other
1969	What is your racial background? (Mark one)	• White/Caucasian • Black/Negro/Afro-American • American Indian • Oriental
1970	Are you: (Mark one)	• White/Caucasian • Black/Negro/Afro-American • American Indian • Oriental
1971–1975	Are you: (Mark all that apply)	• White/Caucasian • Black/Negro/Afro-American • American Indian • Oriental • Mexican American/Chicano • Puerto Rican American • Other
1976–1989	Are you: (Mark all that apply)	• White/Caucasian • Black/Negro/Afro-American • American Indian • Asian American/Oriental • Mexican American/Chicano • Puerto Rican American • Other
1990–1992	Are you: (Mark all that apply)	• White/Caucasian • Black/African American • American Indian • Asian American/Oriental • Mexican American/Chicano • Puerto Rican American • Other • Other Latino

(continued)

TABLE 1 (CONTINUED)

Year	Question	Racial/Ethnic Category
1993–1996	Are you: (Mark all that apply)	• White/Caucasian • Black/African American • American Indian • Asian American/Asian	• Mexican American/Chicano • Puerto Rican • Other Latino • Other
1997	Are you: (Mark all that apply)	• White/Caucasian • Black/African American • American Indian • Mexican American/Chicano • Puerto Rican • Other Latino • Chinese American/Chinese	• Filipino American/Filipino • Japanese American/Japanese • Korean American/Korean • Southeast Asian (Vietnamese, Laotian, Cambodian, etc.) • Other Asian American/Asian • Other
1998–2000	Are you: (Mark all that apply)	• White/Caucasian • Black/African American • American Indian • Asian American/Asian	• Mexican American/Chicano • Puerto Rican • Other Latino • Other
2001–2014	Are you: (Mark all that apply)	• White/Caucasian • Black/African American • American Indian/Alaska Native • Native Hawaiian/Pacific Islander • Asian American/Asian	• Mexican American/Chicano • Puerto Rican • Other Latino • Other

Note. Reprinted from N. M. Garcia and Mayorga (2018). Used with permission.

discussing a national model birth certificate that includes R/E classification, Buescher et al. (2005) cautioned that while standard categories increase reliability and facilitates comparisons across states, standardization does not mean R/E will have salience when people do not understand the concept of R/E such that "a broadly defined racial group is at best a crude marker . . . certainly not a risk factor or cause" (Buescher et al., 2005, p. 397). While all administrative data systems in the United States do not currently use a universal R/E classification system (e.g., different states can determine the definition of their R/E measures), the closest measure we have are those utilized by the U.S. Census Bureau as well as other federal agencies.

U.S. Census Bureau and Federal Agency Guidance on Measuring Race/Ethnicity

The U.S. Census has collected data on R/E since 1790 with significant changes in measurement and categories over time (Kilty, 2004; Mays et al., 2003; Rodriguez, 2000). The modern R/E Census categories were based on the Office of Management & Budget Directive 15 from 1977 that specified race should be reported in four mutually exclusive categories: White, Black, American Indian or Alaskan Native, and Asian or Pacific Islander. Ethnicity was categorized as Hispanic or not of Hispanic origin (Mays et al., 2003). Prior to this directive, there was no Census question on Hispanic origin with those who identified as being from Latin America primarily seen as White (Idossa et al., 2018; Mora, 2014). See Table 2 for a visual representation of how R/E categories have changed over time on the U.S. Census.

Race/ethnicity measurement on modern Census forms. Studies on the 1990, 2000, and 2010 Census focused on several specific measurement choices that had greatly affected R/E counts. For all of these Census administrations, two separate questions asked about race and Spanish/Hispanic origin. Those of Spanish/Hispanic origin in the 1990 Census were the largest group to mark "Other" for their race (Mays et al., 2003), with 97% of those who selected "some other race" in 2000 identifying as Spanish/Hispanic/Latino and 42% of Spanish/Hispanic/Latino respondents selecting "some other race" (Campbell & Rogalin, 2006).

Other changes in the 2000 Census were in direct response to advocacy groups lobbying for recognition of specific R/E groups. The biggest change allowed respondents for the first time to select more than one R/E category (Aspinall, 2003; Idossa et al., 2018; Mays et al., 2003; Prewitt, 2005, 2018). While many advocated for this change, civil rights advocates, including the National Association for the Advancement of Colored People (NAACP), were concerned that allowing multi-R/E selection would diminish the size of discrete minority populations (Prewitt, 2005, 2018). While R/E count estimates did not markedly change, almost 2 million people selected Black and another R/E category (Campbell, 2007).

Persistent challenges for race/ethnicity measurement on the Census. After no substantive changes were made to R/E measurement in the 2010 Census, many persistent

TABLE 2

Changes in U.S. Census Race Categories From 1850 to 2000 (No Changes in 2010)

Year	White	Black	Native People	Chinese	Japanese	Other Asian or Pacific Islander	Other
1850		Black, mulatto					
1860		Black, mulatto	Indian				
1870	White	Black, mulatto	Indian	Chinese			
1880	White	Black, mulatto	Indian	Chinese			
1890	White	Black, mulatto, quadroon, octoroon	Indian	Chinese	Japanese		
1900	White	Black	Indian	Chinese	Japanese		
1910	White	Black, mulatto	Indian	Chinese	Japanese	Filipino, Hindu, Korean	Other (+ write in)
1920	White	Black, mulatto	Indian	Chinese	Japanese	Filipino, Hindu, Korean	Other (+ write in)
1930[a]	White	Negro	Indian	Chinese	Japanese	Filipino, Hindu, Korean	Other races, spell out in full
1940	White	Negro	Indian	Chinese	Japanese	Filipino, Hindu, Korean	(Other races, spell out in full)
1950	White	Negro	American Indian	Chinese	Japanese	Filipino	(Other races, spell out)
1960	White	Negro	American Indian	Chinese	Japanese	Filipino, Hawaiian, part Hawaiian, etc.	Other (print race)
1970	White	Negro or Black	Indian (American)	Chinese	Japanese	Filipino, Hawaiian, Korean	Other (specify)
1980	White	Black or Negro	Indian (American), Eskimo, Aleut	Chinese	Japanese	Filipino, Korean, Vietnamese, Asian Indian, Hawaiian, Guamanian, Samoan	
1990	White	Black or Negro	Indian (American), Eskimo, Aleut	Chinese	Japanese	Filipino, Hawaiian, Korean, Vietnamese, Asian Indian, Samoan, Guamanian, other Asian or Pacific Islander	Other race
2000	White	Black, African American, or Negro	American Indian or Alaska Native	Chinese	Japanese	Filipino, Hawaiian, Korean, Vietnamese, Asian Indian, Samoan, Guamanian, other Asian or Pacific Islander	Some other race (specify)

Note. See notes on Table 1 in Mays et al. (2003) for more information. Re-created from Mays et al. (2003) with updates.
[a]In the 1930 Census, Mexican was included as a racial category.

challenges and methodological issues remain that could be remedied in a future Census. Chief among these issues is that asking separately about Hispanic origin and race has consistently led to an inflated "other" race category made up predominately of those of Hispanic origin. Federal surveys in general asked these questions separately to not conflate common ancestry, language, and culture (i.e., ethnicity) with common physical/phenotype characteristics (i.e., race; Campbell & Rogalin, 2006; Eisenhower et al., 2014; Mays et al., 2003). However, those who respond to the Census form and other government surveys have been shown to not make the same distinction (Campbell & Rogalin, 2006; Eisenhower et al., 2014). Despite being part of the Census form for several decades, empirical evidence has shown that this distinction between Hispanic origin and R/E is not resulting in valid data differentiating those of Hispanic origin by R/E.

Two specific recommendations for the 2020 Census were made in the literature reviewed. First, combine the separate Hispanic question with the overall question on race for a single R/E question. Respondents would still be able to mark more than one category and write-in options would still be available. The other recommendation was to add "Middle Eastern, North African" as an option on the R/E question. These groups have traditionally been considered White by federal data sets (Prewitt, 2018). Since Prewitt (2018) published this article, the U.S. Census Bureau has submitted a request to keep two separate questions on Hispanic origin and race. The request also specified there would be no separate Middle Eastern, North African category, instead keeping these categories explicitly as part of the White option (U.S. Census Bureau, Commerce Department, 2018).

Despite the importance of the U.S. Census as a model that other administrative data sets can use, scholars have considered different ways to measure R/E that address these persistent challenges. We review many of these advances below but first highlight the challenges of Hispanic pan-ethnicity.

The Hispanic Pan-Ethnicity Presents Specific Measurement Challenges

As discussed above, asking separately about Hispanic origin and race has not successfully led to differentiating ethnicity from race with the plurality of Hispanic respondents choosing "other" as their race (Eisenhower et al., 2014; Haney López, 2005; Hitlin et al., 2007). If given an open response option, Hispanic respondents tended to write in their country/region of origin (Idossa et al., 2018; Landale & Oropesa, 2002), or, on the Census in particular, they wrote in "Latino" (Haney López, 2005). Studies have suggested that more granular measures of R/E would resolve this issue (Hitlin et al., 2007; Prewitt, 2018). These measures could include country of origin, language, religion, migrant status, nationality, skin color, geographic region, and recency of immigration (Aspinall, 2009; DiPietro & Bursik, 2012; J. A. Garcia, 2017; Haney López, 2005; Idossa et al., 2018; Williams & Husk, 2013). Including all of these various alternative ethnicity measures has proven to be politically sensitive at the federal level with concerns about questions related to nativity and citizenship potentially undermining data accuracy and privacy. At the same time, including more specific questions about language and country of origin likely improve reliability, especially for more recent immigrants, as pan-ethnic identity identification has been shown to be less reliable over time especially for adolescents (Feliciano & Rumbaut, 2018, 2019). In addition, while including measures of color (e.g., hair color, facial features, and skin tone) could be illuminating for differentiating inequality within the Hispanic ethnicity, Haney López (2005) argued that the Census and other administrative data collection efforts are unlikely to include these measures for political reasons.

Reliability and Validity of Race/Ethnicity Measures

Across any measure, it is important to be aware of and explicitly examine the reliability and validity of said measure. From a historical perspective, defining R/E has been entirely reliant on cultural norms and time dependent (Roberts, 2011). Defining what it means to be a valid and reliable measure of R/E is in and of itself a difficult enterprise. The included studies focused on assessments of reliability or validity that gauged how frequently these measures might change over time or be recorded inaccurately. We conceptualize measurement reliability of R/E as how consistently individuals report R/E when asked extremely similar questions about their R/E over time. Measurement validity of R/E measures refers to the accuracy of the R/E measures when comparing R/E measures across multiple sources of data, a form of concurrent validity.

Reliability. Issues of reliability tend to focus on those with multi-R/E identities. While allowing individuals to select more than one R/E hypothetically increases the validity of responses (i.e., more accurately represent how people see themselves), many have expressed the concern that this multi-tick option decreases reliability (Aspinall, 2009; Prewitt, 2018). For example, 40% of individuals who checked multiple boxes on the R/E question on the 2000 Census identified as monoracial in a follow-up survey 1 year later (Prewitt, 2018). Another concern is that many multiracial individuals will be more likely to exclusively check the "White" box as they assimilate (Prewitt, 2018). Open-response R/E measures that are often used in conjunction with multi-tick boxes have been shown to be particularly unreliable (Aspinall, 2001). These reliability challenges often stem from the lack of agreement on what it means to claim certain R/E for those whose R/E identification is culturally and temporally dependent. For instance, Roberts (2011) wrote about how President Barack Obama identified solely as Black on the 2010 Census. At other points in his life, he might have identified as White and Black and in other time periods, he would have been identified by Census data collectors as "mulatto."

Several studies examined R/E responses over time of multiracial individuals to examine reliability. For instance, Harris and Sim (2002) compared R/E measures that were collected at school with those collected at home. Twice as many students self-identified as multiracial at school than at home. This change was mostly due to more students identifying as White–American Indian at school than at home. Less than 2% of students consistently identified themselves as multiracial (Harris & Sim, 2002). Another study examined changes in multiracial identification over time (across 6 years) finding that 6% of adolescents changed their R/E, almost half of which went from being monoracial to being multiracial (Hitlin et al., 2006). Just as with the previous study, self-classification change was often due to changing American Indian self-categorization (Harris & Sim, 2002; Hitlin et al., 2006).

Two studies also compared how R/E identification could differ for children based on the R/E of their parents. Both of these studies found that having parents of different races did not necessarily mean that they identified their children as multiracial, and having parents of the same race did not necessarily mean the child would not be multiracial. Multiracial identification was more common when one parent was White or American Indian and the other parent was not (Bratter, 2007). In families with one Black and one White parent, about half identified their child as Black-White, a quarter as Black, a tenth as White, and a tenth as "other" (Roth, 2005).

Other studies examined reliability of R/E more broadly outside of just multi-R/E identities. For instance, Feliciano and Rumbaut (2018, 2019) examined how ethnic self-identity labels change from adolescence to early adulthood among children of immigrants. They found about half of their sample kept the same ethnic identity over time with changes less likely to occur during adulthood. Using pan-ethnic labels or identifying as "American" was common during adolescence but much less common in adulthood (Feliciano & Rumbaut, 2018, 2019).

Craemer (2010) examined if being reminded of genetic or ancestral information would induce changes in R/E self-identification within a short time (5–90 minutes). He found that about 3% of the sample made short-term self-classification changes with American Indian/Alaskan Native, "other," and multiracial categories tending to lose members while Black, Hispanic, and Asian categories tended to gain members (Craemer, 2010). It is possible that R/E self-identification will lose reliability over time as ancestral genetic research gains popularity and specificity.[6]

Validity. Studies assessing the concurrent validity of R/E measures tended to use data from health records and compared records either across health systems or randomly selected individuals to be surveyed about their R/E to compare with their health records. Overall match rates across data sources tended to be around 60% to 70% when restricted to those with complete information (Eisenhower et al., 2014; Kressin et al., 2003; Moscou et al., 2003; Smith et al., 2010). Accuracy tended to be lower for smaller R/E groups. For instance, Kressin et al. (2003) found that agreement rates were 60% for African American, Hispanic, and White but 15% for American Indians. Smith et al. (2010) found accuracy among White records to be 89% and 18% among American Indian/Alaskan Native. Several studies also found that rates of missingness differed across populations with Hispanic individuals more likely to be missing R/E information in one of the sources of data (Eisenhower et al., 2014; Kressin et al., 2003; Maizlish & Herrera, 2006; Smith et al., 2010). Overall, the agreement on R/E across data sets left much to be desired. Authors of these studies encouraged collecting R/E through self-report whenever possible (since this is health care data, on provider visit or hospitalization), linking records to birth certificates, creating measures with more granularity for Hispanic individuals, and uniform data collection procedures (Eisenhower et al., 2014; Kressin et al., 2003; Moscou et al., 2003; Smith et al., 2010).

Considering Alternative Measurement Approaches

Defining race/ethnicity categories. While many have lamented the limitations inherent in common measures of R/E, especially those utilized by the U.S. Census Bureau, the difficult task remains of how to improve the options available for measuring R/E. When deciding on R/E categories, there was an inherent trade-off between statistical reliability and validity (Aspinall, 2001; Buescher et al., 2005; Eisenhower et al., 2014; Williams & Husk, 2013). For instance, the White category was very reliable but can mask important variation and the disadvantages of certain ethnic groups like those from the Middle East in the United States (Williams & Husk, 2013). At the same time, including measures that were increasingly multidimensional might not be practical due to respondent and administrative burden (Aspinall, 2001; Eisenhower et al., 2014). Likely a solution lies in disaggregating some broad categories and by being mindful of the flaws inherent in the chosen approach (Eisenhower et al., 2014; N. M. Garcia & Mayorga, 2018).

Several studies include recommendations when defining R/E categories. First, it is important to think about whether R/E categories should be defined by color (e.g., Black) or by "racial" group (e.g., African American), and this decision can have important implications for how people self-identify (Davis et al., 2012; Eisenhower et al., 2014; Roth, 2010). Eisenhower et al. (2014) suggested using color, while Roth (2010) noted that this decision should be based on what is intended to be measured. Roth (2010) created a schematic framework where racial self-identification can be based on subjective self-identification, the race you tell others, the race others believe you to be, among other options. While R/E measures often intend to separate color from ethnicity, it was difficult to proxy racial differences for those who solely identify with their ethnicity—namely, for those of Hispanic origin (Eisenhower et al., 2014; Roth, 2010). Second, selecting R/E categories can begin by determining the universe of all R/E categories such that the list represents how the majority of individuals would self-classify if asked their R/E. This process needs to be done sensitively as some differentiation lacks salience like differentiating the White population in the United States by European country of origin (Marquardt & Herrera, 2015). Any list of categories utilized in U.S. administrative data sets will likely focus on race rather than on ethnicity since ethnicity is seen as diverting attention away from issues of structural racism and power (Aspinall, 2001). Also, there are individuals throughout the United States who may not know their exact ethnic origins (e.g., Black descendants of slaves).

Most identify/best represents items. One of the causes of unreliable R/E measurement (different responses being selected in different data sets) was allowing respondents to select multiple categories. A proposed measurement solution in the literature to help ameliorate this reliability issue was to follow up on R/E questions with an additional item asking those with multiple responses the R/E they most identify with, or which R/E best represents their identity (Campbell & Rogalin, 2006; Mays et al., 2003; Parker et al., 2004; Williams & Husk, 2013). An item gauging the strength or importance of each dimension of R/E of that person allows for more reliable data since the respondent is less likely to change their most salient identity over time or across data sets. This type of item can also ease analysis (discussed more below) though it does not help when individuals do not identify with one dimension of their R/E more than others (e.g., if their primary identity is multiracial).

Phenotype. R/E is often assumed to measure some sort of common experience and is useful for identifying disparities and discrimination. However, there is great variation in experiences and discrimination within R/E categories. Prior work has found phenotype to be highly influential in educational outcomes with systemic disparities within racial group by skin tone (see Monroe, 2013). Several studies suggested measures for skin tone or phenotype as a way to better measure these within-R/E disparities (Foy et al., 2017; J. A. Garcia, 2017; J. A. Garcia et al., 2015; Roth, 2010). For instance, J. A. Garcia et al. (2015) utilized the question, "We are interested in how you would describe your appearance. How would you describe your skin color with 1 being very light to 5 being very dark or somewhere in between?" (p. 359). While items such as this one have been utilized, more research on the reliability and validity of self-reported phenotype items would be necessary for inclusion in broader administrative data collection.

It is important to point out that differences by phenotype are distinct from differences between internal (subjective self-identification) and observed (the race others assume you to be) R/E (Roth, 2010; Vargas & Kingsbury, 2016). Racial identity contestation refers to when one identifies as one R/E but is perceived by most others as a different R/E. About 6% to 10% of adults experienced racial identity contestation, and it is most common for American Indians, although could become more common over time with increasing rates of interracial marriage (Vargas & Kingsbury, 2016). While it remains rare for administrative data sets to include phenotype, it might be an area to consider especially if the Hispanic option becomes part of the full list of R/E categories since separate R/E questions were designed to assess whether an individual identified as Hispanic separate from their race/phenotype/physical appearance.

Missing Data: An Analysis and Measurement Concern

When quantitative education researchers utilize administrative data sets, it is a general expectation that R/E data will, at the very least, be included as covariates regardless of the analytical design. One of the key problems that can arise, however, is missing data on R/E. Those analyzing administrative data sets, especially in education, likely treat missing data on R/E like any other missing data problem. This would lead to a set of common solutions to missing data, including complete case analysis (i.e., dropping observations with missing R/E), an indicator variable for "missing R/E" to account for missing observations, and multiple imputation (see Thompson et al., 2018). At the same time, a robust literature base in public health, epidemiology, linguistics, and other similarly situated fields has utilized other personal information from administrative data files often in conjunction with advanced statistical methods to address missing R/E information (e.g., Adjaye-Gbewonyo et al., 2014; Fremont et al., 2016; Kilty, 2004; Mateos, 2007). These methods use lists of common first names and/or surnames sometimes in conjunction with geocoded address block or tract-level information to assign a probability of a certain R/E or even a specific R/E.

The original name-based R/E classification systems utilized surnames to assign individuals to an R/E (Kilty, 2004; Mateos, 2007). The U.S. Census Bureau has maintained a Spanish/Hispanic surname list since the mid-20th century to identify Hispanic individuals (Fiscella & Fremont, 2006; Kilty, 2004; Voicu, 2018). Researchers have also developed surname lists to identify Asian surnames, in general, as well as Chinese, Indian, Japanese, Korean, Filipino, and Vietnamese American surnames, specifically (Fiscella & Fremont, 2006; Mateos, 2007). Surname lists in the United States are limited to identifying those that could potentially be Hispanic or Asian with little to no utility in identifying other R/E categories. In other countries, surname lists have been utilized to identify religious groups and those of Middle Eastern descent (Mateos, 2007). Others have created first-name based lists to identify R/E using first name and surname, finding that first names might more accurately identify White individuals than surnames (Tzioumis, 2018). As reference name lists continue to be created, Mateos (2007) cautions researchers to make sure that these lists were based on a large enough population to make valid inferences and to be aware of temporal differences, regional differences, differences in average ratio of people per surname, history of name adoption, and surnames reflecting only patrilineal descent.

The theory behind identifying geocoded addresses was that block groups or neighborhoods tend to be racially homogeneous for certain R/E groups, particularly in more segregated regions of the United States. The method proxied the probability someone is a certain R/E by examining the R/E composition of those who live in close proximity to the individual. This method has been found to be most accurate when identifying Black and White individuals (Elliott et al., 2008; Fiscella & Fremont, 2006) but inaccurate for identifying American Indian/Alaskan Native and/

or multiracial individuals (Fremont et al., 2016; Voicu, 2018). Using geocoded addresses lacks accuracy in regions of the country with lower residential segregation and with non-White and non-Black populations who tended to live in more integrated neighborhoods.

The majority of recent studies within this literature on using addresses/names to account for missing R/E assessed the accuracy of the RAND Corporation's Bayesian Improved Surname Geocoding (BISG) method. Researchers used this method to combine names and geocoded addresses to produce probabilities that an individual is Hispanic, Black, Asian, or White. The method first calculated probabilities using surnames from the Hispanic and/or Asian surname lists followed by updating those probabilities based on geocoded Census blocks. Work assessing the accuracy of BISG did so by comparing these predicted probabilities from the Bayesian model to actual self-reported R/E from administrative data sets (usually from the health field; Adjaye-Gbewonyo et al., 2014; Elliott et al., 2008; Fiscella & Fremont, 2006; Fremont et al., 2016; Grundmeier et al., 2015; Shah & Davis, 2017; Voicu, 2018). A recent article updated the BISG to incorporate an additional step of updating probabilities based on first names, which marginally improved the accuracy of identifying those whose self-reported R/E is Black (Voicu, 2018).

The accuracy and the reported utility of the BISG somewhat differed depending on study. For instance, Fremont et al. (2016) reported that the correlation between BISG estimates and self-reported race was 0.90 to 0.96 for Black, Asian American/Pacific Islanders, Hispanic, and White individuals, although the authors note that RAND discouraged using BISG probabilities to assign individual R/E. Elliott et al. (2008) stated that the average correlation between BISG probabilities and self-report was 0.70. Both studies, while reporting substantially different correlations, suggested using BISG for aggregating disparities overall, or the probabilities themselves could be utilized in regression in place of binary indicators of R/E (Elliott et al., 2008; Fremont et al., 2016). When aggregating estimates, Adjaye-Gbewonyo et al. (2014) suggested a method for determining probability cutoffs to assign R/E that takes the trade-off between inaccuracy and individuals not being assigned to an R/E into account. In their study, they suggested that when individuals have an R/E probability of at least 0.50 to 0.57, they be assigned that R/E although they caution that these cutoffs could change depending on the population. One study explicitly compared BISG with the traditional methods of handling missing data, finding that BISG-enhanced imputation significantly reduced bias compared with complete case analysis, using indicators for missing values, and multiple imputation (Grundmeier et al., 2015).

Analysis Incorporating Race/Ethnicity

Fewer articles in this synthesis critically engage with questions on how to incorporate R/E into quantitative analysis as compared with the literature on the measurement of R/E (14 articles are reviewed in this section versus the 47 included information on measurement). Several essays and reviews pointed out a common theme in including R/E in analysis: doing so without nuance, description, or thoughtfulness. While R/E were socially constructed, studies tended to include R/E as covariates with the assumptions that these variables are independent or causal (N. M. Garcia & Mayorga, 2018; James, 2001; Lee, 2009; Ma et al., 2007). For instance, James (2001) described how race cannot cause things to occur, "Instead of merely 'controlling' for the difference of the aberrant 'others,' racial differences should be assessed and grounded in the set of historical and social circumstances that give meaning to the race concept" (James, 2001, p. 246).

Several articles encouraged researchers to be intentional about common analysis decisions like including R/E as covariates and examining effect heterogeneity by R/E (N. M. Garcia & Mayorga, 2018; James, 2001; Lee, 2009; Ma et al., 2007). Often diversity in R/E was recoded into falsely homogeneous indicators like non-White or "students of color," and these methodological decisions should be explained and acknowledged (N. M. Garcia & Mayorga, 2018). Other suggestions included clearly stating how R/E was measured and operationalized as well as the relevance of R/E in the study and why R/E is in the models (Lee, 2009). Another suggestion was for fields to enforce consistent definitions. In a review of studies from the four highest impact medical journals, Ma et al. (2007) found a total of 116 terms for R/E categories with at least 10 different terms being utilized to describe each of the major R/E categories, including White, Black, Asian, or Hispanic. Consistent definitions and including information about measurement and operationalization are important for judging the validity and accuracy of the data (Lee, 2009; Ma et al., 2007).

Another important area of concern that Lee (2009) noted is the tendency to claim that the lack of heterogeneity by R/E was solely because of lack of power (i.e., a small sample size too small to detect an effect) or to explain heterogeneity by R/E that utilized biological or genetics-based arguments. As R/E is socially constructed, heterogeneity by R/E has social or environmental components that are rarely acknowledged within the medical field. As Lee wrote,

This biomedical and genetic focus may lead to biomedical solutions and the withdrawal of social, political, or economic approaches to easing social and economic inequalities. Furthermore, we may inadvertently accept the validity and legitimacy of a biological understanding of race. (Lee, 2009, p. 1189)

Two studies focused specifically on ideas for incorporating R/E into analysis in innovative ways. One example was drawn from the critical race theory tradition coining the term Critical Race Quantitative Intersections + Testimonios (CRQI+T). The CRQI+T framework encouraged directly incorporating qualitative information to make data more experiential and to disrupt dominant data mining techniques (Covarrubias et al., 2018). Under CRQI+T, data mining and analysis were guided by personal experiences and testimonios, and informed by qualitative perspectives. Unlike traditional quantitative research, which defines significance based on statistical calculations of the change of type I error (e.g., $p < .05$), the CRQI+T framework defined the significance of findings based on the testimonies or qualitative perspectives (for an example, see Covarrubias et al., 2018). Mayhew and Simonoff (2015a, 2015b) addressed the common decision to make White-only the reference group within models that included a series of binary indicators for R/E. Instead of making White-only the normative category, the authors suggested what they termed an *effect coding* approach of eliminating White-only as the reference group by recoding each binary indicator of R/E to have a value of –1 for White. They argued that this approach takes an assets-driven modeling approach, while traditional White as a reference category approaches were deficits based. This approach can also be useful for incorporating complexity of R/E identity into models. Thus far, this approach has gained some traction within higher education research with fewer inroads into the K–12 education research community based on current citations.

Incorporating Complex Race/Ethnicity Measures Into Analysis

While few studies more generally considered how to analyze R/E, a broader literature has critically examined the analysis of multi-R/E measures of identity. This literature has been spurred by two interrelated, relatively new ways of measuring R/E: having multiple items to measure complexity in R/E identity and allowing respondents to select more than one R/E option (J. A. Garcia, 2017; Prewitt, 2005). These measurement choices have several important implications for analysis. First, allowing for complex self-identification often led to groups that are too small for statistically significant estimates (in frequentist statistics) in addition to privacy concerns (Marquardt & Herrera, 2015; Prewitt, 2005; Saperstein et al., 2016; Williams & Husk, 2013). For instance, having two R/E items and allowing for more than one R/E box to be checked led the 2000 Census to have up to 189 possible R/E combinations (Prewitt, 2005). Second, Marquardt and Herrera (2015) warned that having more complex measures of R/E identity did not mean that all of these identities will be salient to each individual. When analyzing data with complex R/E identities, it could be advantageous for the researcher to consider only the R/E options that were politically relevant for the study. Political relevance was determined by the context and focus of the study. For instance, this could be determined by including only ethnic groups that are represented by a political organization or groups determined to be at risk for conflict (Marquardt & Herrera, 2015). Third, added complexity has the potential to produce tension between model parsimony and validity (J. A. Garcia, 2017). The appropriate analytical techniques for capturing complex R/E identities might not be obvious, and it could be necessary to examine multicollinearity and sample sizes of small cells (J. A. Garcia, 2017; Saperstein et al., 2016).

Several studies tested specific methods for analyzing complex R/E data, including how to bridge across data sets using different techniques, how to assign single-race categories, and how to compare measures of different dimensions of R/E identity. Those analyzing complex R/E data might have a need to assign multi-R/E individuals to a single R/E for analytical reasons or to combine two data sets that utilize different R/E measures. How this reassignment is done can have major implications for the results depending on the context (Campbell, 2007; Mays et al., 2003; Parker et al., 2004; Schenker & Parker, 2003). For instance, Campbell (2007) considered those who identified as multiracial with one racial identity being Black. While these individuals represented 0.6% of the U.S. population, if their other racial identity was a more rare identity like American Indian/Alaskan Native then reassignment can have major implications.

Reallocation methods can take into account a measure of the R/E the person most identified with (if available) or several single-race assignment options using arbitrary decision rules (e.g., choosing Hispanic ethnicity over all other R/E or assigning the rarest R/E; Mays et al., 2003; Parker et al., 2004; Schenker & Parker, 2003). Arbitrary decision rules were discouraged although a measure of which R/E the person most identifies with was often unavailable (Mays et al., 2003) and may not be an appropriate measure. One option when this measure was not available, according to the literature, is to use fractional methods for aggregating data (not for use with individual assignment) where fractions of multiracial individuals were distributed to their various R/E identities either equally or based on an algorithm. Regression models incorporating covariates can be used to create these fractions. These kinds of regression models can be relatively accurate at re-creating aggregated R/E statistics as long as the fractional distributions can vary by R/E identity (Parker et al., 2004; Schenker & Parker, 2003).[7]

As discussed above in this chapter, administrative data sets might also include multiple different measures of R/E identity. Saperstein et al. (2016) wrote about several different methods for analyzing data to account for multidimensionality of R/E, with multidimensionality being measured through self-report, phenotype, observer classification, and how people think others see them. The researcher can purposefully examine differences between the two dimensions of race by having one measure predict the other. Other options include comparing effects in models using the different dimensions of race, examining effects when all measures are included in the model simultaneously, and including a saturated model with indicators for every possible combination of identities. The analyst might use AIC (Akaike's information criteria) and BIC (Bayesian information criteria) statistics to identify which model has the most parsimonious fit to the original data (Saperstein et al., 2016).

DISCUSSION: HOW TO MEASURE AND ANALYZE RACE/ETHNICITY DATA IN ADMINISTRATIVE DATA SETS

Measurement

The reviewed studies paint a complicated picture of how to better measure and analyze R/E data from administrative data sets. A universal measure is unlikely to solve all of the measurement/analysis issues that can arise. However, creating more universal ways of measuring R/E are possible and should incorporate a few key insights from the reviewed studies. First, we clearly need to reconsider how Hispanic origin is measured. While the U.S. Census stagnates, continuing to have two separate R/E questions, those creating measures for administrative data sets in education do not have to follow this model. Overwhelming evidence indicates that those who identify as Hispanic are unlikely to identify a separate R/E, and forcing Hispanic people to identify a separate R/E leads to issues with missing data. The literature suggests one alternative is to create one item listing possible R/E identities, including Hispanic origin, giving respondents the option of selecting more than one option. This alternative may place additional burden on the data administrators if the data must be reported to a federal or state agency with different definitions of R/E.

However, reliability is lessened by allowing respondents to check multiple boxes and giving write-in options since those with multi-R/E identities are the most likely to change their reported R/E over time especially those who are part American Indian/Alaskan Native. Collecting data over time instead of forcing individuals to have static R/E identities can help address this issue with reliability. For example, state educational administrative data sets could collect data on R/E every year to allow researchers to incorporate the fluid nature of R/E identification. This would be especially important for data on students since several reviewed studies found that multiracial and immigrant children often change their reported R/E until they reach adulthood when their reported R/E becomes more stable. Having measures of R/E over time will be especially important for those who can identify as American Indian/ Alaskan Native since this identity is associated with lower reliability of responses.

Including questions that introduce complexity without confusion will be part of a more valid measurement system. For instance, measures of country of origin, language, and recency of immigration are more likely to be reliable and provide important information on R/E, particularly when focused on pan-ethnic measures of R/E.

The studies suggest a few other ways to increase the concurrent validity of R/E measures. Administrative data sets could measure R/E using self-reports whenever possible as well as supplementing R/E measurement with data from valid sources like birth certificates. Those collecting administrative data could use uniform procedures for collecting and recording this information.

When reconsidering or creating measures of R/E, there are a few concrete suggestions to consider. First, be attentive to the list of possible R/E identities. This list should represent the majority of the population, include politically relevant groups, and include heterogeneity to the extent that it will be helpful for identifying disparities. Two measures could be considered as additions. When people are allowed to select more than one R/E identity, a useful follow-up question could be to ask which of these identities best represents how they view their R/E. That said, as we mention above, there are individuals for whom multiple R/E identities equally represent their lived experiences. For these individuals, asking which identity best represents them will not mitigate researchers' issues with multiple categories being selected. For specific R/E identities, it might also be advantageous to consider self-reported phenotype to identify differences in outcomes by skin tone.

Missing Data

A robust literature primarily from public health suggests that when administrative data sets are missing R/E data on individuals, but have information on names and home addresses, the BISG method is potentially useful. However, these types of methods have several notable limitations that we urge others to carefully consider. The BISG methods are useful only for assessing the probability that an individual is Asian, Hispanic, Black, and, in some cases, White with little utility with other R/E categories. In addition, identifying these Black and White individuals relies on residential segregation, which greatly varies depending on the region. Finally, Asian and Hispanic surnames generally reflect patrilineal descent, an increasingly tenuous assumption considering growing rates of those of multi-R/E descent. The mixed evidence of the accuracy of BISG should also be considered before implementing this method.

Analysis

For analysis of R/E data, much of what the analyst can do is to better describe their measures and their analytical choices. When describing quantitative work incorporating R/E, the researchers should explain why R/E is included in a model, why the R/E measures are operationalized the way they are, and/or why they are interested in heterogeneity by race. These explanations should avoid biological or genetics-based theories instead recognizing that race is not a cause, is socially constructed and can signify common social or environmental experiences. The researcher should also be clear about how R/E was measured (e.g., self-report). Research from the medical field also suggests that education researchers consider making fieldwide definitions of R/E that should be used across studies. These standards for R/E measurement and reporting can incorporate much of the measurement advice described above.

When considering analytical choices made during modeling, researchers should attempt to integrate complex R/E identities into their models. While doing so, they should remain aware of issues of multicollinearity, small cell size, and data privacy. When these issues arise, they can consider incorporating information on R/E identities that are more salient for those respondents (if that measure is available). Researchers could also stop focusing on the binary notion of whether an estimate is statistically significant or insignificant and instead focus on the actual p value and interpret it within the context of the study (e.g., Wasserstein et al., 2019).

CONCLUSION

As administrative data sets in education continue to grow in complexity and as more researchers utilize these data sets, it will be increasingly important to attend to measures of R/E and how those measures are incorporated into analysis. While quantitative analysis of R/E brings with it a troubling history of racial subjugation, embracing quantitative methods to study and address R/E inequality can also hold much promise in the future for understanding and lessening inequality especially with the growth of availability and analysis of big data (see Dixon-Román, 2017). Much of the work that has been done on R/E measurement and analysis has focused on medical or public health fields where administrative data have been prominent for a longer period of time. Administrators, researchers, and policy stakeholders generally use education administrative data as if each piece of information in the data is an objective fact. However, R/E are subjective, varying, and socially constructed (Covarrubias & Vélez, 2013; N. M. Garcia et al., 2018; Gillborn et al., 2018; Ladson-Billings, 2012), and educational measurement of R/E can and has been sporadically conducted. For example, Ford (2019) found state requirements that missing R/E data in K–12 administrative data sets be supplied by observer identification (as opposed to self report) in several states. However, there is no systematic policy on who can be considered the observer in this scenario or what criteria the observer should use to assign R/E values for students. These data are required for federal and state accountability and are consistently used by researchers, yet there is little clarity around the source of information on R/E measures. The current review has highlighted some of the ways that scholars can approach the use of R/E measures in educational administrative data; however, there is significant work still to be done understanding how this type of information is collected. As administrative data in education continue to grow, researchers might consider conducting studies similar to the medical and public health fields to help inform the education research base.

ACKNOWLEDGMENTS

We are grateful to Elisa Wolf and Devon Lockard for their assistance in preparing this chapter and organizing the articles for the literature synthesis.

ORCID iDS

Samantha Viano https://orcid.org/0000-0002-9229-3597
Dominique J. Baker https://orcid.org/0000-0001-8570-9681

NOTES

[1]While DuBois offered one of the first criticisms of the use of quantitative methods to study differences between racial groups, he also created some of the earliest data visualizations utilizing quantitative data (Battle-Baptiste & Rusert, 2018).

[2]Google Scholar included studies with publication dates in 2019 even though the search was performed in December 2018.

[3]Articles excluded due to a lack of inclusion of quantitative data measurement generally focused on legal analysis and broad-based discussions of survey-based data sets.

[4]Articles excluded due to a lack of discussion about the classification of R/E did not include a focus on the operationalization or measurement of R/E.

[5]Articles excluded due to the discussion of R/E classification not being applicable to administrative databases generally included visual classification (e.g., facial recognition software), specimen collection (e.g., genetic data), or probability-based complex sample survey designs. These designs rely on sampling a portion of the population and using probability weighting

to make that sample's data generalize to the larger population. This literature review is focused on administrative data, which includes the data on the entire population of individuals and requires different statistical assumptions than survey data. Therefore, articles using survey data were excluded.

[6]We recognize that race is not a biological or genetic trait. Genetic testing, at best, reports on ancestry, not race (Roberts, 2011). However, research does show that some individuals shift their self-reported classification of R/E when provided information on genetic ancestry (Craemer, 2010). Roberts (2011) included a particularly in-depth discussion on the use and misuse of genetic ancestry tests to claim a certain R/E, including doing so as a means of claiming certain privileges based on that R/E, like tribal citizenship for American Indian genetic ancestry and Israeli citizenship for Jewish ancestry.

[7]It is important to note that this assessment of accuracy relies on the assumption that the actual distributions in the population are similar to the information available to researchers (which is not always true).

REFERENCES

An asterisk indicates that the reference was one of the 55 studies included in the research synthesis.

*Adjaye-Gbewonyo, D., Bednarczyk, R. A., Davis, R. L., & Omer, S. B. (2014). Using the Bayesian Improved Surname Geocoding Method (BISG) to create a working classification of race and ethnicity in a diverse managed care population: A validation study. *Health Services Research, 49*(1), 268–283. https://doi.org/10.1111/1475-6773.12089

*Aspinall, P. J. (2001). Operationalising the collection of ethnicity data in studies of the sociology of health and illness. *Sociology of Health & Illness, 23*(6), 829–862. https://doi.org/10.1111/1467-9566.00277

*Aspinall, P. J. (2003). Who is Asian? A category that remains contested in population and health research. *Journal of Public Health, 25*(2), 91–97. https://doi.org/10.1093/pubmed/fdg021

*Aspinall, P. J. (2009). The future of ethnicity classifications. *Journal of Ethnic and Migration Studies, 35*(9), 1417–1435. https://doi.org/10.1080/13691830903125901

Battle-Baptiste, W., & Rusert, B. (2018). *WEB Du Bois's data portraits: Visualizing Black America*. Chronicle Books.

*Bratter, J. (2007). Will "multiracial" survive to the next generation? The racial classification of children of multiracial parents. *Social Forces, 86*(2), 821–849. https://doi.org/10.1093/sf/86.2.821

*Buescher, P. A., Gizlice, Z., & Jones-Vessey, K. A. (2005). Discrepancies between published data on racial classification and self-reported race: Evidence from the 2002 North Carolina Live Birth Records. *Public Health Reports, 120*(4), 393–398. https://doi.org/10.1177/003335490512000406

*Campbell, M. E. (2007). Thinking outside the (black) box: Measuring Black and multiracial identification on surveys. *Social Science Research, 36*(3), 921–944. https://doi.org/10.1016/j.ssresearch.2006.07.001

*Campbell, M. E., & Rogalin, C. L. (2006). Categorical imperatives: The interaction of Latino and racial identification. *Social Science Quarterly, 87*(5), 1030–1052. https://doi.org/10.1111/j.1540-6237.2006.00414.x

Carbado, D. W., & Roithmayr, D. (2014). Critical race theory meets social science. *Annual Review of Law and Social Science, 10*(1), 149–167. https://doi.org/10.1146/annurev-law-socsci-110413-030928

Connelly, R., Playford, C. J., Gayle, V., & Dibben, C. (2016). The role of administrative data in the big data revolution in social science research. *Social Science Research, 59*, 1–12. https://doi.org/10.1016/j.ssresearch.2016.04.015

*Covarrubias, A., Nava, P. E., Lara, A., Burciaga, R., Vélez, V. N., & Solorzano, D. G. (2018). Critical race quantitative intersections: A testimonio analysis. *Race, Ethnicity and Education, 21*(2), 253–273. https://doi.org/10.1080/13613324.2017.1377412

Covarrubias, A., & Vélez, V. (2013). Critical race quantitative intersectionality. In M. Lynn & A. D. Dixson (Eds.), *Handbook of critical race theory in education.* Routledge Handbooks Online. https://doi.org/10.4324/9780203155721.ch20

*Craemer, T. (2010). Ancestral ambivalence and racial self-classification change. *Social Science Journal, 47*(2), 307–325. https://doi.org/10.1016/j.soscij.2009.11.001

*Davis, S. N., Jackson, R., & Aicardi, C. (2012). "What race do you consider yourself?" Factors influencing use of color in racial self-classification. *Sociation Today, 10*(1). http://www.ncsociology.org/sociationtoday/v101/race.htm

Denton, N. A., & Deane, G. D. (2010). Researching race and ethnicity: Methodological issues. In P. H. Collins & J. Solomos (Eds.), *The SAGE handbook of race and ethnic studies.* Sage. https://doi.org/10.4135/9781446200902.n5

*DiPietro, S. M., & Bursik, R. J. (2012). Studies of the new immigration: The dangers of pan-ethnic classifications. *ANNALS of the American Academy of Political and Social Science, 641*(1), 247–267. https://doi.org/10.1177/0002716211431687

Dixon-Román, E. J. (2017). *Inheriting possibility: Social reproduction and quantification in education.* University of Minnesota Press.

DuBois, W. E. B. (1899). *The Philadelphia Negro: A social study* (No. 14). University of Pennsylvania Press.

*Eisenhower, A., Suyemoto, K., Lucchese, F., & Canenguez, K. (2014). "Which box should I check?" Examining standard check box approaches to measuring race and ethnicity. *Health Services Research, 49*(3), 1034–1055. https://doi.org/10.1111/1475-6773.12132

*Elliott, M. N., Fremont, A., Morrison, P. A., Pantoja, P., & Lurie, N. (2008). A new method for estimating race/ethnicity and associated disparities where administrative records lack self-reported race/ethnicity. *Health Services Research, 43*(5 Pt. 1), 1722–1736. https://doi.org/10.1111/j.1475-6773.2008.00854.x

*Feliciano, C., & Rumbaut, R. G. (2018). Varieties of ethnic self-identities: Children of immigrants in middle adulthood. *RSF: The Russell Sage Foundation Journal of the Social Sciences, 4*(5), 26–46. https://doi.org/10.7758/rsf.2018.4.5.02

*Feliciano, C., & Rumbaut, R. G. (2019). The evolution of ethnic identity from adolescence to middle adulthood: The case of the immigrant second generation. *Emerging Adulthood, 7*(2), 85–96. https://doi.org/10.1177/2167696818805342

Figlio, D., Karbownik, K., & Salvanes, K. (2017). The promise of administrative data in education research. *Education Finance and Policy, 12*(2), 129–136. https://doi.org/10.1162/EDFP_a_00229

*Fiscella, K., & Fremont, A. M. (2006). Use of geocoding and surname analysis to estimate race and ethnicity. *Health Services Research, 41*(4 Pt. 1), 1482–1500. https://doi.org/10.1111/j.1475-6773.2006.00551.x

Ford, K. S. (2019). Observer-identification: A potential threat to the validity of self-identified race and ethnicity. *Educational Researcher, 48*(6), 378–381. https://doi.org/10.3102/0013189X19860803

*Foy, S. L., Ray, V., & Hummel, A. (2017). The shade of a criminal record: Colorism, incarceration, and external racial classification. *Socius: Sociological Research for a Dynamic World, 3.* Advance online publication. https://doi.org/10.1177/2378023116689567

*Fremont, A., Weissman, J. S., Hoch, E., & Elliott, M. N. (2016). When race/ethnicity data are lacking. *Rand Health Quarterly, 6*(1). https://www.ncbi.nlm.nih.gov/pmc/articles/PMC5158280/

*Garcia, J. A. (2017). The Race Project: Researching race in the social sciences researchers, measures, and scope of studies. *Journal of Race, Ethnicity and Politics, 2*(2), 300–346. https://doi.org/10.1017/rep.2017.15

*Garcia, J. A., Sanchez, G. R., Sanchez-Youngman, S., Vargas, E. D., & Ybarra, V. D. (2015). Race as lived experience. *Du Bois Review: Social Science Research on Race, 12*(2), 349–373. https://doi.org/10.1017/S1742058X15000120

Garcia, N. M., López, N., & Vélez, V. N. (2018). QuantCrit: Rectifying quantitative methods through critical race theory. *Race Ethnicity and Education, 21*(2), 149–157. https://doi.org/10.1080/13613324.2017.1377675

*Garcia, N. M., & Mayorga, O. J. (2018). The threat of unexamined secondary data: A critical race transformative convergent mixed methods. *Race Ethnicity and Education, 21*(2), 231–252. https://doi.org/10.1080/13613324.2017.1377415

Gillborn, D., Warmington, P., & Demack, S. (2018). QuantCrit: Education, policy, "Big Data" and principles for a critical race theory of statistics. *Race, Ethnicity and Education, 21*(2), 158–179. https://doi.org/10.1080/13613324.2017.1377417

Grissom, J. A., & Redding, C. (2015). Discretion and disproportionality: Explaining the underrepresentation of high-achieving students of color in gifted programs. *AERA Open, 2*(1). https://doi.org/10.1177/2332858415622175

*Grundmeier, R. W., Song, L., Ramos, M. J., Fiks, A. G., Elliott, M. N., Fremont, A., Pace, W., Wasserman, R. C., & Localio, R. (2015). Imputing missing race/ethnicity in pediatric electronic health records: Reducing bias with use of U.S. Census location and surname data. *Health Services Research, 50*(4), 946–960. https://doi.org/10.1111/1475-6773.12295

Haney López, I. (2005). Race on the 2010 census: Hispanics & the shrinking White majority. *Daedalus, 134*(1), 42–52. https://doi.org/10.1162/0011526053124479

*Harris, D. R., & Sim, J. J. (2002). Who is multiracial? Assessing the complexity of lived race. *American Sociological Review, 67*(4), 614–627. https://doi.org/10.2307/3088948

*Hitlin, S., Brown, J. S., & Elder, G. H. (2006). Racial self-categorization in adolescence: Multiracial development and social pathways. *Child Development, 77*(5), 1298–1308. https://doi.org/10.1111/j.1467-8624.2006.00935.x

*Hitlin, S., Brown, J. S., & Elder, G. H. (2007). Measuring Latinos: Racial vs. ethnic classification and self-understandings. *Social Forces, 86*(2), 587–611. https://doi.org/10.1093/sf/86.2.587

*Idossa, D., Duma, N., Chekhovskiy, K., Go, R., & Ailawadhi, S. (2018). Commentary: Race and ethnicity in biomedical research: Classifications, challenges, and future directions. *Ethnicity & Disease, 28*(4), 561–564. https://doi.org/10.18865/ed.28.4.561

*James, A. (2001). Making sense of race and racial classification. *Race and Society, 4*(2), 235–247. https://doi.org/10.1016/S1090-9524(03)00012-3

Jones, R. S. (1998). Proving Blacks inferior: The sociology of knowledge. In J. A. Ladner (Ed.), *The death of White sociology: Essays on race and culture* (pp. 114–135). Black Classic Press.

*Kilty, K., M. (2004). What's in a name? Racial and ethnic classifications and the meaning of Hispanic/Latino in the United States. *Ethnic Studies Review, 27*(1), 32–56. https://doi.org/10.1525/esr.2004.27.1.32

King, J. E. (2016). We may well become accomplices: To rear a generation of spectators is not to educate at all. *Educational Researcher, 45*(2), 159–172. https://doi.org/10.3102/0013189X16639046

Kobrin, J. L., Sathy, V., & Shaw, E. J. (2007). *A historical view of subgroup performance differences on the SAT Reasoning Test* (Research Report No. 2006-5). College Board.

*Kressin, N. R., Bei-Hung, C., Hendricks, A., & Kazis, L. E. (2003). Agreement between administrative data and patients' self-reports of race/ethnicity. *American Journal of Public Health*, *93*(10), 1734–1739. https://doi.org/10.2105/AJPH.93.10.1734

Ladson-Billings, G. (1998). Just what is critical race theory and what's it doing in a nice field like education? *International Journal of Qualitative Studies in Education*, *11*(1), 7–24. https://doi.org/10.1080/095183998236863

Ladson-Billings, G. (2012). Through a glass darkly: The persistence of race in education research & scholarship. *Educational Researcher*, *41*(4), 115–120. https://doi.org/10.3102/0013189X12440743

Ladson-Billings, G., & Tate, W. F. (1995). Toward a critical race theory of education. *Teachers College Record*, *97*(1), 47–68.

*Landale, N. S., & Oropesa, R. S. (2002). White, Black, or Puerto Rican? Racial self-identification among mainland and island Puerto Ricans. *Social Forces*, *81*(1), 231–254. https://doi.org/10.1353/sof.2002.0052

*Lee, C. (2009). "Race" and "ethnicity" in biomedical research: How do scientists construct and explain differences in health? *Social Science & Medicine*, *68*(6), 1183–1190. https://doi.org/10.1016/j.socscimed.2008.12.036

Liebler, C. A., Porter, S. R., Fernandez, L. E., Noon, J. M., & Ennis, S. R. (2017). America's churning races: Race and ethnicity response changes between Census 2000 and the 2010 Census. *Demography*, *54*(1), 259–284. https://doi.org/10.1007/s13524-016-0544-0

*Ma, I. W. Y., Khan, N. A., Kang, A., Zalunardo, N., & Palepu, A. (2007). Systematic review identified suboptimal reporting and use of race/ethnicity in general medical journals. *Journal of Clinical Epidemiology*, *60*(6), 572–578. https://doi.org/10.1016/j.jclinepi.2006.11.009

*Maizlish, N., & Herrera, L. (2006). Race/ethnicity in medical charts and administrative databases of patients served by community health centers. *Ethnicity & Disease*, *16*(2), 483–487.

*Marquardt, K. L., & Herrera, Y. M. (2015). Ethnicity as a variable: An assessment of measures and data sets of ethnicity and related identities. *Social Science Quarterly*, *96*(3), 689–716. https://doi.org/10.1111/ssqu.12187

*Mateos, P. (2007). A review of name-based ethnicity classification methods and their potential in population studies. *Population, Space and Place*, *13*(4), 243–263. https://doi.org/10.1002/psp.457

*Mayhew, M. J., & Simonoff, J. S. (2015a). Effect coding as a mechanism for improving the accuracy of measuring students who self-identify with more than one race. *Research in Higher Education*, *56*(6), 595–600. https://doi.org/10.1007/s11162-015-9364-0

*Mayhew, M. J., & Simonoff, J. S. (2015b). Non-White, no more: Effect coding as an alternative to dummy coding with implications for higher education researchers. *Journal of College Student Development*, *56*(2), 170–175. https://doi.org/10.1353/csd.2015.0019

*Mays, V. M., Ponce, N. A., Washington, D. L., & Cochran, S. D. (2003). Classification of race and ethnicity: Implications for public health. *Annual Review of Public Health*, 24, 83–110. https://doi.org/10.1146/annurev.publhealth.24.100901.140927

McGuinn, P. (2015). Schooling the state: ESEA and the evolution of the U.S. Department of Education. *RSF: The Russell Sage Foundation Journal of the Social Sciences*, *1*(3), 77–94. https://doi.org/10.7758/rsf.2015.1.3.04

Mihoko Doyle, J., & Kao, G. (2007). Are racial identities of multiracials stable? Changing self-identification among single and multiple race individuals. *Social Psychology Quarterly*, *70*(4), 405–423. https://doi.org/10.1177/019027250707000409

Monroe, C. R. (2013). Colorizing educational research: African American life and schooling as an exemplar. *Educational Researcher*, *42*(1), 9–19. https://doi.org/10.3102/0013189X12469998

*Mora, G. C. (2014). Cross-field effects and ethnic classification: The institutionalization of Hispanic panethnicity, 1965 to 1990. *American Sociological Review, 79*(2), 183–210. https://doi.org/10.1177/0003122413509813

*Moscou, S., Anderson, M. R., Kaplan, J. B., & Valencia, L. (2003). Validity of racial/ethnic classifications in medical records data: An exploratory study. *American Journal of Public Health, 93*(7), 1084–1086. https://doi.org/10.2105/AJPH.93.7.1084

Pang, V. O., Han, P. P., & Pang, J. M. (2011). Asian American and Pacific Islander students: Equity and the achievement gap. *Educational Researcher, 40*(8), 378–389. https://doi.org/10.3102/0013189X11424222

*Parker, J. D., Schenker, N., Ingram, D. D., Weed, J. A., Heck, K. E., & Madans, J. H. (2004). Bridging between two standards for collecting information on race and ethnicity: An application to Census 2000 and vital rates. *Public Health Reports, 119*(2), 192–205. https://doi.org/10.1177/003335490411900213

*Prewitt, K. (2005). Racial classification in America: Where do we go from here? *Daedalus, 134*(1), 5–17. https://doi.org/10.1162/0011526053124370

*Prewitt, K. (2018). The census race classification: Is it doing its job? *ANNALS of the American Academy of Political and Social Science, 677*(1), 8–24. https://doi.org/10.1177/0002716218756629

Roberts, D. (2011). *Fatal invention: How science, politics, and big business re-create race in the twenty-first century.* New Press.

Rodriguez, C. E. (2000). *Changing race: Latinos, the census, and the history of ethnicity in the United States.* New York University Press.

*Roth, W. D. (2005). The end of the one-drop rule? Labeling of multiracial children in Black intermarriages. *Sociological Forum, 20*(1), 35–67. https://doi.org/10.1007/s11206-005-1897-0

*Roth, W. D. (2010). Racial mismatch: The divergence between form and function in data for monitoring racial discrimination of Hispanics: Racial mismatch. *Social Science Quarterly, 91*(5), 1288–1311. https://doi.org/10.1111/j.1540-6237.2010.00732.x

Sablan, J. R. (2019). Can you really measure that? Combining critical race theory and quantitative methods. *American Educational Research Journal, 56*(1), 178–203. https://doi.org/10.3102/0002831218798325

Santelices, M. V., & Wilson, M. (2010). Unfair treatment? The case of Freedle, the SAT, and the standardization approach to differential item functioning. *Harvard Educational Review, 80*(1), 106–134. https://doi.org/10.17763/haer.80.1.j94675w001329270

*Saperstein, A., Kizer, J. M., & Penner, A. M. (2016). Making the most of multiple measures: Disentangling the effects of different dimensions of race in survey research. *The American Behavioral Scientist, 60*(4), 519. https://doi.org/10.1177/0002764215613399

*Schenker, N., & Parker, J. D. (2003). From single-race reporting to multiple-race reporting: Using imputation methods to bridge the transition. *Statistics in Medicine, 22*(9), 1571–1587. https://doi.org/10.1002/sim.1512

*Shah, P. R., & Davis, N. R. (2017). Comparing three methods of measuring race/ethnicity. *Journal of Race, Ethnicity and Politics, 2*(1), 124–139. https://doi.org/10.1017/rep.2016.27

*Smith, N., Iyer, R. L., Langer-Gould, A., Getahun, D. T., Strickland, D., Jacobsen, S. J., Chen, W., Derose, S. F., & Koebnick, C. (2010). Health plan administrative records versus birth certificate records: Quality of race and ethnicity information in children. *BMC Health Services Research, 10*, 316. https://doi.org/10.1186/1472-6963-10-316

Stoskopf, A. (1999). The forgotten history of eugenics. *Rethinking Schools, 13*(3), 12–13.

Tatum, B. D. (2017). *Why are all the Black kids sitting together in the cafeteria? And other conversations about race.* Basic Books.

*Thompson, C. A., Boothroyd, D. B., Hastings, K. G., Cullen, M. R., Palaniappan, L. P., & Rehkopf, D. H. (2018). A multiple-imputation "forward bridging" approach to address changes in the classification of Asian race/ethnicity on the US death certificate. *American Journal of Epidemiology, 187*(2), 347–357. https://doi.org/10.1093/aje/kwx215

*Tzioumis, K. (2018). Demographic aspects of first names. *Scientific Data, 5*, Article 180025. https://doi.org/10.1038/sdata.2018.25

U.S. Census Bureau, Commerce Department. (2018). *2018 End-to-end census test: Race and Hispanic origin questions* (OMB Control Number: 0607-0999).

*Vargas, N., & Kingsbury, J. (2016). Racial identity contestation: Mapping and measuring racial boundaries. *Sociology Compass, 10*(8), 718–729. https://doi.org/10.1111/soc4.12395

*Voicu, I. (2018). Using first name information to improve race and ethnicity classification. *Statistics and Public Policy, 5*(1), 1–13. https://doi.org/10.1080/2330443X.2018.1427012

Wasserstein, R. L., Schirm, A. L., & Lazar, N. A. (2019). Moving to a world beyond "p< 0.05." *The American Statistician, 73*(Suppl. 1), 1–19. https://doi.org/10.1080/00031305.2019.1583913

*Williams, M., & Husk, K. (2013). Can we, should we, measure ethnicity? *International Journal of Social Research Methodology, 16*(4), 285–300. https://doi.org/10.1080/13645579.2012.682794

Winfield, A. G. (2007). *Eugenics and education in America: Institutionalized racism and the implications of history, ideology, and memory* (Vol. 18). Peter Lang.

Zuberi, T. (2001). *Thicker than blood: How racial statistics lie.* University of Minnesota Press.

Zuberi, T., & Bonilla-Silva, E. (2008). *White logic, White methods: Racism and methodology.* Rowman & Littlefield.

Chapter 12

Qualitative Comparative Analysis in Education Research: Its Current Status and Future Potential

SEBNEM CILESIZ
University of Louisiana at Lafayette

THOMAS GRECKHAMER
Louisiana State University

Qualitative comparative analysis (QCA) is a set-theoretic configurational approach that uses the logic of Boolean algebra to conceptualize and empirically examine potentially complex causal relations. The potential of this methodological innovation to draw innovative insights toward answering enduring questions and to foster novel research has increasingly been realized in several social science disciplines. However, to date, limited education research has taken advantage of this potential. The purpose of this review is to facilitate an education research agenda that capitalizes on the strengths of QCA and its set-theoretic approach. We introduce the foundations of QCA, outline the promise it holds for education research, systematically review and appraise empirical education research that has applied QCA, and complement this review with a review of research from outside the field that may serve as inspiration for education researchers. In doing so, we highlight areas of improved research designs in education research practice and point education researchers to promising research directions. We conclude with suggestions for researchers to weigh QCA's strengths and limitations in comparison with other methods.

Qualitative comparative analysis (QCA), a set-theoretic configurational approach based on Boolean algebra, was initially introduced more than 30 years ago and has since been developed largely through the work of Charles Ragin (1987, 2000, 2008). QCA constitutes one of the few genuine methodological innovations in the social sciences over the past decades (Gerring, 2001), and its potential has increasingly been recognized and harnessed through empirical research in fields such as political science, sociology, and management (Rihoux et al., 2013). QCA conceptualizes causal

Review of Research in Education
March 2020, Vol. 44, pp. 332–369
DOI: 10.3102/0091732X20907347
Chapter reuse guidelines: sagepub.com/journals-permissions
© 2020 AERA. http://rre.aera.net

relations as complex, that is, as marked by conjunction, equifinality, and asymmetry. In contrast, the correlational thinking underlying most forms of conventional quantitative analysis (e.g., multiple regression analysis, factor analysis, and structural equation models) conceptualizes causal relations as additive, unifinal, and symmetrical (Abbott, 1988; Fiss, 2007; Grandori & Furnari, 2008; Mahoney, 2004). QCA's alternative approach to causal relations, combined with its set-theoretic configurational approach to unraveling causal complexity, enables researchers to reconsider existing theoretical frameworks that were shaped by a correlational understanding of causality, take a fresh look at both established empirical findings and inconclusive research, and tackle novel research questions regarding phenomena marked by complex causality (Misangyi et al., 2017). Indeed, QCA has enabled the re-envisioning of causal relations informing policy-oriented research in sociology, political science, and organizational research (e.g., Fiss et al., 2013; Ragin, 2006a; Ragin & Fiss, 2017). Despite this potential, QCA's utilization in education has lagged behind that in other fields.

The purpose of our review is to facilitate education research that capitalizes on the unique characteristics of QCA and its set-theoretic approach. To enable a wider utilization of QCA among education researchers, we begin by systematically reviewing, synthesizing, and appraising education research using QCA and present its current range of application in education. Additionally, we identify and present research on education topics from outside the field that may serve as inspiration for education researchers.

Our review (a) systematically documents the current state of empirical education research using QCA by summarizing primary areas of research that have applied QCA and by identifying gaps as well as highlighting promising future directions for these research streams; (b) documents and evaluates the methodological practices of education QCA research based on current methodological recommendations, including identifying exemplary QCA applications in education research; (c) points to the challenges and limitations of empirical QCA research highlighted by education researchers and identifies possible areas of improvement in QCA research designs that would help education researchers to address empirical challenges; and (d) reviews research on education topics published in noneducation journals to identify QCA research to draw inspiration from for future education research.

QCA AND ITS PROMISE FOR EDUCATION RESEARCH

Below we offer a concise introduction to QCA and its set-theoretic configurational approach. For detailed introductions to QCA and its foundations in set-theoretic analysis and Boolean algebra, we refer readers to several comprehensive texts (Ragin, 1987, 2000; Ragin & Fiss, 2008; Rihoux & Ragin, 2009; Schneider & Wagemann, 2012) as well as to shorter tutorials that provide overviews and illustrations of the approach (e.g., Cooper & Glaesser, 2011; Fiss, 2011; Greckhamer et al., 2008).[1]

In his seminal work introducing QCA, Ragin (1987) highlighted two fundamental challenges social science researchers face in conducting empirical cross-case analyses. The first challenge was how to identify types of cases that coherently capture the similarities and differences of cases being studied. The second challenge was that outcomes of interest may be caused by combinations of case attributes rather than by the independent influence of case attributes. Additionally, Ragin (1987, 2000) aimed to address the qualitative/quantitative divide by developing an approach that could analyze samples that were too small to apply conventional quantitative approaches to, such as regression analysis, and too large for qualitative cross-case comparisons.

To address these challenges, Ragin's (1987) central methodological innovation was to develop QCA, which uses the logic of sets and Boolean algebra to map the diversity of cases in a sample and to provide a systematic approach to unravel causal complexity by identifying different combinations of attributes that are consistently linked to the occurrence of an outcome as well as to its absence. QCA transcends the division between qualitative and quantitative research by offering an innovative way to synthesize the strength of qualitative research to focus on in-depth examination of specific cases and the strength of quantitative research to focus on relationships between variables across many cases (Ragin, 1987; Rihoux, 2003). These tenets became the bases for QCA's evolution into a viable and flourishing set-theoretic configurational approach and its recognition across the social sciences (Ragin, 2000, 2008; Rihoux & Marx, 2013).

Before presenting QCA's main tenets and illustrating how they can be applied in education research, we note that QCA has not been without critiques in the social sciences. Because QCA is based on a set of assumptions that differ fundamentally from those of conventional quantitative as well as qualitative research approaches in the social sciences, some scholars repudiate its assumptions and theoretical basis. For example, Lucas and Szatrowski (2014) claimed that both the theoretical foundations and the methodological procedures of QCA were fundamentally inadequate and should be rejected. However, this critique was rebuked based on arguments that it was founded on misunderstanding of QCA's theoretical foundations and its conceptualization of causal relations as necessary and sufficient (Ragin, 2014; Olsen, 2014) as well as on empirical analyses that were erroneous and flawed (Ragin, 2014; Vaisey, 2014). To give another example, Hug (2013) problematized that inductive uses of QCA could be plagued by unaccounted measurement errors. However, Thiem (2014) contended that Hug's arguments were based on a distorted representation of QCA, misunderstanding of its primary objective, and decontextualized interpretations of the role of measurement errors and missing data in QCA.

Cases and Set Attributes

To study their phenomenon of interest, researchers begin a QCA inquiry by determining what should constitute cases. To give a few examples, depending on the outcome of interest, for education research, cases could be schools, school districts, units or departments within schools, individuals such as students, teachers, or school administrators, and countries. Researchers should then select attributes of cases that may be expected to explain the outcome, based on available theory and/or their knowledge of the cases (Berg-Schlosser & De Meur, 2009), which may involve an iterative process of model building and analysis. Key attributes of the cases under study are then conceptualized in terms of sets that capture both the outcome researchers' wish to explain and key attributes they believe to be causally linked to these outcomes. Sets may capture any attributes of these cases that are deemed important in a given setting, such as sets of successful students, large schools, failing school districts, high–socioeconomic status neighborhoods, or high-performing teachers.

Sets in QCA may be "crisp" or "fuzzy" sets[2] (Ragin, 1987, 2000). A crisp set is dichotomous and distinguishes cases' membership only as either "in" or "out" of the set (with respective membership values of 1 or 0), thus capturing *differences in kind.* For example, schools may be classified as either fully in (1) or fully out (0) of the set of high-performing schools. On the other hand, fuzzy sets distinguish *differences in degree* among cases in addition to differences in kind. They permit gradations of set membership by allowing various grades of partial membership from 0 to 1, in addition to full membership and full nonmembership. For example, in addition to designating clearly successful and clearly failing schools, researchers can classify schools as having partial membership in the set of high-performing schools; a relatively well performing school may be considered more in than out of the set of high-performing schools, with a set membership score of .75, whereas another school with mediocre performance may be considered more out than in the set of high-performing schools, with a set membership score of .25.

Calibration: Determining Set Membership of Cases

The process of determining cases' membership in sets, referred to as calibration, aims to capture variation in cases' attributes in a manner that is relevant to the study purpose as well as the cases studied. Calibration involves establishing and applying rules for cases to qualify for full membership, full nonmembership, or (for fuzzy sets) intermediate degrees of set membership (Ragin, 2008). It is a critical part of a QCA research design that requires careful consideration of the theoretical and empirical knowledge about case attributes and outcomes of interest to include in the study. Researchers may use the "indirect" or the "direct" method (for detailed descriptions, see Ragin, 2008) for calibrating different types of fuzzy sets (e.g., fuzzy sets with three, four, five, or six values, or continuous fuzzy sets; see Ragin, 2000, 2008). For example a three-value fuzzy set would include anchors that designate full membership (1), full nonmembership (0), and a crossover point of maximum ambiguity of membership (.5). Likewise, a five-value fuzzy set would include anchors that designate full membership (1), full nonmembership (0), more out than in membership (.25), more in than out membership (.75), and a crossover point indicating "neither in nor out" (.5). A researcher applying the indirect method uses theoretical and substantive knowledge to determine criteria for grouping cases according to their degree of membership; for example, calibration of a five-value fuzzy set requires criteria for each of the five degrees of membership in this set. A researcher applying the direct method to calibrate continuous fuzzy sets uses theoretical and substantive knowledge to identify fixed numerical values linked to three qualitative anchors—one each to designate full membership (1), full nonmembership (0), and a crossover point of maximum ambiguity of membership (.5)—to rescale interval variables into fuzzy sets, using estimates of the log of the odds of full membership as an intermediate step.

Cases as Set-Theoretic Configurations of Attributes and Complex Causality

QCA's logic is configurational in that once sets deemed relevant for the study are defined, all cases' membership in these sets is determined and cases are viewed as configurations defined by their (degrees of) membership in the sets (see below for a discussion of this process, called *calibration*). The combinatorial logic of Boolean algebra can then be used to study patterns of relations among cases' set memberships (Ragin, 1987; Smithson & Verkuilen, 2006). The three basic Boolean operators—logical AND, logical OR, and logical NOT—are used to identify combinations of the presence or absence of attributes that are potentially causally relevant to an outcome and thereby provide the basis for unpacking causal complexity. Put differently, cross-case patterns of set membership are analyzed to identify combinations of sets that are consistently linked to an outcome in order to shed light on causal relations (Ragin, 2000).

In doing so, QCA assumes that the causality underlying many social and organizational phenomena is complex. Complex causality implies that outcomes rarely have a single cause, causes rarely operate in isolation from one another, and specific case attributes may cause opposite effects depending on the context (Ragin, 1987, 2008). Put differently, complex causality involves three key dimensions—conjunction, equifinality, and asymmetry—and QCA provides the analytical tools to empirically explore each of these three dimensions of complex causal relations (Ragin, 2008). We note here that similar to conventional correlational methods, QCA findings provide empirical evidence of association, whereas inferences regarding causal relationships should be based on theory and the study's research design (e.g., Mahoney, 2004; Misangyi et al., 2017). Researchers can strengthen causal inferences from QCA findings through detailed case analyses of "typical" and "deviant" cases (see Rohlfing & Schneider, 2013; Schneider & Rohlfing, 2013, 2016).

The first dimension of causal complexity is conjunctural causality, which means that outcomes rarely have a single cause but, rather, attributes combine to produce an outcome. To capture these interdependencies, QCA draws on one of the key strengths of a case-oriented approach and considers cases holistically as configurations of conditions (Rihoux & Marx, 2013). In contrast, conventional correlational methods including regression approaches aim to isolate the "net effects" of individual "independent" variables on outcomes (Ragin, 2006a). The conjunction (or intersection) of sets is captured through the Boolean operator AND.

The assumption of causal conjunction is consistent with many phenomena in education. For example, the notion of intersectionality is based on the assumption that dimensions of individuals' identity (e.g., race, gender, class) have compounding effects and should not be treated as mutually exclusive categories (Agosto & Roland, 2018; Crenshaw, 1989; Schudde, 2018). Rather, "intersectionality refers to the interaction between gender, race, and other categories of difference in individual lives, social practices, institutional arrangements, and cultural ideologies and the outcomes of these interactions in terms of power" (Davis, 2008, p. 68). The literature on intersectionality has long emphasized that research should treat individuals holistically and focus on how aspects of individual identity intersect (Crenshaw, 1989), even though it is methodologically challenging to do so (Schudde, 2018; Tefera et al., 2018). Ragin and Fiss (2017) demonstrated the potential of QCA to advance empirical research on intersectionality by reevaluating the conditions that lead individuals to either avoid or experience poverty.

The second dimension of complex causality is equifinality, meaning that there may be multiple paths to a given outcome, whereas conventional regression analysis is designed to determine the "unifinal" net effects of independent variables on a dependent variable across all values of other independent variables (Ragin, 2006a). Equifinality is captured through the Boolean operator OR, which describes alternative combinations of sets. The notion of equifinality is consistent with knowledge about many educational phenomena. For example, the argument that there are multiple alternative pathways for students' educational attainment would not be disputed by many education researchers. Indeed, in a study applying QCA, Glaesser and Cooper (2012b) found that alternative paths to students' success included either (a) having high ability (measured by placement in the top quartile on a cognitive ability test) or (b) being a female student with highly educated parents and ability above the median as measured by a cognitive ability test.

The third dimension of causal complexity is asymmetry, which implies that the presence versus absence of attributes may play different roles in the occurrence of outcomes depending on which other conditions they occur with. It also implies that researchers should separately analyze the paths that lead to an outcome, such as success, and those that lead to its absence, such as failure, which are not assumed to be each other's inverse. This again is in contrast to conventional correlational approaches, which conceptualize relations between causes and outcomes as positive or negative linear correlations. QCA captures asymmetric relations through the Boolean operator NOT, which indicates the absence of conditions or of the outcome. The notion of causal asymmetry can potentially lead to important insights by enabling education researchers to identify combinations of attributes linked to the occurrence of an outcome or to its absence. For example, Bandaranayake (2016) used QCA to juxtapose the configurations of attributes that are linked to high-performing versus low-performing secondary schools in Australia.

Truth Table Analysis and Causal Sufficiency and Necessity

The next step following calibration of case attributes and outcome(s) into sets is to construct a data matrix called a "truth table," representing all logically possible configurations of attributes in 2^k rows (k = the number of attributes included in the truth table; therefore, each additional attribute exponentially increases the number of possible configurations and thus the model's complexity). All cases in the study sample are associated with rows of this truth table based on their membership in the attribute sets (Ragin, 1987, 2000). Because the attributes of many cases tend to occur in coherent patterns, some logically possible configurations may not be observed at all in an empirical sample. The assumption that many social phenomena will display this feature of limited diversity, meaning that not all logically possible configurations will be empirically observed (Meyer et al., 1993), is built into QCA's methodology (Ragin, 1987). To give a hypothetical example, in a sample of high school students, students in well-funded schools who take advantage of dual enrollment and whose parents are college graduates may be observed frequently, whereas students in poorly funded schools who take advantage of dual enrollment and whose parents are college graduates may not be observed. These unobserved configurations in a sample, called *logical remainders* or *counterfactual configurations*, require theoretical and empirical evaluation to contribute to the overall solutions, as briefly discussed below.

In contrast to correlational quantitative approaches that aim to isolate independent effects of independent variables on dependent variables (outcomes), in QCA the truth table is analyzed using Boolean algebra to empirically investigate the relationships between combinations of attributes and outcomes by conceptualizing causality in terms of set relations of necessity and sufficiency (Ragin, 2000, 2008). Attributes are deemed *necessary* for observing an outcome when they must be present for the outcome to occur. Empirical evidence for necessity means that all (or almost all[3]) cases displaying the outcome also display the necessary attribute(s), whereas not all cases displaying the necessary attribute(s) must exhibit the outcome. For example, if high cognitive ability is observed in (almost) all high-performing students and (almost) all students lacking high performance also lack high cognitive ability, the case could be made that high cognitive ability is a necessary attribute for high student performance. This does not mean that a necessary condition will also be sufficient, as all students with high cognitive ability may or may not perform highly.

Attributes or attribute combinations are deemed *sufficient* for observing an outcome if they consistently produce the outcome. Empirical evidence for sufficiency would involve that (almost) all cases that display the configuration of attributes also exhibit the outcome. Sufficiency implies that there may be cases other than the ones sharing the sufficient configuration that also display the outcome. Indeed, equifinality presumes that a number of alternative attribute configurations could be sufficient for the occurrence of an outcome. For example, a combination of high–socioeconomic status family background and high cognitive ability may be sufficient for college admission, but this does not rule out that students may be admitted to college due to "causes" other than this combination.

It is at this stage of analysis that counterfactual analyses—that is, evaluation of what outcome any given unobserved configuration would be expected to exhibit if it did exist—are conducted (Ragin, 2008). The current standard analysis distinguishes between "easy" counterfactuals, which are consistent with empirical evidence and theoretical knowledge, and "difficult" counterfactuals, which are consistent with empirical evidence but not with theoretical knowledge (see Ragin, 2008; Ragin & Sonnett, 2005; Soda & Furnari, 2012). As a result, for sufficiency analyses, QCA enables researchers to produce three solutions that are differentiated by integrating (a) no counterfactuals (complex solution), (b) only easy counterfactuals (intermediate solution), or (c) easy as well as difficult counterfactuals (parsimonious solution) (Ragin, 2008). While a recent common practice is to use a configuration chart introduced by Ragin and Fiss (2008) to report a combination of intermediate and parsimonious solutions (e.g., Fiss, 2011), a debate regarding which of these solutions (i.e., complex, intermediate, or parsimonious) should be reported is ongoing (Baumgartner & Thiem, 2017; Duşa, in press; Schneider, 2018); regardless of the decision, researchers should clearly document which solutions they report and why.

REVIEW METHODOLOGY

In this section, we describe our procedures for systematically identifying, selecting, and reviewing relevant articles based on recommendations for literature reviews (Cooper, 2010; Short, 2009; Triandis, 2004; Wolfswinkel et al., 2011). The primary purpose of our review was to assess the current state of research using QCA in education as a basis for providing methodological and substantive suggestions for future research. For this purpose, we searched for peer-reviewed journal articles using QCA methodology published from 1987 to 2018 (1987 was the year of publication of Ragin's first QCA book) in the Web of Science[4] (WoS) and Education Resources Information Center (ERIC) databases. We searched for the terms "qualitative comparative analysis," "QCA," "fsQCA" (fuzzy set QCA), and "csQCA" (crisp set QCA) in the title, abstract, and keywords of articles. In WoS, we operationalized *articles in the field of education* as those published in journals indexed in the "education and education research" and "education scientific disciplines" categories, and in ERIC, the authors independently concluded that all the included articles were published in education journals.

Our secondary purpose was to identify research related to education using QCA methodology from outside the field to serve as inspiration for future education research. For this purpose, we searched the WoS using the same QCA search terms and combined them with education-related keywords (i.e., "education*," "learn*," "teach*," "instruction*," "school*," "student*"), without limiting the search to a subject category. While this sample might not exclusively cover all QCA articles relevant to education, it fulfills our purpose of identifying relevant research for potential inspiration.

Our screening was based on PRISMA (2018) guidelines, whereby we reviewed articles' titles, abstracts, and (when needed) full texts according to predetermined inclusion/exclusion criteria. Specifically, we applied the following criteria to determine an article's eligibility: (a) the article reports an empirical study; (b) QCA is used as a method, either solely or alongside other methods; and (c) education is part of the article's focus. By the same token, we excluded articles if (a) they were not empirical studies, (b) they used the term "qualitative comparative analysis" or the acronym "QCA" to refer to another method or concept,[5] (c) they mentioned QCA in passing but did not use it for any analysis, (d) they mentioned one of our related keywords but education was not part of the article's focus, and (e) their full text was not written in English. As a result of this process, we constructed Set I, consisting of 26 articles published in education journals. After removing overlaps with Set I and screening via the same criteria, we constructed Set II, containing 30 articles published in noneducation journals. Table 1 shows the number of articles identified throughout the search and screening processes. Full references of all articles included in both samples are included in the reference list and indicated with asterisks and daggers, respectively.

In the next step, we closely reviewed all articles in Set I, representing our education sample, and captured bibliographic information, the outcomes studied, the purpose, key findings, and key aspects of the QCA research design (i.e., the type of QCA methodology used, inductive or deductive application of QCA, and whether the study used QCA only or included multiple methods, as well as the sample sizes and nature of the cases). Furthermore, we systematically reviewed the articles' research designs according to currently recommended methodological practices (Greckhamer et al., 2018), and based on this review, we identified studies we considered methodological exemplars of QCA applications in education. For the articles in Set II, representing our noneducation sample, we coded bibliographic information, the discipline of origin (as categorized in the WoS database), the topics studied, and the broad area(s) of education to which the study may contribute.

QCA RESEARCH IN EDUCATION

In Table 2, we provide an overview of key characteristics of the articles we reviewed from the field of education. Complete citations for those articles can be found in the reference list indicated with an asterisk).

Although we searched the period from 1987 to 2018, all of our eligible articles were published between 2009 and 2018, showing that the uptake of QCA in education started more than two decades after the method was introduced. Within this time period, we observed a moderate increase in the number of QCA applications in education research. Compared with the early adoption of QCA in political science and sociology starting in the late 1980s and its rapid increase in the early 2000s (Rihoux et al., 2013) or its proliferation in management and organization studies over the course of the past decade (Misangyi et al., 2017), the adoption of QCA in education research is still at an early stage. Additionally, among the 44 authors associated with the identified articles, few authored more than one article (i.e., Barry Cooper, Judith Glaesser, Richard Gott, Trinn Lauri, Ros Roberts, and Sarah Woulfin), suggesting that QCA expertise among education scholars is at a stage of relative infancy.

TABLE 1
Construction of the Article Sets for Review

Article Sets	WoS Education	ERIC	WoS Noneducation
Records identified through database search	58	101	222
Records after duplicates (i.e., overlapping with previous sample) removed	58	72	168
Records remaining after screening (title and abstract) for eligibility	29	7	42
Studies included in the review after assessing full-text articles for eligibility	23	3	30
	Set Ia	Set Ib	Set II
Total	Set I: Education (26)		Set II: Noneducation (30)

Note. WoS = Web of Science; ERIC = Education Resources Information Center.

Education Topics Studied Using QCA

Our review revealed that QCA studies are somewhat scattered across different domains of education research. Educational administration is the only area where a body of research applying QCA appears to be evolving. Specifically, studies focused on instructional changes within educational reforms (Coburn et al., 2012; Farrell & Marsh, 2016; Trujillo & Woulfin, 2014; Woulfin, 2015) and teacher professional development associated with reforms (Kintz et al., 2015; Woulfin & Jones, 2018). Other research in educational administration includes studies on school leadership and classroom participation (Sebastian et al., 2014), school organization (Lee, 2013), school performance (Bandaranayake, 2016), school choice policy (Lauri & Põder, 2013), persistence in STEM (science, technology, engineering, and mathematics; Pappas et al., 2017), and international aid (Birchler & Michaelowa, 2016). The comparatively stronger presence of QCA in educational administration research may be due to its intellectual proximity to the field of management, which has been one of the earlier adopters of QCA (Misangyi et al., 2017; Rihoux et al., 2013). This is supported by education scholars' references to the management literature to develop their QCA studies (e.g., Sebastian et al., 2014).

QCA applications spanning different domains of education research and different units of analyses demonstrate the wider potential of QCA for education research. For example, Glaesser and Cooper (2012a, 2012b) used QCA to tackle core questions in the sociology of education by investigating how combinations of factors such as students' gender, class, ability, and type of schooling can shed new light on their educational achievement. To give another example, Toots and Lauri (2015) tackled a

TABLE 2

Summary of Education Articles Using Qualitative Comparative Analysis (QCA)

First Author, Year	Outcome	Key QCA Findings	Sample Size and What Is a Case	Crisp/Fuzzy Set (cs/fs)	QCA Only/ Multimethod
Bandaranayake, 2016	High- and low-performing secondary schools	Identified combinations of school and student background characteristics linked to high and low school performance	49 schools	fs	QCA only
Birchler, 2016	Primary education enrollment and quality	Explored combinations of net enrollment rates, equal distribution of aid, and amount of aid that are linked to education quality improvement	15 countries	cs	Regression
Coburn, 2012	High-quality, reform-related instruction	Explored configurations of teachers' social network characteristics linked to high-quality, reform-related instruction and its absence	12 teachers	cs	Qualitative social network analysis
Farrell, 2016	Teachers' instructional responses to data	External data without internal data, or a compliance culture without external data, or no capacity-building intervention sufficient for no change in delivery; internal data, external data, and capacity-building intervention, and the absence of a compliance-oriented data-use culture sufficient for change in delivery	245 responses to data	cs	QCA only
Glaesser, 2012a	Student achievement	Combinations of students class, ability, and gender that are linked to high achievement	2,366 students	cs	QCA only
Glaesser, 2012b	Educational achievement	In both selective and nonselective schools, high ability is sufficient for obtaining certain levels of qualification, but at lower ability levels, students also have to be female and/or have highly educated parents	11,990 students	cs	QCA only

(continued)

TABLE 2 (CONTINUED)

First Author, Year	Outcome	Key QCA Findings	Sample Size and What Is a Case	Crisp/Fuzzy Set (cs/fs)	QCA Only/ Multimethod
Glaesser, 2009a	Competently conducting open-ended science investigation	Substantive understanding and understanding of ideas about evidence jointly are the path to competent science investigations; substantive and procedural understanding paired with prior attainment are another path to competent science investigation	124 students	cs	QCA only
Glaesser, 2009b	Ability to carry out open-ended science investigation	Procedural understanding is a necessary condition to carry out open-ended science investigation; when combined with substantive understanding and/or prior attainment, it is sufficient for the outcome	72 students	cs	Descriptive (pretest posttest) statistics
Hsieh, 2017	Level of rural-urban education divide	Explores relationships between digital characteristics of online learning courses and level of rural/urban education divide	15 students	Unclear	Grey relational analysis
Hsieh, 2018	Effective, efficient, comprehensive online education competitive evaluation model	Explores the determinants of effective and efficient online education	267 individuals	fs	Factor analysis and entropy compared analysis
Jain, 2018	Whether or not students choose elective courses	For most elective courses, rational and emotional factors together influence course selection	101 students	fs	QCA only
Kintz, 2015	Depth of discussions in teacher communities of inquiry	Combinations of clear purpose, coach questioning, and connection of theory to practice were linked to in-depth discussion; absence of two or more of these resulted in lack of deep discussions	17 communities of inquiry	fs	Qualitative data analysis
Lauri, 2013	Countries' education systems' efficiency and equity	Institutional conditions linked to educational systems that are both efficient and equitable	20 countries	fs	QCA only
Lee, 2013	Instructional consistency	Identified the diversity of elementary schools in one school district based on combinations of organizational elements of coordination and control	346 elementary schools	cs	Linear regression (QCA not used for analysis)

(continued)

TABLE 2 (CONTINUED)

First Author, Year	Outcome	Key QCA Findings	Sample Size and What Is a Case	Crisp/Fuzzy Set (cs/fs)	QCA Only/ Multimethod
Olufadi, 2015	College students' academic performance	Identified combinations of mobile phone use behaviors linked to high academic achievement, including students' awareness of the potential effect of mobile phones as a necessary condition	268 students	fs	Linear (blocked) regression
Pappas, 2017	Intention to continue studies in computer science	Absence of barriers and low grades were linked to high intention to continue; when barriers were present, motivation, interest in computer science, or career opportunities mattered	344 students	fs	Contrarian case analysis
Roberts, 2010	Ability to carry out open-ended investigation	Joint presence of procedural ideas, substantive ideas, and prior attainment is sufficient for ability to carry out open-ended science investigation	91 students	fs	Descriptive statistics
Schneider, 2010	Departments' academic job placement of PhD graduates	Combinations of governance factors linked to successful and to unsuccessful departments	14 economics departments	cs	QCA only
Sebastian, 2014	High classroom participation and its absence	Principal instructional leadership necessary for high classroom participation; to be sufficient, it needs to combine with college expectations or high teacher influence in school policy	98 public schools	fs	Descriptive statistics
Snelson-Powell, 2016	Tight and loose coupling of sustainability policies and practices	Combinations of organizational and expertise characteristics of business schools linked to tight vs. loose coupling of sustainability policies and practices	40 business schools	fs	QCA only

(continued)

TABLE 2 (CONTINUED)

First Author, Year	Outcome	Key QCA Findings	Sample Size and What Is a Case	Crisp/Fuzzy Set (cs/fs)	QCA Only/ Multimethod
Tho, 2017	Teaching quality	Teaching investment combined with signal clarity, consistency, and credibility are sufficient for high perceived teaching quality	352 MBA students	fs	Structural equation modeling
Toots, 2015	Students' achievement of high civic knowledge (HCK)	Human development is necessary to achieve HCK; six configurations of contextual and institutional factors, representing accountability or participatory paths, are sufficient for HCK	30 countries	fs	QCA only
Trujillo, 2014	Standards-based curricular content; English learner–specific pedagogical strategies; culturally relevant pedagogy	Specialized trainings, lengthy reform work, and intense engagement with teachers are a dominant path to standards-based curricular content; no results found for English learner–specific pedagogies or culturally relevant pedagogy	64 instructional tasks	cs	Qualitative data analysis
Woulfin, 2015	Reading mini-lessons	Combinations of independent reading with conference and/ or instructional materials were linked with enactment of mini-lessons	36 workshops with 12 teachers	cs	Qualitative data analysis/coding
Woulfin, 2018	Reform-oriented instructional coaching	Combination of principal prioritization of coaching, principal framing of coaching, and principal–coach collaboration was linked to reform-oriented instructional coaching	11 schools	cs	Qualitative data analyses
Zorio-Grima, 2018	Universities' sustainability reporting	Combinations of universities' innovation profile, political situation, and internal factors that are linked to high-sustainability reporting experience	49 universities	fs	QCA only

cross-national comparative education question by studying how countries' institutional environments shape the quality of citizenship education.

Approaches to QCA

In our review of education research, both crisp and fuzzy set approaches were represented about equally (one article was unclear regarding the type of sets used). Following a review of QCA applications in management (Misangyi et al., 2017), we differentiated between inductive and deductive uses of QCA. We classified studies as deductive or theory testing (Lee, 1999) if they empirically examined relationships derived from extant theory—typically articulated in the form of hypotheses, although a priori propositions could serve the same purpose. We classified studies as inductive if they emphasized developing, generating, or elaborating theory from empirical observations (Lee, 1999). Three studies formulated broad a priori propositions or hypotheses regarding the expected configurational nature of their findings (Lauri & Põder, 2013; Pappas et al., 2017; Tho, 2017), while the remaining studies were based on the inductive use of QCA for theory generation or elaboration.

We also evaluated whether studies used QCA as a stand-alone approach or alongside other (qualitative or quantitative) methods; about one half of the education articles used QCA alone, whereas the other half used it in combination with qualitative or quantitative research. For example, Kintz et al. (2015) used qualitative analysis and descriptive statistics alongside their application of QCA. Woulfin and colleagues' studies on educational reform are especially noteworthy in this respect (Trujillo & Woulfin, 2014; Woulfin, 2015; Woulfin & Jones, 2018) as they are based on extensive qualitative data (e.g., observations, interviews, and document analysis) and combine qualitative analysis with QCA. For example, in her study investigating classroom-level policy implementation, Woulfin (2015) used qualitative analyses to derive the cases of mini-lessons and then applied QCA to "re-analyze qualitative data on the most common combinations of conditions resulting in a mini-lesson" (p. 544). In other studies, QCA was used with multiple regression (Lee, 2013; Olufadi, 2015), structural equation modeling (Tho, 2017), or descriptive statistics based on hierarchical linear modeling–based empirical Bayes estimates (Sebastian et al., 2014). These examples demonstrate the versatility of QCA for multimethod research designs.

Sample Sizes and Types of Cases

As noted above, one of Ragin's (1987) original motivations for developing QCA was to enable analyses of data sets with a small to intermediate number of cases (e.g., 12–50; Marx et al., 2014; Ragin, 2000). However, even studies including very few attributes in their model should have samples with 12 or more cases to enable a valid sufficiency analysis (Marx & Dusa, 2011); scholars with smaller numbers of cases should consider primarily focusing on in-depth case analyses (Ragin, 2000), although QCA might still be useful to qualitative researchers to map the diversity of cases in a systematic manner. Additionally, QCA's utility extends beyond smaller sample sizes as a methodological alternative to regression approaches using moderate- to large-N samples (Cooper, 2005; Greckhamer et al., 2013) and as a viable method for building and testing theories with large-N samples (Amoroso & Ragin, 1999; Fiss, 2011; Greckhamer et al., 2008; Ragin & Bradshaw, 1991; Ragin & Fiss, 2008). In our review, the sample sizes of studies[6] ranged from 11 (Woulfin & Jones, 2018) to 11,990 (Glaesser & Cooper, 2012b) cases, with a median of 91 cases. This indicates that education researchers recognized QCA as a viable methodological approach both for small-N and for large-N empirical settings.

What constitutes appropriate cases in a QCA study depends on the phenomenon being studied, and the reviewed articles nicely capture how QCA can be applied to a variety of cases to study different phenomena in set-theoretic terms. Examples of relatively small samples included 12 teachers (Coburn et al., 2012), 11 (Woulfin & Jones, 2018) and 49 (Bandaranayake, 2016) elementary and secondary schools, 40 business schools (Snelson-Powell et al., 2016), 14 economics departments (Schneider & Sadowski, 2010), 17 communities of inquiry (Kintz et al., 2015), and 15 countries and their education systems (Birchler & Michaelowa, 2016). Examples of large-N QCA applications included studies with samples of 344 (Pappas et al., 2017), 2,366 (Glaesser & Cooper, 2012a) and even 11,990 (Glaesser & Cooper, 2012b) individual students. Additional examples of phenomena defined as cases in QCA studies included practices or routines based on codes that resulted from initial qualitative data analyses, such as teachers' responses to data (Farrell & Marsh, 2016), reading workshops (Woulfin, 2015), and instructional tasks (Trujillo & Woulfin, 2014).

Review of Methodological Practices

Our review of education articles included an evaluation of their methodological rigor. Recognizing that QCA and its application in the social sciences continue to evolve and that QCA applications in education are still in their infancy, our objective is not to critique individual articles but rather to understand the extent to which the empirical articles we reviewed reflect current recommendations for QCA research designs. We relied on Greckhamer et al.'s (2018) recent synthesis of recommended practices and established and applied methodological principles to provide guidance for each stage of a QCA research design that enables theoretically sound, empirically well-executed, and analytically rigorous research (for related suggestions of good practices for QCA, see also Schneider & Wagemann, 2010, 2012). Additionally, we developed a rubric (see Table 3) to assess the degree to which the articles applied the aforementioned methodological recommendations either explicitly or implicitly, thereby identifying methodological exemplars in education. However, we emphasize that any recommended practices should not be applied in a mechanistic manner (Greckhamer et al., 2018) and "should not and cannot turn Qualitative Comparative Analysis into a point-and-click method" (Schneider & Wagemann, 2016, p. 320).

TABLE 3
Evaluation Rubric for QCA Applications

Application of QCA	Score
Most or all recommended practices are followed, explicitly or implicitly.	5
Most key recommended practices are followed, explicitly or implicitly, but there are minor issues in implementation.	4
Some recommended practices are followed implicitly, but there is no clear discussion or presentation of QCA analysis.	3
Most key recommended practices are not followed; the analysis and reporting are largely not consistent with recommended practices.	2
Discussion of QCA is very brief; implementation and research design are inadequate.	1

Note. The underlying evaluation of articles' application of QCA assesses the extent to which they reflect current recommended methodological practices as synthesized by Greckhamer et al. (2018). QCA = qualitative comparative analysis.

We identified several studies as *methodological exemplars* (i.e., rated 4 or 5 according to our criteria; e.g., Bandaranayake, 2016; Glaesser & Cooper, 2012a, 2012b; Glaesser et al., 2009a; Pappas et al., 2017; Sebastian et al., 2014; Toots & Lauri, 2015). We find it encouraging to have several exemplars from within education despite the method's relative novelty in education. In the following section, we highlight key points of the aforementioned current methodological recommendations, illustrate their application by way of the exemplars we identified in our sample, and provide recommendations for future research.

Model Building

A QCA research design begins with establishing a configurational theoretical model as a basis for meaningful analysis. This theoretical model should clearly define the researchers' outcome of interest, present a clear rationale for selecting the case attributes included in the model that is rooted either in theory or in case knowledge, establish a clear rationale as to why the conditions should be studied as configurations, and consider the maximum number of conditions that may be included in the study based on the sample at hand to generate valid and parsimonious results.

In our review, about half of the studies built a configurational model that reflected a rationale explaining why the conditions should be studied in combination rather than independently; however, only a handful of studies explicitly pursued configurational theorizing. Pappas et al. (2017) provide a good example: They built a conceptual model that explicitly defined the outcome of interest and attributes as sets, focused on the combinations of case attributes to explain the occurrence of the outcome, and used Venn diagrams to depict the set-theoretic nature of the model. Sebastian et al.'s (2014) study is another excellent example that explicitly articulated a set-theoretic approach to school leadership and organization by drawing on well-established configurational theory in the management literature.

Related to model building, our review also indicates that education researchers should consider the maximum number of attributes they should include in a study based on sample size. Marx and colleagues (Marx, 2010; Marx & Dusa, 2011) provide instructive guidelines that can help balance the number of conditions with the number of cases to ensure that the QCA analysis produces highly valid results. As a reminder, the number of logically possible combinations is 2^k, where $k =$ the number of included attributes; thus, the complexity of QCA models increases exponentially with each additional attribute included. For example, increasing the number of attributes included in a QCA model by two (e.g., from five to seven) raises the number of logically possible attribute combinations fourfold (e.g., from 32 to 128). An increasing number of attributes increases the complexity of findings and thus the difficulty of interpreting them, hence authors should carefully consider the number of included attributes, even in large-N studies (Greckhamer et al., 2013).

Although it appeared that a limit on the number of conditions and model parsimony were not common considerations in the articles we reviewed, Toots and Lauri (2015) explicitly limited the number of conditions to keep the complexity of their model and findings manageable. Indeed, some authors recognized limitations resulting from the number of conditions included in their model relative to the small number of cases in their sample (Bandaranayake, 2016; Lauri & Põder, 2013). In sum, education researchers would benefit from consulting the methodological literature discussed above for guidance on appropriate model complexity or how to balance the number of attributes with the study's sample size to ensure interpretable findings with bounded complexity.

Building a Proper Sample

A critical part of a QCA research design is to build an empirical sample that is suitable for the study's purpose. Building a purposeful empirical sample should begin with identifying the population of cases of interest based on the outcome researchers want to study. Where possible, the study sample could involve the entire population. If that is not possible, researchers should strive to construct a sample that represents the diversity of cases in the population to make interpretation of the results meaningful. Several of the reviewed articles clearly documented a purposeful sampling strategy to build the sample. For example, Bandaranayake (2016) clearly built a purposeful sample targeted to study the identified outcome. With an interest in exploring the paths linked to success versus failure of schools, the author selected a sample based on clear definitions of high-performing and low-performing schools in the population of schools studied and selected all schools that met the criteria for high or low performance. If this were not the case, it would have been important to otherwise draw a sample that clearly represented the diversity of high-performing and low-performing schools. To give another example, Sebastian et al. (2014) studied the link between school leadership and classroom performance by constructing a purposeful sample of schools from archival data for the population of schools in a large urban school district.

Transparent Calibration

Given its set-theoretic foundations, QCA requires empirical data in the form of case set membership. Qualitative or quantitative case data must therefore be transformed into set data through a process of assigning cases' membership in (crisp or fuzzy) sets through calibration. Recommendations include starting with clear definitions of the sets included in a study's model, making transparent decisions regarding what constitutes membership of cases in these sets, and when using the direct method of calibration providing clear rationales for the anchor points chosen. For example, Pappas et al. (2017) clearly explained the process of calibration in their study, explicitly indicated that they followed Ragin's (2008) direct method of calibration, and described how they anchored the three thresholds required for this method of calibration. To give another example, Bandaranayake (2016) transparently described his calibration of fuzzy sets by including a table that describes the calibration thresholds used for each of the four-value fuzzy sets. Given QCA's relatively early state in education, it is understandable for researchers to have difficulty finding theory to support their calibration decisions (e.g., Olufadi, 2015). Drawing on the larger QCA literature may help education researchers navigate these difficulties.

Truth Table Analysis for Necessity and Sufficiency

An essential analytical step in QCA is the construction and analysis of a truth table as the basis for identifying attribute combinations that may be necessary and/or sufficient for the occurrence of outcomes of interest. Truth table analysis requires researchers to choose consistency and case frequency thresholds as well as to articulate any simplifying assumptions grounded in theory to analyze counterfactual cases. For proper interpretation and representation of findings, researchers should report the diversity of cases in their data set if feasible, by presenting the truth table, as well as the results of both necessity and sufficiency analyses. These analyses should ideally be supplemented by case-level evidence, particularly for bolstering arguments regarding causal relationships.

Truth tables were not commonly presented in the articles in our sample. Bandaranayake's (2016) study includes the partial truth table for empirically existing configurations for both the high-performance and the low-performance outcomes; this suffices because with the information provided an interested reader could reconstruct the logically possible but empirically unobserved configurations and thus the complete truth table. Bandaranayake also includes the complete fuzzy set data table for data transparency, which was feasible due to the study's moderate sample size. Similarly, Toots and Lauri (2015) included several truth tables, including combinations of remote and proximal conditions as well as their respective outcomes, also linking them back to cases by listing which countries in their sample represented a respective configuration.

Regarding necessity and sufficiency analyses, few articles reported explicit necessity analyses, whereas a large majority of articles reported some sufficiency analyses results. Necessity analysis is particularly recommended if, based on prior theory and/ or knowledge of cases, researchers suspect one or more case attributes to be necessary for an outcome to occur. Exemplars of necessity analyses include Toots and Lauri's (2015) necessity tests; these authors apply high raw consistency thresholds as recommended and identify human development as a necessary remote condition for high civic knowledge. To give another example, Bandaranayake (2016) found that scoring high on an index of community socio-educational advantage is a necessary condition for high school performance by the recommended benchmarks.

Sufficiency analysis is at the heart of set-theoretic analysis because the notions of conjunctural and equifinal causality, respectively, imply that individual causes, even if necessary, may not be sufficient to be linked to an outcome and alternative combinations of attributes may be sufficient for the same outcome. For example, Glaesser and Cooper (2012b) demonstrated the power of sufficiency analysis by showing how students' ability, gender, and cultural capital combine to enable high educational achievement. Specifically, they found that in both selective and nonselective schools, to reach certain levels of educational success, students' high ability is quasi-sufficient but at lower levels of ability, students also need to be either female or have highly educated parents, or both. In another study along similar lines, Glaesser and Cooper (2012a) found two combinations of student characteristics to be consistently linked to obtaining A-level qualifications in a sample of British secondary school students: Either students with a higher social class background and high ability OR male working-class students with high ability who attended selective schools were consistently attaining A-level qualifications.

A key element of sufficiency analysis regards the consistency benchmarks applied to determine sufficient configurations. With respect to recommended practices, consistency scores should be as close to 1 as possible (Ragin, 2006b), particularly for studies with small sample sizes, and a minimum consistency benchmark of .80 to consider subset relations as sufficient has been fairly well established since it was recommended by Ragin (2008). Researchers facing low consistency of their model should reconsider the attributes included; indeed, the process of selection of attributes may involve an iterative process of model building and analysis, as noted above. Moreover, configurations with consistencies $\leq.75$ should not be interpreted as sufficient because their levels of inconsistency are too high to maintain an argument that even a rough set relation exists (Ragin, 2008; Schneider & Wagemann, 2010). Put differently, configurations with such low consistency scores defy the logic that they should be sufficient to cause the outcome.

Our review suggests that the recommendations for establishing consistency thresholds have not yet penetrated QCA research in education. To begin with, a number of studies did not report sufficiency analyses for the applied raw consistency thresholds to identify sufficient configurations. In addition, some articles we reviewed did not report their findings' overall solution consistency, without which readers cannot evaluate whether the results are sufficiently consistent to be meaningfully interpreted. Furthermore, our review sample included articles that reported sufficiency results with solution consistencies as low as .71 and even .63. For consistency scores that are substantially below the recommended thresholds, appropriate researcher judgment would be to refrain from interpreting these results as substantive sufficiency relationships and instead revisit the configurational model. This caution is especially valid for small-*N* studies. Our sample included an example in which the authors noted that because a solution only approaches the recommended level of consistency with a score of .63, the solution should be interpreted with caution. However, the methods literature would recommend that configurations with such levels of (in)consistency should not be interpreted (Ragin, 2008; Schneider & Wagemann, 2010). To be clear, a .80 consistency threshold should not be applied mechanically. Within the range between the minimum recommended threshold (.80) and perfect consistency of 1, researchers may consider varying consistency thresholds to evaluate how these changes influence the results of sufficiency analyses.[7] Indeed, as we will discuss below, doing so is recommended for evaluating the robustness of a study's results. Typically, choosing a higher consistency threshold leads to lower sufficiency solution coverage, and vice versa.

Analysis of Causal Asymmetry

As noted above, QCA recognizes that the occurrence and the nonoccurrence of an outcome may constitute two qualitatively different phenomena and thus enables researchers to explore causal asymmetry. Thus, researchers should analyze the configurations linked to the presence as well as those linked to the absence of outcomes (Greckhamer et al., 2018; Ragin, 2008; Schneider & Wagemann, 2012). Several studies in our sample took advantage of QCA's ability to report analyses of conditions linked to the absence of the studied outcome. To give some examples, Bandaranayake (2016) reported the configurations linked to both high and low school performance. Similarly, Sebastian et al. (2014) analyzed both the configurations linked to high classroom participation and those linked to the absence of high classroom participation, and Snelson-Powell et al. (2016) investigated the institutional conditions that lead business colleges to tightly couple their espoused sustainability commitments with their practices versus decoupling these commitments from their practices.

Robustness

Because, as in any empirical analysis, the decisions QCA researchers make affect the results, recommendations also involve an evaluation of the robustness of findings—including how changes in the chosen thresholds and different simplifying assumptions would change the results. Of the articles reviewed, few gave some consideration to the robustness of their findings. Among our exemplary studies, Glaesser and Cooper (2012b) discussed and demonstrated how setting different raw consistency thresholds led to different configurations. Similarly, Toots and Lauri (2015) provided an appendix documenting the results of a sensitivity analysis by changing the thresholds of their outcome condition of high civic knowledge and the condition the study identified as necessary, which was presence of high human development. Overall, our review highlights that going forward education researchers using QCA would benefit from being more transparent about their analysis decisions and discussing the robustness of their reported results.

REVIEW OF RESEARCH FROM OTHER FIELDS

In addition to our purpose of tracing the current state of QCA research, our review also aims to offer recommendations for how QCA can be used in future research. For this purpose, we now turn to our review of articles outside the field of education. The 30 articles in Set II (included in the reference list and indicated with a dagger symbol) are intended to capture studies related to education topics published in noneducation journals that could serve as inspiration for education research. While disciplinary divisions are not clear-cut,[8] we assume that education researchers tend to primarily stay abreast of developments within education. Clearly, disciplinary theories and assumptions may differ even when scholars study the same phenomena and/or use the same concepts. Thus, education scholars should keep in mind that these articles were written from the vantage point of and/or for the audience of another discipline. Accordingly, the substantive elements of these articles may be interpreted differently by and have limited use for education scholars. Nonetheless, we believe that considering their methods and research designs could provide inspiration for education researchers focusing on similar phenomena. Therefore, we highlight a few select examples here and provide summaries of all the studies' topics and disciplines in Table 4.

The studies in Set II were concentrated in journals in the sociology (9), business and management (8), public health and health care (4), and psychology and applied psychology (3) categories of the WoS. In addition to discipline of origin, in our review we noted articles' topics and the domain(s) of education research for which each article is most likely to be relevant as inspiration. Overall, the domains of education research that we identified as most pertinent to those articles were educational policy, administration, and leadership (16); higher education (12); diversity, equity, and sociology of education (14); and educational technology (6).

To begin with examples of studies relevant to educational policy, administration, and leadership, Chatterley et al.'s (2014) public health study used QCA with in-depth qualitative data from 16 schools in Bangladesh to identify necessary and sufficient conditions that lead to either well-managed or poorly managed school sanitation, offering insights for policies aimed at encouraging well-managed school

TABLE 4

Summary of Noneducation Articles Using QCA

First Author, Year	Discipline Category	Topic	Relevant Education Subspecialty(ies)
Alon, 2007	Sociology	Graduation rate of students with intersecting disadvantages at elite colleges	Diversity and equity; higher education
Borgna, 2016	Sociology	Inequality of educational opportunity for second-generation immigrants in Europe	Comparative education; educational administration; diversity and equity
Borgna, 2017	Public administration	Social stratification of young adults' literacy skills in OECD countries	Comparative education; educational policy; diversity and equity
Capatina, 2018	Computer science	Game-based learning progress within a collaborative learning environment	Educational technology
Chatterley, 2014	Public health	Management of school sanitation services	Educational administration
Cooper, 2005	Sociology	Role of class, gender, and ability in educational achievement	Educational policy; diversity and equity; sociology of education
Cooper, 2008	Sociology	Role of class origin, gender, and qualifications in adulthood social class	Diversity and equity; sociology of education
Crecente-Romero, 2018	Business	Entrepreneurship as an alternative to seeking employment for overqualified university graduates	Economics of education; higher education
Dai, 2015	Business	Comparison of the effectiveness of e-learning, blended learning, and traditional instruction for remedial instruction	Educational technology
Dill, 2014	Public health	Workers' efficacy and satisfaction in career ladder programs	Higher education

(continued)

TABLE 4 (CONTINUED)

First Author, Year	Discipline Category	Topic	Relevant Education Subspecialty(ies)
Freitag, 2009	Political science	Conditions of regional education systems associated with social inequality in education	Education policy; diversity and equity; sociology of education
Glaesser, 2011	Sociology	Equality of opporunity in tracking in the German educational system	Education policy; diversity and equity
Gonzalez-Serrano, 2017	Applied psychology	Factors influencing adolescents' intention of being physically active after completing their education	Curriculum and instruction; physical activity
Guidi, 2016	Political science	Students' participation in university student organizations	Higher education
Henriques, 2018	Business	Factors that affect undergraduates' choice of a higher education institution	Higher education
Holvoet, 2016	Development studies	Role of incentives in increasing primary school enrollment of females in sub-Saharan African countries	Education policy; diversity and equity
Jiang, 2016	Business	Role of perceived ease of use and attitude in the degree of behavioral intention in multimedia teaching materials	Educational technology
Kien, 2018	Public health	Combinations of teacher and implementation process characteristics affecting the emotional and social school experience of students participating in a school-based health promotion program	Curriculum and instruction; educational administrtion
Lee, 2018	Business	Organizational justice and faculty engagement conditions that contribute to educational value	Higher education
Martí-Parreño, 2018	Psychology	Students' characteristics and their attitude toward the use of educational video games to develop competencies	Educational technology

(continued)

TABLE 4 (CONTINUED)

First Author, Year	Discipline Category	Topic	Relevant Education Subspecialty(ies)
Mostaghel, 2017	Social sciences; gerontology	Conditions that affect senior citizens' acceptance of technology	Educational technology
Nelson, 2017	Sociology	Role of reward bundling and job fit in teacher turnover	Educational administration; education policy
Plewa, 2016	Business	Resources associated with higher education institutions' reputation	Education policy; higher education
Pullum, 2016	Sociology	Conditions for teachers' unions not seeking a vote to overturn state legislature limiting teachers' employment rights	Educational administration; education policy
Rezaev, 2017	Sociology	Drivers of organizational diversity and transformation of the Soviet comprehensive university into a "post-Soviet research university" or "general education organization"	Education policy; higher education
Sergis, 2018	Psychology	Educational leaders' data use to identify conditions for fostering students' digital skills	Educational leadership; educational technology
Shanahan, 2008	Sociology	Role of genetic factors and social context in educational continuation beyond secondary school	Diversity and equity; higher education; sociology of education
Sim, 2018	Management	Interdependence among students' engagement with lecturer, university, and study context	Higher education
Tho, 2015	Business	Factors affecting the transfer of knowledge from business schools to business organizations	Educational administration; higher education
Williams, 2018	Health care	Role of medical training environment in students' racial and gender biases toward patients	Curriculum and instruction; diversity and equity; higher education

Note. QCA = qualitative comparative analysis; OECD = Organisation for Economic Co-operation and Development.

sanitation. Additionally, Sergis et al.'s (2018) study in psychology could be insightful for researchers in education policy and leadership because it demonstrated the utility of QCA for deriving insights that can inform school leaders' strategic school planning as an alternative to school analytics approaches based on data visualization or variance-based analyses.

Studies that may offer ideas for higher education research focused on areas such as faculty affairs, student life, and career programs. For example, a study that utilized QCA to identify the resource configurations underlying the reputations of higher education institutions (Plewa et al., 2016) revealed that combining learning resources either with facilities and campus life or with administrative staff support and industry linkage resulted in strong reputations. Alternatively, in the absence of learning resources, institutions can still achieve high reputations by offering certain combinations of other resources. A sociology article on the change of the Soviet comprehensive university into a "post-Soviet research university" or "general education organization" in post-Soviet countries could stimulate comparative research on educational institutions (Rezaev & Starikov, 2017), for example, for studying the links between institutional changes and universities' research productivity.

QCA studies exploring the links between schooling systems and inequality (Cooper, 2005; Cooper & Glaesser, 2008; Freitag & Schlicht, 2009; Glaesser & Cooper, 2011) could inform research on diversity and equity, and in the sociology of education. For example, a study of the institutional contexts that shape educational opportunities for second-generation immigrants in Europe analyzed educational systems as configurations of interconnected elements (Borgna, 2016). Another article in sociology (Alon, 2007) that investigated the links between college students' backgrounds and graduating from elite educational institutions represents an example of using QCA to study issues of intersectionality as it highlights the compounding effects of disadvantages stemming from the intersection of students' gender, race, and class.

Finally, our review identified several studies that could serve as models for research in educational technology. For example, Mostaghel and Oghazi (2017) investigated the factors influencing technology acceptance among the elderly, noting that technology could provide innovative solutions to deal with the complex care demands of this population. To give another example, Dai and Huang (2015) applied QCA as part of their research design to study the effectiveness of different remedial instruction models, and as such, their study could be of use to research at the intersection of educational technology and instructional design.

DISCUSSION AND POTENTIAL FUTURE DIRECTIONS

This chapter offers a systematic review, synthesis, and appraisal of education research using QCA, presenting its current state of application in education as a basis to facilitate an education research agenda that utilizes the potential benefits and contributions of QCA's set-theoretic approach; it therefore adds to reviews of QCA research in specific disciplines (Kan et al., 2016; Misangyi et al., 2017; Rihoux et al., 2013). Our review indicates that compared with some other social science fields (Misangyi et al., 2017; Rihoux & Marx, 2013) the potential of this innovative approach has yet to be fully harnessed in education. More specifically, our review indicates that empirical education research to date has remained limited to certain areas, that future QCA research in education would benefit from adopting methodological recommendations that are currently represented by a few exemplary studies, and that education researchers could benefit from an awareness of relevant empirical studies in fields that are closely related to their respective domain of education research. Below we provide suggestions for education researchers that follow from our review.

Promising Future Research Directions

Education research is rife with empirical phenomena that may be marked by complex causality. Research that capitalizes on QCA's features to conceptualize and empirically study the conjunction, equifinality, and asymmetry potentially underlying educational phenomena could complement more established methodologies by offering a new approach for established research venues as well as by enabling new research questions based on an understanding of causal complexity.

To give a few examples, empirical and policy analyses approaching educational issues through a lens of intersectionality would be particularly suitable for a QCA approach because social inequalities tend to be interdependent and disadvantages exacerbate other disadvantages while advantages can also be compounded; thus, QCA's assumption that outcomes (here, outcomes of social inequality) are shaped by conjunctive causality is consistent with the position of intersectionality (Ragin & Fiss, 2017). Likewise, QCA's notion of causal asymmetry holds substantial promise for research areas that should not readily assume symmetric outcomes because QCA assumes that the occurrence of an outcome and its absence may be caused by different conditions and may potentially even require different causal models (Schneider & Wagemann, 2012). For example, the causes underlying students' dropping out of school may well be different from the opposite of the causes underlying students' persistence. Likewise, the conditions facilitating women leaders' career advancement in higher education may not equal the absence of barriers hindering their success. Also, any research area where multiple alternative "causal recipes" are suspected—or sought for policymaking purposes—would benefit from QCA research. For example, identifying equifinal paths to student achievement would have implications for creating policies that are practical in different contexts.

Our review also shows that education researchers are taking advantage of QCA's applicability to both large-N and small-N empirical settings (Greckhamer et al., 2013). It is worth reiterating that QCA was originally designed for and is well suited for analyzing relatively small-N samples (12–50) that are not appropriate for conventional quantitative approaches (Ragin, 1987), which holds potential for areas of education research that typically rely on small sample sizes. This includes comparative education research at the country level, special education research that has few students with relevant characteristics eligible for the study, and organizational studies at the school or district level. However, researchers should keep in mind that sample size and the number of attributes included are interrelated, as discussed above.

Using QCA for Multilevel Analyses

QCA also offers an alternative approach for empirical studies of multilevel phenomena (Greckhamer et al., 2008; Lacey & Fiss, 2009). This is especially relevant for education research because of the importance of multilevel contexts in this field (Raudenbush, 1988; Raudenbush & Bryk, 1986). For example, understanding student performance nationally requires researchers to attend to variation among states, local school districts, and/or individual schools in terms of educational resources, processes, and outcomes (Raudenbush, 1988). The importance of multilevel phenomena has resulted in a large body of research using hierarchical linear modeling. Lacey and Fiss (2009) elaborate on QCA's potential to study multilevel phenomena and detail how QCA's set-theoretic approach to multilevel issues and to conceptualizing cases as configurations across levels differs from conventional statistical approaches to multilevel analysis.

Our review illustrated examples of QCA studies that used cases at various levels of analysis, including students, departments, schools, and countries. Building on this previous research, future education research can analyze empirical phenomena spanning multiple levels of analysis by properly defining the cases of interest and the relevant case attributes. For example, multilevel research using QCA could study the joint effect of teachers, schools or school leaders, districts, and/or larger geographic divisions on student outcomes. QCA offers a theoretical and methodological approach to hierarchical multilevel models that enables researchers to combine data from multiple levels in a way that can disentangle the causal complexity resulting from the interrelations of attributes across different levels. However, we note that because multilevel research would potentially need to consider more attributes, it may be particularly challenging to theorize parsimonious models, making sample size considerations vital.

Using QCA for Research Syntheses

While we only included primary empirical research in our review, during our search and screening of studies for eligibility, we noted several articles that used QCA as a meta-analytic method for literature syntheses. For example, Burchett et al. (2018) used QCA to conduct a systematic review of research on the effectiveness of lifestyle weight management programs for children, synthesizing 11 qualitative studies. Similarly, Forman-Hoffman et al. (2017) used QCA to synthesize the literature on mental health care for children and adolescents to identify consistent relationships between combinations of strategy components and improvements in mental health outcomes. We also offer a few examples outside our review that may be inspirational for education researchers who might consider using QCA to conduct meta-analyses. First, Hodson and Roscigno (2004) used QCA to synthesize the findings from more than 80 workplace ethnographies. Second, Joshi et al. (2015) first used traditional meta-analysis to examine whether occupation-, industry- and job-level factors individually affect gender pay gaps and then used QCA to explore whether and how these factors combined to affect gender pay gaps. While these examples demonstrate QCA's promise, as with any meta-analysis, researchers should ensure that the studies underlying the synthesis combine studies that share similar features (Cooper, 2010; Kepes et al., 2013), meaning that for the purposes of QCA they should study comparable cases, outcomes, and attributes.

Concluding Notes

Our review is intended to facilitate applications of QCA in education research and to contribute toward building the requisite expertise for reaping QCA's potential for education research. Although we focused on presenting the strengths and potential contributions of QCA to education research, we emphasize that QCA is not a panacea for all research problems and, like any other approach, has limitations. Researchers considering whether they should choose QCA or other approaches should evaluate the respective strengths and appropriateness of each approach for their study. First, as we discussed above, QCA fundamentally differs from correlational and linear regression analysis approaches in its assumption of causal relations. Whereas QCA is well suited for studies focused on unraveling causal complexity, it is ill suited to identify the independent effects of individual attributes (i.e., independent variables) on a dependent variable or to explain variance in the dependent variable. Thus, researchers interested in the latter research objectives should choose an appropriate regression analysis or variance decomposition approach over QCA. For researchers interested in a more detailed discussion of the differences between QCA and regression analyses, we recommend several studies offering in-depth demonstrations and discussions of these differences (Grofman & Schneider, 2009; Katz et al., 2005; Thiem et al., 2015; Vis, 2012).

Similarly, researchers considering the appropriateness of QCA relative to qualitative analyses should consider the research questions they aim to answer. Although a strength of QCA is to systematically identify cross-case patterns of a limited number of attributes while also preserving the integrity of cases as complex configurations of key attributes, this involves reducing the complexity of cases to a relatively small number of attributes rather than exploring the detailed and idiosyncratic richness of individual cases (Ragin, 2000). Put differently, researchers who are primarily interested in an in-depth interpretative understanding of a small number of cases rather than a systematic cross-case comparison of key patterns should choose qualitative research approaches over QCA. Furthermore, qualitative research encompasses a wide variety of methods with different purposes and assumptions (Crotty, 1998;

Guba & Lincoln, 1994), including interpretation of individuals' lifeworlds and subjective experiences and deconstructing taken-for-granted realities. Relatedly, as noted above, QCA would not be a good fit for studies with samples smaller than 12. It is generally advisable to complement QCA findings with in-depth qualitative, within-case analysis of selected cases to build strong arguments of causal relations (Mahoney, 2004; Rohlfing & Schneider, 2013; Schneider & Rohlfing, 2013).

We conclude with a note of caution that as an innovative method (Gerring, 2001) that fundamentally breaks from the common quantitative and qualitative methodological traditions in the social sciences and that is still evolving, QCA continues to provoke debates between its proponents and opponents, such as those introduced above. A review of the arguments suggests that the debates stem from diverging assumptions and perspectives of proponents or opponents of QCA and that QCA is not merely a method but a fundamentally different way of conceptualizing and empirically studying social science phenomena. Therefore, we recommend that researchers interested in QCA who review these debates pay close attention to understanding and appreciating how QCA differs in its assumptions and goals from other traditions of research so that they can judge whether QCA is suitable for their research goals. Our hope is that more education researchers will take interest in this underutilized approach, weight its merits, and consider its application as a means to bridge exchanges across different research traditions (Mahoney & Goertz, 2006) to answer key questions in education research. We also hope that researchers who decide not to pursue QCA research will do so as informed sceptics rather than uninformed dismissers (Mahoney, 2004).

ORCID iDs

Sebnem Cilesiz https://orcid.org/0000-0001-8779-4197
Thomas Greckhamer https://orcid.org/0000-0002-5766-556X

NOTES

[1]A comprehensive QCA bibliography across disciplines is available at www.compasss.org.

[2]Multivalue sets, a less commonly used third type of sets, are an extension of crisp set QCA and allow capturing of multicategorical, nominal-scale conditions. For an introduction to mvQCA [multivalue set QCA], see Cronqvist and Berg-Schlosser (2009) and Vink and van Vliet (2009), and for an example relevant to higher education, see Rezaev and Starikov (2017).

[3]Because in QCA researchers usually apply consistency benchmarks to evaluate whether empirical results support inferences regarding necessity and sufficiency, attributes that surpass these benchmarks may also be described as "usually" or "quasi" necessary or sufficient.

[4]WoS may be referred to by alternative names (including Web of Knowledge, Social Sciences Citation Index, Thompson Reuters, and Clarivate Analytics) due to ownership and name changes over time. We searched the WoS Core Collection, which covers the four indexes SSCI, SCI-EXPANDED, A&HCI, and ESCI.

[5]Our decision to use "QCA" as an inclusive search term resulted in an initial sample that included articles using the acronym to refer to other terms such as "qualifications and curriculum authority," "quantitative content analysis," "qualitative content analysis," or other medical,

legal, or informatics terms. As a result, articles that are not relevant to the QCA method accounted for 60% of the articles that were eliminated from the initial search records in ERIC.

[6]For articles combining QCA and other methodologies with differing sample sizes for the QCA portion and the other portions, we only report sample sizes relevant to the QCA portion.

[7]Future education research will also benefit from integrating the relatively new fuzzy set analysis measure of proportional reduction in inconsistency, which helps researchers strengthen sufficiency analysis by avoiding simultaneous subset relations of configurations in both the presence and the absence of the outcome (Greckhamer et al., 2018).

[8]For example, Glaesser and Cooper's QCA research on topics in sociology of education appears in both education and sociology outlets.

REFERENCES

References marked with an asterisk indicate articles reviewed in education journals.
References marked with a dagger indicate articles reviewed in noneducation journals.

Abbott, A. (1988). Transcending general linear reality. *Sociological Theory, 6*(2), 169–186. https://doi.org/10.2307/202114

Agosto, V., & Roland, E. (2018). Intersectionality in educational leadership: A critical review. *Review of Research in Education, 42*(1), 255–285. https://doi.org/10.3102/0091732X18762433

†Alon, S. (2007). Overlapping disadvantages and the racial/ethnic graduation gap among students attending selective institutions. *Social Science Research, 36*(4), 1475–1499. https://doi.org/10.1016/j.ssresearch.2007.01.006

Amoroso, L. M., & Ragin, C. C. (1999). Two approaches to understanding control of voluntary and involuntary job shifts among Germans and foreigners from 1991 to 1996. *Vierteljahreshefte zur Wirtschaftsforschung, 68*(2), 222–229.

*Bandaranayake, B. (2016). Polarisation of high-performing and low-performing secondary schools in Victoria, Australia: An analysis of causal complexities. *Australian Educational Researcher, 43*(5), 587–606. https://doi.org/10.1007/s13384-016-0213-8

Baumgartner, M., & Thiem, A. (2017). Often trusted never (properly) tested: Evaluating qualitative comparative analysis. *Sociological Methods & Research*. Advance online publication. https://doi.org/10.1177/0049124117701487

Berg-Schlosser, D., & De Meur, G. (2009). Comparative research design: Case and variable selection. In B. Rihoux, & C. Ragin (Eds.), *Configurational comparative methods: Qualitative comparative analysis (QCA) and related techniques* (pp. 19–32). Sage.

*Birchler, K., & Michaelowa, K. (2016). Making aid work for education in developing countries: An analysis of aid effectiveness for primary education coverage and quality. *International Journal of Educational Development, 48*, 37–52. https://doi.org/10.1016/j.ijedudev.2015.11.008

†Borgna, C. (2016). Multiple paths to inequality. How institutional contexts shape the educational opportunities of second-generation immigrants in Europe. *European Societies, 18*(2), 180–199. https://doi.org/10.1080/14616696.2015.1134801

†Borgna, C. (2017). Different systems, same inequalities? Post-compulsory education and young adults' literacy in 18 OECD countries. *Journal of European Social Policy, 27*(4), 332–345. https://doi.org/10.1177/0958928717719197

Burchett, H. E. D., Sutcliffe, K., Melendez-Torres, G. J., Rees, R., & Thomas, J. (2018). Lifestyle weight management programmes for children: A systematic review using qualitative comparative analysis to identify critical pathways to effectiveness. *Preventive Medicine, 106*, 1–12. https://doi.org/10.1016/j.ypmed.2017.08.025

†Capatina, A., Bleoju, G., Rancati, E., & Hoareau, E. (2018). Tracking precursors of learning analytics over serious game team performance ranking. *Behaviour & Information Technology, 37*(10/11), 1008–1020. https://doi.org/10.1080/0144929X.2018.1474949

†Chatterley, C., Javernick-Will, A., Linden, K. G., Alam, K., Bottinelli, L., & Venkatesh, M. (2014). A qualitative comparative analysis of well-managed school sanitation in Bangladesh, *14*(6). https://doi.org/10.1186/1471-2458-14-6

*Coburn, C. E., Russell, J. L., Kaufman, J. H., & Stein, M. K. (2012). Supporting sustainability: Teachers' advice networks and ambitious instructional reform. *American Journal of Education, 119*(1), 137–182. https://doi.org/10.1086/667699

†Cooper, B. (2005). Applying Ragin's crisp and fuzzy set QCA to large datasets: Social class and educational achievement in the National Child Development Study. *Sociological Research Online, 10*(2). https://doi.org/10.5153/sro.1068

†Cooper, B., & Glaesser, J. (2008). How has educational expansion changed the necessary and sufficient conditions for achieving professional, managerial and technical class positions in Britain? A configurational analysis. *Sociological Research Online, 13*(3), 2. https://doi.org/10.5153/sro.1703

Cooper, B., & Glaesser, J. (2011). Paradoxes and pitfalls in using fuzzy set QCA: Illustrations form a critical review of a study of educational inequality. *Sociological Research Online, 16*(3), 1–14. https://doi.org/10.5153/sro.2444

Cooper, H. M. (2010). *Research synthesis and meta-analysis: A step-by-step approach* (4th ed.). Sage.

†Crecente-Romero, F., Giménez-Baldazo, M., & Rivera-Galicia, L. F. (2018). Can entrepreneurship channel overqualification in young university graduates in the European Union? *Journal of Business Research, 89*, 223–228. https://doi.org/10.1016/j.jbusres.2018.01.056

Crenshaw, K. (1989). Demarginalizing the intersection of race and sex: A Black feminist critique of antidiscrimination doctrine, feminist theory and antiracist politics. *University of Chicago Legal Forum, 140*, 139–167.

Cronqvist, L., & Berg-Schlosser, D. (2009). Multi-value QCA (vmQCA). In B. Rihoux, & C. Ragin (Eds.), *Configurational comparative methods: Qualitative comparative analysis and related techniques* (pp. 69–86). Sage.

Crotty, M. (1998). *The foundations of social research.* Sage.

†Dai, C.-Y., & Huang, D.-H. (2015). Causal complexities to evaluate the effectiveness of remedial instruction. *Journal of Business Research, 68*(4), 894–899. https://doi.org/10.1016/j.jbusres.2014.11.048

Davis, K. (2008). Intersectionality as buzzword: A sociology of science perspective on what makes a feminist theory successful. *Feminist Theory, 9*(1), 67–85. https://doi.org/10.1177/1464700108086364

†Dill, J. S., Chuang, E., & Morgan, J. C. (2014). Healthcare organization-education partnerships and career ladder programs for health care workers. *Social Science & Medicine, 122*, 63–71. https://doi.org/10.1016/j.socscimed.2014.10.021

Duşa, A. (2019). Critical tension: Sufficiency and parsimony in QCA. *Sociological Methods & Research.* Advance online publication. https://doi.org/10.1177/0049124119882456

*Farrell, C. C., & Marsh, J. A. (2016). Contributing conditions: A qualitative comparative analysis of teachers' instructional responses to data. *Teaching and Teacher Education, 60*, 398–412. https://doi.org/10.1016/j.tate.2016.07.010

Fiss, P. (2007). Towards a set-theoretic approach for studying organizational configurations. *Academy of Management Review, 32*(4), 1180–1198. https://doi.org/10.5465/amr.2007.26586092

Fiss, P. (2011). Building better causal theories: A fuzzy set approach to typologies in organization research. *Academy of Management Journal, 54*(2), 393–420. https://doi.org/10.5465/amj.2011.60263120

Fiss, P., Cambré, B., & Marx, A. (Eds.). (2013). *Configurational theory and methods in organizational research* (Vol. 38, Research in the Sociology of Organizations). Emerald Group.

Forman-Hoffman, V. L., Middleton, J. C., McKeeman, J. L., Stambaugh, L. F., Christian, R. B., Gaynes, B. N., Kane, H. L., Kahwati, L. C., Lohr, K. N., & Viswanathan, M. (2017). Quality improvement, implementation, and dissemination strategies to improve mental health care for children and adolescents: A systematic review. *Implementation Science, 12*(93), 1–21. https://doi.org/10.1186/s13012-017-0626-4

†Freitag, M., & Schlicht, R. (2009). Educational federalism in Germany: Foundations of social inequality in education. *Governance: An International Journal of Policy Administration and Institutions, 22*(1), 47–72. https://doi.org/10.1111/j.1468-0491.2008.01421.x

Gerring, J. (2001). *Social science methodology: A criterial framework.* Cambridge University Press.

†Glaesser, J., & Cooper, B. (2011). Selectivity and flexibility in the German secondary school system: A configurational analysis of recent data from the German socio-economic panel. *European Sociological Review, 27*(5), 570–585. https://doi.org/10.1093/esr/jcq026

*Glaesser, J., & Cooper, B. (2012a). Educational achievement in selective and comprehensive local education authorities: A configurational analysis. *British Journal of Sociology of Education, 33*(2), 223–244. https://doi.org/10.1080/01425692.2011.649833

*Glaesser, J., & Cooper, B. (2012b). Gender, parental education, and ability: Their interacting roles in predicting GCSE success. *Cambridge Journal of Education, 42*(4), 463–480. https://doi.org/10.1080/0305764X.2012.733346

*Glaesser, J., Gott, R., Roberts, R., & Cooper, B. (2009a). The roles of substantive and procedural understanding in open-ended science investigations: Using fuzzy set qualitative comparative analysis to compare two different tasks. *Research in Science Education, 39*(4), 595–624. https://doi.org/10.1007/s11165-008-9108-7

*Glaesser, J., Gott, R., Roberts, R., & Cooper, B. (2009b). Underlying success in open-ended investigations in science: Using qualitative comparative analysis to identify necessary and sufficient conditions. *Research in Science & Technological Education, 27*(1), 5–30. https://doi.org/10.1080/02635140802658784

†González-Serrano, M. H., Moreno, F. C., Hervás, J. C., & Prado-Gascó, V. (2017). Why are you passive? Understanding teen's sports intentions by QCA and LM. *Revista de Psicología del Deporte, 26*(Suppl. 3), 91–96.

Grandori, A., & Furnari, S. (2008). A chemistry of organization: Combinatory analysis and design. *Organization Studies, 29*(3), 459–485. https://doi.org/10.1177/0170840607088023

Greckhamer, T., Furnari, S., Fiss, P., & Aguilera, R. (2018). Studying configurations with qualitative comparative analysis: Best practices in strategy and organization research. *Strategic Organization, 16*(4), 482–495. https://doi.org/10.1177/1476127018786487

Greckhamer, T., Misangyi, V., Elms, H., & Lacey, R. (2008). Using qualitative comparative analysis in strategic management research: An examination of combinations of industry, corporate, and business-unit effects. *Organizational Research Methods, 11*(4), 695–726. https://doi.org/10.1177/1094428107302907

Greckhamer, T., Misangyi, V., & Fiss, P. (2013). The two QCAs: From a small-N to a large-N set-theoretic approach. *Research in the Sociology of Organizations, 38*, 49–75. https://doi.org/10.1108/S0733-558X(2013)0000038007

Grofman, B., & Schneider, C. (2009). An introduction to crisp set QCA, with a comparison to binary logistic regression. *Political Research Quarterly, 62*(4), 662–672. https://doi.org/10.1177/1065912909338464

Guba, E., & Lincoln, Y. (1994). Competing paradigms in qualitative research. In N. K. Denzin, & Y. S. Lincoln (Eds.), *Handbook of qualitative research* (pp. 105–117). Sage.

†Guidi, R., Bonetti, M., & Popolla, M. (2017). Differently collective: Youth activism in Italian university associations. *Partecipazione e Conflitto, 9*(3), 857–892. https://doi.org/10.1285/i20356609v9i3p857

†Henriques, P. L., Matos, P. V., Jerónimo, H. M., Mosquera, P., da Silva, F. P., & Bacalhau, J. (2018). University or polytechnic? A fuzzy-set approach of prospective students' choice and its implications for higher education institutions' managers. *Journal of Business Research, 89*, 435–441. https://doi.org/10.1016/j.jbusres.2017.12.024

Hodson, R., & Roscigno, V. J. (2004). Organizational success and worker dignity: Complementary or contradictory. *American Journal of Sociology, 110*(3), 672–708. https://doi.org/10.1086/422626

†Holvoet, N., & Inberg, L. (2016). Do gender targets and gender working groups contribute to more gender-sensitive budget support? Evidence from 14 sub-Saharan African countries. *European Journal of Development Research, 28*(5), 875–892. https://doi.org/10.1057/ejdr.2015.58

*Hsieh, M.-Y. (2017). An empirical study of education divide diminishment through online learning courses. *EURASIA Journal of Mathematics, Science & Technology Education, 13*(7), 3189–3208. https://doi.org/10.12973/eurasia.2017.00712a

*Hsieh, M.-Y. (2018). Exploring the most decisive online education determinants as impacted by Taiwan's New Southbound Policy. *Eurasia Journal of Mathematics, Science & Technology Education, 14*(5), 1945–1962. https://doi.org/10.29333/ejmste/83608

Hug, S. (2013). Qualitative comparative analysis: How inductive use and measurement error lead to problematic inference. *Political Analysis, 21*(2), 252–265. https://doi.org/10.1093/pan/mps061

*Jain, V., & Jain, P. (2018). Affect vs cognition as antecedents of selection behaviour of elective courses using fsQCA. *Journal of Applied Research in Higher Education, 10*(4), 443–455. https://doi.org/10.1108/JARHE-12-2017-0164

†Jiang, T.-H., Chen, S.-L., & Chen, J. K. C. (2016). Examining the role of behavioral intention on multimedia teaching materials using FSQCA. *Journal of Business Research, 69*(6), 2252–2258. https://doi.org/10.1016/j.jbusres.2015.12.038

Joshi, A., Son, J., & Roh, H. (2015). When can women close the gap? A meta-analytic test of sex differences in performance and rewards. *Academy of Management Journal, 58*(5), 1516–1545. https://doi.org/10.5465/amj.2013.0721

Kan, S., Adegbite, E., El Omari, S., & Abdellatif, M. (2016). On the use of qualitative comparative analysis in management. *Journal of Business Research, 69*(4), 1458–1463. https://doi.org/10.1016/j.jbusres.2015.10.125

Katz, A., Hau, M., & Mahoney, J. (2005). Explaining the great reversal in Spanish America: Fuzzy set analysis versus regression analysis. *Sociological Methods & Research, 33*(4), 539–573. https://doi.org/10.1177/0049124104266002

Kepes, S., McDaniel, M., Brannick, M., & Banks, G. (2013). Meta-analytic reviews in the organizational sciences: Two meta-analytic schools on the way to MARS (the Meta-Analytic Reporting Standards). *Journal of Business Psychology, 28*(2), 123–143. https://doi.org/10.1007/s10869-013-9300-2

†Kien, C., Grillich, L., Nussbaumer-Streit, B., & Schoberberger, R. (2018). Pathways leading to success and non-success: A process evaluation of a cluster randomized physical activity health promotion program applying fuzzy-set qualitative comparative analysis. *BMC Public Health, 18*, Article 1386. https://doi.org/10.1186/s12889-018-6284-x

*Kintz, T., Lane, J., Gotwals, A., & Cisterna, D. (2015). Professional development at the local level: Necessary and sufficient conditions for critical colleagueship. *Teaching and Teacher Education, 51*, 121–136. https://doi.org/10.1016/j.tate.2015.06.004

Lacey, R., & Fiss, P. (2009). Comparative organizational analysis across multiple levels: A set-theoretic approach. *Research in the Sociology of Organizations, 26*, 91–116. https://doi .org/10.1108/S0733-558X(2009)0000026006

*Lauri, T., & Põder, K. (2013). School choice policy: Seeking to balance educational efficiency and equity. A comparative analysis of 20 European countries. *European Educational Research Journal, 12*(4), 534–552. https://doi.org/10.2304/eerj.2013.12.4.534

*Lee, L. C. (2013). The diversity of school organizational configurations. *International Journal of Research & Method in Education, 36*(4), 309–340. https://doi.org/10.1080/17437 27X.2012.705274

†Lee, M. T., & Raschke, R. L. (2018). Freeing "workplace prisoners" in higher education: Configurations for collective knowledge building and educational value decisions. *Journal of Business Research, 88*, 443–448. https://doi.org/10.1016/j.jbusres.2018.01.022

Lee, T. W. (1999). *Using qualitative methods in organizational research.* Sage.

Lucas, S. R., & Szatrowski, A. (2014). Qualitative comparative analysis in critical perspective. *Sociological Methodology, 44*, 1–79. https://doi.org/10.1177/0081175014532763

Mahoney, J. (2004). Reflections on fuzzy-set/QCA. *Newsletter of the American Political Science Association, 2*(2), 17–21.

Mahoney, J., & Goertz, G. (2006). A tale of two cultures: Contrasting quantitative and qualitative research. *Political Analysis, 14*(3), 227–249. https://doi.org/10.1093/pan/mpj017

†Martí-Parreño, J., Galbis-Córdova, A., & Miquel-Romero, M. J. (2018). Students' attitude towards the use of educational video games to develop competencies. *Computers in Human Behavior, 81*, 366–377. https://doi.org/10.1016/j.chb.2017.12.017

Marx, A. (2010). Crisp-set qualitative comparative analysis (csQCA) and model specification: Benchmarks for future csQCA applications. *International Journal of Multiple Research Approaches, 4*(2), 138–158. https://doi.org/10.5172/mra.2010.4.2.138

Marx, A., & Dusa, A. (2011). Crisp-set qualitative comparative analysis (csQCA), contradictions and consistency benchmarks for model specification. *Methodological Innovations Online, 6*(2), 103–148. https://doi.org/10.4256/mio.2010.0037

Marx, A., Rihoux, B., & Ragin, C. (2014). The origins, development, and application of qualitative comparative analysis: The first 25 years. *European Political Science Review, 6*(1), 115–142. https://doi.org/10.1017/S1755773912000318

Meyer, A. D., Tsui, A. S., & Hinings, C. R. (1993). Configurational approaches to organizational analysis. *Academy of Management Journal, 36*(6), 1175–1195. https:// doi.org/10.2307/256809

Misangyi, V., Greckhamer, T., Furnari, S., Fiss, P., Crilly, D., & Aguilera, R. (2017). Embracing causal complexity: The emergence of a neo-configurational perspective. *Journal of Management, 43*(1), 255–282. https://doi.org/10.1177/0149206316679252

†Mostaghel, R., & Oghazi, P. (2017). Elderly and technology tools: A fuzzyset qualitative comparative analysis. *Quality & Quantity: International Journal of Methodology, 51*(5), 1969–1982. https://doi.org/10.1007/s11135-016-0390-6

†Nelson, J. (2017). Pathways to green(er) pastures: Reward bundles, human capital, and turnover decisions in a semi-profession. *Qualitative Sociology, 40*(1), 23–57. https://doi .org/10.1007/s11133-016-9348-1

Olsen, W. (2014). Comment: The usefulness of QCA under realist assumptions. *Sociological Methodology, 44*(1), 101–107. https://doi.org/10.1177/0081175014542080

*Olufadi, Y. (2015). A configurational approach to the investigation of the multiple paths to success of students through mobile phone use behaviors. *Computers & Education, 86*, 84–104. https://doi.org/10.1016/j.compedu.2015.03.005

*Pappas, I. O., Giannakos, M. N., Jaccheri, L., & Sampson, D. G. (2017). Assessing student behavior in computer science education with an fsQCA approach. *ACM Transactions on Computing Education, 17*(2), 1. https://doi.org/10.1145/3036399

†Plewa, C., Ho, J., Conduit, J., & Karpen, I. O. (2016). Reputation in higher education: A fuzzy set analysis of resource configurations. *Journal of Business Research, 69*(8), 3087–3095. https://doi.org/10.1016/j.jbusres.2016.01.024

PRISMA. (2018, September 13). *PRISMA 2009 flow diagram.* http://www.prisma-statement.org/PRISMAStatement/FlowDiagram

†Pullum, A. (2016). Social movements, strategic choice, and recourse to the polls. *Mobilization, 21*(2), 177. https://doi.org/10.17813/1086-671X-21-2-177

Ragin, C. (1987). *The comparative method: Moving beyond qualitative and quantitative strategies.* University of California Press.

Ragin, C. (2000). *Fuzzy-set social science.* University of Chicago Press.

Ragin, C. (2006a). The limitations of net-effects thinking. In B. Rihoux, & H. Grimm (Eds.), *Innovative comparative methods for policy analysis* (pp. 13–41). Springer.

Ragin, C. (2006b). Set relations in social research: Evaluating their consistency and coverage. *Political Analysis, 14*(3), 291–310. https://doi.org/10.1093/pan/mpj019

Ragin, C. (2008). *Redesigning social inquiry: Fuzzy sets and beyond.* University of Chicago Press.

Ragin, C. (2014). Comment: Lucas and Szatrowski in critical perspective. *Sociological Methodology, 44*(1), 80–94. https://doi.org/10.1177/0081175014542081

Ragin, C., & Bradshaw, Y. (1991). Statistical analysis of employment discrimination: A review and critique. *Research in Social Stratification and Mobility, 10,* 199–228.

Ragin, C., & Fiss, P. (2008). Net effects versus configurations: An empirical demonstration. In C. Ragin (Ed.), *Redesigning social inquiry: Fuzzy sets and beyond* (pp. 190–212). University of Chicago Press.

Ragin, C., & Fiss, P. (2017). *Intersectional inequality: Race, class, test scores, and poverty.* University of Chicago Press.

Ragin, C., & Sonnett, J. (2005). Between complexity and parsimony: Limited diversity, counterfactual cases, and comparative analysis. In S. Kropp, & M. Minkenberg (Eds.), *Vergleichen in der Politikwissenschaft* (pp. 180–197). VS Verlag fuer Sozialwissenschaften.

Raudenbush, S. (1988). Educational applications of hierarchical linear models: A review. *Journal of Educational Statistics, 13*(2), 85–116. https://doi.org/10.3102/10769986013002085

Raudenbush, S., & Bryk, A. (1986). A hierarchical model for studying school effects. *Sociology of Education, 59*(1), 1–17. https://doi.org/10.2307/2112482

†Rezaev, A. V., & Starikov, V. S. (2017). The transformation of higher education systems in six post-Soviet countries: Causes and consequences of organizational change. *Comparative Sociology, 16*(1), 127–146. https://doi.org/10.1163/15691330-12341418

Rihoux, B. (2003). Bridging the gap between qualitative and quantitative worlds? A retrospective and prospective view on qualitative comparative analysis. *Field Methods, 15*(4), 351–365. https://doi.org/10.1177/1525822X03257690

Rihoux, B., Álamos-Concha, P., Bol, D., Marx, A., & Rezsöhazy, I. (2013). A comprehensive mapping of QCA applications in journal articles from 1984 to 2011. *Political Research Quarterly, 66*(1), 175–184. https://doi.org/10.1177/1065912912468269

Rihoux, B., & Marx, A. (2013). QCA, 25 years after "The Comparative Method": Mapping, challenges, and innovations—mini-symposium. *Political Research Quarterly, 66*(1), 167–235. https://doi.org/10.1177/1065912912468269

Rihoux, B., & Ragin, C. (2009). *Configurational comparative methods: Qualitative comparative analysis (QCA) and related techniques.* Sage.

*Roberts, R., Gott, R., & Glaesser, J. (2010). Students' approaches to open-ended science investigation: The importance of substantive and procedural understanding. *Research Papers in Education, 25*(4), 377–407. https://doi.org/10.1080/02671520902980680

Rohlfing, I., & Schneider, C. (2013). Improving research on necessary conditions: Formalized case selection for process tracing after QCA. *Political Research Quarterly, 66*(1), 220–235. https://doi.org/10.1177/1065912912468269

Schneider, C. (2018). Realists and idealists in QCA. *Political Analysis, 26*(2), 246–254. https://doi.org/10.1017/pan.2017.45

Schneider, C., & Rohlfing, I. (2013). Combining QCA and process tracing in set-theoretic multi-method research. *Sociological Methods & Research, 42*(4), 559–597. https://doi.org/10.1177/0049124113481341

Schneider, C., & Rohlfing, I. (2016). Case studies nested in fuzzy-set QCA on sufficiency: Formalizing case selection and causal inference. *Sociological Methods & Research, 45*(3), 526–568. https://doi.org/10.1177/0049124114532446

Schneider, C., & Wagemann, C. (2010). Standards of good practice in qualitative comparative analysis (QCA) and fuzzy-sets. *Comparative Sociology, 9*(3), 397–418. https://doi.org/10.1163/156913210X12493538729793

Schneider, C., & Wagemann, C. (2012). *Set-theoretic methods for the social sciences.* Cambridge University Press.

Schneider, C., & Wagemann, C. (2016). Assessing ESA on what it is designed for: A reply to Cooper and Glaesser. *Field Methods, 28*(3), 316–321. https://doi.org/10.1177/1525822X15598977

*Schneider, P., & Sadowski, D. (2010). The impact of new public management instruments on PhD education. *Higher Education, 59*(5), 543–565. https://doi.org/10.1007/s10734-009-9264-3

Schudde, L. (2018). Heterogeneous effects in education: The promise and challenge of incorporating intersectionality into quantitative methodological approaches. *Review of Research in Education, 42*(1), 72–92. https://doi.org/10.3102/0091732X18759040

*Sebastian, J., Allensworth, E., & Stevens, D. (2014). The influence of school leadership on classroom participation: Examining configurations of organizational supports. *Teachers College Record, 116*(8), 1–36.

†Sergis, S., Sampson, D. G., & Giannakos, M. N. (2018). Supporting school leadership decision making with holistic school analytics: Bridging the qualitative-quantitative divide using fuzzy-set qualitative comparative analysis. *Computers in Human Behavior, 89*, 355–366. https://doi.org/10.1016/j.chb.2018.06.016

†Shanahan, M. J., Vaisey, S., Erickson, L. D., & Smolen, A. (2008). Environmental contingencies and genetic propensities: Social capital, educational continuation, and dopamine receptor gene DRD2. *American Journal of Sociology, 114*(Suppl. 1), S260–S286. https://doi.org/10.1086/592204

Short, J. (2009). The art of writing a review article. *Journal of Management, 35*(6), 1312–1317. https://doi.org/10.1177/0149206309337489

†Sim, M., Conduit, J., & Plewa, C. (2018). Engagement within a service system: A fuzzy set analysis in a higher education setting. *Journal of Service Management, 29*(3), 422–442. https://doi.org/10.1108/JOSM-08-2016-0232

Smithson, M., & Verkuilen, J. (2006). *Fuzzy set theory: Applications in the social sciences.* Sage.

*Snelson-Powell, A., Grosvold, J., & Millington, A. (2016). Business school legitimacy and the challenge of sustainability: A fuzzy set analysis of institutional decoupling. *Academy of Management Learning & Education, 15*(4), 703–723. https://doi.org/10.5465/amle.2015.0307

Soda, G., & Furnari, S. (2012). Exploring the topology of the plausible: Fs/QCA counterfactual analysis and the plausible fit of unobserved organizational configurations. *Strategic Organization, 10*(3), 285–296. https://doi.org/10.1177/1476127012452826

Tefera, A. A., Powers, J. M., & Fischman, G. (2018). Intersectionality in education: A conceptual aspiration and research imperative. *Review of Research in Education, 42*(1), vii–xvii. https://doi.org/10.3102/0091732X18768504

Thiem, A. (2014). Mill's methods, induction, and case sensitivity in qualitative comparative analysis: A comment on Hug (2013). *Qualitative & Multimethods Research, 12*(2), 19–24.

Thiem, A., Baumgartner, M., & Bol, D. (2015). A correction of three misunderstandings between configurational comparativists and regression analysts. *Comparative Political Studies, 49*(6), 742–774. https://doi.org/10.1177/0010414014565892

*Tho, N. D. (2017). Using signals to evaluate the teaching quality of MBA faculty members: fsQCA and SEM findings. *Education + Training, 59*(3), 292–304. https://doi.org/10.1108/ET-03-2016-0060

†Tho, N. D., & Trang, N. T. M. (2015). Can knowledge be transferred from business schools to business organizations through in-service training students? SEM and fsQCA findings. *Journal of Business Research, 68*(6), 1332–1340. https://doi.org/10.1016/j.jbusres.2014.12.003

*Toots, A., & Lauri, T. (2015). Institutional and contextual factors of quality in civic and citizenship education: Exploring possibilities of qualitative comparative analysis. *Comparative Education, 51*(2), 247–275. https://doi.org/10.1080/03050068.2014.985926

Triandis, H. C. (2004). Dimensions of culture beyond Hofstede. In H. Vinken, J. Soeters, & P. Ester (Eds.), *Comparing cultures: Dimensions of culture in a comparative perspective* (pp. 28–42). Brill.

*Trujillo, T. M., & Woulfin, S. L. (2014). Equity-oriented reform amid standards-based accountability: A qualitative comparative analysis of an intermediary's instructional practices. *American Educational Research Journal, 51*(2), 253–293. https://doi.org/10.3102/0002831214527335

Vaisey, S. (2014). Comment: QCA works—when used with care. *Sociological Methodology, 44*(1), 108–112. https://doi.org/10.1177/0081175014542083

Vink, M. P., & van Vliet, O. (2009). Not quite crisp, not yet fuzzy? Assessing the potentials and pitfalls of multi-value QCA. *Field Methods, 21*(3), 265–289. https://doi.org/10.1177/1525822X09332633

Vis, B. (2012). The comparative advantages of fsQCA and regression analyses for moderately large-N analyses. *Sociological Methods & Research, 41*(1), 168–198. https://doi.org/10.1177/0049124112442142

†Williams, R. L., Vasquez, C. E., Getrich, C. M., Kano, M., Boursaw, B., Krabbenhoft, C., & Sussman, A. L. (2018). Racial/gender biases in student clinical decision-making: A mixed-method study of medical school attributes associated with lower incidence of biases. *JGIM: Journal of General Internal Medicine, 33*(12), 2056–2064. https://doi.org/10.1007/s11606-018-4543-2

Wolfswinkel, J., Furtmueller, E., & Wilderom, C. (2011). Using grounded theory as a method for rigorously reviewing literature. *European Journal of Information Systems, 22*(1), 45–55. https://doi.org/10.1057/ejis.2011.51

*Woulfin, S. L. (2015). Highway to reform: The coupling of district reading policy and instructional practice. *Journal of Educational Change, 16*(4), 535–557. https://doi.org/10.1007/s10833-015-9261-5

*Woulfin, S. L., & Jones, B. (2018). Rooted in relationships: An analysis of dimensions of social capital enabling instructional coaching. *Journal of Professional Capital and Community, 3*(1), 25–38. https://doi.org/10.1108/JPCC-07-2017-0017

*Zorio-Grima, A., Sierra-García, L., & Garcia-Benau, M. A. (2018). Sustainability reporting experience by universities: A causal configuration approach. *International Journal of Sustainability in Higher Education, 19*(2), 337–352. https://doi.org/10.1108/IJSHE-07-2016-0142

Chapter 13

Bifurcating Worlds? A Systematic Review of How Visual and Language Data Are Combined to Study Teachers and Their Teaching

Rachel E. Schachter (iD)
University of Nebraska, Lincoln

Donald Freeman
Naivedya Parakkal
University of Michigan

Connecting teachers' perspectives with their practice is an enduring challenge shaping what and how we understand teaching. Researchers tend to bifurcate teachers' work between their private and their public lives. These "worlds" bring particular meanings that are rendered through the analyses of visual documentations of teaching and teachers' language-based accounts of their teaching. Combining these two forms of data is a basic research challenge both operationally and conceptually. Operationally, the researcher determines how the forms are connected and which decisions reflect (and are anchored in) conceptual warrants. This review identified 52 studies that combine visual and language data to study teachers and teaching to examine how data were collected and analyzed in the studies and what types of the theoretical frameworks were used to warrant the interpretations resulting from the connections. The review found only seven studies that balanced both worlds by explicitly warranting how the two forms of data were interconnected. Otherwise, most studies foregrounded one form of data and drew on the other to support or explain the first. Whereas most of the authors rationalized the connection between the forms of data in their studies, few took the more complex step of theorizing how the two worlds were connected. We argue that such incomplete connections risk inaccurately representing the work of teaching. We propose some design questions and research procedures that researchers may use to avoid bifurcating teachers' worlds.

Review of Research in Education
March 2020, Vol. 44, pp. 370–402
DOI: 10.3102/0091732X20903305
Chapter reuse guidelines: sagepub.com/journals-permissions
© 2020 AERA. http://rre.aera.net

The mind is so near itself
It cannot see distinctly.
And I have none to ask,
Should you think it breathed
And had you the leisure to tell me,
I should feel quick gratitude.
—Poet Emily Dickinson writing to General Thomas Wentworth Higginson to solicit his comments
on several of her poems[1]

FRAMING THE PROBLEM CONCEPTUALLY AND METHODOLOGICALLY

Uncovering what another is thinking, and how that thinking is connected to what they do, has been a central undertaking in the creative arts as well as in research. In education, identifying procedures that enable researchers to connect teachers' perspectives to how they enact their classroom practices presents a continuing conceptual and methodological challenge. The poet Emily Dickinson's eloquent phrasing, "The mind is so near itself/It cannot see distinctly," expresses a version of this conceptual problem that is rooted in the Cartesian mind–body problem in philosophy: How to gain access to another person's thoughts? In research, the methodological problem comes to the fore when researchers look to document the relationship between thinking and actions in order to study the connection. "Documenting the relationship" includes the procedures that are used, as well as the warrants researchers use to connect thinking with actions, to make claims, and to anchor findings. This chapter addresses one specific procedural context of this challenge: How education researchers have documented teachers' perspectives on their *own* classroom teaching. We argue that, although there has been attention to the "world" of teachers' "mental lives" (Walberg, 1977) and a recognition that classroom teaching and learning cannot be fully understood from the public world alone, research procedures for studying these worlds have not kept pace conceptually.

How education researchers relate thinking and action specifically in the context of teachers' work in classroom teaching entails a cluster of conceptual and methodological decisions. The decisions about research procedures determine "what we see" about the inner and outer worlds of teaching being studied. Decisions about conceptualizing the relationship between teachers' thinking and knowing and what is observed in their actions determine "what we get" from employing those procedures. This chapter reviews studies to examine these relationships between what we see and what we get: How specifically do research procedures capture, document, and reflect teachers' perspectives on their own classroom instruction?

Speaking broadly about methodology, researchers have used interviews (e.g., Kvale, 2008; Mishler, 1991), surveys (e.g., Becker, 2000; McMillan et al., 2002), or explicit measures of teacher knowledge (e.g., Hill et al., 2008; Moats, 1994) to document the inner world of teachers' thought processes. These procedures hinge on the conceptual and methodological assumption that these aspects of teachers' thinking—their private world—can be rendered indirectly through language. Thus, asserting that researchers can gain access to teachers' thinking and perspectives through the language exchanged in interviewing or through responses to survey questions. Researchers can document the inner world of what teachers know through the explicit measures of teaching such as surveys of teachers' knowledge that are expressed in language. In these ways, *language data* are supposed to provide access to, or to capture and represent the private worlds of teachers' thinking. For the purposes of this review, we define language data as teachers' verbal expressions of their thinking. Meanwhile, the external world of classroom activity and instruction is usually documented visually, generally through observational instruments and field notes, and sometimes through images and recordings of practice. These *visual data* are held to directly document the public world of teaching.

Making the connections between language and visual data methodologically introduces assumptions about how these worlds relate to each other. We refer to private and the public as "worlds" inasmuch as each brings a particular set of meanings that are rendered through these analyses of visual or language data. We argue that education research in this area has usually focused on (or foregrounded) the meanings of one world and drawn on the meanings from the other to support or "explain" the first. Perhaps because it seems more immediate and accessible, studies have tended to focus more on the visual world of teaching rather than on the thinking or intentions behind actions (Kennedy, 2016). We refer to this disconnect between the private worlds of teachers and the public worlds of classroom activity as "bifurcating worlds."

This systematic review examines how the worlds of teachers' thinking can become connected to their public actions through the methodological procedures that researchers use and the conceptual assumptions they make. Writing about this issue in qualitative work more broadly, Maxwell (2013) has admonished fellow researchers to

think about what particular sources of error or bias might exist, and look for specific ways to deal with this, rather than relying on your selection of methods to do this for you. In the final analysis, validity threats are made implausible by evidence, not methods. (p. 128)

Although this problem is not limited to education research, it becomes centrally important to understanding and improving classroom practice. Research that focuses exclusively—or even primarily—on the public world of teaching risks building interpretations, explanations, and findings about classroom practice that omit the private world of the teacher as a principal protagonist. To rely on what can be observed and documented in this public world as evidence essentially tells only part of the story. In contrast, research that relies, through interviews, for example, on the private world of teaching risks making assumptions about how the perspectives expressed are linked to practice without evidence of this connection. Connecting the public and private worlds then, treating them as complementary, can create a fuller, more complex, though often messier understanding of how classroom teaching unfolds. Overcoming this bifurcating of worlds is more than a methodological undertaking, however. It involves more than how the language and visual data are collected. The challenge entails working on how the meanings of the two forms of data are positioned relative to one another in analysis and how the connections asserted by the researcher are grounded theoretically.

AIM OF THIS CHAPTER

In this review, we examine data collection methods that purport to connect the two worlds and thus to allow the researcher to make and warrant, through analysis, connections between visual data with language data. Importantly, we have focused on the methods used to solicit in-service teachers' perspectives on their *own* classroom instruction. The particular focus on *in-service* teachers' perspectives rules out work using video in preservice teacher preparation or in-service teacher education, in which the recordings and the visual data they produce are used for pedagogical purposes (e.g., Abell et al., 1998; Masingila & Doerr, 2002; Xiao & Tobin, 2018). We recognize that much of this work is often anchored in similar assumptions about how teachers' thinking and their actions are connected; however, this review sought to examine research that involved the ongoing, established practices of teachers. Whereas there are a variety of research methods that elicit perspectives, we focused particularly on methods for connecting the public and private work of the individual teacher. We were specifically interested in three dimensions of these data collection methods: (1) the collection procedures themselves, (2) the frameworks on which these procedures are anchored explicitly or implicitly to theorize or justify the connection, and (3) the assumptions about what is represented in visual and language data that these methods make.

In examining studies that use data collection procedures of in-service teachers' practices that combine data from the public and private worlds of their teaching, the review asks the broader research question: *What can be understood about teaching through the use of data collection and analyses procedures that integrate language data and visual data?* Within this question, we are specifically concerned with the following:

Research Question 1 (RQ1): Which *data collection procedures* are used to combine visual and language data to study teaching?

Research Question 2 (RQ2): Which *theoretical frameworks* support the collection and integration of these two types of data in these procedures?

Research Question 3 (RQ3): What *assumptions* are made in linking or "warranting" the analyses of the visual and language data, and how do these assumptions vary by data collection procedure?

We address each of these subquestions in the Findings section and then return to the overarching question at the close of the discussion.

METHOD

Article Search

To address these specific research questions, we undertook a systematic literature review to assemble and describe a set of empirical studies, including those using quantitative, qualitative, and mixed methods, which met predetermined criteria (Gough, 2015). We began by searching for research studies published in refereed sources that used procedures that combined language data with visual data to understand teachers' perspectives as linked to their public practice. We followed procedures used by other researchers who had reviewed literature on the use of videos (Gaudin & Chaliès, 2015) as well as procedures used by the authors in previous work (Schachter, 2015; Schachter & Freeman, in press). We started by searching common education research databases, including ERIC, Education (SAGE), PsycINFO, Wiley Online Library, and Social Science Citation Index; however, we found that these search results were not as thorough or exhaustive as we had anticipated. After consulting with an education research librarian, we expanded our search to ProQuest, which draws from the above databases and included access to a total of 95 databases at the second author's institution.

We undertook multiple steps in conducting this search and narrowing the data set. We began by combining the terms "thinking" AND "teaching" to broadly capture research on the private processes involved in teaching. Then, based on preliminary searches, we developed a Boolean search query with variations on terms related to "language data," "visual data," "teach*," "thinking," and "reflection." We then narrowed the search by limiting it to articles in peer-reviewed journals. We set a date range from January 1, 1975, to December 31, 2018.[2] To further bound the search, we excluded document and source types that were not explicitly empirical articles, such as "conference papers and proceedings" and "literature reviews." We also did not include articles in languages other than English. Both of these parameters resulted in a very small reduction in the total. The entire process resulted in 607 articles.

Exclusion and Inclusion Coding

To be included in this study, each article had to meet the criteria presented in Table 1. To identify the final data set, these criteria were applied sequentially to the 607 articles. The coding then proceeded in two phases.

Phase 1 Coding

Articles were excluded that did not meet the specific characteristics related to the research questions, described subsequently. The three authors and a graduate student researcher read the abstracts of each article and excluded articles that were (1) not empirical studies; (2) not about teaching and learning in pre-K to 12th-grade settings *with in-service teachers*; (3) not about classroom practices, in which we included the activities that teachers initiate, direct, manage, or take part; and (4) did not specifically study teachers (see Table 1). The latter criterion is central to this review as we are

TABLE 1

Criteria for Including or Excluding Articles in the Search

Phase 1	Phase 2
1. Does not meet criteria for rigorous quantitative or qualitative research (based on criteria outlined in Brown & Lan, 2015; Schachter, 2015).	1. Must contain visual and language data.
2. The participants in the study are not teachers.	2. Must include in-service teachers.
3. The study does not examine some form of classroom practice.	3. Must elicit teachers' accounts or perspectives on practice. The focus must be on teachers and not on students.
4. The study does not take place in a pre-K to 12th-grade setting.	4. Must specify collection methods of visual and language data.
	5. Must be published in 1975 or later.
	6. Must be peer-reviewed.
	7. If professional development (PD) is involved, the study must focus on uptake of PD in the classroom or on understanding PD-related changes in the classroom.

concerned with how visual and language data about classroom teaching can capture and represent teachers' perspectives. Thus, articles that focused on students in classrooms were excluded, whereas those that involved teacher–student interactions and data on the teacher's views on that activity were included. For example, Vetter (2010) studied how a teacher facilitated student identities during English language arts (ELA), thus examining the teacher's role and practice although the outcome was connected to students. In total, 87 articles remained after this process.

Phase 2 Coding

The processes of exclusion coding ruled out articles, but we then needed to confirm that the final data set only included articles that were relevant to our research questions. To this end, the remaining 87 articles were each read in their entirety by the three authors and the graduate research student to confirm suitability for inclusion in the study (see Table 1). Only articles that specified the collection and the analysis of both language and visual data in their data methods and findings were included. Furthermore, articles were included only if the language and visual data elicited teachers' thinking or perspectives about their own teaching. For example, Vetter (2010) discussed previously used language data from teacher interviews and visual data from recorded observations to understand how the teacher facilitated student identity development. This process resulted in 18 articles that were relevant to our search.

Additional Searches

Based on best practices in such reviews (Gough, 2015; Schachter, 2015), the third author and the graduate research student used the references listed in the included articles to search for other studies that met the criteria. The main authors of the included publications were also searched to locate additional studies from their work that might be relevant. To make these determinations, we first examined the article titles and then, as needed, the abstracts and even the full texts of articles themselves. The two phases of coding criteria described previously were then applied to the articles from this secondary search. In total, 27 additional articles were located through this process and included in the final data set. As the chapter was being prepared, expert reviewers also suggested additional authors or publications to examine as part of the search. This process added 10 articles to the review.

Article Coding and Analyses

The final data set included 52 articles that used both visual and language data to examine the public and private worlds of teaching. We conducted a content analyses (Hsieh & Shannon, 2005) to review the contents of the included articles, using both inductive and deductive coding to address the research questions. A priori codes were generated to identify the research design and data collection procedures (RQ1) and to identify how researchers connected the visual and language data to understand teaching (RQ2 and RQ3).

Additional grounded codes related to the research questions, use of language data, and data sources were developed based on patterns identified in the data via inductive analysis (Corbin & Strauss, 2008; Schachter, 2015). As with most grounded analyses, this combined coding strategy supported a nuanced approach in addressing the research questions. Specifically, we noted that in some of the studies it was difficult to identify theoretical frameworks that connected the visual and language data (RQ2). Thus, we developed codes based on how researchers used theory to support the collection of language data more generally. Additionally, codes related to the purpose of the studies as well as codes that foregrounded the different forms of data (i.e., visual or language) also emerged (RQ3). Table 2 provides a list of codes, definitions, and, when appropriate, the number of studies meeting the code.

FINDINGS

In total, 52 articles were included in the analyses for this review. We had initially intended to exclude articles that integrated visual data with language data elicited before or after their enacted instruction (i.e., in the teacher's planning or post hoc reflections on their teaching). Invoking this criterion would have significantly reduced the final data set, however. Therefore, we chose to broaden the scope of this study beyond in-the-moment practice to consider practice more generally (Lampert, 2010). Given our focus on understanding how researchers connect the public and private worlds in the act of teaching, we only included these articles if the researchers used the data to elicit teachers' perspectives about their own practice.

The resulting set of 52 articles included research from 1991 to 2018 that studied preschool (e.g., Alanís, 2018; Baker, 2019; Schachter, 2017), elementary (e.g., Drake

TABLE 2

Coding Categories by Research Question (RQ)

Code	Definition	Number of Studies
RQ1: Procedures		
Research design	Researchers' description of their design	See Table 3
Visual data collection procedures	Identified from data methods	See Table 3
Language data collection procedures	Identified from data methods	See Table 3
Explicit connection	Two types of data were explicitly linked to understand connections between the public and private worlds of teaching from the teacher's perspective.	21
Implicit connection	No explicit description of how visual and language data were combined to understand connections between the public and private worlds of teaching.	31
RQ2: Theoretical frameworks		
Knowledge	Researchers providing theory regarding teachers' knowledge—must use the word "knowledge."	17
Beliefs	Researchers providing theory regarding teachers' beliefs—must use the word "belief."	17
Teacher or student identities	Researchers providing theory regarding the role of identity for teachers or students.	11
Classroom practices	Researchers focusing on the inner world as a way to understand classroom activities that teachers initiate, direct, manage, and participate in.	37
RQ3: Assumptions or warrants		
Foregrounding visual data and backgrounding language data	Research design/presentation of findings favors or foregrounds visual data or the public world of teaching.	18
Foregrounding language data and backgrounding visual data	Research design/presentation of findings favors or foregrounds language data or the private world of teaching.	21
Balanced	Research design/presentation of findings ascribes similar importance to the public and private sides of teaching.	13

377

& Sherin, 2006; Henderson & Palmer 2015b; Levitt, 2002), middle (e.g., Hofer & Swan, 2008; Martin et al., 2001), and secondary (e.g., Alazzi, 2008; Chiodo & Tsai, 1997; Vetter, 2010) teachers. Among these studies, multiple content areas were investigated, including ELA (e.g., Camburn & Barnes, 2004; Flynn & Schachter, 2017; Hamel, 2003; Maloch, 2002; Worthy et al., 2015), science (e.g., Diezmann & Watters, 2015; Levitt, 2002; Savasci & Berlin, 2012), and social studies (e.g., Alazzi, 2008; Hofer & Swan, 2008), with researchers examining a variety of practices such as grouping students (e.g., Maloch et al., 2013), using technology in the classroom (e.g., Hughes & Ooms, 2004; Swan & Hofer, 2011), and working with dual language learners (DLL; e.g., Gersten, 1999; Musanti, 2017; Musanti et al., 2009; Palmer et al., 2014). In terms of topical focus, we noted three broad groups of research questions that guided the studies: questions focused on classroom practices ($n = 33$), particular groups of teachers (e.g., novice, Latinx; $n = 16$), or the implementation or uptake professional development ($n = 10$). The following section presents the findings by research question.

RQ1: Procedures

The first question asked which *data collection procedures* were used to combine visual and language data to study teaching. The majority of studies in the sample collected a range of data to build cases or to address their research questions descriptively. These procedures were often discussed in the context of the broader research design; other times they were simply mentioned in describing the data collection. Researchers reported a variety of study designs; the most common design was some form of "case study" ($n = 22$). The next most frequent research paradigm and design was "qualitative" ($n = 9$). A variety of other research designs were used less frequently and are presented in Table 3. Notably, all the studies included qualitative components in their research designs with some researchers collecting quantitative descriptive data (e.g., through surveys). Although these research approaches did allow for the concurrent collection of language and visual data, very few researchers described explicitly how they combined both visual and language data in data collection; the exceptions are described subsequently.

Researchers used a variety of data collection procedures to collect visual and language data as presented in Table 3. The majority of these procedures depended on observations of classroom practice ($n = 44$) and teacher interviews ($n = 49$). Indeed, only three studies did not use interviews to gather language data; relying on group discussions of some form to elicit teacher perspectives (de Vocht, 2015; Kullberg et al., 2016; Runesson, 2013). Generally, the interviews were semistructured, yet researchers noted a variety of interview types, also displayed in Table 3. For instance, in some cases researchers mentioned "debriefing" interviews or "informal" conversations with teachers before or after observing instruction ($n = 6$), which raises an interesting question about whether researchers simply saw these interactions as procedural or included data from such informal debriefings in their studies. In addition to interviews, researchers collected language data through teacher logs (e.g., Camburn

TABLE 3
Included Articles and Their Data Types

Author(s)	Year	Instructional Context	Research Method With Relevant Procedure	Visual Data	Language Data
Aguirre & Speer	1999	Secondary teachers' mathematics instruction	Qualitative study	Classroom observations (recordings, field notes)	Interviews
Alanís	2018	Preschool teachers' work with DLLs	Qualitative study	Class observations (recordings, field notes)	Interviews
Alazzi	2008	Secondary social studies teachers	Qualitative study	classroom observations (video recordings)	Interviews
Baker	2019	Preschool teachers' work with DLLs	Multiple case study	Classroom observations (recordings and field notes)	Semistructured interviews, structured debrief conversation about video-recorded lesson or activity
Baker	2018	Preschool teachers participating PD	Qualitative case study	Classroom observations (field notes)	Semistructured interviews, surveys
Camburn & Barnes	2004	Elementary teachers' ELA instruction	Log validation study	Classroom observations (field notes)	Teacher logs, interviews
Celedón-Pattichis	2010	ESL mathematics teacher	Case study	Classroom observations (field notes), textbooks, teacher records	Interviews
Chiodo & Tsai	1997	Chinese secondary social studies teachers' critical thinking instruction	*Not specified*	Classroom observations (recordings), ministry guidelines, teacher manuals	Interviews
Crockett	2002	Elementary school teachers participating in a mathematics PD	Clinical case study	Classroom observations (recordings)	Formal and informal interviews, teacher inquiry group sessions
de Vocht	2015	Preschool teachers' teacher–child interactions	Dialogic research	Classroom observations (recordings)	Teacher–researcher discussion of video-recordings
Diezmann & Watters	2015	Novice secondary teachers' science instruction	Case study	Classroom observations (recordings)	Semistructured interviews
Drake & Sherin	2006	Elementary teachers' mathematics instruction	*Not specified* w/ narrative inquiry	Classroom observations (recordings and field notes)	Interviews, personal narrative generation
Flynn & Schachter	2017	Preschool teachers' ELA instruction	Exploratory study w/ stimulated recall	Classroom observations (recordings)	Stimulated recall interviews
Friesen & Butera	2012	Preschool teachers' ELA instruction	Multiple case study	Classroom observations (field notes)	Semistructured interviews, questionnaires
Gersten	1999	Elementary teachers' work with DLLs	*Not specified*	Classroom observations (field notes)	Semistructured interviews

(continued)

TABLE 3 (CONTINUED)

Author(s)	Year	Instructional Context	Research Method With Relevant Procedure	Visual Data	Language Data
Hamel	2003	Secondary teachers' ELA instruction	Qualitative case study	Classroom observations (field notes), classroom artifacts of student learning, video-recorded student think-alouds	Semistructured interviews, surveys
Henderson & Palmer	2015a	Preschool teachers' work with DLLs	Ethnographic approach	Classroom observations and weekly planning meetings (recordings, field notes)	Semistructured interviews
Henderson & Palmer	2015b	Elementary teachers' work with DLLs	Ethnographic approach	Classroom observations (recordings, field notes)	Semistructured and informal interviews
Hofer & Swan	2008	Middle school ELA and social studies teachers using technology	Interpretive case study	Classroom observations (field notes), teachers' project plans	Open-response survey questions, interviews
Hughes et al.	2005	Middle school humanities teachers participating in a technology PD	Longitudinal embedded multiple-case study	Classroom observations (field notes)	Pre- and poststructured interviews
Hughes & Ooms	2004	Middle school arts-humanities teachers participating in a technology PD	Longitudinal, multiple case, embedded research design	Classroom observations (field notes)	Interviews, inquiry group discussions
Jiménez & Gersten	1999	Latina elementary school teachers' ELA instruction	Qualitative study	Classroom observations (field notes)	Semistructured interviews
Kullberg et al.	2016	Secondary teachers participating in mathematics PD	Phenomenographic research w/ learning study	Classroom observations (recordings)	Teacher discussions during lesson planning and after lesson implementation
Levitt	2002	Elementary teachers' science instruction	Not specified	Classroom observations (field notes)	Semistructured interviews
Machado et al.	2017	Middle school teacher's ELA instruction	Case study	Classroom observations (recordings and field notes), class artifacts	Semistructured interviews
Maloch	2002	Elementary teacher's ELA instruction	Qualitative study	Classroom observations (recordings and field notes), recorded literature discussion groups	Formal and informal interviews, teacher logs/notes
Maloch	2004	Elementary teacher's ELA instruction	Qualitative study	Classroom observations (recordings and field notes), lesson plans, student work	Formal and informal interviews
Maloch	2005	Elementary teacher's ELA instruction	Qualitative study	Classroom observations (recordings and field notes), planning notes, class artifacts	Formal and informal interviews
Maloch	2008	Elementary teacher's ELA instruction	Case study	Classroom observations (recordings and field notes), class artifacts	Formal and informal interviews

(continued)

TABLE 3 (CONTINUED)

Author(s)	Year	Instructional Context	Research Method With Relevant Procedure	Visual Data	Language Data
Maloch et al.	2013	Elementary teachers' ELA grouping practices	Interpretive study w/cross case comparison	Classroom observations (recordings and field notes)	Formal and informal interviews
Martin et al.	2001	Beginning middle school teachers	Case study	Classroom observations (field notes)	Formal and informal interviews
Musanti	2017	Novice elementary teacher's bilingual practices	Case study	Classroom observations (field notes)	Semistructured interviews, unstructured debriefing conversations
Martínez et al.	2015	Elementary teachers' work with DLLs	Qualitative study	Classroom observations (recordings and field notes)	Semistructured interviews
Musanti & Celedón-Pattichis	2013	Bilingual elementary teachers' mathematics instruction	Case study	Classroom observations (recordings and field notes)	Interviews
Musanti et al.	2009	Elementary teachers participating in DLL instruction PD	Case study	Classroom observations (recordings and field notes)	Semistructured interviews, unstructured debriefings
Palmer et al.	2014	Preschool and elementary teachers' work with DLLs	Ethnographic methods w/ discourse analysis	Classroom observations (recordings)	Interviews
Runeson	2013	Elementary teachers participating in a mathematics PD	*Not specified*	Classroom observations (recordings)	Audio recordings of planning and debriefing meetings
Riojas-Cortez et al.	2013	Early childhood teachers	Qualitative design	Classroom observations (field notes)	Interviews, oral reflections, focus groups
Savasci & Berlin	2012	Middle and secondary teachers' science instruction	Multiple, cross case study	Classroom observations via researcher tool (field notes), class documents	Interviews, questionnaire
Schachter	2017	Preschool teachers' ELA instruction	Phenomenological w/ stimulated recall	Classroom observations (recordings and field notes)	Planning interviews, stimulated recall interviews
Souto-Manning	2010	Preschool teachers in Head Start program	Action research and ethnographic practices	Classroom observations (recordings and field notes), photographs, and notes taken by teachers during home visits	Interviews, informal debriefings
Swan & Hicks	2007	Secondary social studies teachers' integration of technology	*Not specified*	Classroom observations (field notes), instructional artifacts	Pre- and postinterviews
Swan & Hofer	2011	Secondary social studies teachers' technology use	*Not specified*	Classroom observations, teacher's project plans	Interviews

(continued)

TABLE 3 (CONTINUED)

Author(s)	Year	Instructional Context	Research Method With Relevant Procedure	Visual Data	Language Data
Tobin	1988	Japanese preschool teachers	Visual anthropology and multivocal ethnography	School observations (recordings)	Teachers' autoethnographic discourse
Vetter	2010	Secondary teacher's ELA instruction	Micro-ethnography	Classroom observations (recordings and field notes)	Formal and informal interviews
Vetter	2013	Elementary teacher's ELA instruction	Qualitative study	Classroom observations (recordings and field notes)	Formal and informal interviews
Watters & Diezmann	2016	Beginning elementary teacher's science discourse	Single embedded explanatory case study w/ stimulated recall	Classroom observations (recordings & field notes)	Interviews and semistructured debriefing sessions
Watters & Ginns	1997	Elementary school teachers participating in a science PD	Problem-based methodology w/ case studies	Classroom observations (recordings and field notes)	Semistructured interviews
Westerman	1991	Novice and experienced elementary school teachers	*Not specified* w/ stimulated recall	Classroom observations (recordings)	Prelesson structured interviews, stimulated recall interviews
Whitney et al.	2008	Middle school teachers' participating in a writing PD	Case studies	Classroom observations (field notes), teacher-selected collection of documents from classroom activities	Interviews
Worthy et al.	2015	Elementary teachers' ELA instruction	*Not specified*	Classroom observations (field notes), video recordings of guided reading lessons	Formal and informal interviews
Zuniga et al.	2018	Preschool and third-grade teachers	Ethnographic methods	Classroom observations (recordings), class artifacts	Semistructured and informal interviews

Note. PD = professional development; ELA = English language arts; DLL = dual language learner.

& Barnes, 2004, Maloch, 2002), recording teacher meetings (e.g., Crockett, 2002; Hughes & Ooms, 2004; Kullberg et al., 2016; Souto-Manning, 2010), researcher–teacher discussions of videos (e.g., de Vocht, 2015), by gathering teachers' autoethnographic and oral reflections (e.g., Riojas-Cortez et al., 2013; Tobin, 1988), or administering questionnaires (e.g., Friesen & Butera, 2012; Hofer & Swan, 2008). Among these, researcher-teacher discussions of videos, reflective writing, or questionnaires were used much less frequently as collection procedures.

Visual data were collected through video recordings of practice (e.g., Drake & Sherin, 2006; Machado et al., 2017; Worthy et al., 2015), field notes regarding classroom practices (e.g., Levitt, 2002; Musanti & Celedón-Pattichis, 2013; Watters & Ginns, 1997), and photographs taken by teachers (e.g., Souto-Manning, 2010). Some researchers also collected visual documentation of products of practice, such as student work (e.g., Hofer & Swan, 2008; Maloch, 2008; Palmer et al., 2014), lesson plans (e.g., Hofer & Swan, 2008; Maloch, 2004), or curriculum standards (e.g., Alazzi, 2008). Importantly, just over half of the studies utilized audio and/or video recordings of classroom practice ($n = 32$); the rest relied solely on researcher observation via field notes ($n = 20$). Only 16 studies used both recordings and field notes to collect visual data.

The procedures for observing and interviewing teachers varied across studies. For example, Gersten (1999) used "open-ended qualitative classroom" observations (p. 41) to study the ELA practice of four teachers working with DLLs. These teachers were observed at least six times for an hour each time, and observers recorded segments of lessons deemed to be representative of practice. Teachers were formally interviewed twice via semistructured interview protocols and then were debriefed informally by the researchers after the observations. In their study of a technology professional development delivered via inquiry groups, Hughes and Ooms (2004) interviewed teachers once, observed in the classroom and collected field notes once a month, and then relied on recordings of the teachers' inquiry meetings to collect their data.

In most studies, particularly those identified by authors as qualitative or case studies, data were gathered without making explicit connections between the two data forms or making clear how these two forms might be capturing both the private and the public worlds of teaching. For example, Martin et al. (2001) were interested in investigating the experiences of new teachers. They conducted interviews and observations and engaged teachers in formal conversations. Although they collected visual and language data, they did not explicitly discuss the affordance of these forms of data in connecting teachers' perspectives with their public practice. In 31 studies, the connection between the forms of data was drawn implicitly; this general approach seemed the default approach, a point to which we return in the Discussion section.

Some procedures were explicitly intended to combine the visual and language data, such as the stimulated recall procedure used by Watters and Diezmann (2016) in their case study of a career-change teacher. Working with recorded examples of classroom practice, the researchers and the teacher selected salient instances to use to "stimulate" discussion of the teacher's perspectives on the practices they saw. Here the two forms of data were explicitly linked in the collection process to understand connections between the public and the private worlds of teaching from the teacher's perspective. The stimulated recall procedure was used in four articles (Flynn & Schachter, 2017; Schachter, 2017; Watters & Diezmann, 2016; Westerman, 1991) in this review.

Other procedures also connected visual and language data. In her researcher-teacher dialogue study, de Vocht (2015) engaged in reflective exchanges with two preschool teachers after she had watched recordings of their interactions with children, thus using the videos to elicit teachers' perspectives. Camburn and Barnes's (2004) log validation study offered a final example of explicit collection and use of the two forms of data. In this study, the researchers collected four types of data: observer log data and observer narratives of classroom practice—and combined these with language data from teacher logs and interviews. All four data sources were focused on a single classroom observation. The aim was to examine differences in how classroom practices were documented from researcher and teacher perspectives in the two types of logs. These data were connected through the teacher interviews that were used to explain differing interpretations of the public observations of teaching in the two logs. These three procedures—stimulated recall, dialogic exchanges, and the log-interview analyses—each explicitly linked visual and language data and came the closest to capturing teachers' in-the-moment thinking. These procedures were in contrast to the default approach mentioned above that combined interviews with field notes or other types of visual data to interpret classroom practices.

RQ2: Theoretical Frameworks

The second question was directed at understanding how *theoretical frameworks* anchored the collection of both visual and language data. It asked which theoretical frameworks support the collection and integration of these two types of data in these procedures. However, there were few examples of theoretical frameworks that explicitly supported both types of data collection. In one example, Maloch et al. (2013) examined how ELA teachers grouped students within the context of guided reading. The authors organized their study around the concept of teachers as sensemakers whose "enactments of practices necessarily take into account their background, their experiences, their beliefs, and their local contexts" (p. 284). With this conceptualization, the researchers needed to elicit language data to understand this sensemaking process and how it was connected to the teachers' enacted practice.

In a second example, Schachter (2017) developed a phenomenological framework that explicitly outlined the connection between the two types of data in order to understand participants' experience of the phenomenon. She stated,

There are two important components to phenomenological work: describing the phenomenon of interest, in this case, teaching young children, and describing the participants' experiences of the phenomenon. In the context of this study, phenomenology is used as a way to understand how teachers reason about their practice as it is enacted. (p. 97)

In a third instance, Levitt (2002) made the theoretical claim that beliefs comprised part of the private world of teaching, which she called "non-observable," and influenced their "observable" public practice. Using observations as a starting point, she interviewed teachers to elicit their beliefs about science teaching, arguing that "teachers' actions in the classroom and the *observable* effects of those actions can be better understood if the *non-observable* phenomena of their thought processes, including their beliefs, are made public" (italics added; p. 5).

In many of the studies, the research designs often implicitly linked the two forms of data. As described earlier, about half of the studies ($n = 22$) in the review characterized themselves as "case studies." In working to build these cases, the researchers collected robust data (Yin, 2014) that usually included observations or field notes and language data via interviews. In this sense then, these methodological moves, which were inherent in the research design, played the role of a de facto theoretical framework that linked the two forms of data.

We do not mean to say that the reviewed studies lacked theoretical frameworks to support their research; indeed, they were generally well theorized. For example, Friesen and Butera (2012) were interested in early childhood teachers' reading practices and the role that beliefs played in informing these practices. Their theory held that beliefs mattered in practice and therefore it was necessary to capture this private world of teaching to understand the public classroom practice. They explained that "[they] sought to find examples of how the teachers made instructional decisions about reading and the professional, practical, and personal experiences that contributed to these choices" (p. 363). In this way, like many other researchers they foregrounded the language data and drew on the visual data to interpret the private world it represented. Generally, however, researchers focused solely on the need to elicit language data separate from the visual data, providing different rationalizations for this dichotomous focus. Somewhat ironically though, the rationalizations that supported dichotomous data collection procedures were often similar to the rationalizations made by researchers who explicitly connected the two forms of data.

We noted four principal rationalizations for trying to access teachers' perspectives. These rationalizations were connected to teachers' knowledge ($n = 17$), teachers' beliefs ($n = 17$), classroom practices ($n = 37$), and teacher or student identities ($n = 11$). Thirty-four studies included multiple rationales; the majority of these combined understanding classroom practices and teachers' knowledge. An example of this is from Friesen and Butera (2012), described previously, who differentiated beliefs, which included "professional, practical and personal experiences," and the knowledge gained through those experiences, thus nominating beliefs and knowledge as two dimensions of teachers' private worlds.

The studies included in this review recognized the role of teachers' private worlds in the work of teaching; however, the ways in which they linked teachers' perspectives to the public world of their practice were often tacitly assumed. These assumptions seemed to turn on how the two forms of data were interrelated in both collection and analysis. In the data collection process, what each form of data was actually capturing and how those were interconnected was often tacit or unexplained by the researchers. Similarly, in data analysis, the ways in which the two forms of data were linked entailed assumptions made by researchers. These assumptions hinged on which form of data was foregrounded. The process of foregrounding one form of data led to how both forms of data were interpreted and to the claims that the authors could make in their findings. We return to these issues regarding connecting and foregrounding data in the Discussion section. At this juncture, however, we are simply highlighting the relative lack of clear theoretical framing of the relationship between the two forms of data in most of the studies reviewed.

RQ3: Assumptions or Warrants

The issue of assuming an ambiguous connection between the public and private worlds of teaching goes to the core of the problem in this systematic review—that is, how researchers *warranted* the connection and what they could reasonably say about teaching from their studies. Interestingly, and perhaps to be expected, these warrants were not generally laid out in the theoretical frameworks in the studies. Rather, the warrants were often evident in the way in which the researchers foregrounded one or the other form of data.

One can argue that a researcher's assumptions are, by definition, inaccessible to others, as Dickinson writes of poetry in the epigraph. How data are collected and analyzed do reflect theoretical positions, however. Thus, we use the term "assumption" to refer to this underlying rationale, whether or not it is explicitly stated. The way in which researchers presented their findings, what they directed the reader to focus on, and which type of data seemed to play a larger role in their efforts to address their research questions all reflect these assumptions. Some studies in the review foregrounded the public practice of teaching and used language data to explain the teachers' thinking about these public phenomena. Other studies did the reverse: They foregrounded the private world as captured in the language data and placed it in the context of the public practice of teaching as documented in visual data, which often included field or observation notes.

For example, Vetter's (2013) study of how a secondary ELA teacher supported the language interactions of students speaking African American language (AAL) foregrounded the data on these classroom practices while using the teacher interview data to elaborate them. In the data analysis, she used discourse analyses to examine the classroom interactions, focusing heavily on the visual data of the classroom dialogue and interactions through field notes and recordings. Vetter then used the teacher interview data, which elicited the private world of teaching, to deepen and broaden her understanding and interpretations of the visual. She explained,

I examine how Gina leveraged AAL in ways that contributed to her expectations for the literacy community. Second, I investigate how Gina leveraged AAL that appeared to conflict with her expectations for the literacy community. (p. 185)

Here, she foregrounds the public world of teaching and categorizes how it fits within the teacher, Gina's, thinking about her teaching. Vetter states explicitly that "discourse analysis framed around positioning theory [was used] to interpret classroom interactions" (pp. 179–180), thus indicating how she led with the visual data in analyzing and presenting teaching.

In contrast, Savasci and Berlin's (2012) study of teachers' reported beliefs about science and constructivist practices relied heavily on the language data to describe teachers' perspectives. Their findings included many excerpts from teachers' interviews with short summaries of their visual data to demonstrate how public practices did or did not align with these reported beliefs. In describing their findings, they stated, "In summary, teacher expressed beliefs were not consistent with their classroom practice" (p. 76). Their study exemplifies how the language data representing the beliefs was foregrounded in the presentation with discussion of public practices. Furthermore, their statement, "Expressed beliefs were not consistent with their classroom practice," defaults to the visible world as the "correct" view of their teaching, in their use of the word "consistent," in spite of the fact the researchers emphasized the language data in their findings.

In most instances, we observed that the research design favored or foregrounded one form of data over the other. In studies in which the connection was theorized, the findings and interpretations were warranted through that theorization. In other cases, where the theoretical connection was not explicit, the connection was often drawn implicitly in the data analyses. Consider two examples discussed previously, Vetter (2013) and Savasci and Berlin (2012): Neither provided an explicit theorization of how the visual and language data were connected. Instead, the connections were assumed in the analysis and interpretation of their findings. For Vetter, the assumption was operationalized in using the language data to elaborate the visual data, whereas for Savasci and Berlin it was operationalized in using their observations to contrast with what teachers said in their interviews. In so doing, each focused more heavily on one form of data and then used the other form to support the claims they were making about the foregrounded data. We would argue that without a theoretical connection, combining the visual and language data occurs in the interpretation process, which usually leads to the foregrounding of one form of data over the other. There is an important implication here: If the two forms of data are not treated equivalently, and therefore an explicit connection drawn between them as parallel and interrelated versions of the phenomenon, researchers run the risk of misrepresenting one of the two worlds in their interpretation of teaching.

That said, a quarter of the reviewed articles balanced the language and visual data more or less evenly ($n = 13$), thus ascribing similar importance to the public and private worlds of teaching. For example, Drake and Sherin (2006) observed teachers multiple times as they taught a new mathematics curriculum. The researchers then interviewed teachers either before or after the lessons to understand their goals and to address questions that arose regarding practice. They also observed and recorded the teachers' participation in a monthly mathematics professional development and conducted mathematics life story interviews with teachers. They were able to link the pre- and postconversations with teachers to the visual data of the classroom practice and interweave their mathematics life stories with teachers' accounts of their overall practice. They supported this balanced connection with their theorization of teachers whose "sensemaking about a mathematics reform curriculum and about their own mathematics teaching practices is situated in their identities as learners and teachers of mathematics" (p. 157). Their claim regarding teachers' "sensemaking about a mathematics reform curriculum and about their own mathematics teaching practices" anchored data collection strategies and the ways they interpreted and presented their data to warrant their claims and represent the thinking and actions of teachers.

In a second example, Aguirre and Speer (1999) used teacher interviews to identify different types of beliefs connected to teaching mathematics. They then mapped these beliefs onto observations of the teachers' practice to represent how beliefs were informing practice. This balance was achieved when they both theoretically and procedurally specified the connection between the two forms of data. From the start, the authors had a clear vision of how the two forms of data were connected in the study and therefore each was given equal weight in both the analyses and the presentation of the findings. From the standpoint of this review, the data analyses used by Aguirre and Speer did not use either data source to document teachers' in-the-moment perspectives on their teaching. Rather, the researchers used data gathered through more general interviews to link teacher beliefs with public practice. The study did, however, portray an integrated view that connected the private and public worlds of teachers.

As we examined the foregrounding of data sources, we recognized that researchers were making analytic decisions in designing their studies and in analyzing their data. Most often, the research design drove how data were analyzed and integrated to address the research questions. This use of research design to establish the connection de facto may make sense in terms of general research quality (Creswell & Creswell, 2018), however, it can prove problematic. In our review, we found that often researchers did not make explicit to their readers (and possibly to themselves) how they were justifying or warranting these connections between the public and private worlds of teaching. This was the opposite case in the studies that balanced the two forms of data: Most of these were also more explicit about the connection between the two forms of data and the warrants that were used to argue for those connections.

The use of stimulated recall as a data collection procedure was a notable exception to this analytic balancing act. This may be because in using stimulated recall, the researcher needs to determine who is connecting the visual data in the video and the language data in recalling what was captured on it. Hence, the procedure itself introduces a set of explicit choices and decisions (Schachter & Freeman, 2015) about why both visual and language data matter in the study and how they are to be interwoven in collecting and analyzing the data. These decisions include whether and how to deliberately allow the teacher to control the visual data (recorded observation) to elicit (or "stimulate") the language data. For example, Westerman (1991) used stimulated recall interviews to look at the in-the-moment decision-making processes of novice and expert teachers. This procedural decision allowed the teachers to make the connection between what was documented in the visual data on the video and what was happening privately for them during the process of teaching. This decision about who made the connection illuminated how the private and the public worlds connected by identifying the decision-making processes from the teachers' perspectives.

DISCUSSION

This chapter has examined how researchers combine visual and language data to understand teachers' perspectives on their own teaching and to identify data collection and analysis procedures and theoretical frameworks that support this type of research. We found that relatively few articles—only 52 studies—met the criteria for this review. Furthermore, even fewer articles were explicit, either procedurally or theoretically, about how the two forms of data were connected. It would seem fair to say based on this review that, to date, research connecting the private and the public worlds of teachers' teaching is limited.

Expanding this type of research is important in light of the current U.S. education context, however. Many teacher evaluation systems and reform efforts, either in use or contemplated, are based on teachers' observable practice (Cohen & Goldhaber, 2016). Although these aspects of instruction may be more amenable to measurement schemes, they do not present the entire picture of the teaching process. For this reason alone, there is a risk of oversimplifying the work of teaching and not effectively improving classroom practice. Furthermore, there is a growing body of research that identifies the risk of using observation measures as the sole mechanism for interpreting quality of practice (e.g., Bailey et al., 2016; Campbell & Ronfeldt, 2018; Hill & Grossman, 2013). The policies that focus on observable teaching only position teachers within deficit or punitive orientations (Holloway, 2019) and do not account for the specialized knowledge that is necessary to bring about successful teaching (Ball et al., 2008; Shulman, 1987). In this education context, it is critically important that the research community pursues work that presents the complexity of the work of teaching by highlighting and examining how the private and public worlds are interwoven. Simply put, one cannot document—let alone seek to improve—the public activity of teaching without accounting for, and indeed highlighting, the private world of teachers' thinking.

Affordances of Combining Visual and Language Data to Study Teaching

Before turning to the particular methodological challenges in conducting research that combines visual and language data to study teaching, it is important to note the contributions these studies can—and do—make to understanding of teaching. Although the ways in which language and visual data are combined varied across studies in this review, we saw patterns that support the continued combination of these two types of data in research designs. Posing research questions about a range of issues in student and teacher learning, including how particular classroom practices are being enacted or about teachers' experiences in, and uptake from, professional development all turn to some degree on combining visual and language data. Studies can also focus on instruction in relation to specific types of teaching or content areas, as well as on how teacher or student identities shape teaching and learning. Furthermore, it can be argued that simply through collecting language data in conjunction with visual data, researchers are recognizing the private worlds of teachers, even if these connections are not drawn explicitly. Studies of this nature underscore the critical point that practice does not happen in a vacuum. To separate classroom practices from teachers' beliefs, knowledge, intentions, or their identities leads to partial and incomplete accounts of the work of teaching.

Warranting Data Collection Designs and Procedures

The chapter findings identify a broader pattern of what seem to be established norms for studying teachers' thinking about their work. Each study involved at least some form of qualitative data collection, either through observations of the public world of teaching or interviews to gain access to the private world of teaching. In fact, all but three studies ($n = 49$) used interviews to collect language data, and all the studies we reviewed included observations, although these were documented in various ways (e.g., recordings, field notes). These are common research procedures employed by qualitative researchers (Marshall & Rossman, 2006). However, the majority of researchers were not explicit in stating why they used the procedures they chose, or how the data generated in using these procedures were connected to represent both worlds of teaching. It may be that, given the prevalence of these procedures in the field, researchers are simply assuming the warrants or reasons for using both visual and language data in their studies. As Booth et al. (2016) have argued, "Experienced researchers rarely state their warrants explicitly when they write for specialized readers in their fields because they can safely assume that these readers already know them" (p. 158). Although it is true that readers may know the value of these research procedures, this review indicates that the field may be oversimplifying the research process when combining procedures to collect multiple forms of data.

The implicit assumptions about warrants and research design is borne out in the finding that nearly half of the reviewed articles ($n = 22$) were designed to be some form of case study. Case studies afford researchers the decision to bound their foci of study while also collecting robust data to understand their research question and build their "case" (Yin, 2014). In terms of data collection, these studies draw on both visual and language data, often combining observations and document collection with interviews and member checking. The implicit warrant seems to be that all the data combine to elucidate the particular case. However, we found that researchers often used the case study as the research design to serve as a proxy for defining how the research procedures and warrants connected the visual and language data they had gathered. In this fashion then, the overall study design served researchers as a warrant in and of itself.

Maxwell (2012) makes a similar observation in his argument about causation or "causal realism"[3] in qualitative work more broadly. He argues that such research "identifies process as a necessary and central aspect of causation . . . makes context intrinsic to causal explanation . . . [and] extends causal efficacy to beliefs, values, intentions, and meanings, not just to physical objects and events" (p. 657). In that case studies are often used to examine processes, social contexts, and "beliefs, values, intentions, and meanings," it seems to make sense that researchers would use case studies as research designs to draw causal connections between the private and public worlds of teaching. Our concern is that case study designs can often skirt the central issue of how the two forms of data are connected. Many of these studies still rely on foregrounding one form of data in their designs and analyses and then drawing on the other form of data to confirm, disconfirm, or extend findings that have been developed from the first. Although these types of studies were proposed as "cases" of teachers' perspectives on their classroom teaching (e.g., Diezmann & Watters, 2015; Friesen & Butera, 2012), when organized in this way they tended in fact to reify the assumption that all the data contributed to defining the case without the need to theorize the interconnection between the two forms (e.g., Martin et al., 2001).

This overall lack of explicit theorization about how visual and language data connected was striking across the studies in this review; in fact, only seven studies (13%) were explicitly theorized. We had anticipated that since the core problem in this work involves connecting worlds of teaching, theory would be used regularly to make these connections explicit. We did not find this to be the case. Although most researchers provided a rationale for the need to understand the private processes of teachers, they did not connect these to the public process of teaching. Only a few researchers referenced specific theorizations (e.g., sensemaking, Maloch et al., 2013; phenomenology, Schachter, 2017; sociocultural theory, Henderson & Palmer 2015a) to connect visual and language data. The other 45 studies left this relationship unarticulated or assumed, foregrounding of one or the other forms of data in various ways.

We want to underscore a distinction that has emerged in this review that we believe could be useful going forward. It is the distinction between *rationalizing* the need to collect both forms of data and *theorizing* how language and visual data in a study are connected. *Rationalizing* entails the researcher acknowledging that there are data to be gathered about both the public and private worlds of teaching, and that both forms can be related to the research questions and contribute in the analyses and findings. In these cases, the two forms of data are usually linked de facto when one form is foregrounded in the analysis and the other is used to amplify, extend, or even explain it. For example, Martin et al. (2001) foregrounded language data (interviews) to gain insight into "what new teachers experience in their first three years of teaching" (p. 60). The collection of visual data (classroom observations) was rationalized as a way to triangulate the findings.

In *theorizing*, the researcher goes a step further to determine that the connection between the two forms of data is integral to the claims they are seeking to make and to warrant. This determination happens in the design of the study, when the researcher recognizes that how these data are to be collected, how they are to be integrated in analysis, and how they will be represented in findings are essential decisions both conceptually and procedurally (Freeman, 1996). For example, de Vocht's (2015) study in this review used Bakhtinian concepts of dialogue and moral answerability, as well as a "dialogic research methodology" (p. 323) to make explicit connections between the visual and language data in the research design and procedures, as well as in the findings. She theorized the relationship between the two forms of data claiming that, through dialogue and "collaborative meaning making of video-recorded encounters between teacher and children," the teacher and the researcher "gained a deeper understanding of the complexity of teacher-child dialogue" (p. 329).

The foregrounding of one form of data in favor of the other is a de facto manifestation of rationalizing the need for the forms in a particular study without fully working out the connection between them or what that connection may warrant in the claims of the study. Theorizing, on the other hand, entails actively working to avoid bifurcating worlds in designing the procedures of the study and in warranting the claims in the findings. Although there are procedural and methodological dimensions to these decisions, at their core they are determinations of whose version of the phenomenon gets told in the study. We refer to this determination as "authoring" the connection between language and visual data.

Connecting Language and Visual Data as an Authoring Continuum

When we embarked on this review, we hypothesized that connecting visual and language data was a temporal problem that necessitated understanding teachers' perspectives in-the-moment as they enacted instruction. In this sense, stimulated recall as a data collection procedure addressed this temporal issue head-on. Our understanding has evolved over the course of the review, however. We now would argue that combining the visual and the language data can actually be framed as a question of positionality in who "authors" the connection between the two forms. Indeed, who connects the two forms of data, and how, matters considerably in bridging the two worlds. When the researcher is the primary author of the connection, the work is told from the third-person perspective. When the teacher authors the link, the first-person account comes to the fore.

Authoring is a way of positioning the bifurcation between the worlds and managing it within the research study. In the review, we found there was a continuum of how the connection between the two forms of data was authored. In almost every case, the researchers were the main authors, making the connections between—and thus making meaning of—the language and the visual through the analytic and descriptive processes they used. In these cases, the researchers made the decisions about how the data were connected and authored those connections either explicitly or implicitly. At times, the decisions asserted the primacy of the researchers' interpretations as, for example, in the Savasci and Berlin (2012) study cited earlier. Here, the researchers decided to use observational data to demonstrate how practice did not align with teachers' stated beliefs about the teaching practice the researchers had observed.

These moves tend to align with more traditional research methods in which researchers tend to maintain teacher-researcher boundaries. The distinction in roles is structured into the research process, although this line can typically be more fluid in qualitative research (Creswell & Creswell, 2018; Marshall & Rossman, 2006). Researchers seemed aware of this possibility with all incorporating qualitative procedures in their studies and many being explicit and reflexive about their roles in shaping the research process. This reflexivity included the researchers as participants/ providers of a professional development, co-teaching, or having taught a study participant in a preservice program. But it is noteworthy that this reflexivity did not translate into how the researchers analyzed and connected the visual and language data. In fact, such studies often tended to cleave to a more conventional positioning in which researchers "studied" what teacher-participants were doing and thinking.

At the other end of the continuum were the few articles (e.g., de Vocht, 2015; Schachter, 2017; Watters & Diezmann, 2016) in which the teachers authored the connection between the two forms of data. This was accomplished through the use of a few particular procedures: stimulated recall, teacher study logs, or dialogic research study designs. In each of these studies, the researchers asked the teachers to language their perspectives on the visual data. For instance, during interviews, Hamel (2003) asked teachers to explain and assess artifacts that demonstrated students' understanding of literature. These artifacts, which included papers, journals, tests, and video/audio tapes, led to teacher discussion about the kind of teaching practices that might support student learning. In this way, the teachers were able to decide when and how to make the connections between the two forms of data. This move offered teachers the possibility of authoring the meaning of the observed practices.

There are several other nuances in the continuum in which researchers provided teacher-participants opportunities to author the connection between the forms of data, albeit in a more circumscribed role. This authoring could occur procedurally through the use of debriefing meetings that followed observations of teaching ($n = 6$), which allowed teachers to express perspectives on the observation even though they did not explicitly connect the language directly to the visual data (e.g., recorded observations, field notes). It was also not always clear how researchers accounted for these debrief data in the overall analytic process of the study. A second procedural strategy involved the explicit inclusion of member checking (Patton, 1980) to triangulate findings ($n = 12$). In essence, member checking allowed teachers to proofread the written analyses that were authored by the researcher. A third type of authoring on this continuum involved research design–related or genre-related protocols that engaged teachers in authoring their experiences through the use of narratives. However, these procedures were limited to the language data. It is intriguing, and worth noting, that the search process did not surface any teacher-research studies, which would be the logical extension of the authoring continuum (see Freeman, 1996).

Decisions about who gets to make meaning of the language and visual data depend on the layering of research design, data collection procedures, and analytic strategies. These decisions, which can allow or inhibit teachers from making meaning through the connection of data on their public and private worlds, are very much dependent on the theoretical frameworks and warrants that researchers use to rationalize and implement their studies. Recognizing that qualitative research is an iterative process (Maxwell, 2013), sometimes these decisions are made by researchers as they implement the study design to address their research questions. However, it is critical to point out that the initial conceptualization of a study and the ultimate analyses are not separate. As long as researchers tend to default to rationalizing rather than theorizing how visual and language data connect in their studies, the work they produce will be dominated by the researchers' views and interpretations. This fact has consequences for how teachers as the central protagonists are positioned in generating knowledge about classroom teaching and learning (Freeman, 1996).

Other researchers have likewise identified the challenge of negotiating power dynamics between the researcher and participants in education research, both in studying teachers (e.g., Adair, 2011; Souto-Manning, 2010; Tobin, 1988) and students (e.g., Martínez, 2010; Orellana & Bowman, 2003). Furthermore, a growing number of researchers have also explored these topics within the context of teacher education, particularly with preservice teachers (e.g., Abell et al., 1998; Masingila & Doerr, 2002; Xiao & Tobin, 2018). The connection between the private and the public introduces another way to consider these dynamics of positioning and authoring. In doing so here, our emphasis fits solidly within these orientations to research methods.

Limitations

In undertaking a review of this complexity, limitations are bound to emerge; we note two principal ones here. The first concerns how we bounded the search to conduct the review. Through the specific focus on in-service teachers, we have potentially excluded research studies that examine preservice teacher education. Although preservice teachers are certainly an important population to consider, we chose to narrow the focus for two reasons. Inasmuch as video is increasingly part of teacher preparation, the pedagogical procedure is often paired with research on its use and impact, as noted earlier in this chapter. This dual focus could potentially confound our particular interest in how connections between visual and language data are warranted. Additionally, we set the parameter on in-service teachers in order to consider established practitioners and how these two forms of data are connected in studies that have documented ongoing practices in teaching. For in-service teachers, these practices are shaped by the social contexts of schools and their communities, whereas preservice teachers are often in more constrained settings. Practically speaking, this parameter led us to identify a manageable body of literature. Politically speaking, we would argue that the focus on practicing teachers is important in identifying a current gap in the research that combines both visual and language data at a time when there is an increasing focus on evaluating teachers through observation, as noted previously.

The second limitation was operational; it lay in the instability of the ProQuest database over time. The inability to replicate searches, even from one day to the next, was a challenge. It was a problem that several expert librarians with whom we worked at the two institutions noted was not uncommon in using ProQuest. Although we were able to address our concerns about locating relevant articles through backward searches and checking for additional works from authors we had already included, this problem of stability does raise larger questions about the replicability of these types of reviews. Whereas one wants the universe of studies to be permeable and to be refreshed by new work, the apparent fungibility of search parameters and terms does introduce challenges to replicating searches.

Avoiding the Bifurcation of Worlds: Implications and Recommendations

In designing their studies, researchers have the possibility of basing findings on what can be publicly observed in classrooms. They can also draw out what is private and therefore not directly accessible to them, and ascribe meaning to it. In making these decisions, researchers have the possibility of addressing the problem of bifurcating worlds head-on through intentionally designing their studies and focusing on authoring practices. These decisions blend the private and public worlds as Dickinson wrote in the epigraph to Higginson as the potential reader of her poems, "And I have none to ask/Should you think it [the mind] breathed/And had you the leisure to tell me."

We argue that to address potentially bifurcating of these worlds researchers need to consider both private and public aspects of teaching throughout the research process: from how they orient the study and frame the questions that drive it, to what they designate as the data and what those data represent, to how data are gathered and analyzed, to how the findings are authored. We offer the following questions, which can bring to bear teachers' perspectives, for consideration:

1. Why, as researcher, am I collecting visual and language data? How do these two forms of data elucidate the research aims or questions?
2. How do I connect the two types of data in the study? What will the connection provide? Am I theorizing the link or am I rationalizing the apparent need for both forms of data?
3. How will I connect these data in analysis such that they document the work of teaching?
4. Who, the researcher or the teachers, is the primary voice in authoring the findings? Are there ways in the study design to engage with participants to author the connection between the private and the public worlds of teaching?

The review identified several procedures that highlight the potential for avoiding bifurcating the public and the private worlds. Regarding data collection, the stimulated recall interview is a procedure that offers theoretical, procedural, and analytic grounds to conceptualize the connection between visual and language data. Depending on the decisions of who manages the recall process, stimulated recall also has the potential to engage teachers in authoring the connection between them. But fundamentally, as a data collection procedure stimulated recall sets up a set of decisions that can—and indeed probably ought to—be applied in any study that draws on the two forms of data (Schachter & Freeman, in press). In this sense then, stimulated recall offers both a template for thinking through the questions posed above and a specific means of addressing them.

Photovoice is a second potentially promising data collection method (Wang & Burris, 1997). The procedure engages participants in creating their own visual data in the photos they take. The procedure often includes then connecting these images to language data as the participants explain those images. This procedure has been used with students in efforts to increase their agency in the research process (e.g., Smith et al., 2012; Warne et al., 2013). Interestingly, although the same principles can be applied with teachers, our review did not find any studies in which teachers used photovoice about their teaching. There are also ethnographic approaches that use video data (e.g., autoethnography, Tobin, 1988; video-cued ethnography, Adair, 2011). These procedures can allow the teacher to author the connection between their teaching and their thinking about it, thus decentering the researcher. Finally, teacher action research (Carr & Kemmis, 2003; Mills, 2000) allows teachers to investigate and interpret their teaching solely from their perspectives, thereby authoring the entire process. Researchers can both support teachers in engaging in this type of work and support the publication and dissemination of their findings (Freeman, 1998).

CONCLUSION

We trust that this chapter contributes useful insights to this developing concern of melding public and private in education research. The aim is to collect data that can meaningfully deepen the study of teaching through combining data on the public life in classrooms (visual data) and the private lives of teachers (language data). Central to this deepening, we argue, is becoming more systematic about assumptions of how visual and language data connect a priori in the research design and the choice of research procedures. Through illuminating these connections between teachers' perspectives and how they enact their classroom instruction and by highlighting the rather limited roles of teachers in authoring these connections, we hope readers of this review will identify new ways of thinking about and addressing an enduring problem in education practice and research: how to support teachers in improving instruction.

Although the use of visual data to investigate the public world of teaching has become a mainstay of education research, it only tells part of the story. From field or observational notes (e.g., Patton, 2005) to video (e.g., Learning How to Look & Listen, 2016), visual data do not speak for themselves; they generally need to be expressed in language. This dynamic between what is visual and what is language is elemental in how we study teaching. How these two forms of information are connected and who authors that connection shape what is told and therefore what is understood about the work of teaching. The research challenge brings myriad possibilities for exposing the complexities of teachers' work and thereby advancing the teaching profession. It is fundamentally important to represent teachers' thinking about what they do to understand the relationship between what is public and what is private in their work. Operationally, this means connecting what is seen and observed with what is said. Epistemologically, it means warranting what is assumed in drawing those connections and thus in making research claims about them.

The work of teaching is paradoxical: It is at once individual, private, and performative, while it is simultaneously social, public, and interactive. These paradoxical qualities are at the core of the challenge of bifurcating worlds. Addressing and overcoming this bifurcation needs to be a collaborative endeavor between the researcher and the teacher. To borrow from the words of Dickinson in the epigraph, teachers often "have none to ask" to "see distinctly" what they are doing. The "leisure" of telling and hearing from another, perhaps in the role of researcher, may bring "gratitude" for the other's show of interest. More important though, it can open up a fuller understanding of the work itself, which, in turn, can support desired changes and needed improvements.

ACKNOWLEDGMENTS

We would like to thank Heyang Chen for his contribution to this work.

ORCID iD

Rachel E. Schachter https://orcid.org/0000-0003-3951-858X

NOTES

[1]Quoted from Thomas Wentworth Higginson's (1891) essay in *The Atlantic*.
[2]This date was selected based on prior work of the authors identifying 1975 as the year of the first stimulated recall research publication focusing on pre-K to 12th-grade teachers.
[3]Maxwell quotes this term from Little (2010, p. 218).

REFERENCES

References marked with an asterisk indicate studies included in the review.

Abell, S. K., Bryan, L. A., & Anderson, M. A. (1998). Investigating preservice elementary science teacher reflective thinking using integrated media case-based instruction in elementary science teacher preparation. *Science Teacher Education*, *82*(4), 491–509. https://doi .org/10.1002/(SICI)1098-237X(199807)82:4%3C491::AID-SCE5%3E3.0.CO;2-6

Adair, J. K. (2011). Confirming *Chanclas*: What early childhood teacher educators can learn from immigrant school teachers. *Journal of Early Childhood Education*, *32*(1), 55–71. https://doi.org/10.1080/10901027.2010.547652

*Aguirre, J., & Speer, N. M. (1999). Examining the relationship between beliefs and goals in teacher practice. *Journal of Mathematical Behavior*, *18*(3), 327–356. https://doi .org/10.1016/S0732-3123(99)00034-6

*Alanís, I. (2018). Enhancing collaborative learning: Activities and structures in a dual language preschool classroom. *Association of Mexican American Educators Journal, 12*(1), 5–26. https://doi.org/10.24974/amae.12.1.375

*Alazzi, K. F. (2008). Teachers' perceptions of critical thinking: A study of Jordanian secondary school social studies teachers. *Social Studies, 99*(6), 243–248. https://doi.org/10.3200/TSSS.99.6.243-248

Bailey, J., Bocala, C., Shakman, K., & Zweig, J. (2016, October). *Teacher demographics and evaluation: A descriptive study in a large urban district* (REL 2017-189). U.S. Department of Education, Institute of Education Sciences, National Center for Education Evaluation and Regional Assistance, & Regional Educational Laboratory Northeast & Islands. https://ies.ed.gov/ncee/edlabs/regions/northeast/pdf/REL_2017189.pdf

*Baker, M. (2018). Early childhood teachers at the center: A qualitative case study of professional development in an urban district. *Early Childhood Education Journal, 46*(2), 231–240. https://doi.org/10.1007/s10643-017-0858-6

*Baker, M. (2019). Playing, talking, co-constructing: Exemplary teaching for young dual language learners across program types. *Early Childhood Education Journal, 47*(1), 115–130. https://doi.org/10.1007/s10643-018-0903-0

Ball, D. L., Thames, M. H., & Phelps, G. (2008). Content knowledge for teaching: What makes it special? *Journal of Teacher Education, 59*(5), 389–407. https://doi.org/10.1177/0022487108324554

Becker, H. J. (2000). Findings from the teaching, learning, and computing survey. *Education Policy Analysis Archives, 8*, 51. https://doi.org/10.14507/epaa.v8n51.2000

Booth, W. C., Colomb, G. G., Williams, J. M., Bizup, J., & Fitzgerald, W. T. (2016). *The craft of research* (4th ed.). University of Chicago Press.

Brown, C. P., & Lan, Y. C. (2015). A qualitative metasynthesis comparing US teachers' conceptions of school readiness prior to and after the implementation of NCLB. *Teaching and Teacher Education, 45*, 1-13. https://doi.org/10.1016/j.tate.2014.08.012

*Camburn, E., & Barnes, C. A. (2004). Assessing the validity of a language arts instruction log through triangulation. *Elementary School Journal, 105*(1), 49–73. https://doi.org/10.1086/428802

Campbell, S. L., & Ronfeldt, M. (2018). Observational evaluation of teachers: Measuring more than we bargained for? *American Educational Research Journal, 55*(6), 1233–1267. https://doi.org/10.3102/0002831218776216

Carr, W., & Kemmis, S. (2003). *Becoming critical: Education knowledge and action research.* Falmer Press. https://doi.org/10.4324/9780203496626

*Celedón-Pattichis, S. (2010). Implementing reform curriculum voicing the experiences of an ESL/mathematics teacher. *Middle Grades Research Journal, 5*(4), 185–198.

*Chiodo, J. J., & Tsai, M. H. (1997). Secondary school teachers' perspectives of teaching critical thinking in social studies classes in the Republic of China. *Journal of Social Studies Research, 21*, 3–12.

Cohen, J., & Goldhaber, D. (2016). Building a more complete understanding of teacher evaluation using classroom observations. *Educational Researcher, 45*, 378–387. https://doi.org/10.3102/0013189X16659442

Corbin, J., & Strauss, A. (2008). *Basics of qualitative research.* Sage.

Creswell, J. W., & Creswell, J. D. (2018). *Research design* (5th ed.). Sage.

*Crockett, M. D. (2002). Inquiry as professional development: Creating dilemmas through teachers' work. *Teaching and Teacher Education, 18*(5), 609–624. https://doi.org/10.1016/S0742-051X(02)00019-7

*de Vocht, L. (2015). Reconceptualising teacher–child dialogue in early years education as a moral answerability. *International Journal of Early Childhood, 47*(2), 317–330. https://doi.org/10.1007/s13158-015-0140-2

*Diezmann, C. M., & Watters, J. J. (2015). The knowledge base of subject matter experts in teaching: A case study of a professional scientist as a beginning teacher. *International Journal of Science and Mathematics Education, 13*(6), 1517–1537. https://doi.org/10.1007/s10763-014-9561-x

*Drake, C., & Sherin, M. G. (2006). Practicing change: Curriculum adaptation and teacher narrative in the context of mathematics education reform. *Curriculum Inquiry, 36*(2), 153–187. https://doi.org/10.1111/j.1467-873X.2006.00351.x

*Flynn, E. E., & Schachter, R. E. (2017). Teaching for tomorrow: An exploratory study of prekindergarten teachers' underlying assumptions about how children learn. *Journal of Early Childhood Teacher Education, 38*(2), 182–208. https://doi.org/10.1080/1090102 7.2017.1280862

Freeman, D. (1996). To take them at their word: Language data in the study of teachers' knowledge. *Harvard Educational Review, 66*(4), 732–762. https://doi.org/10.17763/haer.66.4.3511321j38858h69

Freeman, D. (1998). *Doing teacher research: From inquiry to understanding.* Heinle & Heinle.

*Friesen, A., & Butera, G. (2012). "You introduce all of the alphabet . . . But I do not think it should be the main focus": Exploring early educators' decisions about reading instruction. *Early Childhood Education Journal, 40*(6), 361–368. https://doi.org/10.1007/s10643-012-0530-0

Gaudin, C., & Chaliès, S. (2015). Video viewing in teacher education and professional development: A literature review. *Educational Research Review, 16*, 41–67. https://doi.org/10.1016/j.edurev.2015.06.001

*Gersten, R. (1999). Lost opportunities: Challenges confronting four teachers of English-language learners. *Elementary School Journal, 100*(1), 37–56. https://doi.org/10.1086/461942

Gough, D. (2015). Qualitative and mixed methods in systematic reviews. *Systematic Reviews, 4*, Article 181. https://doi.org/10.1186/s13643-015-0151-y

*Hamel, F. L. (2003). Teacher understanding of student understanding: Revising the gap between teacher conceptions and students' ways with literature. *Research in the Teaching of English, 38*(1), 49–84.

*Henderson, K. I., & Palmer, D. K. (2015a). Teacher scaffolding and pair work in a bilingual pre-kindergarten classroom. *Journal of Immersion and Content-Based Language Education, 3*(1), 77–101. https://doi.org/10.1075/jicb.3.1.04hen

*Henderson, K. I., & Palmer, D. K. (2015b). Teacher and student language practices and ideologies in a third-grade two-way dual language program implementation. *International Multilingual Research Journal, 9*(2), 75–92. https://doi.org/10.1080/19313152.2015.1016827

Higginson, T. W. (1891, October). Emily Dickinson's letters. *The Atlantic.* Retrieved from https://www.theatlantic.com/magazine/archive/1891/10/emily-dickinsons-letters/306524/

Hill, H. C., Ball, D. L., & Schilling, S. G. (2008). Unpacking pedagogical content knowledge: Conceptualizing and measuring teachers' topic-specific knowledge of students. *Journal for Research in Mathematics Education, 39*(4), 372–400.

Hill, H. C., & Grossman, P. (2013). Learning from teacher observations: Challenges and opportunities posed by new teacher evaluation systems. *Harvard Educational Review, 83*(2), 371–384. https://doi.org/10.17763/haer.83.2.d11511403715u376

*Hofer, M., & Swan, K. O. (2008). Technological pedagogical content knowledge in action: A case study of a middle school digital documentary project. *Journal of Research on Technology in Education, 41*(2), 179–200. https://doi.org/10.1080/15391523.2008.10782528

Holloway, J. (2019). Risky teachers: Mitigating risk through high stakes teacher evaluation in the USA. *Discourse: Studies on the Cultural Politics of Education, 40*(3), 399–411. https://doi.org/10.1080/01596306.2017.1322938

Hsieh, H., & Shannon, S. (2005). Three approaches to qualitative content analysis. *Qualitative Health Research, 15*(9), 1277–1288. https://doi.org/10.1177/1049732305276687

*Hughes, J. E., Kerr, S. P., & Ooms, A. (2005). Content-focused technology inquiry groups: Cases of teacher learning and technology integration. *Journal of Educational Computing Research, 32*(4), 367–379. https://doi.org/10.2190/2N87-8AGA-BJ3D-46Q8

*Hughes, J. E., & Ooms, A. (2004). Content-focused technology inquiry groups: Preparing urban teachers to integrate technology to transform student learning. *Journal of Research on Technology in Education, 36*(2), 397–411. https://doi.org/10.1080/15391523.2004.10782422

*Jiménez, R. T., & Gersten, R. (1999). Lessons and dilemmas derived from the literacy instruction of two Latina/o teachers. *American Educational Research Journal, 36*(4), 265–301. https://doi.org/10.3102/00028312036002265

Kennedy, M. (2016). Parsing the practice of teaching. *Journal of Teacher Education, 67*(1), 6–17. https://doi.org/10.1177/0022487115614617

*Kullberg, A., Mårtensson, P., & Runesson, U. (2016). What is to be learned? Teachers' collective inquiry into the object of learning. *Scandinavian Journal of Educational Research, 60*(3), 309–322. https://doi.org/10.1080/00313831.2015.1119725

Kvale, S. (2008). *Doing interviews.* Sage.

Lampert, M. (2010). Learning teaching in, from, and for practice: What do we mean? *Journal of Teacher Education, 61*(1–2), 21–34. https://doi.org/10.1177/0022487109347321

Learning How to Look & Listen. (2016). *Building capacity for video based social & educational research.* https://www.learninghowtolookandlisten.com/futuredirections

*Levitt, K. E. (2002). An analysis of elementary teachers' beliefs regarding the teaching and learning of science. *Science Education, 86*(1), 1–22. https://doi.org/10.1002/sce.1042

Little, D. (2010). *New contributions to the philosophy of history* (Vol. 6). Springer Science & Business Media. https://doi.org/10.1007/978-90-481-9410-0

*Machado, E., Vaughan, A., Coppola, R., & Woodard, R. (2017). "Lived life through a colored lens": Culturally sustaining poetry in an urban literacy classroom. *Language Arts, 94*(6), 367–381.

*Maloch, B. (2002). Scaffolding student talk: One teacher's role in literature discussion groups. *Reading Research Quarterly, 37*(1), 94–112. https://doi.org/10.1598/RRQ.37.1.4

*Maloch, B. (2004). On the road to literature discussion groups: Teacher scaffolding during preparatory experiences. *Literacy Research and Instruction, 44*(2), 1–20. https://doi.org/10.1080/19388070409558424

*Maloch, B. (2005). Becoming a "WOW Reader": Context and continuity in a second grade classroom. *Journal of Classroom Interaction, 40*(1), 5–17.

*Maloch, B. (2008). Beyond exposure: The uses of informational texts in a second grade classroom. *Research in the Teaching of English, 42*(3), 315–362.

*Maloch, B., Worthy, J., Hampton, A., Jordan, M., Hungerford-Kresser, H., & Semingson, P. (2013). Portraits of practice: A cross-case analysis of two first-grade teachers and their grouping practices. *Research in the Teaching of English, 47*(3), 277–312.

Marshall, C., & Rossman, G. B. (2006). *Designing qualitative research.* Sage.

*Martin, L. A., Chiodo, J. J., & Chang, L. H. (2001). First year teachers: Looking back after three years. *Action in Teacher Education, 23*(1), 55–63. https://doi.org/10.1080/01626620.2001.10463055

Martínez, R. A. (2010). Spanglish as a literacy tool: Towards an understanding of the potential role of Spanish-English code-switching in the development of academic literacy. *Research in the Teaching of English, 45*(2), 124–149.

*Martínez, R. A., Hikida, M., & Durán, L. (2015). Unpacking ideologies of linguistic purism: How dual language teachers make sense of everyday translanguaging. *International Multilingual Research Journal, 9*(1), 26–42. https://doi.org/10.1080/19313152.2014.977712

Masingila, J. O., & Doerr, H. M. (2002). Understanding pre-service teachers' emerging practices through their analyses of a case study of practice. *Journal of Mathematics Teacher Education, 5*(3), 235–263. https://doi.org/10.1023/A:1019847825912

Maxwell, J. (2012). The importance of qualitative research for causal explanation in education. *Qualitative Inquiry, 18*(8), 655–661. https://doi.org/10.1177/1077800412452856

Maxwell, J. A. (2013). *Qualitative research design: An interactive approach* (3rd ed.). Sage.

McMillan, J. H., Myran, S., & Workman, D. (2002). Elementary teachers' classroom assessment and grading practices. *Journal of Educational Research, 95*(4), 203–213. https://doi.org/10.1080/00220670209596593

Mills, G. E. (2000). *Action research: A guide for the teacher researcher.* Prentice Hall.

Mishler, E. G. (1991). *Research interviewing.* Harvard University Press.

Moats, L. C. (1994). The missing foundation in teacher education. *Annals of Dyslexia, 44*(1), 81–102. https://doi.org/10.1007/BF02648156

*Musanti, S. I. (2017). A novice bilingual teacher's journey: Teacher's noticing as a pathway to negotiate contradictory teaching discourses. *International Journal of Multicultural Education, 19*(2), 146–162. https://doi.org/10.18251/ijme.v19i2.1305

*Musanti, S. I., & Celedón-Pattichis, S. (2013). Promising pedagogical practices for emergent bilinguals in kindergarten: Towards a mathematics discourse community. *Journal of Multilingual Education Research, 4,* Article 4. https://fordham.bepress.com/jmer/vol4/iss1/4/

*Musanti, S. I., Celedón-Pattichis, S., & Marshall, M. E. (2009). Reflections on language and mathematics problem solving: A case study of a bilingual first-grade teacher. *Bilingual Research Journal, 32*(1), 25–41. https://doi.org/10.1080/15235880902965763

Orellana, M. F., & Bowman, P. (2003). Cultural diversity research on learning and development: Conceptual, methodological, and strategic considerations. *Educational Researcher, 32*(5), 26–32. https://doi.org/10.3102/0013189X032005026

*Palmer, D. K., Martínez, R. A., Mateus, S. G., & Henderson, K. (2014). Reframing the debate on language separation: Towards a vision for translanguaging pedagogies in the dual language classroom. *Modern Language Journal, 98,* 757–772. https://doi.org/10.1111/j.1540-4781.2014.12121.x

Patton, M. Q. (1980). *Qualitative evaluation methods.* Sage.

Patton, M. Q. (2005). Qualitative research. In B. S. Everitt & D. C. Howell (Eds.), *Encyclopedia of statistics in behavioral science.* John Wiley. https://doi.org/10.1002/0470013192.bsa514

*Riojas-Cortez, M., Alanís, I., & Flores, B. B. (2013). Early childhood teachers reconstruct beliefs and practices through reflexive action. *Journal of Early Childhood Teacher Education, 34*(1), 36–45. https://doi.org/10.1080/10901027.2013.758536

*Runesson, U. (2013). Focusing on the object of learning and what is critical for learning: a case study of teachers' inquiry into teaching and learning mathematics. *Perspectives in Education, 31*(3), 170–183.

*Savasci, F., & Berlin, D. F. (2012). Science teacher beliefs and classroom practice related to constructivism in different school settings. *Journal of Science Teacher Education, 23*(1), 65–86. https://doi.org/10.1007/s10972-011-9262-z

Schachter, R. E. (2015). An analytic study of the professional development research in early childhood education. *Early Education and Development, 26,* 1057-1085. https://doi.org/10.1080/10409289.2015.1009335

*Schachter, R. E. (2017). Early childhood teachers' pedagogical reasoning about how children learn during language and literacy instruction. *International Journal of Early Childhood, 49*(1), 95–111. https://doi.org/10.1007/s13158-017-0179-3

Schachter, R. E., & Freeman, D. (2015). Using stimulated recall to study teachers and teaching: A brief introduction to the research methodology. In P. O. Lucas & R. L. Rodrigues (Eds.), *Temas e Rumos nas Pesquisas em Linguistica (Aplicada): Questos empiricas, eticas e praticas* (Vol. 1, pp. 223–243). Pontes Editores.

Schachter, R. E., & Freeman, D. (in press). Bridging the public and private in teaching: An argument for revisiting stimulated recall as a research procedure. *Harvard Educational Review.*

Shulman, L. (1987). Knowledge and teaching: Foundations of the new reform. *Harvard Educational Review, 57*(1), 1–23. https://doi.org/10.17763/haer.57.1.j463w79r56455411

Smith, L., Bratini, L., & Appio, L. M. (2012). "Everybody's teaching and everybody's learning": Photovoice and youth counseling. *Journal of Counseling & Development, 90*(1), 3–12. https://doi.org/10.1111/j.1556-6676.2012.00001.x

*Souto-Manning, M. (2010). Challenging ethnocentric literary practices: (Re)positioning home literacies in a Head Start classroom. *Research in the Teaching of English, 45*(2), 150–178. www.jstor.org/stable/40997088

*Swan, K., & Hicks, D. (2007). Through the democratic lens: The role of purpose in leveraging technology to support historical inquiry in the social studies classroom. *International Journal of Social Education, 21*(2), 142–168.

*Swan, K., & Hofer, M. (2011). In search of technological pedagogical content knowledge: Teachers' initial foray into podcasting in economics. *Journal of Research on Technology in Education, 44*(1), 75–98. https://doi.org/10.1080/15391523.2011.10782580

*Tobin, J. J. (1988). Visual anthropology and multivocal ethnography: A dialogical approach to Japanese preschool class size. *Dialectical Anthropology, 13*, 173–187. https://doi.org/10.1007/BF00704329

*Vetter, A. (2010). Positioning students as readers and writers through talk in a high school English classroom. *English Education, 43*(1), 33–64.

*Vetter, A. (2013). "You need some laugh bones!" Leveraging AAL in a high school English classroom. *Journal of Literacy Research, 45*(2), 173–206. https://doi.org/10.1177/1086296X12474653

Walberg, H. (1977). Decision and perception: New constructs for research on teaching effects. *Cambridge Journal of Education, 7*(1), 33–39. https://doi.org/10.1080/0305764770070105

Wang, C., & Burris, M. A. (1997). Photovoice: Concept, methodology, and use for participatory needs assessment. *Health Education & Behavior, 24*(3), 369–387. https://doi.org/10.1177/109019819702400309

Warne, M., Snyder, K., & Gådin, K. G. (2013). Photovoice: An opportunity and challenge for students' genuine participation. *Health Promotion International, 28*(3), 299–310. https://doi.org/10.1093/heapro/das011

*Watters, J. J., & Diezmann, C. M. (2016). Engaging elementary students in learning science: An analysis of classroom dialogue. *Instructional Science, 44*(1), 25–44. https://doi.org/10.1007/s11251-015-9364-7

*Watters, J. J., & Ginns, I. S. (1997). An in-depth study of a teacher engaged in an innovative primary science trial professional development project. *Research in Science Education, 27*(1), 51–69. https://doi.org/10.1007/BF02463032

*Westerman, D. A. (1991). Expert and novice teacher decision making. *Journal of Teacher Education, 42*(4), 292–305. https://doi.org/10.1177/002248719104200407

*Whitney, A., Blau, S., Bright, A., Cabe, R., Dewar, T., Macias, R., Rogers, P., & Levin, J. (2008). Beyond strategies: Teacher practice, writing process, and the influence of inquiry. *English Education, 40*(3), 201–230.

*Worthy, J., Maloch, B., Pursley, B., Hungerford-Kresser, H., Hampton, A., Jordan, M., & Semingson, P. (2015). What are the rest of the students doing? Literacy work stations in two first-grade classrooms. *Language Arts, 92*(3), 173–186.

Xiao, B., & Tobin, J. (2018). The use of video as a tool for reflection with preservice teachers. *Journal of Early Childhood Teacher Education, 39*(4), 328–345. https://doi.org/10.1080/10901027.2018.1516705

Yin, R. K. (2014). *Case study research design and methods.* Sage.

*Zuniga, C. E., Henderson, K. I., & Palmer, D. K. (2018). Language policy toward equity: How bilingual teachers use policy mandates to their own ends. *Language and Education, 32*(1), 60–76. https://doi.org/10.1080/09500782.2017.1349792

Chapter 14

Research on Continuous Improvement: Exploring the Complexities of Managing Educational Change

Maxwell M. Yurkofsky

Amelia J. Peterson (iD)

Jal D. Mehta

Rebecca Horwitz-Willis

Kim M. Frumin

Harvard Graduate School of Education

As a result of the frustration with the dominant "What Works" paradigm of large-scale research-based improvement, practitioners, researchers, foundations, and policymakers are increasingly embracing a set of ideas and practices that can be collectively labeled continuous improvement (CI) methods. This chapter provides a comparative review of these methods, paying particular attention to CI methods' intellectual influences, theories of action, and affordances and challenges in practice. We first map out and explore the shared intellectual forebears that CI methods draw on. We then discuss three kinds of complexity to which CI methods explicitly attend—ambiguity, variability, and interdependence— and how CI methods seek a balance of local and formal knowledge in response to this complexity. We go on to argue that CI methods are generally less attentive to the relational and political dimensions of educational change and that this leads to challenges in practice. We conclude by considering CI methods' aspirations for impact at scale, and offer a number of recommendations to inform future research and practice.

We are in the midst of an exciting shift in education research and practice. As a result of increasing frustration with the dominant "What Works" paradigm of large-scale research-based improvement (Bryk et al., 2015; Penuel et al., 2011), practitioners, researchers, foundations, and policymakers are beginning to favor good

Review of Research in Education
March 2020, Vol. 44, pp. 403–433
DOI: 10.3102/0091732X20907363
Chapter reuse guidelines: sagepub.com/journals-permissions
© 2020 AERA. http://rre.aera.net

practice over best practice, local proofs over experimental evidence, adaptation over faithful implementation, and a focus on practitioners' problems over researchers' solutions. These ideas are embodied in a number of educational improvement methods that range in their origin and theory of action but are increasingly being labeled *continuous improvement* (CI) methods.

On initial inspection, CI methods have important differences. Some emerge out of the research–practice partnership (RPP) and design-based research traditions, therefore placing greater value on the role of researchers in supporting larger scale and multiyear research and improvement efforts. Others have developed from a focus on data-based decision making and professional learning communities, and therefore see smaller teams of educators as the core drivers of research and improvement. But underneath these differences, CI methods share a number of common characteristics that make them useful to analyze as a group. In particular, we are interested in four shared commitments:

1. Grounding improvement efforts in local problems or needs
2. Empowering practitioners to take an active role in research and improvement
3. Engaging in iteration, which involves a cyclical process of action, assessment, reflection, and adjustment
4. Striving to spur change across schools and systems, not just individual classrooms

These similarities also reflect the fact that, as illustrated in this chapter, CI methods share a similar intellectual lineage, one rooted in John Dewey's pragmatism and often connected to theories of organizational learning, quality improvement, action science, improvement science, design-based research, and teacher research.

In light of their alignment around these four pillars and their divergence across a number of other dimensions, we believe there is much to be learned by putting different CI methods into conversation with one another. With a few important exceptions that we discuss later (e.g., Coburn et al., 2013; Lochmiller & Lester, 2017; Peurach et al., 2018), much of the writing about these methods has (a) been written by proponents, (b) examined a single method only, or (c) emphasized the similarities among the methods as part of an effort to build a case for these approaches as a whole (Penuel et al., 2018). We offer an external examination of the methods in relation to each other and to their intellectual forebears, as well as the empirical evidence about their successes and challenges in practice.

We approach this task as a critical friend of the movement, sharing many of its aspirations but also seeking to clearly see the challenges, all in the hope of helping those who use these methods land in a better place. If we had to capture our main message in a sentence, it would be that CI methods as a whole are still too steeped in ideas from their forebears in industry, and if they are going to be successful in transforming educational systems, they need to more consciously attend to the political and relational dimensions of systemic change. Doing so would make these methods more human; more attentive to issues of race, gender, and power; and more responsive to the rhythm and demands of public school systems, all of which are critical if these methods are going to contribute to a more just and equitable educational future. We did, however, find some examples where methods had more consciously attended to these dimensions, which we explicate in more detail below.

We develop this argument in six parts. First, we define the scope and method of our inquiry. We describe the steps we took to identify the CI methods that align with the definition above and the literature that sheds light on these methods in theory and practice, as well as some emergent patterns relating to the methods' differing theories of action and intellectual origins. This review illuminated how most CI methods are intended as responses to the complexity of education. In the second section, we elaborate on three kinds of complexity to which these methods explicitly attend: ambiguity, variability, and interdependence. Synthesizing across the intellectual forebears of CI methods, we discuss some of the perennial challenges of responding to these three types of complexity in the third section, particularly the challenges of balancing and interweaving local and expert knowledge. In Sections 4 and 5, we introduce two additional kinds of complexity stemming from the uniquely relational and political character of educational systems that are less attended to by the forebears and progenitors of CI methods. We highlight the challenges that relational and political dynamics pose for CI methods in practice and discuss the (often implicit) strategies used to grapple with these challenges. In the sixth section, we discuss how these forms of complexity pose unique challenges when considering the longer-term aims of CI methods to spur systemic change, and offer some recommendations and pathways forward. We conclude by discussing the implications of our analysis for the broader educational field.

MAPPING THE LANDSCAPE: CI METHODS AND THEIR INTELLECTUAL FOREBEARS

In approaching this chapter, we engaged in a systematic review of the literature on CI methods. We first drew on the ERIC database to search for research on CI methods that met the criteria in the introduction: methods that were grounded in local problems of practice, practitioner-centered, iterative, and focused on systems change. Through this process, we identified 14 methods that meet our criteria, and 110 empirical and theoretical publications over the past 25 years about these methods published in peer-reviewed journals and academic presses (see Supplemental Appendix A available in the online journal for additional information).[1] Table 1 provides a brief description of each method.

We used the theoretical articles to understand the similarities and differences across these methods' theories of action, and then drew on the empirical articles to understand the successes and challenges these methods faced in realizing their theories of action. Our reading of the literature also allowed us to organize CI methods into some rough groupings (see Figure 1). While the discussion of these methods

TABLE 1

A Brief Description of the 14 CI Methods That Served as the Focus for Our Analysis

CI Method	Target User	Description
Cycles of inquiry	Teachers	A focused, short-term, iterative process of defining a question, analyzing evidence, determining an inquiry focus, implementing an intervention, and evaluating impact
Data Teams	Teachers	A collaborative model for implementing data-driven decision making at the instructional level
The Data Wise improvement process	Teachers, teacher teams, often with school leader involvement	An eight-step process where teams of educators build a foundation for collaborative work, inquire into problems of learning and practice, and develop, implement, and continuously assess and adjust an action plan
Design-based implementation research	Combination of teachers, school leaders researchers, and district leaders	An approach to connecting research and practice that is grounded in collaborative, iterative, systematic inquiry to develop effective, scalable, and sustainable policies and programs in schools and school districts
Design-based school improvement	School leaders	A systematic, disciplined, and design-based form of problem solving in educational organizations that involves developing and refining theories of action
Design thinking	Various	A set of mind-sets and a multistep process for redesigning a product, practice, or service around the specific needs of a user
Instructional rounds	District leaders and, school-based teams	An approach to improving instruction that involves a group of educators meeting together on an ongoing basis to define a problem of practice, visit classrooms, discuss what they saw, and identify next levels of work
Lesson study	Teachers	Originating in Japan, lesson study is a process in which teacher teams research, plan, publicly enact, discuss, and then refine intended improvements to instruction
The National Center on Scaling Up Effective Schools	Combination of teachers, school leaders, and district leaders	A continuous improvement model where researchers and practitioners codesign innovations based on outlier schools, adaptively integrate that innovation using plan-do-study-act cycles in a subset of schools, and scale up the innovation across the district
Networked Improvement Communities	Combination of teachers, school leaders, district leaders, and often outside researchers or facilitators	A network that works across sites and draws on the principles of improvement science to address a shared problem of practice using system-mapping tools and plan-do-study-act cycles
The Strategic Educational Research Partnership	Researchers, designers, teachers, and school leaders	A research-practice partnership between researchers and designers to develop new tools or routines through iterative cycles of practitioner feedback
Spirals of inquiry	Teachers	A fluid six-phase inquiry process directing practitioners toward understanding how their students experience learning and how their own practice affects that experience
Teacher research	Teachers	Action-based research that enables educators to investigate questions related to teaching and learning by systematically collecting and analyzing data, reflecting on changes to their assumptions and practices, and sharing their learning
Total quality management	Combination of teachers, school leaders, and district leaders	A management approach that involves employees working on cross-department teams to continuously improve internal processes in order to enhance customer satisfaction

Note. CI = continuous improvement.

FIGURE 1
A Venn Diagram of Some of the Continuous Improvement Methods in Our
Sample, Based on the Typical Level at Which the Method Focuses and the Extent
of the Involvement of External Expertise

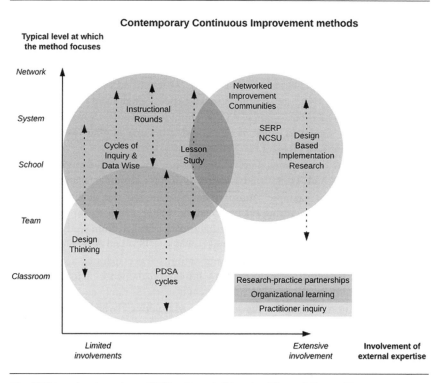

Note. PDSA = plan-do-study-act; SERP = Strategic Educational Research Partnership;
NCSU = National Center on Scaling Up Effective Schools. The placement of methods is intended to
illustrate some potential differences but cannot be conclusive due to the range of examples within any
given method. Note that methods can be nested inside each other, for example, PDSA cycles are part of
Networked Improvement Communities.

sometimes gets subsumed under the "RPP" frame, we thought that the methods fell
into three broad buckets: RPPs, organizational improvement, and practitioner
inquiry. We array these as a Venn diagram to illustrate areas of overlap.[2]

We organized Figure 1 around two dimensions of difference that play important
roles in the theories of action for each method: (a) the typical level at which the
method focuses (e.g., a teacher applying the method to their own classroom vs. a
whole system using the method to address a more systemic problem) and (b) the
involvement of external expertise (typically researchers).

We were also interested in understanding the intellectual origins of these methods. To do this, we selected up to four articles for those methods that developed an explicit, research-based argument for their process. We identified and reviewed the major bodies of knowledge on which these methods drew (see Supplemental Appendix B available in the online journal for details on this process), keeping track of which methods cited one another and each body of knowledge. We used this analysis to identify central influences (hereafter called "forebears") across many methods (e.g., improvement science, organizational learning), and then drew on these bodies of work to inform our analysis of these methods' theories of action.

To create a visual representation of the themes we identified when engaging in this process, we used UCINET to conduct a social network analysis of the citation patterns between each method and these different bodies of work (Borgatti et al., 2002), which includes the extent to which these methods cited one another. We present the results of this analysis in Figure 2.

From the many connections here, we highlight a few notable themes. First, the forebears of CI methods come from a variety of sectors, disciplines, and epistemological traditions. For example, improvement science and the quality movement originated in the manufacturing sector (Deming, 1982) and then spread to health care (Cohen-Vogel et al., 2015), sociocultural theory emerged from study of apprenticeships (Lave & Wenger, 1991), and Argyris et al.'s (1985) and Argyris and Schön's (1997) work in organizational learning and action science spanned across sectors. Interestingly, although these forebears draw heavily on the work of John Dewey— hence his centrality in our network diagram—CI methods rarely cite Dewey's work directly. In addition, writing on "the complexity of teaching" (which represents work by scholars like David Cohen and Magdalene Lampert) was as an unexpectedly central influence across a variety of methods.

This prompted us to focus in on a couple of questions as we engaged in our review of the research:

- How do the different origins of CI methods inform their theories of action and their particular affordances in the context of American education?
- What characteristics of schooling do CI methods convey when using the term *complexity*, and how have CI methods evolved from their roots in other sectors to grapple with this complexity?

We turn now to this set of questions.

CONCEPTUALIZING AND MANAGING COMPLEXITY

Our review of CI methods' theories of action supports the finding that most methods share a conception of schooling as "complex." This conception underpins their turn away from a "What Works" approach to education research and toward approaches that ground improvement efforts in local problems or needs, put practitioners and their perspectives at the center of research and improvement, and include

FIGURE 2
Social Network Analysis of the Citation Patterns Between and Among CI Methods and With Intellectual Forebears

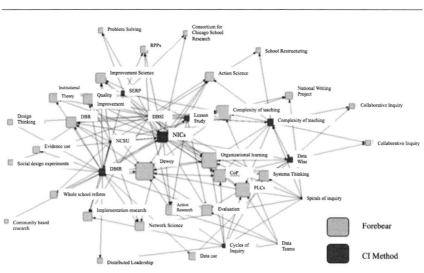

Note. CI = continuous improvement; CoP = communities of practice; DBR = design-based research; DBSI = design-based school improvement; DBIR = design-based implementation research; NCSU = National Center on Scaling Up Effective Schools; NIC = Networked Improvement Community; PLCs = professional learning communities; RPP = research–practice partnership; SERP = Strategic Educational Research Partnership. More cited forebears or methods are larger in size.

cycles of iteration. We found, however, that as we looked beyond rhetorical references to complexity to more detailed descriptions, method developers described complexity in different ways. Across the various methods we have identified three types of complexity that are inherent in the problems they seek to address. They argue that these problems are the following:

1. *Ambiguous and wicked*: Method progenitors frequently invoke complexity as it relates to ambiguity—more specifically that educational problems are often "wicked" in the sense of being ill-defined and involving competing goals or value systems (Churchman, 1967). Many progenitors ground their analysis in the complexity of teachers' daily work, including Lampert (1985), Cohen (2011), and Dewey's (1929/2011) earlier conception of the multiplicitous nature of teaching. Mintrop and Zumpe (2019) build on this argument, discussing how design-based approaches are particularly useful in education where "complexity and uncertainty produce ill-defined problems with unknown solution paths, unclear constraints, and ambiguous goals" (p. 304). Design methods, they argue, offer processes for "defining and framing the problem itself and considering

multiple solution paths" (p. 304). Likewise, Retna (2016) studying teachers adopting design thinking, describes design as being developed to address "ill-structured problems" (p. 6).

2. *Variable and context-specific*: A second source of complexity that progenitors seek to address is the variability within and across education systems. Variability stems from the diverse and changing needs and assets of teachers and students across grades, schools, and districts (Bryk et al., 2015; Cohen, 2011), as well as the unique local environment in which schools and classrooms are situated. For example, Penuel et al. (2011, p. 331) ground their justification for design-based implementation research (DBIR) in the varying effects of treatments across settings due to these differing local contexts.

3. *Interdependent and nested*: A third conception of complexity focuses on how the various elements of educational systems are interconnected. As a result, efforts to solve any one problem can quickly implicate many other aspects of school systems. For example, citing Rowan (2002), Penuel et al. (2011, p. 331) argue that improving educational systems "demands alignment and coordination of the actions of people, teams, and organizational units within a complex institutional ecology." One implication of this form of complexity is that each member of the system has an inherently limited view of the problem they are trying to solve (Bryk et al., 2011). Interdependence also implies that outcomes are the product of multiple factors that interact, creating nonlinear and often unpredictable patterns of outcomes. Some methods attempt to grapple directly with this form of complexity, viewing systems as mappable and manipulable combinations of interdependent elements, such as those found in engineering (Dolle et al., 2013).

CI methods have developed many similar approaches in response to these forms of complexity. For example, they respond to variability by focusing on local problems, and address interdependence and ambiguity by gradually uncovering and provisionally addressing the inevitable unexpected outcomes within a particular context.

But these shared approaches also create numerous challenges. First, they require a delicate interweaving of formal and local knowledge—an aspiration that forebears have grappled with over the past century. In addition, they underemphasize two other aspects of complexity—which we label as the *undiscussability* of change that goes "below the green line" (Wheatley & Dalmau, 1983) and *the political fragmentation* of school systems—resulting in challenges to implementing these methods in practice. Finally, CI methods' attention to complexity can be in tension with their ambition for scaled impact. We develop these themes in more detail below.

FORMAL AND LOCAL KNOWLEDGE: HOW SHOULD THEY RELATE?

CI methods all recognize the need to move away from an epistemology that privileges the knowledge that comes from formal, generalizable research, working instead to weave in local knowledge that can apply more closely to the specific variabilities, interdependencies, and ambiguities of particular educational contexts. Nevertheless, they offer a range of contrasting approaches to interweaving formal and local knowledge, building on a century-long discussion about science, epistemology, and change.

Contrasting Approaches to External Knowledge

At one end of a continuum are those who are quite skeptical of the role of external knowledge. Design thinking, as a methodology, for example, celebrates the ingenuity of its practitioners, and suggests that through close observations, empathy interviews, brainstorming, and prototyping, fresh new ideas will be generated that meet the needs of the context and the moment. From this perspective external "expertise" can actually be a constraining force, as it represents the authority of the established and inhibits the creation of new insights (Kelley, 2002, pp. 64–65).

Likewise, work that emphasizes the importance of local practitioner reflection and iteration is more skeptical about formal external knowledge. Donald Schön, whose book *The Reflective Practitioner* has been highly influential in the field, argued that in the training of professionals the technical rationality of the university was overemphasized and that local craft knowledge was underemphasized (Schön, 2017). He argued that the epistemology that dominated the university, grounded in technical rationality and "application of research-based theory and technique," was ill-suited to the kinds of problems that were most relevant to practitioners. University professors maintained their status by focusing on elegant problems and formal techniques, but real problems existed in a "swampy lowland" of ambiguity that was known to practitioners but largely invisible to most university faculty. Thus, he argued that students should apprentice under master teachers who had both extensive craft and formal knowledge, and for practitioners to engage in iterative cycles of learning and reflection as they worked.

Others have been skeptical of formal university knowledge because of its connection to histories of racism, oppression, and use to reify the educational status quo. Cochran-Smith and Lytle (1999) urge teachers to engage in ongoing critique of, and revision to, dominant ideas and resources—not only on grounds of usefulness but also on grounds of ethics, justice, ideology, and values. Much of the work on teacher action research and participatory action research (Duncan-Andrade & Morrell, 2008) takes this stance, arguing that this kind of research requires a Freirian stance to break from dominant ideologies and work with students and communities to develop alternative frames and cycles of inquiry.

More toward the middle of the spectrum are methods like Data Wise and Instructional Rounds. They do not take an explicit stance on the role of formal versus local knowledge but in practice assume that there is much local knowledge that could be mobilized to address a problem, if only a rigorous process were used to examine assumptions and generate new possibilities (Boudett et al., 2013; City et al., 2009). In so doing, they are elevating the importance of organizational knowledge *about* the process of improvement—what Deming called profound knowledge (1994)—and assuming that appropriate improvement processes will bring in both local and external knowledge as needed.

Others articulate a model that interweaves formal knowledge with local, contextual knowledge. John Dewey, for example, offered an integrative view, arguing that both were essential in supporting the variable and complex work of teaching. Dewey was opposed to simplistic ideas of knowledge transfer; anticipating much of the modern debate, he argued that local conditions were simply too complex and variable for scientific findings to be simply "applied." He writes in *The Sources of a Science of Education* (Dewey, 1929/2011),

> No conclusion of scientific research can be converted into an immediate rule of educational art. For there is no educational practice whatever which is not highly complex; that is to say, which does not contain many other conditions and factors than are included in the scientific finding. (p. 9)

Thus, he concludes, there is no substitute for the judgment and wisdom of the teacher in the moment.

At the same time, Dewey (1929/2011) argues, this judgment can be informed by the development of formal knowledge. He gives the example of a study suggesting that girls mature earlier than boys during puberty. This fact does not predetermine practice, but it helps the thoughtful teacher conceptualize his work:

> The teacher who really knows this fact will have his personal attitude changed. He will be on the alert to make certain observations which would otherwise escape him; he . . . will be enabled to interpret some facts which would otherwise be confused and misunderstood. This knowledge and understanding render his practice more intelligent, more flexible and better adapted to deal effectively with concrete phenomena of practice. (p. 9)

Dewey (1929/2011) concludes therefore that while some mistakenly see science as creating uniformity: "The opposite is the case. Command of scientific methods and systematized subject-matter liberates individuals; it enables them to see new problems, devise new procedures, and, in general, makes for diversification rather than for set uniformity" (p. 6).

DBIR similarly foregrounds the interweaving of formal and local knowledge. DBIR is frequently grounded in disciplinary communities of university experts, who have spent many years thinking about how those disciplines are structured and what methods would enable teachers to teach in ambitious ways (Fishman et al., 2013). Although these experts begin with a fairly well-defined set of priors about what good instruction would look like (Penuel et al., 2011), they use codesign and adaptation processes to develop interventions that integrate their formal knowledge with the local knowledge embedded in the contexts they support (e.g., Kwon et al., 2014; Penuel et al., 2007; Severance et al., 2016).

Networked improvement communities (NICs) are perhaps the most synthetic method, offering a role for formal expertise but drawing on empathy interviews and local knowledge that comes with design thinking, and using their network structures to identify and develop positive deviants that can offer workable answers to local problems (Bryk et al., 2015). Compared to DBIR, NICs are also more flexible; they apply profound knowledge (through the use of tools like driver diagrams, plan-do-study-act cycles [PDSAs], and root cause analysis) and then draw on different bodies of knowledge as the definition of the problem requires (Russell et al., 2017).

Which Approach Under Which Circumstances?

Three dimensions seem particularly important in thinking about which of the approaches are best suited to the problem at hand: (a) whether the local knowledge available is sufficient to tackle the problem, (b) whether the problem is clearly bounded within a single domain of existing knowledge or moves across content areas, and (c) whether the broader system authorities have an important role to play in addressing the problem.

Specifically, early research on these methods suggests that different processes are appropriate depending on whether or not local knowledge is sufficient to tackle the problem. Methods that foreground local expertise and profound knowledge can help teachers to identify problems, but those teachers can be stymied in learning about new solutions in the absence of external expertise, resulting in more superficial changes to instruction (Allen & Calhoun, 1998; Bocala, 2015; Copland, 2003; Gallimore et al., 2009; Lockwood, 2017). Methods like DBIR and lesson study that provide this external expertise but also allow for iterative adaptation have a stronger track record of addressing problems related to classroom instruction (e.g., Connor et al., 2017; Lewis & Perry, 2017).

A second dimension is flexibility. Methods like design thinking, Instructional Rounds, Data Wise, and cycles of inquiry are flexible in that they do not preassume any particular problem or any preset content expertise. Design thinking—intentionally developed in the field of design to be deployed in a great variety of different domains (Buchanan, 1992)—may be a good choice for schools and districts that are trying to innovate in more fundamental ways. From our own research, we have the example of Cowichan Valley, a district in British Columbia, which is seeking to question virtually every aspect of conventional schooling—should there be desks and chairs? what should the schedule look like?—and have found that using the design process offers a collaborative way for teachers, students, parents, and community members to develop new ideas on a variety of fronts. Methods like DBIR that foreground disciplinary content expertise are less appropriate for districts that are seeking open-ended change across a variety of dimensions.

A third dimension is the extent to which other elements of the system are implicated in the problem CI methods are seeking to address. Methods like teacher action research, Data Wise, and design thinking can be conducted locally without buy-in, coordination with, or support from top-level administrators in the system. These more local methods can energize teachers around change; can be adapted to meet the needs, interests, and goals of individual teachers; and can produce high commitment and thoughtful reflection upon practice (Copland, 2003; Goodnough, 2010; Schildkamp et al., 2016; Scribner et al., 1999; Zeichner, 2003). However, in the absence of administrator support these efforts may be limited to coalitions of the willing, and may run into conflicts with broader policies and demands, limiting the ability to create systemic change (Artiles, 2015; Goodnough, 2010).

Conversely, larger scale RPPs are better suited to addressing more systemic problems that have garnered significant administrator buy-in. For example, NICs—with their emphasis on building system maps and driver diagrams, as well as developing diverse teams to ensure that "sufficient interest, influence, and expertise exist to address the problem" (Dolle et al., 2013, p. 447)—are well set up to support changes that require coordination across different actors in the system. However, defining problems at the system level also risks alienating teachers who have a different understanding of their most pressing needs. A fairly common challenge among RPPs that bring formal expertise to bear on a district- or network-wide problem of practice is that there are typically some practitioners who are less bought in to the framing of the problem or the pathway forward (e.g., Hannan et al., 2015; Penuel et al., 2007; Redding et al., 2018; Tichnor-Wagner et al., 2017).

In sum, like their forebears, CI methods interweave different combinations of formal and local knowledge as a way of managing the complexities of educational change. Also like their forebears, the available research on CI methods does not suggest a single "right" way of balancing or integrating formal and local knowledge. Instead, we found that different approaches may be more and less appropriate depending on the characteristics of the problem at hand. As a result, we recommend more careful consideration of and research into the fit between CI methods and the specific complexities of the problem they are trying to solve.

THE RELATIONAL ELEMENTS OF SYSTEMIC CHANGE: GOING "BELOW THE GREEN LINE" AND SURFACING THE UNDISCUSSABLE

Most CI methods acknowledge that educational improvement, relative to other domains, is a human-centric endeavor (Cohen, 1988). Indeed, the core "technology" of schooling is the ongoing interaction among teachers and students in the service of human improvement. And yet, there is little conceptualization of how CI methods might support improvement in light of the relational character of education. This absence seems to be a key consequence of the fact that many CI methods stem from fields outside of education where this relational dimension is less core to the work of improvement.

Our review suggests that to be effective, improvement efforts need to attend not simply to data, evidence, and iterative cycles but also to the relational elements of schools, which can serve as invisible enablers and barriers to change. By relational elements we refer more specifically to intersubjective understandings of teaching and learning, as well as practitioners' individual beliefs, mind-sets, and identities, which can be replicated or disrupted through their everyday work-related actions and inter-actions (Smets & Jarzabkowski, 2013). In the studies of communities of practice, Wenger (1998) describes these relational elements in terms of "negotiation of meaning": the process by which the nature and explanation of things is defined among individuals. Relational elements also include the nature of the relationships and levels of trust among and across the different actors in the system (Bryk & Schneider, 2002). Wheatley and colleagues use the metaphor of the "green line" to distinguish between elements of organizations residing "above the green line" that are typically the focus of interventions—such as structures, operations and strategy— and the more invisible aspects of organizations (e.g., identities and relationships) that fall "below the green line" but are vital to organizational change (Wheatley, 2006; Wheatley & Dalmau, 1983).

The Necessity and Challenge of Attending to the Relational Elements of Change

As a result of a number of historical and structural features of American educational systems, the relational elements of schools can often serve as barriers to change. In particular, school systems are (a) riven with mistrust of those above in the hierarchy, especially in recent years as a result of climates of accountability and teacher evaluation (Mehta, 2013), which engenders reluctance to engage in new change efforts (Payne, 2007); (b) saddled with assumptions about teaching, professional collaboration, and racial equity that conflict with many aspirations of current reform movements (Lortie, 1975; Pollock, 2009); and (c) organized as street-level bureaucracies, wherein the impossibility of monitoring or prescribing every aspect of teachers' work results in de facto autonomy for teachers, whose substantive participation in new change efforts is therefore difficult to ensure (Weatherly & Lipsky, 1977).

Unfortunately, CI methods are often not well positioned to attend to the relational elements of schools. We illustrate the tensions with examples from two educational issues that are top priorities for many using CI methods: racial equity and student-centered instruction.

First, CI methods prioritize practitioner generation and framing of problems, but issues that are in conflict with stated goals, values, and identities may not be surfaced (Argyris & Schön, 1997). Educators who believe in supporting equitable schools can still carry implicit biases that affect their practices, and teachers who aspire to improve their pedagogy may in practice have trouble giving up the belief that external factors (e.g., parental and neighborhood influence)—as opposed to their own actions as teachers—are the primary determinants of students' achievement (Timperley & Robinson, 2001; Warikoo et al., 2016). As a result of this misalignment, the problems educators surface may not reflect the most important areas for improvement.

This challenge is compounded by the difficulty of directly observing and measuring the relational elements of schools, which can undermine CI methods' focus on analyzable problems (Argyris et al., 1985). It is difficult to collect data on how teachers' ongoing relationships and encounters with students can contribute to racial achievement gaps. This ambiguity allows for practitioners to suggest alternative causes of racial disparities in achievement, resulting in avoidance or confusion over the topic (Pollock, 2009; Safir, 2017). Similarly, the differences between more and less effective approaches to student-centered learning are not easily detected through traditional assessments or brief classroom visitations (National Research Council, 2001; Spillane & Jennings, 1997).

These two challenges, combined with the value-laden nature of educators' work, make it difficult to discuss relational elements of schools openly and transparently. This poses challenges given the emphasis in CI on collaborative inquiry and decision making. For example, educators may adhere to a color-blind ideology that cautions against explicit discussions of race and the ways in which one's own biases and actions might contribute to disparate outcomes (Bonilla-Silva, 2017; Pollock, 2009). Though less fraught, it can also be difficult for teachers to surface in public discussion the ways their own and their colleagues' actions may cut against their learner-centered goals (Horn & Little, 2010; Rait, 1995). In sum, the relational elements of schools that fall "below the green line" are less visible, analyzable, and discussable, thus posing challenges for CI methods.

Going Below the Green Line: Warm and Cool Approaches

When examining the intellectual influences of CI methods, we found two strands of thinking that target "below the green line" elements of change. The first, which we characterize as the *warmer*, or *socializing*, approach, is grounded in the idea that people naturally strive to improve their craft, and the only reason they do not is because of the structures and culture of their organization. For example, Deming's (1982) theory of quality improvement tasks management with harnessing workers' natural inclination to improve by giving them opportunities to create, learn, and adjust. Theories of situated learning also reflect this approach, proposing that mindset and behavior shifts involve a gradual and natural socialization of individuals into a community with shared identity, norms, and practices (Lave & Wenger, 1991).

The second, *cooler*, or *problematizing*, approach is grounded in the idea that humans are generally resistant to change and require uncomfortable interventions to spur changes in behavior (Mezirow, 1991). Argyris and Schön (1997) find that most people in organizations prioritize winning, achieving goals, appearing rational, and minimizing negative feelings, which collectively leads to defensive behaviors and limited risk taking. They argue that real learning requires changing practitioners' assumptions, which necessitates targeting their "theories in use": making them visible, noting how they depart from their espoused theories of action, and using this disequilibrium to prompt change. Teaching on adaptive leadership often takes a similar approach (e.g., Heifetz et al., 2009).

In theory, these two approaches can and should be integrated. Building trust and shared norms creates the space and psychological safety that enables people to have hard conversations about problematic assumptions, norms, and practices (Edmondson & Lei, 2014; Safir, 2017). However, in practice, we found that CI methods rarely attended explicitly to both warmer and cooler approaches to change. A number of methods, particularly those structured as RPPs, prioritize building shared norms and trust between researchers and practitioners and creating a climate where educators feel safe to take risks in trying out new ideas (Coburn & Penuel, 2016; Donovan et al., 2013; Penuel, 2015). However, these methods rarely utilize that foundation to push educators to reevaluate existing beliefs about their work. For example, Roegman et al. (2017) described how the efforts of university-based facilitators to lead inquiry into more sensitive topics were stymied by a prevailing "culture of nice" that limited discussions of systemic inequities.

In contrast, the PDSA process embedded in NICs and the National Center on Scaling Up Effective Schools, as well as many data use protocols, helps make visible and challenge educators' assumptions but includes fewer explicit strategies for building shared norms and culture. For example, educators engaged in PDSA cycles often assimilate the cycles into their existing, less well developed, approach to improvement, which can prevent them from using the process to destabilize and address other assumptions about their practice (Hannan et al., 2015; Tichnor-Wagner et al., 2017). PDSA cycles are a form of counternormative work (Hannan et al., 2015), and educators are not used to seeing their own successes and challenges as important knowledge that could guide others' work, if well documented (Tichnor-Wagner et al., 2017). One study of design-based school improvement similarly found that educators struggled to use the process in a way that did not just confirm their existing ideas about improvement, despite sustained support from researchers around this challenge (Mintrop & Zumpe, 2019). And in a review of data use in schools, Datnow and Park (2018) found that efforts to use data for CI often focused instead on using it only to group students or meet narrow accountability demands.

There are some exceptions to this either/or pattern. Traditions of teacher research (e.g., Cochran-Smith & Lytle, 1990) support teacher teams in taking on fundamentally different practices, norms, and identities that relate to their roles as knowledge producers in order to support more critical inquiry into their own practice and prevailing educational ideas and values. Data Wise transitions from a socializing approach early on to a problematizing approach later in the cycle (Boudett et al., 2013). For example, Data Wise offers activities for educators to better understand who they are in relation to their team (e.g., the "compass points" protocol) so that in later steps, with the help of protocols designed to minimize risk or vulnerability for individual teachers, teams are better able to have difficult conversations about instructional problems of practice. But little research has examined the success of these methods in garnering shifts in teachers' thinking and practice (for exceptions, see Allen & Calhoun, 1998; Goodnough, 2010).

Overall, CI methods could benefit from attending more to the relational elements of schooling that fall "below the green line" but are necessary for deep and sustained change (Safir, 2017). This might best be accomplished by intentionally fostering both socializing (warmer) and problematizing (cooler) approaches to change, striking a balance between safety and challenge (Edmondson, 2002). This could involve drawing more explicitly on forebears that integrate these approaches to change, including traditions of teacher research, and adapting methods that were designed in other sectors to better meet the relational demands of educational contexts.

POLITICAL FRAGMENTATION: HIGH DEMAND, TURBULENCE, AND INCOHERENCE

A second source of complexity overlooked by CI progenitors is political fragmentation. The American political context of local democratic control over education produces layers of educational governance that offer competing and often conflicting imperatives (Cohen & Spillane, 1992; Chubb & Moe, 1990). Perhaps because CI methods stem in part from manufacturing, on the one side, or classroom-based design, on the other, the methods have to date provided less guidance in how to manage the political complexities that are an inevitable feature of change efforts in a democratic public school system. The particular challenges with which CI methods must grapple can be summarized as high demand, turbulence, and incoherence.

High demand stems from the need for educators to be responsive not only to the needs of their students and families but also to the expectations stemming from other layers of the fragmented educational system (Chubb & Moe, 1990). As a result, the already demanding work of teaching is often compounded by a torrent of time-consuming external expectations (e.g., frequent interim and state assessments, evaluation procedures, school improvement planning, mandatory professional development), all in the context of limited preparation and collaborative time (Johnson, 2013; Kraft et al., 2015). In this time- and energy-scarce environment, CI methods ask teachers and leaders to take on new roles and responsibilities that, however potentially rich and meaningful, may risk as being seen as another distraction if not carefully integrated into their existing work. This in turn may contribute to burnout (Martin & Gobstein, 2015) or more superficial engagement with CI methods, as practitioners prioritize those demands that are familiar or come with sanctions (Leary et al., 2016).

Turbulence enters into school systems, particularly those in underresourced communities, through the high rates of teacher, principal, and superintendent churn, and with it waves of partially implemented reforms (Hess, 2011; Payne, 2008). Such changes cut against the stability needed for CI methods to flourish (Glazer & Peurach, 2013), and may contribute to reform fatigue and ceremonial compliance, while also impeding efforts to build a culture supportive of CI methods (Coburn et al., 2013 Englert et al., 1977; Rosenquist et al., 2015). CI methods may unintentionally exacerbate this turbulence because funding for this work is often temporary, in which case it risks becoming yet another briefly implemented reform (Detert et al., 2000; Leary et al., 2016; Martin & Gobstein, 2015).

A final challenge is *incoherence*. As a result of the contested purposes of education and the varied stakeholders whom schools are meant to serve, educators often experience an incoherent environment that pulls them in many competing directions at once (Cohen & Spillane, 1992; Ingersoll, 2005; Lampert, 1985). These competing values and priorities can push against improvement efforts, such as when districts and states implement CI methods in ways that conform to the piecemeal, rushed, and compliance-oriented approach of educational bureaucracies that methods are meant to subvert (Akiba & Wilkinson, 2016).

CI method progenitors have not explicitly attended to how their methods address these challenges of political fragmentation. However, our review identified three different, more implicit ways these methods try to manage fragmentation, each with certain weaknesses.

Approach 1: Head Down, Ignoring the System: Equipping Educators With Inquiry Tools

This approach attempts to isolate improvement efforts from broader political dynamics, equipping educators with inquiry tools needed to understand and improve the core work of teaching and learning. Methods like Data Wise, Data Teams, and lesson study seek to build certain organizational preconditions for successful inquiry work but then direct the bulk of their attention toward teaching practice and student understanding, with a focus on problems of practice that are within a teacher's immediate control (Boudett et al., 2013).

This approach is vulnerable to political fragmentation. At the school level, educators' take-up of inquiry processes is frequently constrained by a multiplicity of other initiatives (Tichnor-Wagner et al., 2017), lack of ongoing access to relevant data (Hannan et al., 2015), and districts' history with past reforms (Scribner et al., 1999), which can create a climate of distrust that makes inquiry and learning more difficult (Allen & Calhoun, 1998; Ingram et al., 2004). For example, despite a competitive application process, coaches in Russell et al.'s (2019) study struggled to document their PDSA cycles due to the number of other expectations they had to manage. Copland (2003) found that teachers facing external pressure for improvement who had limited time to engage in inquiry would often jump to solutions before understanding the problems they were trying to solve. As a result of these challenges, many studies have pointed to the important role of school-based leadership and advocacy in supporting this work (e.g., Copland, 2003; Hannan et al., 2015; Perry & Lewis, 2009), which in turn can be cultivated by having district leaders directly engaging in these methods as well (Cannata et al., 2017; Lockwood et al., 2017; Rigby et al., 2018; Roegman et al., 2015).

Approach 2: Designing Coherent Niches or Subsystems

A second approach to managing fragmentation involves the creation of niches (Cohen & Mehta, 2017) or subsystems that are both coherent and adaptable to teachers' local context. This approach is typically used among methods in the DBIR tradition (Frumin, 2019). For example, Anderson et al. (2018) described their aim as "creating 'tool kits' for a curricular activity system" that includes aligned teacher and students guides, professional development and assessments. This approach takes on a fairly narrow slice of the work of a school system such as a biology curriculum or earth science unit and then develops the kind of coherent and adaptable infrastructure that school systems typically lack around that "slice." Lesson study takes a similar approach, frequently coupling together the lesson study cycle with the kinds of conceptually rich curriculum materials that are present in Japan but lacking in the United States (Lewis & Perry, 2017).

To manage the political environment, such niches frequently have to engage in *buffering*—protecting their work from the demands of the larger systems—and *bridging*— finding ways to connect their work to the demands of the larger system. For example, when an RPP in Denver Public Schools began piloting a biology curriculum aligned to the Next Generation Science Standards, teachers initially received lower ratings on their formal evaluations due to evaluators not being familiar with the new standards. The RPP developed a new observation protocol but had to continuously engage in this kind of bridging and buffering in order to create coherence for teachers (Frumin, 2019; Honig & Hatch, 2004; Penuel, 2015).

Scholars have also stressed that these kinds of subsystems require a stable and supportive system environment—a precondition less likely to be available in low-performing districts (Debarger et al., 2013). Researchers in the design-based tradition emphasize the importance of engaging in CI to better negotiate these challenges (e.g., Anderson et al., 2018), but the methods and process for this kind of second-order CI are less fleshed out (for an exception, see Peurach et al., 2016).

Approach 3: Systematic Attention to the Environment

The third, and most comprehensive, approach is to work directly with actors in the larger education system. For example, in a NIC, network members are asked to map out the entire system contributing to the problem of practice and potential drivers of improvement. By bringing together a variety of critical stakeholders, NICs also aim to bridge communication and coordination problems that arise as a result of fragmentation. The NCSU model is similar in many ways to NICs, except that rather than mapping out the full system, they focus on identifying distinguishing practices from positive outlier schools and using those to inform the district-level and school-level plans (Cohen-Vogel et al., 2016). When there is buy-in across the system, there are clear advantages to this approach in terms of comprehensiveness and reducing some of the conflicting imperatives described above.

But this approach also comes with trade-offs. Given the tacit and relational dimensions of change, building a shared driver diagram or coordinated approach to improvement does not necessarily ensure that teachers and those actually implementing the reforms are fully on board with the change. Indeed, a persistent difficulty across NICs and NCSUs is for educators to connect their school-level improvement work with the broader aims of the network (Cannata et al; 2017; Martin & Gobstein, 2015; Tichnor-Wagner et al., 2017). Understanding that these maps will be used in politicized contexts with multiple, competing interest groups, we also wonder if they privilege what is legible, politically safe, and representative of dominant interests. For example, in our study of an early-literacy NIC, we found participants turned away from a focus on the impact of trauma on students' engagement with literacy toward data-driven guided reading groups. The latter approach enabled the NIC to focus on a well-bounded problem of practice that was well aligned to the political aims of the county department of education, but it also resulted in a lost opportunity to fully address literacy challenges stemming specifically from students' experience with trauma.

In sum, CI methods operate not in closed systems but instead in systems that must be responsive to a dynamic and complex ecosystem of policies, reforms, and intermediary organizations (Burch, 2007; Rowan, 2002). We worry that without explicitly attending to this environment, CI methods risk contributing to the very incoherence they are trying to ameliorate. This risk is particularly great as CI receives increased attention from funders and policymakers, which increases the temptation to use these methods in ritualized or ceremonial ways that may please external stakeholders while exacerbating demands on educators (Yurkofsky, 2017; Peurach et al., 2018). Avoiding this outcome will likely require more explicit attention to how CI methods operate given fragmentation. For example, we have wondered whether it is preferable to intentionally embed CI methods within district or state governance as a way of minimizing incoherence and multiple demands, or if that risks corruption of the CI process by politics and accountability (e.g., Datnow & Park, 2018).

IMPACT AMID COMPLEXITY: CHALLENGES AND PATHWAYS FORWARD

Challenges

CI methods face an immense challenge in their efforts to address educational problems that manifest the five forms of complexity—ambiguity, variability, interdependence, indiscussability, and political fragmentation—that we have laid out in this chapter. When looking across CI methods' theories of action, we identified four different visions for influencing the educational sector despite this complexity. As above, these different visions are implied rather than explicitly justified:

- One vision for large-scale impact involves embedding collaborative inquiry processes into the work of teaching and leadership. We see this approach in most localized CI methods. For example, Lewis et al. (2006) articulate how lesson study is *not* about developing increasingly refined interventions but rather about deepening educators' knowledge, commitment, and learning resources through ongoing communal inquiry.
- A second vision involves school systems drawing on improvement science to enhance reform efforts. This approach is best seen in NICs and the NCSU, and involves educators using PDSA cycles to modify new tools or initiatives so that they are better integrated into educators' work (Hannan et al., 2015), and

network leaders using these insights to improve the reform effort (Redding et al., 2018).

- A third vision involves using collaborative processes like codesign to develop interventions that are better tailored to the needs of teachers (Penuel et al., 2007). This approach involves designing interventions (and complementary systems of adult learning) that support educators in making productive adaptations (Scherrer et al., 2013). This allows for interventions to be scaled up while still being useful to teachers with varied needs and in diverse contexts.

- A fourth vision, which often runs alongside the others described, involves the spread of RPPs, such that practitioners have better access to research as they embark on improvements, and researchers can generate better theory through sustained and iterative collaboration.

These methods thus imply substantial changes in the roles of teachers, leaders, and researchers; the way districts organize for improvement; the process by which instructional materials are designed; and the relationship between school systems and universities. Even though most of these methods are still in their first or second decade, there is already some promising evidence that each of these approaches to large-scale impact could be successful. Evidence from a randomized control trial of lesson study across 39 educator teams suggests that collaborative inquiry processes can improve teaching and learning when coupled with instructional resources (Lewis & Perry, 2017). Yamada et al. (2018) used propensity score matching to demonstrate the positive impact of their NIC on improving completion rates of remedial math courses for more than 4,000 students across 10 community colleges. In addition, a number of interventions that have come out of DBIR (all of which are RPPs) have also led to improved teaching practice and student outcomes (Connor, et al., 2017; Debarger et al., 2017; Donovan & Snow, 2018; Wright & Gotwals, 2017).

Inattention to these five forms of complexity, however, may frustrate CI methods' efforts at larger scale impact. Efforts to scale up collaborative inquiry have faced challenges related to education's ambiguous causal relationships and flawed outcome measurements (Copland, 2003; Ingram et al., 2004), sensitive and value-laden topics of inquiry (Roegman et al., 2017), and conflicting external demands (Hubers et al., 2017). In practice, this can result in educators departing from CI's core principles, such as in making decisions via intuition over evidence, not assessing the effectiveness of chosen interventions, or acting and identifying solutions before understanding the problem (Allen & Calhoun, 1998; Copland, 2003; Detert et al., 2000; Hubers et al., 2017; Mintrop & Zumpe, 2019; Nelson, 2009). Efforts to use improvement science to support the scaling up of reforms have similarly been constrained in practice by political fragmentation (Hannan et al., 2015; Russell et al., 2019; Tichnor-Wagner et al., 2017). For example, Redding and Viano (2018), studying a networked partnership, found that in the hopes of garnering staff buy-in and addressing the prior histories of reform efforts, teacher leaders developed less disruptive changes that were also less likely to substantially improve teaching.

Efforts to collaboratively design more educator-centered interventions also struggled to confront these different sources of complexity. Anderson et al. (2018) offer one of the few accounts of an attempt to codesign tools that would scale up to the level of "thousands of classrooms" (p. 1028), finding that implementation varied across classrooms and that the prior classroom culture prevailed in determining whether tools were implemented as intended. In the Strategic Education Research Partnership with the Boston Public Schools, researchers found that only "internally coherent" schools could integrate their initially designed literacy tools. This led to a refocusing around the design of additional tools to measure and improve internal coherence (Donovan & Snow, 2018).

Pathways Forward

Across the different visions for scaling impact, CI methods often struggle to integrate into the complex systems they are seeking to transform. We see four necessary steps to take this field forward.

The first tasks researchers with clarifying and testing out the different mechanisms by which CI methods yield improvements in teaching and learning (Lochmiller & Lester, 2017). Underlying each CI method is an organizational theory of change (however implicit or incomplete) that is grounded in assumptions about how people learn, work together, and solve problems of varying complexity. Drawing on Weiss's (1995) work on theory-driven evaluation, we believe much can be learned by making these theories explicit and then evaluating them (e.g., Perry & Lewis, 2009), focusing not just on the overall effect of CI methods on student outcomes but also on the effects of certain components of a CI method's theory of action on more intermediate outcomes (e.g., related to internal coherence, professional community, or social network structure). Although there are not yet many areas of sustained and comparative investigation into the key mechanisms by which CI methods improve teaching and learning, we reviewed a number of stand-alone studies that serve as great starting points for such research. For example, in studying CI in a school district, Redding and Viano (2018) tested the theory that teacher ownership of a scale-up process improves implementation. Likewise, Hatch et al. (2016) draw on social network analysis to evaluate the mechanisms by which instructional rounds might support the development of a community of practice.

Second, we recommend investigating CI methods in terms of the combination of protocols and routines that make them up. This would involve fewer research questions about the impact of a given CI method, and more questions about which components of methods are most appropriate for a given context or problem. We believe more openness toward *cross-pollination* could be helpful. By cross-pollination, we mean thinking of CI methods as bundles of different routines, processes, and strategies, each with a particular purpose that could be appropriate depending on the context or problem. For example, PDSAs are a prominent protocol for iteration across CI methods, but educators have struggled to use PDSAs in certain contexts, particularly when problems are less well defined and data sources more problematic. We therefore would encourage exploring other methods of iteration that might be better tailored to more ambiguous educational contexts, such as the research lesson process of lesson study. A cross-pollination approach would also help to leverage the complementary strengths and weaknesses of different CI methods that we have identified in this chapter.

Cross-pollination might also allow for greater flexibility in the role of researchers and a questioning of RPPs as a defining feature of many CI methods. Although there are certainly contexts in which the prominent role of researchers seems essential (e.g., the codesigning of new curriculum and assessments), researcher involvement brings unique challenges (Coburn et al., 2013). Depending on the problem at hand, these challenges may outweigh the expertise researchers offer.

Clarifying the role researchers should play in CI methods across different contexts and over time relates to our third recommendation, which is to specify—even as tentative hypotheses—the underlying theory of action for how CI methods will yield impact in the long-term. Although many CI methods are funded through generous and short-term grants, we found little discussion of how improvement efforts might persist or expand when these additional funds run out.[3] Moreover, empirical research into CI methods tends to focus on whether and how these methods work under ideal conditions, rather than how they might scale into new contexts or with less funding. For example, while there is quasi-experimental evidence that the Carnegie Math Pathways—an intervention that includes courses, professional development, student support, and participation in an NIC—increased completion of developmental math requirements (Yamada et al., 2018), we now wonder how this intervention could be scaled up without losing integrity. How essential is it that the program continues to exist as part of a network, or to draw on improvement science? More broadly, while much research has documented the early stages of RPP work (Cobb et al., 2013; Debarger et al., 2017; Penuel et al., 2007; Wright & Gotwals, 2017), less is known about how well designers can foresee and design for the variable contexts in which educators may use these materials as it spreads out and/or scales up over time.

A final recommendation is for leaders in the CI tradition to recognize their dual roles as institutional entrepreneurs working to build a new field of research and improvement that runs counter to many of the structures, norms, and assumptions of the status quo (Peurach et al., 2018), and researchers engaging in rigorous work of advancing knowledge and improving outcomes within this new field. These two roles are essential, but they often push in competing directions. Our worry is that too much of a field-building orientation might divert attention from identifying and improving upon the limitations of these methods, which we believe is necessary for the long-term success of this movement (Peterson, 2016).

CONCLUSION

Continuous improvement, in all its guises, is becoming increasingly influential in education reform, including state and federal policy, district and school improvement plans, as well as in the language of many foundations and educational nonprofits. While the roots of it are old, and connect to industry and design as well as education, its logic has been newly embraced in recent years. But while in one sense what it offers is anodyne—who could be against "continuous improvement"?—our excavation suggests that its underlying ideas are actually quite radical in their intentions and aspirations. The purveyors of such movements are seeking to move away from top-down policy, to help teachers and school leaders embrace evidence and work more scientifically, to change the relationship between researchers and practitioners, and to surface and confront deep underlying issues of inequity. These more radical goals are at odds with many of the structural and cultural features of the American educational system, and thus despite the unexceptionable name, what we are really witnessing is a deeply countercultural movement that challenges, and seeks to transform, many aspects of this system.

We foresee two possible scenarios. The first is that the language of CI gets assimilated into existing ways of doing things. Districts adopt "continuous improvement" but do so within a paradigm of compliance and control, teachers adopt inquiry cycles but inquire in ways that are consistent with their pedagogical priors, and researchers and schools work together in ways that allow them to win grants and produce publications but do not lead to deep improvements in practice. This pattern of assimilation would be consistent with previous countercultural efforts at instructional reform (Cohen, 1990), and it is the most likely outcome. We fear that what would happen under this scenario is that data and inquiry cycles would become the myth and ceremony of the modern age, widely institutionalized but leading to little change either in practice or in the fundamental routines, structures, processes, and culture that govern the sector (Yurkofsky, 2017).

A second scenario is more hopeful. Under this view, CI processes recognize that what they are promoting is counter to dominant logics but gradually and practically create new ways of working that are consistent with the deeper aspirations of the movement. As people experience these new routines, identities, and roles, they experience greater success and efficacy than they did in the past, and, in so doing, their appetite for doing more work under this new paradigm increases. That creates the motivation for more work of this new type, and over time, the work deepens as people become more familiar with the new way of working and become increasingly knowledgeable and skilled.

For this second scenario to come to pass, this review suggests that movement proponents will need to become more forthright than they have been so far in taking on the challenges that the educational sector presents. In particular, they need to work actively to manage the political turbulence, incoherence, and conflicting demands that are so characteristic of the American education sector, and they will need to create humane CI processes that mix warm and cool approaches, and go "below the green line" to address many of the unseen, adaptive elements that are critical to deep and sustainable change. In so doing, they could help CI processes become the disruptive force that is inherent in their deepest aspirations, as opposed to becoming yet another reform that is swallowed by the forces it is seeking to transform.

ACKNOWLEDGMENTS

We would like to thank the reviewers and editors for their invaluable feedback throughout the revision process. The ideas in this chapter were originally presented at the 2019 Meeting of the American Educational Research Association, during which time we received helpful feedback from our discussant, Christopher Redding, as well as many others who attended. We are also grateful to David Sherer who provided feedback on an earlier draft of this chapter. Work on this chapter was supported by a research grant from the Spencer Foundation (No. 256554).

ORCID iD

Amelia Peterson   https://orcid.org/0000-0002-7225-9068

NOTES

[1]We limited our sample to published research, excluding conference papers. While conference papers can be useful at illustrating ideas that have not yet made it into published research, for this review we were interested in taking stock of the field and its evolution over time, and thus limited our scope to work that has been published.

[2]This map displays a subset of the CI methods in our sample in order to illustrate our argument. This map is not intended to be comprehensive.

[3]These observations were informed by a discussion at the 2019 American Educational Research Association session "Building Knowledge About Research-Practice Partnerships" where we presented an early draft of these arguments. Christopher Redding and Joshua Glazer, in particular, provided insight on this point.

REFERENCES

Akiba, M., & Wilkinson, B. (2016). Adopting an international innovation for teacher professional development: State and district approaches to lesson study in Florida. *Journal of Teacher Education, 67*(1), 74–93. https://doi.org/10.1177/0022487115593603
Allen, L., & Calhoun, E. F. (1998). Schoolwide action research: Findings from six years of study. *Phi Delta Kappan, 79*(9), 706–710. https://www.jstor.org/stable/20439316
Anderson, C. W., de los Santos, E. X., Bodbyl, S., Covitt, B. A., Edwards, K. D., Hancock, J. B., Lin, Q., Thomas, C. M., Penual, W. R., & Welch, M. M. (2018). Designing educational systems to support enactment of the Next Generation Science Standards. *Journal of Research in Science Teaching, 55*(7), 1026–1052. https://doi.org/10.1002/tea.21484
Argyris, C., Putnam, R., & Smith, D. M. (1985). *Action science* (Vol. 13). Jossey-Bass.

Argyris, C., & Schön, D. A. (1997). Organizational learning: A theory of action perspective. *Rei: Revista Española de Investigaciones Sociológicas,* (77/78), 345-348. https://doi .org/10.2307/40183951

Artiles, J. A. (2015). *The Education DesignShop: Broadening non-designers' solutions for big issues* [Master's thesis, Massachusetts Institute of Technology]. http://dspace.mit.edu/ handle/1721.1/103568

Bocala, C. (2015). From experience to expertise: The development of teachers' learning in lesson study. *Journal of Teacher Education, 66*(4), 349–362. https://doi .org/10.1177/0022487115592032

Bonilla-Silva, E. (2017). What we were, what we are, and what we should be: The racial problem of American sociology. *Social Problems, 64*(2), 179–187. https://doi.org/10.1093/ socpro/spx006

Borgatti, S. P., Everett, M. G., & Freeman, L. C. (2002). *UCINET for Windows: Software for social network analysis* [Computer software]. Analytic Technologies.

Boudett, K. P., City, E. A., & Murnane, R. J. (2013). *Data wise: A step-by-step guide to using assessment results to improve teaching and learning.* Harvard Education Press.

Bryk, A. S., Gomez, L. M., & Grunow, A. (2011). Getting ideas into action: Building networked improvement communities in education. In M. T. Hallinan (Ed.), *Frontiers in sociology of education* (pp. 127–162). Springer. https://doi.org/10.1007/978-94-007-1576-9_7

Bryk, A. S., Gomez, L. M., Grunow, A., & LeMahieu, P. G. (2015). *Learning to improve: How America's schools can get better at getting better.* Harvard Education Press.

Bryk, A. S., & Schneider, B. (2002). *Trust in schools: A core resource for improvement.* Russell Sage Foundation.

Buchanan, R. (1992). Wicked problems in design thinking. *Design Issues, 8*(2), 5–21. https:// doi.org/10.2307/1511637

Burch, P. (2007). Educational policy and practice from the perspective of institutional theory: Crafting a wider lens. *Educational Researcher, 36*(2), 84–95. https://doi .org/10.3102/0013189X07299792

Cannata, M., Cohen-Vogel, L., & Sorum, M. (2017). Partnering for improvement: Improvement communities and their role in scale up. *Peabody Journal of Education, 92*(5), 569–588. https://doi.org/10.1080/0161956X.2017.1368633

Chubb, J. E., & Moe, T. M. (1990). *Politics, markets, and America's schools.* Brookings Institution Press.

Churchman, C. (1967). Wicked problems [Guest editorial]. *Management Science, 14*(4), 141–146. https://doi.org/10.1287/mnsc.14.4.B141

City, E. A., Elmore, R. F., Fiarman, S. E., & Teitel, L. (2009). *Instructional rounds in education.* Harvard Education Press.

Cobb, P., Jackson, K., Smith, T., Sorum, M., & Henrick, E. (2013). Design research with educational systems: Investigating and supporting improvements in the quality of mathematics teaching and learning at scale. *National Society for the Study of Education Yearbook, 112*(2), 320–349.

Coburn, C. E., & Penuel, W. R. (2016). Research–practice partnerships in education: Outcomes, dynamics, and open questions. *Educational Researcher, 45*(1), 48–54. https:// doi.org/10.3102/0013189X16631750

Coburn, C. E., Penuel, W. R., & Geil, K. E. (2013). *Practice partnerships: A strategy for leveraging research for education.* W. T. Grant Foundation.

Cochran-Smith, M., & Lytle, S. L. (1999). Chapter 8: Relationships of knowledge and practice: Teacher learning in communities. *Review of Research in Education, 24*(1), 249–305. https://doi.org/10.3102/0091732X024001249

Cohen, D. K. (1988). Teaching practice: Plus ça change. In P. W. Jackson (Ed.), *Contributing to educational change: Perspectives on research and practice* (pp. 27–84). McCutchan.

Cohen, D. (1990). A revolution in one classroom: The case of Mrs Oublier. *Education Evaluation and Policy Analysis, 12*(3), 311–329.

Cohen, D. K. (2011). *Teaching and its predicaments.* Harvard University Press. https://doi.org/10.4159/harvard.9780674062788

Cohen, D. K., & Mehta, J. D. (2017). Why reform sometimes succeeds: Understanding the conditions that produce reforms that last. *American Educational Research Journal, 54*(4), 644–690. https://doi.org/10.3102/0002831217700078

Cohen, D. K., & Spillane, J. P. (1992). Policy and practice: The relations between governance and instruction. *Review of Research in Education, 18*, 3–50. https://doi.org/10.2307/1167296

Cohen-Vogel, L., Cannata, M., Rutledge, S. A., & Socol, A. R. (2016). A model of continuous improvement in high schools: A process for research, innovation design, implementation, and scale. *Teachers College Record, 118*(13).

Cohen-Vogel, L., Tichnor-Wagner, A., Allen, D., Harrison, C., Kainz, K., Socol, A. R., & Wang, Q. (2015). Implementing educational innovations at scale: Transforming researchers into continuous improvement scientists. *Educational Policy, 29*(1), 257–277. https://doi.org/10.1177/0895904814560886

Connor, C. M., Dombek, J., Crowe, E. C., Spencer, M., Tighe, E. L., Coffinger, S., Zargar, E., Wood, T., & Petscher, Y. (2017). Acquiring science and social studies knowledge in kindergarten through fourth grade: Conceptualization, design, implementation, and efficacy testing of content-area literacy instruction (CALI). *Journal of educational psychology, 109*(3), 301–320. https://doi.org/10.1037/edu0000128

Copland, M. A. (2003). Leadership of inquiry: Building and sustaining capacity for school improvement. *Educational Evaluation and Policy Analysis, 25*(4), 375–395. https://doi.org/10.3102/01623737025004375

Datnow, A., & Park, V. (2018). Opening or closing doors for students? Equity and data use in schools. *Journal of Educational Change, 19*(2), 131–152. https://doi.org/10.1007/s10833-018-9323-6

Debarger, A. H., Choppin, J., Beauvineau, Y., & Moorthy, S. (2013). Designing for productive adaptations of curriculum interventions. *National Society for the Study of Education Yearbook, 112*(2), 298–319.

Debarger, A. H., Penuel, W. R., Moorthy, S., Beauvineau, Y., Kennedy, C. A., & Boscardin, C. K. (2017). Investigating purposeful science curriculum adaptation as a strategy to improve teaching and learning. *Science Education, 101*(1), 66–98. https://doi.org/10.1002/sce.21249

Deming, W. E. (1982). *Out of the crisis.* MIT press.

Deming, W. E. (1994). *The new economics for industry, government, education.* MIT press.

Detert, J. R., Kopel, M. B., Mauriel, J., & Jenni, R. (2000). Quality management in U.S. high schools: Evidence from the field. *Journal of School Leadership, 10*(2), 158–87. https://doi.org/10.1177/105268460001000203

Dewey, J. (2011). *The sources of a science of education.* Martino Fine Books. (Original work published 1929)

Dolle, J. R., Gomez, L. M., Russell, J. L., & Bryk, A. S. (2013). More than a network: Building professional communities for educational improvement. *National Society for the Study of Education Yearbook, 112*(2), 443–463.

Donovan, M. S., & Snow, C. (2018). Sustaining research–practice partnerships: Benefits and challenges of a long-term research and development agenda. In B. Bevan & W. R. Penuel (Eds.), *Connecting research and practice for educational improvement* (pp. 33–50). Routledge. https://doi.org/10.4324/9781315268309-3

Donovan, M. S., Snow, C., & Daro, P. (2013). The SERP approach to problem-solving research, development, and implementation. *National Society for the Study of Education Yearbook, 112*(2), 400–425.

Duncan-Andrade, J. M. R., & Morrell, E. (2008). *The art of critical pedagogy: Possibilities for moving from theory to practice in urban schools* (Vol. 285). Peter Lang. https://doi .org/10.3726/b12771

Edmondson, A. C. (2002). The local and variegated nature of learning in organizations: A group-level perspective. *Organization Science, 13*(2), 128–146. https://doi.org/10.1287/ orsc.13.2.128.530

Edmondson, A. C., & Lei, Z. (2014). Psychological safety: The history, renaissance, and future of an interpersonal construct. *Annual Review of Organizational Psychology and Organizational Behavior, 1*(1), 23–43. https://doi.org/10.1146/annurev-org-psych-031413-091305

Englert, R. M., Kean, M. H., & Scribner, J. D. (1977). Politics of program evaluation in large city school districts. *Education and Urban Society, 9*(4), 429–450. https://doi .org/10.1177/001312457700900403

Fishman, B. J., Penuel, W. R., Allen, A.-R., Cheng, B. H., & Sabelli, N. (2013). Design-based implementation research: An emerging model for transforming the relationship of research and practice. *National Society for the Study of Education, 112*(2), 136–156.

Frumin, K. (2019). Researchers and practitioners in partnership: Co-design of a high school biology curriculum [Unpublished doctoral dissertation]. Harvard Graduate School of Education.

Gallimore, R., Ermeling, B. A., Saunders, W. M., & Goldenberg, C. (2009). Moving the learning of teaching closer to practice: Teacher education implications of school-based inquiry teams. *The Elementary School Journal, 109*(5), 537–553. https://doi.org/10.1086/597001

Glazer, J. L., & Peurach, D. J. (2013). School improvement networks as a strategy for large-scale education reform: The role of educational environments. *Educational Policy, 27*(4), 676–710. https://doi.org/10.1177/0895904811429283

Goodnough, K. (2010). Teacher learning and collaborative action research: Generating a "knowledge-of-practice" in the context of science education. *Journal of Science Teacher Education, 21*(8), 917–935. https://doi.org/10.1007/s10972-010-9215-y

Hannan, M., Russell, J. L., Takahashi, S., & Park, S. (2015). Using improvement science to better support beginning teachers: The case of the building a teaching effectiveness network. *Journal of Teacher Education, 66*(5), 494–508. https://doi .org/10.1177/0022487115602126

Hatch, T., Hill, K., & Roegman, R. (2016). Investigating the role of instructional rounds in the development of social networks and district-wide improvement. *American Educational Research Journal, 53*(4), 1022–1053. https://doi.org/10.3102/0002831216653205

Heifetz, R. A., Grashow, A., & Linsky, M. (2009). *The practice of adaptive leadership: Tools and tactics for changing your organization and the world.* Brighton, MA: Harvard Business Press.

Hess, F. M. (2011). *Spinning wheels: The politics of urban school reform.* Washington, DC: Brookings Institution Press.

Honig, M. I., & Hatch, T. C. (2004). Crafting coherence: How schools strategically manage multiple, external demands. *Educational Researcher, 33*(8), 16–30. https://doi.org/10.31 02/0013189X033008016

Horn, I. S., & Little, J. W. (2010). Attending to problems of practice: Routines and resources for professional learning in teachers' workplace interactions. *American Educational Research Journal, 47*(1), 181–217. https://doi.org/10.3102/0002831209345158

Hubers, M. D., Schildkamp, K., Poortman, C. L., & Pieters, J. M. (2017). The quest for sustained data use: Developing organizational routines. *Teaching and Teacher Education, 67*, 509–521. https://doi.org/10.1016/j.tate.2017.07.007

Ingram, D., Louis, K. S., & Schroeder, R. G. (2004). Accountability policies and teacher decision making: Barriers to the use of data to improve practice. *Teachers College Record, 106*(6), 1258–1287. https://doi.org/10.1111/j.1467-9620.2004.00379.x

Johnson, C. C. (2013). Educational turbulence: The influence of macro and micro-policy on science education reform. *Journal of Science Teacher Education, 24*(4), 693–715. https://doi.org/10.1007/s10972-012-9333-9

Kelley, T. (2002). *The art of innovation: Lessons in creativity from IDEO, America's leading design firm: Success through innovation the IDEO way* (Main ed.). Profile Books.

Kraft, M. A., Papay, J. P., Johnson, S. M., Charner-Laird, M., Ng, M., & Reinhorn, S. (2015). Educating amid uncertainty: The organizational supports teachers need to serve students in high-poverty, urban schools. *Educational Administration Quarterly, 51*(5), 753–790. https://doi.org/10.1177/0013161X15607617

Kwon, S. M., Wardrip, P. S., & Gomez, L. M. (2014). Co-design of interdisciplinary projects as a mechanism for school capacity growth. *Improving Schools, 17*(1), 54–71. https://doi.org/10.1177/1365480213519517

Lampert, M. (1985). How do teachers manage to teach? Perspectives on problems in practice. *Harvard Educational Review, 55*(2), 178–195. https://doi.org/10.17763/haer.55.2.56142234616x4352

Lave, J., & Wenger, E. (1991). *Situated learning: Legitimate peripheral participation.* Cambridge University Press. https://doi.org/10.1017/CBO9780511815355

Leary, H., Severance, S., Penuel, W. R., Quigley, D., Sumner, T., & Devaul, H. (2016). Designing a deeply digital science curriculum: Supporting teacher learning and implementation with organizing technologies. *Journal of Science Teacher Education, 27*(1), 61–77. https://doi.org/10.1007/s10972-016-9452-9

Lewis, C., & Perry, R. (2017). Lesson study to scale up research-based knowledge: A randomized, controlled trial of fractions learning. *Journal for Research in Mathematics Education, 48*(3), 261–299. https://doi.org/10.5951/jresematheduc.48.3.0261

Lewis, C., Perry, R., & Murata, A. (2006). How should research contribute to instructional improvement? The case of lesson study. *Educational Researcher, 35*(3), 3–14. https://doi.org/10.3102/0013189X035003003

Lochmiller, C. R., & Lester, J. N. (2017). Conceptualizing practitioner-scholarship for educational leadership research and practice. *Journal of Research on Leadership Education, 12*(1), 3–25. https://doi.org/10.1177/1942775116668525

Lockwood, M., Dillman, M., & Boudett, K. P. (2017). Using data wisely at the system level. *Phi Delta Kappan, 99*(1), 25–30. https://doi.org/10.1177/0031721717728275

Lockwood, M. G. (2017). *Refining the art of coaching: Organizational learning on a district data inquiry team* [Unpublished doctoral dissertation]. Harvard Graduate School of Education.

Lortie, D. C. (1975). *Schoolteacher: A sociological study* (Vol. 21). University of Chicago Press.

Martin, W. G., & Gobstein, H. (2015). Generating a networked improvement community to improve secondary mathematics teacher preparation: Network leadership, organization, and operation. *Journal of Teacher Education, 66*(5), 482–493. https://doi.org/10.1177/0022487115602312

Mehta, J. (2013). *The allure of order: High hopes, dashed expectations, and the troubled quest to remake American schooling.* Oxford University Press.

Mezirow, J. (1991). *Transformative dimensions of adult learning.* Jossey Bass.

Mintrop, R., & Zumpe, E. (2019). Solving real-life problems of practice and education leaders' school improvement mind-set. *American Journal of Education, 125*(3), 295–344. https://doi.org/10.1086/702733

National Research Council. (2001). *Knowing what students know: The science and design of educational assessment.* National Academies Press.

Nelson, T. H. (2009). Teachers' collaborative inquiry and professional growth: Should we be optimistic? *Science Education, 93*(3), 548–580. https://doi.org/10.1002/sce.20302

Payne, C. M. (2008). *So much reform, so little change: The persistence of failure in urban schools.* Cambridge, MA: Harvard Education Press.

Payne, C. M. (2007). *I've got the light of freedom: The organizing tradition and the Mississippi freedom struggle.* University of California Press.

Penuel, W. R. (2015, September 22–25). *Infrastructuring as a practice for promoting transformation and equity in design-based implementation research* [Keynote presentation]. International Society for Design and Development in Education Conference, Boulder, CO, United States.

Penuel, W. R., Fishman, B. J., Haugan Cheng, B., & Sabelli, N. (2011). Organizing research and development at the intersection of learning, implementation, and design. *Educational Researcher, 40*(7), 331–337. https://doi.org/10.3102/0013189X11421826

Penuel, W. R., Peurach, D. J., LeBoeuf, W. A., Riedy, R., Barber, M., Clark, T., & Gabriele, K. (2018). *Defining collaborative problem solving research: Common values and distinctive approaches.* LearnDBIR.

Penuel, W. R., Roschelle, J., & Shechtman, N. (2007). Designing formative assessment software with teachers: An analysis of the co-design process. *Research and Practice in Technology Enhanced Learning, 2*(1), 51–74. https://doi.org/10.1142/S1793206807000300

Perry, R. R., & Lewis, C. C. (2009). What is successful adaptation of lesson study in the US? *Journal of Educational Change, 10*(4), 365–391. https://doi.org/10.1007/s10833-008-9069-7

Peterson, A. (2016). Getting 'What Works' working: Building blocks for the integration of experimental and improvement science. *International Journal of Research & Method in Education, 39*(3), 299–313. https://doi.org/10.1080/1743727X.2016.1170114

Peurach, D. J., Lenhoff, S. W., & Glazer, J. L. (2016). Large-scale high school reform through school improvement networks: Exploring possibilities for "developmental evaluation." *Teachers College Record, 118*(13).

Peurach, D. J., Penuel, W. R., & Russell, J. L. (2018). Beyond ritualized rationality: Organizational dynamics of instructionally-focused continuous improvement. In M. Connolly, D. H. Eddy-Spicer, C. James, & S. D. Hruse (Eds.), *The Sage handbook of school organization* (pp. 465–488). Sage. https://doi.org/10.4135/9781526465542.n28

Pollock, M. (2009). *Colormute: Race talk dilemmas in an American school.* Princeton University Press. https://doi.org/10.1515/9781400826124

Rait, E. (1995). Against the current: Organizational learning in schools. In S. B. Bacharach & B. Mundell (Eds.), *Images of schools: Structures and roles in organizational behavior* (pp. 71–107). Corwin.

Redding, C., & Viano, S. L. (2018). Co-creating school innovations: Should self-determination be a component of school improvement? *Teachers College Record, 120*(11).

Redding, C., Cannata, M., & Miller, J. (2018). System learning in an urban school district: A case study of intra-district learning. *Journal of Educational Change, 19*(1), 77–101. https://doi.org/10.1007/s10833-017-9310-3

Retna, K. S. (2016). Thinking about "design thinking": A study of teacher experiences. *Asia Pacific Journal of Education, 36*(Suppl. 1), 5–19. https://doi.org/10.1080/02188791.2015.1005049

Rigby, J. G., Forman, S., Fox, A., & Kazemi, E. (2018). Leadership development through design and experimentation: Learning in a research–practice partnership. *Journal of Research on Leadership Education, 13*(3), 316–339. https://doi.org/10.1177/1942775118776009

Roegman, R., Hatch, T., Hill, K., & Kniewel, V. S. (2015). Relationships, instruction, understandings: One district's implementation of rounds. *Journal of Educational Administration, 53*(5), 625–641. https://doi.org/10.1108/JEA-07-2014-0078

Roegman, R., Allen, D., & Hatch, T. (2017). The elusiveness of equity: Evolution of instructional rounds in a superintendents network. *American Journal of Education, 124*(1), 127–159. https://doi.org/10.1086/693957

Rosenquist, B. A., Henrick, E. C., & Smith, T. M. (2015). Research–practice partnerships to support the development of high quality mathematics instruction for all students. *Journal of Education for Students Placed at Risk, 20*(1–2), 42–57. https://doi.org/10.1080/10824669.2014.988335

Rowan, B. (2002). The ecology of school improvement: Notes on the school improvement industry in the United States. *Journal of Educational Change, 3*(3–4), 283–314. https://doi.org/10.1023/A:1021277712833

Russell, J. L., Bryk, A. S., Dolle, J. R., Gomez, L. M., Lemahieu, P. G., & Grunow, A. (2017). A framework for the initiation of networked improvement communities. *Teachers College Record, 119*(5).

Russell, J. L., Correnti, R., Stein, M. K., Bill, V., Hannan, M., Schwartz, N., Booker, L. N., Pratt, N. R., & Matthis, C. (2019). Learning from adaptation to support instructional improvement at scale: Understanding coach adaptation in the TN Mathematics Coaching Project. *American Educational Research Journal.* https://doi.org/10.3102/0002831219854050

Safir, S. (2017). *The listening leader: Creating the conditions for equitable school transformation.* John Wiley.

Scherrer, J., Israel, N., & Resnick, L. B. (2013). Beyond classrooms: Scaling and sustaining instructional innovations. *Yearbook of the National Society for the Study of Education, 112*(2), 426–442.

Schildkamp, K., Poortman, C. L., & Handelzalts, A. (2016). Data teams for school improvement. *School Effectiveness and School Improvement, 27*(2), 228–254. https://doi.org/10.1080/09243453.2015.1056192

Schön, D. A. (2017). *The reflective practitioner: How professionals think in action.* Routledge. https://doi.org/10.4324/9781315237473

Scribner, J. P., Cockrell, K. S., Cockrell, D. H., & Valentine, J. W. (1999). Creating professional communities in schools through organizational learning: An evaluation of a school improvement process. *Educational Administration Quarterly, 35*(1), 130–160. https://doi.org/10.1177/0013161X99351007

Severance, S., Penuel, W. R., Sumner, T., & Leary, H. (2016). Organizing for teacher agency in curricular co-design. *Journal of the Learning Sciences, 25*(4), 531–564. https://doi.org/10.1080/10508406.2016.1207541

Smets, M., & Jarzabkowski, P. (2013). Reconstructing institutional complexity in practice: A relational model of institutional work and complexity. *Human Relations, 66*(10), 1279–1309. https://doi.org/10.1177/0018726712471407

Spillane, J. P., & Jennings, N. E. (1997). Aligned instructional policy and ambitious pedagogy: Exploring instructional reform from the classroom perspective. *Teachers College Record, 98*(3), 449–81.

Tichnor-Wagner, A., Wachen, J., Cannata, M., & Cohen-Vogel, L. (2017). Continuous improvement in the public school context: Understanding how educators respond to plan–do–study–act cycles. *Journal of Educational Change, 18*(4), 465–494. https://doi.org/10.1007/s10833-017-9301-4

Timperley, H. S., & Robinson, V. M. (2001). Achieving school improvement through challenging and changing teachers' schema. *Journal of Educational Change, 2*(4), 281–300. https://doi.org/10.1023/A:1014646624263

Warikoo, N., Sinclair, S., Fei, J., & Jacoby-Senghor, D. (2016). Examining racial bias in education: A new approach. *Educational Researcher, 45*(9), 508–514. https://doi.org/10.3102/0013189X16683408

Weatherly, R., & Lipsky, M. (1977). Street-level bureaucrats and institutional innovation: Implementing special-education reform. *Harvard Educational Review, 47*(2), 171–197. https://doi.org/10.17763/haer.47.2.v870r1v16786270x

Weiss, C. H. (1995). Nothing as practical as good theory: Exploring theory-based evaluation for comprehensive community initiatives for children and families. In J. P. Connell, A. C. Kubisch, L. B. Schorr, & C. H. Weiss (Eds.), *New approaches to evaluating community initiatives: Concepts, methods, and contexts* (1st ed., pp. 65–92). Aspen Institute.

Wenger, E. (1998). Communities of practice: Learning as a social system. *Systems Thinker, 9*(5), 2–3.

Wheatley, M. J. (2006). *Leadership and the new science: Discovering order in a chaotic world* (3rd ed.). Berrett-Koehler.

Wheatley, M. J., & Dalmau, T. (1983). *Below the green line or the 6 circle model* [Unpublished manuscript].

Wright, T. S., & Gotwals, A. W. (2017). Supporting kindergartners' science talk in the context of an integrated science and disciplinary literacy curriculum. *The Elementary School Journal, 117*(3), 513–537. https://doi.org/10.1086/690273

Yamada, H., Bohannon, A. X., Grunow, A., & Thorn, C. A. (2018). Assessing the effectiveness of Quantway®: A multilevel model with propensity score matching. *Community College Review, 46*(3), 257–287. https://doi.org/10.1177/0091552118771754

Yurkofsky, M. M. (2017). *The restructuring of educational organizations: From ceremonial rules to technical ceremonies* [Unpublished doctoral dissertation]. Harvard Graduate School of Education.

Zeichner, K. M. (2003). Teacher research as professional development for P–12 educators in the USA [1]. *Educational Action Research, 11*(2), 301–326. https://doi.org/10.1080/09650790300200211

About the Editors

Jeanne M. Powers, PhD, is an associate professor in the Mary Lou Fulton Teachers College at Arizona State University. Her research focuses on school segregation, school choice, teacher retention, the educational experiences of immigrant students, and the factors that shape the implementation of complex educational reforms.

Gustavo E. Fischman, PhD, is a professor of educational policy and comparative education in the Mary Lou Fulton Teachers College at Arizona State University. His research focuses on understanding and improving the processes of scholarly production and knowledge mobilization. His research interests also include sustainability and education and the uses (and misuses) of global learning metrics and international large-scale assessments in educational reform projects.

Margarita Pivovarova, PhD, is an assistant professor in the Mary Lou Fulton Teachers College at Arizona State University. Her research focuses on the relationship between student achievement, teacher quality, and school contextual factors. Her research interests also include teacher labor markets and factors that influence teachers' decision to enter, stay in, or leave the profession.

Review of Research in Education
March 2020, Vol. 44, p. 434
DOI: 10.3102/0091732X20909343
© 2020 AERA. http://rre.aera.net

About the Contributors

Jee Bin Ahn is a PhD candidate in the Department of Education Policy Studies at the Pennsylvania State University. Her research examines socioeconomic disparities in various student outcomes using comparative and international perspectives.

Dominique J. Baker is an assistant professor of education policy in the Annette Caldwell Simmons School of Education and Human Development, Southern Methodist University. Her research focuses on the way education policy affects and shapes the access and success of underrepresented students in higher education.

Rachel Baker is an assistant professor of education at the School of Education at the University of California, Irvine. She studies how institutional and state policies affect student behavior and decision making in higher education. Her work focuses on how to support student success, particularly for underrepresented groups, through policy and instruction.

Ryan Shaun Baker is an associate professor at the University of Pennsylvania and the director of the Penn Center for Learning Analytics. His lab conducts research on engagement and robust learning within online and blended learning, seeking to find actionable indicators that can be used today but predict future student outcomes. He was the founding president of the International Educational Data Mining Society, is currently serving as editor of the journal *Computer-Based Learning in Context*, is the associate editor of two journals, was the first technical director of the Pittsburgh Science of Learning Center DataShop, and currently serves as codirector of the MOOC Replication Framework.

W. Douglas Baker is a professor of English education in the Department of English Language and Literature and the associate dean of the College of Arts & Sciences at Eastern Michigan University. His research investigates classroom discourse as epistemology for learning disciplinary knowledge. His recent work explores interdisciplinary differences as resources for learning.

Review of Research in Education
March 2020, Vol. 44, pp. 435–441
DOI: 10.3102/0091732X20909399
© 2020 AERA. http://rre.aera.net

Arnetha F. Ball, PhD, is the Charles E. Ducommun Professor (Emerita) in the Graduate School of Education at Stanford University. Her research advances socio-cultural theories through studies that integrate sociolinguistic and ethnographic approaches to investigate ways in which semiotic systems serve as a means for mediating teaching and learning in linguistically complex settings and the processes of teacher change and development.

Efrat Blumenfeld-Lieberthal is the head of the David Azrieli School of Architecture at the Tel Aviv University. She received her BArch, MA, and PhD from the Technion–Israel Institute of Technology. Her research interests include applying theories of complexity to urban environments, and complex networks and smart cities and the way they influence urban development.

Alisha Butler, MA, is a doctoral candidate studying education policy at the University of Maryland, College Park College of Education. Her research examines how gentrification influences parents' school selection processes and the politics of parent engagement in urban public schools.

Monaliza Maximo Chian is a postdoctoral fellow in the Faculty of Education at the University of Hong Kong. Her PhD in education at the University of California, Santa Barbara, focused on teaching-learning relationships and qualitative-interpretive research. Her current research focuses on interdisciplinary collaborations and innovative curriculum design in higher education.

Sebnem Cilesiz, PhD, is the Patrick Rutherford/BORSF Associate Professor at the University of Louisiana at Lafayette. Her research focuses on qualitative research methodology, critical perspectives on educational policy and leadership, and social and cultural contexts of educational technology.

Casey D. Cobb, PhD, is the Raymond Neag Professor of Educational Policy at the Neag School of Education at the University of Connecticut. He is a National Education Policy Center Fellow and a member of the Research Advisory Panel for the National Coalition on School Diversity. His current research interests include policies on school choice, accountability, and school reform, where he examines the implications for equity and educational opportunity. He is former editor of *Educational Administration Quarterly* and serves on the editorial boards for *Education Policy Analysis Archives* and *Education Research International*, among others. He is coauthor of *Fundamentals of Statistical Reasoning in Education* (Wiley/Jossey Bass, 4th ed.) and *Leading Dynamic Schools* (Corwin Press). He is a former member of Connecticut's Region 19 School Board. He holds an AB from Harvard University, an MS from the University of Maine, and a PhD from Arizona State University.

Christian Fischer is an assistant professor of educational effectiveness at the Hector Research Institute of Education Sciences and Psychology at the Eberhard Karls University of Tübingen, Germany. His research examines approaches to improve

STEM teaching and learning. In particular, he is interested in how digital technologies may help increase educational effectiveness for all learners.

Donald Freeman is a professor of education at the School of Education, University of Michigan. His work focuses on understanding and supporting language teacher learning at scale. He directs the Learning4Teaching Project, a group of transnational research studies of public sector teachers' experiences in professional development. He is author, most recently, of *Educating Second Language Teachers* (Oxford University Press, 2016).

Dominik E. Froehlich, PhD, is a postdoctoral researcher and senior lecturer at the University of Vienna. His research focuses on mixed-methods social network analysis and informal learning.

Kim M. Frumin, EdD, is a postdoctoral fellow at the Harvard Graduate School of Education. Her research explores research-practice partnerships and online teacher professional learning.

Maithreyi Gopalan, PhD, is an assistant professor of education at the Pennsylvania State University. Her research examines the causes and consequences of racial and socioeconomic disparities in student outcomes using interdisciplinary perspectives.

Heela Goren is a PhD candidate at University College London Institute of Education. Her research interests include global citizenship education, social justice, internationalization, and comparative education. Her work is currently focused on local and national interpretations and adaptations of concepts promoted by global and international organizations.

Thomas Greckhamer, PhD, is the Catherine Rucks Professor of Management at Louisiana State University. His research focuses on configurational and discourse-oriented approaches to strategic management, qualitative research methodology, and qualitative comparative analysis.

Judith L. Green is a distinguished professor emerita in the Gevirtz Graduate School of Education at the University of California, Santa Barbara. Her research investigates ways of studying the social and discursive knowledge in classrooms. Her recent work explores overtime construction of processes and practices afforded students in preK–20 education.

Ayush Gupta is an associate research professor in physics and keystone instructor in engineering at the University of Maryland, College Park. His research aims to model the dynamics of learners' cognition and the role of emotions and ideologies in learning, especially in how engineering students think about technology and society.

J. W. Hammond is a postdoctoral research fellow at the University of Michigan, where he studies assessment history and technology, as well as the ethics, politics, and rhetorics of research synthesis. This work reexamines the past for insights regarding how to promote a more socially responsible and responsive future for education.

LeeAnna Hooper is an elementary school teacher and elementary science educator. Her research and practice explore classroom discourse and elementary science learning communities. Her primary research interest centers on the integration of discipline-specific literacy practices as a means to shape epistemic practices and support student sensemaking in elementary science.

Rebecca Horwitz-Willis, JD, is a PhD candidate in culture, institutions, and society at Harvard University. Her research focuses on cultural, institutional, and legal factors that impact racial justice in schools.

Minh Q. Huynh is a PhD candidate in Educational Foundations and Policy at the University of Michigan. He studies international organizations and global education policy.

Melinda Z. Kalainoff, PhD, Colonel (Retd.), served as an assistant professor and deputy department head in the Department of Chemistry and Life Science at the United States Military Academy at West Point. Her research focuses on studies of how disciplinary content knowledge is socially constructed through discourse in science and engineering learning environments.

Gregory J. Kelly is senior associate dean and distinguished professor at the College of Education at Pennsylvania State University. His research investigates classroom discourse, epistemology, and science learning. His recent work examines epistemic practices in science and engineering education.

Carl Lagoze is an associate professor at the University of Michigan School of Information. His research focuses on knowledge infrastructures, especially in the context of scholarly communication and the transformation of traditional institutions in the networked digital era.

Katrina Liu, PhD, is an assistant professor of Teaching and Learning at the University of Nevada, Las Vegas. Focusing on theory, practice, and innovation in preparing quality teachers for diverse contexts, her current research includes critical reflection for transformative learning in teacher education and preparing and supporting teachers and teacher educators of color. Her interdisciplinary work appears in journals such as *Review of Research in Education, Educational Review*, and *Reflective Practice*.

Claire Maxwell is a professor of sociology at University of Copenhagen. Her research expertise lies in the field of internationalization of education and how this is reshaping tracks through education systems, aspirations for higher education, and employment. Her work has recently focused specifically on the practices of globally mobile professional families in relation to schooling and notions of belonging.

Jal D. Mehta is a professor of education at the Harvard Graduate School of Education. He is the author, most recently, of *In Search of Deeper Learning: The Quest to Remake the American High School* (Harvard University Press, 2019), with Sarah Fine.

Richard Miller, PhD, is an assistant professor of Ethnomusicology at the University of Nevada, Las Vegas. In addition to historical work on music and music education in East and Southeast Asia, his research focuses on technology, race, ethnicity, and language issues in teaching and teacher education.

Pamela A. Moss is the John Dewey Collegiate Professor of Education at the University of Michigan. Her scholarship engages the critical potential of methodological pluralism in education research: how it is and might be theorized, practiced, taught, supported by organizational and governmental policies, and embedded in the evolving infrastructures through which knowledge is produced and used to orient action.

Naivedya Parakkal is a doctoral student at the University of Michigan. Her research focuses on understanding how legacies of imperialism shape the identities, subjectivities, and educational experiences of youth in the global South, and how they are (un)learning, resisting, and transforming dominant practices and discourses around globalization, development, and modernity.

Zachary A. Pardos is an assistant professor in the Graduate School of Education and School of Information at the University of California, Berkeley. He directs the Computational Approaches to Human Learning research lab and teaches courses on data mining, digital learning environments, and machine learning in education. His focal areas of study are knowledge representation and recommender systems in education.

Amelia J. Peterson is a PhD candidate in education policy and program evaluation at Harvard University and a fellow in social policy at the London School of Economics. Her research examines from a comparative perspective how education systems change, with a particular focus on upper secondary schooling.

Thomas M. Philip is an associate professor and the director of teacher education in the Graduate School of Education at University of California, Berkeley. His research is focused on teacher learning, teacher ideology, the political and ethical dimensions of learning, and the coconstruction of power in learning environments through digital technologies.

Kelly Rosinger, PhD, is an assistant professor in the Department of Education Policy Studies and a research associate in the Center for the Study of Higher Education at the Pennsylvania State University. Her research examines the barriers students face going to and through college and how postsecondary policies, practices, and interventions shape educational outcomes.

Rachel E. Schachter, PhD, is an assistant professor in the Child, Youth and Family Studies Department, College of Education and Human Development, at the University of Nebraska, Lincoln. Her research focuses on understanding early childhood teachers' experiences and how to build from these experiences in order to bring about meaningful changes in practice and improved outcomes for children.

Hannah Schäfer, BA, is a master's degree student and research assistant at the University of Vienna. Her research interests include history of education, philosophy of education, and mixed methods.

Kristin A. Sinclair, PhD, is an assistant teaching professor at Georgetown University. Her research uses critical theories of spatial justice and youth sociopolitical development to examine whether, how, and under what conditions teachers and schools might use place- and community-based education to engage young people in activism and social change.

Audra Skukauskaite is an associate professor in the College of Community Innovation and Education at the University of Central Florida. Her research focuses on teaching and learning of research methodologies and application of discourse-based ethnographic approaches in interdisciplinary fields, such as invention education.

Stefan Slater is a PhD student at the University of Pennsylvania's Graduate School of Education, working in the Penn Center for Learning Analytics with Dr. Ryan Baker. His research includes evaluations of model goodness and model power and the modeling of player learning and player behavior in video games, both educational and noneducational.

Padhraic Smyth is a Chancellor's Professor in the Department of Computer Science at the University of California, Irvine, with co-appointments in the Department of Education and the Department of Statistics. He is a fellow of the Association for Computing Machinery and the Association for the Advancement of Artificial Intelligence. His research interests are in machine learning, pattern recognition, and applied statistics.

Carmen Vanderhoof teaches science methods classes at the Pennsylvania State University and supervises student-teachers in the local school district. She takes an ethnographic perspective to research multiple literacies and the intersection of science and engineering practices across grade levels.

Sara Van Waes, PhD, is a visiting professor at the Faculty of Social Sciences, University of Antwerp. Her research interests include social networks, professional development, and higher education.

Samantha Viano is an assistant professor of education in the College of Education and Human Development at George Mason University. Her research focuses on evaluating policies and assessing school contexts that predominantly affect at-risk or traditionally marginalized student populations and their teachers.

Mark Warschauer is a professor of education at the University of California, Irvine, where he directs the Digital Learning Lab, and the editor in chief of *AERA Open*. His research focuses on the use of digital media to promote diverse learners' literacy development and academic achievement.

Joseph Jay Williams is an assistant professor in the Department of Computer Science at the University of Toronto. His research combines human-computer interaction and psychology by conducting randomized A/B comparisons in real-world settings. He applies statistics and machine learning methods like multiarmed bandit algorithms to dynamically adapt randomized A/B comparisons to enhance and personalize the experience for people in the future, balancing practical impact with conducting scientific research.

Miri Yemini is an established comparative education scholar, tenured at Tel Aviv University, with interests in internationalization of education in schools and higher education, global citizenship education, and education in conflict-ridden societies. She has also developed a strong research contribution around the involvement of external actors in schools.

Renzhe Yu is a PhD student in education at the University of California, Irvine. His research uses large-scale data analytics to understand and support college students' day-to-day learning and life experiences, with the goal of promoting success and equity in higher education. He was a Data Science for Social Good Fellow at the Alan Turing Institute and the University of Chicago.

Maxwell M. Yurkofsky is a doctoral candidate in education policy, leadership, and instructional practice at the Harvard Graduate School of Education. His research draws on institutional and organizational theory to understand how school systems organize for continuous improvement and deeper learning.